HISTORY IN DISPUTE

ADVISORY BOARD

HISTORY IN DISPUTE

Volume 9

World War I: Second Series

Edited by **Dennis Showalter**

A MANLY, INC. BOOK

GALE®

THOMSON

GALE

Detroit • New York • San Diego • San Francisco • Cleveland • New Haven, Conn. • Waterville, Maine • London • Munich

History in Dispute
Volume 9–World War I, Second Series

Editorial Directors
Matthew J. Bruccoli and Richard Layman

Senior Editor
Karen L. Rood

Series Editor
Anthony J. Scotti Jr.

ISBN 1-55862-448-1

Printed in the United States of America
10 9 8 7 6 5 4 3 2 1

CONTENTS

CONTENTS

CONTENTS

CONTENTS

ABOUT THE SERIES

History in Dispute is an ongoing series designed to present, in an informative and lively pro-con format, different perspectives on major historical events drawn from all time periods and from all parts of the globe. The series was developed in response to requests from librarians and educators for a history-reference source that will help students hone essential critical-thinking skills while serving as a valuable research tool for class assignments.

Individual volumes in the series concentrate on specific themes, eras, or subjects intended to correspond to the way history is studied at the academic level. For example, early volumes cover such topics as the Cold War, American Social and Political Movements, and World War II. Volume subtitles make it easy for users to identify contents at a glance and facilitate searching for specific subjects in library catalogues.

Each volume of *History in Dispute* includes up to fifty entries, centered on the overall theme of that volume and chosen by an advisory board of historians for their relevance to the curriculum. Entries are arranged alphabetically by the name of the event or issue in its most common form. (Thus, in Volume 1, the issue "Was detente a success?" is presented under the chapter heading "Detente.")

Each entry begins with a brief statement of the opposing points of view on the topic, followed by a short essay summarizing the issue and outlining the controversy. At the heart of the entry, designed to engage students' interest while providing essential information, are the two or more lengthy essays, written specifically for this publication by experts in the field, each presenting one side of the dispute.

In addition to this substantial prose explication, entries also include excerpts from primary-source documents, other useful information typeset in easy-to-locate shaded boxes, detailed entry bibliographies, and photographs or illustrations appropriate to the issue.

Other features of *History in Dispute* volumes include: individual volume introductions by academic experts, tables of contents that identify both the issues and the controversies, chronologies of events, names and credentials of advisers, brief biographies of contributors, thorough volume bibliographies for more information on the topic, and a comprehensive subject index.

ACKNOWLEDGMENTS

James F. Tidd Jr., *Assistant in-house editor.*

Philip B. Dematteis, *Production manager.*

Kathy Lawler Merlette, *Office manager.*

Ann M. Cheschi, Amber L. Coker, Linda Dalton Mullinax, and Angi Pleasant, *Administrative support.*

Ann-Marie Holland, *Accounting.*

Sally R. Evans, *Copyediting supervisor.* Phyllis A. Avant, Brenda Carol Blanton, Melissa D. Hinton, Charles Loughlin, Rebecca Mayo, Nancy E. Smith, Elizabeth Jo Ann Sumner, *Copyediting staff.* Brenda Cabra, *Freelance copyeditor.*

Janet E. Hill, *Layout and graphics supervisor.* Zoe R. Cook, *Lead layout and graphics.* Karla Corley Brown, *Layout and graphics.*

Scott Nemzek, Paul Talbot, *Photography editors.*

Jason Paddock, *Permissions editor.*

Joseph M. Bruccoli and Zoe R. Cook, *Digital photographic copy work.*

Marie L. Parker, *Systems manager.*

Kathleen M. Flanagan, *Typesetting supervisor.* Patricia Marie Flanagan, Mark J. McEwan, and Pamela D. Norton, *Typesetting staff.*

Walter W. Ross, *Library researcher.* Tucker Taylor, *Circulation department head, Thomas Cooper Library, University of South Carolina.* John Brunswick, *Interlibrary-loan department head.* Virginia W. Weathers, *Reference department head.* Brette Barclay, Marilee Birchfield, Paul Cammarata, Gary Geer, Michael Macan, Tom Marcil, and Sharon Verba, *Reference librarians.*

PREFACE

The stalemate confirmed on the Western Front in 1916 was sustained in other theaters as well. In the Balkans an initial Allied commitment of two divisions, based on the Greek port of Salonika, increased to more than a dozen during 1916 but failed to do any more than maintain themselves in what cynics called "the war's largest internment camp." Allied diplomacy persuaded Romania to enter the conflict in August, but the kingdom's army was ill prepared for the kind of war the Central Powers had learned to wage. It was smashed in a lightning German-Austrian offensive commanded by Erich von Falkenhayn who, dismissed as Chief of Staff for his failure at Verdun, demonstrated unexpected competence in field command.

The Romanian fragments withdrew to their eastern border, joining a Russian army that had made a surprising recovery from the debacles of 1915 and was ready—at least at the level of the high command—to try the battlefield once more. An ill-planned attack around Vilna in the spring dampened enthusiasm at the same time French demands for an attack to relieve the pressure on Verdun increased. When the new commander of the Southwestern Front, General Alexander Brusilov, proposed an attack in his sector with the resources currently available, he was authorized to go ahead. The "Brusilov offensive" that began in June represented a significant departure from accepted practice in that it struck a simultaneous set of blows instead of concentrating in a single sector. Against Germans, with their flexible command and administrative systems, the result might have been immediate disaster. Against an overextended and demoralized Austro-Hungarian army, the Russians achieved remarkable initial successes. Within a month, however, the arrival of German reinforcements and the lack of Russian reserves restored a status quo confirmed by several disastrous attacks further north.

Even at sea the stalemate endured. On 31 May a sortie by the German High Seas Fleet was intercepted by the British, in part because of skillful use of radio intelligence. The resulting battle in the North Sea, Jutland to the British and Skagerrak to the Germans, was tactically indecisive, with neither side suffering significant losses. British admiral Sir John Jellicoe has been sharply criticized for a caution reflecting a widespread sense that he was, in Winston Churchill's words, "the only man who could lose the war in an afternoon." Strategically, the battle put the cork into the bottle: never again would the German fleet, built at such high costs, come out to challenge its rival directly. On the other hand, Jutland created no new way for the Royal Navy to force the issue without facing unacceptable losses.

In 1916 all the major combatants accepted a de facto attritional model of victory. In France, already mobilized to the limit, that view did not mean much. Verdun became a symbol of determination to endure and overcome at any cost. By year's end it was becoming clear that the war's price might just be France's continued existence as a great power. In Great Britain, still committed in principle to voluntarism, conscription was introduced. Also, a reorganization of government occurred as well as the creation of an increasing number of agencies of government control. Individuals, communities, and interest groups nevertheless remained the principal sources of action in a society continuing to believe it was fighting by its own will in a righteous cause. Russian attempts at systematization and belt-tightening increasingly foundered as a semimodern society proved unable to produce enough competent midlevel officials and administrators to maximize available resources. An overstrained economy depended more and more on muscle power as opposed to machines—and the men and women who did the work had neither money to spend nor food to buy with it, as inflation soared and distribution systems gridlocked.

Matters were much the same on the other side of the line in Austria-Hungary, where ethnic and nationalist rivalries were fueled by privation and in turn contributed to economic breakdown. Antagonism between labor and industry flourished as food costs outstripped an inflation that mocked both wage increases and direct government subsidies. Agricultural production declined as men and animals were drawn into an army that only returned physical and emotional cripples to a civilian life growing increasingly desperate.

Germany, by contrast, took matters in hand. The appointment in August of Paul von Hindenburg as Chief of Staff was more than a military change. Hindenburg, riding high on the glory of Tannenberg (1914) and the other German triumphs on the Russian Front, was by now an emotional substitute for a Kaiser systematically kept away from any important decisions. With Quartermaster-General Erich Ludendorff, Hindenburg was expected to bring victory to a sorely tried Fatherland. The "1916 Program" provided in principle for complete mobilization of German resources under government control. Hindenburg and Ludendorff demanded massive increases in munitions production and a civilian population entirely subject to regulation for the sake of the war effort. They paid no attention to the actual state of the country's resources. The result was a failure, compounded by administrative bungling, unenforceable regulations, and levels of interference in daily life that proved excessive even for people accustomed to regimentation.

By 1917, in other words, the indicators of collapse were plain to see in every major combatant. They were neutralized, at least temporarily, by an increasing effectiveness in the techniques of war making. The process began with a German Army that took stock of its experiences and began developing a system of flexible defense in depth that would defy every effort to break it for the next year. That was accompanied by a strategic withdrawal from some of the more exposed sectors of the Western Front—movement to more defensible positions that nevertheless fired Allied imaginations that this time the Hun was definitely on the run.

The British Expeditionary Force (BEF) had also demonstrated a high learning curve in the later stages of the Somme campaign (1916). Its staff work was significantly improved in every category from evacuation of casualties to fire-support coordination. In April 1917 the Third Army mounted a set-piece attack at Arras whose ultimate prolongation has obscured the relative effectiveness of the initial operations. The same point can be made about the simultaneous, and often-excoriated, French attacks in the Chemin des Dames. The "Nivelle Offensive," named for its advocate and commander, was an initial, limited success, accounting for thirty thousand prisoners and advancing as much as four miles on a sixteen-mile sector. General Robert-Georges Nivelle, however, had promised far more: a decisive breakthrough that would be the beginning of the war's end. For a large part of the French army the disappointment, on top of two and a half years of huge losses for little gain, led to widespread mutiny.

It was not mutiny in the classic sense, with officers shot and the red flag hoisted as the soldiers marched on Paris. It amounted rather to a struggle for power within the military system, with the soldiers ultimately reaccepting authority in return for affirmation of their status as citizens of a representative democracy. In practice, the French army spent a year restoring its equilibrium as its new commander, Philippe Pétain, promised to "wait for the tanks and the Americans."

Meanwhile the British soldiered on, assuming primary responsibility for keeping the Germans under pressure in a sector that promised much strategically but delivered little tactically. Since 1914 the Germans had held the high ground around the Belgian city of Ypres. A successful attack there would also threaten German communications in the Flanders sector and—with a little luck—open the way to the Channel coast and its submarine bases. In June a successful local attack took advantage of two years' worth of mining the German position to clear the Messines Ridge. This assault was a preliminary one to the Battle of Third Ypres, better known as Passchendaele.

Dismissed for years as a triumph of British butchery and bungling, the Passchendaele campaign has been significantly reinterpreted by a new generation of British military historians. These scholars make the case that British minor tactics were skillful and the military command was competent. The possibility of gaining important strategic objectives was not a mere chimera. The "bite-and-hold" technique of limited attacks for limited objectives significantly eroded the fighting power of a German Army already stretched to its limits. What went wrong was the enduring pattern of sustaining the operation for too long after its diminishing returns were obvious—particularly in the context of an abnormally heavy rainfall that checked and mated British reliance on firepower by transforming the battle zone to a sea of sticky mud, virtually impassable by guns, trucks, and wagons.

The revisionists' well-supported case cannot entirely deny the sense of malaise affecting both the French and British armies at the turn of the year—a sense that the war would continue until nothing and no one was left to wage it. Germany was no less war weary—in good part because of the failure of one of the strategic initiatives it undertook at the start of 1917. Submarines had done significant damage to British commerce in 1915, until protests by neutral nations—especially the United States—caused the campaign's suspension. In January 1917 the U-boats were again turned loose. The risks of bringing the United States into the war were by then considered acceptable, balanced against the expectation of starving Britain into making peace by sinking the merchantmen that were the island kingdom's lifeline.

The U-boats enjoyed striking success in early going—though never coming close to the stated objective. The introduction of a convoy system in May did much to counter the undersea campaign simply by creating a much larger ratio of empty space in the North Atlantic. Moreover, American president Woodrow Wilson was finally convinced German victory posed an unacceptable strategic and ideological threat and the United States entered the war on 6 April. American mobilization was head over heels. Its primary military strength was a battle fleet the Allies did not need. Wilson and his field commander, General John J. Pershing, were determined to assert an independent diplomatic and military presence, complicating an already-strained alliance. Yet, millions of Americans were donning army uniforms and flooding into training camps that were designed to produce fighting divisions on an assembly-line basis. That situation made it worthwhile to give the new "associated power" the autonomy it demanded—especially given developments in the east.

By early 1917 the government of Tsar Nicholas II had sacrificed any legitimacy it once might have possessed. A revolution supported by both moderates and radicals overthrew the Empire in March. The new government in part sought to establish its own validity by continuing the war. A major offensive, named after War Minister Alexander Kerensky, began on 1 June and collapsed in a matter of days. The Germans counterattacked and this time kept moving. Russia collapsed into chaos, with the Bolsheviks under Vladimir Lenin seizing power in November by a coup in Petrograd. The result was civil war and the end of the Eastern Front.

Meanwhile, Germany sought its own solutions. Austria-Hungary's request for assistance on the Italian front led to the transfer of enough men and guns to inflict a heavy defeat on the Italians at the Battle of Caporetto, beginning on 24 October. The front, however, once again stabilized with the help of British and French reinforcements. Though Russia's revolutionary government resisted anything like negotiations as the Germans understood them, its collapse as a military threat freed troops for the Western Front. Most of the divisions transferred were second-rate but could take over quiet sectors and enable the concentration of the German Army's best men and formations for a final blow.

During 1917 the Germans had developed new offensive tactics, based on intense artillery barrages designed to neutralize rather than destroy, followed by infantry assaults based on the principle of infiltration: finding and exploiting weak spots. In the spring of 1918 they massed against the British front weakened by recent extension and the BEF that had been so long on the offensive its defensive skills had atrophied. On 21 March the offensive went forward. Its architect, Ludendorff, had never paid much attention to establishing objectives. "Punch a hole and see what happens" had been his guiding principle. The German Army, however, lacked the mobility and striking power to convert its initial successes into breakthroughs. The British bent in some areas and broke in others, but the line held to a point where the German High Command began improvising, shifting its rapidly eroding strike forces from sector to sector in an ultimately vain effort to replicate their initial successes.

Vain it may have been, but the German offensive frightened the Allies enough to appoint a supreme commander, French marshal Ferdinand Foch. His powers, limited essentially to those of a coordinator, nevertheless enabled a more rational use of reserves—a process also facilitated by the Americans' willingness to suspend their demand for autonomy and throw their resources, albeit temporarily, into a common pool. German tactics grew less effective, and casualties increased as Allied resistance stiffened. A revivified French army played the key role in holding the final series of offensives, which brought the Germans almost to the gates of Paris but left them with a front line that amounted to a series of large salients with exposed flanks.

The Allied response began in July with a series of small counterstrokes: Soissons by the French and Americans; Hamel by the Australians—smaller in scale but a cameo of effectiveness in its staff work and its coordination of arms. The day 8 August, however, marked the beginning of the war's end. On what Ludendorff called "the black day of the German Army," the BEF launched an army-strength attack on the German positions east of Amiens. Tanks, aircraft, artillery, and infantry combined in a "managed battle" that pushed the front back eight miles on the first day and threw the Germans permanently off balance.

The Germans' failure to recover was in good part the consequence of a series of coordinated Allied offensives: the British in the north, around Arras and in Flanders; the French and British at Bapaume/Peronne; and the Americans at Saint-Mihiel and in the Meuse-Argonne region. These attacks were all tactical triumphs. The tanks that so often facilitated them were still essentially one-shot, throwaway weapons. Aircraft were vulnerable to ground fire. Radios were still bulky, fragile instruments. The internal combustion engine was as yet too undeveloped to be useful in forward areas, let alone convert tactical successes to operational ones. Moreover, in that context of mobility, not least of the Allies' problems was an increasing shortage of draft animals, with the survivors often too weak to keep pulling guns and wagons at the pace necessary to sustain even limited advances over open country.

Instead of being a continuous operation, the "Advance to Victory" during the "Hundred Days" of autumn 1918 was rather a series of hammer blows, each requiring time in between to prepare the next strike. As its casualties mounted and its morale declined, the German Army was no longer able to mount the ripostes its operational doctrine demanded. It fell back, covering and counterpunching like an over-matched boxer inexorably forced into a corner. Peace with Russia, finally concluded in March, brought no immediate gains. On the contrary, its harsh terms confirmed Allied belief that the Central Powers merited no consideration when their turn came. A final Austro-Hungarian offensive in Italy stalled in June; the Dual Monarchy began dissolving from internal tensions well before the Italian counterattack at Vittorio Veneto four months later. Turkey capitulated in the face of a British offensive in Palestine during September and October. The gardeners of Salonika left their cultivation long enough to smash through the weakened Bulgarian Army and drive up the Danube River into the vitals of what were rapidly becoming Austria-Hungary's successor states.

By midsummer, Allied aircraft were regularly bombing strategic targets in Germany. The High Seas Fleet, on which so much had been lavished, retained value only as a sacrificial pawn, and that was removed when its sailors refused to make a final sortie even the officers regarded as a suicide mission. On 1 October, Ludendorff declared the war lost. Two days later, Prince Max of Baden became Chancellor and requested peace on the basis of Wilson's Fourteen Points. First announced in January 1918, this plan called for, among other things, arms reduction, open diplomacy, and freedom of the seas—none of them previously attractive to the Second Reich. On 28 October, Germany officially became a constitutional monarchy—a case of too little, far too late. On 9 November the Kaiser fled to Holland, and a republic was proclaimed in Berlin. That republic finally signed an armistice on 11 November 1918, and the guns of August finally fell silent.

The reconstruction of Europe that began at Versailles a few weeks later lies outside the scope of these volumes. After almost one hundred years' analysis, it is generally concluded that the Versailles settlement was an intermediate solution. Neither an act of reconciliation nor a punitive "Carthaginian Peace," it combined desire for retribution and concern for security on one hand with recognition on the other that Western civilization had come too close to hurling itself off a cliff and that eventually some form of reintegration was necessary. With the United States retreating into isolationism, Russia pursuing world revolution as the Soviet Union, and Germany nursing a sense of betrayal, that reintegration would only begin three-quarters of a century, and another total war, later. That story, however, is told in other volumes of *History in Dispute*.

—DENNIS SHOWALTER,
COLORADO COLLEGE,
COLORADO SPRINGS

CHRONOLOGY

Boldface type indicates an entry in this volume.

1914

JUNE: Austrian foreign minister Leopold Berchtold schemes to gain German support for an Austrian-Hungarian-Bulgarian-Turkish alliance to encircle Serbia. (*See* **Structural Flaws**)

25 JUNE: Austrian archduke Francis "Franz" Ferdinand, nephew of Emperor Francis Joseph, arrives in Bosnia to supervise summer maneuvers by the Habsburg army. (*See* **Habsburgs**)

28 JUNE: Ferdinand and his wife, Sophia Chotek, are shot and killed in Sarajevo, Bosnia, by Gavrilo Princip, a Bosnian Serbian nationalist who is identified as being a member of *Narodna Odbrana* (National Defense) and part of a six-man assassination team. (*See* **Habsburgs** *and* **Yugoslavia**)

5 JULY: An Austrian emissary travels to Berlin to inform the Germans that Austria will ask for a guarantee of good conduct from the Serbs or that they will make them face military action. Kaiser Wilhelm II agrees to support Austria.

7 JULY: Berchtold, who does not believe that the Russians will respond to Austrian aggression in the Balkans, proposes to the Imperial Council of Ministers that Austria mobilize against Serbia. Hungarian prime minister Kálmán Tisza insists that a note be sent first, rather than an ultimatum setting conditions, including the right of Austrian investigators to supervise the investigation of the assassinations.

16 JULY: French president Raymond Poincaré makes a state visit to France's ally Russia, which supports Serbia. (*See* **Imperial Russia**)

23 JULY: The Austrian note, dated to expire on 25 July, arrives in Belgrade. The Serbs reject the demands.

26–27 JULY: Serbia mobilizes its forces; Russia calls up its military reservists. (*See* **Russian Logistics**)

26–27 JULY: Turkish minister of war Enver Paşa, who had served as the military attaché to Germany in 1909–1911, speaks with German diplomats about the possibility of an alliance between their two countries.

28 JULY: Austrian border guards fire on a Serbian patrol that strays across the border. Austria-Hungary declares war on Serbia. Russian military leaders decide to order a formal mobilization of their army, but they are held in check by Tsar Nicholas II. (*See* **Tsar Nicholas II**)

28 JULY: The Ottoman Empire declares war on Bosnia.

29 JULY: Austrian gunboats on the Danube River bombard Belgrade.

30 JULY: Russia formally mobilizes its troops and orders reservists to report to depots on 31 July. German officials respond by ordering a "State of Danger of War." (*See* **Imperial Russia** *and* **Russian Logistics**)

AUGUST: Great Britain calls for enlistments, which will become the nucleus of the New Army. These troops will be ready for action by 1915.

1 AUGUST: Germany orders the mobilization of its armies and declares war against Russia.

2 AUGUST: Germany demands that Belgium allow German troops the right to transverse its territory for operations against France. Germany invades Luxembourg. (*See* **Belgian Neutrality** *and* **German Tactics**)

2 AUGUST: Great Britain mobilizes its naval fleet.

3 AUGUST: Germany formally declares war on France.

4 AUGUST: The German Tenth Army Corps, under the command of Otto von Emmich, invades Belgium and faces resistance at Liège. Civilians, including priests, are killed, and the town of Battice is burned. Larger massacres occur during the next three weeks, as German

reservist units arrive in the country; the killings are known as the "Rape of Belgium," reports of which stir anti-German sentiment in the United States. (*See* **Belgian Neutrality** and **German Tactics**)

4 AUGUST: President Woodrow Wilson declares that the United States will remain a neutral country. (*See* **U.S. Entry**)

4 AUGUST: The British navy begins blockading sea traffic to German ports. (*See* **High Seas Fleet**)

5 AUGUST: Great Britain, France, and Russia are officially at war with Germany. Austria declares war on Russia.

5 AUGUST: The German minelayer *Königin Luise* is sunk by the HMS *Amphion* off the coast of eastern England.

6 AUGUST: The HMS *Amphion* hits a mine and sinks in the North Sea.

7 AUGUST: Liège surrenders to the Germans.

7 AUGUST: The French Seventh Corps, ordered forward by General Joseph Joffre, attack Mulhouse in Alsace. The French are beaten back by a German counterattack three days later.

7 AUGUST: HMS *Gloucester* engages the German cruisers *Goeben* and *Breslau* in the Mediterranean Sea, after the cruisers leave the port of Messina in Italy. The German ships had just three days earlier bombarded French-held ports in Algeria, allegedly while flying Russian flags.

8 AUGUST: The British Parliament passes the Defense of the Realm Act, which prohibits spying and the spread of disinformation and gives the government the right to confiscate factories and property deemed necessary to prosecute the war. (*See* **British War Economy**)

8 AUGUST: British and French African colonial troops invade Togoland, West Africa, and destroy a communications center in the Battle of Kamina, which is over by 26 August. The two countries divide control of the colony between themselves. (*See* **French African Troops**)

8 AUGUST: British forces shell the towns of Bagamoyo and Dar es Salaam on the German East African coast.

9 AUGUST: The Germans lose their first submarine, the *U–15*, which is rammed and sunk by the HMS *Birmingham*.

10 AUGUST: Austrian troops invade Poland.

12 AUGUST: Great Britain and France declare war on Austria. Italy asserts its neutrality.

12 AUGUST: Fort Pontisse in Belgium is bombarded by a huge German artillery gun, a Krup 420, which fires two-thousand-pound shells. The garrison surrenders on 13 August,

as do the defenders of several other local forts that come under fire from the Germans. (*See* **Belgian Neutrality**)

12 AUGUST: The *U–13*, which is probably sunk after striking a mine, goes down in Heligoland Bight.

12–21 AUGUST: Austrian troops cross the Drina River and engage the Serbians in the Battle of the Jadar. The Serbs, however, are successful in pushing the Austrians back.

13 AUGUST: British fighter aircraft of the Royal Flying Corps (RFC) arrive in France. (*See* **Aircraft**)

14 AUGUST: The French First Army, under the command of Auguste Dubail, advances toward the city of Sarrebourg. The Germans stoutly defend against this incursion but gradually fall back. The twelve-day battle that follows is called the Battle of the Frontiers (Lorraine).

14 AUGUST: The British Expeditionary Force (BEF) disembarks at Boulogne and marches toward Belgium. (*See* **British Strategy**)

15 AUGUST: Fort Loncin, headquarters for Belgian general Gérard Leman, explodes after a German shell hits a munitions magazine. Leman is knocked unconscious in the blast and is captured by the Germans. (*See* **Belgian Neutrality**)

15 AUGUST: The Panama Canal is officially opened to traffic, although barges have been regularly traversing the waterway since mid May.

15 AUGUST: The Japanese insist that the Germans leave China. (*See* **End of Imperialism** and **Japan**)

18 AUGUST: Sarrebourg is captured by the French.

18–19 AUGUST: German forces defeat Belgian opposition in the Battle of Tirlement; German general Heinrich von Kluck leads his troops into Brussels on 20 August. (*See* **Belgian Neutrality**)

19 AUGUST: Mulhouse is recaptured by the Germans. Dubail orders a night attack on German positions to restore communications with other French corps along the front.

20 AUGUST: A frontwide counterattack is undertaken by eight German corps, which smash French opposition. The French Seventh Corps is pushed back; only the Twentieth Corps, under the command of Ferdinand Foch, holds firm. The remainder of the French army, which lost more than 140,000 men, retreats behind the Meurthe River by 23 August. (*See* **Foch**)

20 AUGUST: Russian troops, under the command of Pavel Rennenkampf, attack the German Eighth Army in East Prussia, forcing it to withdraw to the Vistula River. The German commander is replaced by Generals Paul von Hindenburg and Erich Ludendorff. (*See* **Imperial Russia**)

22 AUGUST: The French Third Army, which had been advancing into the Ardennes Forest, collapses under a German counterattack. French colonial troops, part of the Fourth Army, are encircled by the German army. The Third Colonial Division loses more than eleven thousand soldiers of its fifteen-thousand-man complement. The Third and Fourth Armies are pushed back across the Meuse River by 25 August. (*See* **French Colonial Troops**)

22 AUGUST: Admiral Maximilian Graf von Spee commands the German Far Eastern Squadron in the Pacific Ocean. His fleet bombards Papeete in Tahiti and then heads for South America. (*See* **High Seas Fleet**)

23 AUGUST: German and British soldiers fight for the first time in the war at the Battle of Mons. Approximately seventy thousand British, positioned alongside the French Fifth Corps, are forced to retreat by the German First Army, which is nearly double the size of its opponents. (*See* **British Strategy**)

23 AUGUST: Japan, realizing an opportunity to enlarge its empire at the expense of the heavily engaged Central Powers, declares war against Germany. The Japanese, supported by the British, lay siege to Tsingtao, a German-controlled port on the Chinese coast. (*See* **Japan**)

24 AUGUST: Forts in the vicinity of Namur, Belgium, are reduced by German artillery.

25 AUGUST–7 SEPTEMBER: The Germans attack the Allied front established along the Meurthe River, breaking through French defensive lines. (*See* **German Tactics**)

26 AUGUST: British troops under the command of General Horace Smith-Dorrien, while retreating from their defeat at Mons, fight a defending action at Le Cateau. Nearly eight thousand casualties are suffered by the British. A combined Belgian and French counterattack slows the German advance and allows the weary British troops to withdraw. (*See* **British Command Structure** *and* **British Strategy**)

26 AUGUST: The German light cruiser *Magdeburg* is beached in the Baltic Sea, and the Russians are able to capture its code books and key. These items are sent to England where, along with other materials confiscated from German ships, British intelligence is able to read German naval transmissions.

26–31 AUGUST: The Russian Second Army, under the command of Alexandr Samsonov, enters East Prussia and engages German troops, who are initially forced to retreat. After a change of leadership and the arrival of fresh troops, the Germans surround the Russian army; the Russians are defeated; Samsonov commits suicide (29 August); and the invading force is destroyed or captured. Only 1 out of every 15 Russian soldiers of the original 150,000-man force are able to withdraw from the engagement. The Allies censor information about the battle to avoid a collapse of confidence. (*See* **Russian Logistics**)

28 AUGUST: British admiral David Beatty leads his fleet of two cruisers and twenty destroyers against a German fleet at Heligoland Bight. The HMS *Arethusa* and *Ariadne* are seriously damaged; the Germans lose the *Mainz* and *Köln,* and their fleet is forced back into port. (*See* **High Seas Fleet**)

29 AUGUST: The French Fifth Army, commanded by Charles Lanrezac, engages the German Second Army. Known as the Battle of Guise, in this engagement the Germans attack during a foggy morning, but a surprise French counterattack throws them back.

29 AUGUST: German Samoa is captured by a New Zealand force of 1,400 men. (*See* **End of Imperialism**)

30 AUGUST: German troops reach positions just west of Paris, but General Kluck realizes his units have lost contact with other elements of the German army, and he stops the advance. The Germans take Amiens. (*See* **German Tactics**)

30 AUGUST: German planes attack Paris. (*See* **Aircraft** *and* **Strategic Bombing**)

2 SEPTEMBER: The French government is moved to Bordeaux in the face of a potential assault on Paris by the Germans.

5 SEPTEMBER: The light cruiser HMS *Pathfinder,* the first British warship sunk by a submarine, is torpedoed and sunk off the Firth of Forth by the *U–21.* (*See* **Maritime Technology**)

5–9 SEPTEMBER: In an effort to protect Paris, the French, led by Joffre, plan an attack on the German Second Army, commanded by Karl von Bülow. The engagement is known as the Battle of the Marne (First Marne). The Germans inadvertently leave their flank exposed after turning their army to the southeast. Beginning on 6 September, a combined French and British assault forces the Germans into a retreat across the Aisne River. Reportedly, the overall German commander, Helmuth von Moltke (the Younger), suffers a mental breakdown and is replaced by General

Erich von Falkenhayn. The battle effectively ends the German drive to conclude the war quickly. (*See* **German Tactics**)

5–9 SEPTEMBER: The first use of aerial photography by the RFC for military purposes occurs during the Battle of the Marne. (*See* **Aircraft**)

8–17 SEPTEMBER: Austrian and Serbian troops clash at the Battle of Drina, as the Serbs enter Bosnia. The occupation is both short-lived and costly. (*See* **Yugoslavia**)

9 SEPTEMBER: The Germans shift their troops, who have defeated the Russian Second Army, against Rennenkampf's army at the Battle of Masurian Lakes. The Russians suffer heavy losses and retire from East Prussia by 14 September. (*See* **Imperial Russia**)

13 SEPTEMBER: Australian troops capture Bougainville, Solomon Islands.

13 SEPTEMBER: Lemberg (Lvov), Ukraine, is captured by the Russians, who push the Austrians out of the area. Russian troops continue to advance, capturing towns and forts, as they move toward the Carpathian Mountains.

15–18 SEPTEMBER: British and French troops attempt to push the Germans back from their placements along the Aisne River. The Germans are entrenched, however, beginning a pattern of trench warfare that becomes the mainstay of World War I engagements; frontal attacks against the Germans, dug in on the high ground, are repulsed with heavy losses. A strategy of gradual western movement, as each army tries to outflank their opponent, becomes known as "The Race to the Sea." (*See* **Trench Warfare**)

20 SEPTEMBER: The German cruiser *Königsberg* destroys the cruiser HMS *Pegasus* off Zanzibar. The German raider had captured and scuttled the freighter *City of Winchester*, which was carrying the tea crop for that year from Ceylon, on 6 August.

21 SEPTEMBER: The Australians capture New Guinea from the Germans.

22 SEPTEMBER: Three British cruisers (HMS *Aboukir*, *Hogue*, and *Cressy*), on patrol in the North Sea, are attacked and sunk by the *U–9*, commanded by Otto Weddigen. More than 1,400 sailors perish. The entire crew of the submarine wins the Iron Cross for their action. (*See* **Maritime Technology**)

22 SEPTEMBER: Madras, a port on the Indian coast, is shelled by the German cruiser *Emden*, captained by Karl von Müller.

25–29 SEPTEMBER: The French Second Army, commanded by Noel de Castlenau, a leading proponent of offensive war and a participant in the development of the French order of battle called Plan XVII, attacks the German trench lines in the Battle of Albert. The French are stopped short of capturing the town of Albert. (*See* **Trench Warfare**)

26 SEPTEMBER: The Indian Expeditionary Force arrives in Marseilles.

26–27 SEPTEMBER: Duala (Cameroon) is captured by the British. Germany had been expanding its territorial interests in West Africa, but by February 1916 they are pushed out of the colony. (*See* **End of Imperialism**)

27 SEPTEMBER: The Russians invade Hungary. (*See* **Russian Logistics**)

27 SEPTEMBER–10 OCTOBER: British and Belgian forces engage the Germans in the Battle of Artois. The town falls to the BEF.

OCTOBER: Turkish authorities place restrictions on its Armenian population, confiscate their weapons, arrest Armenian leaders, and impose censorship of news about its activities.

1–2 OCTOBER: The French Tenth Army attempts to flank the Germans at the Battle of Arras. They manage to capture and hold Arras, but most of their initial gains are pushed back by the German Sixth Army.

4 OCTOBER: The Austrians begin an offensive into Galicia, forcing the Russians out of the Carpathian Mountains.

6 OCTOBER: The Germans, who want to stop the flow of British troops into the theater of battle, attack Antwerp in an attempt to reach the North Sea. British and Belgian troops provide a stiff defense but are forced to withdraw from the city on 10 October.

7 OCTOBER: The Japanese capture the Marshall Islands. (*See* **Japan**)

7 OCTOBER: British pilots from the Royal Naval Air Service (RNAS) destroy a German zeppelin hangar in Dusseldorf. They try a similar attack on 22 September but are foiled by foggy weather. (*See* **Aircraft** *and* **Strategic Bombing**)

11 OCTOBER: The Germans capture Ghent.

11 OCTOBER: The *U–26* sinks the Russian cruiser *Pallada* in the Gulf of Finland, while the *U–9* makes another score, sinking the light cruiser HMS *Hawke* off the coast of Aberdeen. (*See* **Maritime Technology**)

12 OCTOBER: The Germans advance to Warsaw but are pushed back by Russian counterattacks.

14 OCTOBER: Bruges, in West Flanders, falls to the Germans.

14 OCTOBER: The Canadian Expeditionary Force (CEF) arrives in France.

15–21 OCTOBER: The Austrians move northward against the Russians in the Battle of Warsaw but are forced back.

19 OCTOBER–24 NOVEMBER: The Germans attempt to dislodge the Allies from positions along the Yser River, in order to gain cities along the North Sea, in what becomes known as the Battle of Ypres. British, Belgian, and French troops block a much larger German army. (*See* **Ypres**)

20 OCTOBER: Just south of Norway, the *U–17* sinks the first merchantman destroyed by a submarine, the British steamer *Glitra*. The crew is allowed to abandon ship before it is sent to the bottom. (*See* **Convoys** *and* **Maritime Technology**)

27 OCTOBER: The Belgians, as ordered by King Albert I, open their dikes and flood the Yser region.

30 OCTOBER: The German battle cruisers *Goeben* and *Breslau*, flying the colors of the Ottoman Empire, which joined the conflict on the side of the Central Powers on the previous day, bombard Russian ports along the Black Sea. Although they have new names and are officially owned by the Turkish government, the two ships retain their German crews. German and Ottoman control of the Dardanelles constricts the flow of supplies from the Allies to Russia.

31 OCTOBER: The British aircraft carrier HMS *Hermes* is sunk in the English Channel by the *U–27*.

1 NOVEMBER: Admiral Spee's fleet, which is disrupting sea traffic along the South American coast, engages and defeats the British Fourth Cruiser Squadron, commanded by Sir Christopher Cradock, off of Coronel, Chile. HMS cruisers *Monmouth* and *Good Hope* are sunk; Cradock goes down with the *Good Hope*. (*See* **High Seas Fleet**)

2 NOVEMBER: Russia invades Prussia again. Russia declares war on the Ottoman Empire. (*See* **Russian Logistics**)

2–5 NOVEMBER: An Indian and British invasion force is defeated by the Germans at the Battle of Tanga, in German East Africa.

5 NOVEMBER: Great Britain declares war on Turkey and captures Cyprus. (*See* **British Strategy**)

7 NOVEMBER: British and Indian troops land in Mesopotamia, which is part of the Ottoman Empire. The British hope to protect vital oil supplies and quickly capture Basra.

7 NOVEMBER: Japanese and Allied troops capture Tsingtao. (*See* **Japan**)

8 NOVEMBER: Austria invades Serbia. (*See* **Yugoslavia**)

9 NOVEMBER: The German raider *Emden* is sunk by the Australian cruiser *Sydney* after an engagement off of the Cocos Islands in the Indian Ocean.

10 NOVEMBER: The Russian army recaptures Przemysl and turns toward Hungary.

11–25 NOVEMBER: German and Russian armies, each alternately reinforced, struggle to gain an upper hand in the Battle of Lõdz. Eventually the Germans push the Russians back and capture Lõdz on 6 December. (*See* **Russian Logistics**)

14 NOVEMBER: Russian ships engage the *Goeben* in the Black Sea, inflicting serious damage, killing 115, and wounding 59 aboard the German cruiser.

19 NOVEMBER: In addition to increasing its attacks on Armenian civilians, the Turkish army arrests and kills its Armenian soldiers in mass executions.

21 NOVEMBER: RNAS pilots carry out a successful bombing mission against Friedrichshafen, Germany. (*See* **Aircraft** *and* **Strategic Bombing**)

23 NOVEMBER: The *U–18* is captured by British destroyers off Pentland Firth, between the Orkney Islands and Scotland.

2 DECEMBER: Belgrade is captured by the Austrians. (*See* **Yugoslavia**)

5 DECEMBER: Austrian and Russian armies fight at the Battle of Limanova, outside of Krakow, Poland.

8 DECEMBER: Despite his victory at Coronel, Spee's five-ship fleet is caught near the Falkland Islands and destroyed by the British, commanded by Frederick Sturdee. Low on shells, the Germans also faced a superior British fleet. The Germans lose the *Scharnhorst*, *Gneisenau*, *Nürnberg*, and *Leipzig;* only the *Dresden* escapes. (*See* **High Seas Fleet**)

14 DECEMBER: The Turkish battleship *Messudieh* is sunk in the Dardanelles, off Canakkale, by a British submarine.

15 DECEMBER: The Serbians recapture Belgrade from the Austrians. (*See* **Yugoslavia**)

16 DECEMBER: The Germans bombard Hartlepool, Whitby, and Scarborough, England, killing or wounding more than five hundred civilians.

18 DECEMBER: In an attempt to block German aid to the forces engaged in Arras, Indian troops are sent against the German lines in the Battle of Givenchy. They capture two trenches but are pushed back by German counterattacks. On the following day the Germans retake, then lose, the town to a British counterattack. When the battle is over, the

combatants are essentially in the same positions in which they had started, with the exception of having suffered nearly six thousand combined dead. (*See* **Trench Warfare**)

20 DECEMBER: Former German chancellor von Bülow travels to Rome to try to keep the Italians neutral by offering some territorial concessions. A similar mission is sent to Vienna to see if the Austrians will likewise placate the Italians.

21 DECEMBER: Dover, England, is attacked by German seaplanes, although the bombs land in the sea. A more successful bombing run is carried out by the same plane four nights later. (*See* **Aircraft** *and* **Strategic Bombing**)

21 DECEMBER: The Ottoman Third Army attacks the Russians in the Caucasus Mountains.

25 DECEMBER: An unofficial truce is established across no-man's-land in France. Lasting in some cases for several days, but opposed by the commanders, the truce allows enemy troops to talk with each other, trade food and souvenirs, and play sports during the lull. (*See* **Trench Warfare**)

25 DECEMBER: British seaplanes, launched from tenders in the North Sea, attack Cuxhaven, a German seaport on the mouth of the Elbe River. The bombing achieves little success, although it boosts the morale of the British. (*See* **Aircraft** *and* **Strategic Bombing**)

25 DECEMBER: The French battleship *Jean Bart* is sunk by an Austrian submarine in the Straits of Otranto.

25 DECEMBER: British colonel Ernest Swinton suggests to Secretary of State for War Horatio Kitchener that the British develop a tank.

29 DECEMBER: The Russians counterattack near Kars in northeastern Turkey in the Battle of Sarikamish. The Turkish army is forced to surrender on 2 January 1915; only 20 percent of the nearly one-hundred-thousand-man Turkish army survives, with many of the deaths caused by freezing. (*See* **Russian Logistics**)

1915

1 JANUARY: The HMS *Formidable* is sunk in the English Channel. More than five hundred sailors lose their lives.

3 JANUARY: Gas-filled artillery shells are fired by the Germans on Russian positions along the Rawka River near Warsaw, Poland. The gas is a nonlethal tear-producing chemical.

10 JANUARY: American women's rights activists and social reformers Jane Addams and Carrie Chapman Catt organize the Woman's Peace Party.

14 JANUARY: South African leader Louis Botha captures Swakopmund on the Orange River and puts down an Afrikaner revolt. By 9 July 1915, Botha has defeated German interests in South-West Africa. (*See* **End of Imperialism**)

15 JANUARY: The French lose a submarine, the *Saphir,* in an attempt to break through the Dardanelles.

24 JANUARY: Beatty commands an English fleet at the Battle of Dogger Bank. The German cruiser *Blücher* is sunk; the HMS *Lion* is damaged. (*See* **High Seas Fleet**)

3 FEBRUARY: Fifteen thousand Turkish troops cross the Sinai Peninsula and attack the Suez Canal, but they are defeated by Allied defenders.

18 FEBRUARY: The German submarine blockade of England begins, though it was officially announced on 4 February. (*See* **Convoys**)

19 FEBRUARY: Allied naval forces bombard and send raiding parties against Turkish forts in the Dardanelles. These assaults continue into March.

19–20 FEBRUARY: German airships bomb Kings Lynn and Great Yarmouth, in the English province of Norfolk, during a night attack. (*See* **Aircraft** *and* **Strategic Bombing**)

9 MARCH: The Austrians agree to cede Trentino to Italy, but only after the war is finished, which angers the Italians.

9–10 MARCH: The Germans attempt to push the Russians out of East Prussia.

10 MARCH: The British carry out their first aerial attack on enemy installations by bombing a railyard and enemy headquarters in France. (*See* **Aircraft** *and* **Strategic Bombing**)

10–15 MARCH: Sixty thousand British and Indian troops assault and take German lines at the Battle of Neuve Chappelle, forcing a wide breach in the front. The British halt their advance, however, and the Germans recover. A counterattack on 12 March results in high casualties for the Germans.

14 MARCH: The *Dresden* is caught and forced to be scuttled by the British fleet about four hundred miles off the coast of Chile, near the Juan Fernandez Islands.

18 MARCH: The *U–29,* with Captain Weddigen aboard, is rammed and sunk off Pentland Firth by HMS *Dreadnought.*

18 MARCH: A combined French and British fleet suffers major damage while trying to open the Dardanelles. Most of the ships are sunk by mines. The French lose the battleship *Bouvet;* the English, the *Irresistible.*

Other battleships are damaged and have to retire for repairs.

22 MARCH: Russian troops recapture Przemysl and move to face the Austrians in the Carpathian Mountains. (*See* **Russian Logistics**)

28 MARCH: The SS *Falaba*, a passenger ship, is sunk by the *U–28;* an American traveler, Leon Thrasher, is killed in the attack.

2–25 APRIL: A combined Austrian and German force pushes the Russians out of the Carpathian Mountains.

22 APRIL–25 MAY: The Second Battle of Ypres ends in a stalemate. During the engagement the Germans employ poisonous gases (chlorine gas) against enemy troops for the first time. The Allies use wet cloths across their faces to counter the effect of the gas and hold their lines. The Germans lose more than thirty-five thousand men; the Allies, twice that number. The Germans will later employ other gases, including phosgene and mustard, in the war. (*See* **Ypres**)

25 APRIL: Thirty-five thousand British soldiers and seventeen thousand Anzacs (members of the Australian and New Zealand Army Corps) land at Gallipoli, a peninsula jutting out between the Aegean Sea and the Dardanelles. The Anzacs immediately encounter a Turkish force that pins them down along the coastline. More than two thousand soldiers die on the first day. Within two weeks, while making little advance, the Allies lose one-third of their strength.

26 APRIL: Italian leaders who favor intervention on the side of the Allies gain the upper hand and join a secret pact in London (with England, France, and Russia) that promises to obtain for Italy many territorial and colonial additions should the Allies win.

27 APRIL: The French cruiser *Léon Gambetta* is sunk in the Adriatic Sea by an Austrian submarine performing a submerged night attack. More than six hundred sailors perish.

28 APRIL: Austrian and German troops advance into Galicia.

1 MAY: The *Gulflight* is sunk, and two Americans are killed in a U-boat attack in the Atlantic Ocean.

2 MAY: German and Austro-Hungarian troops attack the Russians in Poland. Centered around the cities of Gorlice and Tarnów, the assault catches the Russians by surprise and forces them to retreat, beginning a four-month withdrawal that costs them nearly two million casualties, control of Poland, valuable military stocks, and removal of their commander, Grand Duke Nicholas. (*See* **Russian Logistics**)

7 MAY: The Cunard passenger liner *Lusitania*, passing through the Irish Sea, is torpedoed by the *U–20*. The ship sinks with the loss of 1,198 lives, including 128 U.S. citizens. The Germans claim that banned war supplies were being transported to England, and that they had warned passengers before they left New York of the danger of traveling aboard the ship; U.S. sentiment, however, is enraged against the Germans.

9 MAY: The British fail to push German troops off the high ground in the Battle of Aubers Ridge; they lose more than 11,000 men during the assault.

10 MAY: The Italians agree to a naval convention with Britain and France.

13 MAY: HMS *Goliath* is torpedoed and sunk off Cape Helles, Greece, by a Turkish destroyer. More than five hundred men perish.

13 MAY: President Wilson and Secretary of State William Jennings Bryan send a note of complaint to Germany about the series of U-boat attacks that have resulted in American deaths.

15 MAY: British and Indian troops suffer nearly sixteen thousand casualties in a night attack on German lines at the Battle of Festubert.

23 MAY: Italy declares war on Austria-Hungary. Germany severs diplomatic relations with Italy.

24 MAY: The Allies send a diplomatic note to Turkey, holding it responsible for massacres of Armenian citizens. Since the beginning of the year, hundreds of thousands of Armenians had been arrested, raped, killed, or deported. Many of the people deported are sent to the Syrian desert. Hundreds of Armenian villages and businesses are obliterated. The warning, however, does not stop the atrocities.

25 MAY: The battleship HMS *Triumph* is sunk in the Mediterranean Sea by the *U–21*.

27 MAY: While serving in the Dardanelles, the battleship HMS *Majestic* is sunk by the *U–21*.

31 MAY–1 JUNE: A German zeppelin drops bombs and grenades on London, the first such raid on the capital. (*See* **Aircraft and Strategic Bombing**)

6–7 JUNE: A German zeppelin attacks the English towns of Hull and Grimsby. Twenty-four civilians are killed. (*See* **Aircraft and Strategic Bombing**)

7 JUNE: A zeppelin is shot down over Ghent by a British fighter. (*See* **Aircraft and Strategic Bombing**)

29 JUNE–7 JULY: The Italians and Austrians fight the Battle of the Isonzo (the first of eleven such engagements that bear the same name). The opposing sides pushed each other back and forth across a sixty-mile front in northeastern Italy, seldom more than ten miles in either direction.

4 JULY: The Germans make an official protest to the Turkish government about the atrocities carried out against the Armenian population. Their entreaty is ignored.

9 JULY: German forces in Southwest Africa surrender to Allied forces.

11 JULY: The German raider *Königsberg,* which had been forced to stay in port for eight months, is destroyed by British naval fire in the Rufiji River in East Africa.

18 JULY–10 AUGUST: The Second Battle of the Isonzo is fought.

21 JULY: President Wilson directs his cabinet to begin preparations for possible participation in the war. (*See* **U.S. Entry**)

24 JULY: British troops, led by John Nixon, capture Nasiriya in Mesopotamia (modern Iraq) from Turkish forces. The British army moves northward along the Euphrates River.

5 AUGUST: The Germans enter Warsaw, while their allies, the Austrians, capture Ivangorod (Deblen) in eastern Poland.

8 AUGUST: A British landing on the Gallipoli Peninsula, in an attempt to control the Dardanelles, ends in a failure in the Battle of Suvla Bay.

12 AUGUST: The first torpedo attack from an airplane occurs when a British seaplane hits a Turkish merchant vessel in the Sea of Marmara. (*See* **Aircraft**)

18 AUGUST: *The New York Times* reports on the Armenian massacres.

19 AUGUST: The White Star liner *Arabic* is sunk off the coast of southern Ireland by the *U–24.* Forty-four people die, including two Americans.

19 AUGUST: British jurist, former ambassador to the United States, and member of the International Court of Justice, Lord James Bryce reports that more than five hundred thousand Armenians have been massacred in Turkey.

30 AUGUST: In order to placate the Americans, the Germans pull back from the policy of unannounced U-boat attacks.

1 SEPTEMBER: The Germans pledge not to attack unarmed passenger ships.

21 SEPTEMBER: British and French troops land in Macedonia.

25–28 SEPTEMBER: As part of a planned strategy to break the German lines in three places, the British engage the Germans at the Battle of Loos. On the first day, a British gas attack is blown back upon their own troops, slowing their advance and leading to high casualties against concentrated German machine-gun fire. On the second day, several British attacks are repelled, with high casualties. The two concurrent attacks, against Artois and Champagne, also fail and are completed by 8 October. The British suffer more than sixty thousand casualties. (*See* **British Strategy**)

25–28 SEPTEMBER: British and Indian troops, fighting in 120-degree heat, assault Turkish lines and capture the city of Kut-al-Amara. The Turks withdraw and set up defensive lines nearly four hundred miles to the north at Ctesiphon, the site of an ancient city located approximately halfway between Baghdad and Kut.

29 SEPTEMBER: The French take Vimy Ridge.

OCTOBER: Americans raise money to aid Armenian deportees. Reports claim that as many as eight hundred thousand Armenians have been killed. The deportations and murders, however, continue.

3–5 OCTOBER: British and French forces land at Salonika, Greece. (*See* **Salonika**)

8–9 OCTOBER: The Austrians capture Belgrade. (*See* **Yugoslavia**)

11 OCTOBER: The Bulgarians invade Serbia. (*See* **Yugoslavia**)

14 OCTOBER: The Allies declare war on Bulgaria.

18 OCTOBER–3 NOVEMBER: Third Battle of the Isonzo

10 NOVEMBER–10 DECEMBER: Fourth Battle of the Isonzo

22 NOVEMBER–3 DECEMBER: Nixon's army, as it advances toward Baghdad, attacks Turkish lines defending Ctesiphon. Although they initially push back the Turks, who lose nearly ten thousand men, the British are forced to withdraw to Kut, as they suffer nearly five thousand casualties, including more than half of one Indian division. Poor planning and inefficient medical preparation hurts British morale and prestige. The Turks bottle up the British at Kut and harass their lines during December.

4 DECEMBER: The *Oskar II,* a ship carrying peace activists from the United States, leaves the port of Hoboken, New Jersey, for a trip to Europe. Financed by American industrialist and peace activist Henry Ford, the group hopes to sponsor a peace conference to end the conflict. The ship arrives in Stockholm, and a conference is arranged; however, no representatives from the warring nations attend.

19 DECEMBER: General Douglas Haig is appointed commander of the BEF, replacing John French. (*See* **BEF Command Structure**)

20 DECEMBER: The withdrawal of Allied troops from Gallipoli is completed. The British suffer 33,512 killed, 7,636 missing, and 78,000 wounded, while the Anzacs lose 8,000 killed and 18,000 wounded in the attempt to capture the peninsula.

31 DECEMBER: By this time, a Jewish underground in Palestine, called the Nili, is formed to aid the British in the battle against the Turks in the Middle East. The British utilize their intelligence and espionage but are wary of their motives.

1916

JANUARY: The British Secret Service Bureau becomes MI5, overseeing counterespionage efforts.

1 JANUARY: Yaunde (Cameroon) is captured from the Germans by Allied forces. By 18 February all German troops in Cameroon have surrendered to the Allies. (*See* **End of Imperialism**)

6-7 JANUARY: A British relief force, moving up the Euphrates to help embattled troops at Kut, are defeated by the Turks at Sheikh Sa'ad. More than four thousand Allied soldiers are killed. Another attempt to relieve the troops at Kut is defeated on 13 January.

31 JANUARY-1 FEBRUARY: During the night a large force of German airships raid England, but they fall short of hitting their designated target, Liverpool. Nearly four hundred bombs are dropped; seventy civilians are killed. (*See* **Aircraft** and **Strategic Bombing**)

21 FEBRUARY: The German Fifth Army, led by General Falkenhayn, assaults the fortress at Verdun, an important symbolic marker for the French. The Germans shell the area for nearly a full day prior to their assault. The Battle for Verdun lasts until December 1916. (*See* **Verdun**)

21 FEBRUARY: The Germans inform the Americans that armed merchantmen can be sunk because they will be considered navy vessels. (*See* **Q-ships**)

25 FEBRUARY: The French fort at Douaumont falls to the Germans. General Philippe Pétain takes over the defense of Verdun. (*See* **Verdun**)

26 FEBRUARY: The French cruiser *Provence*, sailing off the coast of Kithria Island, Greece, is sunk by the *U-35*.

27 FEBRUARY: President Wilson begins a national tour to promote military preparedness. (*See* **U.S. Entry**)

9 MARCH: Germany declares war on Portugal.

9 MARCH: A group of Mexican bandits, led by Pancho Villa, cross the United States-Mexico border and raid Columbus, Mexico.

18 MARCH-14 APRIL: The Russian Second Army goes on the offensive east of Vilna (Vilnius), Lithuania, but it loses nearly one hundred thousand men at the Battle of Lake Naroch, which stalls the advance.

24 MARCH: More Americans perish because of the submarine war, this time aboard the French passenger liner *Sussex*, which is sunk in the English Channel.

9-14 APRIL: A five-day barrage, launched by more than 2,500 British artillery pieces, rains down on German positions at Vimy, but it fails to dislodge the enemy. A gas attack, followed by a Canadian advance, allows Allied troops to capture the ridge with few casualties. (*See* **Verdun**)

29 APRIL: British and Indian forces at Kut surrender to the Turks. More than thirteen thousand men are taken captive in one of the worst defeats suffered by British arms; many prisoners of war are killed by the Turks or die on forced marches. During this battle the defenders are resupplied by air drops from the RFC and the RNAS.

10 MAY: The Germans promise to back off unrestricted submarine warfare.

29 MAY: The French are pushed off Le Mort Homme, a hill overlooking the town of Verdun. (*See* **Verdun**)

31 MAY: The German High Seas Fleet and British Grand Fleet face each other in the North Sea at the Battle of Jutland. German admiral Reinhard Scheer is tasked with destroying the English fleet, commanded by John Jellicoe. The British had broken German naval codes and knew of their plans. In the following battle, which many historians judge a draw, the British lose the *Indefatigable, Invincible,* and *Queen Mary,* as well as four cruisers and eight destroyers; the Germans lose the *Derfflinger,* four cruisers, and five destroyers, while the *Seydiltz* is badly damaged. The High Seas Fleet retires to port and never again puts to sea to engage the Grand Fleet. (*See* **High Seas Fleet**)

2-13 JUNE: Canadian troops fight at the Battle of Mount Sorrel. The highest-ranking Canadian soldier to die in the war, a major general, perishes during the engagement.

3 JUNE: The American Board of Commissioners for Foreign Missions issues a report on the Armenian massacres.

3 JUNE: The U.S. Congress passes the National Defense Act, raising the size of the army to 175,000 men and the National Guard to 450,000 men. (*See* **U.S. Entry**)

4 JUNE: A large Russian offensive, with more than forty divisions led by Aleksey Alek-

seyevich Brusilov, invades Galicia and attacks Austro-Hungarian forces, pushing them rearward for approximately sixty miles. The Germans respond by pulling troops away from their assaults on Verdun. (See **Brusilov Offensive** and **Russian Logistics**)

5 JUNE: Lord Kitchener dies at sea near the Orkney Islands, off the northeast coast of Scotland. He is on a mission to confer with the Russians when his ship, the cruiser *Hampshire*, is sunk by a German U-boat.

7 JUNE: Fort Vaux, which is just three miles outside of Verdun, falls to the Germans. (See **Verdun**)

22 JUNE: The Germans renew their attacks on Verdun, trying to capture two bridges leading to the city, but they do not achieve any success. More than seven hundred thousand men, from both sides, die during the contest to control Verdun. (See **Verdun**)

1 JULY: Originally planned to commence on 29 June, and designed to take pressure off the French at Verdun, the Battle of the Somme begins late because of poor visibility for pilots to direct artillery strikes. British and French divisions attack, with the French achieving a greater level of surprise. British losses are high in the initial assaults; they lose nearly 1,000 officers and more than 18,000 enlisted men. South African and Australian troops also participate in the battle. On 14 July a surprise German night counterattack recaptures lost territory and seals a gap in their lines. The Battle for the Somme lasts until 19 November. More than 1.2 million men from both sides lose their lives in this engagement. (See **Verdun**)

3 JULY: A synchronized propeller/machine gun is introduced on British aircraft. (See **Aircraft**)

7 JULY: British forces in Africa capture Tanga from the Germans as well as gain control of Lake Tanganyika. (See **End of Imperialism**)

30 JULY: Munitions and dynamite stored in barges and railcars are blown up in a freight terminal at Black Tom Island, south of the Statue of Liberty in New York harbor, allegedly by German agents. The shock from the blast is said to be felt as far away as Philadelphia. Facilities at nearby Ellis Island suffer $400,000 in damage.

1 AUGUST: The Italians are heavily involved along the Isonzo Front.

3 AUGUST: British and Turkish forces clash at the Battle of Rumani in Egypt. The Turks make an advance on the Suez Canal, which was blunted by British and Australian troops, who build false trenches and utilize cavalry attacks. (See **Cavalry**)

6–9 AUGUST: The Italians take the town of Gorizia from the Austro-Hungarians.

15 AUGUST: Bitlis, a town in eastern Turkey, is captured from the Russians by the Turkish army. The Russians will recapture the town nine days later.

15 AUGUST: Bagamoyo, in German East Africa, falls to the British.

27 AUGUST: Hindenburg and Ludendorff are given command of the German armies.

28 AUGUST: Romania declares war on Austria; Italy declares war on Germany; Germany declares war on Romania the following day.

2–3 SEPTEMBER: A zeppelin attack on England results in little damage, but the Germans lose a zeppelin to English aircraft. (See **Aircraft** and **Strategic Bombing**)

4 SEPTEMBER: Dar es Salaam falls to the English.

15 SEPTEMBER: Twenty-four British, Canadian, and Scottish tanks are employed during the Battle of the Somme, which is their first such use in combat.

18 SEPTEMBER: Florina, in Macedonia, is captured by the British.

25 SEPTEMBER: The British Fourth Army, including New Zealand troops, attacks German lines around the towns of Morval and Les Beoufs, France. The army succeeds in taking several miles of trenches. (See **Trench Warfare** and **Verdun**)

26–28 SEPTEMBER: Four divisions of British troops attack the strong German entrenchments along Thiepval Ridge. They suffer heavy casualties in the assaults. German soldiers in the trenches reportedly taunt their enemy as they advance. (See **Trench Warfare** and **Verdun**)

4 OCTOBER: The Austrians and Germans begin major incursions, which will last until December, into Romania.

8–9 OCTOBER: President Wilson proclaims two "Armenian Relief Days."

10 OCTOBER: The Eighth Battle of the Isonzo is fought.

24 OCTOBER: The French counterattack at Verdun, pushing back the Germans, who are weakened by reductions of their forces because of manpower needs on the Eastern Front. Fort Douaumont is recaptured by the Allies. (See **Verdun**)

26 OCTOBER: A German destroyer raids into the Dover Straits.

5 NOVEMBER: The Germans and Austrians proclaim the creation of the kingdom of Poland. Józef Piłsudski, who led an army of ten thousand Poles against the Russians, is made the

head of a military commission but is later imprisoned when he holds back his troops after the Germans refuse to provide assurances of independence.

1–14 NOVEMBER: The Ninth Battle of the Isonzo is fought.

7 NOVEMBER: President Wilson, a Democrat, wins reelection by defeating Republican candidate Charles Evans Hughes.

9–18 NOVEMBER: British forces attempt to dislodge German positions at the Battle of the Ancre, which ends the Somme offensive. The British capture Beaumont-Hamel.

28 NOVEMBER: German planes attack London for the first time. (*See* **Aircraft** *and* **Strategic Bombing**)

1–4 DECEMBER: German and Austrian troops defeat the Romanians at the Battle of the Argesul River. The Romanians lose Bucharest.

7 DECEMBER: David Lloyd George, the former Minister of Munitions and Secretary of State for War, becomes Prime Minister of England, replacing Herbert Asquith. Lloyd George reforms the War Cabinet.

31 DECEMBER: The Russian mystic and confidant of the royals, Grigory Rasputin, is assassinated by Russian noblemen. (*See* **Imperial Russia**)

1917

8–9 JANUARY: The British forces under Archibald Murray gain control of the Sinai from the Turks. This victory opens the war for further British attacks in the Middle East.

9 JANUARY: The Germans resume unrestricted submarine attacks on all shipping to Great Britain, although this decision is not announced until the last day of the month. (*See* **Convoys**)

FEBRUARY: The Dutch exotic dancer Margaretha Geertruida "Zelle" MacLeod, better known to history as Mata Hari, is executed by a French firing squad for allegedly spying for the Germans.

3 FEBRUARY: The United States ends diplomatic relations with Germany. (*See* **U.S. Entry**)

22–24 FEBRUARY: The British force a Turkish withdrawal from Kut.

23–27 FEBRUARY: Food riots break out in Petrograd (formerly St. Petersburg), Russia. Some of the city garrison troops mutiny and burn down government buildings. (*See* **Imperial Russia, Russian Logistics,** *and* **Russian Revolution**)

1 MARCH: The contents of the Zimmermann telegram are released to the public. This secret diplomatic note from German foreign minister Arthur Zimmermann to the Mexican government, intercepted and decoded by British intelligence, suggests that Mexico might be interested in joining Germany in opposition to the United States, should the Americans join the war on the side of the Allies. Mexico is offered the opportunity to regain territory in the continental United States that it had lost to the Americans. Sentiment in the United States rises against the Germans. (*See* **U.S. Entry**)

5 MARCH: President Wilson is sworn in for his second term in office. He won reelection largely on his promise to keep the United States out of the war.

11 MARCH: Baghdad is captured by the British.

12 MARCH: President Wilson orders that merchant ships be armed. (*See* **Convoys**)

13 MARCH: A provisional government, led by Aleksandr Kerensky, is established in Russia. (*See* **Russian Revolution**)

15 MARCH: Tsar Nicholas II abdicates. He and his family are imprisoned on 21 March. (*See* **Tsar Nicholas II** *and* **Russian Revolution**)

APRIL: Germany is hit by several work stoppages and strikes by workers upset about food shortages and inflation.

2 APRIL: President Wilson, in a speech to Congress, calls for war against Germany. (*See* **U.S. Entry**)

6 APRIL: The United States declares war on Germany; the following day the United States declares war against Austria-Hungary. (*See* **U.S. Entry**)

7 APRIL: The U.S. Navy takes control of all wireless stations in the United States. (*See* **U.S. Entry**)

9 APRIL: British and Canadian troops, including remnants from the Gallipoli campaign, participate in an assault against the Germans in the Second Battle of Arras. The Canadians distinguish themselves by capturing the Vimy Ridge.

14 APRIL: President Wilson establishes the Committee on Public Information, better known as the Creel Commission (after its chairman, newspaperman George Creel), which utilizes propaganda to increase prowar sentiment in the United States and also materials to dishearten the enemy. The board even helps change traditional Germanic words in the English language: for example, sauerkraut becomes "liberty cabbage." (*See* **U.S. Entry**)

16 APRIL: Allied troops under the command of Robert Nivelle attack the Germans, who are entrenched behind the Hindenburg Line, in what becomes known as the Second Battle of the Aisne River or Chemin des Dames offensive. The assaulting troops are slaughtered, raising the ire of French soldiers and citizens; many regiments refuse to engage the enemy. (*See* **Trench Warfare**)

20–21 APRIL: Turkey ends diplomatic relations with the United States. (*See* **U.S. Entry**)

20–21 APRIL: The destroyers HMS *Broke* and *Swift* engage a German force of twelve destroyers as they make a raid into the Dover Strait. The *Broke* rams one German ship, and hand-to-hand combat follows while the ships are engaged. The British ships are badly damaged, and the Germans lose two destroyers.

24 APRIL: U.S. secretary of the treasury William McAdoo authorizes the Liberty Loan Act to raise money by public subscription to fund wartime activities. (*See* **Allied Economics**)

24 APRIL: The first U.S. naval squadron, made up of destroyers, leaves Boston for service in the European theater.

28 APRIL: The Canadians capture the city of Arleux.

MAY: The British institute the convoy system to protect shipping crossing the Atlantic Ocean from German U-boat attacks. (*See* **Convoys**)

MAY: Wilson establishes the War Industries Board, which controls raw materials and war production; investor Bernard Baruch serves as chairman. The agency guarantees profits for manufacturers. (*See* **Allied Economics**)

15 MAY: General Pétain takes command of the French army from Nivelle and calms his mutinous army.

15 MAY: British and Italian naval vessels engage in a two-hour fight with Austrian ships in the Strait of Otranto, which connects the Adriatic Sea with the Ionian Sea. The Austrians, who had initiated the engagement by attacking barrage vessels stationed in the straits, suffer some damage to one of their cruisers, which is towed from the battle to a safe port; a British cruiser is badly damaged in a torpedo attack.

18 MAY: The Selective Service Act is passed by the U.S. Congress. Men from the age of twenty-one to thirty years of age are required to register. Nearly 10,000,000 men register, and a lottery selects around 700,000 names in the first draft. By the end of the war more than 2,800,000 men have been inducted. (*See* **U.S. Entry**)

26 MAY: The British hospital ship *Dover Castle*, carrying wounded from Malta to Gibraltar, is sunk by the *U-67* in the Mediterranean Sea.

5 JUNE: The Germans carry out a daylight air raid on Folkestone in Kent, England. (*See* **Aircraft** *and* **Strategic Bombing**)

7 JUNE: British troops, using nineteen massive underground mines detonated beneath the enemy's lines, take a stretch of heights near the town of Messines, which gives them a commanding position against German positions, at a cost of twenty-four thousand casualties.

12–18 JUNE: Tenth Battle of the Isonzo

13 JUNE: London is the target of another daylight German bombing raid. More than 160 civilians are killed. London, and other parts of England, will be repeatedly attacked in the coming months in similar raids. (*See* **Aircraft** *and* **Strategic Bombing**)

15 JUNE: The Espionage Act is passed by the U.S. Congress, outlawing espionage carried out by agents for foreign countries.

26 JUNE: U.S. troops arrive at St. Nazaire, France. The American Expeditionary Force (AEF) is commanded by John Pershing. Only four divisions arrive in France during the year. When African American divisions land, Pershing detaches them to the French, who supply them with arms and helmets and send them into battle. (*See* **African Americans**)

27 JUNE: The Allies help form a new government in Greece, led by Prime Minister Eleuthérios Venizélos. Greece declares war on Germany.

1 JULY: The Second Brusilov offensive begins as Russians attack Austrian forces in Galicia. The Russians experience good initial results but then are pushed back by Austrian counterattacks by the end of the month. (*See* **Brusilov Offensive**)

2 JULY: Pershing asks for a million-man army, later moving the target figure to three million.

11 JULY: Kerensky is named prime minister of Russia.

31 JULY–10 NOVEMBER: The Third Battle of Ypres (also known as the Battle of Passchendaele) is fought. Over extremely soggy and muddy territory, which has been churned up by constant bombardment, the British army charges into machine-gun fire and poisonous gas attacks from hardened defensive positions, and the attackers suffer severe casualties. Some of the troops actually drown in the mud. Canadian troops succeed in taking the town of Passchendaele. A total, from both sides, of nearly five hundred thousand men become casualties. (*See* **Ypres**)

2 AUGUST: British pilot E. H. Dunning conducts the first landing on a moving aircraft carrier, HMS *Furious,* which is a converted

cruiser. Dunning dies five days later attempting to land on the ship. (*See* **Aircraft**)

10 AUGUST: President Wilson issues an executive order creating the Food Administration. The agency, headed by Herbert Hoover, is tasked with assuring supply and conservation of food, supervising transportation, and preventing monopolies and hoarding. (*See* **Allied Economics**)

14 AUGUST: China declares war on Germany and Austria-Hungary.

15–16 AUGUST: Mustard gas is used by the Germans against the Canadians, who are attacking Hill 70, north of Lens. The Canadians beat back three days of counterattacks (18–20 August).

16–18 AUGUST: British and Irish troops, weary from several weeks of constant shelling and rainy weather, engage the Germans in heavy fighting at the Battle of Langemarck. The Allied troops suffer severe losses as soldiers get bogged in the mire and are raked by concentrated enemy fire. (*See* **Shell Shock**)

18 AUGUST–20 SEPTEMBER: Italy attacks on the Isonzo-Carso front in the Eleventh Battle of the Isonzo.

23 AUGUST: Racial tension explodes in Texas when approximately one hundred African American troops, stationed at Camp Logan, after being provoked by citizens of Houston, march on the town and open fire on the police station, killing sixteen whites and wounding twelve. Sixty-four men are court-martialed: forty-two are given life sentences, and thirteen are condemned to die. The condemned are executed on 11 December. (*See* **African Americans**)

30 AUGUST: The American Field Service (AFS), an ambulance corps staffed mostly by young American college students who volunteer to serve in Europe, is merged with the U.S. Army. More than 2,500 drivers serve in the AFS; more than 150 perish. Other organizations, including the American Red Cross, supply drivers. Many of these volunteers become famous later as writers, including John Dos Passos, Ernest Hemingway, W. Somerset Maugham, and E. E. Cummings. (*See* **Cultural Watershed**)

1 SEPTEMBER: The Germans begin an offensive on the Eastern Front and capture Riga, Latvia (3 September).

2–30 SEPTEMBER: German air raids are carried out on London and southeast England. (*See* **Aircraft** and **Strategic Bombing**)

20 SEPTEMBER: British and Anzac troops in the Second and Fifth Armies engage the Germans in the Battle of Menin Road. The Allied price for capturing roughly five square miles of territory is twenty-one thousand casualties.

26 SEPTEMBER–3 OCTOBER: In an attempt to gain momentum on the victories earned at the Battle of Menin Road, the Allies continue their attack, with much success, against German lines at the Battle of Polygon Wood.

3 OCTOBER: The U.S. Congress passes the War Revenue Act, which increases revenues from $809 million in 1917 to $3.6 billion in 1918.

4 OCTOBER: Anzac troops attack German trenches and pillboxes at Broodseinde and capture more than five thousand enemy soldiers. (*See* **Trench Warfare**)

14 OCTOBER: Six hundred thirty-nine African American army officers graduate from officer training school and are commissioned at Fort Dodge, Des Moines, Iowa. (*See* **African Americans**)

15 OCTOBER: The destroyer USS *Cassin* is torpedoed by the *U–105* off the coast of Ireland, but there is only one casualty.

15–18 OCTOBER: German troops defeat the Allies at the battle of Mahiwa. They then begin to invade Portuguese territory in East Africa along the Zambezi River.

24 OCTOBER–12 NOVEMBER: Austrian-German attacks break through Italian defenses, held by the Second Army, at Caporetto, Austria. The Italians, who lose nearly three hundred thousand men, are pushed back to the Piave River.

2 NOVEMBER: British foreign secretary Arthur Balfour issues a declaration that Great Britain will support the establishment of a homeland for Jews in Palestine.

3 NOVEMBER: U.S. troops engage the enemy for the first time in trench warfare along the Rhine-Marne Canal. Three soldiers are killed and eleven are captured. (*See* **Trench Warfare**)

6 NOVEMBER: Passchendaele is captured by Canadian troops.

6 NOVEMBER: The Bolsheviks, led by Vladimir Lenin, depose the provisional government in Russia. The new government includes Leon Trotsky as commissar for foreign affairs and Joseph Stalin as commissar for national minorities. (*See* **Russian Revolution**)

7 NOVEMBER: Gaza is taken by the British from the Turks.

13 NOVEMBER: The U.S. Army Nurses Corps accepts eighteen black nurses on an "experimental" basis. (*See* **African Americans**)

15 NOVEMBER: Georges Clémenceau again becomes the premier of France. (*See* **European Leadership**)

17 NOVEMBER: Jaffa, northwest of Jerusalem, is captured by the British.

20 NOVEMBER: The British mass more than three hundred tanks to spearhead an infantry attack against German lines. The assault, called the Battle of Cambrai, proves successful, and deep breaches are punched through German positions, but the British fail to take advantage of the situation. Aircraft are used to bomb advance positions.

29 NOVEMBER: The U.S. War Department authorizes the creation of the first large all-black unit, the 92nd Division. (*See* **African Americans**)

6 DECEMBER: U.S. warships join the Allied fleet off the northern coast of Scotland. The destroyer USS *Jacob Jones* is torpedoed and sunk by the *U-53*, east of Start Point, England; sixty-four sailors are killed.

6 DECEMBER: After a collision with the Belgian "relief" ship *Imo*, the French munitions transport *Mont Blanc*, catches fire and explodes in Halifax harbor. The blast causes 1,600 deaths and wounds an additional 9,000 people. An entire Indian village situated up a nearby river is wiped out by a wave caused by the explosion, and pieces of the bulkhead are blown several miles inshore.

9 DECEMBER: The British Egyptian Expeditionary Force, led by Edmund Allenby, captures Jerusalem from the Ottoman Empire.

15 DECEMBER: Peace negotiations between Russia and Germany at Brest-Litovsk result in an armistice between the two countries, though the sides clash over terms.

1918

1 JANUARY: The 369th Infantry, the first African American combat unit in France, arrives. (*See* **African Americans**)

4 JANUARY: The British hospital ship *Rewa* is sunk in the Bristol Channel; three lives are lost.

8 JANUARY: President Wilson announces his Fourteen Points, a plan for establishing a lasting peace in Europe, to a joint session of Congress. His plan calls for open diplomacy among nations, self-determination of nationalities, freedom of the seas, free trade, and a reduction of armaments. Foreign troops are to leave Russia, France, Belgium, Turkey, the Balkans, and several other occupied regions. He also calls for a general association of nations to guarantee the independence and territorial integrity of all countries. (*See* **League of Nations**)

20 JANUARY: After leaving port and sinking two British monitors, the *Goeben* hits several mines and is forced to run aground. The cruiser is later pulled off the shoal and returns to port but is out of commission for the rest of the war. The *Breslau* hits five mines and sinks, with the loss of most of its crew, in the Dardanelles.

3 MARCH: The Treaty of Brest-Litovsk is signed by Russia and the Central Powers. Russia is out of the war and is forced to cede lands in the Baltic, Poland, and Ukraine to the Germans. (*See* **Russian Revolution**)

4 MARCH: British marines land at Murmansk, a Russian city on the Barents Sea, beginning an occupation that lasts until 1920. The British fear that the Finns, who were allied with the Germans, might capture large stores of arms in the city. Trotsky also invites the British in, as he hopes to gain arms for his Red Army.

21 MARCH: With Russia out of the war, Ludendorff orders an offensive, featuring 190 divisions, against the Allies in a bid to capture the city of Amiens. The British Fifth Army is destroyed, but 2 Australian divisions blunt the German attack.

22 MARCH: The Germans reach the Somme. Péronne is lost; the following day, Albert and Noyon are captured. On 27 March the Germans are checked at the Scarpe River. French counterattacks on the next day hold Germans in the Somme region. The final German offensive is checked east of Villers-Bretonneux on 4–5 April by Australian troops.

26 MARCH: The Allies hold an emergency conference at Doullens to discuss the most recent attack, to plan strategy, and to form an oversight council. General Foch is appointed to coordinate actions of the Allies on the Western Front. Foch convinces Pershing to allow the use of American troops. (*See* **Foch**)

APRIL: The assassin Princip dies of tuberculosis at Theresienstadt, Bohemia.

1 APRIL: The Royal Air Force (RAF) is created, along with a women's auxiliary.

2 APRIL: The Germans attack Lys, Arras, and Aisne in a Spring Offensive. Although initially successful, with more than 160,000 casualties suffered, the Germans halt their advance in June.

9 APRIL: The Germans attack in Belgium and capture Bailleul on 15 April; they take Wytschaete and Meteren on 16 April, and Kemmel and Dranoutre on 17 April.

14 APRIL: General Foch is appointed commander in chief of all Allied armies in France. (*See* **Foch**)

15 APRIL: Bailleul is captured by the Germans.

17–19 APRIL: German counterattacks recapture lost ground around Kemmel.

21 APRIL: German fighter ace Manfred von Richthofen, "The Red Baron," credited with downing eighty enemy airplanes, is killed when his aircraft is shot down in action over France. (*See* **Aircraft**)

22–23 APRIL: The British raid Zeebrugge, a coastal city that defends a canal from Bruges to the North Sea, which provides greater access to German U-boats to the North Sea. HMS *Vindictive* lands a raiding party to occupy the Germans, while a submarine torpedoes the locks. Three concrete-filled warships are then sunk in the harbor to block U-boat traffic.

23 APRIL: Heavy German attacks help gain the town of Villers-Bretonneux.

23 APRIL: The USS *Stewart* attacks a German U-boat off the coast of France. The submarine is under assault by French air and sea forces, and the *Stewart* comes alongside and drops depth charges; although initially listed as a kill, the *U–108* survives the attack.

1 MAY: U.S. troops join the front line at Amiens. (*See* **American Impact**)

7 MAY: The Peace of Bucharest ends hostilities between the Central Powers and Romania.

16 MAY: The U.S. Espionage Act is amended to include the outlawing of sedition acts, including prohibitions on anyone who would "wilfully utter, print, write, or publish any disloyal, profane, scurrilous, or abusive language about the form of government of the United States, or the Constitution of the United States, or the military or naval forces of the United States, or the flag." (*See* **U.S. Entry**)

23 MAY: German artillery shells Paris.

27 MAY–2 JUNE: The Germans attack along the Aisne River.

28 MAY: An Armenian republic is declared.

28 MAY: U.S. troops, under French control, engage in a limited counterattack—their first offensive action—on German positions at Cantigny. (*See* **U.S. Entry**)

29 MAY: The French are driven back across Aisne, and the Germans capture Soissons.

30 MAY: The Germans reach the Marne River.

31 MAY: The first of three American troop transports is sunk by German submarines. The USS *President Lincoln* is torpedoed six hundred miles off the French coast, with the loss of twenty-six. One month later, on 1 July, the USS *Covington* is sunk off Brest, France, with the loss of six. On 5 September the *Mount Vernon* is sunk, with the loss of thirty-six lives, off the coast of France.

2–4 JUNE: U.S. troops stop a German advance at the Battle of Chateau-Thierry. (*See* **American Impact** *and* **U.S. Entry**)

6–24 JUNE: U.S. Marines, attached to the Second Division of the AEF, attack entrenched German positions in Belleau Wood (11–12 June), northwest of Chateau-Thierry. After nearly two weeks of fighting and nearly eight thousand casualties, the Americans succeed in capturing the territory. (*See* **American Impact, Trench Warfare,** *and* **U.S. Entry**)

9–13 JUNE: The Germans attack toward Compiègne in the Gneisenau offensive.

11 JUNE: The German advance is checked.

15–23 JUNE: The Austro-Hungarians suffer heavy casualties during attacks on the Italians along the Piave River and are forced to withdraw.

27 JUNE: The Canadian hospital ship *Llandovery Castle* is sunk without warning by the *U–86* near Fastnet, with the loss of 234 lives. The ship is sailing from Halifax to Liverpool; the Germans claim that U.S. pilots and ammunition are being ferried to Europe. The submarine crew also fires upon the lifeboats. Among the dead are 14 female Canadian nurses. Two of the German officers, but not the captain, who cannot be found, are tried for war crimes and given four-year prison sentences after the war ends.

4 JULY: Anzac and American troops take ground from the Germans at Hamel. (*See* **American Impact**)

15 JULY: The Second Battle of the Marne begins with a final German attack. More than eighty-five thousand U.S. troops fight alongside French contingents. (*See* **American Impact**)

16 JULY: Tsar Nicholas and his family are executed by their Bolshevik guards at Yekaterinburg. (*See* **Tsar Nicholas II**)

18 JULY: A massive Allied counterattack begins southwest of the Marne; by 22 July the Germans are in retreat. The first major American offensive, with around 250,000 troops, attacks German positions at Soissons and pushes the enemy out of the region. (*See* **American Impact**)

1 AUGUST: The Allied Expeditionary Force lands at Avkhangelsk, Russia, and captures the city from its defenders. The army is composed of troops from fourteen allied countries, including the United States. More than 8,000 U.S. troops remain on Russian soil until April 1920.

2 AUGUST: The French retake Soissons.

3 AUGUST: Allied expeditionary soldiers, including Japanese troops, land at Vladivostok. (*See* **Japan**)

6-12 AUGUST: A massive Allied attack, supported by more than two thousand artillery guns and two hundred tanks, strikes the Germans along a fifteen-mile front.

8 AUGUST: A British attack, led by five hundred tanks, smashes into German lines along the Somme River. German troops become disillusioned and mutinous during the battle. (*See* **German Collapse**)

9-16 AUGUST: The French advance and capture Lassigny.

17-20 AUGUST: The French drive the Germans from the Aisne Heights.

18 AUGUST: The German retreat from Ancre begins.

21-31 AUGUST: British troops push back German lines in the Second Battle of Bapaume. They recapture Albert on 22 August, Bapaume on 29 August, and Péronne on 30 August. Nearly thirty-five thousand German soldiers are captured. (*See* **German Collapse**)

26 AUGUST-3 SEPTEMBER: British and German troops struggle for the Hindenburg Line in the Battle of the Scarpe. On 31 August the British capture Bellecourt.

26 AUGUST: The British capture Monchy-le-Preux.

3-9 SEPTEMBER : The Germans are forced to fall back behind the Hindenburg Line. (*See* **German Collapse**)

6 SEPTEMBER: American troops reach the Aisne River.

12-16 SEPTEMBER: A massive U.S. attack, supported by the French and more than 1,400 airplanes, commences on German lines around St. Mihiel. The entire salient quickly collapses, and the Germans are expelled. (*See* **Aircraft** *and* **German Collapse**)

14 SEPTEMBER: The Germans retreat to an area between Meuse and Moselle. (*See* **German Collapse**)

19-30 SEPTEMBER: The British begin an offensive in Palestine and Syria. They are aided by an Armenian legion. The Turkish armies are defeated and Damascus is captured on 1 October.

26 SEPTEMBER: The U.S. Coast Guard cutter *Tampa* is sunk in the Bristol Channel, probably by a U-boat attack, with the loss of its complete crew—118 men are killed.

26-29 SEPTEMBER: The U.S. First Army attacks the German Fifth Army in the Argonne Forest. By 16 October the Germans are pushed out of the forest. More than 600,000 U.S. troops participated, losing 117,000 killed or wounded. (*See* **American Impact**)

26-30 SEPTEMBER: French troops attack German forces in the Champagne region.

26 SEPTEMBER-5 OCTOBER: British troops attack on a thirty-mile front between St. Quentin and the Sensée.

28 SEPTEMBER: British, French, and American divisions attack on the twelve-mile front, cross the St. Quentin Canal, and capture Bellecourt.

29 SEPTEMBER: Bulgaria signs an armistice with the Allies and surrenders the following day.

3 OCTOBER: The Hindenburg Line is crossed by Allied troops.

6-12 OCTOBER: During an offensive movement, the British capture Cambrai (8 October) and Le Cateau (10 October).

7 OCTOBER: Beirut is captured by the British.

9 OCTOBER: The Germans evacuate the Argonne Forest. (*See* **German Collapse**)

14 OCTOBER: Turkey makes diplomatic overtures of peace to the United States. (*See* **American Impact**)

17 OCTOBER: The Belgians enter Ostend and liberate Zeebrugge and Bruges.

21-31 OCTOBER: American and French troops are involved in fierce fighting against the Germans north of Verdun and along the Meuse River.

24-30 OCTOBER: Italian troops attack and rout the Austro-Hungarians in the Battle of Vittorio Veneto.

25-30 OCTOBER: The Turkish army surrenders to the British in Mesopotamia.

26 OCTOBER: Ludendorff resigns after he disagrees with the German government over the acceptance of President Wilson's ideas for peace. (*See* **German Collapse**)

26 OCTOBER: Aleppo is captured by the British; 125,000 deported Armenians are saved.

27 OCTOBER: Austria-Hungary applies to the United States for an armistice.

28 OCTOBER: The Czechs and Slovaks form the independent country of Czechoslovakia.

29 OCTOBER: Yugoslavia announces its independence. (*See* **Yugoslavia**)

30 OCTOBER: The Allies sign an armistice with the Ottoman Empire, which reopens the Dardanelles and allows Allied forces onto its territory.

30 OCTOBER: Austria is declared an independent nation, and its soldiers seek an armistice with the Allies.

31 OCTOBER: A revolution breaks out in Hungary, leading to its independence as a nation.

1–11 NOVEMBER: A Franco-American attack on Forêt de Bourgogne sparks a rapid advance against the Germans.

1–11 NOVEMBER: The British advance between Sambre and Scheldt.

2 NOVEMBER: The British enter Valenciennes, clear Forêt de Mormal, and by 11 November liberate Avesnes, Maubeuge, and Mons. The Canadians are heavily involved in the capture of Valenciennes.

2 NOVEMBER: German troops begin an invasion of Rhodesia.

2 NOVEMBER: The *Surada* and *Murcia* are the last British merchant ships sunk by U-boats in the war.

3 NOVEMBER: German sailors, fearing they are to be sacrificed in a senseless attack on the enemy, mutiny at Kiel. Some mutinous activity may have been initiated as early as 28 October. (*See* **German Collapse**)

4 NOVEMBER: Hostilities between Austria-Hungary and the Allies come to an end.

4 NOVEMBER: The New Zealand Rifle Brigade scales the sixty-foot ramparts at Le Quesnoy.

6 NOVEMBER: The French enter Rethel and the Americans enter Sedan.

8 NOVEMBER: German peace delegates confer with Marshal Foch near Compiègne, France. (*See* **Foch** *and* **German Collapse**)

9 NOVEMBER: Revolts break out in Berlin. (*See* **German Collapse**)

10 NOVEMBER: Kaiser Wilhelm II abdicates and flees to Holland. Germany is proclaimed a republic, under the leadership of the socialist Friedrich Ebert. (*See* **German Collapse**)

11 NOVEMBER: A general armistice between the Allies and Germans is signed, and hostilities cease.

11 NOVEMBER: Poland is declared an independent, sovereign state. The country was devastated by the war, suffering more than one million casualties and the nearly complete destruction of its infrastructure.

21 NOVEMBER: The German Battle Fleet surrenders to the British off the Firth of Forth. (*See* **High Seas Fleet**)

1 DECEMBER: Allied troops enter Germany.

20 DECEMBER: New Zealand troops enter Cologne.

31 DECEMBER: By this time an influenza epidemic works its way around the globe, killing an estimated twenty-two million people (possibly as many as forty million), more than were killed as a result of combat in the war. The first cases in the United States are discovered among returning soldiers at Boston, and during the pandemic even the draft is suspended. More than six hundred thousand Americans die from the disease.

1919

18 JANUARY: Peace talks begin in Paris.

7 FEBRUARY: British delegates to peace talks insist that alleged war criminals be arrested and brought to trial.

14 FEBRUARY: President Wilson presents his plan for the League of Nations, a group of sovereign states who agree to pursue common policies and to submit all differences among themselves to arbitration. (*See* **League of Nations**)

21 JUNE: The German fleet, interned by the Allies in Scapa Flow, is scuttled by its own crews. (*See* **High Seas Fleet**)

28 JUNE: The Treaty of Versailles is signed, and under Article 231 Germany accepts responsibility "for causing all the loss and damage to which the Allied and Associated Governments and their nationals have been subjected as a consequence of the war imposed upon them." Germany loses substantial territory, including Alsace-Lorraine (given to France) and Posen and West Prussia (given to Poland). The region west of the Rhine and fifty kilometers east of it becomes a demilitarized zone. Danzig is declared a free port, and the French are allowed to operate the coal mines of the Saar for fifteen years. The German army is limited to a one-hundred-thousand-man force without the support of tanks, heavy artillery, and aircraft; the navy is reduced to a small coastal force. Finally, Germany is required to pay an indemnity to the Allies (estimated in 1921 at $33 billion).

AFRICAN AMERICANS

Was the position of African Americans in U.S. society improved by the war experience?

Viewpoint: Yes. Wartime service enabled African Americans to receive greater political and economic opportunities.

Viewpoint: No. World War I exacerbated racism.

The entry of the United States into the Great War had a galvanic effect on an African American community that had been increasingly marginalized and essentially regionalized since 1865. The black experience for a half century has been essentially definable as Southern, rural, and deferential. Unwanted in a northern industrial economy that drew its labor force from immigrants and whites forced from rural areas, blacks were correspondingly valued as a source of cheap labor in the South—to a point where they were frequently deterred by both legal and illegal means from leaving. Handbills describing job opportunities elsewhere had to be passed from hand to hand surreptitiously; labor recruiters operated at some risk to limb, if not to life.

Black communities nonetheless existed north of the Mason-Dixon Line—they were relatively small and were usually connected with specific work situations, such as the packing houses of Omaha and Kansas City. Large black communities were established in Chicago, New York, Detroit, and Cleveland. National mobilization changed that residential pattern by making occupational mobility virtually a patriotic duty. Blacks moved north and west, seeking job opportunities that often proved illusory or disappointing, as well as finding discrimination that usually proved all too real. Nevertheless, the Great War began processes of demographic shift and cultural transformation, from the Harlem Renaissance in New York to the earthier but no less vibrant manifestations along Twelfth Street and Vine in Kansas City.

African Americans in uniform had been similarly marginalized: they were confined to four regiments of the regular army and virtually excluded from naval service. World War I highlighted a paradox. On one hand, there were too many black men in the United States, around 10 percent of the eligible males, to be systematically excluded from war service. On the other hand, racist-fueled opinion in white society held that blacks collectively were unpromising military material and could be expected to perform effectively only under white officers. The result was a segregated army that utilized blacks overwhelmingly in labor units. Whether given fancy titles such as the "Pioneer Infantry" or just called stevedores, the soldiers carried out the same work: dig and carry.

Of far more concern to senior American Expeditionary Forces (AEF) leadership was a "social question" based on alleged French disregard for American racial customs—especially the sexual taboos. The French, while by no means as liberal as myth continues to assert, were less worried about interracial relationships and treated blacks more as equals than they were treated in the United States, which caused alarm and despondency among white generals who would have been better advised to see to the training, command, and morale of their black soldiers. The black regular units were not assigned to the AEF. Two black divisions were organized. One, comprising primarily prewar National Guard units, was parceled out by regiments to a French army starved for manpower, and these troops fought well. The other, the Ninety-second, was formed from draftees and had a high percentage of black junior officers, trained separately from their white counterparts. Institutional and personal racism characterized the experience of this division from its organization, culminating in a poor initial performance by one of its regiments that the postwar army establishment used to discredit the fighting ability of black troops and the leadership ability of black officers—canards that persisted into World War II.

Viewpoint:
Yes. Wartime service enabled African Americans to receive greater political and economic opportunities.

Historians generally view the period between World War I and the Great Depression, from 1919 to 1929, as a bleak time for African Americans. Sanctioned disenfranchisement, segregation, and lynching characterized a period described by Allen D. Grimshaw, in *Racial Violence in the United States* (1969), as one of endemic interracial violence. Despite valiant service in World War I, black Americans continued to suffer the status of second-class citizenry. When W. E. B. Du Bois commemorated the three-hundredth anniversary of the arrival of blacks on the North American continent, he lamented: "In sackcloth and ashes we commemorate this year, lest we forget a single drop of blood, a single moan of pain, a single bead of sweat. . . ."

When Du Bois wrote this passage in 1919, the civil rights legislation that ended discrimination and obstacles to voting was still more than four decades in the future. The atmosphere of fear and suspicion caused by Jim Crow laws and D. W. Griffith's epic movie *The Birth of a Nation* (1915) generated more separation and violence. In 1919 alone, there were twenty-five major race riots, two hundred Ku Klux Klan meetings across the nation, and eighty-three lynchings. All this violence led poet James Weldon Johnson to refer to that year as the red summer. These sad events, however, overshadow the fact that despite the barriers of segregation, World War I led to some positive changes to the status and plight of black Americans. Black organizations, culture, and economic opportunity grew as a result of the war and laid the groundwork for the emergence of the black movement that changed the United States in the twentieth century.

World War I initiated modest, yet symbolically important, changes in the status of blacks in the military. The number of black brigades grew to four in the regular army and eight in the National Guard. More than six hundred African Americans were commissioned as officers, and even though most black units in the war were relegated to rear-area labor, the first two American soldiers recognized for bravery in France, Henry Johnson and Needham Roberts, were black. Regiments of the black Ninety-third Division earned the Croix de Guerre unit citation while serving with the French. In an effort to prevent racial violence such as that which took place in Houston in August of 1917, Secretary of War Newton D. Baker appointed Emmet J. Scott of Tuskegee as special assistant for Negro affairs. Leaders of the National Association for the Advancement of Colored People (NAACP), founded in 1910, such as Du Bois and Joel Spingarn, hoped that such accomplishments would raise the status of blacks and open the door to more opportunity at home.

Such doors were indeed opened to blacks, but not in a manner envisioned by the NAACP and National Urban League (also founded in 1910). As industrial production geared up to meet the demands of war, other groups sought to improve their political and economic lot. Unions attempted to organize the growing unskilled labor pool of the mass-production industries that began to dominate the U.S. economy. When the secretary of the National Committee for Organizing Iron and Steel Workers, William Z. Foster, led a major strike against the steel industry in 1919, the steel magnates hired more than thirty thousand black workers to cross the picket lines. This action was a major blow to steel workers and led to the collapse of the strike. Booker T. Washington's offering of a docile, strike-free black working class to American industry seemed to be coming true.

This strike was not the first time industry recruited blacks, nor were they brought in solely as scabs. With the onset of World War I, immigration, an important source of cheap unskilled labor, dried up. The draft also reduced the manpower available to factories. Starting in 1916, labor agents invaded southern states and recruited blacks with promises of good wages, free transportation, and secure jobs. The result

Lieutenant Colonel Otis B. Duncan of the 370th Infantry (center), the highest-ranking African American officer in France at the end of the war, and two decorated junior officers

(National Archives, Washington, D.C.)

was a dramatic exodus of black workers from southern states to northern cities such as Chicago, Gary, Cleveland, and Detroit. Southern cities with industry such as Birmingham, Charleston, and Mobile also saw an influx of blacks looking for work. By 1920, 25 percent of Southern blacks lived in urban areas, compared to only 6 percent in 1910. More than 10,000 blacks went to work for the Pennsylvania Railroad. As a result of this new employment black Americans gained a foothold in a sector of the economy that was previously denied them. The transition, however, proved to be painful. Race riots in cities such as East St. Louis and Chicago left dozens of blacks and whites dead, but the violence did not stem the enormous demographic shift spawned by the material needs of World War I.

Besides opening a new economic door of opportunity for blacks, albeit a narrow one, the migration to the urban North had a tremendous political and cultural impact on the African American community. By 1920, 3.5 million blacks lived in northern cities, mostly in urban slums and factory villages in places such as East St. Louis, Harlem, and Newark; more than 800,000 had moved north during World War I. While NAACP leaders of the time, such as Du Bois, Spingarn, and William Trotter, appealed to middle-class blacks and white liberals, the enlarged urban black underclass did not have a voice regarding their particular social and economic problems. Filling this vacuum was Jamaican-born activist Marcus Garvey, who urged blacks to take pride in their African heritage and

AFRICAN AMERICANS

even encouraged black immigration to Africa. More importantly, Garvey, who formed the Universal Negro Improvement Association (UNIA) in 1914 and started branches in New York in 1916, urged blacks to do for themselves and not wait for "whites to give them the scraps from their plates." The UNIA organized child care and youth centers, as well as many enterprises that were owned by, and employed only, blacks. Although Garvey's movement ultimately collapsed, and he died broke in a European tenement, his movement created a new dimension of self-reliance in the black movement that did not exist before. It laid the groundwork for the black power movement that characterized the 1960s. Garvey's promotion of racial self-awareness within the growing black urban population and the disillusionment generated by the apparent return to pre–World War I segregation did not sit well with the new black proletariat.

At Prohibition-era speakeasies and clubs, new forms of expression and artistic growth focusing on the black experience and contemporary issues emerged. Black writers, poets, musicians, and actors—congregating in Chicago, St. Louis, and most notably in the New York neighborhood of Harlem—created a new era of black history known as the Harlem Renaissance. The strength and originality of these artists appealed to a growing white audience and established black music, literature, and art as permanent fixtures of American culture. Musicians such as Louis Armstrong, Duke Ellington, Cab Calloway, and Ethel Waters attracted international attention as they created jazz and swing. White musicians such as Harry James, Benny Goodman, and Tommy Dorsey popularized this new genre that characterized an entire generation. Black writers such as poet Langston Hughes and novelist Zora Neale Hurston emerged as important voices, and much like authors of the Lost Generation (such as Ernest Hemingway and John Dos Passos), a new generation of expatriates, most of them black Americans, began to attract followings in Paris, London, and even Moscow. Black actors emerged from stereotypical and degrading roles to leading parts on Broadway. Charles Gilpin introduced Americans to the potential of black thespians by capturing the lead role in Eugene O'Neill's play *Emperor Jones* and earning positive reviews in 1921.

Black political aspirations also gained momentum in the years during and preceding World War I. Black communities in northern cities, free of the Jim Crow limitations in the South, made their presence felt in the polling booths. From 1917 to 1925 black politicians were elected to state assemblies in regions where blacks had not held public office since Reconstruction (1865–1877). Edward Johnson became the first black ever elected to the New York State Assembly. Black activism, building on the growing strength of these urban constituencies, began to challenge openly the tenets of racial discrimination and oppression. Groups such as the National Liberty Congress of Colored Americans actively campaigned to make lynching a federal crime. The NAACP sent investigators into the South to gather information on mob violence and petitioned for federal antilynching laws. Between 1918 and 1921 the U.S. House of Representatives passed antilynching laws such as the Dyer Bill, but they were filibustered away by the U.S. Senate. Still, the debate elevated the crime of lynching to national attention.

An example of this new attention took place in September 1919 in Phillips County, Arkansas. Black farmers in that region, many of them World War I veterans, organized and petitioned for detailed accounting reports from white landlords. The farmers incorporated and hired white lawyers from Little Rock to represent them. At a large meeting to discuss their plans, a local deputy sheriff shot at the farmers. The farmers fired back and killed the deputy and one other person. Reaction was swift as the sheriff deputized more than three hundred men, and the governor of Arkansas mobilized five hundred National Guard troops. They spent a week rounding up all black farmers in Phillips County, killing twenty-five of them in the process. Seventy-nine farmers were indicted; after the first few trials, which lasted less than an hour and returned guilty verdicts after five minutes of jury deliberation, the remainder pled guilty to second-degree murder and were given life sentences.

Walter White, assistant secretary of the NAACP, investigated these cases and wrote about them for the *Chicago Daily News*. The situation received national attention through White's reporting, and soon the NAACP had more than $50,000 in contributions, enabling it to appeal the cases successfully. In *Moore* v. *Dempsey* (1923), citing the mob mentality of the lower courts, Justice Oliver Wendell Holmes wrote the U.S. Supreme Court decision that reversed the verdict and set all the farmers imprisoned in Phillips County free.

The early twentieth-century urbanization of the black movement, brought about largely by African Americans migrating to the cities in large numbers to seek factory work during World War I, is arguably the most important event between emancipation (1865) and the civil rights movement of the 1950s and 1960s. As early as 1916 the *New Republic* argued that blacks moving to the North would increase black economic and political power to levels unimaginable in the South. The Urban League held a special conference in 1917 to assess the effect of this urban migration and resolved to organize and protest exploitive practices by industrialists against black labor.

A new black proletariat made of industrial and service workers supported such resolutions. Between 1918 and 1920 black laborers went on strike to unionize in several northern cities, and between 1918 and 1919 the NAACP enjoyed a huge increase in membership. The growing strength of black urban communities became the foundation of efforts to gain equality for all African Americans. Early efforts by blacks to organize during the years surrounding World War I were repressed, sometimes with great violence and loss of life. However, as historian George M. Fredrickson pointed out in *Black Liberation: A Comparative History of Black Ideologies in the United States and South Africa* (1995), black groups and white liberals succeeded in holding the Red Scare–generated tide of repression in check. Through expanding economic opportunity brought on by war industry; self-discovery and organization in urban environments; and the strengthening of newly founded civil rights organizations, black Americans widened their political and economic existence. They planted the seeds of activism that helped African Americans campaign for equality, with greater success, almost a half century later.

–VANCE R. SKARSTEDT, U. S. AIR
FORCE ACADEMY

Viewpoint:
No. World War I exacerbated racism.

World War I occurred during one of the worst eras of race relations in American history. During the 1890s and 1900s the Jim Crow system, which increasingly separated blacks from whites in virtually all spheres of society, was established—most notably in the South. African Americans at the same time were gradually disenfranchised. Despite the creation of this racist system, many African Americans saw World War I as a chance to improve their own lot in life while also helping the larger African American community. Given the creation of the Jim Crow system, it is remarkable that the vast majority of African Americans heeded the call of leaders such as W. E. B. Du Bois to close ranks and support the U.S. government in its war against Germany. Despite the service of blacks, both inside and outside the military, however, the African American community realized few, if any, tangible benefits. While the lives of Afri-

can Americans changed substantially as a result of World War I, it is hard to argue that their daily existence generally improved. Race relations were no better in 1920 than they had been in 1910.

Prior to World War I, the rampant and rabid racism of American society permeated the military as well. By 1900 the U.S. Navy and Marine Corps had started to segregate crews and limit enlistments by African Americans. For the navy, these policies represented a significant change; since the Early Republic period, the navy had been the most integrated of the American military services. Nevertheless, as race relations deteriorated, the navy limited acceptance of African Americans and assigned black sailors almost exclusively to the mess deck and engine room. Similarly, the army accepted black soldiers in the smallest numbers possible and assigned them to the worst jobs in the service, most commonly to labor units. Discipline in all services was normally much harsher for blacks than for whites. Many white communities, especially in the South, objected when black units were sent to nearby bases.

Two incidents in Texas particularly inflamed racial tensions within the military. The first occurred in Brownsville in 1906 when local whites unjustly accused black soldiers of assaulting white women. On the night of 13–14 August shots rang out, and 1 white man died. Local townspeople reported to authorities that they had seen black troops doing the firing. Despite a lack of concrete evidence pointing to the men and serious irregularities in the testimony of the townspeople, President Theodore Roosevelt decided to take executive action. Since the evidence pointed to no specific individuals, the president dismissed from the service all black soldiers from three companies of the 26th Infantry, save those on leave or detached duty at the time of the incident. The executive order dismissed 167 men in all and banned them from future employment with the U.S. government.

The hasty executive action, conducted without due process, angered many Americans, black and white. Subsequent investigations by Senator Joseph Foraker (R.–Ohio) concluded that no black soldiers had fired their rifles. Foraker, who had emerged as a candidate for the Republican presidential nomination in 1908, further concluded that the incident was a conspiracy of townspeople who wanted to influence the War Department to assign only whites to Fort Brown. Despite these findings, the War Department agreed to reinstate only 14 of the dismissed soldiers (not until 1972 did the Nixon administration offi-

BULLETIN NO. 35

On 28 March 1918 Major General Charles Ballou, commander of the Ninety-second Division, while stationed at Camp Funston, Kansas, issued the following orders to his African American troops:

1. It should be well known to all colored officers and men that no useful purpose is served by such acts as will cause the "Color Question" to be raised. It is not a question of legal rights, but a question of policy, and any policy that tends to bring about a conflict of races, with its resulting animosities, is prejudicial to the military interests of the 92nd Division, and therefore prejudicial to an important interest of the colored race.

2. To avoid conflicts the Division Commander has repeatedly urged that all colored members of his command, and especially the officers and non-commissioned officers should refrain from going where their presence will be resented. In spite of this injunction, one of the sergeants of the Medical Department has recently precipitated the precise trouble that should be avoided, and then called on the Division Commander to take sides in a row that should never have occurred, and would not have occurred had the sergeant placed the general good above his personal pleasure and convenience. This sergeant entered a theatre, as he undoubtedly had a legal right to do, and precipitated trouble by making it possible to allege race discrimination in the seat he was given. He is entirely within his legal rights within this matter, and the theatre manager is legally wrong. Nevertheless the sergeant is guilty of the greater wrong of *doing* anything, no matter how legally correct, that will provoke race animosity.

3. The Division Commander repeats that the success of the Division with all that that implies, is dependent upon the good will of the public. That public is nine-tenths white. White men made the Division, and can break it just as easily as it becomes a trouble maker.

4. All concerned are again enjoined to place the general interest of the Division above personal pride and gratification. Avoid every situation that can give rise to racial ill-will. Attend quietly and faithfully to your duties, and don't go where your presence is not desired.

Source: Addie W. Hunton and Kathryn M. Johnson, Two Colored Women With the American Expeditionary Forces *(Brooklyn, N.Y.: Brooklyn Eagle Press, 1920), pp. 46–47.*

blacks, who had been firm supporters of the party of Abraham Lincoln.

Before the war, General Leonard Wood had banned blacks from training at the Plattsburg, New York, camps on the grounds that if they gained equality and intermarried with whites the nation would produce a race of "mongrels." Nevertheless, upon American entry into World War I, African Americans did indeed close ranks with whites. More than 380,000 blacks eventually served, but the army remained suspicious of them. It created segregated training, dining, and housing facilities and assigned black troops to the most remote outposts as often as possible to avoid inflaming local whites. The army assigned 89 percent of all African American soldiers in labor units.

The army, moreover, never placed black officers in positions of authority over whites. Most black units had white (and often Southern) officers. The War Department believed that Southern whites best knew how to "handle" blacks. Colonel Charles Young, who graduated from West Point in 1889, before its resegregation in 1898, was on track to become the first black general in the United States. His distinguished service in the 1898 war with Spain and in the 1916 expedition into Mexico against Pancho Villa qualified him for the promotion. Instead of giving him a general's star (and, by virtue of his rank, significant authority over whites), the army placed him on the retired list, ostensibly because of ill health. To prove the blatant racism that motivated this claim, Young rode on horseback from his home in Ohio to Washington, D.C., but the War Department did not reinstate him until the end of the war. The maintenance of segregation by the army during World War I led to the second Texas incident, this one in Houston in 1917. Two African American soldiers intervened to stop a Houston policeman from beating a black woman. Black regulars, already chafing under the Jim Crow system of the city, responded to the arrest of the 2 men and, as tempers flared, went on a shooting spree on 23 August, killing 17 whites. The all-white investigation teams from the War Department responded by ending all conscription of blacks, and, before appeals could be arranged, the army hanged 13 of the troopers (6 other soldiers would later be executed). The shooting spree terrified white Americans, every bit as much as the summary justice angered black Americans. The War Department soon concluded that African Americans should be used only in labor units.

As a result, only two black units served in combat, and one of those served in a French

cially admit the mistake by the army and grant the dismissed soldiers honorable discharges). The Brownsville incident soured relations between the African American community and the military, as well as those between the Republican Party (despite Foraker's self-serving, but well-intentioned, efforts) and northern

AFRICAN AMERICANS

division despite President Woodrow Wilson's otherwise fierce opposition to placing American soldiers under French and British command. The other unit, the 92nd Division, suffered from poor training, harsh discipline, and (exclusively white) officers who treated them with contempt and fear. Because of white fears after the Houston riot, the 92nd trained with weapons as seldom as possible. As a result they did not perform well. By contrast, the formations that served under French officers distinguished themselves in battle at the Meuse-Argonne in September 1918 (an entire regiment received the French Croix de Guerre), though French officers were counseled to temper their praise of black troops in the presence of white American officers.

African Americans fared no better at home. No African Americans sat on draft boards, and few served in important roles in the administration of the intensely racist President Wilson. In addition to those in government service, tens of thousands of African Americans served their country by moving north to take industrial jobs. The war had cut off the flow of immigration from Europe, creating a labor vacuum that northern industry hoped to solve by recruiting African Americans to cities such as Chicago (which gained 70,000 new black residents), Pittsburgh, and Detroit. The so-called Great Migration eased the labor crisis, but it also created tensions, as African Americans moved into traditionally white factories and neighborhoods.

African Americans who made the Great Migration faced hostility in the areas they left as well as in their new homes. White Southerners angrily, and sometimes violently, opposed the depletion of their labor force. The Department of Labor acceded to white Southern demands and stopped a program designed to assist those African Americans willing to move north, despite the obvious benefit the program brought to the war effort. In the North, whites often protested at having to work alongside blacks, and many unions would not register them. After the war, African Americans were often the first fired.

Racial tensions also turned violent. In July 1917 a riot in East St. Louis, Illinois, left 9 whites and 40 blacks dead. The riot occurred as thousands of African Americans were moving from Mississippi and Tennessee to take industrial jobs in the region. White rioters chased more than 6,000 African Americans from their homes. They also set fire to many houses, devastating the still fledgling black community and poisoning race relations in the area for decades.

After the war, conditions did not significantly improve. Indeed, by many accounts they became significantly worse. Whereas white lynching parties killed 38 blacks in 1917 and 58 blacks in 1918, the number of lynchings actually increased after the war to seventy in 1919. The war did not produce an antilynching bill nor a general desire to improve the lives of black Americans. By 1924 the renewed Ku Klux Klan (inspired by the blatantly racist 1915 movie, *The Birth of a Nation*) reached its peak membership with 4 million members. Two years later, the Klan demonstrated its new power with an open march down Pennsylvania Avenue in Washington, D.C.

After the war, the military curtailed African American opportunities significantly. The navy continued its policy of marginalizing African Americans. In 1934 the navy had just 441 black sailors. The army assigned blacks almost exclusively to labor battalions and banned them from high-profile fields such as aviation. In 1940 the army had just 5 black officers. It was not until that year that the nation promoted its first black general, Benjamin O. Davis Sr.

The most obvious and compelling evidence that World War I did not improve the lives of African Americans lies in the similarity of American mobilization for World War II. Once again, the government asked blacks to close ranks, this time to fight for a war against racism while they were forced to serve in segregated units. That war, however, produced more tangible gains for African Americans. In 1948 another Southern president (and World War I) veteran, Harry S Truman, signed an executive order desegregating the U.S. armed forces. The war for racial equality was not yet over, however, and the first real battlefield victory did not come until 1948, but the tide had finally begun to turn in favor of equal treatment for all Americans.

–MICHAEL S. NEIBERG, U.S. AIR
FORCE ACADEMY

References

Arthur E. Barbeau and Florette Henri, *The Unknown Soldiers: Black American Troops in World War I* (Philadelphia: Temple University Press, 1974).

William Brink and Louis Harris, *The Negro Revolution in America: What Negroes Want, Why and How They are Fighting, Whom They Support, What Whites Think of Them and Their Demands* (New York: Simon & Schuster, 1964).

Jack Foner, *Blacks and the Military in American History: A New Perspective* (New York: Praeger, 1974).

George M. Fredrickson, *Black Liberation: A Comparative History of Black Ideologies in the United States and South Africa* (New York: Oxford University Press, 1995).

Kenneth W. Goings, *The NAACP Comes of Age: The Defeat of Judge John J. Parker* (Bloomington: Indiana University Press, 1990).

Peter Gottlieb, *Making Their Own Way: Southern Blacks' Migration to Pittsburgh, 1916–30* (Urbana: University of Illinois Press, 1987).

Allen D. Grimshaw, ed., *Racial Violence in the United States* (Chicago: Aldine, 1969).

James R. Grossman, *Land of Hope: Chicago, Black Southerners, and the Great Migration* (Chicago: University of Chicago Press, 1989).

Charles Flint Kellogg, *NAACP: A History of the National Association for the Advancement of Colored People* (Baltimore: Johns Hopkins University Press, 1967).

David M. Kennedy, *Over Here: The First World War and American Society* (New York: Oxford University Press, 1980).

Carole Marks and Diana Edkins, *The Power of Pride: Stylemakers and Rulebreakers of the Harlem Renaissance* (New York: Crown, 1999).

August Meier and Elliott Rudwick, *From Plantation to Ghetto,* third edition (New York: Hill & Wang, 1976).

Bernard C. Nalty, *Strength for the Fight: A History of Black Americans in the Military* (New York: Free Press; London: Collier-Macmillan, 1986).

Charles E. Silberman, *Crisis in Black and White* (New York: Random House, 1964).

Irving J. Sloan, *Blacks in America: 1492–1970: A Chronology & Fact Book,* third edition (Dobbs Ferry, N.Y.: Oceana, 1971).

Arnold H. Taylor, *Travail and Triumph: Black Life and Culture in the South Since the Civil War* (Westport, Conn.: Greenwood Press, 1976).

Allen Weinstein and Frank Otto Gatell, eds., *The Segregation Era, 1863–1954: A Modern Reader* (New York: Oxford University Press, 1970).

AFRICAN AMERICANS

AIRCRAFT

Did aircraft play a significant role in the Great War?

Viewpoint: Yes. As the war progressed, aircraft assumed more importance in ground attacks, interdiction, and strategic bombardment.

Viewpoint: No. Aircraft were used primarily for observation and reconnaissance.

Military aircraft during the Great War underwent a more rapid development than at any later time in history. A few airframes—the Spitfire and Me–109, the B 17 and JU 88—served until the end of World War II. Modern aviation designs endure for decades, with some planes being older than their crews, but in World War I, six months was a long operational life for an airplane design.

Missions evolved almost as rapidly. In August 1914, aircraft were regarded as suitable for operational reconnaissance and liaison. In 1915 air-to-air combat was added to their repertoire. By 1916 tactical bombardment and strategic reconnaissance were part of the mix for a state-of-the-art air force. In 1917 purpose-built strategic bombers joined the orders of battle. The Germans introduced ground-attack aircraft, including the J I, a partially armored machine prefiguring the U.S. Air Force's A-10. At the armistice, the Royal Air Force was taking delivery of heavy bombers able to strike Berlin from English airfields.

Tactics changed as well. By the final year of the war the lone-wolf fighter pilot, the archetypical ace, gave way to mass formations that sometimes included fifty single-seaters. France built an "air division" around tactical bombers, the aluminum-framed Breguet 14s, and employed it with devastating effect against German rear areas. German attack squadrons provided close-air support to front-line units in Erich Ludendorff's March and April 1918 offensives. Planes were used for supply, free-dropping food and ammunition; the French even adapted Breguets for a medevac role. For all the sound and fury of aerial combat, the bread and butter of the air war remained observation. Position warfare put a premium on knowing the details of enemy positions. Offensives depended on accurate delivery of supporting artillery fire, and that in turn depended increasingly on aerial photographs and aerial observation. Fighter planes existed essentially to protect the observation machines that directed the ground war. The bombers and strike aircraft remained in the "nice to have" category, but the unglamorous, cumbersome aircraft that took the pictures, spotted the targets, and reported the positions of friends and enemies were at the heart of air force orders of battle until the Armistice.

Viewpoint:
Yes. As the war progressed, aircraft assumed more importance in ground attacks, interdiction, and strategic bombardment.

As the Great War progressed, combat airpower matured to the point of becoming autonomous in nature. In their technology, mission, and organization, the offensive and defensive aspects of the air war grew in significance—comparable to reconnaissance and observation—and yet, in part, separate from contributing to the ground war. The technology of flight evolved dynamically to where new types of aircraft reached the front, tipped the balance of airpower, but were obsolete within a season of flying. The prewar doctrine of employing aircraft for reconnaissance led to contesting the skies for air superiority, attacking ground targets, and bombing areas beyond the front lines. In the expediency of war, air services revolutionized the role of the airplane beyond observation and reconnaissance resulting in a fundamental change in the nature of war.

From the opening ground offensives in August 1914, reconnaissance and observation aircraft overflew the front lines and contributed to the stalemated condition. Reconnaissance flights increased dramatically, and aircraft were a ubiquitous presence above the stagnant trench lines. The intelligence-gathering planes, however, were not the only form of airpower employed above the battlefield. Airmen expanded their role to one of information denial, which led to the more consequential change in the nature of aerial warfare—achieving air superiority.

By the spring of 1916 the "Fokker scourge" sparked the cyclical development of improved technology, new organizations, and strategic air doctrine by the Allies. Armed with Fokker *Eindecker* monoplanes, mounting a machine gun capable of synchronous fire through the propeller arc, the Germans claimed air superiority over the battlefront. They grouped these planes into special single-seat fighter detachments called *Kampfeinsitzer Kommando (KeK)* in order to dominate the skies. As the monumental attack on Verdun erupted on 21 February 1916, twenty-one *Eindeckers* attempted to enforce a *Luftsperre* (aerial blockade) to keep the French from prying behind German lines. While the *KeKs* defended German lines, the chief of the German air service, Colonel von der Lieth-Thomsen concentrated two aerial combat groups, *Kampfgeschwader* of the *OHL*, or *Kagohls*, to bomb the French rear area and the *Voie Sacre*, the only line of resupply to Verdun.

French airmen, armed with the new, technologically advanced Nieuport XI "Bebe," but without gun synchronization, began to contest the Germans for air superiority by flying in groups, offensively, behind German lines. Commandant Tricornot de Rose organized the *pilotes de chasse* into the famous *Groupe des Cigognes,* a unit consisting of the best French aces to counter the three dominant *Eindecker KeKs.* Employing offensive patrols and flying in larger formations with the purpose of fighting German aircraft, the French ultimately emerged in control of the skies over Verdun. By April the Germans felt aerial supremacy slipping from their grasp. Not only had French pursuit pilots forced the German bomber *Kagohls* from the skies, but ten *Feldflieger Abteilungen* aerial photography units and six *Artillerie Flieger Abteilungen* were denied their primary roles in directing German field artillery. This consequence of French airmen wresting air superiority from the Germans was a crucial turning point in the Verdun ground battle.

As the Verdun battle expended its energy, General Fritz von Below reflected on the air war over his lines at the Somme: "With the help of air spotting, the enemy neutralized our artillery, and was able to range his own guns with the utmost accuracy on our infantry trenches; the enemy aircraft gave our own troops a feeling of helplessness, such was [the British] mastery of the air." Von Below was characterizing the aggressive spirit of the Royal Flying Corps (RFC) under Major-General Hugh Trenchard, who amassed more than 420 aircraft in 27 squadrons to take the air war behind the German lines. He accomplished this feat by achieving a three-to-one advantage over German air service. Equipped with the DeHavilland D. H. 2, aerodynamically outfitted with aileron controls, and the synchronized machine-gun carrying Sopwith 1½ Strutter aircraft, the RFC flew in large formations as offensive escorts for army observation and reconnaissance aircraft. In mounting the offensive over the Somme (1916), the RFC lost some 140 aircraft in the contest for aerial dominance.

The Germans responded to the massing of French pursuit aircraft and British offensive air doctrine with a new organization and new aircraft. The more advanced Albatross D-1 gained a reputation of technical superiority during "Bloody April" (1917). More important, the Germans introduced a provisional *Jagdgeschwader* consisting of four *Jagdstaffeln* to concentrate their pursuit aircraft to challenge the Allied fighters. Air superiority became the key ingredient in the air war. Airmen made attacks deliberately directed against infantry deployed in the trenches by dropping explosives and strafing with machine guns.

From the extension of aerial reconnaissance, air services developed opportunities for aircraft to intervene in the ground war. Ground-attack aircraft improved the combat value of artillery-spotting aircraft by directly strafing and dropping high explosives on ground positions. In a sense, a marked psychological advantage was gained over the ground troops as both sides made concerted efforts to attack from the air. During the Battle of the Somme, the RFC employed modified pursuit aircraft for the ground-support role, therefore, fighters, equipped with high explosives, bombed German rear areas and strafed their front-line trenches during the same mission. Loss rates were extremely high for these fliers, approaching 30 percent in some cases, a gruesome measure indicating the effectiveness of infantry attempting to defend themselves with small-arms fire.

The Germans adopted the tactic of attacking trenches by creating aircraft specifically for that purpose. The *Junkers* J 1 in particular was unique in construction: it was made of metal with additional armor plating around vulnerable engine components, the fuel tank, and the cockpit for protection against ground-to-air defensive fire when flying at low altitude in the close infantry support role. Indeed, during the March 1918 "Michael" offensive, the German air service employed thirty-eight ground-attack *stafflen* to support the new "stormtrooper" tactics, providing much needed integral fire support to the highly mobile light-infantry units. Thus, while the British employed fighter aircraft in a multi-purpose role, the Germans used aircraft designed and built specifically for close-air support and trench-strafing missions. Soon, aircraft used to attack entrenched troops had their mission expanded to battlefield interdiction, disrupting enemy rear echelons and supply lines, destroying munitions depots, and harassing troop concentrations. Armed aircraft, akin technologically to the reconnaissance birds, ranged deeper behind enemy communication trenches to strike troop concentrations, lines of communications, and munitions and supply depots, as well as to interdict movement and resupply routes emanating from the rear areas of the battlefield.

In September 1918, U.S. brigadier general William Mitchell employed his air armada in support of the reduction of the St. Mihiel salient by the First American Army by attacking the escaping flow of German troops and war matériel. Mitchell's reconnaissance aircraft detected the Germans withdrawing before Allied ground forces could encircle them in the salient. While the Germans retreated, Allied pursuit, ground-attack, and bomber aircraft achieved air superiority and pummeled the fleeing troops. In an attempt to block their escape, the First Day Bombardment Group struck at road and rail junctions within the salient at such places as Vigneulles, Mars-la-Tour, and Conflans. During this air operation German motor-truck convoys and troop concentrations were bombed; German infantry in their trenches were strafed; and German pursuit aircraft were overwhelmed by Allied aircraft. Rail stations and bridges across the Moselle River were destroyed with high explosives to prevent German reinforcements from coming into the area and to disrupt their retreat out of the salient. French air units under Mitchell's command flew against similar lines of communication targets while the Independent Air Force (IAF) attacked major rail junctions located deeper at the base of the salient: Metz, Hagendingen, and Thionville. The International Allied Force consisted of 696 pursuit, 366 reconnaissance, 323 day bombers, and 91 night bombers, totaling 1,476 aircraft with a ratio of three-to-one combat planes to reconnaissance craft. With his combat air force, Mitchell struck the salient from either side resulting in the successful attack against St. Mihiel. American airmen destroyed 60 enemy aircraft and 12 balloons, dropped 75 tons of explosives, interdicted the movement of enemy troops to and from the salient, and continuously scouted the progress of the offensive.

Hitting the production centers of weapons, chemicals, and munitions by aircraft was undertaken almost immediately after the war became stagnant, while bombing rail lines used to transport raw resources between industrial areas proved a measure of how airpower became a factor not directly related to the battle lines. Trenchard, while General Officer Commanding Royal Flying Corps in France, in September 1916 indicated that "an aeroplane is an offensive and not a defensive weapon. . . . Our machines have continually attacked the enemy on his side of the line, bombed his aerodromes, and carried out attacks on places of importance far behind the lines. The sound policy, then, which should guide all warfare in the air would seem to be this: to exploit the moral effect of the aeroplane on the enemy." On 1 April 1918, when the Royal Air Force (RAF) came into being, the British immediately recognized the great possibilities of strategic interdiction as well as opportunities for conducting counter-air operations by attacking airfields and thereby directly undermining German morale through air raids. Trenchard's employment of airpower to strike German airfields was as important as disrupting their transportation network and industry. Every effort was made to build up and maintain a powerful striking force to execute a series of systematic raids on the key munitions and chemical factories of Germany. Accordingly, on 8

AIRCRAFT

June 1918, the IAF was constituted with the three bomber squadrons from the original Eighth Brigade RFC. This force increased to ten squadrons, five of which had Handley Page aircraft, designed to "carry out powerful and intensive bombardment, from the air, on enemy territory, both for the object of destroying military objectives and, in case of need, to execute reprisals on German towns."

As part of the Inter-Allied Independent Air Force (IIAF), the British made the Ruhr a primary target, but their planes also ranged deep into Germany with attacks against Mainz, Frankfurt am Main, Ludwigshafen, and Aschaffenburg from July to October 1918. During this period, the Allied air forces made 353 raids on Germany, dropping 7,717 bombs and killing 797 Germans while injuring another 380. The damage inflicted on German industry was 15,522,000 reichmarks (approximately $3.6 million).

In monetary terms the results of IIAF bombing during 1918 inflicted damage to the value of less than one-tenth of 1 percent of German war expenditures. A British Air Ministry report after the war substantiated this fact; for example, mainly because of air-raid alarms, the Roechling factory at Volkslingen suffered a production shortfall of 15,803 tons of steel in 1918. This deficit, while considerable, represented less than 5 percent of the 1913 production. More important, the report stipulated that material effects did not constitute the main objective for the IIAF.

In attacking as many population centers as could be reached, the psychological effect was intensified since no townspeople felt safe. Likewise, continued and thorough defensive measures became necessary in areas in which the IIAF was operating. The report concluded: "At present the moral effect of bombing stands undoubtedly to the material in proportion of 20 to 1 and therefore it was necessary to create the greatest moral effect possible."

The effect, both morally and materially, of the raids on German territory carried out during the latter half of 1918 can hardly be overstated. The air offensive contributed to a serious drain on German resources as they were forced to provide large numbers of anti-aircraft guns, searchlights, balloons, and pursuit squadrons for its *Heimatlustschutzes* (home defense), created on 8 December 1916. The German High Command was compelled to recall at least twenty pursuit squadrons from the Western Front and to immobilize a large number of ground troops to man anti-aircraft batteries and an elaborate system of searchlights. At the outbreak of World War I, German air defenses consisted of only 6 motorized guns and 12 horse-drawn 77-millimeter guns. By the end of the war, the Germans employed a sophisticated system for defense of their western cities; they divided the region into five defensive districts, manned by air-defense forces totaling 2,800 officers and 55,000 enlisted personnel crewing 2,770 guns and 718 searchlights. In addition, tens of thousands of men in the observer force and signal corps supported the air-defense effort. In fact, the Allied air-offensive policy was so successful that when the Armistice was signed on 11 November 1918, the bomber force was slated to be increased to a total of forty-eight squadrons by the end of May 1919. In a wider scope, the influence of air combat and aerial bombing profoundly affected the perceptions of war, speeding up the shift toward total war involving civilian populations and whole economies.

A distinctly separate phase of the air war was the First Battle of Britain involving the great German aircraft, the Gotha and Staaken bombers. The large Gotha bombers of *Kagohl* 3, deadly offspring of the disbanded *Brieftauben Abteilung Ostende,* began raiding England from bases around Ghent, Belgium, in the summer of 1917. *Kogohl* 3, comprised of 6 *Bombenstaffeln (Bosta),* conducted raids of 10 to 20 planes over London and southern England. The largest single raid consisted of 43 aircraft, while the deadliest caused 162 British deaths. Giant Staaken R.VI bombers of squadron *Riesen-Flugzeug Abteilung 501* later joined the strategic force and flew night raids in conjunction with the *Gotha* bombers.

General Erich Ludendorff considered the London raids to be primarily a strategic propaganda weapon. Major von Bulow, the historian who analyzed the London raids from the German point of view, wrote:

The main purpose of the bombing attacks was the intimidation of the morale of the English people, the crippling of their will to fight and the preparation of a basis for peace. The secondary purpose of the raids was to disrupt the British war industry, disorganize the communication between coastal ports and London, attack supply dumps of coastal ports and hinder transport of war materials across the Channel. The target of the raids was confined principally to London because it was the heart of England, the operational head quarters of the Allies and the center of its war industry.

During the war German bomber aircraft dropped nearly 2,426 bombs totaling 241 tons on British soil in the course of thirty-two concerted air attacks. London was bombarded sixteen times by airplanes. In all, 838 persons were killed and 1,975 others were wounded as the result of these raids, London suffering more than half of the casualties. Purposely executed during Operations *Turkenkreuz* and Harvest

AIRCRAFT

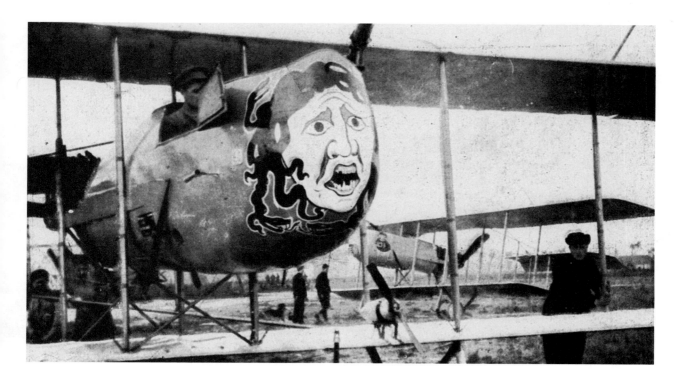

Belgian biplane with the head of Medusa painted on the nose, fall 1916

(from The Illustrated War News, 20 September 1916, page 38, Joseph M. Bruccoli Great War Collection, Thomas Cooper Library, University of South Carolina)

Moon between 25 May 1917 and 19 May 1918, these raids served the underlying motive of unnerving the British public by destroying their homes and by inflicting heavy casualties in order to defeat their national will and force them to sue for peace rather than endure continual air attacks. In this strategy the Germans failed. Along with the costly offensive against England, where the "English Wing" of the *Luftstreitkräfte* lost 62 Gotha and Riesen aircraft (only 19 were lost to British defensive aircraft and ground fire), the German bomber force was relegated to other uses and employed constantly for the duration of the war in attacking Allied airfields and interdicting British and French marshaling yards and supply depots.

British response to these assaults differed from the zeppelin airship defense. No magic bullet could flame a Gotha, so public outcry for protection caused the British military to station 12 RFC squadrons around London. Enough men to outfit a full division on the Western Front were diverted from the Continent as air-defense troops required to man searchlight companies, anti-aircraft batteries, and balloon sections ringing the British capital. Included in this drain of resources and manpower were the attached observer corps that gave England the first truly integrated air defense.

On the Western Front in August 1918 there was relative parity in missions flown between pursuit and bombardment to reconnaissance. At the end of the war the front-line air strengths of the major combatants numbered approximately 9,672 aircraft. Of the 2,820 planes deployed with the French, 988 were pursuit types while 424 aircraft flew in the bombardment role, which was roughly equal to the 1,438 reconnaissance and observation aircraft. The British, with 1,644 aircraft, more heavily favored their offensive air doctrine. They used 904 aircraft in the pursuit role and 362 as bombers compared to 378 as observation aircraft. The British air arm favored pursuit and bombardment almost three-to-one over reconnaissance. The Germans deployed 2,592 airplanes and the Austro-Hungarians had 717. The German *Luftstreitkrafte* used 1,089 pursuit planes, 207 bombers, and 1,289 reconnaissance aircraft, and divided among 81 pursuit *Jastas*, 38 ground-attack *Staffels*, 26 bombing *Staffels*, and 153 artillery and reconnaissance flying units. By the Armistice, the U.S. Air Service had 740 planes in 45 squadrons at the front distributed as follows: 20 pursuit, 7 bombardment, 12 corps, and 6 army observation. The lesser powers of Italy and Russia held in their respective air services, 614 and 545 (Russian numbers from February 1917). Of those planes, the Russian air service had 229 pursuit, 278 observation, and 38 bombardment aircraft (42 percent, 51 percent, and 7 percent, respectively) while the Italians roughly balanced their aerial force between pursuit and reconnaissance each with 46 and 45 percent, respectively, and only 9 percent in the bomber arm.

Aircraft became sufficiently important in combat roles, ground attack, interdiction, and strategic bombardment so that by the Armistice there was a measure of parity among the multiple forms of the air mission. The 17 August 1917 report by General Jan Smuts regarding British

AIRCRAFT

air defense stipulated this progression to the point of declaring that "[an Air Service] can be used as an independent means of war operations [and] unlike artillery, an air fleet can conduct extensive operations far from, and independently of, both Army and Navy." Smuts predicted that "As far as presently can be foreseen, there is absolutely no limit to the scale of its future independent war use. And the day may not be far off when aerial operations with their devastation of enemy lands and destruction of industrial and populace centers on a vast scale may become the principle operations of war, to which the older forms of military and naval operations may become secondary and subordinate."

By 1918 there were specialized types of aircraft: strategic bombers, carrier-based fighters, seaplanes for antisubmarine patrol, interceptors, and ground-attack craft besides reconnaissance and observation planes. Air operations developed during World War I remain the basis of modern airpower applications.

—MICHAEL TERRY, U.S. AIR FORCE ACADEMY

Viewpoint:
No. Aircraft were used primarily for observation and reconnaissance.

The most common image of the World War I aviator found in motion pictures, books, and popular articles is that of the fighter ace, who is one of the last true romantic heroes of warfare. In fact, this popular image is largely myth. Of course, like all myths, there is some element of truth in the portrayal of these pilots. There were indeed many brilliant fighter aces of the war and their effort stands out as a rare flash of individualism in a conflict characterized by great masses of men and matèriel. The fighter ace, however, was not the typical World War I aviator; most airplanes produced during the Great War on both sides were for, and most pilots served in, reconnaissance and observations units—not in the fighter arm. Indeed, the fighter arm was generally considered to be a support arm to aid the efforts of the more vital reconnaissance and observation missions.

One of the most valuable commodities in warfare is intelligence, and the side with a clearer picture of their own and of the enemy's forces has an enormous advantage. Wars, campaigns, and battles have been won because one side had better intelligence than the other. This mission is so important that collecting information was a primary role of the cavalry during the nineteenth century and all the major armies put a great deal of their resources toward creating effective cav-

alry arms. The Germans and French especially learned the value of accurate reconnaissance during the Franco-Prussian War (1870–1871). The reconnaissance of the Germans and French was poor and both armies fought largely "in the dark." At Spicheren (1870), Fröschwiller (1870), and Beaumont (1870) major battles occurred when the two armies simply blundered into each other. The Germans won the battles more by perseverance and by making fewer gross mistakes than the French. Yet, the French could have triumphed in each of these battles if they had possessed a clearer picture of the German forces. Postwar studies by both armies emphasized the need for good reconnaissance.

A further development of the late nineteenth century had a major effect on the requirement for reconnaissance and observation. New long-range, breechloading heavy artillery pieces appeared that could fire projectiles for distances of several miles. The longer range and more rapid fire of artillery made it a far more important arm on the battlefield than ever before. Huge amounts of destructive firepower could now be delivered at considerable distance—more than ten miles for some heavy howitzers. The highly effective new guns, however, were useless unless some means were found to observe well behind enemy lines, spot the fall of shells, and adjust fire.

Driven by the requirement for operational reconnaissance and artillery observations, both the Germans and the French developed balloon units for artillery spotting and spent considerable sums on building maneuverable gas-filled airships that would have the ability to cruise behind enemy lines and gather information. When the airplane was invented, both the German and French general staffs became strong supporters of the new technology. The airplane was the perfect answer to both the reconnaissance requirements and the artillery-spotting mission. By 1914 Germany and France each had more than three hundred airplanes in service, virtually all of them organized into observation and reconnaissance flights utilizing two-seat airplanes. These aircraft, usually biplanes, carried a pilot and an observer. Airplanes were relatively cheap, could be flown from any level field, could be used to observe enemy forces and activity deep behind their lines, and could get information quickly back to headquarters by dropping messages or simply landing the plane near the headquarters and reporting in person. The other combatant nations had smaller air forces, which also consisted mostly of the ubiquitous two-seat observation craft.

At the start of the war, the reconnaissance airplanes proved decisive on the battlefield. In the East, the Germans were greatly outnumbered

BALLOON LANDINGS

In addition to aircraft, manned balloons were utilized during World War I as forward observation platforms from which to direct artillery fire and observe troop movements. Bernard Oliver, a British observer with No. 23 Balloon Section, Royal Flying Corps, recalls some of his experiences:

My turn came to fly with Captain Machin and up we went about four thousand feet. Suddenly a mighty crash and a flash of an exploding shell very close. Captain cooly remarked, "That's the German gun on rails—9.2 weighs a ton, find and tell me when to expect the shell burst and report any damage to us, I'll carry on with the observation." At intervals the gun fired, time of flight, twenty-seven seconds. I gave the Captain roughly where the shell burst and damage, if any. My word, he didn't bat an eyelid, another of these Public School boys!

Major Cochran, MC, from Company Headquarters, phoned us with the warning of trouble ahead. The winch below reported very high tension on the cable. Reluctantly, Captain Machin told the winch to haul us down, as we were still being shelled. The winch, owing to the tension, was unable to haul us down, so the crew resorted to the spider. This was a pulley which fitted around the cable. The crew could walk us down. The slow operation started. When we were down to about 1,000 feet hardly any wind blew so the balloon crumpled up and down we came. The basket fell on a clump of trees, through which the basket landed gently on the ground, with us hanging safely above. After climbing from the balloon, we walked a distance away from the escaping gas and had a smoke. It seemed a long wait before the crew arrived. I shall never forget how they very cautiously looked in the basket to see the state of the bodies, which they assumed they would find within. We had vanished—it was not Easter Sunday. This was my first flight with Captain Machin.

The officer who flew with me on the next flight, we will call Officer No. 3. Soon after reaching our observation height about 4,000/5,000 feet, we were informed on the telephone to look out for Richthofen's flying circus, who had attacked one of us. Very soon we noticed the fourth one north of us in flames, then the third one went down. It was a cloudy day so the planes could easily hide. All was quiet for a while, we settled down and got to work. Suddenly machine-gun bullets were flying all around in all directions. I saw one of the red-marked planes of Richthofen's, very close to us. Looking to my officer for orders to get out, I found myself alone. Not another Easter Sunday! Like a shot, I was over the side, closed my eyes and dropped into space. On my downward journey I opened my eyes and, behold, the pilot of the plane was flying very close to me waving his hand. I gladly waved back. I landed on the edge of a hop field.

As I was heavier than Officer No. 3, I had passed him on the way down. He landed in a stream of dirty water and the wind in the chute carried him quite a way through it. Yes! I think I may have smiled a little to see him! A motor car from the section soon picked us up and No. 3 Officer said, on arriving back at camp, "You heard me tell you to jump?" "Yes, Sir," I replied.

Source: *Lyn MacDonald, 1914–1918: Voices & Images of the Great War (London: Joseph, 1988), pp. 292–293.*

and faced an invasion of East Prussia by the Russian army. However, the Germans had one advantage in the form of a far more effective air service. German aircraft shadowed the Russian forces and gave the German Eighth Army a fairly accurate picture of their dispositions. On the other hand, the Russian army was largely fighting without good intelligence. At Tannenberg in August 1914, the Germans surrounded and destroyed the entire Russian Second Army in one of the most decisive victories in the history of warfare. It was a disaster that the Russians never really recovered from. As for the role of the reconnaissance aircraft, Field Marshal Paul von Hindenburg, commander of the Eighth Army, said "without the airplane there would have been no Tannenberg."

On the Western Front, the reconnaissance airplane proved just as decisive. In early September 1914, as the Germans advanced on Paris and the French and British fell back before the seemingly inexorable onslaught, an Allied reconnaissance plane reported that a large gap had appeared between the two German armies located to the west of Paris. Provided with this information, the British and French were able to

AIRCRAFT

stage a successful counterattack on the Marne River into the exposed gap and outflank the German army. The Germans were sent reeling and lost their best chance to take Paris and quickly win the war.

As the war on the Western Front evolved, the primary and most lethal weapon on the battlefield became the heavy artillery gun. Defensive fortifications were so strong that some offensives were preceded by artillery bombardments lasting weeks that consumed hundreds of trainloads of munitions. Aerial observation became essential for the guns to be worked with maximum effect. In the German attack at Verdun (February 1916), care was taken to amass fighter units and gain control of the air over the battlefield in order to assure effective observation for the more than 1,200 German heavy guns and to deny artillery observation to the French. The French, in turn, deployed the mass of their air service to regain control of the air and provide effective observation for hundreds of their heavy guns. Verdun, one of the greatest battles of history, can be best characterized as an artillery engagement, in which aerial reconnaissance and observation was key. In every campaign after Verdun both sides employed fighter aircraft in large numbers to gain aerial superiority over the front. Control of the air made the artillery far more lethal.

By 1917 Germany and the Allies had developed heavy bombers capable of relatively long-distance missions in order to attack each other's cities and important facilities behind the lines. In 1917 the modern concepts of strategic bombing and interdiction attacks were introduced. Both of these new forms of warfare showed a great deal of promise but the small bombloads of the aircraft, limited range, and technical difficulties of long-distance navigation in 1917–1918 meant that planes did not yet have a decisive effect on the battlefield. In 1917 the Germans introduced heavily armed and armored aircraft, with pilots specifically trained and organized for close-air support of the ground forces. While the British and French did not employ specialized ground-attack units, their air services also began to provide close-air support. There were several cases in which the assault aircraft had a major impact on some battles, such as in the German counterattack at Cambrai (December 1917) or in the French counterattack at Soisson (July 1918). The number of aircraft devoted to this mission, however, was still too small; not until World War II would close-air support play a decisive role on a battlefield.

Yet, throughout the course of the war, the two-seater observation/reconnaissance biplane remained the most common type of aircraft and was used by all the major air forces. In 1917–1918 approximately 50 percent of all the German aircraft were observation planes; bombers, fighters, and ground-attack planes comprising the other 50 percent. Probably one reason why the observation plane retained the central role in the air war was the fairly well-developed state of aerial photography in World War I. By the advent of the airplane, the camera was already a mature technology. While aircraft armament and munitions were only in the first stages of development, aerial cameras were able to reliably take superb photos at high altitudes. The combatant air forces took millions of aerial photographs during the war and many survive as impressive testaments to the technology of the early twentieth century. Photos taken in 1916 and 1917 from 15,000 to 20,000 feet provided clear and sharp images that were invaluable to army planners and artillerymen directing long-range fire. By 1915 it was unthinkable to mount a major operation without careful aerial photography of the front.

Reconnaissance and observation aircraft also proved their worth in maneuver warfare as well as in trench operations. By the time of the great German Spring offensive in 1918 the German air service had developed a heavily armored, all-metal aircraft able to fly low over the battlefield and survive the inevitable heavy ground fire. These planes, dubbed "infantry aircraft," had the mission of flying over the front lines during the offensive at low altitude in order to determine the exact location of German and enemy forces. The radios of 1918 were heavy and unreliable, field-telephone wires were quickly cut by artillery, and runners were simply too slow. In order to conduct offensive operations, forward reinforcements, and redeploy artillery the army headquarters needed accurate information from the front. The "infantry planes" were the best means of getting this information to the rear. The Allies soon picked up this tactic, and following the action on the front lines was added to the mission of the observation and fighter aircraft.

Since World War I, air-force missions such as strategic bombing, interdiction, and close-air support have become the key missions that one thinks of in aerial warfare. Yet, aerial reconnaissance and observation (now largely done by spacecraft or by small unmanned aircraft) still take up a large part of the attention of all military forces. It may not be as glamorous work as that of the fighter ace, but obtaining accurate information has always been one of the primary elements of victory on the battlefield. In World War I, aircraft came to play the central role in intelligence gathering.

–JAMES CORUM, USAF SCHOOL OF
ADVANCED AIRPOWER STUDIES

References

John Buckley, *Air Power in the Age of Total War* (London: UCL Press, 1999; Bloomington: Indiana University Press, 1999).

James S. Corum, *The Luftwaffe: Creating the Operational Air War, 1918–1940* (Lawrence: University Press of Kansas, 1997).

Edgar S. Gorrell, *The Measure of America's World War Aeronautical Effort* (Northfield, Vt.: Norwich University Press, 1940).

Richard Hallion, *Rise of the Fighter Aircraft, 1914–1918* (Annapolis, Md.: Nautical and Aviation Publishing Company of America, 1984).

James J. Hudson, *Hostile Skies: A Combat History of the American Army Air Service in World War I* (Syracuse, N.Y.: Syracuse University Press, 1968).

H. A. Jones, *The War in the Air: Being the Story of the Part Played in the Great War by the Royal Air Force: Appendices* (Oxford: Clarendon Press, 1937).

Lee Kennett, *The First Air War: 1914–1918* (New York: Free Press, 1991).

Kennett, *A History of Strategic Bombing* (New York: Scribners, 1982).

Eric and Jane Lawson, *The First Air Campaign, August 1914–November 1918* (Conshohocken, Pa.: Combined Books, 1996).

John H. Morrow Jr., *German Air Power in World War I* (Lincoln: University of Nebraska Press, 1982).

Morrow, *The Great War in the Air: Military Aviation from 1909 to 1921* (Washington, D.C.: Smithsonian Institution Press, 1993).

Mark K. Wells, ed., *Airpower: Promise and Reality* (Chicago: Imprint Publications, 2000).

George Kent Williams, *Biplanes and Bombsights: British Bombing in World War I* (Montgomery, Ala.: Air University Press, 1999).

AIRCRAFT

ALLIED ECONOMICS

Was the economic contribution of the United States a decisive factor in World War I?

Viewpoint: Yes. Beginning in 1917 the United States provided an essential flow of men, money, and munitions to Europe.

Viewpoint: No. The United States functioned in a secondary role as a banker, a supplier of raw materials, and a manufacturer of products designed elsewhere.

As the Great War moved closer to an avowed attritional model, the Allies correspondingly sought U.S. men, money, and material resources. Yet, along with American entry into the conflict in 1917 came a real concern: could the economy be mobilized in time to prevent Allied defeat at the hands of the final German offensives? To date, American material and financial contributions had been unsystematic, depending on French and British ability to negotiate loans and place contracts with private institutions. National mobilization, however, meant public involvement—and the Wilson administration, with its strong Progressive ambience, was not particularly known as a friend to either industry or finance.

Interaction between public and private enterprise remained contentious, but both sides made concessions for the sake of the war effort. The Marxist image of capitalism that still permeates the modern academy makes it worth emphasizing that the profit motive does not exclude patriotism. Businessmen and financiers were as anxious as the next American to see Germany crushed—arguably more so, from a widespread sense of noblesse oblige. The Wilson administration for its part was willing not only to work with private enterprise but also to bring qualified bankers and businessmen into the burgeoning administrative apparatus as expansion swamped existing bureaucratic systems.

The resulting synergy invites description as the beginning of the military–industrial complex. It certainly facilitated the development of financial transatlantic connections. It also stimulated industrial production, though the War Industries Board (WIB), created in July, remained relatively ineffective until after the turn of the year. The voluntaristic approach of the WIB, and its refusal to set prices by fiat, nevertheless facilitated production increases, albeit at the cost of some inflation. The Allies continued to depend heavily on shells made in the United States. The often-remarked failure of the United States to arm its expeditionary force with American-made weapons reflected not production shortcomings but the Wilson administration's decision to manufacture indigenous designs wherever possible, eschewing the experience gained in previous years of delivering material to France and Britain.

Mobilization was more successful in increasing and coordinating food production, despite increasing shortages of labor—a particular tribute to the administrative skill of Herbert Hoover, head of the U.S. Food Commission, and to the American people's ready acceptance of rationing. Deliveries to the Allies correspondingly increased, with positive effects on both prices and morale. More successful still was the mobilization of American manpower. A draft brought four million men into uniform, with the possibility of millions more to come. A training system provided the essentials of organization and instruction. Mobilization of shipping brought the new soldiers to France, where their contribution to morale was as significant as their physical presence—on both sides of the trenches. The relatively quick end to the conflict in November 1918 has somewhat obscured the significance of even the incomplete American mobilization for Allied victory.

Viewpoint:
Yes. Beginning in 1917 the United States provided an essential flow of men, money, and munitions to Europe.

The United States was ill prepared for an armed conflict when the events of July 1914 immersed the European powers in the Great War. Though the establishment acknowledged a dominant British heritage and increasingly accepted an "English connection" in social terms, the American people were significantly averse to European alliances and their mutual defense clauses. Threefold blessed with an abundance of natural resources, a burgeoning populace, and a border secured by two great oceans, with memories still bright from the devastation of the Civil War (1861–1865), Americans hoped never again to experience a major war—especially not one fought for the gain of an imperialist nation. From a democratic, transatlantic perspective, the Great War was solely a European affair. Yet, as an emerging world power, the United States could not long ignore the widening conflict. In 1917 President Woodrow Wilson's nation reorganized its sociopolitical thinking, economic infrastructure, and military resources to enable swift, intelligent, and decisive action to end the conflict.

Initially a minor phenomenon in the American sociopolitical system, the Quaker tenets of nonviolent behavior and arbitration found increasing acceptance in the aftermath of the Civil War and in the decades leading into World War I. The United States, having suffered greatly in the first modern war, was still nursing deep social wounds. The country had suffered two million casualties by the end of the Civil War. According to Russell F. Weigley, in *A Great Civil War: A Military and Political History, 1861–1865* (2000), the heavy price exacted from the American public was largely accepted as a necessary evil that resolved key points of contention that were fundamentally destabilizing the democratic nation—especially federalism and the charged issue of slavery. In the early twentieth century there were no issues of equal gravity around which or against which the general populace would rally to the defense of any European empires or their political maneuvers.

The American pacifist and populist movements garnered correspondingly broad public support for American nonintervention in the Great War. In 1912 the peace lobby strongly influenced the recently elected president, Woodrow Wilson, to take on a leading pacifist and anti-imperialist, William Jennings Bryan, as his secretary of state. Himself a strong noninterventionist, at least in European contexts, Wilson watched with appreciation as Bryan utilized every opportunity to present the United States as a state neutral "in thought, word, and deed," while simultaneously jockeying for an exploitable diplomatic position to curb the war through either international law or diplomatic discourse.

Bryan's, and his supporters', convictions were strengthened with the revelation in early 1915 that, in the first year of the war, the combined warring powers of Europe had suffered more than one million military dead—a loss far eclipsing the bloodiest battles of the Civil War. European suffering deepened the mainstream American's aversion to the war—but also offered the country certain substantive advantages. Propelled by the noninterventionists, President Wilson concentrated on internal matters, addressing perceived social and economic injustices by such policies as the mandatory eight-hour work limit for railroad workers, a progressive income tax, and progressive legislation against child labor; he narrowly won reelection on the noninterventionist platform. Wilson's actions appealed to the working class, but his efforts also held several unseen benefits. In a short amount of time, the president's measures had bolstered an American economy teetering on the edge of recession by providing regulated hours and job availability for adults, as well as a more-focused business structure and a reliable transportation infrastructure.

While pacifist organizations such as the American Friends Service Committee began actively engaging in relief and reconstruction efforts, other more-powerful forces were working behind the scenes toward securing their international economic future. As early as 1914 several influential American businessmen, most notably Andrew Carnegie and J. P. Morgan, entreated President Wilson to allow their companies to loan large sums of money to the warring factions in Europe. Though the president

ALLIED ECONOMICS

Poster encouraging civilian financial support of the Allied war effort

(Joseph M. Bruccoli Great War Collection, Thomas Cooper Library, University of South Carolina)

had initially demurred, questioning the morality of selling munitions, Wilson held little hope of legally curtailing such transactions. Once cleared to proceed, the loans initiated an economic boom for the United States. The French and British, with nowhere else to turn, poured their newly acquired funds back into the coffers of American corporations, ordering supplies they needed to continue the war.

Termed "War Babies" by historian Charles Seymour, industrial enterprises rapidly expanded production to meet the new demand for brass, copper, steel, gunpowder, and other war necessities. This newfound market, a product of long-standing American neutrality, had indeed galvanized the U.S. economy, but the new business sector largely consisted of precariously maintained, disorganized suppliers working individually. In peacetime, some might have considered the design an asset, but, as suppliers of essential war goods, many considered the situation an untenable problem as the United States approached intervention.

President Wilson supported several legislative plans, including the Webb-Pomerence Bill (1916), hoping to relax antitrust laws for businesses engaged in production and the export trade, but the incentives instead produced a mild economic stimulus. With the creation of the War Industries Board (WIB) in 1917, men such as New York financier Bernard Baruch; vice president of the Hudson Motor Car Company, Howard Coffin; notable statistician for the American Telephone and Telegraph Company, Walter Gifford; and Drexel Institute president, Hollis Godfrey, collectively induced the more independent-minded businesses to follow new methods of production standardization and to cooperate with government instead of resisting it.

The two reorientations reflected a foreign policy fundamentally altered as the German Empire embarked upon a policy of mercantile interdiction and commerce destruction, threatening not only their European adversaries but also the rebounding American economy. Though the U.S. population largely continued to hold to their noninterventionist resolve of years past, their beliefs did little to prevent the deaths of their fellow citizens traveling abroad. Since the sinking of the passenger ship *Lusitania* (1915) and the deaths of several Americans, the hawks had called for war. Those public figures championing the cause of the British Empire against "the Hun" had been silenced—first, upon learning of the brutal actions taken by the British against the small band of rebels during the Easter Rising (1916) in Ireland, and second, by the near-deafening cries of American noninterventionists. With the sinking of the

Arabic (1915), calls for retribution again grew louder. When the *Sussex* was sent to the bottom (1916), the public outcry warranted President Wilson to ask Congress for permission to arm merchant ships, hoping to discourage future German U-boat attacks. Since Bryan had already resigned his cabinet position in protest of Wilson's allowance of American business loans to the warring factions, there was no one within the administration either to privately challenge the political hawks' machinations for open warfare or publicly focus a counterresponse.

Cautiously, the United States moved toward war. Though President Wilson was at heart a pacifist, he took public offense at the unprecedented attacks by Germany on civilian liners. Unlike, moreover, the great European powers, the United States still possessed a small and ill-equipped military. Reelected to the presidency in 1916, Wilson embarked on a policy of militarization. Supported by the revelation of the Zimmerman Telegram, a German attempt at coercing Mexico to join the Axis Powers and destabilize the Americas with a war against the United States, and the sabotage efforts of German spies in destroying munitions-loading docks on Black Tom Island in New Jersey, on 2 April 1917 Wilson requested and received a declaration of war from Congress. The United States instituted an unprecedented military draft. In less than one year, the new U.S. Army had reached 1.75 million strong.

By the end of 1917 Allied efforts had also reduced losses per month to German U-boats from nine hundred thousand tons to three hundred thousand tons, allowing the bulk of U.S. cargoes of supplies and men to arrive relatively unmolested on the continental battlefield of Europe. Though the British and French had repeatedly beseeched Wilson to combine the U.S. troops with theirs, once General John Pershing's forces had committed his American Expeditionary Force (AEF) to battle, the sorely needed strength allowed the U.S. Army the convenience of ignoring Allied calls for an integrated command structure. Within six months, the United States, as the American populace had hoped, began the process of producing a resolution to the conflict.

As the universally recognized decisive force in ending the bloody stalemate, the United States won a position of global influence at the formal Versailles Conference (1919), and as the key industrial power in the future reconstruction of postwar Europe. Yet, without the initial influence of the pacifist and nonintervention movements, the United States might well have been absorbed into the conflict as a secondary power to be utilized by the European alliances as a source of expendable resources in the execution of their imperialistic plans. Instead, the United States entered the conflict as a focused world power bent on ending the nationalist war in Europe and, with well-honed economic, social, and military might, possessed the means to drive that aim to a successful conclusion.

–PAUL A. THOMSEN,
NEW YORK, NEW YORK

Viewpoint:
No. The United States functioned in a secondary role as a banker, a supplier of raw materials, and a manufacturer of products designed elsewhere.

Although there had been some movement toward a new type of warfare in the German wars of unification (1864–1871) and the American Civil War (1861–1865), World War I heralded the advent of total warfare. In a total war a nation had to fight in the following way: mobilize all available people and material resources on both the home and war fronts; retool industry and agriculture to produce supplies for the war effort; direct military operations against enemy combatants and noncombatants, and at the enemy's logistical infrastructure; and achieve a convincing victory and postwar peace. The United States contributed to the Allied victory, but not to as great a degree as has sometimes been suggested. Americans did not die by the millions, starve because of wartime food shortages, or fight the war in their homeland. The United States did not serve as the "arsenal for democracy" that it would in World War II (1939–1945). The European nations built many of their own military machines. Instead, the United States slowly offered more and more financing, raw materials, and manufacturing resources to the Allied nations, particularly to France and Great Britain.

The United States leaped into the full swing of industrialization in the decades before World War I. Millions of Americans moved from agriculture and rural areas to manufacturing and urban areas. The United States gradually emerged as a high-tech, industrial nation rivaling Great Britain and Europe in terms of production and commerce. The use of new technological innovations such as electricity, the internal-combustion engine, and the assembly line had dramatically increased the amount of manufactured goods. At the same time, prices for cutting-edge items such as Ford automobiles fell from $850 per vehicle in 1908 to $350 per vehicle in 1916. Manufactur-

ing also benefited from new management techniques such as those of Frederick Taylor, who favored the efficient use of less-skilled workers with standardized tasks over the use of highly skilled workers with specific tasks. As a result of so-called Taylorism, production levels of American factories increased still more. By 1914 no limit for possible increases of the quantity and quality of U.S. products was in sight.

When World War I started in 1914, the United States carried on trade with all the combatant nations, though the largest proportion was with Great Britain. Trade with the Central Powers, Germany and the Austro-Hungarian Empire, dropped off precipitously as the war progressed. Trade with the Allied powers, particularly France and Great Britain, increased at a geometric rate.

In total, the United States spent $33 billion on World War I. It therefore appears the United States provided an absolutely essential contribution to the Allied war effort. It may also appear that American industry, agriculture, finances, and eventually its military played primary roles in the Allied war effort. On balance, however, the United States played secondary, albeit decisive, roles in supporting the Allies. These roles include that of banker, supplier of raw materials, and manufacturer of hardware designed elsewhere.

American financial institutions and the U.S. government helped pay for the Allied cause in World War I. In the early stages of the war effort, the European nations called in their own debts to pay for war materials. Then, as the need for production of those war materials increased, the European nations turned to their imperial colonies for raw materials to be brought to the home nations. Indeed, the Europeans brought colonial laborers to work in their factories. This policy did not relieve shortages in food, clothing, ammunition, weapons, and other supplies. With the Allies desperate for an influx of investments, the United States loomed large as the potential bank for the Allies. U.S. loans were in turn used to pay for war materials manufactured by Americans.

In 1915 the American business Bethlehem Steel contracted with Great Britain for $80 million to manufacture ammunition. Du Pont, another large U.S. corporation, received a $96-million contract to produce gunpowder. Total trade with the Allied Powers rose from $825 million in 1914 to $3.2 billion in 1916 and even higher by 1918. Finances also shifted toward the United States away from Europe during World War I. The United States was a debtor nation in the amount of $3.7 billion in 1914. In 1917 alone, for example, the United States loaned $2.7 billion to the Allies. The United States emerged a creditor nation in the amount of

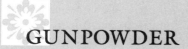

GUNPOWDER

In 1921 Bernard Baruch, former chairman of the War Industries Board (WIB), prepared a report on the control of raw materials and industrial production, including the manufacture of explosives, during World War I. A portion of that report appears here:

The explosives industry in the United States jumped from a $50,000,000 output in 1913 to a $500,000,000 output in 1917, which in turn had nearly doubled by November, 1918, and the year 1919 would have seen it more than doubled. . . .

Our development of military smokeless powder and military explosives during this period is unparalleled in history. In 1914 our smokeless powder capacity was 450,000 pounds per month. On November 10, 1918, we had facilities in operation producing nearly 2,500,000 pounds per day, and plants were nearly completed sufficient for 3,500,000 pounds per day. The developments in the production of ammonium nitrate, picric acid, and T.N.T., while not quite so great, followed an analogous course. We made a few thousand pounds of each of them before the war.

The problem before our government was to provide for the American program without robbing the allied program here. In fact, increasing difficulties in shipping were making it necessary for the Allies to close down some of their plants at home and depend upon America for increasing requirements. The vast plant facilities in this country in the spring of 1917, while they were owned by our nationals, had been built at the expense of the allied Governments. While our Government had a legal right to commandeer their output and use it for the American forces, such action would have been hostile to the common purpose. At the very beginning the President announced the policy that we would assist the Allies in taking full advantage of the properties which they had amortized here. . . .

Under this program America would have supplied the bulk of the propellant powder used on our side of the lines in 1919. In order to simplify the placing of contracts and the control over the flow of raw materials to the plants, the policy was adopted during the summer of 1918 of having the Ordnance Department purchase the entire American output for 1919, the department to resell in turn to the Allies such quantities as their respective programs required. On this theory a contract for 234,000,000 pounds, to be delivered during the first six months of 1919, was placed with the DuPont Co. On September 24, 1918, at a base price of 43 1/4 cents per pound. This was the lowest figure at which they had ever sold smokeless powder. This gives a notion of the dimensions of the American program for the production of propellent powder.

Modern warfare requires for high explosives, used as shell filler, a tonnage equal to about 85 per cent of that of the propellents. Raw materials for high explosives weigh about 20 pounds to 1 pound of the finished product. While England had some of these materials, France and Italy had practically none. Shipping conditions required that America should take the burden of the manufacture, and she set about to do it.

Source: *Bernard M. Baruch,* American Industry in the War: A Report of the War Industries Board (March 1921), *edited by Richard H. Hippelheuser (New York: Prentice-Hall, 1941), pp. 185–187.*

almost $4 billion, excluding government loans, by the end of the conflict. Conversely, European nations had neared bankruptcy because of their wartime debts.

In addition to loans, the United States also supplied massive amounts of raw materials to the Allied war effort. Early on, the necessities for warfare overwhelmed Allied industries. For example, some 16,000 soldiers and horses required twenty railroad cars full of food and fodder for each day on the front and still more during battles. Raw materials such as coal, pig iron, steel, cotton, and agricultural products were exported in huge quantities to France and Great Britain. Together with Canada, the United States led the world in production of all these materials. American exports increased from $2 billion in 1913 to $6 billion in 1916. For the most part, though, these exports included non-military items. Even when the United States entered the war in spring 1917, production of military arms and equipment remained low.

Acting as the breadbasket and bank for the Allied war effort put strains on American industry and transportation. In North America, transportation bottlenecks occurred because unloaded railroad cars clogged the tracks and switching yards in the East. This problem in turn caused a severe shortage of railroad cars—leaving food, coal, and other materials stacked up elsewhere in the nation. Only the U.S. government could bring order and rationality to this chaotic mess. In late 1917 President Woodrow Wilson established the U.S. Railroad Administration. This super-agency relieved and reformed the American transportation and supply network. By spring 1918 American railroads moved 625,000 soldiers per month on nine thousand special trains while maintaining other wartime transportation levels.

French and British industries took raw materials from North America and manufactured them into finished war products such as airplanes, tanks, artillery, clothing, trains, automobiles, and other equipment. It has been argued by Gerd Hardach, in an article in *The French Home Front, 1914–1918* (1992), edited by Patrick Fridenson, that World War I stimulated French industrial development. Following the principles of Taylorism and employing auxiliary workers such as women and colonials, the production of steel, coal, and pig iron increased to help France meet wartime demands. Reduced supplies of raw materials during periods of active German submarine warfare caused declines in French production.

American development of war equipment, in contrast, remained low throughout the war. The U.S. Army did not help increase the production levels because of archaic and inefficient procurement methods. No rational system of research and development on new weapons systems existed. Consequently, soldiers who served in the American Expeditionary Force (AEF) in 1917 and 1918 used European-developed and -manufactured weapons and equipment already on hand in France.

The influx of American manpower into the Allied war machine was the most important "raw material" that the United States provided to the war effort. The American soldier received advanced training, equipment, and supplies not from American but from French and British sources. The AEF purchased a higher percentage of its supplies from the French and British than it brought from the North American continent. For example, only 20 percent of the aircraft flown by American pilots were manufactured in the United States;

instead, Americans flew French and British planes. Of the 3,500 artillery pieces used by the AEF, less than 500 were manufactured in the United States; in fact, Americans depended so much on French artillery that the U.S. Army adopted the metric system to designate barrel diameter. Many of the rifles used by American infantry, although manufactured in the United States, were actually based on a British design. The American arms manufacturers Remington and Winchester adapted the Model 1917 Enfield from the British Model 1914 Enfield. Even the helmets worn by Americans were copies of those used by the British soldiers.

The United States played a secondary, yet important economic role in the Allied war effort. Americans also made another noneconomic contribution to the Allied war effort as a whole. The entry into the conflict in spring 1917 increased Allied morale, which was significant, especially in light of the massive mutinies in 1917 that left the French army crippled and ineffective. American manpower, that overlooked raw material, helped tip the scales in the Allies' favor in 1918. Knowing that millions more Yanks would be coming to fight for the Allied cause also dashed German hopes for victory.

–DAVID J. ULBRICH, TEMPLE UNIVERSITY

References

Bernard M. Baruch, *American Industry in the War: A Report of the War Industries Board (March 1921)*, edited by Richard H. Hippelheuser (New York: Prentice-Hall, 1941).

Herbert J. Bass, ed., *America's Entry Into World War I: Submarines, Sentiment, or Security?* (New York: Holt, Rinehart & Winston, 1964).

Paul S. Boyer, ed., *The Oxford Companion to United States History* (Oxford & New York: Oxford University Press, 2001).

Harvey A. DeWeerd, *President Wilson Fights His War: World War I and the American Intervention* (New York: Macmillan, 1968).

Dennis M. Drew and Donald M. Snow, *The Eagle's Talons: The American Experience at War* (Maxwell Air Force Base, Ala.: Air University Press, 1988).

Gerd Hardach, "Industrial Mobilization in 1914–1918," in *The French Home Front, 1914–1918*, edited by Patrick Fridenson, translated by Bruce Little (New York: Berg, 1992), pp. 57–88.

David M. Kennedy, *Over Here: The First World War and American Society* (New York: Oxford University Press, 1980).

Paul A. C. Koistinen, *Mobilizing for Modern War: The Political Economy of American Warfare, 1865–1919* (Lawrence: University Press of Kansas, 1997).

James T. Patterson, *America in the Twentieth Century: A History* (New York: Harcourt Brace Jovanovich, 1976).

Charles R. Shrader, "'Maconochie's Stew': Logistical Support of American Forces with the BEF, 1917–1918," in *The Great War, 1914–18: Essays on the Military, Political, and*

Social History of the First World War, edited by R. J. Q. Adams (College Station: Texas A&M University Press, 1990), pp. 101–131.

Russsell F. Weigley, *A Great Civil War: A Military and Political History, 1861–1865* (Bloomington: Indiana University Press, 2000).

Robert H. Zieger, *America's Great War: World War I and the American Experience* (Lanham, Md.: Rowman & Littlefield, 2000).

Phyllis A. Zimmerman, *The Neck of the Bottle: George W. Goethals and the Reorganization of the U. S. Army Supply System, 1917–1918* (College Station: Texas A&M University Press, 1992).

ALLIED ECONOMICS

AMERICAN IMPACT

Was American participation in the Great War decisive?

Viewpoint: Yes. The material and moral impact of U.S. intervention and the subsequent rapid deployment of troops to Europe both sustained the Allies and disheartened the Germans in the crucial early months of 1918.

Viewpoint: No. The German empire collapsed under the weight of the combined efforts of the British and French from 1914–1918, not because of the arrival of American troops.

The decisive nature of American participation in World War I has been affirmed by both its allies and its enemies. French general Philippe Pétain informed his exhausted, mutinous soldiers in 1917 that France would wait "for the Americans and the tanks." A German army initially skeptical of U.S. ability to raise an effective force came grudgingly and increasingly to respect the fighting power of the men in flat helmets, who just kept coming in ways no soldiers had done since Verdun (1916) and the Somme (1916). The masses of people who crowded the streets of France and Britain to cheer American troops, their commanding general, John Pershing, and their commander in chief, Woodrow Wilson, were perfectly willing to allow the Yanks all they wanted of the credit for bringing to an end four years of unparalleled horror.

More than images were involved. U.S. participation on the Allied side was a major morale boost in itself, and Wilson's rhetoric of a new international order revitalized Allied populations desensitized by millions of casualties. U.S. contributions of men and matériel heavily tipped the balance of an attritional war in the Allied favor. The mere presence of the doughboys in the hundreds of thousands was a tonic to exsanguinated Allied armies—and to their generals, who eagerly sought to integrate these fresh troops into their own ranks. In combat the Americans made all the mistakes of inexperience, but they showed an increasingly steep learning curve. Even the initial chaos of the Argonne campaign (1918) was in the process of being sorted out when the Armistice ended the fighting. Had the war continued into 1919, conventional wisdom long asserted, the Yanks would have played the foremost role in achieving an Allied victory that became inevitable with their arrival in France.

That rosy and flattering picture has been challenged in recent years by an emerging school of French and British—primarily British—historiography interested in reclaiming ownership of the Great War experience. These scholars present American participation as having its principal positive consequences in frameworks already established. French and British armies bore the main brunt of stopping a 1918 German offensive that was a last-ditch effort by an already exhausted Reich. In the fall counterattack the British Expeditionary Force (BEF) forced the Germans off balance and sent them slowly staggering backward toward the Rhine and capitulation. American intransigence, especially in the matter of an independent army, was understandable, but it also prolonged the war and cost lives—including thousands of American ones. The unctuous moralizing of President

Wilson so influenced the negotiations at Versailles that a commonsense peace settlement proved impossible—and then the Americans refused to sustain the fragile agreement that in fact resulted. Is this position Euro–sour grapes or justified revisionism?

**Viewpoint:
Yes. The material and moral impact of U.S. intervention and the subsequent rapid deployment of troops to Europe both sustained the Allies and disheartened the Germans in the crucial early months of 1918.**

Before the United States entered World War I in April 1917, its status as a world power had scarcely been recognized in the international arena. Even after it became a combatant, the effectiveness of its military contribution was called into question. Had not France and Britain lost the flower of their manhood over the previous three years? Yet, American historians have persisted in claiming that U.S. involvement in World War I was decisive in precipitating the German defeat. Although the sacrifices of the other Allies were surely enormous and worthy of honor, it is entirely correct to say that American involvement—which began in earnest in 1918—tipped the balance at a critical moment and won the war.

Unlike the outcome of World War II (1939–1945), the conclusion of World War I remained uncertain until the last months of the conflict. Until 1918 the overall military situation was characterized by an apparently unbreakable stalemate on the Western Front and by Allied reverses on the more peripheral fronts—in Italy, in the Middle East, in the Balkans, and worst of all, on the Eastern Front. While the United States prepared its growing civilian army for combat, the Western Front campaigns of 1917 showed that there was little hope for the British and French forces if they were to continue fighting without assistance from the United States. Within weeks of the American declaration of war, the French army was paralyzed by near-mutiny conditions when soldiers of nearly half of its combat divisions refused to take the offensive. Although they remained willing to defend against German attacks, the French army was for all practical purposes incapable of carrying on an active role for nearly a year. British forces on the Western Front, almost completely on their own, hardly acquitted themselves with success. A major offensive centered around the town of Passchendaele in western Belgium went on for more than three months (31 July–10 November 1917) and cost the British a quarter of a

million casualties without any palpable result. In November 1917 another costly British attack near the French town of Cambrai was repulsed despite some initial gains achieved by the limited use of tanks.

The turn of 1918 was even less encouraging for the Allied war effort. The Bolsheviks' seizure of power in Russia in November 1917 led to their swift conclusion of a three-month armistice with Germany and to negotiations for a separate peace on the Eastern Front. Knowing well that Russia no longer had the means or the inclination to remain a combatant, the Germans were free to relocate an enormous number of troops and huge stores of military supplies to the West for a new offensive. Long-standing Anglo-French fears that Russia would depart permanently from the war were confirmed by the peace treaty signed at Brest-Litovsk in March 1918.

By the time it had concluded peace with Soviet Russia, Germany was ready for a major offensive in the West. Less than three weeks after the Brest-Litovsk Treaty was signed, reinforced German armies in France, enjoying a considerable numerical advantage, slammed into weakly held British positions. In sharp contrast to most previous offensives on the Western Front, the first phase of the German attack in the spring of 1918 broke through the front and moved twenty miles forward in a matter of days. The weak British forces opposing it only succeeded in reestablishing a stable front because the German High Command made strategic mistakes that caused their troops in the field to lose momentum and stall in difficult terrain. A series of renewed German attacks pushed back the Allied positions even further. By late May 1918, German troops stood just forty miles from Paris, almost as close as they had at the height of their first offensive in 1914.

Whether the British and French could have held their positions by themselves is an unanswerable question because, of course, they did not have to face that situation. Although the United States had been a belligerent for more than a year, its first major formations only began to see action as German troops approached Paris. French observers liked to point out that the Americans achieved military triumphs only because the Germans had already lost their momentum and had suffered too many casualties to continue. Their

"THE AMERICANS KILL EVERYTHING!"

German soldier Kurt Hesse, a grenadier with the 36th Infantry Division, recounts fighting against American troops in mid July 1918 while the Germans made a last push against Allied lines in the Battle of the Marne:

The railroad tracks are crossed, the railroad station Varennes taken after a short fight, we go on past the road Moulins-Varennes—already 1,000 m. south of the Marne!—and up the southern slopes of the valley. Suddenly from the right there are sounds of sharp fighting and screams. In the morning mist, in the high grain field, one can see storm columns advance, dressed in brown—Americans!

Now and then they stand still and shoot. Our men come running back. The situation is extremely critical. Where are our neighbors, the 6th grenadiers? The attack must have been given up. The grenadiers are blindly shooting their volleys "according to program." This is to last until 11 o'clock in the morning, then they will be free for other tasks. But these they could hardly have carried out anyway, for observation of the battle is very hard; low mists veil the landscape, the grain is high, and movements are covered by the many little woods and orchards. The commanders of the Second battalion of the fusileers, Cavalry Captain von Plehwe and Captain Eben who are far at the front of their companies, realize that there is extreme danger in delay. All able to shoot, aim against the enemy on the right flank.

One must admit he is courageous unto death. Not till the machine-gun fire and the desperate shooting of our infantry had reaped a bloody harvest in his lines, did he halt and run back. But we take breaths of relief. Yet it is clear to each one of us: our own attack has failed! We must see to it that we can hold the position we have won with our weak forces, numerically much smaller than the enemy's.

The railroad line seems adequate for the defense. It is situated somewhat high and offers protection against fire, although on the other hand it is naturally a good target for the enemy artillery. Methodically the parts which are farther front are drawn back to this point. The right endangered flank is strongly reenforced. . . .

On the afternoon of July 15th it was possible to improve the line somewhat, as the enemy on the Marne, probably from fear of a double flanking movement, drew back its position somewhat; but this did not change anything in the final result of the day. *It was the severest defeat of the war!*

One only had to descend the northern slopes of the Marne: *never have I seen so many dead, nor such frightful sights in battle. The Americans on the other shore had completely shot to pieces in a close combat two of our companies. They had lain in the grain, in semicircular formation, had let us approach, and then from 30 to 50 feet had shot almost all of us down.* This foe has nerves, one must allow him this boast; but he also showed a bestial brutality. "The Americans kill everything!" That was the cry of horror of July 15th, which long took hold of our men. At home meanwhile they were sarcastic about the imperfect training of this enemy, about the American "bluff" and the like. The fact that on July 15th more than 60 per cent of our troops led to battle were left dead or wounded upon the battlefield may substantially be charged to his credit.

Source: Charles F. Horne, ed., Source Records of the Great War, volume 6 (Indianapolis: American Legion, 1930), pp. 255–256.

British counterparts tended to view the American troops as enthusiastic and overconfident yet too unprepared and inexperienced to be decisive. Both of these views, however, were ultimately irrelevant and self-serving. The hard fact was that American troops took up the line when the British and French had been driven to exhaustion and had lost more ground to the Germans than at any other time since the autumn of 1914. U.S. troops were instrumental in turning back the German advance at Soissons and Château-Thierry in early June 1918. The spirited resistance and pursuit of an enemy retreat at Belleau Wood by the U.S. Marine Corps denied the Germans access to the strategic city of Rheims and thus deprived them of the key to the railway network east of Paris. It may interest revisionist critics of U.S. military power to know that French troops around Belleau Wood actually urged the Marines there—without success—to join in their retreat. One Marine officer replied "Hell, we just got here!" Overconfidence can be a wonderful thing, even if armchair strategists dismiss it later out of national pride. In mid July a force of 140,000 American troops threw the vanguard of the German attack back across the Marne, repeating the much-revered success of the French in 1914.

The most decisive feature of American involvement in the war, however, remained the potential to fight, a factor that the abrupt end of the war in November 1918 prevented from reaching its full manifestation. The arrival of U.S. troops in France was relatively slow. The United States fielded the seventeenth largest army in the world. It declared war and required several months of training and preparation to put into uniform a field army comparable to those of France and Britain. Nevertheless, the drafting of several million men and the reorganization of the American economy for war production was achieved with a great deal of efficiency. The first round of the draft called almost 4 million men into training for active service. By March 1918 there were more than 300,000 American troops in France, and nearly as many fresh U.S. troops arrived in each and every subsequent month. By the end of the war 2 million Americans were serving in France. When the French commander in chief, Marshal Joseph Joffre, said earlier in the war that what the Allies needed most was "men, men, men," he could not possibly have asked for a better answer than what the U.S. government was prepared to provide.

These crushing numbers made all the difference, for as the American military presence in France grew, the British and French armies could barely tread water. Replacing their losses to the German spring offensive was an insuperable task. Large sections of the French army remained inactive until the summer of 1918, and the French government could only refill weakened units by drafting the next class of eighteen-year-old recruits. Between the summer of 1917 and the summer of 1918, the size of the British contingent in France shrank by one-third and had no immediate prospect of replenishing itself. By September 1918 there were more American servicemen at the front than British.

The wholesale introduction of U.S. troops into the battle line by the late summer of 1918 proved even more decisive than their timely and skillful defense of the approaches to Paris earlier in the year. With more than six hundred thousand American combat troops massed on the Western Front, the Allies could afford to launch a major offensive not just in one sector or another but along its entire length. When the American commander, General John Pershing, began his attack on 12 September, the frontal positions of the German army collapsed everywhere from the Belgian coast to Luxembourg. All German gains of 1918 were erased, and in many places the Germans lost territory they had held firmly since the first weeks of the war. Once again British and French observers tried to argue that the Germans had been preparing to retreat anyway, but the fact remains that Pershing's campaign was an American success that the British and French were, by their own quiet admission, incapable of achieving.

No one saw the importance of American involvement more clearly than the German High Command. Even before the crucial September offensive, the largely American successes on the Marne had created a near-panic situation at German headquarters. Although the de facto chief of military planning, General Erich Ludendorff, appeared determined to stay the course, his associates on the German General Staff began to call for either a purely defensive war or for armistice negotiations. German losses between March and August 1918 totaled nearly a million men, and adequate replacements simply did not exist. The next eligible group of draftees was expected to replenish less than a third of German losses, and the more creative General Staff officers put forward macabre plans to maximize the number of wounded soldiers who could be sent back into the line. As the American presence in France grew from seemingly limitless reserves, even Ludendorff had to admit that the buildup was the single largest cause for the declining morale of the German army.

The events of September 1918 broke all remaining German resolve. On 28 September, only sixteen days after Pershing's offensive began, the stalwart Ludendorff, who had never flinched at the carnage of the previous four years, suffered a nervous breakdown in his office (which his subordinates prudently closed off for the day) and tried to blame everyone but himself for the "looming defeat." He finally conceded that the time had come to call for an armistice. The war was over six weeks later.

The facts illustrate with little ambiguity that this outcome would not have been the case without decisive American involvement. Critics have said that the United States lay dormant for more than a year after its original declaration of war and became an active combatant only after Germany had spent its last resources, but they ignore several important points. First, American troops played a crucial, if not unilateral, role in checking the German advance toward Paris in the summer of 1918. Without their presence at crucial moments, the Allies would have had a significantly more difficult time resisting the five separate German offensives launched on the Western Front between March and July 1918. Second, the introduction of a huge number of fresh American troops, even if they were less experienced than their British and French counterparts, created an enormous psychological impact on the German military, from the demoralized foot soldiers who heard rumors of it to the top commanders who had to reconcile it with their strategic plans. Would Ludendorff have pitched his fit and thrown in the towel so readily if he did not have to think about the prospect of four million fresh American troops arrayed against his bleeding army? Finally, if the Allies had been forced to continue the war beyond Armistice Day, their potential to carry the war forward, drive the Germans all the way out of France and Belgium, and carry the war across the German frontiers did not exist independently of American military involvement. France could barely muster a sizable portion of its army to fight for its own soil, while Britain could no longer replace its battlefield losses. Without the decisive contribution of the United States, a speedy and favorable end of the war in 1918 would have been impossible.

–PAUL DU QUENOY,
GEORGETOWN UNIVERSITY

Viewpoint:
No. The German empire collapsed under the weight of the combined efforts of the British and French from 1914–1918, not because of the arrival of American troops.

It is a typical American belief that the arrival of the American Expeditionary Force (AEF) in France in 1917 brought Imperial Germany to its knees, thereby bringing World War I to its end. This perspective, however, overlooks the simple fact that Russia, France, Britain, and its allies had fought Germany and Austria-Hungary for three years before General John Pershing's troops began to trickle onto the battlefields of the Western Front in the last part of 1917. Surely, three years of the bloodiest combat to date had their effect upon the ability of Germany to continue the war.

Napoleon Bonaparte was finished at Waterloo (1815) and his nephew, Napoleon III, at Sedan (1870). Yet, World War I was not decided in a single battle—it was won by the long, drawn-out losses of fighting on two fronts. Consider the death totals: at least 8.6 million men were killed in the war, some 1.8 million of them German. An average of 5,600 men were killed on both sides each day of the war.

This bloodletting proved to be the end for Germany. Changes in technology and logistics produced an operational stalemate early in the war. Heavily supplied defensive positions, ranging back several miles, fortified with barbed wire and defended by colossal artillery barrages and machine guns had produced this condition. Trench warfare of the Western Front still stands as a metaphor for costly and futile slaughter. Britain had destroyed its prewar army and had pretty much sacrificed the one built to replace it in 1916 in the Fields of Flanders. Losses on the opposing side were similar: the Germans had suffered some 1,500,000 battlefield casualties by the end of 1915, and the battle of the Somme produced some 630,000 additional casualties.

Not until 1918 did military thinkers devise a solution to this impasse. The answer came not from technology in the form of still–nascent British and French experiments in armor. Rather, a way to defeat defense in depth was found by using the oldest of all military specialities, the foot soldier. Moreover, this doctrinal change was successfully implemented not by the eventual victors but by the German Imperial Army. Using small, individually operating infantry teams armed with grenades, rifles, and submachine guns, the German army managed to counter defense in depth with deep penetrating attacks that took ten times more territory from the Allies from March to June 1918 than the Allies had taken from the Germans in all of 1917, a year that had been seen as successful for the Allied powers. While the gains of the 1918 "Ludendorff Offensive" were impressive, they came at a tremendous cost: nearly 1 million German casualties. If Germany had used this technique earlier, it might have won the war.

By the middle of 1918, however, Germany had nothing left to fight with. What remained was to salvage the best possible settlement. Though Berlin had practically no power to launch another offensive, the experience of 1914–1918 indicated that the defensive was still heavily favored. Moreover, German territory was still untouched by actual fighting.

Yet, holding off long enough to gain a reasonable settlement was easier said than done. Time was not on the side of Berlin because the British had managed to inflict other losses upon Germany. Though Britain had sent a sig-

AMERICAN IMPACT

1918 poster by Herbert Paus that provided a slogan used as a justification for the war

(Joseph M. Bruccoli Great War Collection, Thomas Cooper Library, University of South Carolina)

nificant army to the Western Front, one cannot overlook the contributions of the Royal Navy in sapping the German will to resist. From 1914 an ever-tightening blockade of German and neutral ports had gradually lowered German consumption to low levels. Germany was left to rely on its own resources to meet the needs of both industry and of its population. However, this goal was a nigh-impossible task, and it led to a high degree of suffering and social unrest. The Germans were reduced to eating dogs and cats, and improvising a kind of bread from potato peels and sawdust. Naturally, disease followed malnourishment, and the Spanish influenza epidemic hit Germans just as hard, if not harder, than anyone else. In January 1918 some 400,000 workers in Berlin went on strike, demanding peace, and the protests spread to six other German cities. Martial law was declared in Berlin and Hamburg. Yet, this upheaval was only a foretaste of the unrest that would break out in the autumn.

Another way that time was running out for the Germans was that by 1919 the Americans would be on the Western Front in appreciable numbers. When the United States declared war on Germany in April 1917, the U.S. Army did not have a single division in its force structure. As one might expect, its contributions in 1917 were negligible; only in January 1918 did the American Expeditionary Force (AEF) deploy a division to the front lines. In September 1918 the United States

successfully carried out its own offensive on the St. Mihiel salient, but against German units that in fact were withdrawing from the sector. Similarly, the attacks in the Argonne were against German formations that were pulling back. A considerable increase in the American army on the Western Front was planned, and no doubt the German General Staff worried about the prospect.

As things turned out, however, the German General Staff would not be given the opportunity to worry for long. Four years of losses on the front, of blockade and economic strain, and of a leadership that promised a victory worthy of the hardships all combined to create a collapse of the home front. Germany in September and October 1918 was in a state of chaos. Perhaps fittingly for a country whose leadership was always out of touch with its population, the collapse started with the decision of the North Sea Fleet leadership to launch a last heroic suicide mission at sea against the Royal Navy. The enlisted ranks, suffering an arrogance of power much like the average German, mutinied. Their example inspired a series of other rebellions across the country. Railway, industrial, and urban centers were seized by rebels inspired not just by war fatigue but also by the promises of Vladimir Lenin's example and of President Woodrow Wilson's calls for a just peace. In September the Kaiser authorized negotiations with the Americans for an armistice. The German army began its constant withdrawal under the pressure of the Allied attacks. On 9 November the Kaiser's abdication was announced by Prince Max of Baden, who named Socialist politician Friedrich Ebert as chancellor. Under the conditions of a total collapse of his regime, Kaiser Wilhelm II abdicated and left for exile in the Netherlands. No other option remained but surrender. A long war of attrition had reached its logical conclusion, and the German regime fell apart to the advantage of the Allies. Though the Americans would have been a tremendous force had the war continued in 1919, they had arrived too late to make the difference in 1918. British and French efforts on land and sea had succeeded in forcing a collapse of Germany.

—PHIL GILTNER, U.S. MILITARY ACADEMY

References

John Keegan, *The First World War* (London: Hutchinson, 1998).

Walter LaFeber, *The American Age: Foreign Policy at Home and Abroad,* volume 2, *Since 1896,* second edition (New York: Norton, 1994).

John Terraine, *To Win a War: 1918, the Year of Victory* (London: Sidgwick & Jackson, 1978).

David F. Trask, *The AEF and Coalition Warmaking, 1917–1918* (Lawrence: University Press of Kansas, 1993).

BEF COMMAND STRUCTURE

Was the British Expeditionary Force command structure too rigid?

Viewpoint: Yes. Throughout the war, the bureaucratic nature of the BEF command structure hindered the realization of plans and policies.

Viewpoint: No. The British command structure demonstrated a capacity to integrate human resources and matériel into a war-winning system.

The historiography of the British high command in World War I has developed around opposing poles. One is expressed in the title of a book by Australian John Laffin: *British Butchers and Bunglers of World War One* (1988). This position depicts a senior officer corps not merely culpably ignorant of contemporary developments in the craft of war, but in a sense proud of its ignorance. From before the war the British army emphasized conformity, privileged physical over intellectual activity, and focused its energies on securing top appointments in an institution whose small size turned predictable competition into brutal infighting. Authors such as Norman Dixon in *On the Psychology of Military Incompetence* (1976) present the British army of the World War I era as a petri dish cultivating military incompetence by rewarding psychological dysfunction. Historians interpreting modern British history in class warfare contexts insist a system of incestuous privilege by its nature could not produce the spectrum of talents required to lead a national army in a total war. The generals were out of their depths from start to finish—and Britain paid the price of privilege in dead and maimed.

In specific terms, the wartime high command is denounced for its inability to see any possibilities of victory other than the Western Front. It is pilloried as favoring its own kind over talented outsiders such as Canadian general Arthur Currie and Australian general John Monash. It is attacked for emphasizing moral force over physical factors, for remoteness from the actual battlefields, and for disinterest in new weapons and methods. Tim Travers in particular makes a case in *How the War Was Won: Command and Technology in the British Army on the Western Front, 1917–1918* (1992) that by 1917 the British Expeditionary Forces (BEF) command structure, down to division levels, was paralyzed. Unable and unwilling to communicate internally, it initiated operations such as Passchendaele (1917) and Cambrai (1917) without clear objectives and continued them too long. The German successes of 1918 reflected the failure of the BEF to understand and apply a concept of defense-in-depth foreign to its "groupthink." The final British victory later in the year was attained at the cost of high casualties, incurred in good part because of failure to understand the potential of even early versions of the tank.

The counterpoint to that position emphasizes the institutional unfamiliarity of the British army with war on continental scales and contextualizes its command problems by making the case that no other army was more successful in solving the firepower/mobility conundrum so starkly posed by the Western Front. Military decisions, moreover, were strongly influenced by the fact of British participation in a coalition with France, and that a good part of French territory was German-occupied. The abortive attacks of 1915, the Somme (1916), and Passchendaele were all strongly shaped by French circumstances.

As for alleged obsession with the Western Front, nowhere else could an army capable of mounting a serious offensive find an infrastructure sufficiently developed to support its operations. In Russia, Italy, and the Middle East alike, traditional factors such as terrain and disease were by themselves enough to gridlock campaigns.

Within those limits the British high command maintained the loyalty of its men, engaged an increasingly high proportion of the German army, and demonstrated a remarkably steep learning curve. If anything the BEF from Sir Douglas Haig downward was too quick to innovate, with the result that firepower- and mechanical-based approaches jostled for place until the Armistice. At least, assert defenders of the high command, the BEF bore the brunt of the fighting in the last hundred days of World War I, using manpower, firepower, and mobility in a tactical/operational synergy that for the first time kept the Germans off balance past the point where they could rally and consolidate.

Viewpoint:
Yes. Throughout the war, the bureaucratic nature of the BEF command structure hindered the realization of plans and policies.

For some time, particularly in the half century after 1930, much British writing on the British Expeditionary Force (BEF) focused on the supposed personal qualities—moral, intellectual, and social—of the commanders and the degree to which they were responsible for the heavy casualties suffered by the army during the war. Since the mid 1980s, historians have sought to analyze events on the Western Front more dispassionately and from different angles. As a result, they have emphasized British success: the creation over four years, from a tiny nucleus, of a mighty, modern, combined-arms force that learned from its early errors and became a war-winning weapon.

The rapid expansion of the British army inevitably caused difficulties in command and control, not the least that of inexperience. Furthermore, the technological and environmental conditions of the Western Front—the lack of good radio communications, the often poor state of the ground—combined with the scale of the conflict, posed a serious challenge to command structures of all nations that fought in World War I. Notwithstanding a recognition of all these factors, however, any objective assessment of the BEF command structure over the course of the war must still conclude that it was overly hierarchic and rigid, and that this limited potentially useful discussion.

In the years before World War I, the British army began a difficult period of transition toward a fully professional status. Although improvements had been made, in many ways it

had not fully completed this change by 1914. Its officer corps remained an almost feudal institution, with advancement depending as much on good connections and patronage as on military ability. It also reflected many of the faults of the wider society from which it was drawn. It emphasized the value of deference and obedience within a strict hierarchy and strong group loyalty, and tended to be suspicious of over-professionalism or intellectualism. As the BEF expanded into the largest army Britain had ever put in the field, it perpetuated, particularly in its upper echelons, many of these prewar characteristics.

In planning and in combat, the BEF tended to operate on a "top-down" basis. Both orders and information came from above, down the chain of command, in writing rather than verbally. It was difficult for information to flow back up the chain to the top in order to influence the planning or the fighting of battles. Although subordinates might be aware of mistakes or lack of understanding among their senior officers, they were not encouraged to make these known. For example, even when liaison officers were introduced, as a means of keeping general headquarters (GHQ) in touch with battlefield conditions, the reports these officers produced tended to be ignored in favor of the more optimistic versions produced by more-senior officers at army headquarters.

These problems were compounded by the nature of the war being fought, which tended to isolate senior commanders even more, and by the personalities of the commanders in chief. The difficulties of communication and transport meant that it was all but impossible for commanders above divisional level to visit frontline troops, quite apart from the possible danger involved. To do so removed them from the center of command for too long. But in the absence of detailed firsthand reports, it is arguable that senior officers tended to accept simplistic bureaucratic measures of success without criticism. For example, heavy casualty figures seem

BEF COMMAND STRUCTURE

French children accompanying British infantrymen as they march through Lille, France, on 18 October 1918

(Imperial War Museum, London)

often to have been seen at GHQ as a sign of successful, "thrusting" generalship, without regard for any practical results achieved. Conversely, low casualty rates were evidence of lack of keenness in the assault. Certainly, the necessary separation of senior officers from the front line, as well as the heavy emotional burden they had to withstand, seems to have resulted in a distancing from their troops that often strikes the modern observer as callous.

Neither Sir John French nor Sir Douglas Haig possessed either the sort of character or the inclination to challenge the established hierarchical system. Indeed, their personal traits tended to exacerbate the situation, although whether this is grounds for criticism of them is perhaps another matter: since they had risen to the top of the tree, they could hardly be expected to behave otherwise. French was a man overpromoted and out of his depth, rightly afraid of challenges from below. Famously, when Sir Horace Smith-Dorrien questioned whether French meant to stand on the defensive or to attack at the battle of Mons in 1914, French told him: "You do as you are ordered and don't ask questions."

Haig, who took over from French at the end of 1915, might at first seem to have preferred a system which, if rigid, was at least nonprescriptive. Instead of formulating precise plans for his army commanders to follow, he preferred to give them a general plan and objectives, allowing them to work out the precise details of operations. Indeed, he deemed this noninterference in subordinates' plans a crucial element in his method of command. However, when combined with the complications of hierarchy and patronage already identified, as well as Haig's own character, which was forbidding and taciturn to the point of Trappism, this apparent flexibility in fact resulted in an absence of discussion. This led to, if not command paralysis, at least considerable confusion. Haig's subordinates were too fearful of him, or too indebted to him, to wish to disturb his equilibrium, either by giving him information that did not fit in with his preconceptions, by debating the suitability of the outline plans they had been given, or by confessing their incomprehension. Haig himself found it difficult to accept information that did not fit in with his preconceptions and tended to become angry if challenged.

The results of this command structure were most obvious precisely during the planning for the great battles of 1916 and 1917. While planning for the Battle of the Somme in early 1916, Sir Henry Rawlinson, commander of the Fourth Army, appears to have been too apprehensive of his chief's negative reaction to stand up to him over the issue of whether the offensive should aim for a breakthrough or for more limited objectives. The result was that during the planning for the Third Battle of Ypres, confusion again existed over the scale, style, and objectives of the assault. Not only was Sir Hubert Gough, commander of the Fifth Army, too intimidated to confront Haig with his lack of understanding, but Gough's subordinates also seemingly existed in an atmosphere of terror, unable to tell their chief about the flaws in his plan. It has been argued that this breakdown in command at the highest level allowed senior commanders to continue fighting battles according to an outmoded paradigm, which emphasized human valor and morale, to the detriment of more-modern technological solutions to battlefield problems. Although new weapons, such as tanks and gas, were accepted with alacrity, commanders then attempted to integrate them into existing operations and tactics, rather than use them to their best advantage.

The hierarchy that limited the flow of information and discussion at a senior level was also apparent in the BEF's rigidity lower down the structure of command. As the army expanded, it attempted to keep up many of its prewar traditions in terms of hierarchy and deference. There was good-natured, but heartfelt, suspicion of other units and arms—so-called regimentalism—which restricted the effectiveness of cooperation. Junior officers and NCOs were encouraged not only to be obedient, but also constantly to look for orders from above before taking action. In a battlefield environment where communications were liable to sudden breakdown, flexibility and individual initiative by junior commanders were at a premium. At no point in the war did the BEF consistently display these characteristics; certainly it never encouraged them, even though it did improve its officer training as the war went on. Those senior regimental officers who either did not trust or understand technical innovations tended to shunt responsibility for these onto their least favorite junior officers, thus inhibiting the integration of new weapons technologies.

Again thanks to the policy of only a general setting of objectives, small-unit commanders were often able to experiment and innovate to find the tactics that worked best: a situation of constructive anarchy with potentially great rewards in terms of speeding up a "learning-curve." During the battles of 1916 and 1917,

even neighboring units might employ very different tactics. However, the failure of communications higher up the command ladder meant that tactical developments were often not effectively passed on to other units. This could mean that lessons had to be repeatedly and painfully learned by many units, rather than just one.

The best example of the failings inherent throughout the BEF's structure of command was the inadequate implementation of "defense in depth" in early 1918. It seems that few British commanders at any level fully comprehended the new elastic defensive system, in particular the need for tactical withdrawal from the outpost line. Although expressed at the time, such apparent lack of understanding did not lead to the discussion that might have clarified a workable system of defense. Instead, officers implemented "defense in depth" because it was ordained from above, often attempting to fit it into their preconceived image of the need to contest every yard of ground. The result was defensive failure and near disaster. It was notable that at the small-unit level, many British troops lacked the flexibility to successfully implement the impromptu counterattacks that had been a feature of the elastic German defense they were supposedly copying.

At a high level, the BEF's command structure prevented the free flow of information and ideas that might have led to more efficient operations. Plans were laid down from above without the potentially valuable input of subordinates. This situation occurred because the army as a whole had a system of command that was rigid and hierarchic, even though it had elements—the doctrine of noninterference in subordinates' detailed plans—that might seem to be more democratic. In these characteristics it reflected not only the society from which it was drawn but also more particularly the prewar colonial army out of which it grew. The rigidity of the BEF's command structure had a negative effect on its war-fighting ability.

—DANIEL TODMAN, PEMBROKE COLLEGE, CAMBRIDGE UNIVERSITY

Viewpoint:
No. The British command structure demonstrated a capacity to integrate human resources and matériel into a war-winning system.

The British army, like most armies, went into World War I convinced morale was the key to victory. This point of view makes sense, to a

HAIG ON ARTILLERY

British field marshal Douglas Haig, in a report originally published in The London Gazette *on 8 April 1919 and republished by the U.S. War Department in 1919, comments on the use of artillery in World War I:*

The growth of our artillery was even more remarkable, its numbers and power increasing out of all proportion to the experience of previous wars. The 486 pieces of light and medium artillery with which we took the field in August, 1914, were represented at the date of the armistice by 6,437 guns and howitzers of all natures, including pieces of the heaviest caliber.

This vast increase so profoundly influenced the employment of artillery and was accompanied by so intimate an association with other arms and services that it merits special comment.

In the first place, big changes were required in artillery organization, as well as important decisions concerning the proportions in which the different natures of artillery and artillery ammunition should be manufactured. These changes and decisions were made during 1916, and resulted in the existing artillery organization of the British armies in France.

In order to gain the elasticity essential to the quick concentration of guns at the decisive point, to enable the best use to be made of them, and to facilitate ammunition supply and fire control, artillery commanders, acting under army and corps commanders, were introduced, and staffs provided for them. This enabled the large concentrations of guns required for our offensives to be quickly absorbed and efficiently directed. The proportions required of guns to howitzers and of the lighter to the heavier natures were determined by certain factors, namely the problem of siting in the comparatively limited areas available the great numbers of pieces required for an offensive; the "lives" of the different types of guns and howitzers, that is the number of rounds which can be fired from them before they become unserviceable from wear, and questions of relative accuracy and fire effect upon particular kinds of targets.

The results attained by the organization established in 1916 is in itself strong evidence of the soundness of the principles upon which it was based. It made possible a high degree of elasticity, and by the full and successful exploitation of all the means placed at its disposal by science and experience, insured that the continuous artillery battle which began on the Somme should culminate, as it did, in the defeat of the enemy's guns.

The great development of air photography, sound ranging, flash spotting, air-burst ranging, and aerial observation brought counterbattery work and harassing fire both by day and night to a high state of perfection. Special progress was made in the art of engaging moving targets with fire controlled by observation from aeroplanes and balloons. The work of the field survey sections in the location of hostile battery positions by resection and the employment of accurate maps was brought into extended use. In combination with the work of the calibration sections in the accurate calibration of guns and by careful calculation of corrections of range required to compensate for weather conditions it became possible to a large extent to dispense with registration, whereby the chance of effecting surprise was greatly increased. In the operations east of Amiens on August 8, 1918, in which over 2,000 guns were employed, practically the whole of the batteries concentrated for the purpose of the attack opened fire for the first time, on the actual morning of the assault.

The use of smoke shell for covering the advance of our infantry and masking the enemy's positions was introduced and employed with increasing frequency and effect. New forms of gas shell were made available, and their combination with the infantry attack carefully studied. The invention of a new fuze known as "106," which was first used in the Battle of Arras, 1917, enabled wire entanglements to be easily and quickly destroyed, and so modified our methods of attacking organized positions. By bursting the shell the instant it touched the ground and before it had become buried, the destructive effect of the explosion was greatly increased. It became possible to cut wire with a far less expenditure of time and ammunition, and the factor of surprise was given a larger part in operations.

Great attention was paid to the training of personnel, and in particular the Chapperton Down Artillery School, Salisbury Plain, was formed for training artillery brigade commanders and battery commanders, while artillery schools in France were organized for the training of subalterns and noncommissioned officers.

A short examination of our principal attacks will give a good idea of the increasing importance of artillery. On the first day of the Somme Battle of 1916 the number of artillery personnel engaged was equal to about half the infantry strength of the attacking divisions. On this one day a total of nearly 13,000 tons of artillery ammunition was fired by us on the western front. Our attacks at Arras and Messines, on April 9 and June 7, 1917, saw the total expenditure of artillery ammunition nearly doubled on the first days of those battles, while the proportion of artillery personnel to infantry steadily grew.

Source: *"Field Marshal Sir Douglas Haig, Features of the War,"* The World War I Document Archive, <http://raven.cc.ukans.edu/~kansite/ww_one/comment/haigvue.htm>.

BEF COMMAND STRUCTURE

degree: a soldier with a better weapon who is unwilling to fight will lose to a motivated foe. It was taken to an extreme, however, with some generals believing that they only needed to demolish the obstacles to a charge (barbed wire or trenches) for the superior morale of the British infantry to ensure victory. In addition, there was a xenophobic assessment of morale. Field Marshal Douglas Haig (especially) felt that British morale was always high and German morale was always declining. In truth, the morale of both sides fluctuated, and a more sophisticated commander would have taken steps to sustain the morale of his own men rather than simply assuming it was good. Gradually, the necessity of using technical arms (gas, tanks, aircraft, and, above all, artillery) was recognized by British commanders, although a special place was always reserved for morale.

The command structure of the British Expeditionary Force (BEF) was also far from perfect. There was no good system to choose commanders or staff officers, so at all levels some men performed poorly. Even so, by the end of the war, experience had weeded out most incompetent officers. More important, by the middle of the war, strong support had been given to key new technologies that would be used alongside the traditional morale factor. The BEF won several important battles in 1918 because of these combinations.

Gas was one of the important new technologies. It was immediately recognized as a useful weapon, quickly adopted (less than six months after the Germans first used gas on the Western Front, the British returned the "favor"), and gradually improved. At first it was badly used because of severe production and technical limitations and downright muddled thinking. Once the factories got going, however, Britain produced a string of gases with different properties, so there was a gas appropriate for most tactical situations.

Better gases were complemented with improved tactics. Experience showed what worked and what did not, and there were enough intelligent staff officers to sift through the reports and spread the news. A comparison of the 1916 and 1918 editions of the General Headquarters (GHQ) pamphlet, "Instructions on the Use of Lethal and Lachrymatory Shell," shows what happened. In the latter version there are more detailed numbers on how many shells are needed to cover an area and how long the gas will linger in different weather. Various gases are identified as appropriate for different British goals (harassment, area denial, or causing casualties) and to defeat distinct German objectives.

Despite its usefulness, gas warfare had too many drawbacks to be decisive. Good antigas discipline would minimize casualties; the weather could intervene at almost any time and dilute the best-laid plans; and lethality was actually relatively low. Senior officers used gas when and where they could, but as a supplement rather than a centerpiece.

Aircraft (balloons as well as airplanes) was another developing technology, and one the BEF enthusiastically embraced throughout the war. Although the first aircraft had no weapons with which to intervene in the ground fighting—they were used as observers—these scouts brought back vital information through aerial photography that led to the Miracle of the Marne (the blocking of the German advance, in September 1914, into France). While both sides quickly started to arm aircraft, even before "fighters" became common there was a more important aerial predator: the artillery spotter. By mid September 1914 the BEF was using aircraft to select tactical targets and adjust artillery fire onto the unlucky ones.

Soon aircraft were sprouting guns, bombs, cameras, and wireless sets. Nevertheless, there were real limits on their direct effect on the battlefield. Underpowered engines meant payloads (especially bomb loads) were small, and the complexity of production and fragility of the aircraft themselves meant there were never vast numbers in service. There was no possibility of massive aerial bombardments, as there would be in World War II. Instead, the deadliest thing an aircraft (here including balloons) could take aloft was an artillery observer. With a real-time connection to the guns below, an observer could direct them to demolish either an already-known target or one of opportunity. (Sometimes the German fighter ace Manfred von Richthofen, "The Red Baron," has been criticized for attacking mainly observation aircraft, which were generally easier targets, but the German infantry would probably have thanked him all the more.)

The BEF, recognizing the importance of good air-to-ground liaisons, linked observation squadrons and artillery headquarters so that the people involved could gain familiarity and work together better. They also recognized the benefits of a standardized system, and once experience showed the best methods, they were adopted both by the Royal Flying Corps (RFC) and the Royal Artillery. The RFC had an aggressive, morale-based ethos that attacking was better than defending, as if a pilot could impose his will on an aircraft and then the enemy. Probably too much was made of the morale idea, but even modern fighter pilots are aggressive—or, it is said, they have no business being fighter pilots!

While aircraft became increasingly important, the World War I tank was a chancy weapon. Mechanical reliability was always a problem (up to one-third often broke down before entering action), mobility was low (as much as another third bogged down, got caught on stumps, or ended up in ditches), and they were frighteningly vulnerable to decent antitank weapons. Nevertheless, they made a huge difference in small-unit tactics because they were essentially invulnerable to machine-gun fire.

The BEF is often savaged, first for lack of enthusiasm about tanks and then for the poor use of the tanks it got. In fact, in early 1916 (before the first tank entered battle) Haig had asked for one thousand tanks, but production was slow, and it was not until 1917 that the one thousandth tank was finished; he never had one thousand of them at any one time. Nor was he slow to use them in battle. Instead, although the point is hotly debated, he may have committed them too soon, before substantial numbers were available. In mid September 1916, with forty-nine tanks on hand, he threw them into the battle of the Somme. At the end of their first day, about a dozen were still running—and these needed overhaul. Even so, Haig was encouraged and two weeks later began planning a surprise dawn attack using tanks to grab a small sector of the German line.

Conservatives at GHQ are often blamed for seeing the tank as a supporting weapon and not recognizing its potential. To be sure, Haig and GHQ explicitly saw tanks as "auxiliary" to the infantry, but that view did not stop innovations and improvements. Throughout 1917 and 1918 the Tank Corps developed tactics that responded to their own vehicles, evolving British infantry/artillery tactics, and improved German defenses. They also had to devise plans to operate in unfamiliar environments, such as the plans for an amphibious operation on the Flanders coast.

Some visionary officers could see the long-term potential of the tank to change the face of battle, but from 1916 to 1918 the tanks available were not revolutionary. Grinding at three miles per hour or less, frequently breaking down, and exhausting their crews with heat and carbon monoxide, tanks were not yet a breakthrough weapon. Nor were they anything like invulnerable: the Germans quickly reacted and introduced antitank weapons. In fact, by 1918 the Tank Corps was asking the artillery to deal with "all anti-tank devices," testimony of how much support was needed by the tanks before they could support others. So the "visionary" plans for a massive tank breakout in 1919 were more like mirages than visions: industry could not produce tanks fast enough, and those they could build could not move far enough or fast enough to execute the plans.

Artillery, although not a new technology, developed into the most important weapon system in World War I, probably inflicting more than half of all wounds suffered in combat. Indeed, by 1918 the Royal Artillery was probably the most effective artillery in the world, largely because the BEF understood how to integrate these weapons into a combined-arms battle. While it was obviously effective, artillery by itself was not a war winner but instead a support for the troops actually in action. Initially it was a struggle to get enough guns and shells (and then, because of production problems and profiteers, reliable shells) to implement new tactics. Other problems cropped up: training the vast influx of new men (and some of the older officers) and devising a command system to handle the influx of artillery.

By 1916 most of the initial problems were solved. A new command system was in place, and while it naturally needed improvement over time, from the beginning it provided a framework for adjustments, rather than needing individual brilliance to get results. Indeed, it proved so satisfactory that it lasted through World War II and is the basis of the modern artillery command system. There were enough guns and shells during World War I to finally try some of the ideas that had emerged in the lean years of 1914–1915, and the gunners were a bit better trained.

The Battle of the Somme was an ugly engagement, with little finesse and hundreds of thousands of casualties, but it proved that enough artillery fire could indeed blast a line of defenses to the point that friendly infantry could capture them—although this strategy usually took long enough that the enemy could gather men and guns for a counterattack. In the opening battles of 1917 this pattern was repeated with increasing efficiency: the Allies employed heavy-artillery bombardments, followed by an infantry advance; the process was repeated as desired. Both the infantry and artillery gained experience and refined their tactics. Artillery officers realized some of the limitations inherent in the bludgeoning tactics and started thinking ahead for new ways to achieve the same results, but they had to wait for the infantry—the troops who had the final say because they were the ones risking their lives—to become comfortable with the new methods.

Over time the technical problems were solved, allowing first the artillerymen, and then the rest of the army, to implement tactics that took advantage of the new capabilities. By 1918 the BEF was using artillery much more effectively. At times it was even used as a semi-independent element of battle, no longer being assigned directly to support a given infantry unit. Yet, it was still integrated into the battle as a whole because the formation commander decided how to use his artillery.

Even in 1918 infantry were still seen as the centerpiece, and morale still played a role, making it possible for conservatives to say "I told you so." Gas, tanks, and aircraft all had serious technological limitations; artillery was considered a combat support arm rather than engaged in combat directly. After the war there was a backlash against the strategies employed in the Western Front, and many useful lessons were thrown out because they were tainted with the experience of combat in the trenches; as a result, the army of the 1920s and 1930s does not adequately reflect the competence and tactical sophistication of 1917 and especially 1918. At the end of the war the BEF had a sophisticated combined-arms doctrine, incorporating a wide array of weapons, tactics, and operational plans that could be customized depending on the circumstances they faced.

–SANDERS MARBLE,
SMITHSONIAN INSTITUTION

References

Brian Bond, *The Victorian Army and the Staff College, 1854–1914* (London: Eyre Methuen, 1972).

Norman Dixon, *On the Psychology of Military Incompetence* (London: Cape, 1976).

Paddy Griffith, *Battle Tactics of the Western Front: The British Army's Art of Attack, 1916–18* (New Haven, Conn.: Yale University Press, 1994).

Griffith, ed., *British Fighting Methods in the Great War* (London: Cass, 1996).

J. P. Harris, *Men, Ideas and Tanks: British Military Thought and Armoured Forces, 1903–1939* (Manchester, U.K. & New York: Manchester University Press, 1995).

John Laffin, *British Butchers and Bunglers of World War One* (Gloucester, U.K.: Sutton, 1988).

Donald Richter, *Chemical Soldiers: British Gas Warfare in World War I* (Lawrence: University Press of Kansas, 1992).

Gary Sheffield, *Forgotten Victory: The First World War, Myths and Realities* (London: Headline, 2001).

Tim Travers, *How the War Was Won: Command and Technology in the British Army on the Western Front, 1917–1918* (London & New York: Routledge, 1992).

Travers, *The Killing Ground: The British Army, the Western Front, and the Emergence of Modern Warfare, 1900–1918* (London & Boston: Allen & Unwin, 1987).

BELGIAN NEUTRALITY

Was the violation of Belgian neutrality in 1914 the reason for Great Britain's declaration of war on Germany?

Viewpoint: Yes. The international treaty of 1839 had formally acknowledged that Belgian neutrality was an important element in European stability and British strategic interests.

Viewpoint: No. The British had already determined to declare war once Germany had mobilized its military forces.

For three-quarters of the nineteenth century the neutrality of Belgium was one of the constants of European diplomacy. The perceived risks involved in its violation were seen by all the powers as exceeding any gains that could be reasonably calculated. For the first time in centuries the traditional "cockpit of Europe" had been removed from the military and political calculations of its neighbors. Belgium provided for its own security less by creating a field army than by constructing and updating major fortress systems at Liege, Namur, and Antwerp: they were designed to be deterrents to an invader from either east, south, or west across the English Channel.

The situation changed in 1904. In that year Count Alfred von Schlieffen, Chief of the Prussian General Staff, first proposed openly the violation of Belgian neutrality as part of the German war plan. Schlieffen increasingly recognized the restrictions on tactics and operations created by the firepower of modern weapons. He understood too the increasing strength of the fixed defenses of France. His solution was to go around them, strengthening the German right wing and swinging it through Belgium in a strategic envelopment, bypassing Liege and Namur and driving straight toward Paris.

This idea had been discussed in German General Staff circles since the 1890s. Previously it had been rejected on grounds of risk. Schlieffen was willing to take that risk. He assumed that Belgian neutrality would have already been broken by the French, going so far as to postulate Belgium responding by becoming an ally of Germany. His successor, Helmuth von Moltke the Younger, was more realistic and less sanguine. Moltke expected Britain to intervene on the French side in any Franco-German conflict and did not believe France would be so obliging as to breach Belgian neutrality before the first German troops crossed the frontier. He responded by engaging civilian political authorities more deeply in planning for a contingency Moltke considered increasingly necessary if there were to be any chance of the short war he regarded as vital to the survival of the Second Reich.

Both Chancellor Theobald von Bethmann Hollweg and the Foreign Office had reservations. Bethmann openly acknowledged in 1914 that Germany was wrong in invading Belgium and promised to make good the wrong at the first opportunity—not a usual statement from a head of state at the start of a war. Moltke himself said it was "unpleasant" to begin a war by invading a neutral neighbor. Moral questions and diplomatic anxieties, however, took second place to operational concerns that in turn were defined in a context of military necessity.

Was Germany constrained by circumstances to invade Belgium in 1914? Sources and opinions differ. What is certain is that the decision to violate Belgian neutrality was worse than a crime. It was a mistake with dire consequences for everyone involved.

Viewpoint:
Yes. The international treaty of 1839 had formally acknowledged that Belgian neutrality was an important element in European stability and British strategic interests.

The small kingdom of Belgium appears marginal in the story of the vast conflagration caused by World War I, but the violation by Germany of its neutrality in 1914 contributed a great deal to unleashing the conflict on a global scale. The march of the German army through Belgian territory was the direct cause for the decisive entry of Great Britain into the conflict and was a major step in extending the consequences of the Balkan crisis into a world war.

Despite the protection provided by the international treaty of 1839 guaranteeing its neutrality, the widening of World War I depended on the involvement of Belgium. When the German General Staff drew up war plans in the pre-war period, the existence of a Franco-Russian military agreement forced it to plan for a two-front conflict. Since it was widely believed that Russia could not pose a military threat for at least six weeks after the declaration of hostilities, the chief of the German General Staff, Count Alfred von Schlieffen, planned to deliver a knockout blow against France during those critical first six weeks and then turn the might of the German army against Russia. Schlieffen realized that in order to carry out a lightning campaign, the German army would need excellent lines of communication to move and supply a large and rapidly advancing army. The hilly, forested, and heavily defended territory that lay across the Franco-German border could not have fulfilled this prerequisite. The only suitable topography for Schlieffen's plan was to be found to the north, on the Belgian plain. With no serious natural obstacles, excellent roads and railways, and a Belgian army that was believed to be inconsequential, the small kingdom was the perfect route for German troops embarking on an invasion of France. A flanking move through Belgium also offered the strategic opportunity to envelop most of the French army, which was expected to be deployed in forward defensive positions along the German border. When Schlieffen finalized his plan in 1906, it called for

a major drive through Belgium that would turn south between Paris and the English Channel and then move east to encircle the main body of the French army.

Belgium was critical to German strategic thinking, and the French high command knew it. French intelligence could not produce any hard evidence suggesting the details of the Schlieffen Plan, but it was not at all difficult for French military planners to deduce the advantages to Germany of an advance through Belgium. After 1907 several French war-plan variants called for a heavy concentration of troops along the Franco-Belgian frontier in anticipation of the flanking maneuver that Schlieffen had planned. The French general staff even flirted with the idea of a direct deployment of troops into Belgium to forestall a German advance through that country.

The Belgians were not unaware that their country would become a battleground in a Franco-German conflict. As early as 1904, two years before Schlieffen developed the final draft of his plan, Kaiser Wilhelm II told the Belgian king Leopold II that in the future "you will be with us or against us." Leopold's successor Albert I also had to listen to German cajoling, but neither king compromised the neutrality of his country under pressure from Berlin. The Germans, however, were not alone. The French government also suggested deploying troops on Belgian territory if the Germans invaded, but Belgium refused to compromise its neutrality even if it meant its own defense. Brussels responded in the same way to British hints of sending an expeditionary force into Belgium in the event of a German attack, and in 1912 Belgium expressly declined a concrete British offer to come to the aid of the small country if Germany violated its neutrality.

Why would Britain defend Belgium? Although it was one of the signatory powers of the 1839 Belgian neutrality treaty, British interests extended far beyond the mere principle of holding up an arcane international agreement to defend a marginal European nation. One of the few constants in British diplomacy was that London always refused to tolerate the control of the Low Countries by any major power. This position was especially true for the strategic estuary of the Schelde River and the efficient, high-volume ports that the Kingdom of Bel-

GERMAN ULTIMATUM

On 2 August 1914 Germany sent the following ultimatum to Belgium:

Reliable information has been received by the German Government to the effect that French forces intend to march on the line of the Meuse by Gîvet and Namur. This information leaves no doubt as to the intention of France to march through Belgian territory against Germany.

The German Government cannot but fear that Belgium, in spite of the utmost goodwill, will be unable, without assistance, to repel so considerable a French invasion with sufficient prospect of success to afford an adequate guarantee against danger to Germany. It is essential for the self-defence of Germany that she should anticipate any such hostile attack. The German Government would, however, feel the deepest regret if Belgium regarded as an act of hostility against herself the fact that the measures of Germany's opponents force Germany, for her own protection, to enter Belgian territory.

In order to exclude any possibility of misunderstanding, the German Government make the following declaration:

1. Germany has in view no act of hostility against Belgium. In the event of Belgium being prepared in the coming war to maintain an attitude of friendly neutrality towards Germany, the German Government bind themselves, at the conclusion of peace, to guarantee the possessions and independence of the Belgian Kingdom in full.

2. Germany undertakes, under the above-mentioned condition, to evacuate Belgian territory on the conclusion of peace.

3. If Belgium adopts a friendly attitude, Germany is prepared, in co-operation with the Belgian authorities, to purchase all necessaries for her troops against a cash payment, and to pay an indemnity for any damage that may have been caused by German troops.

4. Should Belgium oppose the German troops, and in particular should she throw difficulties in the way of their march by a resistance of the fortresses on the Meuse, or by destroying railways, roads, tunnels or other similar works, Germany will, to her regret, be compelled to consider Belgium as an enemy.

In this event, Germany can undertake no obligations towards Belgium, but the eventual adjustment of the relations between the two States must be left to the decision of arms.

The German Government, however, entertain the distinct hope that this eventuality will not occur, and that the Belgian Government will know how to take the necessary measures to prevent the occurrence of incidents such as those mentioned.

In this case the friendly ties which bind the two neighbouring States will grow stronger and more enduring.

Source: Hugh Gibson, A Journal From Our Legation in Belgium *(Garden City, N.Y.: Doubleday, Page, 1917), pp. 16–17.*

gium controlled after its creation in 1830. Even in the days of Elizabeth I, more than three centuries before 1914, British troops had been sent to the region to support its population's uprising against the hegemonic Spanish Empire. In the seventeenth and eighteenth centuries, Britain had gone to war several times specifically to keep the Netherlands out of French control. When Germany threatened to seize control of the area in the twentieth century, British intervention—whether it was welcomed by the Belgians or not—was a sure bet.

British insistence on the absence of any major power from the Low Countries was an essential catalyst for its involvement in World War I. Apart from a direct threat to its interests, there was no rationale for the British government to enter the war. Although it had settled its strategic differences with France in 1904 and Russia in 1907, it did not maintain a military alliance with either country. It had only an informal agreement with France to carry out joint military operations if the interests of both countries were threatened. If there were no such threat, however, Britain was neither obliged nor inclined to go to war. Even as Britain came to view Germany as the greatest threat to its security, they scrupulously resisted any upgrading of their relationship with France to a military alliance. They were even reluctant to engage in joint military planning with the French to establish a tactical contingency plan in the event of a crisis. The precise nature and details of British participation in the event of war were kept deliberately vague right up to the outbreak of conflict. British reluctance to go to war was so earnest that its government hesitated to make any firm commitment even when Germany declared war on France on 3 August 1914. Although France was the victim of direct German aggression, for the moment the parameters of the conflict included no direct threat to British interests. Paul Cambon, the French ambassador in London, recorded his enormous frustration with the real possibility that Britain might not find a reason to come to aid his country.

The situation changed fundamentally when German troops crossed the Belgian frontier, but even at that crucial time the British government still held out the hope that war might be averted. Rather than instantly declaring war, the British first issued an ultimatum calling for the Germans to withdraw their forces from Belgium and gave them a full day to comply. Had Germany for some reason backed down and withdrawn its forces from Belgium, the threat to British interests would have been neutralized and the state of war that took effect when the ultimatum expired would never have existed. Although the use of an ultimatum was a relatively common gesture (Britain issued a similar ultimatum calling for Germany to withdraw its forces from Poland in 1939), the extension of a grace period belies the notion that Britain was just waiting for the slightest pretext to go to war. If the British government were truly committed to fighting Germany for larger reasons in 1914, why would it have wasted a crucial day of war preparations and mobilization time to allow its opponent to avert confrontation?

This argument is not to say that the British would have remained indefinitely aloof from a general European war if the Germans had stayed out of Belgium. Any number of other German military actions might have presented a threat to British security requirements significant enough to provoke its entry into the conflict. Germany, for example, could have used its fleet to blockade French ports on the English Channel and thus would have posed an unacceptable threat to British control of its home waters. London specifically warned Berlin that this action would lead to war. The essential point, however, is that Britain was only willing to wage war against Germany if it perceived an unambiguous threat to its vital strategic interests. The execution of military operations by Germany in Belgium fulfilled that condition, while its declaration of war on France did not.

Did the Germans realize what their operational plans in Belgium would mean? All of the

evidence indicates that they did not. No one in the German government or military high command seriously believed that Britain would commit itself to a destructive general European war, and risk the stability of its empire and commercial wealth, to protect a seventy-five-year-old agreement on the neutrality of a small kingdom. The German strategists were almost certainly not ignorant of the importance of a neutral Netherlands in British diplomatic history, but they soberly calculated that the costs of maintaining that convention in modern times could not outweigh common sense. One aim of Wilhelm II's diplomacy before World War I was to convince Britain that its natural interests would be served by an Anglo-German alliance. German planners also comforted themselves with the wily but legally correct argument that since only the Kingdom of Prussia had signed the neutrality treaty of 1839, the unified Germany that emerged in 1871 was not bound to honor it. Successive drafts of the Schlieffen Plan dismissed the possibility of British intervention outright, and this assumption was reflected in the attitudes of the government. The Imperial German chancellor, Theobald von Bethmann Hollweg, could not have made the point more clearly when he declared that the neutrality treaty was nothing but a "scrap of paper."

Furthermore, the German leadership did not believe that even the Belgians would take the neutrality of their country seriously. Before the war, German diplomacy toward Belgium was driven by the desire of Berlin to secure transit rights, an approach that included Wilhelm II's coercive, heavy-handed interactions with Leopold II and Albert I. Since the Belgian royal house was a branch of the minor German Saxe-Coburg-Gotha dynasty—the same principality that gave its name to the British royal family from the death of Queen Victoria in 1901 until George V changed the name to Windsor in 1917—many responsible German officials refused to believe that it would ultimately resist the ambitions of their country. This view was augmented by German military hubris, which held—incorrectly as it turned out—that the tiny and poorly equipped Belgian army was too weak to offer any substantive resistance to a German invasion. The German leadership patronized Belgium further by regarding its proud adherence to neutrality as an empty and self-flattering expression of national pride. Even when Belgian troops fought back in the first days of the war, the German high command viewed their resistance as a symbolic gesture that would evaporate as soon as the political leadership of Belgium recognized the futility of the situation and rolled over. On 2 August 1914, when Berlin issued a twelve-hour ultimatum requiring the Belgians to allow German troops to pass through their country, many German officials believed they would give in.

The German violation of Belgian neutrality tripped a wire that brought Britain and all the might of its empire into the emerging continental conflict. Far from being a mere pretext or an alliance-triggering accident, the situation presented the British government with a direct threat to its strategic interests. Historically, it had gone to war several times to defend the very same interests, and its attitude toward them had not changed by 1914. The German high command surely miscalculated the British—and for that matter the Belgian—reaction to its military plans, but this error does not change the fact of British perceptions. Although the Germans believed it was an acceptable risk, they began the war with a military operation that ended the early, noncommittal British approach to the emerging conflict and assured its wholehearted involvement of Britain.

–PAUL DU QUENOY,
GEORGETOWN UNIVERSITY

Viewpoint:
No. The British had already determined to declare war once Germany had mobilized its military forces.

In 1839 France, Prussia, and Great Britain signed a treaty with Belgium mutually guaranteeing Belgian neutrality. This treaty stipulated that none of the signatory nations, each of whom had either a land or water boundary with Belgium, would allow their armed forces to enter Belgian territory, recruit troops, interdict its borders, or even come to its aid without specific expressed permission. This inviolability of Belgian soil was upheld for seventy-five years and was one of the landmarks of nineteenth-century diplomacy.

Since the Congress of Vienna (1815) at the close of the Napoleonic Wars, diplomacy trumped force in all of the capitals of Europe, successfully preventing a major continental war from occurring and successfully containing the midcentury conflicts that restructured central Europe. It was a trade of aristocrats whose upbringing was to be civilized and who all belonged to the same privileged social circle in that extremely stratified atmosphere that characterized the century. The diplomats frequented the same salons, took the waters at the same spas, and while they remained faithful to the interests of their respective countries, they saw few problems that could not be straightened out among gentlemen over port and cigars. After all, most of the reigning monarchs were related. Queen Victoria at her Silver Jubilee (1862) counted six heads of state, including the tsar of Russia and the emperor of Germany, as kin. The trouble began when the Foreign Offices began talking more to each other than with their own military staffs. At the outbreak of the Great War (1914) the only nation that had anything like a National Security Council that contained politicians and diplomats as well as military officers was Great Britain. Even here the army dominated: the navy declined participation, dreaming its own dreams of a new Trafalgar (1805).

By the end of the century there was a clear chasm between the strategic views of European foreign offices and their armed forces—in particular, the general staffs. The aim of the diplomatic corps was to ameliorate and reconcile crisis situations; that of the general staff was to put their respective national forces in the most favorable position to win the war should crisis management fail.

Armies have always been involved in contingency planning, but two forces drove the development of the modern general staff. First was the explosive growth in the size of the national armies, a legacy of Napoleon Bonaparte. Second was the development of the railroads. Before the age of railroads the size of armies had been restricted by logistics. Now that barrier had, to a great extent, been lifted. The result was that strategic planning was largely reduced to railroad timetables. General staffs were created to make contingency plans for various war scenarios so when war threatened the appropriate response could be plucked from its pigeonhole and immediately implemented. All of this planning was done with extreme secrecy, not only from the prying eyes of foreign spies but from members of their own governments. The Schlieffen Plan of Germany was not revealed to the emperor for more than thirty years after its initial formulation. Plan XVII was shown to the French president only in July 1914. The Italian Chief of Staff presented his war plans to the premier on the afternoon of the declaration of war. It is no wonder the diplomatic and military corps were less and less on the same page—or arguably even in the same book.

At the epicenter of the increasingly hostile European great powers was Belgium. The neutrality treaty, to the diplomats, stood as an inviolable wall that no nation would be such a dastard as to break or more pragmatically would run the risks of breaking first. To the military, the German military in particular, it was little more than an obstruction, a river to be bridged, a planning

Belgian troops with dog-drawn machine guns retreating to Antwerp in August 1914

(Imperial War Museum, London)

complication. Once the Anglo-French alliance was struck, the Germans knew they would have to fight England regardless.

When Count Alfred von Schlieffen began work on his fateful plan in 1892, he was trying to solve three problems: first, how to penetrate the line of fortified defenses France had built along their common border; second, how to fight a two-front war with Russia and France; third, what was the most efficient means of moving millions of men and tons of supplies to the battle zone. By 1897 he had decided that a direct assault on the French forts was impractical. He and his analysts worked ceaselessly at the sandbox, trying out various ideas. At first, he decided to send a relatively small force around the French left flank, just nipping a corner of Belgium in order to flank the forts. With each annual revision of the plan, Schlieffen began nipping more and more territory until he was sending 70 percent of his troops through the heart of Belgium.

This planning was the ultimate war game; an intellectual exercise examining the outer limits of what is possible without regard for what is probable. The plan called for the complete defeat of France forty days after the mobilization of German forces and then the transfer of the entire army back across Germany to meet the Russians who, according to the estimates of the General Staff, would take the full forty days to mobilize.

With stereotypical monomania, Schlieffen and his successor Helmuth von Moltke the Younger modified and refined this offensive plan for forty years and year by year sanctified it as scripture.

The French, in contrast, dithered. They produced a succession of seventeen different plans, each superseding the last. As implemented, the final one sent the bulk of the army through Alsace, while the German army flanked them on the left—through Belgium. An earlier version had called for massing troops on the Belgian border with instructions to meet the German force near Antwerp. That plan was discarded because France did not wish to bear the international stigma and approbation of being the first country to violate Belgian neutrality. The Germans were made of sterner stuff.

The British faced a different problem—how to land their troops on the Continent in order to get them into battle as quickly and as fresh as possible. The most logical spot was Antwerp, one of the best deepwater ports along the channel and the most strategically situated by far. Both the British Foreign Office and the military pleaded with Belgium on many occasions to allow them the use of the harbor and/or permission to allow the British army to cross the border in defense of Belgium should the Germans attack. Belgium continually refused in hope that Germany would continue to honor its neutrality despite hints and threats to the contrary and from fear that such an arrangement would automatically violate the neutrality treaty. The primary response of Belgium was to build two huge modern fortresses outside Liege and Antwerp, whose only purpose was to deter and delay possible German aggression. Since these fortifications took more than a decade to construct, it is evident that Germany had been on the Belgian mind for some time.

The deliberate violation of a county's neutrality was viewed by the international community most seriously. Not only did it call into question all of the violating country's treaty commitments, but also it was generally an automatic act of war against the other signers of the guaranteeing treaty—in this case, France and Great Britain. Belgian neutrality was not the trip wire of war; that was dependent on the general mobilization of Germany. The elaborate timetables of calling up reserves and getting everybody in the correct unit and on the correct train to the proper sector of the front did not allow for the traditional overt war-creating act. By the time German troops reached the Belgian border, French troops were moving toward Alsace in accordance with Plan XVII. Great Britain, moving a bit slower, did not declare war until after the German assaults on the Liege fortifications. Although that violation was numbered among the *causus belli*, the real reason for Britain joining the conflict was that they had a secret agreement with France to man the French left flank, for example on the Belgian border, in case of war.

Belgian neutrality did not serve as a "trip wire" for the commencement of hostilities. That was effectively accomplished by the declaration of war by Austria-Hungary against Serbia and the subsequent general mobilization. This action triggered the mobilization plans, which had occupied so many hours of meticulous planning on paper by the General Staffs of the affected nations. In the end it was not the nobility of defending a neutral nation but the dictatorship of railroad timetables.

–JOHN WHEATLEY,
BROOKLYN CENTER, MINNESOTA

References

Roger Chickering and Stig Förster, eds., *Great War, Total War: Combat and Mobilization on the Western Front, 1914–1918* (Cambridge & New York: Cambridge University Press, 2000).

John Keegan, *The First World War* (London: Hutchinson, 1998).

Daniel H. Thomas, *The Guarantee of Belgian Independence and Neutrality in European Diplomacy, 1830's–1930's* (Kingston, R.I.: Thomas, 1983).

Barbara W. Tuchman, *The Guns of August* (New York: Macmillan, 1962).

BELGIAN NEUTRALITY

BRITISH STRATEGY

Did Britain commit an error in deploying the BEF to France in 1914?

Viewpoint: Yes. The half-dozen divisions of the BEF were no more than a flank guard in northern France. Deployed through Antwerp, or even directed against the German Baltic coastline, they could have had a much greater effect.

Viewpoint: No. Developments in technology and the increased size of armed forces had long since rendered "strategies of the indirect approach" ineffective against major powers.

In the aftermath of World War I, among the questions most hotly debated in Britain was that of the deployment of the British Expeditionary Force (BEF). The decision to commit these six combat-ready divisions on the left flank of the French structured the entire course of the war for Britain. That move included participation in the Somme (1916) and Passchendaele (1917), and left hundreds of thousands of dead and maimed. Meanwhile, Royal Navy dreadnoughts, built at great expense, swung at anchor in Scapa Flow, absorbing a disproportionate share of resources and at best deterring the sorties of a German navy that hindsight suggested had been more *frisson* than actual threat.

Was there another way? Might the BEF and its follow-up divisions have been better employed in what military writer Basil H. Liddell Hart called a "strategy of the indirect approach"? Instead of falling in on the left of the line, like a dutiful client, suppose the British army had fulfilled its historic role of being "a bullet fired by the British Navy"? Perhaps in the Baltic, perhaps somewhere in the Mediterranean—perhaps above all in Belgium, that traditional theater of operations for British land forces—the army might have found an alternative to the stagnation of the Western Front.

British strategy before 1914 was predicated on an assumption of "business as usual." Since the turn of the twentieth century the government accepted the impossibility of avoiding involvement in a major European war. The challenge was how best to come through the conflict with minimal loss and minimal risk. The response was an intention—not quite a developed plan—to make Britain the bank and the factory of an alliance including France and Russia. German military preponderance guaranteed that those states would from the beginning be fighting for their lives. Britain would supply "gunpowder and guineas": weapons, food, and money—the latter at suitable rates of interest—while simultaneously taking over first the German world markets, then, conceivably, those of its allies as well. The Royal Navy would hold the German fleet in check, eventually fighting and winning a decisive victory over its upstart rival. The key role, however, would be played by the British army, which was both Britain's ante and pawn. Put in line with the French, it would be a proof of good faith that "perfidious Albion" was not once more preparing to take as much or as little of the war as it willed.

It was a realistic, not to say a cynical, strategy. It might have succeeded in a short conflict. But as World War I continued and British generals began raising "New Armies" to swing the balance in favor of the Allies, the concept of a limited continental commitment gave way to an acceptance of a strategic paradigm focused on the Western Front—one with no room for arabesques and sideshows.

Viewpoint:
Yes. The half-dozen divisions of the BEF were no more than a flank guard in northern France. Deployed through Antwerp, or even directed against the German Baltic coastline, they could have had a much greater effect.

Up until the start of World War I, traditional British military strategy relied primarily on the navy, with the army as the secondary branch of service. Except on rare occasions, the British followed a policy, codified by American historian Alfred Thayer Mahan, of projecting power through the use of the fleet, with the army then serving as the ground projection of that power beyond the high-tide line. The brilliant Peninsula Campaign (1808–1814) during the Napoleonic War was predicated upon this fundamental principle: that the ability to transport men and equipment by sea to an enemy's weak spot, in this case Spain and Portugal, could overcome the ability of any land-based power to respond effectively. The additional keys to British victory were the wretched condition of Spanish roads and the deadly threat of guerillas, while the "road" of the sea was wide open. It was a card the British knew how to play brilliantly and had resulted in their creation of an empire.

Thus, British adoption of the role of a land-force power in World War I was a clear reversal of strategic principles that best served the empire and in fact set the stage for the collapse of that empire. Throughout the nineteenth century the role of the British army was a secondary one, even though it saw far more action than the navy. After Trafalgar (1805) the Royal Navy simply maintained the inglorious task of blockading Napoleon Bonaparte's maneuvers and dealing with the pesky upstart—the United States. It saw only limited action in the Crimean War (1853–1856) and occasional police-type actions such as the Chinese Opium Wars (1839–1843, 1856–1860) and the bombardment of Alexandria (1882). One reason it saw so little action was its unchallenged supremacy.

The British army, however, though small by the standards of France, Germany, Russia, and Austria, was active around the world as it was busy conquering and holding an empire.

Therefore, like any bureaucracy, it constantly envisioned a bigger piece of the appropriations pie, especially when the great arms race heated up prior to the start of World War I. Admiral John Fisher was getting millions for his new dreadnought-class battleships. Should not the army, its officers argued, receive the same consideration?

As the emphasis of war planning shifted from possible confrontations with France or Russia to one with Germany, the army aggressively pushed for a major role and, like the proverbial curse, it got what it wished for. Thus, one sees the beginnings of the ill-fated strategy of direct and immediate intervention into Belgium if the Germans should advance across this neutral country, which had been in large part created by England to serve as a buffer against France.

The idea ran that a small, elite force, the cream of the old traditional volunteer army, landing ahead of a German advance could secure the left flank of the defensive line, ensuring that key ports would be held to support future actions and the influx of additional troops once new regiments were raised. It was classic circular logic: an intervention to hold ports so that ports could be held to support an intervention. The appeal of the army to the navy was that by holding the channel ports, access would be denied to the enemy. The British navy, however, waited four years trying to coax the German fleet out of port for a confrontational battle. In retrospect, it is highly improbable even if the Germans had seized the channel ports that they would have dared to move their main battle fleet to these facilities.

The result is well known. The "Old Contemptibles" were annihilated in Flanders in the first six weeks of the war. With the commitment of England to full-scale land intervention in France, this small nucleus, so heroically sacrificed, could have been far better used to form the backbone of the mass mobilization of 1915–1916. Such a use might possibly have spared England many casualties later. Instead, much of the mobilization to create the largest land force in the history of England was directed by amateurs who knew little of the realities of running an army, let alone how to properly use that army in the field.

Far more important, though, was the question of whether such use of its elite professional force was well thought out and properly implemented. In 1914 the small British force had lit-

SOLDIERS OF THE KING

Field Marshal Horatio Kitchener, who organized the British army prior to its departure for action on the Continent, here addresses his troops:

You are ordered abroad as a soldier of the King to help our French comrades against the invasion of a common enemy. You have to perform a task which will need your courage, your energy, your patience. Remember that the honour of the British Army depends on your individual conduct. It will be your duty not only to set an example of discipline and perfect steadyness under fire but also to maintain the most friendly relations with those whom you are helping in this struggle. The operations in which you are engaged will, for the most part, take place in a friendly country, and you can do your own country no better service than in showing yourself in France and Belgium in the true character of a British soldier.

Be invariably courteous, considerate and kind. Never do anything likely to injure or destroy property, and always look upon looting as a disgraceful act. You are sure to meet a welcome and to be trusted; your conduct must justify that welcome and that trust. Your duty cannot be done unless your health is sound. So keep constantly on your guard against any excesses. In this new experience you may find temptations both in wine and women. You must entirely resist both temptations, and, while treating all women with perfect courtesy, you should avoid any intimacy.

Source: *"1914: Kitchener's Address to the Troops,"* War and Military History, <http://www.lib.byu.edu/~rdh/wwi/1914/kitchner.html>.

---

tle true impact on the final turn of events. France would have held against the Germans whether the British were there or not, though for three-quarters of a century the dwindling number of survivors of the battles in Flanders maintained that their heroic sacrifice gave the less-well-prepared French the time to properly mobilize against the invasion. Such a response, however, is rooted in issues of national pride and self-justification rather than military realities. As for the French response to this assumption, it takes no imagination to reach a conclusion: the British actually muddled things up through poor communications.

If the British had not landed their army but instead kept it as a force to be deployed later, the German high command would have been forced to respond throughout the opening weeks of the war, detailing additional resources to guard against a possible strike on its flank. Thus, the result would have, in relationship to the Battle of the Marne (1914), been basically the same, with the key factor for England being that the nucleus of its army would still be intact.

The great days of amphibious warfare were yet to come, but in 1914 the potential was there. The invasion of Gallipoli (1915) clearly demonstrated this fact when the British put a Commonwealth force of more than seventy-five thousand men onto the beaches within a couple of days. The failure at Gallipoli was not in the initial implementation of the plan but rather in the loss of nerve on the part of the high command to drive forward aggressively to victory. It should be noted as well that Gallipoli was carried out at the end of a long logistical support line, in an alien environment, and against a position that was poorly reconnoitered. That campaign was far different from the potential of a major amphibious assault launched from the heart of the empire against a nearby shore that was territory long familiar to those who would go to fight there.

As an alternative to the initial deployment into Flanders (1914), one should consider the prospect of Britain husbanding its forces; keeping them at Dover, East Anglia, and Southampton; and poising them as an amphibious threat that could strike anywhere along the Belgian coast, or perhaps strike even into the north German coast and the key prize of the Kiel Canal. Mahan maintained that the mere existence of a fleet, "the fleet in being," was power in and of itself that an enemy must be forced to respond to. An "army in being" would have forced the German army to reconsider its strategic deployment.

Throughout history, any nation that controls the sea and thus maintains a clear and viable threat of amphibious assault, either as a raid designed to disrupt or as a full-scale invasion, has a distinct advantage over its adversaries. Defensive forces far outnumbering the actual aggressor army must be maintained at any potential point of contact, while the offensive force can sit back, wait, pick the weakest link in the defensive chain, and then go in to break it.

It could have been the same situation with the British in 1914 and perhaps for the entire length of World War I. The losses, both human and financial, which drained the empire, might thus have been avoided, with England emerging from the conflict as a strong global power still to be reckoned with rather than as a nation going into steady decline. Combine this offensive threat with the immense hitting power of a fleet of dreadnoughts, and such an invasion strike along the coast would undoubtedly have forced a sortie by the German Fleet, thus opening the opportunity for a Battle of Jutland that might have been fought to the finish in 1914 or 1915 rather than the stalemated battle of 1916.

The military policy of a country and the resulting strategic deployments must always be based upon the fundamental principle of advancing a national cause; anything less is a tragic waste of precious national resources. The British commitment to defend France in a ground war against Germany served no truly significant goals for Britain other than satisfying a misplaced hubris and then afterward filling a need to somehow justify the blood already spilled. How different history might have been if instead England had kept its army close to home, propagandizing that it would indeed be used at the appropriate place and time, threatening and dodging, and then when presented with a reasonable prospect, finally going in to do maximum damage to the enemy.

The result of such a strategy for England would have been a nation not bled white by the struggle but a nation still capable of maintaining a dominant position throughout the twentieth century. Even if the result had been fundamentally different, if the Old Contemptibles had not died in Flanders and the Germans eventually marched down the Champs Elysèe in 1914 . . . would it have been any different for England in the long run? Undoubtedly so, and for the better most likely, with England maintaining its financial balance, an entire generation spared the nightmare of the trenches, and no second edition of a world war inevitably bearing down to finish off what was left of the empire.

–WILLIAM R. FORSTCHEN,
MONTREAT COLLEGE

Viewpoint:
No. Developments in technology and the increased size of armed forces had long since rendered "strategies of the indirect approach" ineffective against major powers.

The idea of using the British Expeditionary Force (BEF) to operate along the coasts of northern Europe, threatening enemy communications by striking behind German lines, perhaps even enveloping the right flank of the force sweeping through Belgium, was in the operational and tactical contexts of 1914 no more than a tabletop war game. Fortunately, it did not get beyond that stage, or Britain might have faced an early run-through of Dunkirk (1940), with far more disastrous consequences. A large-scale invasion by sea against opposition is rightly regarded as one of the most difficult of military operations—as the British were soon to learn at Gallipoli (1915).

Nevertheless, the idea of basing British future-war strategy on amphibious operations was seriously considered and advocated in the early years of the twentieth century. Its primary supporters came from the Royal Navy, who regarded such landings as a means to a greater end: the drawing out of the German High Seas Fleet for a decisive naval battle. Sir John Fisher went even further, entertaining projects for amphibious operations in the Baltic, supported by a force of specially designed light-draft warships.

If Fisher's visions found little support in either service, the soldiers were favorable to an option of operating independently, particularly as intelligence reports made German intentions to attack through Belgium increasingly plain. Sir John French, who would command the BEF, had originally begun his career in the Royal Navy. He was the highest-ranking army supporter of making the principal British effort go through Belgium—not least because it provided both strategic independence from France and a line of communications that would be under British control. As late as 1912, French urged negotiating with Belgium despite the repeated reiteration by that state of its commitment to complete neutrality.

The British army at home, as it emerged from the Haldane reforms (1906), was organizationally a rationalized restructuring of the forces available in Britain once the demands of the empire had been met: six twelve-battalion infantry divisions and a large cavalry division, plus some surplus artillery. It was not, however, configured exclusively for employment on the French left flank. In principle the BEF was intended as a true strategic reserve, to be sent wherever it was needed in a British and Imperial context.

That plan did not mean landing the force by open boats and then sending it across open beaches. Debarking men from a troop ship into a rowboat in even calm seas is no easy task, to say nothing of provisioning them once they were ashore. For such a landing, specialized training and equipment would be needed. The army had time and money for neither. There was, moreover, no suitable beach-landing site north of Amsterdam that was not in immediate reach of a German army able through the use of railroads to create an insuperable manpower differential in a short period.

Any landing force with the numbers and the firepower to have anything but a temporary tactical impact required a deep-water port, with permanent facilities for quickly unloading large numbers of ships. For practical purposes as well, the port had to be located in a country friendly enough not merely to eschew damaging the facilities but also to make their longshoremen available. The only harbor likely to meet these criteria was Antwerp.

The problem with using Antwerp was that by the time the BEF completed its landing in the ports of northern France, the Germans had occupied Liège, thrust deep into Belgium, and driven the Belgian army back toward, and eventually into, the port city. Had the British landed there, the four divisions they initially committed might initially have faced some of the same German divisions they met at Mons (1914) and Le Cateau (1914). They would have fought, however, not in the company of the French but of a Belgian army badly reduced in numbers and shaken in morale—certainly spent as an offensive force.

Nor was it inevitable that German Chief of Staff Helmuth von Moltke (the Younger) would have directly weakened his striking wing. The Germans were concerned about their Belgian sector. Even in the historical scenario, they kept ten to twelve division-size formations available for siege and screening operations behind their main advance. Most of these troops were second-line units. Even had the British made an unimpaired administrative landing—a highly questionable prospect given the near-chaotic Belgian command and administrative situation in Antwerp—the BEF would have been constrained to advance "into the blue," unsupported and against superior forces capable of immediate reinforcement. German divisions transferred from Alsace-Lorraine to Flanders in October were much closer to their railheads in August. A highly probable result of a British "Antwerp alternate" would have been the abortion of the German Lorraine offensive before it even began, with correspondingly improved prospects for the campaign as a whole.

Nor did the performance of the BEF in offensive operations during the aftermath of the Marne (1914) suggest that the same units and commanders would suddenly have developed into daring and successful open-field warriors in an alternate theater. The most likely scenario was a rapid retirement on Antwerp, perhaps covered by the newly landed Fourth and Sixth Divisions, the actual second wave of the BEF. This time, however, the BEF would have its back to the sea rather than an open route of retreat by land.

On 5 August 1914 Sir John French, as BEF commander, at least considered realizing this hypothetical position, suggesting that his army use Antwerp as a base. Since both banks of the Scheldt River leading into the port were Dutch, that alternative involved violating Dutch neutrality, with corresponding diplomatic and economic advantages to the Germans. The proposal died, however, when Winston Churchill, then First Lord of the Admiralty, said the navy could not support the operation. Again in October, French considered shifting the BEF from the Western Front to Antwerp, which was still in Belgian hands. He was influenced in part by his own mercurial temperament, because he was frustrated by the course of the war to date. His earlier interest in a Belgian initiative had also been rekindled when Churchill promised full support of the move by the Royal Navy.

BRITISH STRATEGY

In fact, Sir John Jellicoe had just taken command of the Grand Fleet on 4 August. The fleet had just moved from its channel bases to Scapa Flow in the Orkney Islands north of Scotland and was in the process of creating a major naval base where none had existed before. The primary objective of the admiral who Churchill declared could "lose the war in an afternoon" was to keep the German fleet bottled up and not allow it to escape to the open sea. Supporting the army at Antwerp, however, would have taken at least a major part of the fleet from Scapa Flow to exactly where its admirals did not want to be—in the narrow confines of the English Channel, subject to U-boat attacks such as those that sank the old cruisers *Cressy, Aboukir,* and *Hogue* on 5 September, and subject as well to a sortie by the German High Seas Fleet, which would be in a good position to catch its enemy on a tactical lee shore. The navy, in short, had no interest in underwriting its First Lord's rhetoric, and the BEF stayed in place.

French's 1914 initiatives favored the same end game: the strategic isolation of the BEF by its entrapment in a fortress complex. An operational military disaster was by no means inevitable. Most probably the bulk of the British troops, like those at Gallipoli, would have been successfully evacuated—to be redeployed in the Flanders sector of the Western Front,

the only place where they would be of strategic and operational use.

–JOHN WHEATLEY,
BROOKLYN CENTER, MINNESOTA

References

David Ascoli, *The Mons Star: The British Expeditionary Force, 5th Aug.–22nd Nov. 1914* (London: Harrap, 1981).

George H. Cassar, *The Tragedy of Sir John French* (Newark: University of Delaware Press; London: Associated University Presses, 1985).

Roger Chickering and Stig Förster, eds., *Great War, Total War: Combat and Mobilization on the Western Front, 1914–1918* (Cambridge & New York: Cambridge University Press, 2000).

Paddy Griffith, ed., *British Fighting Methods in the Great War* (London: Cass, 1996).

Richard Holmes, *Riding the Retreat: Mons to the Marne 1914 Revisited* (London: Cape, 1995).

Hew Strachan, *The Oxford Illustrated History of the First World War* (Oxford & New York: Oxford University Press, 1998).

BRITISH WAR ECONOMY

Was the British war economy characterized by systematic government control?

Viewpoint: Yes. The British government took firm control of the economy and employed a structured plan to conduct the war.

Viewpoint: No. From the beginning Britain relied on the private sphere whenever possible and improvised as the need arose.

Economic mobilization in Great Britain during World War I was a structure of paradoxes. Before the war British strategy was based on repeating the pattern tested in Continental conflicts since the eighteenth century: use Adam Smith's "invisible hand" to increase domestic production in order to sustain European allies. During 1916 it became increasingly clear that the war was becoming an attritional conflict requiring comprehensive economic mobilization under central direction. Nevertheless, systematic plans based on coherent principles did not emerge until 1918.

Earlier introduction of such measures as conscription, the creation of government agencies controlling food and shipping, and even David Lloyd George's Ministry of Munitions all suggest the imposition of state direction of the war effort. In practice, however, these and similar institutions were superimposed on a resilient infrastructure based on property rights, individual freedoms, and voluntary cooperation. Government attempts to impose centralized control over even such an apparent essential as food production ran into constant difficulties. To a degree, Lloyd George's reputation as "the great improviser" reflected the constant need to find ways around an opposition that was less committed to obstructionism and profiteering than it was convinced it could manage better on its own than with the interference of even well-intentioned bureaucrats.

The comprehensively cultivated public sense of participating voluntarily in a just cause remained a key aspect of the war effort even during the crisis of 1918. Where decision making became more centralized, it did so in response to ad hoc social, economic, and political developments. Arguably, indeed, government initiatives had less to do with increasing state intervention into economic affairs than did public sentiment, as individuals, interest groups, and communities responded to a growing conviction that attritional war demanded popular commitment that was focused and directed in pursuit of victory. Consent was more important to the British war effort than control.

Viewpoint:
Yes. The British government took firm control of the economy and employed a structured plan to conduct the war.

Britain did not muddle through World War I with a laissez-faire attitude toward its industrial economy, hoping that all war needs would be met by a wave of Adam Smith's "invisible hand." Just the opposite occurred. The government controlled British industries with a firm hand, structuring factories and distribution to meet its war needs.

Great Britain entered World War I with a nineteenth-century industrial economy that had to supply the products needed to fight a twentieth-century war. Previously, Britain fought colonial wars with a small professional army. This strategy required little support beyond its array of Royal Arsenals and contracts with a chosen few industrial firms with experience in arms manufacture. The Boer War (1899–1902), which was bigger than expected, forced some changes in the way Britain acquired arms for its army. World War I, however, delivered a shock that forced greater changes. The old bureaucratic methods could not be scaled up to meet the demands of total war. Government had to seize the reins of the economy, changing it from its prewar laissez-faire state to a centrally guided command economy with many participants. Furthermore, Britain would have to utilize an industrial base that was in decline relative to its rivals and allies.

World War I started with the British Expeditionary Force (BEF) numbering six infantry divisions and a cavalry division, all drawing arms and supplies through the narrow funnel of the ordnance department of the War Office, governed by a master general of ordnance. Yet, even this force—small compared to larger armies to follow—was running short of artillery shells by the spring of 1915.

While rumors of the shell shortage had earlier percolated among the Conservatives in Parliament, the news broke with a fury in May 1915. BEF commander John French had "leaked" the story to the *Times* of London, bypassing his chain of command to publicize the problem. This revelation came on the heels of First Sea Lord Jackie Fisher's resignation, which prompted a crisis forcing Liberal prime minister Herbert Asquith to bring the Conservatives into his government.

The failure of the War Ministry to provide the BEF with sufficient shells triggered a political response. David Lloyd George, then Chancellor of the Exchequer, headed a Treasury inquiry into the shortage, running into resistance from Secretary of State for War Horatio Kitchener, who withheld information. Kitchener ran the War Ministry as an unquestioned fiefdom, not clearly subordinate to civilians in the government. It was politically impossible to remove Kitchener, but on the question of supplying the army he could be bypassed. Asquith's government formed a new Ministry of Munitions, placing Lloyd George in charge. The Ministry was up and running by June.

Lloyd George seemed an odd choice for the job. A pacifist who opposed the Boer War, he quickly changed course upon the German invasion of Belgium. Untitled and unprivileged, Lloyd George did not go fishing in the shallow hiring pool of the ruling class to staff his ministry, instead turning to the self-made managers of British industry, his so-called men of push and go. It would take technocrats, not bureaucrats, to fashion a government body whose purview eventually encompassed all aspects of weapons design, manufacture, and purchase by the end of the war.

Building this machine was not an act of improvisation but a deliberate delegation of authority to a large number of factory managers, union leaders, and industrialists to get the job done. Lloyd George believed that any firm with an expertise in engineering and manufacturing could make a shell, a fuse, or a gun. It was absurd that the third largest manufacturing economy in the world could not supply its main army in the field, but that was the price the government paid for doing nothing and relying on prewar purchasing practices. Government arsenals and select contractors were not up to the job, and Kitchener had already rejected offers from private industry to help the war effort.

All the major belligerents had to undergo some type of government-guided transition from a peace to a war economy. As armies ballooned from prewar levels, new divisions had to be armed and supplied. Partnership between corporations and government became a corresponding necessity. By July 1915 the Ministry of Munitions was busy building that partnership. It divided Britain into ten districts and selected a mix of labor leaders, manufacturers, and executives to form forty-seven local Boards of Management that reported back to the Ministry. Questionnaires to sixty-five thousand workshops yielded forty-five thousand replies on the amount of machinery and labor available. Each board eventually chose one of three schemes to handle shell manufacture—government-built factories run by the boards, state-financed but privately run factories, or a mix of the first two schemes.

Organizing factories was simple and mechanical compared to organizing labor and

THE MUNITIONS CRISIS

French author and commentator Jules Destrée comments on the manner in which the British government handled the crisis in supplying munitions:

The Government was thus able to reorganize the production works themselves. There were of two kinds. First, there were the munitions works properly so called, where it was necessary to extend the plant or increase the rate of production. Then there were factories which had to be altered so as to adapt them to the new kind of work. Finally, the Government decided to create sixteen large works—a number substantially increased to twenty-six—the equipment of which is being carried out with the utmost dispatch.

The next thing was to organize the labor and recruit fresh hands. There was a choice of two methods, the compulsory and the voluntary. After going into the matter with the Trades union leaders it was the latter method that was decided upon. It was more in accordance with English traditions and sentiment. A vast recruiting campaign was started, the headquarters being the town hall, in one hundred and eighty different centers. It lasted a week, and was an immense success. Mr. Lloyd George stated, on July 23, 1915, that the Government had got together 100,000 workmen, most of whom were experts in machinery and shipbuilding. True, it was not possible to employ them all, some already doing Government work, others being indispensable to the civil life of the country. But when all deductions were made it was found that the number of men was amply sufficient for present needs. To them we must add the skilled workmen who had joined the army and who, as far as possible, were brought home to serve their country in an industrial capacity.

All the workmen were assigned either to the works already in existence—which in many cases were short of hands and unable for this reason to fulfill their contracts—or else they were allotted to new factories.

But in view of influence wielded by the Labor Unions, various provisions were inserted in the Munitions Act. They related to the settlement of labor disputes, and to the prohibition of strikes and lock-outs the grounds for which had not been submitted to the Board of Trade.

To obviate such disputes, which were generally called forth by the excessive profits accruing to the employers and the demands of the wage-earners, the system of "Controlled Establishments" was instituted. Every establishment engaged in munitions work was placed, so far as the regulation of profits and salaries was concerned, under direct Government control. Any modification in the rate of wages had to be submitted to the Ministry of Munitions, which had the power to refer the question to an Arbitration Board specially set up by the Act.

Source: *Charles F. Horne,* The Great Events of the Great War, *volume 3 (New York: National Alumni, 1930), pp. 208–209.*

management to pull together in harness. The Munitions of War Act (1915) relaxed union rules but capped industry profits to one-fifth above the average profit of the previous two years of peacetime. State control still left managers and foremen to organize work—not laissez-faire, but delegation of responsibility after goals were set. Britain had as well to shift from mass production based on skilled labor to greater use of unskilled labor. The October Programme of Dilution implemented the change. If positions for skilled workers could not be filled, invalid veterans and then unskilled workers were brought in to do the simplest tasks. By this stroke, millions of women were brought into the factories to do jobs left vacant by men serving at the front, creating a revolution of a different sort on the home front.

After the Ministry of Munitions took control of shell production, the British army never again suffered a shortage of munitions. During the last half of 1915, production of the most commonly used shells increased fourfold to fivefold. The total shells produced in the second half of 1916 was seventeen times greater than for the first half of 1915, when production was controlled by the War Ministry.

Likewise, the Ministry took over manufacture of artillery, a much-needed move given the impending growth of the army. The six-division BEF, bled white in 1914, was going to be replaced by a seventy-division force drawing from a pool of two million volunteers. Orders placed by the master general of ordnance for delivery of 18-pounder field guns, for example, would only outfit twenty-four of Kitchener's projected divisions. In addition, these guns would not be delivered until June 1915. Yet, the problem was solved by the Ministry of Munitions, which boosted artillery production by orders of magnitude. Production of the 18-pounder gun was up 6.5 times by June 1916, while 4.5-inch howitzer production grew eightfold in the same period. The new divisions were fully outfitted by the time the British army took the offensive at the Somme (1916).

All of Lloyd George's "push and go" could not change the fact that England could not fulfill all of its war needs by domestic manufacture alone. Britain, cradle of the Industrial Revolution, had only 13.6 percent of the world's manufacturing output to call its own in 1913, compared to Germany, with 14.7 percent, and the United States, with 32 percent. It was to the United States that Britain had to turn, eventually fulfilling 40 percent of its war orders there. By April 1917 the Ministry of Munitions had 1,600 of its agents deployed in the United States, contracting with factories, inspecting shells and guns to make sure they met specifications, and supervising shipments to Britain.

That move raised a new question: how to pay? Lloyd George was given broad powers to fulfill war orders at any cost. The British Treasury had to pay for American war goods in dollars. Britain could use its gold to buy dollars at $4.86 to the pound, but after a while the demand for dollars would drive the exchange rate against Britain, making dollars more expensive while cheapening the pound. The solution was to rely on British overseas investments to finance the purchase of American-made war goods. The British share of worldwide overseas investments was 43 percent, or about $19.5 billion. The United States made up 21 percent of this portfolio, totaling about £835 million. While the British Treasury bought American goods with gold and tried to float unsecured loans (with no success before 1917), it was able to compel the sale of British-owned American securities to itself. It then used these dollar-denominated assets as collateral to secure loans from the New York money market. J. P. Morgan and Company, which started the war as the U.S. purchasing agent for Britain until the establishment of the Ministry of Munitions, became the American banker for the English.

By the time the United States entered the war in April 1917, however, Britain found that it had used about $5 billion in its U.S. assets to secure war loans. With little gold left in London, Britain was broke. It would now be dependent on the United States as a source of unsecured credit. U.S. treasury secretary James McAdoo had an unusually free hand here, as President Woodrow Wilson had little interest in financial affairs. The May 1917 Liberty Loan came in at $3 billion, oversubscribed by 50 percent. While a large share of this fund paid for outfitting the American Expeditionary Force (AEF), some of the fund was used to help finance U.S. allies. American loans later cost Britain 40 percent of its budget in the 1920s in order to service the war debt. In the end, the British public-private sector relationship for American finance gave way to direct government-to-government finance for the remainder of the war.

The Ministry of Munitions quickly grew to control other aspects of weapons design and manufacture. The Stokes mortar, a cheap and easily manufactured weapon, was brought into being after being rejected by the War Ministry. Likewise, the Ministry of Munitions took over development of the tank from a navy bureau then developing "land ships." During 1916–1917 the ministry added petroleum allocation to its purview, while in 1917 the ministry took over the supply of tanks, trucks, truck and aircraft engines, railway supplies, and mechanical trans-

port. Agricultural machinery was taken over by mid 1917, with tank design and development brought in-house by the end of the year. Aircraft design and manufacture was taken over by 1918.

By the time Lloyd George left the ministry for the office of prime minister in 1917, it had grown to eighteen departments with a staff of five thousand. At the end of the war, now under the direction of Winston Churchill, the ministry reached fifty departments employing fifteen thousand people. Lloyd George managed to control the department through sheer force of personality, an office door that was always open to anyone, and by bypassing formal channels. After Lloyd George's departure a plan to formalize the department failed after clashing with its more informal corporate culture. Under Churchill in August 1917, the departments were assigned to one of ten groups, and department heads were expected to report to their group leaders. Churchill kept his office door open, too, but the managers essentially took care of most issues coming up from the department level. These leaders constituted the Munitions Council, whom Churchill dealt with regularly.

Nothing fails like success, and the need for the Ministry of Munitions died upon the end of war. The military retrieved many of the powers it surrendered to the ministry. By the early 1920s the ministry was disbanded. Yet, it marked a startling transformation of a private-sector laissez-faire economy to a centrally managed command economy supplying a nation in arms. The brief embrace of "war socialism" by Great Britain would be repeated in World War II with a Ministry of Production firmly seated in the war cabinet. The lessons learned from 1914–1915 prevented a repeat of the shell shortage during the bloody sequel to the Great War.

—WILLIAM TERDOSLAVICH
NEW YORK, NEW YORK

Viewpoint:
No. From the beginning Britain relied on the private sphere whenever possible and improvised as the need arose.

"Muddling through" is a phrase often used to characterize the British way of making war. It implies conditions featuring barely adequate leadership, administrative confusion, blindness to military needs, and a willingness to rely on tenacity and improvisation rather than rational planning to gain the final victory. However appealing to a romantic view of British history

BRITISH WAR ECONOMY

this notion may be, everyone in 1914 understood that making war depended upon the production and distribution of needed materials and the provision of a well-trained fighting force. Nor did the Liberal Party government of Herbert Asquith flinch from asserting the authority of government to supervise the provision of these needs. By the end of 1914, Asquith's government had taken over rail transportation. In March of 1915 the Defense of the Realm Act gave the government authority to manage practically every important aspect of the wartime economy.

Over the course of the war the government used this authority to intervene in the economy as the need arose. Its first test was the 1915 crisis over the supply of munitions. Supplies from the chemical and engineering economic sectors could not keep up with demand, and the War Department, which negotiated contracts with suppliers, was understaffed. In May the government established the Ministry of Munitions, accepting the need to coordinate contracts, build factories, and support the relocation of workers to these work sites. By 1918 more than five hundred thousand workers had been added to munitions production.

The next crisis concerned manpower. When war was declared, voluntary enlistments filled quotas. In October of 1915, as manpower supplies declined, the government introduced a scheme whereby individuals could declare their

willingness to serve—the "Derby Scheme." When this strategy failed to produce the required numbers, a Military Service Act conscripting single men between the ages of eighteen and forty-one was introduced in January of 1916. In May a second act extended conscription to married men. These acts put the government in the business of allocating personnel to both the military forces and private sectors engaged in war production, keeping skilled workers in vital industries, and reenforcing the labor pool with unskilled workers (women played important roles here) by agreements worked out with the trade unions. By the end of the war more than 3.5 million workers had been added to the combined rolls of the military forces and domestic industries.

Overseas trade quickly fell under state supervision. Early in 1915 the government began requisitioning products for the war. These efforts also involved support for the production of shipping, which was suffering heavy losses from German U-boat attacks. The control of trade led inevitably to the rationing of supplies to domestic markets as well as to the imposition, early in 1916, of price controls. This latter move came in recognition that market conditions could not manage the huge demands of war production without driving up prices beyond the ability of domestic consumption to pay.

The failure of grain harvests in 1916 led to the crystallization of earlier plans to control food prices and encourage domestic production. Between February and July of 1917 the government set up a Food Production Department and introduced a Corn [cereal grain] Production Act. The price of the 1917 crop was fixed, and the department negotiated the recruitment of soldiers from the farms with the War Office. To cultivate additional farmlands, tractors were introduced on a large scale and later became a permanent part of British farming. By the end of the war the British government controlled 90 percent of all imports and managed the distribution of 80 percent of all food consumed in the domestic market.

These measures illustrate the willingness of the British state to use its authority to step in to areas where voluntary cooperation and market forces proved inadequate to meet the needs of a war economy. Not only were the leaders willing to act, they were willing to follow through the complex connections between production, manpower, and labor to extend their control as far as was necessary. In other words, they were willing to turn specific controls over the economy into more-general ones.

The timing of these interventions may appear to be too lacking in foresight, reflecting on the inability of the leaders to grasp the nature of the task they had undertaken. In fact, however, these measures evolved as they did because early indicators of the progress of the war suggested that the slogan "business as usual" might prove to be the watchword of government policy. The large number of volunteers for military service was one such indicator. Another was the stability, and even the rise, in the value of the pound sterling; only by mid 1915 did it appear that the balance of trade was consistently turning against Britain. Moreover, the War Office continued to predict and the Ministers to accept that the war would be of short duration—a vision that died in the mud of the Somme (1916). It was in these circumstances that the then-Chancellor of the Exchequer, David Lloyd George, prepared a budget for 1915 that failed to acknowledge that an economic crisis was around the corner. By March 1916, Lloyd George would be Minister of Munitions and demanding more interventionist measures.

The strategic thinking with which the government entered the war also disposed it to steer clear of an all-out commitment to fighting on the European continent. For two hundred years British strategic doctrine had held to the theory of "blue-water" warfare, a notion that Britain would build up its financial reserves, maintain its industrial base, and wage a holding action on the western European front, wearing down the German army until it could intervene with decisive force. This strategy dictated an economic policy of caution and preservation. Throughout 1915 and 1916 Lloyd George's replacement at the Treasury, Reginald McKenna, resisted conscription of labor and the commitment of large and seemingly endless numbers to the trenches in Flanders because he feared that the drain on manpower would erode the industrial base of the nation and ruin its credit abroad.

The war itself overwhelmed all of these assumptions and calculations. The rapidity with which modern industrialized warfare could consume manpower and material had not been grasped—by any statesman. Nor had the terms under which the war was being waged in the west—a combination of stalemate and attrition—been contemplated. An army trained to prefer horsemanship and cavalry charges had to try to adapt to trenches, machine guns, barbed wire, and artillery bombardment. These factors quickly forced British political leaders to rethink the requirements of the war. Thus the novel conditions created a muddle. The leaders, however, accepted its challenges and made their way through the muddle with planning and execution. In difficult circumstances they acquitted themselves well indeed.

–ROBERT MCJIMSEY,
COLORADO COLLEGE

References

Peter Dewey, *War and Progress: Britain, 1914–1945* (London & New York: Longman, 1997).

Bentley Brinkerhoff Gilbert, *David Lloyd George, A Political Life,* volume 2, *The Organizer of Victory, 191½z16* (London: Batsford, 1992).

Sidney Pollard, *The Development of the British Economy, 1914–1990,* fourth edition (London: Arnold, 1992).

John Turner, *British Politics and the Great War: Coalition and Conflict, 1915–1918* (New Haven: Yale University Press, 1992).

BRUSILOV OFFENSIVE

Did the Brusilov Offensive of 1916 demonstrate the vigor of the Russian army?

Viewpoint: Yes. The Russians employed innovative tactical methods to cope with trench warfare.

Viewpoint: No. The initial Russian success reflected the weakness of the Austro-Hungarian opposition; the offensive eventually stalled as much from the incompetence of the Russian High Command as from enemy resistance.

By the spring of 1916 the hard-hammered Russian army had replaced enough of its lost men and equipment for its leaders to think once more about taking the offensive against the Central Powers. The increasingly obvious weakness of the Austro-Hungarians and the concentration of German resources in the West for the attack on Verdun created an opportunity that led the Stavka, the Russian High Command, to plan in April a series of offensives, with their central point a drive on Vilna in the north. As a preliminary, General Aleksey Brusilov, newly appointed commander of the Southwestern Front, was to mount an attack in his sector to draw enemy reserves south.

This move was intended as a secondary operation, but Brusilov put his considerable intellectual and physical energy into galvanizing his discouraged subordinates to get behind a fresh approach. Standard Great War offensives had involved concentrating on a particular sector, what the Germans called a *Schwerpunkt*, and throwing every available man and round into blasting through enemy defenses. Brusilov was as aware as every other senior officer that this method had consistently proved futile. He lacked, moreover, the local superiority of force necessary even to begin it. Instead the Russian commander proposed to attack along almost the entire 350 miles of his four-army sector. This strategy, he argued, would force the Central Powers to disperse their reserves instead of concentrating them to contain an attack at one point. It would also shake the morale of Austrian troops and commanders by keeping them off balance, uncertain of where the next blow would fall. Finally, a full-scale offensive in the south might encourage Romania to enter the war on the Allied side.

Brusilov's approach did not involve an equal dispersion of his forces all along the front. Instead each of the armies on the Southwestern Front concentrated its efforts in a narrow sector. If all went well, the enemy would face four near-simultaneous ruptures of the front, with no clear idea of from where the main effort was coming. In that context, while Brusilov's intention was to focus on his northern right wing and drive for Lutsk, he did not exclude the possibility of pursuing promising alternatives that might develop elsewhere along his front.

The offensive began on 4 June and achieved quick success. By 7 June, Lutsk had fallen and the Russians in that sector had advanced as far as twenty and twenty-five miles as Austrian resistance virtually collapsed. Because of his own strategy, however, Brusilov lacked the sector reserves to exploit the victory. Instead, he hesitated. Stavka ordered him to push on, but neither sent him reinforcements nor launched its originally projected attack toward Vilna. Meanwhile, the Germans moved to restore the front. The Austrians transferred reinforcements from Italy. The Russian offensive slowed, then stopped even though Brusilov finally began receiving more troops. By mid August the drive had ended. Casualties on both sides totaled more than one million. The back of the Austrian army was broken and Romania had come into the war on the Allied side, but the Russian army had also spent its last physical and moral reserves in what proved to be the final military effort of the Tsarist Empire.

Viewpoint:
Yes. The Russians employed innovative tactical methods to cope with trench warfare.

The Russians sustained millions of casualties in the catastrophic 1915 campaign of Gorlice-Tarnow. It appeared that the battered tsarist army had been rendered incapable of serious battle for some time. By summer 1916, however, the Russian army stood on the threshold of what would be its greatest victory of World War I, the Brusilov Offensive. In 1916 the armies of General Aleksey Brusilov were resupplied with such vital military necessities as artillery shells, but their major asset was Brusilov himself. A unique Russian general, Brusilov was adept at learning from his experiences and brought to the battlefield a new Eastern Front strategy (copied from Western Front experiences).

In December 1915 the Russians launched a two-army offensive against the Austro-Hungarian right-flank positions near the Romanian frontier. Following an artillery barrage unprecedented on the Eastern Front for its intensity, the assault commenced on 27 December 1915. The time-consuming transfer and deployment of Russian forces into the designated offensive area quickly caught the attention of the Habsburg intelligence service. Consequently, troops were immediately dispatched to strengthen this threatened Habsburg right-flank position. Austro-Hungarian commanders were successful in utilizing artillery to maintain their troops' perseverance in battle. Much to their advantage, the Austro-Hungarians also made better use of their reserves.

The Russians committed serious errors that negatively affected the outcome of the battle. It was a poor time of the year to launch a major military operation, with winter weather making many roads impassable. The Russian supply and transport system collapsed, leaving its Seventh Army on the brink of starvation. To make matters worse, tsarist operations were poorly planned and ill prepared. Russian losses were severe. Sufficient reserves were lacking. In addition, the chosen attack front was too narrow for the deployed Russian striking force. The failure of field artillery to support infantry advances further weakened the Russian offensive. Tactical errors resulted in premature infantry advances far from the Austrian lines, thereby drawing massive defensive fire.

The Austro-Hungarian victory of December 1915 is critical to understanding the subsequent Brusilov Offensive of June 1916. While Brusilov learned from these earlier mistakes, the Habsburg Supreme Command was misled by the victory and became overly confident in the strength of their defensive positions. Designed specifically to weaken the effect of Russian heavy artillery bombardment, the Habsburg defensive positions appeared to have proven their worth in the December-January battles and led to the extension of their use on the entire Austro-Hungarian eastern front. The major result of Habsburg artillery barrages from close proximity to the front lines was the complete halting of the Russian assaults. Although useful in the described battles, this successful tactic resulted in artillery units being positioned much too close to the front lines during the forthcoming Brusilov Offensive.

In a replay of their earlier mistakes, the Russians began advancing under adverse weather conditions in March 1916 against the Germans at Lake Naroch. Once again, the Russians suffered a terrible battlefield defeat, despite the fact that they greatly outnumbered their opponent.

Plans for coordinated Entente operations in 1916 were discussed at a conference on 14 April, where the Russians announced their intentions to aid the hard-pressed Italians and attack the Germans to relieve the pressure on the French Verdun front. Meanwhile, on the Austro-Hungarian southwest front, Brusilov's armies would attack only once victory was achieved in the north against the German foe. Several Russian generals opposed the plan, arguing that the complete failure of the recent March offensive made it unlikely that the German front could be broken. German defensive positions were much too strong, they contended, and the Russian armies lacked sufficient heavy artillery. Brusilov then argued in favor of launching an offensive on his front, emphasizing that such an attack would pin down Habsburg forces and divert their reserves, thereby greatly assisting the projected northern offensive. Brusilov's proposal was approved; however, because the main emphasis was the German front, no additional troops, artillery, or ammunition would be provided for the effort. Thus, the tsarist armies had a mere 130,000-soldier majority count on a two-hundred-mile front.

Russian soldiers standing among dead Austrians following the Brusilov Offensive

(Robert Hunt Picture Library)

While Brusilov was preparing his offensive, a Habsburg offensive struck against Italy on 15 May. As a result of Italian pressure for assistance, it was decided that Brusilov's attack on the Austro-Hungarian front would commence on 4 June 1916. The Russian main offensive against Germany was set for 14 June. Brusilov immediately informed his four army commanders of the projected offensive. His instructions proved to be both unique and significant. First, enormous numbers of artillery batteries and reserves were to be concentrated on one specific section at the front of each of the four armies. Second, enemy barbed-wire emplacements and defensive trenches had to be destroyed by preparatory artillery barrages. The infantry would then attack with the support of continuing artillery barrages, ultimately resulting in that portion of the front collapsing, which would force other neighboring sections also to withdraw. Massive barrages would cover the entire two-hundred-mile front to keep the enemy off balance and preclude rapid and effective insertion of reserves.

Such innovative tactics, new to the Russian army, stemmed from Brusilov's perception that previous Allied offensives had failed because the days-long artillery preparation destroyed any possibility of surprise. Successful advances were halted quickly by enemy enfilading fire from all sides of the created salient. In addition, Brusilov recognized that after the infantry advanced, supporting artillery could not be moved forward rapidly enough because their earlier barrages had torn up the terrain.

Other innovative tactics put to use on the battlefield by Brusilov included the uniform forward movement of Russian trenches on the entire front to within two or three hundred feet of the enemy positions in order to cloak each specific attack position just before the assault. Large dugouts with high ramparts were constructed along the front to hide the assembling reserve units. This strategy prevented the opposing Habsburg forces from massing troops at any one threatened location as they had successfully done in the 1915–1916 Bukovina campaign.

Each tsarist army commander selected the particular sector (up to thirty kilometers) of his own front where the enemy lines would be breached. A few days before the offensive, shock troops and artillery batteries were shifted under the cloak of darkness to the front lines to achieve complete surprise. Replicas of Habsburg trenches were built far behind the front to allow mock-attack training for the tsarist troops.

THE WAVES OF WAR

An Austrian observer comments on townspeople caught in the Russian advance into Hungary, part of the victories won in 1916 by the armies of General Aleksey Brusilov:

The wide town-square was filled with people, and General von Pfanzer-Baltin himself was expected. But then in the afternoon, whilst the artillery fire in the north, in the direction of Okna and Dobronovtse, was getting louder and louder, a dispatch-rider arrived with the following message, which was read out to the expectant crowds in the square: "His Excellency General von Pfanzer-Baltin is prevented from taking part in the festivities of to-day, and gives notice of his absence."

Six days later crowds were again filling the town square—no longer to "commemorate" the Russian occupation of Czernovitz. On Saturday, June 10th, at 6. p.m, military transports began to traverse the main streets of the town, moving from the direction of the bridgehead of Zhuchka towards Starozhyniets. It was an interminable chain of all kinds of vehicles, from huge, heavy motor lorries down to light gigs driven by army officers. The waves of war were rolling through the city.

As if at a given sign the town square filled with people. Frightened, searching eyes were asking for an explanation. Terrifying news began to circulate, the excited imagination of the crowd was at work. Mysterious information was passed from mouth to mouth, yet no one knew anything definite. A fever got hold of the town. With bags, boxes and baskets people were hurrying to the railway station. "Is an evacuation-train leaving, and when?" they were asking with the persistence of desperation. . . .

Suddenly—no one knows how—the news spread that the army group of General Papp had evacuated its positions and was retreating. Even the hour of the event was known. The information was correct. The greatest optimists now gave up all hope. The safety of the Bukovina was closely connected with the name of General Papp.

The gray dawn found the city in full flight. The streets were filled with crowds, the tram-cars were carrying wounded soldiers, as at the order of the army command the evacuation of the military hospitals had been started. The square before the railway station was closely packed with people, but the police were admitting only railway officials. The women were begging, crying, lifting up their children. They had to wait—the train was not meant for them.

At 8 a.m. the first evacuation train left the city. The next was due at noon, or at 3 p.m. Many people preferred to fly by foot, as the prices of cabs and cars had risen to an incredible height. The artillery fire was drawing closer and closer, and above the heads of the crowd appeared a Russian aviator. Their hearts were shaking with fear.

The prices of goods in the town were falling rapidly. Tobacco and cigarettes, which previously were hardly to be had anywhere, were offered at half price without any restrictions. Women from the suburbs who, not knowing what had happened, had brought their vegetables to the market, were selling them for a third of the usual price, only to be able to return to their homes and children. For the merchants in Czernovitz the evacuation was a catastrophe. As they had been supplying the army with goods, they had gathered stores valued at millions of crowns. None of them could be carried away; only Government property was being removed.

The news that the town would soon come under fire led to a sheer panic. The crowd in front of the station was seized with frenzy. Against the resistance of the officials it forced its way into the station and invaded a half-empty military train. The same happened in the case of the next train, and to all the following ones. In the course of Sunday 6 to 8,000 people left Czernovitz.

Source: Charles F. Horne, Source Records of the Great War, volume 4 (Indianapolis: American Legion, 1930), pp. 202–204.

Air reconnaissance—a novelty for Russian forces—and intelligence gathered from prisoners of war enabled the Russians to chart all opposing Habsburg positions. Such reports indicated that multiple German units had transferred to the French theater at Verdun, that multiple combat-proven Austro-Hungarian divisions had been transferred to the Italian front, and that the Austrians had neither sizable reserves nor the capability of rapidly sending reinforcements. Thus, both Central Powers had removed significant forces from the Eastern Front, their respective actions at Verdun and Italy based upon the assumption that their portion at the front could withstand any Russian threat! This belief proved to be a key factor in the success of Brusilov's offensive.

On 3 June, the eve of the offensive, Brusilov's unorthodox tactics were questioned by the conservative Russian Chief of the General Staff, who insisted that Brusilov postpone the offensive until a concentrated attack could be prepared against the till-now customary tsarist one-front offensive. Brusilov replied that the offensive could not be halted at that late date.

Meanwhile, Brusilov's troops continued to dig closer to the enemy positions while increasing the intensity of harassing artillery barrages, particularly against the Habsburg Fourth and Seventh Armies. The artillery caused extensive damage to the barbed-wire entanglements, which would assist the rapid forward movement of the assaulting tsarist troops. The psychological tension in the Habsburg front lines mounted as the shelling intensified. Habsburg forces did not effectively return fire against the enemy artillery barrages, partially because priority for artillery shells had been allocated to the Italian offensive. This decision left the Habsburg forward lines unprepared for the Russian attack, despite the fact that it had been anticipated for weeks. Feverish Russian preparations and warnings through diplomatic channels, as well as air reconnaissance, left no doubt as to the enemy's intentions. The Russians did not have a significant numerical advantage at the onset of the offensive, though they would have a much greater number of reserves available at the key attack points.

In the early hours of 4 June 1916, Russian artillery fired along the entire Austro-Hungarian front, signaling the commencement of the attack. The intensity of the artillery barrage far exceeded any previous engagement in the east. The Russians had profited from their tactical mistakes of January and March 1916, and they now had amassed superior artillery for the offensive, while the Habsburg High Command had unwisely removed fifteen heavy-artillery batteries and multi-battle-tried divisions from the Russian front for service against Italy.

General Conrad von Hötzendorf's field commanders reacted in confusion to the Russian infantry attacks. Individual corps commanders misrepresented or completely failed to report the actual situation on their fronts, which led to disaster, particularly for the Habsburg Fourth Army. Its defensive positions were reduced to rubble in the first artillery barrages, with "colossal smoke and dust clouds, which hindered observation," while sand filled the breeches of defensive weapons. Russian artillery fire systematically decimated the Austrian frontline positions and then ranged against the second "one hundred meter" lines, as well as the connecting communications trenches and reserve troop-assembly areas. Habsburg reserves were rushed in but hurled into battle in such small

numbers that they proved ineffective. Moreover, for various reasons, the usual counterattacks never materialized. One of Brusilov's main objectives had thus been achieved. Enemy reserves had been rapidly committed, and Russian artillery could decimate the tightly packed Austrian forward trenches—where two-thirds of the manpower was located, as in the earlier 1916 battle. The result was a frightful number of casualties in the Austro-Hungarian lines, producing a "shocked psychological situation with the troops and their commanders." One source cites the Fourth Army strength dropping from 117,000 to 28,000 men in twenty-four hours, much more than the official version of 54 percent losses. These enormous losses, much more than 50 percent of fighting strength of the two armies (the Fourth and Seventh), were a result of the lack of sufficient heavy artillery support, poor coordination between infantry and artillery, and the loss of supporting artillery pieces. At the same time as the Russians surprisingly and rapidly achieved victory over the Austrian Fourth Army near Lutsk, a Russian army launched a successful second pincer movement with an assault between the Dniester and Pruth Rivers. The victory had begun.

Thus commenced the most successful Russian and Allied victory of the war. Brusilov's unorthodox (for the Russian army) strategy not only revenged the terrible Gorlice-Tarnow battle of a year earlier but also almost knocked Austria-Hungary out of the war. The months-long battle slowed only in July when Brusilov outran his supply lines and again reverted to earlier tsarist military techniques. This great victory, the last for Russia in World War I, came at a great cost in terms of human life. Significantly, it also represented a step toward revolution in Russia.

—GRAYDON A. TUNSTALL, UNIVERSITY OF
SOUTH FLORIDA

Viewpoint:
No. The initial Russian success reflected the weakness of the Austro-Hungarian opposition; the offensive eventually stalled as much from the incompetence of the Russian High Command as from enemy resistance.

In his memoirs German Field Marshal Paul von Hindenberg looked back upon the first week of the Brusilov Offensive (1916) and confessed that "For a moment, we were faced with the menace of a complete collapse." German reinforcement and assumption of control over Austrian troops combined with incompetent timidity by Russian commanders not only averted such a collapse but ultimately reversed many of Russian general Aleksey Brusilov's gains by the end of the war.

The initial successes of the Brusilov Offensive stand in such stark contrast to the dismal performance of Russian arms throughout the rest of the war that one is tempted to term them "vital" or "innovative." Bernard Pares, in *The Fall of the Russian Monarchy: A Study of the Evidence* (1939), his account of the demise of the Russian monarchy, credited Brusilov with the notion of an innovative "Tap Along the Wall." Brusilov did indeed open the attack along a broad front, seeking weak points. Nevertheless, the offensive failed for the same reasons as so many Russian efforts throughout the Great War. Brusilov's plan included the same spendthrift waste of troops that characterized other offensives, especially when his initial successes were rewarded by the diversion of troops from other fronts to his own. Repeated failures of coordination among Russian commanders bled the offensive of its energy and of any chance it had to gain synergy along the front.

At the outset of the campaign, no men, munitions, or supplies were transferred from the Western Front to Brusilov. The miserly treatment of Brusilov by the Stavka was classic Russian. Russian commanders on the Western Front, Alexei Evert and Aleksey Kuropatkin, had once been senior to the current Chief of Staff Mikhail Alexeyev. Brusilov believed that Alexeyev therefore husbanded resources to cover their incompetence. They, for their part, simultaneously sidestepped defeat by avoiding offensive action that might have lent support to Brusilov's advance.

As Alexeyev belatedly rewarded Brusilov's initial success and diverted troops and ammunition to the offensive, he shed any pretext at innovation and poured those troops into the cauldron at Kowel, seeking the same type of "decisive breakthrough" so familiar to observers of the Western Front. W. Bruce Lincoln described in *Passage Through Armageddon: The Russians in War and Revolution, 1914–1918* (1986) the tragic slaughter of the cream of the Russian army, its Imperial Guards. Turned over to Brusilov's command by Alexeyev, two Corps of the Guards were marched through a nearly impassable bog before Kowel. With no artillery support, and constantly strafed by German aircraft, 80 percent of these crack units were lost in less than two weeks with no gain for Russia. While Lincoln placed primary responsibility for the debacle on the corps commanders, Brusilov himself reverted to orthodox tactics of massed frontal attacks before Kowel.

Rather than representing any new Russian vigor or vitality, the Brusilov Offensive carried the same old hallmarks of Russian command incompetence as had the first efforts at offensive into East Prussia under Aleksandr Samsonov and Pavel Rennenkampf in 1914. Commanders allowed personal feelings and their desire to keep their records unblemished to supercede the demands of combat and the interests of Russia. Despite repeated orders from Stavka, and despite an enormous advantage in men, munitions, and material, Evert failed for weeks to launch a planned western offensive designed to support Brusilov. When finally prodded into action late in June, Evert used old-style, mass frontal attacks with poor preparation and execution. His botched command led to eighty thousand Russian casualties while inflicting only sixteen thousand on his opponents. Evert's incompetence placed a deadly drain on Russian manpower.

Evert's and Kuropatkin's failures to advance eliminated any chance Brusilov might have had to achieve a strategic breakthrough. Brusilov could not shift his axis of attack to the west, because Evert's and Kuropatkin's immobility would have exposed his northern flanks to decisive counterattack. By the time rain in autumn made any further advance impossible, Brusilov had lost five hundred thousand of the men that the War Ministry had trained so well the previous winter, and with them, the last, best hopes of Russia for victory.

Despite the flawed Russian command, those hopes for victory had been real, as Brusilov's attack unraveled the armies opposing him. His success, however, was based upon the weakness of Austro-Hungarian arms. The reach of the Austrian commander in chief, Franz Conrad von Hötzendorf, constantly exceeded his grasp. Many of the subjects of Emperor Francis Joseph I held much greater affinity for their Slavic Russian brethren than loyalty to him, and the hodgepodge mix of nations and languages that was the Austro-Hungarian Empire created nearly impossible problems of command and control. Finally, the Austrian supply and munitions situation was worse even than that of Russia. These flaws were the critical causes of Brusilov's initial success.

An ardent patriot, Conrad detested the notion that Austria should be overshadowed by Germany. Throughout the fall of 1914 he furiously sought opportunities for Austrian armies to duplicate the success of Hindenberg and Erich Ludendorff at Tannenberg (1914). Instead, his efforts were frustrating failures at Tomaszów, Zlota Lipa, Gnila Lipa, and Lwów in the early days of the war, with the disastrous loss of the Przemysl fortress in March 1915. That debacle convinced General Erich von Falkenhayn of Austrian weakness and inspired him to refocus German attention on the Eastern Front. German general August von Mackensen's steamrolling offensives and the Russian Great Retreat of 1915 followed.

The weakness of Austria was only in part the result of Conrad's ineptitude. Rank-and-file soldiers of the Austro-Hungarian armies surrendered in droves to Brusilov's advancing Russians. Pares noted that "the subjects of Franz Josef had no affection for him." Instead, many of them felt great affinity for their Slavic Russian brethren. Brusilov took 26,000 prisoners on the first day of his offensive, and more than 125,000 prisoners in the first four days. To put these numbers in perspective: one-third of the Austro-Hungarian troops facing Brusilov's armies became prisoners in the first eight days of the offensive. Many of these prisoners were Serbs, Czechs, Poles, Ruthenians, and Slovaks—in short, Slavs who may have looked upon surrender as a step toward Pan-Slavic unity as well as a blow against the oppression of Austria-Hungary.

The multiethnic character of the Austrian army weakened it in other ways as well. Prior to the start of World War I, Austrian officers were always multilingual, with most speaking three or four languages. Such polyglots were essential, given that the common soldiers of the army spoke at least fifteen distinct languages. Those officers died en masse in 1914. General Max Hoffman, commanding Austro-Hungarian forces in Galicia, noted in August 1916 that "Besides, there are all these different races mixed up together—no less than twenty-three distinct languages. No one understands anyone else."

The supply and munitions problem was as complicated as the language situation. At the start of the war, Austrian artillery pieces demanded forty-five different shell types to accommodate the widely varying calibers and types of weapons produced throughout the empire.

Austrian weakness accounted for the initial success of Brusilov's Offensive, but Russian command incompetence, combined with monumental losses in men and material, ensured its ultimate failure. Failed coordination among the Russian armies isolated the advances to the Southwestern Front. The slaughter of the Guards Army bogged down Brusilov's right, which had to limit its advances to avoid exposing its flanks in the absence of any forward drive by Evert and Kuropatkin. But slaughter was not limited to the Guards. Brusilov, who contended that the only offensive action that could proceed without casualties was conducted during training maneuvers, accepted massive losses. In the first days of the offensive, Brusilov's Eighth Army lost thirty-five thousand men and most of his shell reserves. Such casual disregard for loss of life drained Russian manpower and demonstrated that Brusilov's thinking was hardly new and innovative but instead was in concert with that of his peers on the Western Front. Some of Brusilov's other deci-

sions contributed to the gridlock that undermined his success as well. To save fodder, Brusilov turned most of his cavalry into infantry. While this decision meant spare space on supply trains for men and munitions, it also meant that his forces could not pursue the Austrians when they broke into full flight. The offensive finally locked up completely when Romania entered the war as an ally of Russia. As Romanian forces were continually driven to defeat by German and Austrian opponents, Russian troops were diverted to prop them up. By the end of 1916 one Russian soldier out of four on Brusilov's front was engaged not in pursuing the offensive, but in defending the new ally.

Command incompetence doomed the offensive from the start. Its initial successes were the result of the critical weaknesses of Austro-Hungarian forces. Even these successes, however, bogged down into gridlock as Brusilov's initiative failed and he reverted to orthodox, pyrrhic attacks with massive formations against fortified positions. The losses generated were enormous, and by the winter of 1916–1917 the incompetence of Russian commanders finally broke the discipline of the common soldiers, who assumed their place in the front line of the February revolution.

–DAVID L. RUFFLEY,
U.S. AIR FORCE ACADEMY

References

A. A. Brusilov, *A Soldier's Notebook, 1914–1918* (Westport, Conn.: Greenwood Press, 1971).

Martin Gilbert, *The First World War: A Complete History* (New York: Holt, 1994).

John Keegan, *The First World War* (London: Hutchinson, 1998).

Alfred Knox, *With the Russian Army, 1914–1917, Being Chiefly Extracts From the Diary of a Military Attaché,* two volumes (London: Hutchinson, 1921).

W. Bruce Lincoln, *Passage Through Armageddon: The Russians in War and Revolution, 1914–1918* (New York: Simon & Schuster, 1986).

Bernard Pares, *The Fall of the Russian Monarchy: A Study of the Evidence* (London: Cape, 1939; New York: Knopf, 1939).

Norman Stone, *The Eastern Front, 1914–1917* (New York: Scribners, 1975).

CAVALRY

Was cavalry in World War I an antiquated combat arm?

Viewpoint: Yes. Although cavalry had mobility, it was rendered obsolete by the increased firepower of the Great War.

Viewpoint: No. When used properly, cavalry provided tactical and operational mobility that could influence the course of a battle.

Cavalry has been a major scapegoat for everything that went wrong in the Great War. Critics describe armies whose retrograde commanders were inflexibly committed to mounted action and which maintained huge forces of horsemen that clogged rear areas, distorted supply systems because of inexhaustible demands for forage, and then proved helpless under modern firepower.

Reality is less dramatic and more pedestrian. The proportion of cavalry in the European armies had been shrinking for a century before World War I. Large-scale mounted action was generally understood to be unlikely; cavalries instead understood their roles as screening and reconnaissance. The British cavalry was trained to fight dismounted as well as on horseback. German cavalry divisions included rifle battalions with their own motor transport.

In the early weeks on the Western Front, squadron- and regimental-level cavalry charges occurred and occasionally succeeded. In Russia the lower force-to-space ratios also offered opportunities for the maneuver of larger mounted formations. By the end of 1915, however, European cavalry forces were being reduced in size, the regiments dismounted, and the men sent into the trenches. The French and British kept a few mounted divisions but found them more valuable for defensive operations as a mobile reserve of firepower—a role enhanced as cavalry received more heavy and light machine guns. The lack of cavalry in the German army was arguably one factor in the failure of its March 1918 offensive: infantry too easily lost touch with the retreating enemy. The final British offensive has also been described as suffering from a lack of mounted troops to keep pressure on the Germans.

In the Middle East, Mesopotamia, and Palestine the mounted arm played a more significant role at tactical and operational levels. British, Australian, and Indian horsemen conducted the operational pursuit that broke a hard-fighting Turkish army, using aircraft and motorized machine guns to supplement their organic artillery and automatic weapons. Even against machine guns, the broken terrain of Palestine made successful cavalry charges possible by units as diverse as British Yeomanry, Indian lancers, and Australian mounted riflemen. The sword might have been obsolescent, but before the final campaign in 1918 the Australian Mounted Division made them standard issue. By November 1918 the future of cavalry might have been in doubt, but its presence was still welcome.

Viewpoint:
Yes. Although cavalry had mobility, it was rendered obsolete by the increased firepower of the Great War.

During World War I the internal-combustion engine did not alter fundamentally the nature of military operations. Wheeled motor vehicles were unreliable and confined to existing roads, while early tanks proved unable to outpace infantry. Therefore, horse cavalry remained the only component of the belligerent armies that was consistently capable of conducting mobile warfare. Nonetheless, cases of the successful employment of cavalry were few and far between in World War I. By the early twentieth century, modern firepower had drastically reduced the effectiveness of mounted troops on the battlefield. The institutional culture of European cavalry forces, however, inhibited their adaptation to this technological reality. It also left them poorly suited for the combined-arms cooperation necessary to achieve victory during World War I. Thus, while it had yet to be replaced by a weapon of equivalent mobility, cavalry proved to be an antiquated tool that was irrelevant to the outcome of the conflict.

In order to understand the reasons for the impotence of cavalry in World War I, it is useful to begin by briefly examining its institutional development in the preceding decades. Over the course of the nineteenth century, professional competence gradually superseded wealth and social status as the key criterion for the appointment and promotion of officers in European armies, particularly in the infantry and artillery. In the cavalry, however, this trend was less pronounced for two reasons. First, throughout the 1800s, admission to its officer corps remained largely restricted to members of the European upper classes and aristocracy who could bear the considerable expense associated with securing and maintaining a commission in the mounted arm. This policy excluded capable and ambitious individuals without sufficient financial resources. Second, the considerable glamour and romance surrounding the past exploits of European cavalry discouraged analysis of the future role of the arm by those with the means to gain a commission. As a result, cavalry officers were less inclined to serious study of their profession than their counterparts in the infantry and artillery. Hubert Gough, a British cavalry commander in 1914, commented in his memoirs on the other officers in his regiment in the 1890s:

I liked my brother officers personally, from the colonel to my fellow subalterns, but I could not feel much respect for them as serious soldiers. . . . Not one of them had read a book on tactics, Clery's or any other. To know your drill was sufficient. We led a cheerful, care-free life; what duties we had to do, and in which we were thoroughly proficient, were punctiliously attended to, but they did not call for much mental effort. Afternoons were usually free for most of the officers. We played pool and some cricket at the Aldershot Club in the summer.

This lack of study was significant, particularly in light of the growing impact of firepower in wars fought since the mid nineteenth century. The increased use of rifles, machine guns, and modern artillery had profound implications for the role of mounted troops on the battlefield. Nevertheless, European cavalry continued to train in traditional shock tactics using the *arme blanche* (sword or lance), emphasizing the mounted charge by troopers armed with lance or saber. More generally, officers extolled the virtues of a rather ambiguous, but equally time-honored quality known as the "cavalry spirit." Sir John French, the most celebrated British cavalry commander of the South African War (1899–1902), offered a partial definition in 1904, explaining: "It is difficult to determine what one means by the 'cavalry spirit,' but it is a power which is *felt* and realized by those who have served much with the arm. Its attributes are 'élan,' 'dash,' and a fixed determination always to take the offensive and secure the initiative."

Cavalry officers were not entirely oblivious to the implications of technological change. In the British army in particular, in the decade before World War I, there was intense debate regarding the continued efficacy of shock tactics on a battlefield swept by modern firepower. Rather than spurring wholesale reforms, however, serious discussion of the future roles of the mounted arm largely reaffirmed the commitment of cavalry officers to their traditional tactics and modes of behavior. Given the centrality of the *arme blanche* and the "cavalry spirit" in the storied past of the mounted arm, officers perceived that the abandonment of these concepts would threaten the survival of the cavalry in its existing form. Thus, the training of European cavalry did not change significantly in the years immediately before the war. In the French and German armies, the training regimen of mounted troops consisted almost entirely of shock tactics. The German cavalry regularly practiced massed charges by entire divisions. While British troopers were taught marksmanship and dismounted action, shock tactics still consumed 80 percent of their training time as late as 1910. Given the impact of machine guns and artillery on large targets such as charging masses of cav-

A column of German cavalry on the Eastern Front in 1916

(from Grosser Bilderatlas des Weltkrieges [1915–1919], Joseph M. Bruccoli Great War Collection, Thomas Cooper Library, University of South Carolina)

alry, this instruction was of dubious value on the modern battlefield.

Equally problematic was the continued ascendancy of the "cavalry spirit" among officers of the mounted arm. A determination to take the offensive was not necessarily a negative attribute in a cavalry commander. An equally important component of the "cavalry spirit," however, was independence of action, as qualities such as "élan" and "dash" could not be stifled by adherence to preconceived operational plans. The fact that cavalry officers expected considerable freedom in the field held the potential to undermine their cooperation with other units during active operations. Thus, on the eve of World War I, the mounted arm retained dated tactics, habits, and values that were ill suited to the scale and intensity of the impending conflict.

The opening weeks of the war quickly laid bare the inadequacies of cavalry. On 24 August 1914, for example, a disastrous charge by the Ninth Lancers of the British Cavalry Division demonstrated the ineffectiveness of shock tactics against modern weaponry. Galloping across a field without conducting prior reconnaissance,

the cavalry was halted by wire fencing under the sights of enemy artillery. While the charge had little impact on the German infantry at which it was directed, the Ninth Lancers suffered heavily, with their commander reporting to his superiors that his regiment had been "practically annihilated." Heavy casualties were not the only consequence of cavalry officers' affection for shock tactics. In the German army, it encouraged the neglect of the other, less glamorous duties performed by mounted troops assigned to protect infantry formations. As Dennis E. Showalter has observed in *Tannenberg: Clash of Empires* (1991): "Their principal mission of close-range reconnaissance tended to be at best indifferently performed by horsemen seeking opportunities for mounted action on a troop or squadron level."

The danger inherent in the independence exercised by cavalry commanders was also revealed early in the war. On 25 August, as the British Expeditionary Force (BEF) retired toward Paris with the German army in hot pursuit, its Cavalry Division effectively disintegrated, with its commander, Edmund Allenby, losing control of three of the four brigades that

CAVALRY

composed it. While the confusion involved in the retreat did little to facilitate cohesion, neither did the independent mind-set of the brigade commanders. Two of them did not reestablish contact with divisional headquarters until several days later, and one, the aforementioned Gough, deliberately removed his formation from Allenby's control, retiring independently and eventually subordinating himself to another commander. The dispersal of the Cavalry Division and, in particular, Gough's extraordinary actions endangered the BEF at a critical point in the retreat. A similar lack of cooperation prevailed during the Battle of the Marne in early September, as the British took the offensive against the overextended German army. Infantry officers complained repeatedly in this period about the failure of the cavalry to coordinate its movements with the rest of the army. The resulting delays impeded the British advance. Thus, while the open warfare that prevailed in France and Belgium during the initial stages of the war gave cavalry the potential to utilize its mobility, the independence inherent in the "cavalry spirit" rendered the mounted arm a detriment to the effectiveness of European armies.

With the onset of trench warfare on the Western Front in late 1914, cavalry units were required to fight dismounted alongside the infantry and artillery. Given its orientation toward mounted operations and shock tactics, however, the cavalry proved poorly suited to this task. French cuirassiers fought in an archaic uniform consisting of a blue tunic, a breastplate, and a helmet festooned with a horse's tail. They were equipped only with a sword and pistol, hardly adequate armament against German infantry. In addition, their value in the prolonged operations characteristic of trench warfare was circumscribed by the French army policy of relieving cavalry on a daily basis. Moreover, as one British officer complained, "Their fighting hours were from 9am to 4pm only!" Trained in dismounted action, British cavalry performed more creditably in 1914, holding trenches against German attacks during the First Battle of Ypres. This success, however, stemmed from the fact that British troopers performed as infantry, even adopting bayonets to combat the enemy on foot. Thus, rather than a vindication of the mounted arm, the use of British cavalry in the trenches is evidence of its obsolescence.

The German and French armies soon recognized this obsolescence. As early as September 1914, the German army effectively abandoned shock tactics, converting its cavalry divisions into mobile infantry brigades. By 1915 the French had made similar changes. While senior British commanders, many of them cavalrymen, clung to the hope of reviving the *arme blanche,* the British cavalry spent the years after 1914 either in the trenches or in reserve, waiting for an opportunity to exploit a breakthrough by the infantry. Such opportunities proved elusive. Even during the closing British offensives of 1918, when relative mobility had been restored to the battlefield, the cavalry achieved only isolated successes. The British Cavalry Corps in fact spent most of the final two months of the conflict in reserve. According to a leading historian of the British cavalry: ". . . its tactical innovations and contribution to the last offensives of 1918 fade into insignificance compared with those of the artillery, infantry and engineers."

Mounted troops were not entirely without purpose during World War I, particularly during the mobile warfare that prevailed in western Europe during the opening and closing stages of the conflict. Opportunities for the use of cavalry, however, were curtailed severely by modern firepower. The institutional culture of the mounted arm further inhibited its effectiveness. The preference of cavalry officers for traditional shock tactics intensified the impact of modern weapons on mounted troops. It also distracted cavalry from its less prestigious tasks such as reconnaissance. In addition, the independence inherent in the "cavalry spirit" undermined cooperation between arms and formations during a conflict in which it was essential for victory. Throughout the war, mounted troops proved most effective when employed as infantry. Cavalry, in its traditional form, was obsolete.

–NIKOLAS GARDNER, MOUNT ROYAL COLLEGE, CALGARY, ALBERTA

Viewpoint:
No. When used properly, cavalry provided tactical and operational mobility that could influence the course of a battle.

World War I was widely seen, even at the time, as marking the end of cavalry as a viable military arm. Much criticism has been aimed at the armies that went to war in 1914 with regiments of lancers and cuirassiers. This contention is particularly the case in Anglophone military histories of the war, where a tradition has existed that associates the cavalry with a backward-looking mind-set among senior military commanders, which is seen as responsible for high levels of casualties and lack of early tactical, operational, and strategic innovation. The emotional tone of such arguments has often prevented a fair assessment of the role of cavalry in the conflict, which would conclude that they still had a part to play in the successful prosecution of war.

It is clear that technological developments that had taken place over the course of the nineteenth century impacted on all arms in the opening years of World War I. Smokeless powder, magazine-loading rifles, effective machine guns, quick-firing artillery, and barbed wire all forced changes in tactics, most obviously the resort to prolonged trench warfare. Cavalry were particularly vulnerable to the effects of some of these developments, as was made clear by some of the first encounters on both Eastern and Western Fronts. Although perhaps not as susceptible to small-arms fire in the charge as might be assumed—horses do not suffer from reaction shock, so unless their bones were broken they could often complete a charge before collapsing from wounds—concentrated mounted units were an inviting target for machine guns or artillery. Cavalry were easily blocked by barbed wire: this piece of technology had been created, after all, to control the movements of animals. As other arms increasingly sought shelter in fixed defenses, cavalry had little initial role to play. Indeed, it is hard to see cavalry of any era being deployed in the first instance against defensive positions of such complex strength as existed on the Western Front.

Until the front lines of trenches were broken, cavalry seemed useless. Even if this breakthrough was possible, several other factors limited its employment. It was extremely difficult to position the cavalry correctly in order to exploit the small and fleeting breaches that could be created during the early years of the war. If they were placed too close, they would block roads and be devastated by the enemy's artillery. If too far away, they would be unable to react in time to what might be a brief opportunity. The situation was complicated further by the sheer area occupied by cavalry units; by the effect on the ground of heavy bombardments, which further slowed deployment; and by the primitive state of communications. This last factor particularly affected all offensive tactics and operations during the war. Even where the situation was more fluid, cavalry increasingly found their other main battlefield role—as reconnaissance—being usurped by more-modern technologies. Other troops, including cyclists, pilots, and armored-car drivers, could improve on much of the mobility and flexibility of the cavalry in the reconnaissance role.

The cavalry still retained, however, some advantages that other arms could not improve upon. At no point during World War I did a

CAVALRY IN ACTION

British corporal J. G. Mortimer, Tenth Battalion, The York and Lancaster Regiment, recalls the arrival of cavalry during a 1917 attack on the Hindenburg Line:

When zero hour arrived the officer would blow a whistle. If you didn't hear it you saw everybody mounting the parapet, so you did the same and on you went, with the best of luck and a spoonful of rum. On the tenth we went over the top in the second wave and we passed through the first wave when they reached their objective on the Hindenburg Line. We carried on until we reached a network of shallow trenches at the front of Monchy-Le-Preux where we were ordered to stay put and we spent the night in these trenches. It was open ground between these trenches and Monchy-Le-Preux. Just after dawn, we got the surprise of our lives when from a copse on our right there emerged the Cavalry. It was a thrilling sight to see them line up in one long line. Then, with the officer and standard-bearer in the centre they set up a yell and set off hell for leather for Monchy-Le-Preux. We all stood up in the trench and yelled with them. The element of surprise was on their side because they got halfway to Monchy before the Germans realised what was happening—then all hell was let loose and Jerry threw everything he had got at them. They disappeared into the village, where they must have dismounted because groups of about eight to ten horses were brought back to the copse, each group led by one man. They captured Monchy. But at what a price of horses and men!

Source: Lyn MacDonald, 1914–1918: Voices & Images of the Great War (London: Joseph, 1988), pp. 201–202.

mechanical alternative to the horse exist that offered the same opportunities for rapid, all-terrain exploitation of an initial success against an opponent. Early tanks were mechanically unreliable, slow moving, and short-ranged. Although effective in the first assault, they were then difficult to re-muster. While they were faster moving than their tracked brethren, armored cars found it difficult to operate off-road. Neither vehicle had the potential to advance quickly and then have their occupants dismount and hold ground until the arrival of friendly infantry in the way that cavalry could. Moreover, when well supported by covering fire, possibly from their own weapons, cavalry was still capable of effective shock action against infantry or artillery who were disorganized, not heavily entrenched, or surprised. This type of operation was more clearly the case at a tactical, rather than operational, level. Even when it came to reconnaissance, cavalry held the advantage in open warfare; they were able to capture and identify enemy troops, whereas aircraft could often only detect their presence.

In this battlefield environment, any cavalry units that were to be successful had to be well led at all levels, motivated, and tactically adept, as well as capable of performing all aspects of the cavalryman's role: reconnaissance, charging as shock troops with cold steel, fighting dismounted, and "galloping"—charging a position mounted, only to take and hold it on foot. It should not be surprising that those armies whose troops were not capable of this military multitasking abandoned their cavalry relatively quickly. After initial disappointments, the German, Russian, and French armies all reorganized their cavalry units; the Germans and French largely turned them into mounted infantry, who were mobile behind the lines but fought on foot, and the Russians simply dismounted them. Both the Russians and Germans, however, were to some extent to regret these decisions when they finally achieved seemingly decisive breakthroughs—in the offensives of 1916 and 1918—only to be unable to exploit them. It seems likely that both the Brusilov offensive and, more especially, the German assaults of spring 1918, could have achieved even greater success if they could have been developed more quickly. This result was not possible with the troops then available.

Among the major combatants, the only one to retain faith in the cavalry to any degree were the British. It is no coincidence that in 1914 British cavalrymen were a generation ahead of their opponents and their allies in terms of tactical development and training, although the quality of their cavalry on the Western Front declined steadily through the war. The greatest evidence for the effective use of cavalry therefore comes from the British side.

On the Western Front in 1914, the survival of the British Expeditionary Force (BEF) as a fighting unit during the retreat from Mons was the result of the ability of its cavalry division to hold off the German forces attacking it. Although vital information about German troop movements was provided by aircraft, rather than cavalry, the latter won a major defensive victory. In 1916, on the Somme, confusion in planning and difficulties in deployment limited the performance of the cavalry. When it came into action on 14 July, near High Wood, the numbers employed to follow up initial infantry success were so small that it is hard to make a judgment on its success. It was far from disastrous, however, and it is at least arguable that a deployment in greater strength might well have secured in an afternoon objectives that the British infantry were subsequently to spend another month and many casualties attempting to take.

Although 1917 offered further frustration for the British cavalry—particularly an extremely poorly conceived plan for its employment at Cambrai—in 1918 there was vindication. Following the German breakthrough in March, the cavalry provided vital mobile firepower in a defensive role. In small-unit strength, it also performed several mounted charges to retake key positions from the German forces. When British forces returned to the attack that summer, cavalry played a crucial role in the offensive of the Fourth Army on 8 August. Following up a successful infantry and tank assault, it took all its initial objectives by late afternoon, along with many prisoners. Two individual units performed highly successful mounted charges. The ability of the cavalry to move rapidly ahead of accompanying infantry to secure more-distant objectives greatly expanded the depth of penetration of the British assault, effectively carrying it through the German lines. Despite the success of this all-arms approach however, British commanders in 1918 increasingly reverted to offensive tactics based on artillery and infantry, within which there was little place for the cavalry until the final advance before the Armistice.

In the Middle East, during the campaign against Turkish forces in Palestine (1917–1918), the cavalry enjoyed its greatest success. Most of the troops involved were intended originally as mounted riflemen, but by 1917 they were effectively operating as cavalry. Turkish defensive positions were less dense than those on the Western Front and often were unprotected by barbed wire; these factors were central to the success of the cavalry. The most famous engagement was the charge of the Australian Light Horse at Beersheba on 31 October 1917, in which horsemen successfully overran entrenched infantry to swiftly secure vital water supplies. There were also several less-well-publicized, but equally important, actions in which the cavalry made adept use of fire and movement tactics to secure defended positions. Operationally, the mobility and flexibility of the cavalry enabled Allenby to carry through his lightning offensive, resulting in the capture of Damascus in the autumn of 1918.

An analysis of these examples makes it clear that there was still a role for cavalry in World War I, but that there were certain conditions necessary for its use. In the offensive in particular, it required: the destruction or absence of heavy defenses (particularly barbed wire), adequate fire support, the relative dispersion of enemy forces, and correct positioning and planning to enable proper exploitation. This need for particular conditions in order to achieve success was not so different from early tanks. Given these conditions, it was not surprising that the most unambiguous successes for the cavalry came either in defensive situations on the Western Front, where greater fluidity removed many of the limiting factors, or in theaters where the level of technological development or troop concentration was lower, most obviously in Palestine. However, offensive use on the Western Front in August 1918 shows that there was a place for cavalry even outside these situations. Well-trained cavalry could play a crucial part in converting the break-in to a breakthrough. In this case it should be seen as one of several specialist arms that were employed together to create an extremely powerful, indeed war-winning, weapon. Its use was not a military atavism, but a correct appreciation of the potential implementation of the most-effective military technology available at the time.

–DANIEL TODMAN, PEMBROKE COLLEGE,
CAMBRIDGE UNIVERSITY

References

Marquess of Anglesey, *A History of the British Cavalry, 1816 to 1919,* volume 4 (London: Cooper, 1986).

Stephen Badsey, "Cavalry and the Development of Breakthrough Doctrine," in *British Fighting Methods in the Great War,* edited by Paddy Griffith (London & Portland, Ore.: Frank Cass, 1996), pp. 138–174.

Brian Bond, "Doctrine and Training in the British Cavalry, 1870–1914," in *The Theory and Practice of War: Essays Presented to Captain B. H. Liddell Hart,* edited by Michael Howard (London: Cassell, 1965), pp. 95–125.

Nikolas Gardner, "Command and Control in the 'Great Retreat' of 1914: the Disintegration of the British Cavalry Division," *Journal of Military History,* 63 (January 1999): 29–54.

Hubert Gough, *Soldiering On: Being the Memoirs of General Sir Hubert Gough* (London: Barker, 1954).

Dennis E. Showalter, *Tannenberg: Clash of Empires* (Hamden, Conn.: Archon, 1991).

Edward Spiers, "The British Cavalry, 1902–1914," *Journal of the Society for Army Historical Research,* 57 (Summer 1979): 71–79.

CONVOYS

Was Great Britain's failure to introduce a convoy system prior to 1917 a mistake?

Viewpoint: Yes. The loss rates for unescorted merchant ships are proof that the Royal Navy neglected protection of merchant vessels in favor of fleet action against U-boats and raiders.

Viewpoint: No. German U-boats, limited in number and capabilities, were never a serious threat to British merchant shipping.

Well before the outbreak of World War I (1914), the British government and the Royal Navy were concerned about maintaining a steady supply of foodstuffs and raw materials to the British Isles. The major threat, however, was considered to be from surface raiders. Submarine technology was too undeveloped and submarines were too few in number and too short-ranged to pose a serious large-scale threat to British commerce. Even when in 1915 Germany proclaimed an undersea blockade of the British Isles, it proved more of a gesture than a threat—the sinking of the *Lusitania* notwithstanding.

Until the end of 1916, doctrine and experience combined to affirm that sailing individually was the best way to minimize merchant ship losses. The navy lacked escort craft of any kind. Shipowners and captains were reluctant to accept the economic costs and the physical risks of traveling in company under naval command. It was a game of averages, and the British were winning. Submarine sinkings were causing problems, but the loss rates were more acceptable than the alternative of convoy, and on the whole the British economy was functioning well.

To a degree, however, the favorable balance was a function of German restraint: the U-boats were being kept in check to avoid the risk of bringing the United States into the war. When in February 1917 Germany decided to accept that risk, the paradigm shifted. By April the U-boats were sinking a quarter of the tonnage bound for British ports. At that point, shortages and scarcities were still specific—sugar and meat supplies, for example, shrank alarmingly. Britain was not, as some accounts assert, on the brink of starvation. Unless, however, the trend could be reversed, it was all too possible to calculate almost to a day in time when Britain would either have to reconstruct her economy fundamentally or to risk being starved out of the war.

The convoy system introduced in May 1917 was not a panacea, but in company with related developments in the antisubmarine campaign it solved the problem. Considered together, the measures did more to deter attacks than sink U-boats. The results, however, were the same: a steady flow not only of supplies but of American soldiers into Britain and France during 1918—a tide the U-boats were unable to stem.

Viewpoint:
Yes. The loss rates for unescorted merchant ships are proof that the Royal Navy neglected protection of merchant vessels in favor of fleet action against U-boats and raiders.

Losses of shipping caused by German submarine attacks in World War I almost proved fatal to the British war effort. British forces in France demanded massive amounts of logistical support: food, ammunition, weapons, and other matériel. Even with help from its global empire, Great Britain was unable to keep up with these wartime demands. As a result, Britain and France turned to the United States to supply financing, food, raw materials, and manufactured goods. Items in the last three categories had to be transported across the Atlantic Ocean from North America to the British Isles and France. The voyage exposed merchant ships to possible German naval attack.

Although Germany used surface ships for commerce raiding in World War I, their use of submarines, or "U-boats," proved to be more effective. The U-boat sailed on the surface in search of Allied merchant shipping. When an Allied vessel was sighted, the submarine remained on the surface and sank the vessel with its deck cannon, or it submerged and sank the vessel with torpedoes. The latter tactic offered an element of greater surprise with less danger to the U-boat.

Throughout the war German U-boats inflicted heavy losses on Allied shipping, including sinking everything from warships to merchant vessels to luxury liners. In this way so-called total war, with its emphasis on complete mobilization of the resources of a nation for war and with its disregard for noncombatant immunity, extended into naval warfare. During periods of unrestricted submarine warfare, vessels flying neutral flags also fell victim to U-boat attacks.

In total, losses amounted to more than 5,500 Allied and neutral vessels carrying more than 12,190,000 tons of cargo. In 1915 U-boats sank 227 British ships, totaling 850,000 tons of cargo. In the first half of 1916 U-boats destroyed 610,000 tons of shipping of all nations. This first period of unrestricted submarine campaign ended in May 1916. For the next few months, Allied losses declined significantly. Then, in February 1917, Germany reinstituted unrestricted submarine warfare, and shipping losses again rose dramatically. U-boats indiscriminately sank ships sailing for England. German grand admiral Henning von

Holtzendorff bore the prime responsibility for convincing Kaiser Wilhelm II that this naval strategy was a sure means to victory. Holtzendorff hoped to destroy 600,000 tons of shipping per month and thus starve England out of the war. In February 1917 U-boats sank 520,000 tons of Allied and neutral shipping. In March 1917 they sank 560,000 tons. In April 1917 U-boats sank 860,000 tons. The staggering losses in one month surpassed total losses for previous years.

Desperate to reduce these losses and avert defeat, the British Admiralty, composed of the highest-ranking officers in the Royal Navy, debated the possibility of using the convoy system as a possible solution. In a convoy, dozens of merchant ships sailed in a fixed formation while naval ships guarded the outer perimeter. Some merchant ships, it was believed, might fall victim to submarine or surface attack; but it was hoped that most of them would survive the attacks. Convoys therefore offered collective protection to merchant ships in groups, as well as additional protection from escort warships. British admiral David Beatty and U.S. admiral William Sims, the American naval representative in London, strongly supported the use of the convoy system.

Overall, however, the British Admiralty, did not recognize the shipping losses as critical enough to warrant the use of a convoy system, a major change in the naval strategy and fleet allocation. Sir John Jellicoe, Admiral of the Fleet and commander of the British Grand Fleet, fixated on finding offensive solutions to the naval problems. He had hoped to attack the German High Seas Fleet. The Battle of Jutland (1916) had no decisive effect on the outcome of World War I; the strategic value of this battle proved to be limited. The convoy system was too defensive and passive for most officers in the British Admiralty. Diverting the fastest elements of the fleet to escort duty would have reduced the combat effectiveness of the fleet as a whole. The British navy did not possess enough escort vessels for convoys. Jellicoe firmly believed that grouping merchant ships in convoys presented easier targets for the marauding U-boats in the Atlantic Ocean.

Commercial interests also discouraged the employment of the convoy system. Merchant ships, already loaded and ready to sail, would have to be kept in port until a critical mass of merchantmen and escort warships were gathered. The voyage would take extra time because of zigzagging maneuvers used to avoid U-boat contacts. Even if the convoy successfully crossed the Atlantic, the process risked serious delays because of bottlenecks at ports in England or France as the cargo was being unloaded.

American armored cruiser in service to protect transport convoys, circa 1917. The seaplanes on the rear of the vessel were used to spot enemy warships and submarines

(from Collier's New Photographic History of the World's War *[1918], Joseph M. Bruccoli Great War Collection, Thomas Cooper Library, University of South Carolina).*

Instead of employing a convoy system, the British Admiralty ordered a variety of countermeasures to relieve shipping losses. Earlier in the war, the British navy had attempted to place mines outside German submarine bases, but this strategy proved to be largely unsuccessful. Also earlier in the war, the British outfitted "Q-ships," which were heavily armed ships disguised as defenseless merchants. It was hoped that if a German U-boat surfaced and attacked the Q-ship with its deck guns, the Q-ship could in turn destroy the U-boat. The Q-ships achieved some success early in the war, but U-boat captains soon learned to be wary of these dangerous vessels. The British navy also organized offensive patrols, which were comprised of submarine-hunting warships. Once found, U-boats could be tracked to within a few hundred yards with hydrophones and then destroyed with depth charges. When the latter exploded at a particular depth, the concussion exerted explosive force and water pressure against the thin hulls of U-boats. Such force often caused leaks or breaks in the hulls that disabled or sank those U-boats. While offensive-minded and capable of sinking U-boats, these submarine-hunting patrols achieved little success because of time and distance factors along the sea routes. Too few U-boats could be found in too long a period of time and over too large an area. A final part of the problem facing the British Admiralty reflected poor collection and analysis of the data concerning naval transportation. The Admiralty did not grasp the nature of the antisubmarine war and therefore did not recognize that convoys provided a reasonable option.

Shipping losses of 860,000 tons in April 1917 made it apparent that existing countermeasures to German submarine warfare were failures. Commander R. G. H. Henderson, an officer in the British Royal Navy who supported the use of convoys, showed that the logic of the Admiralty in avoiding using convoys had been flawed. Those in favor of the convoy system reasoned that it could not make the already desperate situation worse. Some debate exists among historians about whether British prime minister David Lloyd George actually intervened to help convince the Admiralty to try a convoy in April 1917. Regardless of Lloyd George's involvement or lack thereof, the convoy system was finally tested as a last resort. On 10 May the first experimental Allied convoy sailed from Gibraltar to England without the loss of a vessel.

The convoy system gradually increased in use over time. It was organized and efficient, utilizing more than a dozen sea routes on which hundreds of convoys traveled between summer 1917 and the end of the conflict in November 1918. Eventually, convoys left from ports all over the world, including New York and Sydney, Australia. When U-boats turned to preying on merchant ships leaving English ports, the British Navy utilized convoys for outward-bound shipping. Various convoys, for instance, departed from Liverpool every eight to sixteen days. Convoys offered many advantages and benefits. A convoy of several dozen merchant ships actually possessed a greater chance for success in evading U-boat attacks than those vessels sailing individually. U-boats merely needed to lie in wait for the hundreds of individual ships. Instead, the Allied convoy system forced the U-boats to patrol more actively. Code-breakers in the British Admiralty also increased their efficiency at intercepting German communications and relaying that intelligence information to the convoys en route. Such information gave convoys some prospect of avoiding the U-boats altogether. Finding a convoy may have offered many targets, but the chances of that happening diminished greatly in the large Atlantic Ocean. The escort warships also gained valuable opportunities to hunt and sink the U-boats. German losses increased as the escorts took a heavy toll on the U-boats. The U.S. Navy assisted by sending more than thirty destroyers to augment the British escort force.

The incredible shipping losses of spring 1917 declined. By August, Allied shipping losses had declined to 510,000 tons, still a high number. In October almost 100 convoys with a total of 1,500 merchant ships had arrived in England, while only 24 of these vessels had been lost. By December the total had decreased to 400,000 tons. In June 1918 Allied shipping losses fell below 300,000 tons per month. Another factor yielded still more positive results: the Allies produced merchant ships faster than the U-boats could sink them.

No convoy provided total immunity to those vessels in it. The strategy, however, significantly reduced losses to more acceptable levels. Once the convoy system had been implemented, the U-boats never again achieved their previous levels of success. Not only did Germany fail to achieve the strategic goal of starving the British into submission, the U-boats could not even halt the movement of hundreds of thousands of American soldiers sailing for France.

—DAVID J. ULBRICH, TEMPLE UNIVERSITY

Viewpoint:
No. German U-boats, limited in number and capabilities, were never a serious threat to British merchant shipping.

One of the defining myths of the Great War is that of the convoy. Its essential form describes a Britain brought to the point of strangulation by a German submarine offensive whose success was essentially the product of the blinkered refusal of the Royal Navy to have merchant ships sail in escorted groups. Faced in the summer of 1917 with the collapse of the war effort, the gold-braided excellencies of the Admiralty finally adopted a convoy system and saw the U-boat offensive decline to the point of impotence within months.

The appeal of the legend scarcely requires explanation; the facts of the case, however, were a good deal more complex. Prewar British plans for trade protection were based on con-

centrating naval forces in the North Sea, with the intention of preventing the movements of surface commerce raiders, either warships or converted civilian vessels. Given the vulnerability of German overseas possessions, the strategy was sensible. The few German ships at sea on the outbreak of war would have some initial successes, but their eventual fate was certain. Keeping merchantmen together, moreover, was likely to enhance the effect of surface raiding by multiplying the victims if a convoy was spotted. Instead, merchantmen were instructed that proceeding singly and avoiding the usual cruising routes were the best predictors of safety.

As U-boats began replacing raiders as the principal maritime threat, independent sailing still seemed the safest procedure. U-boats were short-ranged, slow under water, and vulnerable on the surface. Escort vessels were in short supply, especially given the steadily increasing demands of the battle fleet on British matériel and personnel resources. Merchant captains generally believed their chances were better sailing alone, each relying on his seamanship, his judgment, and his crew. Attempting to keep station with a dozen or more other ships of varying ages and speeds was dismissed as an open invitation to the Germans. In the absence of "consumer pressure," any change would have to come from the top.

While troopships and vital matériel cargoes were usually escorted, during the middle of the war the Royal Navy relied instead on an economy-of-force system of patrolling certain specific routes, similar to police beats in dangerous neighborhoods. Going after the U-boats directly, hunting them in areas they were known to be operating, was widely favored in theory, but foundered on the lack—or rather the unavailability—of the fast, destroyer-type craft best suited for that mission, compounded by the inadequate detection instruments then available. Despite its shortcomings, the system worked until the Germans introduced unrestricted submarine warfare in early 1917. Losses in the first half of 1916 were around 600,000 tons. In April 1917 alone the shipping loss was more than 860,000 tons.

The overall effects of the unrestricted submarine campaign were limited. The U-boats were too few and their technologies too underdeveloped to sink a sufficient number of ships quickly enough to cripple the Allied war effort. Entry of the United States into the conflict made available a navy, a merchant fleet, and a shipbuilding system able even in the short run to replace the losses inflicted by undersea attacks. U.S. participation in the war guaranteed even greater Allied access to the substantial food resources of Latin America. British agriculture

CONVOY DEFENSE

American journalist George Edward Creel, chairman of the Committee on Public Information, the agency responsible for wartime propaganda, wrote the following "upbeat" jingoist account of U.S. destroyers protecting a transport convoy to Europe:

German submarines attacked the transports in force. They were outfought by the American escorting destroyers, and at least one submarine was destroyed.

No American ship was hit, and not a life lost. The German submarines attacked twice. On both occasions the U-boats were beaten off with every appearance of loss. One boat was certainly sunk, and there is reason to believe that the accurate fire of our gunners sent others to the bottom.

For the purpose of convenience the expedition was divided into contingents. Each contingent was composed of troopships and a naval escort designed to keep off such German raiders as might be met with. An ocean rendezvous was arranged with the American destroyers now operating in European waters in order that the passage through the danger zone might be attended by every possible protection.

The first attack occurred at 10.30 p.m. on June 22nd. What gives it a peculiar and disturbing significance is that our ships were set upon at a point well on this side of the rendezvous, in a part of the Atlantic which might have been presumed free of submarines.

The attack was made in force, and although the night made it impossible to arrive at an exact count, it was clear that the U-boats had gathered for what they deemed would be a slaughter. The heavy gunfire of the American destroyers scattered the submarines. It is not known how many torpedoes were launched, but at least five were counted.

The second attack was launched a few days later against another contingent, the point of attack being beyond the rendezvous. Not only did the destroyers hold the U-boats at a safe distance, but their speed resulted in the sinking of at least one submarine. Grenades were used, firing a charge of explosives timed to go off at a certain distance under water. In one instance the wreckage covered the surface of the sea after a shot at the periscope, and reports claim that the boat was sunk.

Protected by our high-seas convoy, destroyers, and by French war vessels, the contingent proceeded and joined the others at the French port. The whole nation will rejoice that so great a peril was passed by the vanguard of the men who will fight our battles in France.

Source: *Charles F. Horne, ed.,* Source Records of the Great War, *volume 5 (Indianapolis: American Legion, 1930), pp. 181–182.*

as well responded to the challenge, increasing grain production almost a third in 1917, primarily by converting pastures to cropland.

Had the convoy system not been introduced, British eating patterns might have changed significantly. Privation, comparable to that Germany suffered in the final years of the war, was not a likely option. War, however, is waged in real time, not hindsight. In early 1917 the numbers seemed to be combining in a way that spelled catastrophe for Britain and for the Allied cause.

The response of the Royal Navy, the initial mathematical miscalculations regarding the escorts needed, and the eventual introduction of convoys as a desperation measure, had a limited impact on the naval war. Although the losses to underwater attacks fell off sharply,

they still stood at 400,000 tons as late as December. Convoys were not a magic bullet; in themselves they proved insufficient to halt the hemorrhaging of British and Allied shipping.

The convoy system was, however, only part of a developing, comprehensive campaign against the U-boats. It included such spectacular—and unsuccessful—operations as the April 1918 raid on the Flanders submarine bases. It incorporated the laying of minefields, "barrages" as they were called, in the North Sea—more than 70,000 mines between Scotland and Norway—and the English Channel. It involved increasing patrol activity in the English Channel, the preferred entry/exit route for the U-boats. It extended to using nets and similar devices to ensnare unwary captains. The collective significance of these operations lay primarily in the increasing stress they placed on crews already strained to physical and psychological limits by the primitive conditions of life aboard a U-boat. A crew that had to take hair-raising risks merely to break out into the Atlantic was more likely to be concerned with how to return safely through the barriers than with building a score during their patrol.

An increasing number of warships, specialized escorts and otherwise, became available for antisubmarine operations. By 1918 the building programs of the Royal Navy were turning out dozens of small vessels useful for keeping U-boats below periscope depth. The U.S. Navy sent the best of its new destroyers to reinforce antisubmarine patrols and embarked on its own formidable program of small-craft escort construction. Even the Grand Fleet spared, albeit temporarily and unwillingly, numbers of its carefully husbanded destroyers for particular antisubmarine operations.

Escorts constituted a major deterrent by their presence. Contemporary search and communications technology made locating and tracking convoys as difficult for practical purposes as locating and tracking single ships. Should a U-boat get lucky, the risks of drawing the attention of the escorts deterred attacks even by veteran captains, whose experience had been gained under essentially different conditions. In contrast to their World War II successors, German U-boats in World War I lacked the speed and firepower for night surface attacks of the kind that wreaked such havoc on the North Atlantic convoys. Nor was radio communication sufficiently developed to permit the concentrations of boats, the "wolf packs" that were the basic tactical formation of the later conflict. A typical experience was that of the *U-70*. In May 1918 it encountered a convoy of thirty-eight merchantmen escorted by eight destroyers and three sloops. The weather was good; the sea was smooth; and the wind was favorable. The commander of the *U-70*, however, waited for the convoy to pass, fired two torpedoes (both misses), and performed the classic maneuver called "escape and evasion" but better described as "getting the hell out of the way."

Convoys steaming close to land benefited from another major technical/tactical innovation: air escort. The French had pioneered this development in the Mediterranean and along their Atlantic and channel coasts. During 1918 the British developed a formidable network of patrol and escort routes, using dirigibles, aircraft, and even balloons tethered to ships. The aircraft were a mixed bag, ranging from formidable long-range flying boats, precursors of the Sunderlands and Catalinas of World War II, to training planes. Like the escorts, their main value was as deterrents. A surfaced U-boat was unlikely to take the risk of lingering to determine the exact type of aircraft it confronted—especially since the planes were only supplementary weapons for the sloops and destroyers, with their guns and depth charges.

A gridlocked German industry was correspondingly unable to produce enough boats to restore the relative balance of forces for an increasingly overmatched undersea service. Even had the projected construction programs delivered the boats, opportunities for their effective use were diminishing. By the late summer of 1918, attacking any merchantman under almost any circumstances was understood as involving a high level of risk. What happened was almost less important than what might happen. Increasing numbers of patrols were aborted and attacks unmade because chances of success and survival had sunk below acceptable percentages. The World War I German U-boat fleet, though highly motivated by the standards of its surface counterpart, understood the mathematics of attritional warfare better than its Nazi successors. In particular, the commanders and their crews understood that in an attritional campaign the heroic sacrifices of individuals are unlikely to tip the balances. Percentages are what counts.

–DENNIS SHOWALTER,
COLORADO COLLEGE

References

Julian S. Corbett, *Naval Operations*, 5 volumes (London & New York: Longmans, Green, 1920–1931).

Paul G. Halpern, *A Naval History of World War I* (Annapolis, Md.: Naval Institute Press, 1994).

Arthur Hezlet, *The Submarine and Sea Power* (London: Davies, 1967).

John Keegan, *The First World War* (London: Hutchinson, 1998).

David Kennedy, *Over Here: The First World War and American Society* (New York: Oxford University Press, 1980).

Ronald H. Spector, *At War, at Sea: Sailors and Naval Combat in the Twentieth Century* (New York: Viking, 2001).

John Terraine, *Business in Great Waters: The U-boat Wars, 1916–1945* (London: Cooper, 1989).

CULTURAL WATERSHED

Was World War I a cultural turning point?

Viewpoint: Yes. World War I caused a drastic change in traditional social norms and values.

Viewpoint: Yes. The experience of World War I represented a loss of innocence for Europe.

Viewpoint: No. The great transformation in twentieth-century culture and society came from modernism, a movement intensified and extended by World War I but introduced well before 1914.

The notion that the Great War of 1914–1918 was a cultural and intellectual watershed, as well as a political and military one, has been taken for granted almost since the guns fell silent. Progress made during the nineteenth century in the West had been blown apart by heavy shells and submerged in the mud of the trenches. The artifacts of the Industrial Revolution had been restructured and reconfigured to destroy life instead of improve it. The virtues and values most cultivated prior to 1914—duty, honor, commitment—had been precisely the qualities that sustained the conflict beyond all reason. The states that had been centers of identity fell one by one, as their citizens came to loathe their governments more than they feared their enemies.

The moral and cultural authority of Western civilization itself seemed challenged by a war that mobilized sixty million men and killed ten million of them. As churches and universities answered the call to arms and as authors wrote propaganda and musicians composed marches, it was small wonder that the wartime Dadaists insisted only nonsense made sense. Empiricism and objectivity were snares and deceits. Not surprisingly, the defining toy of the 1920s was the yo-yo: endlessly spinning on its own axis, performing arabesques that led nowhere.

In every aspect of postwar Europe, the conventions of culture were redefined to exclude conventions—particularly those involving structure. Jazz, with its riffs and improvisations, became the defining music of the avant-garde. The cigarette, denounced before 1914 as effeminate, supplanted pipes and cigars as the defining masculine source of nicotine. Women's underwear became loose rather than restrictive. Nor was transgressive behavior entirely an individual or private matter. Societies once priding themselves on their civics now tolerated violence on levels unthinkable before 1914. Politics were increasingly defined by communism and fascism, with their fundamental challenges to the bourgeois order. Governments openly advocated class- or race-based policies that before the Great War had been dismissed as the stuff of deranged fantasy.

Yet, though things might have been changed utterly, they also can be said to have remained the same. Perhaps more accurately, they were normalized. Most men and women resumed ordinary lives—on one level because they had no choice, on another because routine was a welcome relief from chaos. Patterns of spouse selection might have become more flexible, but returned veterans married and war widows remarried. After 1918 Europe's energies were devoted as much to memory and mourning as to pursuing a manic future. Public landscapes and "sacred spaces" commemorated loss and sacrifice. Private behaviors were shaped by grief and nostalgia. In both cases the goal was to process the events of the war and to integrate them into social and emotional structures. Arguably, the defining artifact of the postwar West was the restructured *Arc de Triomphe* in Paris, with the Tomb of the Unknown Soldier placed at the center of the national monument to France's glory. The uneasy juxtaposition of stability and innovation, past and future, continues to structure discourse on the legacy of the Great War.

Viewpoint:
Yes. World War I caused a drastic change in traditional social norms and values.

World War I represented a seismic shift in the cultural values of modern Europe. For people who came of age after 1918, the political, social, and economic consequences of the war had created a radically different world. The horror and dislocation that the conflict inflicted on the European mind forever ended the rational, hierarchical, and traditional ethos of earlier times and set the stage for the ambiguities of the twentieth century. Historian Jacques Barzun wrote disparagingly, yet not inaccurately, in *From Dawn to Decadence: 500 Years of European Cultural Life, 1500 to the Present* (2000), that "the blow that hurled the modern world on its course of self-destruction was the Great War of 1914–18."

Like many cultural changes, the transformation caused by World War I had clear social and political parallels and causes. Before 1914 most European nations that became involved in the conflict were still dominated by a many-centuries-old hierarchy of aristocratic landowners. Despite the relative decline in their economic position, the traditional elite of these countries continued to monopolize state service, social prestige, and cultural leadership. Although this dominance had by varying degrees ceased to be relevant in northwestern Europe, where the governments of Britain, France, the Low Countries, and Scandinavia had moved toward political democratization and the professionalization of state service and public life, it was nevertheless the continuing state of affairs in most of the remaining states of Europe. A casual look through the roster of ministers, diplomats, and army officers of the time reveals the virtually complete domination by aristocrats of those spheres, as does even the most cursory survey of European political and diplomatic history before 1914. In nations where an emerging middle class or other nonpatrician elements aspired to leadership, the parvenus took great pains to ape the attitudes, manners, tastes, mores, prejudices, and affectations of the traditional elite, or at least what they perceived

those qualities to be. Even in Republican France, ownership of a country estate, marriage into a bona fide aristocratic family, establishment in "high society," and a traditionally defined genteel lifestyle were highly prized goals in the prewar business world and professions. In an increasingly democratic Britain, the newly emerging elite not only shared those goals but also aspired to the titles, honors, and even speech patterns that would at least superficially raise their social standing to that of the traditional aristocracy. Indeed, it is not unfair to say that before World War I the ultimate ambition of the so-called new bourgeoisie of Europe was to assimilate into the traditional elite in order to legitimize its enhanced position within a fairly universal and well-established framework of social convention.

Four short years of war shattered this world forever. Within that period all combatant powers suffered horribly from the conflict, and most experienced a radical transformation of their domestic political and social structures. Even those European states that did not suffer violent revolution nevertheless experienced far-reaching changes, as the aristocratic political leadership was swept away, along with the aristocratic foundations of cultural life.

The principal reason for this transformation was that the war thoroughly discredited the values and assumptions of the prewar world. After four years of carnage, in which more people were killed than in all the wars of the previous several centuries combined, it was widely believed that government by "gentlemen amateurs" conducted in an aristocratic milieu was no longer acceptable or desirable. As beautiful as the best scenes of the prewar world may have been, after 1918 the traditional forms of political and social organization seemed woefully inadequate for the needs of the modern state and society. As the war drew to a close, the German, Russian, Austro-Hungarian, and Turkish monarchies collapsed and were replaced with radically different regimes. The dramatically altered geography of Eastern Europe derived from nationalist ideals strong enough to supersede the traditional principle of multiethnic loyalty to a feudal ruler. Even the Western democracies were transformed, as political life there came to involve broad state influence over the economy and society, the advent of universal

A HELL OF A ROW

British poet and writer Robert Graves, who served during World War I, recalls in his autobiography Good-Bye To All That *(1929) a breakdown in discipline during the conflict, when the colonel gathered his officers to complain:*

One day David met me in the village street. He said: "Did you hear the bugle? There's a hell of a row on about something. All officers and warrant-officers are to meet in the village schoolroom at once. Scatter's looking as black as thunder. No one knows yet what the axe is about." We went along together and squeezed into one of the school desk-benches. When the colonel entered and the room was called to attention by the senior major, David and I hurt ourselves standing up, bench and all. Scatter told us all to be seated. The officers were in one class, the warrant-officers and non-commissioned officers in another. The colonel glared at us from the teacher's desk. He began his lecture with general accusations. He said that he had lately noticed many signs of slovenliness in the battalion—men with their pocket-flaps undone, and actually walking down the village street with their hands in their trouser-pockets—boots unpolished—sentries strolling about on their beats at company billets instead of marching up and down in a soldier-like way—rowdiness in the *estaminets*—slackness in saluting—with many other grave indications of lowered discipline. He threatened to stop all leave to the United Kingdom unless discipline improved. He promised us a saluting parade every morning before breakfast which he would attend in person. All this general axe-ing and we knew that he had not yet reached the particular axe. It was this: "I have here principally to tell you of a very disagreeable occurrence. As I was going out of my orderly room early this morning I came upon a group of soldiers; I will not mention their company. One of these soldiers was in conversation with a lance-corporal. You may not believe it, but it was a fact that he addressed the corporal by his Christian name; *he called him Jack.* The corporal made no protest. To think that the First Battalion has sunk to a level where it is possible for such familiarity to exist between N.C.O.'s and the men under their command! Naturally, I put the corporal under arrest, and he appeared before me at once on the charge of "conduct unbecoming of an N.C.O." He was reduced to the ranks, and the man was given field-punishment for using insubordinate language to an N.C.O. And, I warn you, if any further case of the sorts comes to my notice—and I expect you officers to report the slightest instance to me at once instead of dealing with it as a company matter. . . ."

Source: *Robert Graves,* Good-Bye To All That *(New York: Cape & Smith, 1929), pp. 218–219.*

---

suffrage (achieved in Britain only in 1918), meritocratic competition for positions of power and authority, the increased strength of trade unions, and an expanded public role for women.

Throughout the continent the privileged political positions long enjoyed by the traditional elite were thoroughly dismantled. Sometimes this process took extreme forms. In revolutionary Russia the Soviet government sought nothing less than the physical extermination of the old aristocratic elite, first confiscating its property and other assets, and then proceeding to eliminate its members as the inherent "class enemies" of the new society. Certainly the Soviet government also targeted the "upstart" bourgeoisie of Imperial Russia, its clerical estate, and anyone from any social background who opposed the regime, but the displacement and destruction of the aristocracy represented the most thorough and complete change in the power structure.

Other nations dealt with the former masters of the land more benignly but with almost equal effectiveness. The nascent German and Austrian republics instituted truly democratic political systems, abolished all legal distinctions based on birth or social class, thoroughly democratized access to government service, and thus effectively marginalized the aristocracy. The Austrian republic even forbade the use of titles and the word "von" and its variants (prepositions meaning "of" or "from" to denote land ownership) in last names. While the aristocracies of these nations survived, they lost their corporate coherence and privileged positions almost overnight. Individual aristocrats could still occupy high-profile roles in these countries but only by virtue of personal distinction. Field Marshal Paul von Hindenburg was elected president of Germany in 1925 and reelected in 1932 because he was the most distinguished war hero in the country, not because he was a Prussian aristocrat benefiting from access and patronage.

The emerging nations of Eastern Europe, built on the territory of the former empires, adopted discriminatory and economically harmful policies toward much of their aristocracies because they either came from or identified with the predominant ethnic groups of the former Imperial powers. While many of the new states did not develop strong democratic systems and often fell into authoritarian dictatorships, their leaders never shied from attacking the Imperial legacies that a large percentage of their aristocratic populations personified, and generally refused to establish governments by and for their indigenous aristocracies.

Even in mild Great Britain, David Lloyd George's Liberal government carried out a far-reaching postwar program of high taxation and land redistribution that permanently, and purposely, alienated many aristocratic landowners from their traditional sources of independent wealth and political power. Plans to abolish the right of British hereditary aristocracy to sit and vote in the House of Lords, partially carried out in 1999, were originally drafted by a Liberal Member of Parliament in 1918. The introduction of universal suffrage in the same year markedly reduced the electoral prospects for the traditional elite at every level of government, while the aggressive professionalization of state service further reduced their overrepresentation in that sphere, too. At the same time even the British Conservative Party came to the quiet realization that members of the traditional elite were inappropriate figures to lead in an era of mass politics. In the generation after World War I the objectively most qualified candidates in two party-leadership contests—George Curzon, Marquis Curzon, in 1923 and Edward Wood, Viscount Halifax, in 1940—were rejected because of their family backgrounds and passed over in favor of decidedly less distinguished figures.

Another major factor in the decline of the aristocracy stemmed from the war itself. Because traditional aristocracies tended to dominate the officer corps of European armies, perhaps even more thoroughly than they did government and society, they experienced proportionally much heavier casualties than any other social class. In the British army the per-capita losses among the traditional elite were as much as eight times that of the rest of the population. In other national armies, even more heavily dominated by aristocrats and having suffered larger numbers of casualties than the British, losses among the traditional elite were still higher. While death on the battlefield eliminated a significant portion of the rising generation of European aristocrats, the psychological impact such losses had on those who survived—often friends and relatives—diminished their willingness to remain active leaders in the future.

As the war came to consume far more of the resources of Europe than had originally been expected, governments had to adopt economic policies that kept the price of agricultural land and products artificially low, while they kept property and inheritance taxes at unprecedented levels. The all-too-modern world of rationing, shortages, inflation, and requisitions had a direct impact on the luxuries, trappings, pastimes, and general way of life of the traditional elite. Even as the flower of aristocratic manhood was dying in large numbers at the front, the future economic and social position of European aristocracies was under assault at home.

In the aftermath of World War I, aristocratic life in Europe was in a state of collapse. As the emerging nonpatrician leadership of European governments and economies came into their own during and immediately after the war, the changing climate naturally de-emphasized the cultural values of the old world. Their fundamental redefinition, along lines that matched the new social and political order, was unavoidable in postwar Europe. Since the new elite tended to be urban rather than rural, cosmopolitan rather than provincial, commercial rather than agricultural, liberal rather than conservative, and diverse rather than homogeneous, new cultural trends were bound to emerge under their patronage and decidedly different way of life. In the aftermath of the bloodiest war to date, moreover, the premium that the traditional elite had placed on martial qualities, traditional ideas of honor, feats of physical prowess, and ascriptive characteristics such as heredity and bloodlines was not simply inappropriate but anathema to the war-weary masses.

The postwar realm of ideas bore one of the most striking transitions. Like the aristocratic attachment to military ideas, the rationalist philosophies that had a near-monopoly on nineteenth-century Europe seemed unrealistic, irrelevant, and naive after 1918. If shaping government and society with such ideas could lead to the horrors of World War I, what validity could they possibly have for the future of humanity? In an age when traditional philosophical values had no apparent place, European thinkers dreamed up several alternatives, the clash of which came to underlie the new cultural ethos on the Continent. On the extreme Left many advocated a full-scale rejection of all tradition through atheistic communism and extreme forms of socialism. In the place of a semifeudal order or a "bourgeois democracy," a new society based on "scientific" laws of human development and social organization was to lead humanity toward a utopian future. Although this view had triumphed only in Russia by the end of the war, it nevertheless had broad appeal in intellectual circles throughout Europe.

Other varieties of political thought identified the centralized modern state as the proper agent of economic and social organization. In their view a disinterested elite of administrators and technicians would exercise broad powers for the good of the state and society. This core idea inspired socialist thinkers who came to advocate efficient state planning, as well as fascist movements that added rabid nationalism to the list of government prerogatives and priorities.

On the Right, there still survived an anemic tradition focused on reviving or preserving the role of notables and other traditional elites in power. This movement eventually became successful in Antonio Salazar's Portugal, Francisco Franco's Spain, and Vichy France, and somewhat complemented Italian fascism but remained a relic in every other major country. While all of these ideologies had roots in European philosophy and intellectual history before 1914, their practical implementation had been either nonexistent or extremely limited except in the case of traditionalism. The world war and its consequences changed that.

The multiplicity of competing and mutually exclusive ideas created much political turmoil in the 1920s and 1930s, but their influence on the cultural landscape of Europe was truly amazing. In addition to the obvious development of rival political ideologies, new philosophies acquired real currency and inspired many to believe that emerging "social science" disciplines such as sociology, psychology, anthropology, and determinist economics could be used to diagnose and correct the problems of human existence. Structuralist thinkers such as anthropologist Claude Lévi-Strauss argued that outmoded structures of the traditional society had preconditioned human society to act in harmful ways. Sigmund Freud's psychoanalytic school suggested that human neuroses were rooted in sexual dysfunctions, also caused by anachronistic social structures. The economist John Maynard Keynes argued that the economic troubles in the world could be set right by comprehensive programs of state intervention, not unlike those that had characterized European war economies in the recent conflict. These theories and many others led to broad experimentation in virtually every aspect of the human experience to a magnitude that had been unthinkable before World War I.

If culture can be distilled into the artistic representation of society, then surely the era that followed World War I represented another radical break with the prewar world. Even if the culture of mass mourning often clung to traditional frameworks, it proved fleeting, and experimentation in painting, music, architecture, fashion, film, theater, and other media was the rule in the 1920s. Surely there were prewar antecedents, but they were almost always exceptions that flouted established standards of taste and expectations of elegance. To cite the world of music, before the war the German composer Richard Strauss had indeed written two highly experimental operas, *Salome* (1905) and *Elektra* (1909), which presented provocative themes of dementia and sexual deviance through musical scores that departed radically from the accepted rules of composition. Yet, Strauss was so roundly criticized that he had to save his reputation, and virtually apologize to the opera-going public, by composing a much more conventional, melodic, and acceptable opera, *Der Rosenkavalier* (1911), almost immediately thereafter. When the Russian composer Igor Stravinsky's revolutionary *Le Sacre du printemps* (The Rite of Spring) premiered in Paris in 1913, the performance nearly caused a riot. In the postwar world, by contrast, composers such as Alban Berg, Arnold Schoenberg, and Kurt Weill never had to apologize for their indulgence in radical new interpretations of music theory and regularly presented themes of psychosis, alienation, perversion, and social catastrophe in their works. Stravinsky was hailed as a genius only a few years after his Parisian debacle. In the world of popular music the much-maligned American ragtime of the turn of the century evolved into the hugely popular and worldwide jazz phenomenon of the 1920s.

Prewar theater in Germany showed some hints of experimentation in the Expressionist school represented by playwright Frank Wedekind, but performances were limited and, despite marginal critical appeal, public appreciation was not forthcoming. In the 1920s, however, artists such as director Max Reinhardt and playwright Bertolt Brecht revolutionized theater to broad acclaim, largely by emphasizing the newly relevant themes of alienation and psychological instability, and by using art as a medium for political agitation. Works such as Carl Zuckmayer's play *Der Hauptmann von Köpenick* (*The Captain from Köpenick,* 1930) made a laughingstock of the martial values that had commanded respect in the German Empire not long before its production.

At the same time, writers such as Erich Maria Remarque, Henry de Montherlant, Louis-Ferdinand Destouches (Louis-Ferdinand Céline), Robert Graves, Aldous Huxley, and Thomas Mann explored the dark and ever-present theme of alienation in fiction, generally

Pastel drawing by Eric Kennington of the British writer Robert Graves in his World War I uniform in reaction to their impressions of World War I. In architecture, Walter Gropius's Bauhaus school, founded in 1919, rejected the prewar emphasis on "ostentatious" Gothic or neoclassical construction and instead constructed beauty around radical modernity and the principle of form fitting function. In painting, Pablo Picasso went from his difficult bohemian life before the war to international celebrity in the 1920s as Salvador Dali, George Grosz, Käthe Kollwitz and many other artists did. Perhaps the most familiar image of all was the stark contrast between the fashionable Edwardian English aristocratic lady wearing a long dress, corset, and prim hat and the short-skirted flapper sporting a radically new fashion scarcely ten years later.

No matter how one looks at the postwar world, its contrast with the prewar world is stunning. As empires, the traditional elite, exclusionary political traditions, and the cultural values that had long accompanied them fell into retreat, European civilization developed a broad array of new ideas. From politics to social science to the arts, the culture of postwar Europe represented both a departure from and a rejection of traditional norms and values. The descent of traditional Europe into slaughter and calamity produced a new cosmopolitan culture of instability, insecurity, relativism, determinism, and experimentation that forever displaced the rationalism and idealism of the prewar world.

–PAUL DU QUENOY,
GEORGETOWN UNIVERSITY

Viewpoint:
Yes. The experience of World War I represented a loss of innocence for Europe.

In 1927 French poet Paul Valéry reflected on the results of World War I: "One can say that all the fundamentals of our world have been affected by the war, or more exactly, by the circumstances of the war. . . . It changed the lives of individuals, disrupted economies, altered governments and redrew borders." "But," he observed, "among all these injured things is the Mind. The Mind has indeed been cruelly wounded; its complaint is heard in the hearts of intellectual men; it passes a mournful judgment on itself. It doubts itself profoundly." Returning soldiers as well as civilians also testified that the war changed the ways they perceived and thought about the world. Old truths and values lost authority, causing people to develop different and distinctively modern ways

of understanding. Science, philosophy, literature, and art registered the changes, but the altered standards and attitudes also influenced how ordinary people led their lives. The fads, fascinations, and diversions typical of the 1920s, what Robert Graves and Alan Hodge, in *The Long Week-end: A Social History of Great Britain, 1918–1939* (1940), labeled "all the things of a forgettable sort," bore the clear imprint of the war.

To say that the war "utterly changed standards and tastes" minimizes the weight of established ways of thinking, however. Language itself enforced continuity; victims and witnesses made do with words tailored to peacetime in order to describe battles and loss. People also drew on values promoted by schools, families, and the state before the war to deal with new and unexpected realities. The bereaved, for example, sought consolation in religion, Romanticism, and classical ideals. Official initiatives to commemorate the war dead also invoked ideas of sacrifice and patriotic duty to valorize the fallen and validate the costs. Others acknowledged traditional values but puzzled over their relevance to life as they now knew it.

Shaped by an age that believed in progress and the powers of reason, those who lived through the war experienced an acute sense of distance between who they had been and what they had become. J. B. Priestley, an English veteran, in *Margin Released: A Writer's Reminiscences and Reflections* (1962), reflected: "If you were born in 1894, as I was, you suddenly saw a great jagged crack in the looking glass. After that your mind could not escape from the idea of a world which ended in 1914 and another one that began about 1919 with a wilderness of smoke and fury, outside the sensible time, lying between them." Society before 1914 took on the glow of the ideal and unreachable; it seemed a time of calm and peace, clouded only by their knowledge of what it actually all led to. Looking back, they saw their innocence and mourned its loss. In "MCMXIV" (1964), English poet Philip Larkin wrote:

> Never such innocence,
> Never before or since,
> As changed itself to past
> Without word—the men
> Leaving the gardens tidy,
> The thousands of marriages
> Lasting a little while longer:
> Never such innocence again.

British soldiers, Paul Fussell points out in *The Great War and Modern Memory* (1975), responded to the clash between present realities and the carefree past the only way they could—with irony. Civilians followed, adopting a mode of understanding that, according to Fussell, defines modern memory.

The feeling that values and ideals commonly accepted before the war no longer held true contributed to the sense of disjunction. Many no longer felt confidence in the "great words"—in democracy, justice, and truth. When so many people died for so little reason, liberals' hymns to the value of the individual lost something of their resonance. The war called into question the easy equation of science and progress. That human ingenuity produced such destructive engines of war exposed the more malevolent possibilities of technology and industrialization. Confidence in democracy also wavered, particularly toward the end of the war, as liberal governments pursued victory with as much indifference to human life as the autocracies showed. The rigid controls liberals imposed on dissent and on workers confirmed what prewar dissidents had routinely charged—basic freedoms mattered less than the defense of the state.

Belief in progress, the foundation of prewar optimism, also foundered under the impact of the Great War. Progress assumed a linear and upward movement of history; it made the future an improved version of the past. Those who saw the inescapable, destructive impact of the war on values and institutions worried that tomorrow would be as bad as today. Another response insisted that 1918 definitively severed the present from the past. The war and the Bolshevik Revolution (1917) produced an entirely new age, a break in history feared by some and celebrated by others. Hopes for revolution had existed before 1914, as had doubts about the linear, progressive flow of history, but the war gave these views the force of concrete evidence.

The conflict challenged another article of prewar faith: the primacy of reason. Nineteenth-century scientists and social thinkers generally believed that nature and society functioned according to observable laws. Uncovering them permitted rational reform, the key to the steady improvement of life. Moreover, they expected reason to civilize society by defeating ignorance and by allowing individuals to control their primitive impulses. Plenty of voices before the war challenged the assumptions that underlay such a respect for reason. Max Planck and Albert Einstein in physics and Sigmund Freud in psychology, for example, used the methods of science to demonstrate that observation and reason produced only a limited understanding of the universe and the human mind. Friedrich Nietzsche took another step and dismissed laws as artificial inventions. At the same time, avant-garde artists made familiar objects unrecognizable in order, they said, to represent reality more exactly. These thinkers showed that the basic structures of nature, if they existed at all, eluded reason.

The war confirmed the "revolt against reason" and extended its appeal beyond a few intellectuals, as it broke faith in established truths and provided ample evidence of the limits of rationality. New theories in physics and psychology gained support, eroding confidence in a predictable, mechanistically ordered universe and a predictable, rationally ordered mind. Avant-garde writers and artists moved further away from traditional subject matter, aesthetic standards, and stylistic modes after the war. They gave powerful form to the sense of disjunction, to interest in the unconscious, and to questions about conventional truths evident in the aftermath of World War I.

The dissolving certainties reached beyond the lecture halls, learned treatises, art exhibitions, and highbrow novels to undercut traditional social values and shape tastes. The war played a direct role in changing social life by bringing more women into the workforce and by putting a premium on youth and on living. Hemlines went up and respectable women went out unchaperoned. Released from the regimentation and tension of the war and from the restrictions of prewar social conventions, nightlife flourished in the 1920s as the celebration of life became a public ritual. People drank cocktails and gyrated to the syncopated rhythms of jazz and the Charleston; they watched movies and followed Oscar Wilde's dictum "Never resist temptation." They thrilled to the exploits of adventure-seekers and record-breakers such as Charles Lindbergh, who captivated the public imagination with his daring solo flight across the Atlantic (1927).

A conflict as costly, long, and unexpected as this one irreversibly changed views of war and politics and shook deeper, established systems of meaning. It left people looking for explanations and for ways of reaffirming their beliefs or finding new directions. "The war experience," commented Eric J. Leed in *No Man's Land: Combat and Identity in World War I* (1979), "is an ultimate confirmation of the power of men to ascribe meaning and pattern to a world, even when that world seemed to resist all patterning." War did not eradicate the old standards and norms, but it rattled their foundations and made them try to fit new realities. Traditional values surfaced to justify the war and to give the grieving solace; they served to mend rifts in history and in individuals' lives. The existence of these gaps and the sense that prewar values could not stretch to cover or connect them caused the persistent disorientation and anxiety characteristic, in the view of historians such as Modris Eksteins, of the modern sensibility.

The destructive force of World War I also cleared the way for emerging ideas. It reinforced the challenges to dominant values that had appeared before 1914 and that without the war would have remained submerged or have required longer to take hold. In particular, it diminished faith in progress and in reason and entrenched an awareness of the power of contingency and of the nonrational dimensions of the self. As a result, people felt less able to control themselves or to direct society, another feeling said to characterize the modern worldview. The war produced, finally, some changes of its own, primarily a loss of innocence. It left unforgettable landscapes of destruction that marked the rupture with a safer past and produced a sense of foreboding that the next decades amply justified.

–SUSAN A. ASHLEY, COLORADO COLLEGE

Viewpoint:
No. The great transformation in twentieth-century culture and society came from modernism, a movement intensified and extended by World War I but introduced well before 1914.

World War I caused the death of more than nine million soldiers and the collapse of four empires (Austro-Hungarian, German, Ottoman, and Russian). Yet, perhaps the ultimate tragedy of the war was how little European culture changed during and after it. This claim for continuity contradicts writers such as Paul Fussell, who argues in *The Great War and Modern Memory* (1975) that the Great War created a tableau of cynicism and irony, world weariness, and fatalism in which old verities like King and Country became trite and embarrassingly passé. Fussell's concentration on disillusioned "war writers" of arguably exceptional sensitivity overlooks the attitudes of the many Britons who processed their war experiences in conventional ways. As much to the point, it overlooks the fact that these men were themselves relative latecomers to a modernist movement well antedating the turn of the century.

The machine age fostered uncertainty by its acceleration of change. Rudyard Kipling celebrated technology as a transformer, describing the gods of India vainly seeking to destroy a railway bridge over "Mother Ganges." However, Mark Twain suggested a darker side of the picture in *A Connecticut Yankee in King Arthur's Court* (1889), where "the magic of science" is ultimately confounded by older magic

and darker fears. Modris Eksteins in *Rites of Spring: The Great War and the Birth of the Modern Age* (1989) particularly stresses the German contributions to the increasing pace of the nineteenth century. The "restless Reich" was a source of change in everything from industrial techniques to architecture. Self-assertion, rebellion, and innovation were the dominant characteristics of an approach that increasingly challenged empiricism and objectivity in art, history, music, and literature. Jacob Burckhardt and Friedrich Nietzsche argued for history itself as a construction—an exercise similar to poetry or art. Musicians such as Gustav Mahler challenged the parameters of meter and tonality. Generational conventions were turned upside down by a youth movement that increasingly identified with feminist and gay-rights movements—and that was identified, especially by adults and outsiders, as supporting free sexuality.

Allied propaganda in the initial period of the Great War focused strongly on the necessity for returning the German genie to its subjectivist bottle. However, in Paris, philosophers such as Henri Bergson had asserted the importance of intuition, and poets such as Charles Peguy had rhapsodized about the beauty of death in battle. Igor Stravinsky's *Le Sacre du printemps* first challenged the conventions of the ballet in 1913. Pablo Picasso began the Cubist movement in 1907 with his *Les Demoiselles d'Avignon;* two years later, the Italian Filippo Marinetti coined the word *Futurism* to describe art forms that embraced and celebrated modern dynamism and fractious mechanization. Marinetti wrote in 1909 that "We proclaim that the world is the richer for a new beauty of speed, and our praise is for the man at the wheel. There is no beauty now save in struggle, no masterpiece can be anything but aggressive, and hence we glorify war, militarism and patriotism."

Modernism was not necessarily affirmative; the themes of distortion, alienation, and despair were not products of the Western Front. Pre–1914 art was infused with images of apocalypse. The catastrophe of war merely consolidated and intensified their expression. Oswald Spengler began writing *The Decline of the West* in 1911 and finished in 1922. Thomas Mann's *Death in Venice* (1913) used plague as a metaphor for devastation. The war produced nothing as artistically disturbing as Edvard Munch's existential cry of horror *The Scream* (1893), and Ludwig Meidner's urban "landscapes" of chaos and destruction remain compelling a century later.

Outside the realm of fine arts, cultural uneasiness and uncertainty shaped Sigmund

CULTURAL WATERSHED

Freud's *The Interpretation of Dreams* (1900) and *Totem and Taboo* (1913). As Freud deconstructed conventional notions of childhood innocence and human sexuality, the discoveries of physicists such as Max Planck and Albert Einstein demolished the ordered universe of Sir Isaac Newton and the Enlightenment.

Confronting a relativistic universe governed by laws of quantum physics that suggested inherent uncertainty, prewar cultural commentators discovered in Freud's works the irrationality of human behavior and the importance of the subconscious in charting the hidden contours of the human mind. None of these observations were comforting in an environment of growing social and political tension, a climate one American observer described in 1914 as "militarism run mad."

Prewar modernist impulses were not free from posturing, rhetoric, or youth's desire to shock its respectable elders. Yet, Maurice Ravel, best known as the composer of *Bolero* (1928), at thirty-nine and in poor health, pestered French authorities until he donned a uniform as a truck driver for the artillery. Cubist painter Fernand Léger served with the engineers for three years until disabled by gas poisoning. The names could be multiplied at will, along with countries of origin. What was significant is the high number of modernists who served in the front lines—and who frequently found confirmation there of the importance of personal experience.

The trenches challenged every form of logic and paradigm of order. A shell could blow off a man's uniform, toss him ten yards away, and leave him unscratched to marvel at his luck. Or a single small piece of steel could find a vital spot and kill him while his comrades remained unaware. A line of men could be cut down by a machine gun, but a few survivors could be left standing when the weapon jammed or an ammunition belt had to be changed. Such events were seemingly the stuff of legend rather than of fact. They nevertheless epitomized a general perception that survival itself was a random experience, having little to do with individual skills as a soldier and even less with any deeper human qualities. Modernist subjectivity was validated with every frontline tour. Otto Dix embodied the "restless" element of German culture. From a working-class background, he absorbed Nietzschean philosophy and Futurist ideas, celebrating the guns of August in *War* (1924). Experience soon cured his enthusiasm. However, his wartime sketches and postwar paintings continued to incorporate a modernist sensibility—arguably an inversion of Futurism rather than its repudiation, celebrating not war's beauty but its ugliness.

From a deeper perspective, the soldier and the artist were perceived not as opposite poles on a continuum but rather as sharing a common position. Both stood at the limits of rational order; each had the task of imposing meaning on chaos. The "meaning" might be Dadaism's manic denial of meaning or it might be a personal sense of mission, like the one that infused Adolf Hitler in the course of his military career. Hitler was by no means the only veteran who came away convinced that he had survived for a reason and that his postwar life's mission was to discover that reason. Julius Streicher, one of Hitler's early followers, found his rationale for being in a degenerate anti-Semitism. Ernest Hemingway found a place as literary spokesman for a "lost generation." Laurence Stallings became a Broadway playwright, and Karl Wittgenstein a philosopher. Each saw himself as triumphing over his war experiences by making them part of his personal identity.

None of these assertions means that the war had no effect on Western sensibility. The war intensified intellectual patterns that already existed and helped to make sense of an experience that confounded any notion of an ordered universe. The challenges that cultural modernism posed to rationalism and objectivity before the Great War seemed validated beyond criticism by the events of 1914–1918.

–DENNIS SHOWALTER,
COLORADO COLLEGE
AND
–WILLIAM J. ASTORE,
U.S. AIR FORCE ACADEMY

References

Jacques Barzun, *From Dawn to Decadence: 500 Years of European Cultural Life, 1500 to the Present* (New York: HarperCollins, 2000).

David Cannadine, *The Decline and Fall of the British Aristocracy* (New Haven: Yale University Press, 1990).

Gordon A. Craig and others, *World War I: A Turning Point in Modern History, Essays in the Significance of the War,* edited by Jack J. Roth (New York: Knopf, 1967).

Modris Eksteins, *Rites of Spring: The Great War and the Birth of the Modern Age* (Toronto: Lester & Orpen Dennys, 1989).

Sigmund Freud, *Civilization and its Discontents,* translated and edited by James Strachey (New York: Norton, 1961).

Paul Fussell, *The Great War and Modern Memory* (New York: Oxford University Press, 1975).

Robert Graves and Alan Hodge, *The Long Weekend: A Social History of Great Britain, 1918–1939* (London: Faber & Faber, 1940).

Michael Howard and William Roger Louis, eds., *The Oxford History of the Twentieth Century* (Oxford & New York: Oxford University Press, 1998).

Stefan Kühl, *The Nazi Connection: Eugenics, American Racism, and German National Socialism* (New York: Oxford University Press, 1994).

Philip Larkin, "MCMXIV," in *The Soldiers' Tale: Bearing Witness to Modern War,* by Samuel Hynes (New York: John Lane, 1997), p. 106.

Eric J. Leed, *No Man's Land: Combat and Identity in World War I* (Cambridge & New York: Cambridge University Press, 1979).

George Lichtheim, *Europe in the Twentieth Century* (London: Weidenfeld & Nicolson, 1972; New York: Praeger, 1972).

Arno J. Mayer, *The Persistence of the Old Regime: Europe to the Great War* (New York: Pantheon, 1981).

Mark Mazower, *Dark Continent: Europe's Twentieth Century* (New York: Knopf, 1998).

J. B. Priestley, *Margin Released: A Writer's Reminiscences and Reflections* (New York: Harper & Row, 1962).

Zeev Sternhell, and others, *The Birth of Fascist Ideology: From Cultural Rebellion to Political Revolution,* translated by David Maisel (Princeton: Princeton University Press, 1994).

Richard Stites, *Revolutionary Dreams: Utopian Vision and Experimental Life in the Russian Revolution* (New York: Oxford University Press, 1989).

Paul Valéry, *Variety,* translated by Malcolm Cowley (New York: Harcourt, Brace, 1927).

Jay Winter, *Sites of Memory, Sites of Mourning: The Great War in European Cultural History* (Cambridge & New York: Cambridge University Press, 1995).

END OF IMPERIALISM

Did the Great War mark the end of imperialism?

Viewpoint: Yes. After four years of warfare, imperial powers lacked the means and the will to sustain their empires against a rising tide of nationalism.

Viewpoint: No. After the war, imperial powers expanded their control in the Middle East, the Far East, and Latin America.

A casual glance at a map of the world in 1919 might suggest that imperialism was alive and well in the aftermath of the Great War. The system of mandates introduced by the League of Nations invited dismissal as a fig leaf for the indefinite continuation of European rule. In military terms, the war had exponentially increased the gap between "the West and the rest"—to a point where even the Japanese army essentially abandoned hope of matching directly Western firepower and Western mechanization. The British Empire controlled several new territories in 1914. Its writ now ran throughout the Middle East, while in Africa, "Cape to Cairo" had become a political reality. France too had expanded its influence, direct and indirect, in the Middle East and North Africa. Even in those regions where direct rule had not been extended, Latin America and China in particular, Western concepts of free trade, backed where necessary by gunboats and expeditionary forces, bade fair to render political independence a vestigial appendix to economic integration.

Beneath the surface, however, tectonic shifts were beginning. The Great War had diminished the number of serious pretenders to imperial status. Germany was off that board by international treaty. Tsarist Russia had transformed itself from an imperial power to the self-proclaimed leader of an anti-Western nationalist/revolutionary movement that found increasing resonance among Western-educated elites seeking to apply the French, American, and Russian Revolutions to their own systems. The United States loudly denied identification with traditional imperialism, describing its international policies as a non-zero-sum game from which all participants would eventually benefit. The surviving empires were suffering badly from overstretch—moral, military, and financial. Empire had never been a paying proposition; after World War I its direct costs increased, not least from providing even minimum pensions to disabled veterans of the war fought by the mother countries. Military operations grew more complex and more costly from Morocco to the Northwest Frontier of India, again not least as the lessons and the hardware of the Great War diffused throughout the rest of the world. Finally, the number of young Western men willing to spend their lives in service to the overseas possessions of their states had been significantly reduced—not from war casualties alone but from a growing conviction that empire was a losing game and a failing proposition. The challenge of nationalism was moral as well as political: its implied question was what right, after the hecatombs of 1914–1918, did Europe have to any claim outside its own frontiers? Mohandas Gandhi's aphoristic reply, when asked what he thought of Western civilization, that it would be a very good idea, resonated among soldiers and officials as well as students and journalists.

**Viewpoint:
Yes. After four years of
warfare, imperial powers lacked the
means and the will to sustain their
empires against a rising tide of
nationalism.**

If President Warren Harding claimed that the United States in the 1920s desired a "return to normalcy," the wish to return to the old ways was equally strong in London and Paris. This wish also reflected a desire to return to the old colonial system that had grown so dramatically in the fifty years before World War I. However, the war had so drastically damaged the two countries that the old way was simply untenable. In short, World War I marked the beginning of the end for imperialism.

People tend to think of colonies as pure profit centers, assets whose retention was a clear benefit. Nothing, in fact, could be further from the truth. Empires require administrators, police, teachers, and a host of other personnel both at home and abroad. They need infrastructure. These requirements cost money, and it is not entirely clear that the cost of colonies was smaller than the profits derived from them. Consider, too, another less-tangible cost that the imperialists were no longer able to pay. Empire is predicated on the assertion of superiority by the colonial power over the natives. When colonized and colonizer both perceive a superiority of the controlling power, significant economies in government control naturally result. Europeans may have felt that they could not bear the burden in the wake of the catastrophe that was World War I. Just as imperialists could not sustain the illusion of superiority, they were hard-pressed to maintain the manpower and financial demands that empire places on a country.

The losses in manpower caused by the war were staggering. It is estimated that France lost approximately 47 percent of its prewar military manpower strength, while Britain lost 15 percent of its own. This reduction meant, at the least, that the manpower needed to sustain empire was seriously lacking. Already before the war it had become a tenet of policy that the French and British Empires were dramatically overstretched. The costly and drawn-out Boer War (1899–1902), for example, had convinced the Chief of the Imperial General Staff that Britain needed to reduce the threats to empire, which the Foreign Office promptly did by reaching agreements to limit actual and potential colonial disputes with France, the United States, and Russia.

Of course, war casualties had more dramatic effects at home than they did in the empire. Losses in productive capacity represented by the reduction of manpower cannot be accurately calculated, but it is safe to say that economic recovery in France and Britain was far from certain at the end of the war. The worldwide economic crisis of 1929 brought what prosperity there was to a quick halt, although it should be noted that France, with a lower dependence on international trade, was able to put off the disaster a bit longer. Making matters worse, a Damoclean sword hung over the heads of both Britain and France in the form of war debts owed to the United States. The war had essentially depleted the reserves of both countries, and President Calvin Coolidge's laconic response—"They hired the money, didn't they?"—to requests from London and Paris for debt relief did not indicate that there would be any help in this quarter. Only with the Dawes (1924) and Young (1929) Plans would the financial burden of the war be managed, well after the worldwide depression had hurt any prospects of recovery.

The war damage Europe suffered hampered its ability to assert its superiority over foreign natives. As long as Europe could pose as the more-developed, civilized, sophisticated center that it had appeared to be in the last half of the nineteenth century, European powers could count on a grudging acceptance of their control in those places where they had established colonies. However, the storm of 1914–1918 seriously undermined that claim to rule by right. Not only had the Europeans killed each other off by the millions for a cause that no one was entirely sure of, they had done so for only a few yards of mud, in most cases, and right in front of colonial troops shipped to Europe. Africans, Indians, and Asians all saw firsthand the madness of World War I, and no one would ever again be able to persuade them of the superiority of the Europeans.

Nevertheless, in the face of these changes, Britain and France both attempted to return to the colonial game, using the "Mandate System" set up by the League of Nations to dispose of the colonies of Imperial Germany and the now-defunct Ottoman Empire. The idea behind the Mandate System was that the new nonimperialist age heralded by the Fourteen Points would not have new colonies. Rather, the League of Nations would supervise these territories until they were "ready" for self-rule. The results were mixed. Britain jettisoned Iraq and Jordan before too long, while France showed no inclination to rid itself of its costly ventures in Syria and Lebanon. To the south, Britain probably wished for nothing more than to unload troublesome Palestine but in good conscience could not do so until a semblance of order was established between native Palestinians and European Zionist settlers. Meanwhile, India, under the leadership of the Indian National Congress and Mohandas Gandhi, was proving a ceaseless drain on Britain. Both India and Palestine would be dropped quickly after the end of World War II.

In short, while both Paris and London wished for a return to the imperial heyday of the prewar era, such a desire remained chimerical. Losses in manpower, in financial wherewithal, and in political legitimacy fatally undermined the notion of imperial control of the undeveloped world. There was no way to turn the clock back, and the age of European world domination had come to an end.

—PHIL GILTNER, U.S. MILITARY ACADEMY

Viewpoint:
No. After the war, imperial powers expanded their control in the Middle East, the Far East, and Latin America.

Not only did World War I not mark an end of colonialism by the European powers, it furthered the colonial interests of several European countries, primarily France and Britain. The colonial powers refused to grant independence to any of their colonies during and immediately following the war. This policy was followed, in spite of requests from various countries, including Indochina and Ireland, at the Peace Conference at Versailles (1919), to which they sent representatives.

One of the Indochinese delegates at the Versailles Peace Conference was a political cartoonist named Nguyen Tat Thanh, which was the given name of Ho Chi Minh. He tried to broach the topic of Indochinese independence at the conference but was rebuffed by the French, who had no intentions of relinquishing this natural-resource-rich region. This same response occurred when Robert Childers, the Irish delegate, attempted to obtain similar consideration for Ireland.

In what was a serious affront to the disenfranchised European and non-European nationalist groups, the victorious powers created many new European countries through the Treaties of Versailles. They took land from Russia and created the Baltic states of Latvia, Lithuania, and Estonia. From the old Austrian region of Bohemia, they forced the Czechs and Slovaks together, along with some Germans, into the single state of Czechoslovakia. They established Turkey from the main regions of the Ottoman Empire, while Yugoslavia was created as an amalgamation of some twenty ethnic groups under a Serbian king. Finally, after more than one hundred years of nonexistence, they re-created Poland. Clearly, the map of the world was changing.

The colonial powers were willing to use force to maintain their rule. One of the most infamous examples comes from India in 1919. Amid growing political tension, the Indian National Congress, headed by Mohandas Gandhi, continued its agitation for independence. They protested, held work stoppages, and staged public rallies, all in contravention of British orders. On 13 April 1919, in the Jallianwala Bagh (a large open mall) in the Punjab town of Amritsar, approximately 20,000 people gathered for a peaceful protest against repressive British legislation, especially the Rowlatt Act (1919), which authorized the arrest and imprisonment without trial of Indian people. The military commander in the area, General Reginald Dyer, took 100 soldiers onto the grounds where the demonstration was proceeding, lined up his men, and without warning, opened fire on the crowd. Unfortunately, the troops were blocking the only exit. They killed 379 men, women, and children, while wounding another 1,208. Dyer was never actually disciplined for this act but was asked to retire quietly after a board of inquiry.

Similarly, in Ireland during the Anglo-Irish War (1916–1921), the British used a combination of police and army units to try to put down the rebellion beginning in 1919 and ending in July 1921. When this policy proved insufficient, they organized the Auxiliary Division of the Royal Irish Constabulary (1920) from former British soldiers, men who had seen combat in the World War. The Black and Tans, as they were known, became legendary on both sides of the conflict for their brutality. For instance, on Sunday, 21 November 1920, in retaliation for the assassination of some members of a British counterintelligence group by the Irish Republican Army (IRA), a group of Black and Tans entered a crowded stadium at Croke Park in Dublin and fired on the crowd, killing eleven and wounding eleven. This retaliatory strike was the first so-called Bloody Sunday massacre in Irish history. The next month, the Black and Tans set fire to the city of Cork in retaliation for some killings of their comrades. As large parts of the city burned, the Black and Tans allegedly hampered the work of the firemen who came to put out the blaze. Thousands were left homeless. By early 1921 even the Brit-

BROKEN PROMISES

In July 1936 Ethiopian emperor Haile Selassie addressed the League of Nations in Geneva concerning the Italian invasion of his country and the stance of the league.

On October 3rd, 1935, the Italian troops invaded my territory. A few hours later only I decreed general mobilization. In my desire to maintain peace I had, following the example of a great country in Europe on the eve of the Great War, caused my troops to withdraw thirty kilometres so as to remove any pretext of provocation.

War then took place in the atrocious conditions which I have laid before the Assembly. In that unequal struggle between a Government commanding more than forty-two million inhabitants, having at its disposal financial, industrial and technical means which enabled it to create unlimited quantities of the most death-dealing weapons, and, on the other hand, a small people of twelve million inhabitants, without arms, without resources having on its side only the justice of its own cause and the promise of the League of Nations. What real assistance was given to Ethiopia by the fifty two nations who had declared the Rome Government guilty of a breach of the Covenant and had undertaken to prevent the triumph of the aggressor? Has each of the States Members, as it was its duty to do in virtue of its signature appended to Article 15 of the Covenant, considered the aggressor as having committed an act of war personally directed against itself? I had placed all my hopes in the execution of these undertakings. My confidence had been confirmed by the repeated declarations made in the Council to the effect that aggression must not be rewarded, and that force would end by being compelled to bow before right.

In December, 1935, the Council made it quite clear that its feelings were in harmony with those of hundreds of millions of people who, in all parts of the world, had protested against the proposal to dismember Ethiopia. It was constantly repeated that there was not merely a conflict between the Italian Government and the League of Nations, and that is why I personally refused all proposals to my personal advantage made to me by the Italian Government, if only I would betray my people and the Covenant of the League of Nations. I was defending the cause of all small peoples who are threatened with aggression.

What have become of the promises made to me as long ago as October, 1935? I noted with grief, but without surprise that three Powers considered their undertakings under the Covenant as absolutely of no value. Their connections with Italy impelled them to refuse to take any measures whatsoever in order to stop Italian aggression. On the contrary, it was a profound disappointment to me to learn the attitude of a certain Government which, whilst ever protesting its scrupulous attachment to the Covenant, has tirelessly used all its efforts to prevent its observance. As soon as any measure which was likely to be rapidly effective was proposed, various pretexts were devised in order to postpone even consideration of the measure. Did the secret agreements of January, 1935, provide for this tireless obstruction?

The Ethiopian Government never expected other Governments to shed their soldiers' blood to defend the Covenant when their own immediately personal interests were not at stake. Ethiopian warriors asked only for means to defend themselves. On many occasions I have asked for financial assistance for the purchase of arms. That assistance has been constantly refused me. What, then, in practice, is the meaning of Article 16 of the Covenant and of collective security?. . .

Apart from the Kingdom of the Lord there is not on this earth any nation that is superior to any other. Should it happen that a strong Government finds it may with impunity destroy a weak people, then the hour strikes for that weak people to appeal to the League of Nations to give its judgment in all freedom. God and history will remember your judgment.

Source: Haile Selassie, "Appeal to the League of Nations," June 1936, Temple University, Internet website, http://oll.temple.edu/hist249/course/Documents/appeal_to_the_league_of_nations_.htm.

British field marshal Lord Horatio Kitchener reviewing Indian officers, summer 1914

(from The Illustrated War News, *2 September 1914, page 42, Joseph M. Bruccoli Great War Collection, Thomas Cooper Library, University of South Carolina)*

ish government admitted that the Black and Tans were out of control. It was these types of actions that demonstrated just how desperate the British were to retain control of their colony, for that is what Ireland truly was.

Not only did the colonial powers refuse to abandon control of their colonies, they expanded into other regions. Under the Versailles Treaty, France occupied the Saarland and Rhineland states of Germany. The French also had the right to profit from the natural resources and to tax the populations in these areas. Under the guise of readying the colonies

formerly held by their enemies for nationhood, as spelled out in the treaty, the victorious powers, Britain and France, who allegedly fought for democracy and the rights of small nations, finished the war owning or controlling far more of the world than when the conflict began. As directed by the League of Nations, certain former areas of the Ottoman Empire and other regions were to be held as protectorates, called Mandates, until such time as they were ready to assume full independence. Unfortunately for the Mandates, the "protecting" powers were not only responsible for deciding when these areas were "ready" for independence, but they also had the right to exploit the natural resources and raw materials of the Mandates, thus creating the conflict of interest that existed until they succumbed to international pressure. Britain assumed responsibility for Arabia, Egypt, Iraq, Palestine, and Persia, while France did the same for Syria, Lebanon, and Transjordan.

The United States, although it never ratified the Treaty of Versailles nor became a member of the League of Nations, was not immune to the beckoning call of imperialism. Beginning in 1912 the United States undertook a series of "interventions" in Latin America, justified under the Monroe Doctrine (1823), which lasted into the 1930s. The Monroe Doctrine, named after the president who first promulgated it (James Monroe), stated that the United States had the right to prevent foreign aggression in the western hemisphere, with force if necessary, and to promote "stability" in the region. The United States invaded Nicaragua in 1912, Haiti in 1915, the Dominican Republic in 1916, remaining in each country until the mid 1930s. So blatant was this aggression that U.S. Marine major general Smedley Butler, a two-time recipient of the Medal of Honor, stated after his retirement that he

> spent thirty-three years and four months in active military service as a member of this country's most agile military force, the Marine Corps. I served in all commissioned ranks from Second Lieutenant to Major-General. And during that period, I spent most of my time being a high class muscle-man for Big Business, for Wall Street and for the Bankers. In short, I was a racketeer, a gangster for capitalism.

Indeed, it is difficult to justify any of these actions based on the Monroe Doctrine, as the only threats were to the profits of American companies. However, the United States had already been a colonial power for a generation, starting in 1898, when it seized Hawaii. It simply invaded a sovereign nation with whom it had official diplomatic relations and treaties. The United States continued in this vein in 1898 by seizing and keeping the Philippines and other eastern Pacific islands, Cuba, Puerto Rico, and the Virgin Islands. When Filipinos continued their struggle for independence, which they had initiated prior to the American takeover, the United States responded with brutality and beat them into submission during the Philippine Insurrection (1899–1902).

A similar situation existed in China from 1900. Concerned about the deteriorating effects of western influences in their country, the *I-ho ch'üan* or "Society of Righteous (or

Harmonious) Fists" (also called the Boxers) rebelled against this influence by killing foreigners and laying siege to the Legation Quarter in Peking. Many Europeans were able to take refuge in their embassies within the Quarter. The West responded by sending a multinational force to relieve the siege. After ninety days, the force of American, British, French, German, Italian, and Russian troops fought their way through to the city and lifted the siege. With the rebellion crushed, the international intervention forces remained in occupation of China until 1940. Indeed, the American Fourth Marine Regiment remained stationed in Shanghai until 1940, when it was transferred to the Philippines, where it fought the Japanese invasion a year later.

These activities of the major victorious powers after World War I spurred on some of their lesser allies to try the same type of colonial aggrandizement. Italy, with the rise of rabid nationalism in the form of the Fascist movement, embarked on colonial expansion in 1935. Having finished the subjugation of Libya, which began in 1911, *il duce* (the leader), Benito Mussolini, attacked the oldest Christian empire in the world—Ethiopia. Under Emperor Haile Selassie, Ethiopia was one of the only independent African nations (the other being Liberia). With a sophisticated culture that extended back millennia, the Ethiopians were clearly advanced, yet not industrialized. Surprisingly, they performed well against a technologically superior foe, but the outcome was virtually preordained, as Italy triumphed and occupied the country.

The only non-European nation that undertook colonial exploits was Japan, which was operating under its own rabid military dictatorship. No stranger to colonialism, Japan seized Korea in 1905, during its war with Russia, and held it until 1945. Under the provisions of the Versailles Treaty, they took control of the German-administered Shandong province in China in 1920, along with several German colonies in the Pacific. In September 1931 Japan invaded Manchuria to gain, what amounted to, living space; their conquest of this area was exceedingly brutal. The Rape of Nanking (1937), in which at least 370,000 people in the Chinese city were butchered over a six-month period by occupying troops, is still decried as one of the worst crimes committed by Japan.

What is clear is that colonialism did not end with the completion of World War I. Imperialism changed appearances in some cases, but it remained until the 1960s. While it is also true that the war set the stage for future colonial independence, it would take forty years for some colonies to realize this dream. With the later colonial excursions of Japan and

Italy, the League of Nations and the international community as it existed at the time discovered that their protests meant nothing against armed aggression. With the main members of the League also brutally holding colonies, however, their protestations rang hollow. It was not until after World War II that colonialism began to end.

–WILLIAM KAUTT, UNIVERSITY OF ULSTER AT JORDANSTOWN

References

Christopher M. Andrew and A. S. Kanya-Forstner, *France Overseas: The Great War and the Climax of French Imperial Expansion* (London: Thames & Hudson, 1981).

A. Adu Boahen, *General History of Africa,* volume 7, *Africa under Colonial Domination 1880–1935* (London: Heinemann / Berkeley: University of California Press, 1985).

Manfred F. Boemke, Gerald D. Feldman, and Elisabeth Glaser, eds., *The Treaty of Versailles: A Reassessment After 75 Years* (Washington, D.C.: German Historical Institute; Cambridge & New York: Cambridge University Press, 1998).

Michael J. Cohen, *Palestine, Retreat from the Mandate: The Making of British Policy, 1936–45* (London: Elek, 1978).

Alice L. Conklin and Ian Christopher Fletcher, eds., *European Imperialism, 1830–1930: Climax and Contradiction* (Boston: Houghton Mifflin, 1999).

John Darwin, *Britain, Egypt, and the Middle East: Imperial Policy in the Aftermath of War, 1918–1922* (New York: St. Martin's Press, 1981).

Stephen Hemsley Longrigg, *Syria and Lebanon under French Mandate* (London & New York: Oxford University Press, 1958).

EUROPEAN LEADERSHIP

Was World War I caused by inadequate political and military leadership in Europe?

Viewpoint: Yes. Before the July Crisis of 1914, no European leader was able to confront the looming catastrophe.

Viewpoint: No. The men who made European policy decisions in 1914 are best understood as prisoners of events.

A century of perspective on the outbreak of war in 1914 suggests that Europe was sent to its doom by a generation of second-rate leaders. The diplomats, politicians, generals, and admirals who made decisions and signed documents were not as a class incompetent—it might have been better for Europe and the world if they had been. Instead, they were just capable enough to oversee catastrophe without averting it and, correspondingly unequal to the responsibilities they held.

European leaders in 1914 suffer in comparison to their predecessors. No foreign office featured an Otto von Bismarck or a Benjamin Disraeli. The increasingly professionalized armed forces cast up not gifted captains but bureaucrats in uniform—a pattern epitomized by the presence of Helmuth von Moltke (the Younger) as Chief of the German General Staff. When offered the post once held by his uncle, Helmuth von Moltke (the Elder), he allegedly asked Kaiser Wilhelm II if His Majesty proposed to win twice in the same lottery. The sense of wearing shoes a little too large was common in chanceries and general staffs. So too was a reluctance to admit it. The result was a pattern of inflexibility. As decisions went wrong, those who made them were unwilling to risk losing face by changing their minds. The one key figure who attempted flexible policies was Wilhelm II, and he remains pilloried by historians as an indecisive neurotic.

Mediocrity at the top was to a degree facilitated by the relatively limited pool of acceptable candidates for leadership positions. Though merit was an increasing criterion for advancement in Europe generally, foreign offices and armies remained relative strongholds of privilege. This system involved less lineage per se than connections—the right schools, the right regiments, the right friends, and the right accents. A major consequence was decision-making environments strongly susceptible to what is now called "groupthink": collective wisdom expressed in collective discussions.

European decision makers were also overtaken by the sheer pace of events. July 1914 was the first real-time crisis in history: telephones and telegraphs kept armies and governments consistently informed of developments. It can be argued that they did their work too well. There was no lead time and no opportunity to draft a note or dispatch, consider its wording, and allow it to simmer for a day or so. Constant disruption of routines affected the sleep patterns and the digestion of men no longer young, as well as highlighting personal and institutional shortcomings. The July Crisis is a case study in the adverse effects of stress on decision making.

Viewpoint:
Yes. Before the July Crisis of 1914, no European leader was able to confront the looming catastrophe.

Clearly, in the coming of World War I in 1914, civilian and military leadership failed. In 1878 German chancellor Otto von Bismarck and British prime minister Benjamin Disraeli, statesmen with exceptional ability, were able to defuse a similar crisis at the Congress of Berlin. But no one of their caliber was available in 1914, when leaders accepted war because they could not formulate alternatives.

Some of the leaders pursued the military option because it was the only way in which national policy objectives could be secured. Serbia, for example, could only wrest Bosnia-Herzegovina away from Austria-Hungary by military means. France and Italy found themselves in much the same situation, although neither power had hostile intentions against either Germany or Austria-Hungary in the immediate future.

Other leaders, however, did have choices other than war; yet, none pursued them. Among second-rate thinkers was Franz Conrad von Hötzendorff, the bellicose Chief of the Austrian General Staff. He had been spoiling for war with Serbia for some time. While fearful of rising Serbian nationalism, Conrad feared even more a repeat of the Bosnian Crisis (1908–1909), which he felt would have been the most opportune time for war. In any event, Conrad wanted to crush and annex Serbia as soon as possible.

However illogical Conrad's thinking, it enjoyed wide support in Austro-Hungarian military circles. He had the full support of War Minister Alexander von Krobatin and many high-ranking Austrian generals. Mostly of German background, the most notable were the Austrian military attaché in Belgrade and the Austrian commander in Bosnia, General Oskar Potiorek. Aside from his dislike of the Serbians, Potiorek also had a personal motive for war. He had been in charge of the security arrangements for Franz Ferdinand's ill-fated visit to Sarajevo.

Conrad's German counterpart, Helmuth von Moltke (the Younger), nephew of the victor of Königgrätz (1866) and Sedan (1870), was also anxious for war. Gazing upon the world through the dark prism of Social Darwinism, Moltke by 1914 had become convinced that a war was coming "sooner or later." The forces of German culture, lodged in Germany and Austria-Hungary, would be pit-ted against the Slavics threatening to overwhelm them. Moltke preferred that the war came sooner, as he felt that the passage of time worked against Germany. Moltke's attitude was shared by his deputy, General George von Waldersee, and the War Minister, General Erich von Falkenhayn.

Lest anyone think that only the military leaders of the Central Powers were anxious for war, this attitude applied to the civilian leaders as well. German kaiser Wilhelm II, caught up in the "world power or decline" delirium, desired to have a final settling of accounts with both France and Britain, as well as to stamp out the "Slavic peril." Chancellor Theobald von Bethmann Hollweg was also amenable to the idea of war.

Passion for war was even more pronounced in Austria-Hungary. Confronted with what was regarded as the very survival of Austria-Hungary, leaders such as Prime Minister Leopold Berchtold were perfectly willing to follow Conrad's lead, especially after Wilhelm II had given Austria the "blank check." Francis Joseph saw war as a matter of form as much as survival. As the old emperor put it, "If we are to go down, we should at least go down decently."

On the Entente side, a lack of aggressiveness in diplomacy should not be confused with unwillingness to go to war. Nicholas II's advisers were all of a mind to go to war for several reasons. First, the increasing influence of Pan-Slavism made support for Serbia all the more imperative for the position of Russia in the Slavic world. Second, going to war raised the prospect of coming to a definitive settling of accounts with Austria-Hungary, a festering sore in Russian foreign policy since 1854. Finally, Russian leaders, both civilian and military, felt that the tsarist regime could not afford a repeat of the humiliation inflicted by Germany in the Bosnian Crisis (1908–1909).

While France certainly did not aggressively pursue war in 1914, French civilian and military leaders were more than willing to "roll the iron dice" with Germany. In part, French leadership was buoyed by the Russian alliance. Thus, French president Raymond Poincaré could assure his audience in a speech that Russian troops "would be in Berlin by November." French military leaders were more than ready to put Plan XVII, and the offensive theories advocated by Ferdinand Foch and Henri de Grandmaison, to the ultimate test against hated Germany.

British leaders had their own reasons for preferring war with Germany. On the military side, the Admiralty and the leaders of the Royal Navy were anxious to eliminate any potential German challenge to British control

EUROPEAN LEADERSHIP

THE SWORD WILL ALWAYS BE

In 1913 German crown prince Frederick William, son of Kaiser Wilhelm II, and a general in World War I, wrote about militarism and the world position of his country:

. . . we live in a time which points with special satisfaction to the proud height of its culture, which is only too willing to boast of its international cosmopolitanism, and flatters itself with visionary dreams of the *possibility of an everlasting peace throughout the world. This view of life is un-German and does not suit us.* The German who loves his people, who believes in the greatness and the future of our homeland, and who is unwilling to see its position diminished, dare not close his eyes in the indulgence of dreams such as these, he dare not allow himself to be lulled into indolent sleep by the lullabies of peace sung by the Utopians.

Germany has behind her since the last great war a period of economic prosperity, which has in it something almost disconcerting. Comfort has so increased in all circles of our people that luxury and claims to a certain style of life have undergone a rank development. . . .

Then old ideals, even the position and the honor of the nation, may be sympathetically affected; *for peace, peace at any price, is necessary for the undisturbed acquisition of money.* But the study of history teaches us that all those States which in the decisive hour have been guided by purely commercial considerations have miserably come to grief. *The sympathies of civilized nations* are to-day, as in the battles of antiquity, still with the *sturdy and the bold fighting armies;* they are with the brave combatants who, in the words which Lessing puts in the mouth of

Tellheim, are soldiers for their country, and fight out of love which they bear to the cause. Certainly diplomatic dexterity can, and should, postpone the conflict for a time, and at times disentangle the difficulties. Certainly all those in authority must and will be fully conscious of their enormous responsibility in the grave hour of decision. They must make it clear to their own minds that the gigantic conflagration, once enkindled, cannot be so easily or so quickly extinguished. As, however, lightning is an adjustment of the tension between two differently charged strata of the atmosphere, so the sword will always be and remain until the end of the world the decisive factor.

Therefore every one, to whom his country is dear, and who believes in a great future for our nation, must joyfully do his part in the task of seeing that the old military spirit of our fathers is not lost, and that it is not sicklied o'er with the pale cast of thought. For the sword alone is not decisive, but the arm steeled in exercise which bears the sword. Each of us must keep himself fit for arms and also prepared in his mind for the great solemn hour when the Emperor calls us to the standard—the hour when we no longer belong to ourselves, but to the Fatherland with all the forces of our mind and our body; for all these faculties must be brought to the highest exertion, to that "will to victory" which has never been without success in history.

Source: Charles F. Horne, ed., The Great Events of the Great War, volume 1 (New York: National Alumni, 1923), pp. 141–142.

---

of the Atlantic, with its implications for the safety of British trade. The only question the Admiralty had to deal with was how aggressive a course the Royal Navy should pursue in dealing with the German High Seas Fleet once war came. That question was effectively decided when Winston Churchill, First Lord of the Admiralty, replaced the aggressive Sir John Fisher with the more cautious Sir John Jellicoe as commander of the Grand Fleet.

The prospect of going to war also found favor with the British leadership politically. Given the recent two decades of diplomatic tension with Germany and the ensuing naval race, this position was understandable. British leaders viewed going to war as simply another example of Britain pursuing its traditional foreign policy of preventing any power from attaining hegemony in Europe. For all the talk about fair play, in reality, all the German invasion of Belgium did was present the government of Sir Herbert Asquith with a perfect pretext to enter the war. It is also worth noting that the decision by the Asquith government to enter the war was supported by all political parties.

The least critical thing here is motive. All of the great powers had motives, right or wrong. All of the leaders of the major powers in 1914, both civilian and military, fully expected that a war would come. The only thing that remained was timing. Some, most notably Conrad and Moltke the Younger, preferred that war break out sooner than later. All, however, accepted with a sort of unthinking fatalism that a major war was on the horizon. None of the leaders in Europe, either civilian or military, had the vision required to see the kind of cataclysm that would result, or how it could be avoided. As the events of July 1914 unfolded, this acceptance of the certainty of war created an atmosphere in which the prospect of war could be looked on as an opportunity not to be passed up. No one could see that dreams of victory held by all the major powers would turn into the nightmarish reality that was World War I.

–R. L. DINARDO, USMC COMMAND AND
STAFF COLLEGE, QUANTICO, VIRGINIA

Viewpoint:
No. The men who made European policy decisions in 1914 are best understood as prisoners of events.

The European leaders who forged policy and dictated military strategy for their respective nations at the outset of the Great War were among the educated elite of their generation and were equally experienced in administration and negotiation, successful in utilizing a half century of technological and social innovations. Closely attuned to the desires and weaknesses of their nations, these men ably handled the often delicate matters of state and usually tempestuous national security issues, even in the weeks leading to the July 1914 tragedy.

When confronted with an ever-deepening quagmire of flawed perceptions, precarious alliances, munition-fueled deterrence, and what historian John Keegan, in *The First World War* (1998), calls "naked nationalism," European leaders took one of three paths: active deterrence (best typified by Germany), reactive deterrence (as shown by France), or tacit/neutral deterrence (best illustrated by actions taken in Great Britain).

Kaiser Wilhelm II, the third emperor of Germany, sought to model himself strongly after his grandfather Wilhelm I, an unheralded architect of German victories in the Seven Weeks' War (1866) and the Franco-Prussian War (1870–1871). Despite his well-documented shortcomings, Wilhelm II recognized and accepted the inherent social, political, and economic advantages of military power. After the 1890 dismissal of Chancellor Otto von Bismarck, the Kaiser utilized his considerable authority to press for a unilateral German security based not on alliances but on armed force. "The balance of power in Europe," he once allegedly declared, "is me and my twenty-five army corps, and I shit on everything else."

Wilhelm might not have said it, but he acted as though he believed it. His nationalist efforts bore ample fruit in the form of a German High Seas Fleet (developed by naval innovator Grand Admiral Alfred von Tirpitz to nearly rival the vaunted naval supremacy of Great Britain), a broadened industrial base, and an expanded army generally considered the best trained and most effective in the world. German models of military training and planning had been copied by most regional European powers by the turn of the twentieth century and were influential as well in Japan and the United States. Germany had become nearly invulnerable to intimidation and attack—a reasonable goal given its geographic exposure in central Europe.

That drive for security was perceived differently elsewhere. Having survived punitive economic measures at the close of the Franco-Prussian War, decades of political factionalism, and intermittent episodes of bitter civil and religious discord, the Third Republic of France had managed to rise from the brink of German-encouraged self-annihilation. Mindful of what they had lost economically, logistically, and personally to Germany in years past, the French leadership methodically restored the diminished status of their country through diplomatic arrangements with the aloof maritime empire of Great Britain and the reserved continental empire of Tsarist Russia. In response to the rising tide of German nationalism, French leaders and elites increasingly, with almost single-minded determination, prepared as well for what they perceived as an inevitable reckoning with Germany.

Though the reasoning was flawed when viewed in hindsight, the Third Republic maintained a security policy congruent with its perceptions. Realizing the superior military power of Germany, France desperately sought a means to counter what it perceived as its enemy's expected aggression. A veteran of several conflicts including the Franco-Prussian War and the Sino-French War (1884–1885), Marshall Joseph Joffre's Plan XVII provided what seemed the key to French security concerns. As France could not match the Germans man for man and blow for blow, Joffre intended to launch the bulk of French forces against Germany at the commencement of hostilities. An *attaque à outrance* would

General Paul von Hindenburg, Kaiser Wilhelm II, and General Erich Ludendorff (l.-r.) studying maps, circa 1917

(from Grosser Bilderatlas des Weltkrieges *[1915–1919], Joseph M. Bruccoli Great War Collection, Thomas Cooper Library, University of South Carolina)*

force the Germans onto the defensive, ensuring the integrity of French borders and offering the potential of retaking the long-lost provinces of Alsace and Lorraine. By the summer of 1914, France had managed to implement a comprehensive response to the apparently unavoidable challenge of Germany.

As European tensions heightened, British leadership undertook similarly reasonable measures to maintain its naval dominance and to act as a stabilizing influence on its allies. Primarily influenced by Admiral John Fisher and his protégé, Admiral John Jellicoe, the British navy expanded in size, widening its numerical superiority over Germany; modernized its technology, increasing the efficiency of their vessels with the conversion from a coal- to an oil-dominant fleet; and simultaneously increased the tactical assets of the fleet with the creation of several new ship types, including the heavily armed Dreadnought-class battleships and the accompanying battle cruisers. With its signature attached to several key security agreements, a new arsenal of destructive power at sea, and a reorganized army with modernized weapons, including improved artillery pieces, Great Britain created a deterrent force sufficient to underwrite a balance of European power.

The evaluation by each state of its strength and its circumstances came undone in the after-math of inexplicable events: the assassination of a royal couple widely unpopular in their own country (Habsburg archduke Franz Ferdinand and his duchess, Sophia of Hohenberg) by terrorists inspired by a Serbian radical group, the Black Hand. Through a series of unpredictable twists and miscalculations, still best described in Barbara W. Tuchman's seminal work *The Guns of August* (1962), measures meant to bolster national pride and national security instead destabilized the international order that sustained them.

The leadership of Europe found itself factionalized along lines predetermined by treaties that had never been intended as doomsday machines. Yet, if broken, they contained a risk of isolation in an emergency. If followed, they incorporated a growing certainty of general war. The result was a paralysis that left even the best statesmen unwilling to take risks for peace.

While the leaders of an aggressive Serbia and a waning Austro-Hungarian Empire exchanged arguments about responsibility and accountability, other foreign offices attempted to broker a compromise. Events deteriorated far too rapidly. British foreign minister Lord Edward Grey hesitated to apply overt diplomatic political force during the crisis. His uninspired, measured response to the escalating situation reflected British deterrence strategy but was perceived as indifference by critical parties in Berlin and Vienna. Wilhelm II's military and diplomatic subordinates, instead of taking direct counsel of their fears and ambitions for the future of Germany, sidestepped responsibility and offered Austria a "blank check." Austro-Hungarian statesmen and generals in turn were reassured by the silence of major potential adversaries and expressions of support by an ally whose commitment had previously been considered a matter of words on paper. Vienna stepped through the breach and into total war.

With their populations apparently calling for war, with sudden hope of spoils, and underpinned by the conventional wisdom that no war waged with the new and powerful weapons available could last longer than a few weeks, European governors watched with bated breath as military mobilization plans were implemented, each hoping someone else would create room for negotiation. Instead, in less than a month words gave way to cannon, and blood replaced ink as a means of dialogue.

Failure of vision was not limited to the topmost level of leadership. General Helmuth von Moltke (the Younger), the successor of the vaunted German strategist General Alfred von Schlieffen, failed to adapt or apply his predecessor's grand designs in the contexts of the modern battlefield. He also was unable to grasp success in the first weeks of the war with France. French military leaders likewise failed to adjust to the new weapons systems, sacrificed nearly a million men in futile tactical attacks, and found themselves in a position of sacrificing more men to drive the *Boche* from French soil. By contrast, British and German admirals refused to risk their new assets by seeking decisive action against enemy shipping (Germany) or the enemy fleet (Britain). The most imaginative thinker on either side in the opening months of war, First Lord of the British Admiralty and future Prime Minister Winston Churchill, sought one quick fix after another, culminating in the 1915 launch of the disastrous Gallipoli campaign.

The list of leadership failures during the summer of 1914 and the following years is daunting. Yet, European leaders had successfully navigated the treacherous waters of diplomatic and military policy for decades before the Great War, expecting that strong defenses and forthright foreign policies would lead to national security and international stability. Instead, the events of July and August unfolded so rapidly that institutions and systems designed to stabilize the continent began working in reverse and spawned a synergistic escalation of perceived diplomatic and military aggression that led to unimaginable disaster.

Though hindsight tempts one to reevaluate the steps that led to World War I from a postmodern perspective, no one person or group of individuals was likely to develop, under the immense pressures of summer 1914, a means of unraveling the alliance and deterrence systems that spawned the Great War. Policymakers and military men worked with what they held at hand: reacting to situations and utilizing the instruments and symbols of a new era to demonstrate commitment and resolve. They implemented war plans drafted and redrafted over decades—ultimately praying for a swift victory and awaiting their opponents' surrender.

–PAUL A. THOMSEN, NEW YORK, NEW YORK

References

John Horne, ed., *State, Society, and Mobilization in Europe During the First World War* (Cambridge & New York: Cambridge University Press, 1997).

John Keegan, *The First World War* (London: Hutchinson, 1998).

John Maynard Keynes, *The Economic Consequences of the Peace* (London: Macmillan, 1919).

Dwight E. Lee, ed., *The Outbreak of the First World War: Causes and Responsibilities,* fourth edition (Lexington, Mass.: D. C. Heath, 1975).

Barbara W. Tuchman, *The Guns of August* (New York: Macmillan, 1962).

FOCH

Was the appointment of Ferdinand Foch as supreme commander a turning point in the Allied war effort on the Western Front?

Viewpoint: Yes. Foch skillfully thwarted the German offensive of 1918.

Viewpoint: No. Foch was a figurehead, who never directly coordinated Allied offensive operations.

From the beginning of the Great War the Allied effort on the Western Front was undertaken in a coalition context. Britain and France had differing war aims and strategic visions. Both their military and their political cultures clashed unmercifully. British and French policy and strategy were, nevertheless, ultimately determined essentially by the requirements of an increasingly close military alliance. The possibilities for Britain of pursuing an independent strategic path, whether by developing other theaters of war or by undertaking unilateral operations in the West, were essentially limited by the consequences of the initial decision to send its army to the Continent in 1914 and deploy it on the French left wing. France for its part accepted the primary burden of the fighting in the first years of the war with the understanding—indeed, the confidence—that as Britain developed and committed its armed forces, it would assume an increasing share of the operational burden.

That mutual understanding worked sufficiently well in the early years that the respective high commands had been able to coordinate operations at the military level with reasonable mutual satisfaction. Even the British offensive on the Somme (1916) is best understood as reflecting the broader interests of the alliance, as opposed to a unilateral pulling of French chestnuts from the fire of Verdun (1916). Nineteen seventeen, however, strained the informal structures of alliance cooperation to the breaking point. The new British prime minister, David Lloyd George, succeeded in establishing a joint command for a combined offensive under French general Robert Nivelle. The result was not merely a defeat but a fiasco. In its aftermath the French army was shaken to the point of mutiny; the British army bled itself white in the marshes of Passchendaele (1917). Elsewhere, Russia left the war; Italy was eviscerated at Caporetto (1917); the U-boats seemed on the point of starving Britain out of the war; and Germany was clearly preparing for a major offensive of its own. In the fall and winter of 1917, again at the initiative of Lloyd George, the Allies created a Supreme War Council (SWC), including representatives of a new partner: the United States.

The SWC was essentially a political body rather than a military one. Its purpose was to coordinate Allied planning by facilitating joint consultation. Its limits became clear during the German offensive that began on 21 March 1918. Neither the British nor the French would commit the limited reserves they possessed to help the other. The British Expeditionary Force (BEF) at least entertained the possibility of retreating toward the Channel ports instead of into France. The Americans, despite General John Pershing's offer of every man and gun for the duration of the emergency, remained committed to military autonomy. In that context the appointment of Marshal Ferdinand Foch as Generalissimo of the Allied armies was accepted as a necessary emergency measure, providing at least an authority to shift reserves where they were needed, without regard for national origins. Whether the appointment became something more is the subject of the following essays.

Viewpoint:
Yes. Foch skillfully thwarted the German offensive of 1918.

As a result of his great achievement in bringing together American, Belgian, British, Italian, and French forces in 1918, Ferdinand Foch remains one of the best-loved twentieth-century soldiers of France. As a symbol of French admiration for this distinguished man, his tomb rests near Napoleon Bonaparte's under the gold dome of Les Invalides. Foch's ability to convert the disconnected Allied war efforts into a unified whole ensured the failure of the German Spring Offensives (1918) and allowed the Allies to resume their attacks. The offensives that Foch oversaw and coordinated eventually led to the November armistice. No other Allied general could have handled the job of supreme commander with as much tact and wisdom as did Foch. His appointment was a dramatic turning point in Allied fortunes.

The entry of the United States into the war in April 1917 promised to be a major turning point. American troops would, the Allies hoped, balance out German forces that were freed to come west by the collapse of the Russians. The United States would also extend financial credits to help the Allies fund an increasingly expensive war. One problem, however, loomed ominously: President Woodrow Wilson and General John Pershing insisted that the American Expeditionary Force (AEF) retain a separate identity and a completely independent chain of command. Wilson's goals were political. He wanted a starring role at the postwar peace conference. He saw a separate U.S. force as a way to extend his moral and political authority. Pershing, for his part, objected to European tactics and shuddered at the idea of American lives being wasted in frontal assaults (although in reality Pershing's tactics differed little, if at all, from those of European generals). Wilson even insisted that the United States not be called an "ally," but an "associated power."

The firm desire of the Americans to remain apart from European chains of command complicated an already difficult alliance problem. Great Britain, Belgium, France, Italy, and (until 1917) Russia had not been able to agree on any satisfactory method to join their forces into something resembling a coherent whole. As a result, the Allies were really operating several loosely coordinated and sometimes quite separate wars. The few Allied joint operations of the war had either been clearly dominated by one power, as Great Britain directed the Dardanelles campaign (1915), or had amounted to little, such as the ineffective Salonika campaign (1915). Radically different military and political agendas kept the Allies from forming the kind of synergistic coalition that might have multiplied their individual efforts.

The German attack on Caporetto (1917) took advantage of the inability of the Allies to coordinate strategy. It turned into a rout of the Italian army and threatened to knock Italy out of the war entirely. Caporetto finally woke the Allies to the need for joint action. The challenge was to find a man acceptable to all who could oversee and manage coordinated strategy. He would need to be a man of talent and experience, and he would most likely need to be French, as most of the fighting was occurring in France. On top of those qualifications, he would have to be acceptable to the British, Italian, Belgian, and American staffs.

Such men were not exactly common, but Foch fit the job description almost as if it were written exclusively for him. During the confused summer of 1914 the Twentieth Corps, commanded by Foch, had stood firm while others retreated. Foch fought hard, but he quickly gained notoriety for holding too long to outdated offensive doctrines. His 1915 and 1916 offensives gained little ground at great cost, but he nevertheless held to his prewar beliefs in the power of the offensive. He once allegedly sent a telegram reading: "My center is giving way, my right is in retreat, situation excellent. I attack." His costly attacks damaged his reputation in French military circles. When Robert Nivelle replaced Foch's close associate Joseph Joffre as commander in chief of French armies in late 1916, Foch went into semiretirement.

Without an army or corps to command, Foch turned his energies to inter-Allied relations. His skills in this area were already considerable. During the so-called race to the sea in 1914, Foch had been instrumental in coordinating French, British, and Belgian efforts. He took responsibility for enjoining the operations of all three armies during the first battle of Ypres in the fall of 1914 and remained as a kind of informal generalissimo of those forces into 1915. Because of Foch's relatively positive relations with British officers, Joffre (whose own relations with British

FOCH

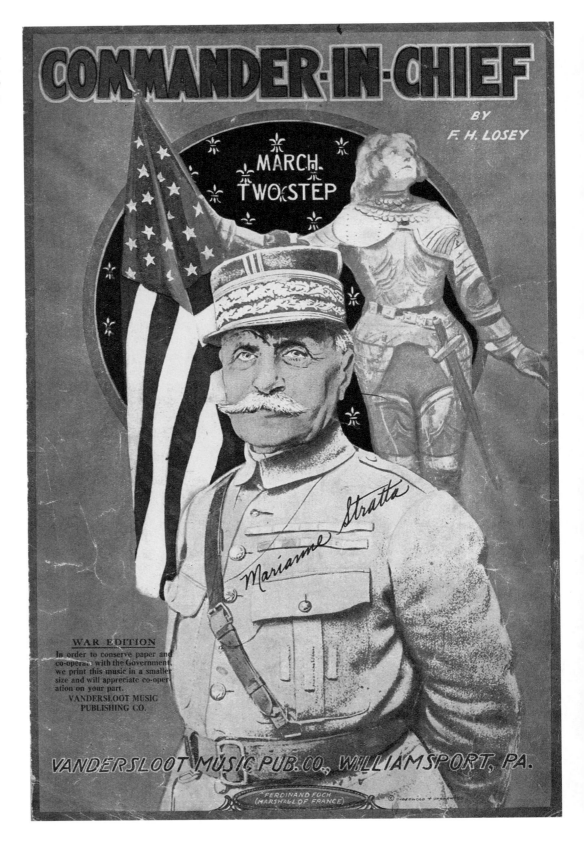

officers were much more strained) chose him to lead the French troops who participated in the disaster at Somme (1916). Even though Foch disagreed with the British plan, he maintained good relations with Field Marshal Douglas Haig's staff throughout. The operation was an unqualified failure, but the experience at least gave Foch an insight into the workings of the British high command, information that few French generals possessed.

In 1917, Foch's diplomatic skills made him ideally suited to plan for ways to help Italy in the event of a major Austro-German offensive there. That offensive came at Caporetto. Foch's planning and diplomacy resulted in a concerted relief effort that helped to bolster the Italians and prevent the defeat at Caporetto from turning into a general rout. Even before Caporetto, Foch had drawn plans for shipping a contingent of French and British units to Italy in the event of a major crisis. After the Caporetto disaster, the Italians used eight divisions of that contingent to hold their positions along the Piave River and keep Venice out of German hands. His advance work may have kept Italy in the war.

By 1918, then, Foch had experience working with all of the powers within the Allied camp. He was thus in an ideal position to take advantage of the Allies' tardy acknowledgment of their need for greater unity of command. That realization came within a few days of the start of the German Spring Offensive. Massive German gains finally scared the Allies into naming Foch the Allied generalissimo on 26 March. He had the crucial support of Field Marshal Haig, his partner from the Somme campaign, meaning that the British would agree to the plan. Even the independence-minded Americans saw the wisdom in the idea of a centralized command. General Pershing supported the idea of a centralized command and, more importantly, the appointment of Foch to fill the job. Pershing offered to place eight U.S. divisions then in France under Foch's authority, thereby greatly enhancing the generalissimo's power. On 3 April, Foch received a tremendous vote of confidence when the Allies authorized him to have full commander-in-chief powers on the Western Front.

With a centralized command, Foch had the authority to control a general reserve and he could quickly move men to deal with German attacks across the Western Front. Instead of fighting a divided foe comprised of four separate chains of command, the Germans were now up against one unified enemy for the first time in the war. Foch thereby ruined the German plan to split the British and French forces, sending the former scurrying north to the Channel ports and the latter rushing south to protect Paris. Instead, coordinated Allied armies stopped the German drive near Montdidier, about fifty miles from the outskirts of the French capital.

With a combined force, Foch also began to plan a combined counteroffensive to drive the Germans back. Foch planned and oversaw four coordinated Allied offensives at the Marne River, the Amiens salient, Flanders, and the St. Mihiel salient. Unrelenting pressure all along the lines continued into September, preventing the Germans from concentrating their few remaining reserves in any one area.

Foch, ever the diplomat, understood the national sensitivities involved in combined operations. He satisfied the desire of the Americans for a separate sector of the front and freed up fourteen U.S. divisions from the strategic reserve and gave them to Pershing, who used those forces, reconstituted into the American First Army, to score a decided (and decidedly American) victory at St. Mihiel. Foch therefore understood the value of centralization as well as the need to respect the desires and fears of national commands under his authority. His tremendous instincts for knowing when not to centralize avoided many perceived insults to national pride that might have threatened the battlefield unity he took such care to nourish.

From 1916 to 1918 Foch went from semiretirement to hero of France. He dictated armistice terms to the Germans in November and served as the chief military adviser of France at the Paris Peace Conference. That transformation was the result of Foch's tremendous performance as Allied generalissimo in 1918. No other Allied officer could have performed the job of commander in chief as skillfully as did Foch. His appointment and his subsequent success must be counted as a key turning point in Allied fortunes. His masterful control of Allied armies kept Germany out of Paris in 1918 and led to an armistice within seven months of his appointment.

–MICHAEL S. NEIBERG,
U.S. AIR FORCE ACADEMY

Viewpoint:
No. Foch was a figurehead, who never directly coordinated Allied offensive operations.

Historians have traditionally represented the appointment of French general Ferdinand Foch to the position of Supreme Allied Commander in March 1918 as a dramatic turning point in the history of the Great War. This conventional view argues that prior to Foch's appointment there was no unity of action between the French and British armies on the Western Front, or in the Allied war effort in general, and that he welded the Allied armies into a cohesive and unified fighting force, for the first time, under his command. Yet, this theory ignores two vital facts. In the first place, there had been inter-Allied cooperation on the Western Front since the earliest days of the war, and there had even been limited success in coordinating French and British operations on the Western Front with Russian operations on the Eastern Front. Although lacking the formal title, General Joseph Joffre and General Robert Nivelle had held similar positions to Foch's in the years 1914–1917, and thus Foch's appointment in 1918 was not as monumental as it is sometimes portrayed. In addition, in spite of his title, Foch had little real authority. Unlike U.S. general Dwight D. Eisenhower in World War II, for example, Foch did not plan and conduct the military campaigns. Rather, the influential and independent personalities who commanded the French, British, and American armies on the Western Front were essentially left to their own devices in terms of planning and conducting military operations. Foch coerced, advised, and provided guidance but lacked the authority to enforce his will. Thus, he had the power to persuade but not the power to command.

From the outset of the Great War, military cooperation between the Entente was of prime importance if an Allied victory was ever to be achieved. This fact was recognized by all of the Allies, and hence, from the beginning of the war until its conclusion, an attempt was made to coordinate their military activities. On the Western Front, where French, British, and Belgian forces operated alongside one another, cooperation was particularly important. The French army was the largest Allied contingent on the Western Front, overwhelmingly so during 1914–1915, and held the longest sector. Hence, the French commander in chief, beginning with General Joffre, always played a leading role in planning and conducting military operations in the West. Joffre did not wield direct power over British or Belgian forces, but their operations were nevertheless closely coordinated with his own and generally followed his lead during 1914–1915. Even the landing at Gallipoli (1915) was an international operation, as was the subsequent occupation of Salonika.

By far the largest and most grandiose inter-Allied operations planned were the Entente offensives where Joffre attempted to coordinate a Franco-British assault at the Somme (1916) with a Russian offensive on the Eastern Front. Although the unexpected German attack at Verdun (1916) upset these plans somewhat, the attacks were still carried out, with the Russians striking in June and the British and French in July. The fact that these operations were all ultimately unsuccessful belies the fact that, considering the communications tech-nology available and the widely divergent fronts on which the battles were fought, they represent an amazing degree of inter-Allied cooperation.

In 1917, following Joffre's dismissal by the French government, General Nivelle succeeded to the position of commander in chief of the French army, albeit with a slightly different title. By this time Field Marshal Douglas Haig had run afoul of British prime minister David Lloyd George, who, lacking the political support to relieve the British Expeditionary Force (BEF) commander, determined to subordinate Haig to his French counterpart. The result was the placing of the BEF under the direct control of Nivelle for the duration of the forthcoming offensive to be launched in April 1917. This appointment made Nivelle the de facto Supreme Allied Commander on the Western Front a full year before that position would be officially created. In many ways, Nivelle's power was far greater than what Joffre had wielded before him, or what Foch would wield after. British military operations were directly subordinated to Nivelle's plans when a British offensive at Arras was designed as the first stage of a general Allied assault, with the main blow being dealt by French armies further south.

The disaster that befell this joint Allied offensive, especially in the French sector, made the British high command extremely leery of ever entrusting their forces to the care of an Allied supreme commander again. The first of the great German offensives in the West that began on 21 March 1918 changed their thinking on this subject. The British were badly defeated in the opening stages of the German attack, and Haig believed that the new French commander in chief, General Philippe Pétain, was slow to provide assistance to his hard-pressed forces. It was to discuss how much French assistance could be sent to the British and how much the French would be willing to lengthen their lines that the celebrated Doullens Conference was held, at which the position of Supreme Allied Commander was created and Foch was named to the post. Yet, was this event as significant as it is sometimes portrayed?

The position of Supreme Allied Commander was not as unique as it is often described. Joffre and Nivelle had already held similar positions, although Foch was granted an actual title. Nevertheless, his authority, first to "coordinate" and later clarified to "command" Allied forces, was in many ways severely restricted. For example, Haig continued to conduct his defensive battle in the north according to his own plans, and Foch only slightly increased the number of French reserve divisions that Pétain, on his own initiative, had already begun deploying to the former British zone of operations. Although Foch's naturally optimistic and combative attitude was certainly refreshing, the dour Haig and his veteran BEF

FIGHTING AN AMERICAN BATTLE

Supreme Allied Commander Ferdinand Foch faced many challenges in holding together the Allied armies, not the least of which was how to deal with the new American contingents arrived in France. In his memoirs, he recalls working Iwith the overall commander of the American Expeditionary Force (AEF), General John Pershing:

To this appeal of the Allies to America, General Pershing very shortly took occasion to respond in an indirect but particularly expressive manner. On July 9th, at the moment when the German Eighteenth Army was launching its attacks in the direction of Compiègne, the Commander of the American Expeditionary Forces, renewing his gesture of March 28th, came to see me at Bombon. He assured me that he associated himself entirely with the common cause and that more than ever he fervently desired to see all his divisions taking part in the battle. At the same time he constituted himself the interpreter of the unanimous sentiment of the American nation which, he said, was absolutely determined to throw its whole force into the contest without counting the cost. . . .

However, the rapid growth of the American forces rendered all the more pressing General Pershing's desire to form them into an autonomous army. On July 10th he came to see me with a request to expedite as much as possible the formation into army corps of American divisions then in the French zone; he also asked me to furnish artillery for those divisions which had none, drawing it, if need be, from French units.

I was emphatic on this occasion in once more assuring General Pershing that no one desired more fervently than myself the constitution of American corps and armies, and sectors in which American troops would fight an American battle, and that my best efforts were being directed to this end. I was, indeed, firmly convinced that the soldiers of any country only give of their best when fighting under their own leaders and under their own colours. National self esteem is then engaged.

General Pershing's experience and character, moreover, were a guarantee that, whenever he might engage American troops, he would only halt after success had been achieved. Unfortunately, the lack of guns still prevented the furnishing of artillery to all the American divisions or army corps which it might have been possible to form.

Source: *Ferdinand Foch,* The Memoirs of Marshal Foch, *translated by T. Bentley Mott (Garden City, N.Y.: Doubleday, Doran, 1931), pp. 344–346.*

---

were more than capable of regaining their feet and making a solid defensive stand without need of much encouragement. At no point did Foch dictate orders directly to the British army or even indirectly through Haig. He encouraged them and urged Haig to prepare for an eventual counteroffensive, but this action was something that Haig had already determined to do. When the British finally attacked on 8 August 1918, it was according to Haig's plan and schedule, even if it did fit into Foch's overall desire for a general Allied offensive.

There is no correlation between Foch as Supreme Allied Commander in World War I and, for example, Eisenhower's role as Supreme Allied Commander in World War II. Foch did not possess the mammoth, multinational staff that Eisenhower later did and, unlike Eisenhower, did little to no actual planning of military operations. Rather, the planning and conduct of military operations was left almost entirely to Haig,

Pétain, and later General John Pershing and their respective staffs. Unlike Eisenhower, Foch never really adopted an "Allied" mind-set. Foch was instrumental in shuttling British and French reserve divisions to bolster threatened sectors during the German offensives. Yet, France and the French army remained his top priorities throughout his tenure as Supreme Allied Commander, and there is no evidence that he ever placed British or American concerns before those of his own country in the spirit of the alliance.

Perhaps the greatest overestimation of Foch's influence committed by historians is the assumption that he dictated policy for the French army during 1918. This conclusion is simply not the case. Pétain remained the recognized, and widely respected, commander of the French army throughout Foch's tenure as Supreme Allied Commander, and when the two men clashed over policy and the conduct of military operations, Foch did not always get his way. Without question, Foch had more influence over the French army than he had over the BEF, or later the American Expeditionary Forces (AEF), but even here he still did not command. It was Pétain who formulated both defensive and offensive doctrine for the French army during 1918, and it was Pétain in particular who waged the defensive battles of June–July 1918 that finally stemmed the tide of the German advance.

Of the three major armies on the Western Front, Foch probably attempted to exercise the most influence over Pershing's AEF. Pershing lacked the experience and reputation that Haig and Pétain had and therefore, theoretically at least, had the least ability to resist Foch's suggestions. Yet, Pershing repeatedly clashed with Foch over the use of American troops, timing of American operations, and other issues. At no point was Foch ever actually able to issue a direct order to the Americans and have them obey it. Rather, he suggested, argued, and cajoled but did not actually command.

This pronouncement does not mean that Foch was never able directly to influence operations on the Western Front, and some have credited him with the successful Allied counteroffensive along the Marne that marked the turning point of the 1918 campaign. Is this credit truly warranted? Although Foch was heaped with accolades for the dramatic Franco-American counterattack of 18 July 1918 against the Germans in the Aisne-Marne pocket—indeed, would win his marshal's baton for it—in fact, Pétain played a major role in planning and executing the attack. It is true that Foch overruled Pétain when the latter wished to delay the counteroffensive until the Germans were more firmly tied down along the Marne, and some have hailed this decision as indicative of Foch's aggressiveness. Indeed, this moment represented one of the few times that Foch was able to use his authority as Supreme Allied Commander to countermand Pétain's orders, but in this case Foch's direct action may have actually caused the attack to miscarry. Foch's decision to launch the attack prematurely has been cited as a primary reason for the failure of the counteroffensive to cut off and destroy the German armies in the pocket, instead of merely pushing them back, which is what actually occurred. Although the Second Battle of the Marne was unquestionably a success, had Pétain's plan been followed it could have been a truly decisive victory that tore open the entire front, rather than the local tactical success that it turned out to be.

Foch coordinated the launching of simultaneous offensives on 26 September 1918 by the French, British, and American armies, but again the operations themselves were planned and executed by the army commanders, not Foch. In terms of his coordination of the attacks, Foch did nothing more than Joffre or Nivelle had done before him. While these operations were overwhelmingly more successful than previous Allied offensives, this success was due more to the exhausted state of the German army, the prolific use of armor by the Allied armies, and the good leadership displayed by Haig, Pétain, and Pershing, rather than to Foch's leadership as supreme commander. In fact, Foch was not directly involved in overseeing any of these offensives, including the French attack. Thus, Foch was more a symbol of Allied cooperation than an actual supreme commander.

–ROBERT B. BRUCE,
SAM HOUSTON STATE UNIVERSITY

References

Jean Autin, *Foch, ou, le Triomphe de la Volonté* (Paris: Perrin, 1987).

Ferdinand Foch, *Memoirs of Marshal Foch,* translated by T. Bentley Mott (New York: Doubleday, Doran, 1931).

Liddell Hart, *Foch, the Man of Orleans* (London: Eyre & Spottiswoode, 1931).

T. M. Hunter, "Foch and Eisenhower: A Study in Allied Supreme Command," *Army Quarterly,* 87 (1963): 33–52.

André Charles Victor Laffargue, *Foch et la Bataille de 1918* (Paris: Arthaud, 1967).

Auguste Marie Emile Laure, *Le Commandement en Chef des Armées Françaises du 15 mai 1917 a l'armistice* (Paris: Editions Berger-Levrault, 1937).

Michael Neiberg, *Foch: Supreme Allied Commander of World War I* (Dulles, Va.: Brassey's, forthcoming).

Guy Pedroncini, "Le Commandement Unique sur le Front Occidental en 1918," *Guerres Mondiales et Conflits Contemporains,* 42 (1992): 31–36.

Pedroncini, *Pétain: Géneral en Chef, 1917–1918* (Paris: Presses Universitaires de France, 1974).

Donald Smythe, *Pershing: General of the Armies* (Bloomington: Indiana University Press, 1986).

John Terraine, *Douglas Haig: The Educated Soldier* (London: Hutchinson, 1963).

David F. Trask, *The AEF and Coalition Warmaking, 1917–1918* (Lawrence: University Press of Kansas, 1993).

FOCH

FRENCH AFRICAN TROOPS

Did the French use of African troops on the Western Front constitute imperialist exploitation?

Viewpoint: Yes. The French army considered African troops as essentially cannon fodder, whose performance did nothing to modify the traditional imperial systems of rule and control.

Viewpoint: No. The French African soldiers were regarded as elite shock troops, and they played an increasingly important role in the war effort as regular manpower reserves declined.

French imperialism as it developed during the nineteenth century stressed increasingly the significance of direct acculturation and assimilation. Under the Third Republic, French expansion was best justified by bringing the benefits of French culture and civilization to peoples deprived of them. Eventually the colonies—or some of them, such as the West Indian islands of Guadeloupe and Martinique or the "Four Communes" of Senegal—might expect to become part of "legal France" itself. Under the Third Republic even Algeria was increasingly integrated into metropolitan administrative and political systems.

A logical extension of that vision was the integration of non-French peoples into the defense of a nation in the process of becoming theirs by cultural ascription. France had recruited volunteers in Algeria since the 1830s and had employed the elite *Tirailleurs Algeriens* in the Crimea, Italy, and finally France, against the Germans in 1870. By the turn of the century a growing systematic imbalance between the populations of France and Germany led the French army to consider seriously turning to the empire for large-scale contributions of manpower. The number of Algerian battalions was steadily increased, with conscription being introduced for Muslims in 1912. Colonel Charles Mangin called for a *Force Noire* (black army) to be raised in sub-Saharan French colonies, among the peoples lumped together as "Senegalese." The number of Africans available in 1914 was, however, still limited—fewer than a hundred thousand—and many of those individuals were engaged in the pacification of Morocco.

French mobilization plans nevertheless called for the immediate dispatch of North African battalions across the Mediterranean. As the Marne campaign (1914) progressed, they were joined by the Senegalese and by a small contingent of Moroccans. (One of the war's small ironies is that the Moroccan Division, arguably the best and certainly the most famous division in the French army, included no Moroccans in its ranks. It was composed of Tunisian and Algerian Muslims, Zouaves from France and the European communities of North Africa, and a regiment of the Foreign Legion.)

The Africans were generally well regarded as soldiers. The North African divisions were regularly used as shock troops. The sub-Saharan "Senegalese" had a more-mixed operational history, but after the abortive offensives of 1917 they too found a place as assault troops, attached by battalions to metropolitan divisions for specific operations.

Doubts and limits persisted. Senegalese units were gradually "whitened" as Frenchmen were assigned or attached to handle communications and operate weapons, such as machine guns and mortars, considered too complex for "natives"—or too dangerous to entrust to them. Sub-Saharan African troops were also considered badly adapted to the winters of northeastern France, and whenever possible, were sent south for labor duties until the weather changed. On the whole, however, the steady decline in the number of European Frenchmen available for the trenches led to a corresponding "darkening" of the army. An increasing number of divisions consisted of one North African and two metropolitan regiments. Had the war persisted into 1919, discussions were afoot to reorganize the entire army on a similar basis, using Senegalese as well as North African formations.

The demand for men for the army strained the French colonial system to its limits. Revolts broke out in Algeria and western Africa over recruitment techniques that were difficult to distinguish from random impressment. The French government was forced to make offers and promises that proved difficult to implement in postwar years. Nevertheless, around a half million Africans served during World War I under French colors, most of them on French soil. It was an unprecedented effort by all participants—one whose consequences still persist.

Viewpoint:
Yes. The French army considered African troops as essentially cannon fodder, whose performance did nothing to modify the traditional imperial systems of rule and control.

The "Doctrine of World Empires" goes back to the beginnings of the imperialist movement. In *Etude sur les colonies et la colonisation au regard de la France* (1877) Pierre Raboisson argued that there had never been a great power without colonies. Colonial expansion by France was influenced by the need to regain prestige. Raboisson asserted that France had to pursue a colonial policy in order to compete with the other great powers. French perceptions of their national history served to reinforce this attitude. Resentment over the loss of French Canada and French India in the eighteenth century set off a paranoiac stance toward Britain. It became that much more important to acquire, and make French, areas in Africa and Asia. This desire was strengthened by the disaster of 1870 when Germany defeated France. Germany emerged as the strongest new political, economic, and colonial power in Europe; it outpaced France in industrial development, population size, and birthrate. The low French birthrate and production capabilities compared to Great Britain and Germany meant that it was less able to meet the needs of continual colonial expansion. Some observers worried that France stood in danger of being unable to produce sufficient soldiers to match the German army should another war occur.

Despite these worries colonialism was a source of fierce debate in France. According to Robert Aldrich, in *Greater France: A History of French Overseas Expansion* (1996), "colonial pro-moters faced a long and uphill battle to convince a skeptical political class and wider electorate of the merits of spending money, risking lives and diverting resources to distant and sometimes unpromising colonies." Governments saw colonies as pawns on the chessboard of diplomacy and did not see in them any intrinsic merits. However, a particularly persuasive argument that even most anticolonialists found compelling was the fighting potential of colonial troops. Additionally, the empire could be a training ground for the French army and navy. Europeans still thought of military campaigns as heroic, military officers as noble, and the use of arms as justified in international conflict.

There had been a growing glorification of war and the spreading notion of its inevitability in the two decades before 1914. In 1899 publicist Harold F. Wyatt described war as the only means, which history had confirmed many times, by which strong nations had replaced weaker ones. Social Darwinist ideas influenced some politicians to believe in the superiority of some races over others. English politician Benjamin Disraeli once said, "All is race: there is no other truth." French premier Jules Ferry stated in his great speech of 28 July 1885, in which he whitewashed French colonial policy: "It must be openly said that the superior races have rights over the inferior races." Some French thinkers, such as Georges Vacher de Lapouge, even predicted that following a period of smaller wars, there would be a great racial war: "Then we will see the yellow race, the white race, the black race at one another's throats." As the philosophical ideas and realities of French colonial expansion converged, military officers in colonial administrations came to see colonies as fiefs to be conquered and controlled.

French officials saw colonial troops as the best agents of imperialism; that the military dimension was critical for the defense of the *metropole*, although not yet permanently sta-

tioned in France. The relationship of Paris to its colonial subjects was a direct chain of command in true military fashion. In fact, it has been argued quite convincingly that the military generals involved in African campaigns had their own agenda. Navy and army officers usually took command of colonies from the initial *prise de possession* (taking of possession) until pacification was complete. Even after civilian governments were in place, a military system of administration was the model for the 118 *cercles* who ruled over day-to-day affairs. In the classic study *France, Soldiers, and Africa* (1988) Anthony Clayton argues "that the military retained very great influence on policy-making and much political leverage, on occasions sufficient to assist in undermining the position of ministers. The overall impact of the French African military and its mystique in the years leading up to 1914 was an enormously important contribution to the national unity and self-respect with which France went to war."

In order to accomplish the goals of conquest, France used slaves, war captives, and a variety of mercenaries. Only France brought about an intense militarization of its African colonies. Yet, many French commanders had a poor opinion of African soldiers. One senior officer argued that African troops needed five months of training in order to spend the rest of the year on campaign. While these troops were, in his opinion, slow to learn and possessed poor memories, their leaders suffered from "weakness of character." Regardless of the negative reputations of

African soldiers during the period of conquest, French officials were forced to learn a basic axiom of military force: that it required more soldiers to occupy conquered territory than it had to win it initially. Despite assurances of French officer Charles Mangin, advocate of the Black Army, that West Africa was easily able to supply military manpower, the shortage of men continued to be a problem.

Mangin's campaign for a Black African army made headway in the years immediately prior to 1914. In *La Force Noire* (1910) he argued for the creation of an army recruited in the black African colonies of France; he believed military service might civilize the Africans and could save France. Moreover, under a government plan that made Blaise Diagne, a black African deputy from Senegal, High Commissioner for Recruitment in Africa, provision was made for the systematic recruitment of Africans. In 1912 a law was passed by Governor-General William Ponty that allowed for partial conscription in West Africa to meet future French military commitments. Propaganda campaigns, largely supported by colonial associations and political lobbies, supported this effort. On the basis of this law 170,000 black Africans served in the *Tirailleurs Sénégalais* during World War I.

When hostilities broke out in November 1914 the French armies in Europe lacked the manpower to defend national interests. French military commanders had made plans for the rapid development of African troops in Europe.

French African troops charging a German position at Soissons, France, in 1914

(postcard in scrapbook, Joseph M. Bruccoli Great War Collection, Thomas Cooper Library, University of South Carolina)

Initially, subject peoples were called upon to defend the empire everywhere, and they responded in surprising numbers. As during its period of conquest and pacification in Africa (1886–1905), France began heavy recruitment of African soldiers for the *Tirailleurs Sénégalais*, which had been created in 1857 by Governor Louis Faidherbe. As demands for military quotas increased, however, the Africans resisted. The French quickly moved to reinstitute conscription to meet the voracious demands of military units bereft of recruits at home. Manpower needs led French authorities to make heavy demands on the populations of North and West Africa. According to Clayton, "Even though the two greatest names in France's 1914–18 Army, Foch and Pétain, were not African generals, and even though criticism was sometimes expressed of the qualities of some of the West African troops, the African regiments graduated from being primarily a potential asset to an accepted indispensability."

French officials in West Africa relied on tried and true methods of labor recruitment and military organization. According to Raymond Betts in *Tricouleur: The French Overseas Empire* (1978), because of labor shortages "France tolerated the principle of forced labor. In the initial phases of colonization, the common social mechanism was the *corvée,* an institution that consisted of compulsory labor, of a set number of days, on the construction and repair of public-works projects, notably roads and railroads. It was the quickest and most effective device by which to construct the 'infrastructure' without which the market system could not function." Colonial administrators had been under immense pressure to keep the supply of labor flowing to the business interests of concessionary companies and private investors. Eventually the *corvée* was abolished or, more accurately, transmuted into a poll or head tax. In fact, labor impressment continued in one form or another to the end of World War II (1945).

The military was one of the largest employers of men in the empire. Recruitment policies mirrored those of labor organizations hired by French corporations. In fact, they were often in competition for young, healthy males. The typical soldier was a physically fit peasant in his twenties—who agreed to serve for five or six years. African soldiers received a salary (in 1910) that was only half of the daily wages of a laborer, and a quarter of their earnings were withheld until their discharge. Volunteers sometimes received a bonus, however, and *Tirailleurs Sénégalais* gained an exemption from the *capitation* and *corvée;* they received a half-pension after fifteen years' service and a full pension after twenty-five years' service.

Although the original intention was to use black African troops in the colonies in order to allow French soldiers stationed there to serve in Europe in a time of national emergency, units of the *Force Noire* served in large numbers in France during the world war. Recruitment often amounted to impressment, as many French authorities were willing to acknowledge; but the action was justified as a "blood price." In the words of A. Messimy, a French parliamentarian writing on the matter in 1909, "Africa has cost us enormous amounts of gold, thousands of soldiers, and seas of blood. We don't expect to get the gold back. But the men and blood must be returned by Africa to us with heavy interest." In 1914 the interests of Africans were in no case given a serious consideration. Always in the background was the assumption that the goal was to be one in which the colony contributed the maximum to French needs in some form. The utilitarian concept was never absent.

Almost from the start of World War I to the Armistice (1918), the *Tirailleurs* were continuously in action. When well-trained and well-led, in reasonable terrain, and not crippled by the west European or Turkish winter, the *Tirailleurs* fought as well as any troops. Those with Moroccan, or later Dardanelles, experience performed especially well, according to Clayton. However, these conditions had to be met for them to do their best, and conditions were often unfavorable; therefore, the performance of African troops was indifferent or poor, which was scarcely surprising in view of the nature of Western Front fighting—bombardments, machine-gun fire, trenches, and mud. From the outset, Germany was outraged that France had brought its black battalions to the front, charging that this action was a serious violation of international law. Great Britain also disagreed with the use of Africans on the Western Front. It was one thing to use native troops in Africa, the British complained, but blacks should not be armed in "white men's wars." In an article published in *Current History Magazine,* Melvin E. Page provides a glimpse into European attitudes with this account by a German officer:

At 7.15 in the morning the French attacked. The black Senegal negroes, France's cattle for the shambles . . . A gas attack! . . . they rushed closer, flickering and sometimes disappearing in their cloud . . . Strong, wild fellows, their log-like, fat, black skulls wrapped in pieces of dirty rags. Showing their grinning teeth like panthers, with their bellies drawn in and their necks stretched forward. Some with bayonets on their rifles. Many armed only with knives. Monsters all, in their confused hatred . . . The black cloud halted, wavered, closed its ranks—and rolled nearer and nearer, irresistible, crushing, devastating.

German newspapers contributed significantly to the perception that Africans were ruthless savages who resorted to barbarism on the battlefield and who took no prisoners. The reality, however, is that the mortality rate of African soldiers was three times that of European troops; more than thirty-three thousand black Africans died in the war, and many other *indigines* suffered injuries that left them incapacitated. Clayton explains that the higher casualty rate was partially the result of the extraordinary racialist view held by Mangin and others that the African Negro's less-developed nervous system rendered him impervious to anticipatory anxiety and was therefore only frightened a little, so Senegalais battalions should be used in an assault shock role. Mangin stated: "The nervous system of the black man is much less developed than that of the white. All surgeons have observed how impassive the black is under the knife." Another cause was the successes of the best prewar units that led French officers to believe hurriedly recruited and trained wartime units could all do the same job in similar terrain.

African troops participated in many of the major campaigns of the war including one of the ugliest debacles of the Allies at Chemin des Dames (1917). For the Senegalais the offensive was perhaps the most appalling experience of the war: poorly trained battalions were poured into the attack in conditions of unusual cold and mud; with inadequate artillery preparation; and with shortages of grenades, ammunition, food, and water. Several units broke under the strain. Casualties were exceptionally severe—6,300 out of 25,000 deployed; critics of Mangin accused him of butchery, and a legend that France deliberately used Africans as cannon fodder was born. By the end of the war, many Europeans were appalled at African casualties and protested "against the barbarism and the duplicity" of French officials whose military policies made "use of black human cannon fodder."

After the war certain Senegalais battalions, as part of Mangin's Tenth Army, were sent to Germany for occupation duties, to the bitter resentment of the Germans, who claimed the selection of African troops was a deliberate racial affront. The Germans named these soldiers *die schwarze Schande* (the black shame), thus reinforcing racialist views of the population. On demobilization in West Africa, African survivors returned to their villages or towns where they sought jobs as policemen, forest guards, postmen, male nurses, and chauffeurs. The French army continued the policy of conscription in West Africa, and African soldiers played a significant role in World War II. It is obvious that the French did nothing to modify their traditional imperialistic views regarding the role of the colonies and their need to provide military manpower in defense of the *metropole*. However, the *Tirailleurs Sénégalais* were not merely cannon fodder in the terrible wastage of war. As they had in the previous conflict, they distinguished themselves both as fighting units and individuals, becoming an integral part of the eventual Allied victory in 1945. On the eve of independence in the 1960s, the black African colonies of France counted 96,000 veterans of the *Tirailleurs Sénégalais*.

–DEBORAH A. SCHMITT,
U.S. AIR FORCE ACADEMY

Viewpoint:
No. The French African soldiers were regarded as elite shock troops, and they played an increasingly important role in the war effort as regular manpower reserves declined.

The French use of colonial soldiers from their overseas empire during World War I has always been a subject of great controversy. In the years after the war some charged that racist French generals had no regard for these non-white troops as human beings and had callously used native contingents as nothing more than cannon fodder. Charges of past historical abuse of colonial forces by the French army, with the Great War being the most popularly cited reference, surfaced again during the wars of decolonization in Indochina and Algeria, when such accusations served the political agenda of antiwar elements inside France. Thus, the notion that native troops were exploited and ruthlessly sacrificed by their white officers during the Great War became a fixture in the historiographic landscape of the French experience in that conflict.

Yet, these arguments ignore the fact that the French army was historically in the forefront of treating their colonial troops as the equal of their counterparts from metropolitan France. At a time when, for example, most American officers did not believe that black soldiers were capable of serving in combat, the French considered their *Tirailleurs Sénégalais* and North African Zouaves to be elite units. Without question, the right to serve in combat has always been viewed as a mark of equality, both in France and elsewhere, and the fact that native troops served in combat alongside soldiers from metropolitan France is a hallmark of equality and not racism. The French colonial units took heavy casualties in battle, but what combat unit did not suffer high casualties in the Great War? There is absolutely no evidence that they suffered a higher percentage of casualties than comparable combat units from metropolitan France.

In assessing the service of colonial troops during the Great War, it must be recalled that throughout its long and illustrious history, the French army has contained foreign contingents. The famous Irish "Wild Geese," as well as soldiers from various German states, served in the French army during the seventeenth and eighteenth centuries. Under Emperor Napoleon I *La Grande Armée* was transformed into a truly international force as large numbers of foreign contingents from throughout Europe served. Napoleon also introduced the first North African unit to the French army when he made the famous Mamelukes part of the Imperial Guard Cavalry and also had a Mameluke serve as his personal bodyguard. The first widespread use of nonwhite soldiers in the French army occurred during the conquest of Algeria, which began in 1830, and by the Second Empire (1848–1870) formations such as the Zouaves and *Chasseurs d'Afrique* became elite formations in the armies of Napoleon III. These colonial troops, commanded by French officers, covered themselves in glory in the Crimea and Italy in the 1850s. In an age not noted for positive attitudes toward indigenous peoples, the various African formations became renowned throughout the world for their skill and ferocity in combat. Indeed, consider the fact that in the American Civil War (1861–1865) there were many "Zouave" regiments in the armies. The irony of Confederates copying the dress and nomenclature of a unit made up of North Africans is revealing of how heroic combat service by a racial minority can influence the popular image of their race.

The defeat of France in the Franco-German War (1870–1871) opened up fresh opportunities for colonial troops. As France sought to assuage the loss of Alsace and Lorraine by expanding its overseas empire in Africa and Asia, native contingents proved a vital component in these new wars of conquest. In fact, approximately one-third of the French colonial army in the late nineteenth century was composed of native troops. These contingents were usually provided as part of an agreement made between the French and a local chieftain. Such military alliances between France and the various indigenous peoples of Africa and Asia were mutually beneficial, at least to an extent. While the indigenous peoples provided military manpower to the French army and also abdicated their political sovereignty, French military power proved a valuable ally in defeating intertribal enemies, and the natives also received a tremendous amount of other forms of aid. French culture and civilization arrived with their soldiers and thus began the integration of millions of people into a modern global society, for all the good and bad that such a transformation wrought upon them.

In the years leading up to the Great War, the increasingly hostile German Empire possessed a much larger population than France. The booming German and sluggish French birthrates—a trend that continued throughout the final decades of the nineteenth century—increasingly exacerbated this situation. By the early 1900s it was obvious to French military planners that in the inevitable coming conflict between the two nations, France would be at a severe disadvantage in terms of the number of men it could place under arms. Although the French government attempted to address the issue through such expedients as extending the length of compulsory military service, these reforms only scratched the surface of the problem.

Colonel Charles Mangin, a veteran of several campaigns in Africa, offered a more radical suggestion. Mangin had fought both with and against indigenous peoples in Africa, and this experience taught him that the warriors of these tribes made fine soldiers. In his book *La Force Noire* (1910) Mangin argued that the solution to the French manpower problem lay in mobilizing vast numbers of natives in North Africa and West Africa. Mangin envisioned a colonial army of more than one million men that would take its place alongside the French army and tip the balance in favor of France in the coming war. Mangin's ideas were highly controversial and soon fell victim to opponents from all sides of the political spectrum. Some politicians charged that conscription of natives for use in a European war violated international agreements, while French colonists in potentially volatile areas of the empire were concerned about the long-term effects that arming and training the indigenous population for war would have. These critics feared that such an action would boomerang by providing radical leaders to native resistance movements. Mangin had some support, mainly from French soldiers who had served overseas, but they were unable to overcome political opposition to the program and only limited numbers of colonial troops were serving when war came in 1914.

Although limited in number, the colonial troops once more proved their value on the battlefield. The performance of the *Tirailleurs Algeriens,* the Turcos, in particular in the opening campaigns of World War I, fully lived up to the legacy of their historic past. As casualties for the French army mounted at a horrifying rate throughout 1914–1915, French policymakers began to rethink their previous attitude toward colonial military service. The first steps toward utilization of colonial manpower came when the French conscripted workers from colonies in Indochina to serve in labor battalions. This unarguably exploitative system offered little-to-no recognition or reward for brutally hard work. Yet, by 1916 the French army, spurred on by former colonial officers such as Joseph Joffre and Joseph Gallieni, who now occupied positions of great power and influence, began to take positive strides toward the use of colonial troops in a combat role.

France began large-scale use of colonial troops as combat soldiers in early 1916, by which time the French had suffered more than two million casualties. In that year also the final available Frenchman mustered into military service as the class of 1917 was called to the colors a year early. Such facts bear stark testimony to the level of sacrifice France had already made before the decision to begin widespread use of colonials as combat troops. In the Great War, death came for all regardless of race or ethnicity, and far more soldiers from metropolitan France lost their lives than did those from the overseas colonies.

The irony of criticism leveled against the French for utilizing colonial troops in battle is that the glory and honor of military service lay in active service at the front. While combat duty was infinitely more hazardous than manual labor, it also offered colonial soldiers the promise of promotion, recognition of valor and service, and the opportunity to be seen as equals by the French. It would be on the battlefield, and not as road-repair crews, where colonials could find equality. Thus, it was through combat service that the popular image of colonials changed from one of brutes fit for nothing but swinging a pick to one of fierce warriors fighting for the glory and honor of France.

French colonial troops participated in large numbers in the battles of Verdun (1916) and the Somme (1916) and quickly established a reputation for excellence and ferocity in combat. Certain colonial units stood out, such as the famous *Régiment d'Infanterie Coloniale du Maroc* (RICM), which emerged as an elite unit in the French army. Composed originally of metropolitan Frenchmen who volunteered for colonial service, this regiment became one of the most decorated French units of the entire war. Its regimental standard, preserved and displayed in the *Musée de l'Armée* (Museum of the Army) in Paris, is covered with battle streamers and decorations from virtually every major engagement. Yet, of all the battles listed on the standard the one of which the regiment was most proud is denoted as "Verdun-Douaumont."

Verdun remains a mystical name to the French army. For France it was the great battle of the Great War and, while certain historians have been less than kind in their appraisal of the

---

DEATH OF A SENEGALESE SOLDIER

In his memoirs, French soldier Henri de Lécluse, Comte de Trévoëdal, recalls the death in 1917 of the Senegalese soldier Badji-Djendo, who died of tuberculosis:

A year ago, in Dakar, he embarked, free and happy, with so many good friends on the big steamship which took them to this magical country, France, and this intoxicating life, the War! Since then, what recollections have filled his memory which he never will retell! The landing in Bordeaux on platforms swarming like anthills, the crossing of France and its wonderful surprises at every turn in the road, then the first contact with the enemy, the bayonet charge across a hurricane of iron and fire, followed by the horrible war of holes, to which it was so hard to get used, the dismal guard duty in the night and in the mud, the rough winter of the Argonne where so many Africans contracted the germs of this sickness which was to mow them down by the hundreds, and all at once, the waning strength, the hoarse cough tearing lungs, the fever which ate at you slowly, and Death which comes to reclaim its prey, all despite the science of doctors and the care of the good women of the Red-Cross. . . . In vain the black man came, as so many of his compatriots, to ask for the pure air of Arcachon to chase from his chest the awful pain which gnawed at it. . . . Following a monotonous rhythm, his large, black head rolled back and forth from one side to the other of the pillow, and his emaciated hands seemed to claw at the white sheet, with the mechanical motion of one who was about to die. . . .

Poor innocent victim of the Great War, you came to offer us your life, loyally, almost happily, perhaps without really understanding why! We had taught you that it was necessary to live and die for a flag of the country of your leaders. You did not question further. The least you deserved, as a brave soldier, was to fall facing the enemy on the battlefield. . . . But your sacrifice was even greater, the most painful of all for a warrior like you: disease, suffering, slow death without glory. With the same resignation of your countrymen, you have accepted it without complaint.

Badji-Djendo, humble black rifleman, France thanks you and blesses you! Its great soul hovers above your death bed and will watch over you at the edge of your tomb. . . . Sleep in peace in the bosom of this new homeland which you barely got to know and for which you gave your life!

Source: Henri de Lécluse, Comrades in Arms: The World War I Memoir of Captain Henri de Lécluse, Comte de Trévoëdal, *edited by Roy E. Sandstrom, translated by Jacques F. Dubois (Kent, Ohio & London: Kent State University Press, 1998), pp. 174–175.*

---

outcome, it was widely viewed at the time as a victory that surpassed even that of the Marne. The focal point of much of the fighting was Fort Douaumont, which was lost to the Germans in the opening days of the battle and became the scene of desperate fighting as the French sought to retake it during several offensives in the months that followed. On 24 October 1916, while under the overall command of the great champion of colonial troops, Mangin, the French launched one more attack against the fort with a force heavily beefed up with colonial troops. This time the French broke through, and the colonial soldiers of the RICM stormed Fort Douaumont and thus sealed a great victory for France. Accolades were heaped upon the regiment by the senior military leadership and by exultant politicians. It was the culminating moment of the battle and arguably the greatest feat of arms by French colonial troops in the war. It is highly significant that in the greatest battle France fought in the war, it was their colonial troops that delivered the coup de grace to the Germans. That North Africans, as well as other colonial troops, shared in the "glory and the misery" that was Verdun is testified to by the thousands of graves marked by crescents in the cemetery outside the famous Ossuaire near Douaumont. Yet, it would be false to presume that these colonial troops had been callously sacrificed because of their ethnicity. There are far more crosses than crescents displayed in the military cemeteries of Verdun, crosses that mark the graves of the conscripted *poilus* (frontline soldier) from metropolitan France

By 1917 colonial troops were an integral part of the French army and were renowned for their ferocity in battle. That year combat units from sub-Saharan Africa were widely introduced into the French army, and these black troops soon gained a formidable reputation. They were known to be ruthlessly aggressive in the attack, and it was rumored that the Germans were terrified of them. Although Senegalais units fared poorly in the Nivelle Offensive (April 1917)—caused by many factors, not the least of which was the abysmal weather, snow mixed with freezing rain, for which they were not properly acclimatized—in later battles they performed magnificently, most notably during the Second Battle of the Marne (July 1918).

The argument that natives were exploited for military service belies the fact that they came from tribes in French West Africa where the highest expression of manhood was to become a great warrior. Military service, whether in inter-tribal warfare in Africa or with the French army on the Western Front, was the road to glory and social advancement not only within the aegis of the French Republic and its empire but also within the individual's own tribe. It would thus be wrong to view these men as helpless victims rather than the warriors that they believed themselves to be. Colonial soldiers of the French army were an elite force that for more than a century fought and died for France. Combat duty was deemed by most colonials to be an honor and an opportunity to advance themselves within their own society as well as that of France. Thus, their military service in the Great War was another proud link in a legacy of valor and honor expressed in the profession of arms. Combat service not only affirmed their own identity as warriors but also served to create and enhance this view in the eyes of the French. This positive image of colonials resulted in a desire by the French to recognize and reward their sacrifice and thus led to political and social reforms within the empire in the postwar era that enhanced the political and social status of colonials.

–ROBERT B. BRUCE, SAM HOUSTON
STATE UNIVERSITY

References

Robert Aldrich, *Greater France: A History of French Overseas Expansion* (Basingstoke, U.K.: Macmillan, 1996; New York: St. Martin's Press, 1996).

Winfried Baumgart, *Imperialism: The Idea and Reality of British and French Colonial Expansion, 1880–1914,* translated by Baumgart and Ben V. Mast, revised edition (New York: Oxford University Press, 1982).

Raymond Betts, *Tricouleur: The French Overseas Empire* (London: Gordon & Cremonesi, 1978).

Anthony Clayton, *France, Soldiers, and Africa* (London & New York: Brassey's Defence Publishers, 1988).

Alain Denizot, *Verdun, 1914–1918* (Paris: Nouvelles Editions Latines, 1996).

Myron Echenberg, *Colonial Conscripts: The Tirailleurs Sénégalais in French West Africa, 1857–1960* (Portsmouth, N.H.: Heinemann, 1991; London: Currey, 1991).

Charles Mangin, *La Force Noire* (Paris: Hachette, 1910).

Louis-Eugene Mangin, *Le Général Mangin* (Paris: Lanore, 1986).

Ministère de la Guerre, *Les Armées françaises d'outre-mer, les grands soldats coloniaux* (Paris: Imprimerie Nationale, 1931).

Melvin E. Page, ed., *Africa and the First World War* (London: Macmillan, 1987; New York: St Martin's Press, 1987).

Douglas Porch, *The March to the Marne: The French Army, 1871–1914* (Cambridge & New York: Cambridge University Press, 1981).

GERMAN COLLAPSE

Was the surrender of Germany in 1918 a consequence of a decisive military defeat?

Viewpoint: Yes. The German Army lost the war on the battlefield.

Viewpoint: No. Germany surrendered because military leaders recognized that German society could not endure wartime conditions any longer.

Modern conscript armies are held together by combinations of compulsion, patriotism, and ideology. Underlying these factors is an implied contract between the soldier and the system. When the nature or conduct of a particular conflict breaks that contract, soldiers are likely to respond negatively.

Recent writing on World War I Germany stresses the importance of the relationship between front and home, military and civil society, in eroding the will of the nation to continue the struggle in 1918. Germany, however, had not yet become a single entity for waging total war. The German army of 1914, like its society, was accustomed to living well. That officers enjoyed certain privileges was tolerable as long as the stew contained meat and a soldier could enjoy a regular cigar, a mug of beer, and a shot of schnapps. As the good things in life, from bread to toilet paper, grew scarcer and coarser, the inequalities of a caste/class society—once taken for granted—became less and less bearable. Words such as "outrage" and "injustice" appeared on an increasing number of latrine walls—and in off-duty gripe sessions and letters home.

The conduct of the High Command in the 1918 offensive was a major step toward the final crisis. Pursuit of temporarily defeated enemies periodically ceased while German units looted dugouts and supply dumps of items they had not seen in months or years. As the "Front Hogs" realized just how well-off their opponents were, morale began to sink past the point of restoration. The new German assault tactics, moreover, did little in the long run to shorten casualty lists. By the time of the great Allied counterattacks in July and August, German combat units were burned out. Between July and November almost a million more men were lost in combat. Hundreds of thousands, undernourished and exhausted, were prostrated by influenza.

Wilhelm Deist describes the result as a "camouflaged strike," with the "proletariat" of the German war machine throwing down their tools in a Marxist model of behavior. One might refer as well to Robert Darnton's model of preindustrial protest: challenging a system by defying its norms. The rear areas contained increasing numbers of soldiers who had drifted away from the war. The will to enforce more than minimum levels of discipline evaporated. By November 1918 the German High Command could count no more than a dozen or so of its divisions as able and willing to fight anyone.

To speak of a "strike" is to minimize the emotional factors, especially the sense of betrayal, that accompanied the dissolution. One might be better advised to talk of alienated affection. Disaffected soldiers were poor material for zealots of the Left or the Right. Their mind-set was not the stuff of revolution. It did, however, stop a war. The Imperial German Army ended its existence with a collective sigh of relief. Simultaneously the Reich it served ended its days with a whimper.

Viewpoint:
Yes. The German Army lost the war on the battlefield.

On 1 October 1918, in the aftermath of the shattering of the Hindenburg Line by the Allies, the final defensive line of the German army on the Western Front, General Erich Ludendorff held a conference of his staff officers. He informed them that Germany could no longer win the war. Bulgaria had already capitulated, the Ottoman Empire was on its last legs, and on the Italian Front the Austrian army was about to collapse. Moreover, fresh U.S. troops continued to arrive at French ports in the tens of thousands, while the German soldier was exhausted and no longer able to resist the relentless blows of the British, French, Belgian, and American forces.

The purpose of the meeting, however, was not to find a military solution to the situation. Instead, Ludendorff used it to begin the process of shifting the blame for the debacle Germany faced away from the army and onto other areas of society. Holger H. Herwig, in *The First World War: Germany and Austria-Hungary, 1914–1918* (1997), has observed that Ludendorff's goal was not to find a way to improve the position of Germany as a whole but to save the army from a catastrophic defeat that would see its complete destruction. This meeting, Herwig continues, was the origin of the "stab in the back myth" or the *Dolchstosslegende*. The next day Ludendorff dispatched a subordinate to Berlin with instructions to tell the government that the war was lost.

A year after the surrender of Germany its commander of the army, Field Marshall Paul von Hindenburg, appeared before a government inquiry on unrestricted submarine warfare. Instead of focusing on the U-boat campaign, he delivered an address in which he laid blame for the loss of the war on the home front, which "stabbed" the frontline soldier "in the back." A domestic conspiracy of Marxists, Socialists, and Jews, he asserted, had undermined the national war effort and betrayed the German soldier. In effect, the German army bore no responsibility for the defeat, nor had it failed on the battlefield. His testimony was a shameless, but nonetheless effective, stratagem for the preservation of the status of the German Army and its existence as a force within the postwar state.

Ludendorff and Hindenburg's "stab in the back" defense was nothing more than a self-serving creation that had no basis in the reality of the performance of the German army in the conflict. The German army lost the war because its leaders failed to understand the requirements of waging battle on the Western Front.

The German army not only failed to win the war but actively contributed to its defeat through its pursuit of poor policies. Germany committed too many strategic and operational mistakes. It is necessary to consider only those deficiencies associated with the critical campaign of early 1918. At that point Germany enjoyed a manpower advantage on the Western Front. The American army had not yet arrived in strength, and the German army had been reinforced with troops from the Eastern Front after the withdrawal of Russia from the war. This period was Ludendorff's best, and last, chance to achieve victory.

In these battles the German soldier demonstrated great tactical ability, but mistakes at the higher levels doomed the attacks to failure. In a series of assaults, commencing on 21 March and lasting into June, the German army gained considerable ground. However, the attacks were without strategic purpose and lacked a means to force the enemy to seek peace. In fact, Ludendorff did not appear to have identified any goals for his plans. On the eve of his first attack, the *Michael* offensive that began on 21 March, Ludendorff simply announced to his subordinates that "we shall punch a hole into [their lines]. For the rest, we shall see." The Germans again demonstrated their disdain for logistics, and advancing troops soon outran their support and had to forage for supplies, thereby slowing the initiative. After several more spring offenses, Ludendorff had not achieved victory and left the German army in a more precarious position than it had been in at the beginning of the year. He now had to defend a longer line with fewer troops—fatigued soldiers to whom Ludendorff had promised a war-ending victory that he was unable to deliver. Moreover, Ludendorff's offensives cost the German army nearly one million irreplaceable casualties.

In contrast, the commander of the British forces, General Douglas Haig, remained focused on a single strategic objective, the destruction of the enemy's army in a decisive battle. As a preliminary step to this objective he followed a policy of wearing them down, both by causing casualties and by weakening the

"NO ILLUSIONS"

British general Frederick Maurice recalls the collapse of German opposition and the state of the German army at the end of World War I:

There is no question but that the German armies were completely and decisively beaten in the field. The German plenipotentiaries admitted it when they met Marshal Foch, and von Brockdorff-Rantzau admitted it at Versailles, when he said after the Allied peace terms had been presented to him: "We are under no illusions as to the extent of our defeat and the degree of our wont of power. . . . We know that the power of the German army is broken."

Even if these admissions had not been made, the condition of the German lines of retreat to the Rhine is conclusive evidence of the condition of their armies. Every road was littered with broken-down motor-trucks, guns, machine-guns and trench mortars. Great stacks of supplies and of military stores of all kinds were abandoned. Every railway line was blocked with loaded trucks which the Germans had been unable to remove. The sixty miles of railway in the valley of the Meuse between Dinant and Mézières was filled from end to end with a continuous line of German freight trains carrying guns, ammunition, engineering equipment, and other paraphernalia. On the Belgian canals alone over eight hundred fully charged military barges were found. It is beyond dispute that on November 11 the lines of communication immediately behind the German armies had been thrown into complete disorder by the streams of traffic which were converging on the Meuse bridges, disorder greatly intensified by the attacks of the Allied airmen. The German armies, unable to resist on the fighting front, could no longer retreat in good order, partly because of the congestion on the roads and railways behind them, which not only hampered the movements of the troops, but prevented the systematic supply to them of food and ammunition, partly owing to the fact that there were not horses left to draw the transport of the fighting troops. . . .

Not less remarkable is a report from the headquarters of one of the divisions of the 17th German Army of the Crown Prince Rupprecht's group. The number of the division is obliterated on the report, which is dated November 8, 1918, and was found in a Belgian farmhouse. I have therefore been unable to identify the division, but it appears to have been one of those which was opposed to our First Army. The report runs: "The division can only be considered as unfit for battle. Owing to the extremely heavy casualties, to sickness and to numerous desertions, the average strength of regiments is under 600. Still more important as regards efficiency in battle is the shortage of officers, of which no regiment of the division has more than twelve, and one regiment has only nine. Almost all the machine-guns in the division have been lost or are out of repair, and half the guns of the artillery are deficient. Owing to the lack of horses, less than half the transport of the division can be moved, and if the retreat continues, many guns and vehicles will have to be abandoned. Owing to the lack of petrol, much of the motor transport of the division cannot be moved. The division has not received rations for two days, and the condition of the horses which remain is becoming very bad, because owing to the constant movement there is no time to collect supplies from the country, and forage for them is not arriving."

Source: *Frederick Maurice,* The Last Four Months: How the War Was Won *(Boston: Little, Brown, 1919), pp. 218–221.*

morale of the German soldier. After the war he emphasized his focus with the observation that the war was "one great and continuous engagement." The success of the British effort is seen in the battles from Amiens on 8 August 1918 to the end of the war. The British, joined by their allies, directed a series of blows against the German army. Already weakened by the enactment of Haig's policy, the enemy staggered backward toward his homeland like a boxer who was no longer able to defend himself.

This success was a direct result of the ability of the British army to negate German defensive strengths with their own superior offensive weapons and techniques. For example, the British army pioneered the tank, which they introduced in September 1916 during the Battle of the Somme. The Germans failed to take up the challenge and managed to field only a handful of these weapons. The British were also leaders in the development of techniques for precision artillery fire, including mastering the arcane art of survey and calibration. Another area of British success was artillery intelligence and counter-battery-fire coordination. They took the lead in this mission through their development of superior equipment for sound-ranging and flash-spotting, and the establishment of a coordination office called the Counter-Battery Staff Office. The result was that the British could locate and neutralize enemy batteries at will. Logistical support was a further British strength. After the near collapse of the rear area during the Somme campaign, the British developed a support service that, unlike that of the German army, was capable of meeting the requirements of modern war.

The British even outmatched their opponent in gas warfare, a form of fighting that the Germans introduced in 1915 and at which they enjoyed a great natural advantage because of their possession of the largest chemical industrial base in Europe. It took Britain and the other Western democracies until mid 1918 to overtake the Germans in gas war, but the fact that they were able to do so at all suggests the inability of the German army to sustain and convert a new concept of fighting into the means of victory. In 1918 the British and French could discharge deadly vapors in such quantities and concentrations that they could overpower the capabilities of the inferior German gas mask, thereby exposing the enemy's troops to lethal doses of gas. In addition, the British and French also added mustard gas to their repertoire, a terrifying agent that the Germans had had a monopoly on producing since they introduced it in July 1917. By mid 1918 there were clear signs that the morale of the enemy's soldiers had begun to crack, which was a result, in part, of the growing ascendancy of the Allied gas campaign, as well as their increasing dominance in other areas.

The Battle of Amiens (8 August 1918) highlights the superiority of the British method of attack and the ease with which they were now able to overwhelm German defenses. The British, Canadian, and Australian troops of General Henry Rawlinson's Fourth Army launched a surprise attack at 4:20 A.M., advancing behind a creeping barrage of shells. Tanks went first, both to clear paths through the enemy's wire and to destroy any defenders who had survived the hurricane of shells. At the same time, British counter-battery guns neutralized the German artillery with barrages of high explosive and gas shells. By the end of the day the British had taken seventeen thousand prisoners and captured four hundred guns. The attack was so successful that Ludendorff would call it the "blackest day" of the German army.

After this defeat the Germans were unable to regain their balance. Instead, the Allies drove them backward, attacking relentlessly and giving them no chance to recover. At the end of September the enemy had retreated into the Hindenburg Line, the strongest defensive system on the Western Front. Ludendorff planned to winter behind its ramparts and rebuild his army. On 29 September the British Fourth Army attacked again. Following several days of hard fighting, Rawlinson's troops overcame enemy resistance, breached the Hindenburg Line, and forced the German army to resume its retreat. At this point, even Ludendorff had to recognize that the war was lost.

Ludendorff's and Hindenburg's resort to the *Dolchstosslegende* was nothing more than an attempt by the most senior German officers to exculpate themselves from blame for the loss of the war and a cunning means to shift responsibility from the army to other elements within German society. It is unfortunate that they were so successful, as the "stab in the back myth" helped to undermine the legitimacy of the postwar Weimar government, and the Nazi regime replicated their pattern of blame with horrific consequences. Clearer analysis, however, demonstrates that the responsibility for its defeat rests on the German army alone. In the end, Germany lost the war simply because the military forces of the other combatants waged the conflict more skillfully and defeated the German army on the field of battle.

–ALBERT PALAZZO,
UNIVERSITY OF NEW SOUTH WALES AT THE
AUSTRALIAN DEFENCE FORCE ACADEMY

Viewpoint:
No. Germany surrendered because military leaders recognized that German society could not endure wartime conditions any longer.

In late October and early November 1918, much to the surprise of Entente military leaders, the once-mighty German army collapsed in the face of repeated assaults. British forces pierced the vaunted Hindenburg defensive line with comparative ease. The French and Americans made similar, if not quite so spectacular, gains to the south. Within the space of a few short weeks in the autumn of 1918, the German kaiser abdicated and Germany sued for peace. To the astonishment of almost everyone, it became clear that

Germany was unable to continue the war and that the conflict was finally over.

The cause of the sudden collapse of German resistance has long been the subject of debate. Recent scholarship has tended to place responsibility for the collapse on the fighting prowess of the British army under the direction of its commander in chief, Field Marshal Douglas Haig. Historians such as Paddy Griffith and Gary Sheffield have noted great improvements in British tactics and techniques during the course of 1918, advances that belatedly introduced combined-arms warfare into the British army. Putting this reform together with the fact that British forces led what turned out to be the final assault upon the seemingly formidable Hindenburg Line, they reach the conclusion that British arms defeated the German army so comprehensively in the field that the German high command and government had no recourse but to sue for peace. Thus, in this interpretation, to the British army fall the laurels of victory in World War I.

This view of the end of the war, however, is seriously flawed. While there can be no doubt that the British advance administered the coup de grâce, their success was less the result of military prowess than German weakness. The Entente offensives in the autumn of 1918 effectively pushed in the door of what had become a rotten edifice and in doing so occasioned its collapse. The German army was a shadow of its former self, worn down by four years of warfare and, crucially, by blockade. By the time of the final Entente offensive, it was having great difficulty maintaining itself in the field. The offensive merely hastened its eventual end. Indeed, with the failure of the German offensives of spring 1918, it had become clear to almost all of the leadership that Germany could not win the war, and from this point forward, they looked for some means of bringing the war to a close.

Indeed, that the German Empire and its allies could have survived four years of continuous warfare and blockade would have shocked prewar German strategists. It was a truism within military circles throughout Europe before 1914 that a modern industrial nation could not withstand the strains of a protracted war. Germany appeared particularly vulnerable to its own military leaders. They expected that a long war would result in economic collapse, as workers were called up into the army and as vital raw materials imported from abroad were cut off by naval blockade. Moreover, they did not believe that German society could withstand the strains

German soldiers drinking water from a trough in September 1916

(from Grosser Bilderatlas des Weltkrieges *[1915–1919], Joseph M. Bruccoli Great War Collection, Thomas Cooper Library, University of South Carolina)*

GERMAN COLLAPSE

of a drawn-out conflict. German soldiers feared that popular discontent would inevitably come from the privations caused by continuous war and believed that the German Social Democratic Party would take advantage of such discontent to preach rebellion. Perhaps most importantly, German strategists recognized that a long war would favor the Entente, with its vast reserves of manpower and access to the resources of overseas empires and markets.

The belief that Germany could not win a protracted conflict led its strategists to plan for a short war. The plan of operations constructed by Alfred von Schlieffen and refined by Helmuth von Moltke the Younger attempted to achieve a rapid battlefield victory first over an enemy on one front and then the other. When this plan failed at the Battle of the Marne (1914), the German High Command was left to improvise a new approach to the prolonged conflict for which they were almost wholly unprepared. Unfortunately for the Germans, however, structural problems within their state, government, and military ensured that they were never able to overcome problems caused by the Entente blockade.

Prior to World War I the German economy was dependent upon international trade, both to provide a market for finished German goods and to provide imports of raw materials not found domestically. In particular, Germany was dependent upon imports of food. While the Germans were able to rationalize their industry and find alternative supplies of raw materials for production of vital war matériel, it was in the area of foodstuffs that the Entente blockade had the greatest effect on their ability to continue to wage war. A commission organized by the government in December 1914 calculated that about 20 percent of the average German diet came from imported foodstuffs. Moreover, agriculture had lost about 60 percent of its workforce to the army and suffered from a shortage in draft animals, imported fodder for livestock, and fertilizer for growing crops. In order to ensure that the population of sixty-eight million did not go hungry, the German government attempted to step in and control the agricultural economy. Their efforts, however, were piecemeal and ineffective.

Rationing was first introduced in the winter of 1915 for fat, sugar, and bread. However, differences in administration from state to state, and an unsophisticated approach to the program, meant that there were gross inequities in the system. While the army was given sufficient food to maintain its soldiers in the field, civil society fared poorly. Inefficient administration of the rationing system ensured that farmers and the wealthy were usually able to find food. On the other hand, ordinary people, particularly those living in big cities, found it increasingly difficult to get enough food to eat, and by 1916 several food riots had occurred. The numbers of such riots grew in 1917 and 1918 as the food situation continued to worsen. After the war it was calculated that the Entente "hunger blockade" had directly accounted for approximately 760,000 German deaths.

The situation eventually began to have an ill effect on the army. Malnutrition of young Germans meant that the army was receiving weaker recruits as the war progressed. More immediately, though, as the food situation deteriorated across Germany, so too were rations to the army cut. During the great German offensives of early 1918, the momentum of the attack was often lost because of men stopping to loot British food depots. The situation became so bad that calls were made for the creation of "looting units," which would ensure a more systematic approach to the practice.

By 1918 the army could not help but be affected by the general war-weariness that gripped the entire German nation. Discontent on the home front adversely influenced army morale. Indeed, the army was increasingly having difficulty keeping its units up to strength, as men found ways to avoid frontline service in the unpopular war. Worryingly for the German High Command, units being shipped from the Eastern Front to the Western Front in 1918 often lost up to 20 percent of their strength in transit, and large groups of deserters shirked behind the lines. The offensives planned by Erich Ludendorff for the spring of 1918 were meant to decide the war before the Americans could reach Europe in significant numbers. They were seen by many as the last roll of the dice for Germany. However, although the German army made significant gains and caused serious damage to the Entente forces, their offensive did not cause the enemy alliance to collapse.

Quite the contrary, Ludendorff's offensives effectively brought the exhausted German army and nation to their knees. By mid July the German army had suffered almost 1,000,000 casualties, including large numbers of crucial small-unit leaders, in these attacks. If the combat losses were not enough, influenza also ravaged the poorly nourished army. More than 500,000 soldiers went down sick in June and July. The fighting strength of German formations reflected these losses. For instance, the LI Corps in the German Second Army had a combat strength of 2,683 men to cover a front 6.5 kilometers long. To make matters worse, the casualties of 1918 came from the best formations of the German army, and what was left was in no position to hold the now-extended front.

The failure of Ludendorff's offensives also severely damaged German morale. Anticipating a decisive victory, German soldiers had geared themselves for one final push in the spring of 1918. When the first push failed, most people believed that there was no reason to prolong the war. When Entente forces counterattacked in August, German soldiers began surrendering in large numbers, and between July and November the German army lost nearly 350,000 troops as prisoners. In a sign of the spirit of the troops, units advancing to the front to meet the Entente offensive were often met by retreating troops with taunts of "war-prolongers" and "strike-breakers." Increasingly, officers had to threaten their men to get them to advance to the front.

By the time of the final Entente offensives, the once mighty German army was a shadow of its former self. Four years of continuous warfare and economic blockade had exhausted the army and society from which it came. Moreover, in the wake of the failure of the spring offensives, both the German army and society increasingly questioned their own leadership. By the end of September even the ever-optimistic German High Command was forced to recognize that the army could no longer be relied upon and asked the political leadership to find a way, any way, to end the war. However, even this act could not come quickly enough—German allies, Turkey and Austria, both collapsed and sued for peace in late October, and revolution broke out in Germany itself. On 9 November a republic was declared by a Germany exhausted of militarism and war, and Kaiser Wilhelm II was forced to abdicate. The armistice was set for 11 November. Thus, in the end, the warnings of prewar strategists had been right all along—German society could not withstand a protracted war.

–ROBERT T. FOLEY,
KING'S COLLEGE, LONDON

References

A. C. Bell, *A History of the Blockade of Germany and of the Countries Associated with Her in the Great War: Austria-Hungary, Bulgaria, and Turkey, 1914–1918* (London: HMSO, 1937).

Ian Malcolm Brown, *British Logistics on the Western Front, 1914–1919* (Westport, Conn: Praeger, 1998).

Wilhelm Deist, "The Military Collapse of the German Empire: The Reality Behind the Stab-in-the-Back Myth," *War in History*, 3 (1996): 186–207.

Paddy Griffith, *Battle Tactics of the Western Front: The British Army's Art of Attack, 1916–18* (New Haven: Yale University Press, 1994).

J. P. Harris and Niall Barr, *Amiens to the Armistice: The BEF in the Hundred Days' Campaign, 8 August–11 November 1918* (London & Washington: Brassey's, 1998).

Holger H. Herwig, *The First World War: Germany and Austria-Hungary, 1914–1918* (London & New York: Arnold, 1997).

Hubert C. Johnson, *Breakthrough! Tactics, Technology, and the Search for Victory on the Western Front in World War I* (Novato, Cal.: Presidio Press, 1994).

Timothy T. Lupfer, *The Dynamics of Doctrine: The Changes in German Tactical Doctrine During the First World War* (Fort Leavenworth, Kans.: Combat Studies Institute, U.S. Army Command and General Staff College, 1981).

Ralph Haswell Lutz, comp., *The Causes of the German Collapse in 1918,* translated by W. L. Campbell (Stanford: Stanford University Press, 1934; London: H. Milford, Oxford University Press, 1934).

Avner Offer, *The First World War: An Agrarian Interpretation* (Oxford: Clarendon Press, 1989; New York: Oxford University Press, 1989).

Albert Palazzo, *Seeking Victory on the Western Front: The British Army and Chemical Warfare in World War I* (Lincoln: University of Nebraska Press, 2000).

Robin Prior and Trevor Wilson, *Command on the Western Front: The Military Career of Sir Henry Rawlinson, 1914–18* (Oxford, U.K. & Cambridge, Mass.: Blackwell, 1991).

Tim Travers, *How the War Was Won: Command and Technology in the British Army on the Western Front, 1917–1918* (London & New York: Routledge, 1992).

GERMAN TACTICS

Did the German General Staff effectively implement tactical and doctrinal innovations during the war?

Viewpoint: Yes. The German General Staff had a highly effective organization that ensured new tactics were rapidly incorporated into military training programs.

Viewpoint: No. Most of the new tactics adopted by the German Army were improvisations made by lower-level staff and field officers.

The German Army is widely credited with being more successful than its counterparts at meeting the complex and demanding requirements imposed by the fundamental imbalance among the historic battlefield triad of fire, movement, and protection during the Great War. Between 1914 and 1918, fire so dominated combat that coping with its effect became both the signifier and the definer of the war. In contrast to other conflicts whose focal points have been at the level of operations, strategy, or policy, the fundamental problem of World War I was tactical: breaking in, breaking through, and breaking out of developed defense systems.

The Imperial German Army was in a sense better adapted to meet that challenge than any other army in Europe. The geography of Germany, and increasingly its policy as well, had created a situation requiring the army to win the first battles and win them convincingly. The gridlock that began in autumn 1914 was a corresponding institutional shock. At the same time, the German army did not face the immediate challenges confronting its rivals on both fronts. Standing in enemy territory, it did not have to develop plans for reconquering the motherland, as did the Russians and the French. Nor did it share the British problem of creating a mass army from whole cloth.

Instead, the German army had enough breathing space to recognize that this new conflict was not the Wars of Liberation (1813–1814) or the Wars of Unification (1866–1871) written large. As early as 1915 the traditional principle of *halten, was zu halten ist* (holding what you've got) to the last extremity was giving way to a concept of trading ground for dead British and French soldiers, for the commonsense reason that Germany had no intention of physically occupying all of France in any case. At the regimental level, innovative junior officers developed new assault tactics based on specially trained and armed small units. These "stormtroops" were not only successful in the patrols and raids that were frontline routine; they provided their members a chance to be something other than trench fodder, with correspondingly positive effects on morale.

By 1917 staff officers had extended to the entire army a tactical doctrine based on "resist, bend, snap back": give ground where necessary; mount local counterattacks as quickly as possible; and break off when the shock effect was gone. At the same time the army had benefited from the grass-roots development of stormtroop tactics that could open the way for larger units, creating lines of least resistance, permeating enemy positions as unobtrusively and effectively as water permeates a porous barrier. In defense and attack these tactics both kept Germany in the war and gave the army hope— at least for a while.

Viewpoint:
Yes. The German General Staff had a highly effective organization that ensured new tactics were rapidly incorporated into military training programs.

At the start of World War I the German army had two distinct advantages on the modern battlefield: a well-developed tactical and operational doctrine and a highly effective organization (General Staff) that allowed for rapid tactical/doctrinal innovation. Although the Germans fought armies that greatly outnumbered and outgunned them, they still racked up a score of grand victories that rank with some of the greatest battlefield successes of all time. Tannenberg (1914), Gorlice (1915), Riga (1917), the campaign against Romania (1916), Caporetto (1917), and the March 1918 offensive that broke a British army were all German victories that resulted from employing battlefield tactics and doctrine that were far superior to that of their enemies. The Germans may have had a poorly conceived strategy for much of World War I, but their tactical/operational effectiveness was so successful that they came close to winning the war—despite many strategic disadvantages.

From the reforms of General Gerhard von Scharnhorst early in the nineteenth century, through the 1866 and 1870 wars, and on to the eve of World War I, the Prussian (later German) officer corps devoted a great deal of energy to studying tactics and operations to modify the standard doctrine of combat arms. When the Germans went to war in 1914, the current doctrine manuals (infantry regulations of 1906, cavalry regulations of 1909, field-artillery regulations of 1907, machine-gun-detachment regulations of 1908, and air-service regulations of 1913) formed a comprehensive body of effective battlefield tactics. The Germans had studied the most recent wars, such as the Russo-Japanese War (1904–1905), for lessons and applied the experiences of other nations to their own approach. As a result of this study, German tactics at the start of the war took into account the importance of machine guns on the battlefield as well as the effect of fast-firing artillery and its lethality. While the offense was the preferred mode of war, there was considerable respect for the defense and defensive firepower. German tactics were far better balanced than French tactics, which placed faith in the "offensive spirit" of the army. German tactics relied on superior training and allowed lower-level commanders considerable flexibil-

ity in accomplishing the mission, known as the concept of *Auftragstaktik*.

The instrument that oversaw tactics and doctrine for the army was the General Staff, a small body of only 650 men in a corps of more than 20,000 officers. General Staff officers were specially selected senior lieutenants or junior captains who underwent a rigorous three-year course of study in tactics and operations. Entry into the General Staff was purely by merit, and these officers were accorded preference in promotions and assignments. Membership meant that even a fairly junior officer, a captain or major, would be accorded considerable respect and listened to by his superiors. General Staff officers were also expected to serve as the eyes and ears of the high command and to observe and report the unvarnished truth about deficiencies and problems within the army. In general, the ethic of the German army was not to punish officers who thought critically or who reported unpleasant facts to the high command. In war, such honest accounting is essential to ensuring that the senior commanders have an accurate picture of the battlefield and can change tactics and doctrine. In general, the German General Staff proved to be more effective at analysis and in communicating battlefield experience than their French, British, Russian, or American counterparts.

Much of the impetus for tactical innovation in the war came from the top. Soon after the war became a stalemate in October 1914, the German high command began looking for solutions to return maneuver to the battlefield. One idea proposed to the General Staff was to use incapacitating gases to break a hole in the enemy lines. The first two attempts to use tear gas to disable the enemy in the front lines failed completely. The cold temperatures rendered the chemicals harmless. The general staff encouraged further experimentation, however, and in April 1915 the German army cracked open the Allied lines at Ypres with the use of lethal chlorine gas. The attack was so successful that the Germans were unprepared to follow up their victory. In any case, the direct intervention of the General Staff had unleashed a new weapon of war, which would become an important part of the German tactical repertoire.

Another example of the ability of the General Staff to foster tactical innovation was in artillery tactics. On the Eastern Front in 1916 Lieutenant Colonel Georg Bruchmüller, a foot artillery officer who had been recalled from retirement at the start of the war, devised a new strategy. Bruchmüller was not a General Staff officer, nor was he well known outside

GERMAN TACTICS

GERMAN TACTICS

his own unit. For the attack upon superior Russian forces at Lake Naroch in April 1916, however, he proposed a plan for centralizing the fire of 30 artillery batteries and using a creeping barrage to cover the German assault. It was an unusual plan because the German army had no tactics for coordinating artillery fire above the division level. Still, the Tenth Army commander agreed to try Bruchmüller's tactics, which contributed to a resounding German success. For the next year Bruchmüller, still a lieutenant colonel, was given more and more authority to command the artillery forces for large operations. By the summer of 1917, while in Galicia, he had 134 artillery batteries placed under his command. He worked out a system of using unregistered fire, adopting centralized artillery control, and preceding attacks with short—but extremely heavy—barrages for shock effect. Under Bruchmüller's system, careful coordination with the advancing infan-

try was achieved, and German artillery shifted targets and displaced forwards under a plan that assured that advancing troops would have uninterrupted fire support.

The new artillery tactics more than proved their worth at Riga. In the attack, which was preceded by a whirlwind barrage under Bruchmüller's direction, the German army broke the Russian lines, captured more than twenty thousand prisoners, and effectively took Russia out of the war. Bruchmüller was soon brought to the Western Front, where his artillery tactics became an important part of the great German offensive of 1918.

After the disastrous campaign at Verdun (1916), a new team of Field Marshal Paul von Hindenburg and General Erich Ludendorff took over the German high command. For all his faults, Ludendorff was a first-rate tactician and understood that German tactics had failed on the Western Front. In the fall of 1916 he toured units all along the front, actively solicited advice from junior officers and demanded unvarnished criticism from general staff officers. The result was a new doctrine for defensive operations outlined by the high command in December 1916. The idea of holding ground at all costs was discarded for a new approach that withdrew as many men as possible from the front lines, away from the enemy artillery. Troops remaining at the front were to be entrenched deeply in concrete bunkers so that the ground could be held with a minimum of men and battles would result in fewer casualties. Enemy attacks that broke into German defense lines were to be dealt with by counterattack, a solution that kept up the aggressive and offensive spirit of the army. In stopping the Nivelle offensive and in holding the British attacks in Flanders in 1917, the new defensive tactics proved their worth.

The most famous example of tactical and doctrinal innovation from World War I was the German use of "stormtroop" tactics to break through Allied defense lines in 1917 and 1918. Essentially, the new offensive tactics employed small units of elite, lightly armed infantry to work their way through the enemy defenses, bypassing strongpoints and ignoring their flanks, in order to break as deeply into the enemy lines as possible. The "storm" units would be followed by heavily armed infantry who would take out the bypassed centers of resistance and hold the flanks against any Allied counterattacks. Stormtroop tactics emphasized surprise and effective artillery support. Exactly who originated the concept is unclear, although experiments with these tactics had been made on a small scale in 1916. General Oskar von Hutier on the Eastern Front is credited with using storm tactics on a large scale in 1917 at Riga, and the Allies often referred to the new system as "Von Hutier tactics." In any case, at Caporetto (November 1917) and in the counterattack at Cambrai the same month the new German tactics proved their worth.

The high command eagerly accepted the new concepts. In a pamphlet issued by the high command on 1 January 1918, "The Attack in Position Warfare," the artillery tactics of Bruchmüller and the infantry tactics of von Hutier were fully combined for use on a grand scale. Entire divisions were pulled from the line and trained in the rear as elite "storm" divisions for the 1918 offensive.

Stormtroop tactics proved a huge step in returning maneuver to the Western Front. The opening attack on the Western Front on 21 March 1918 routed the British Fifth Army, broke a hole in the Allied lines, and captured 140 square miles of territory for a fraction of the losses that the British had incurred at the Somme (1916). The German attack, supported by more than 3,700 guns, managed to capture more than fifty thousand Allied prisoners and 800 guns before the end of the month. The new tactics caused a crisis in the Allied command and brought the Germans to within 50 miles of Paris. The Germans proved unable to sustain the logistics for their offensive, however, as horses and motor vehicles bogged down traversing the shell-churned landscape. By April 1918 the German offensive slowed down; although attacks continued, the German blows became weaker as the Allies, with the arrival of the Americans, increased in strength.

For virtually the whole war the high commands of all major combatants had to deal with the lethality of new technologies such as the machine gun and with a scale of warfare never before imagined. The German General Staff also wrestled with the problem of overcoming the inherent power of the defense. By 1918, through the use of innovative tactics and doctrine, the German army came close to restoring maneuver to the battlefield. The world would have to wait until mechanization solved the stalemate of trench warfare with blitzkrieg tactics in 1939.

Yet, one of the great military accomplishments of the war was the ability of the German General Staff to analyze problems and encourage innovation throughout the army. When tactical solutions were found, the high command ensured that new tactics were rapidly incorporated into the training program. Because of this policy the German army was generally a step or two ahead of the Allied armies throughout the war. It was a primary reason for the impressive combat effectiveness of the German army in World War I.

–JAMES CORUM, USAF SCHOOL OF
ADVANCED AIRPOWER STUDIES

Viewpoint:
No. Most of the new tactics adopted by the German Army were improvisations made by lower-level staff and field officers.

The German army of World War I was successful at adapting to war at the sharp end. Whatever its considerable and well-documented faults in the areas of strategy and operational art, the army showed almost from the beginning of the war a high level of flexibility and a

ONE INFERNAL ROAR

A French officer, who watched the German artillery barrage and infantry attack at Verdun on 21 February 1916, recalls his observations:

Thousands of projectiles are flying in all directions, some whistling, others howling, others moaning low, and all uniting in one infernal roar. From time to time an aërial torpedo passes, making a noise like a gigantic motor car. With a tremendous thud a giant shell bursts quite close to our observation post, breaking the telephone wires and interrupting all communications with our batteries.

A man gets out at once for repairs, crawling along on his stomach through all this place of bursting mines and shells. It seems quite impossible that he should escape in the rain of shell, which exceeds anything imaginable; there has never been such a bombardment in war. Our man seems to be enveloped in explosions, and shelters himself from time to time in the shell craters which honeycomb the ground; finally he reaches a less stormy spot, mends his wires, and then, as it would be madness to try to return, settles down in a big crater and waits for the storm to pass.

Beyond, in the valley, dark masses are moving over the snow-covered ground. It is German infantry advancing in packed formation along the valley to the attack. They look like a big gray carpet being unrolled over the country. We telephone through to the batteries and the ball begins. The sight is hellish. In the distance, in the valley and upon the slopes, regiments spread out, and as they deploy fresh troops come pouring in.

There is a whistle over our heads. It is our first shell. It falls right in the middle of the enemy infantry. We telephone through, telling our batteries of their hit, and a deluge of heavy shells is poured on the enemy. Their position becomes critical. Through glasses we can see men maddened, men covered with earth and blood, falling one upon the other. When the first wave of the assault is decimated, the ground is dotted with heaps of corpses, but the second wave is already pressing on. Once more our shells carve awful gaps in their ranks. Nevertheless, like an army of rats the Boches continue to advance in spite of our "marmites." Then our heavy artillery bursts forth in fury. The whole valley is turned into a volcano, and its exit is stopped by the barrier of the slain.

Source: Charles F. Horne, ed., Source Records of the Great War, *volume 4 (Indianapolis: American Legion, 1930), pp. 54–55.*

---

significant openness to innovation at the tactical level. The evaluation and dissemination of the successive waves of innovation certainly owed much to a staff system institutionally conditioned to seek, collate, and disseminate ideas. The best ideas, however, were overwhelmingly produced by staff and field officers at the lower levels, from divisions and regiments down to companies and platoons.

The process began as early as the turn of the first year of the war, when it became apparent that peacetime doctrines and drill manuals were poor preparation for conducting what amounted to siege operations in the open field. The engineer corps accepted the challenge. In contrast to other European armies, German engineers considered themselves assault troops as well as technicians. Their official name, "pioneers," suggested warriors—as opposed to skilled craftsmen—supervising rough labor. Before the war they had been the specialists in fortress operations, both on attack and in defense. Now the pioneers took the lead in spreading trench technologies: grenades, mortars, flamethrowers, and light cannon.

The pioneers did more than make equipment available. They furnished the manpower for the first "assault detachment," the parent formation of the "stormtroops." Its first real successes, however, came under an infantryman: Major Ernst Rohr. Beginning at Verdun (1916), the stormtroops developed a dual reputation. As their numbers increased, they emerged as elite shock troops, depending on individual initiative underwritten by advanced platoon-level weapons systems. On the other hand, the stormtroop units functioned as school troops, staffing instruction camps throughout the army and spreading the gospel of assault tactics to successive classes of junior officers and

GERMAN TACTICS

enlisted men. These graduates in turn served as a leaven in companies and platoons whose energy had been diminished by too many months in the trenches. Ernst Jünger, the epitome of what the army called "storm-trooper spirit," made his reputation in the assault platoon of a line infantry regiment.

The integration of stormtroops into the army, as opposed to their marginalization as an elite group, in turn reflected the attitude of junior staff officers and commanders. In the fall of 1914 Hans von Seeckt, then a colonel and chief of staff of Third Corps, began experimenting with alternate tactics and formations in attacking fortified positions. Rohr owed his initial success to the free hand he received from the army to which his detachment was first assigned—a hand guided by the staff officers. Arguably the best example of this mid-level flexibility, however, is the wartime career of General Georg Bruchmüller. He had retired in 1913 on medical grounds after three thoroughly undistinguished decades in the heavy artillery—the least-regarded combat branch of the army. Recalled on the outbreak of war, he was assigned as artillery commander of a newly raised reserve division on the Russian front. But his division commander allowed him to develop and test plans for using massed, centrally controlled artillery fire. They worked well enough on a small scale that Bruchmüller took them to the corps level. When the corps artillery commander rejected the idea, Bruchmüller went a level higher. Tenth Army chief of staff Emil Hell gave him a chance, and in April 1916 Bruchmüller's new tactics were the centerpiece of an unusually successful local counterattack at Lake Naroch.

The rest is artilleryman's history. Bruchmüller was allowed to form his own staff of artillery experts, majors, and captains. First in the east, at Riga (1917), then in Erich Ludendorff's spring offensive (1918) on the Western Front, he became the impresario of the most sophisticated systems of fire preparation and fire control seen to date on a battlefield. He never rose above colonel in rank, but his nickname, *Durchbruchmueller* (Breakthrough Mueller), testifies to the respect he enjoyed from Ludendorff to the anonymous *Frontschweine* (front-hogs) who followed his "steel wind" into and across shattered Allied positions.

The British, the French, and even the American armies also demonstrated flexibility and adaptability during the Great War. The Germans, however, were the most successful at recognizing experience based on particular circumstances—to a degree that quality reflected the dominant tactical focus in the years prior to 1914. German war planning was increasingly based on the sovereign importance of the battlefield. Professional military publications concentrated on details of organization, armament, and deployment. It was scarcely unusual to have that concern persist in a war whose problems and challenges, from the perspective of the army, were themselves essentially tactical, especially on the Western Front, where Germany after 1914 was a satiated power, concerned primarily with maintaining its gains.

Important as well to innovation from the bottom up was the emphasis placed by the German army on self-education. The German company officer, especially by comparison to his counterpart in other armies, was a student of his craft. Admission to the higher military schools on which promotion beyond major ultimately depended for most officers was based on passing examinations; the curricula of those institutions was in turn dominated by military subjects in the narrow sense. At least in the infantry and artillery, most regiments of the peacetime army correspondingly expected their junior officers to spend time with books and maps. That training was true even for the elite Prussian Guard, which boasted of the high number of its officers who qualified for advanced schooling almost as much as it bragged about their lineage.

Professional education translated into decentralized responsibility. Unit commanders at all levels were responsible for the effectiveness of their formations. Appealing to doctrinal wisdom was no more acceptable than citing superior orders as an explanation—let alone an excuse—for failure. "His Majesty made you an officer so that you would know when *not* to obey" was a common aphorism of superiors to juniors at all levels of command.

Most armies pay lip service to the concept. The army of the German Empire was able to internalize it in good part because of the aristocratic self-image of its officer corps. By 1914, birth was less important to that concept than attitude. The officer was expected to regard himself as someone above the ordinary interests and rivalries of civil society, justified in his claim to being "the first man in the state" by his readiness to put himself in harm's way when the shooting began. It was a mind-set whose shortcomings have so often been documented that its positive aspects have been submerged. One of them was an expectation that an officer of any rank would stand for his principles and behind his ideas. Related to that was a concept, eroded since its emergence in the days of Frederick the Great but still viable, that all officers, at least all regular officers, were members of a community that ultimately transcended rank.

The ramifications of this mentality must not be overstated. Orders were still meant to be obeyed; juniors still challenged superiors' wisdom at the expense of their careers. Yet, underlying those realities was a sense, older and deeper than any career consciousness, that honor might eventually require an officer to "put his commission on the table" to make a point—and a recognition that honor in turn required a fellow officer's position be respected.

Ultimately, a French regular officer's model was bureaucratic: avoid making waves and transfer responsibility upward. A British officer saw himself as a member of a gentleman's club, with a corresponding responsibility to maintain group harmony and identity. German officers were sharper-edged: carnivores as opposed to their more herbivorous rivals. Their collective values were fundamentally antagonistic to an emerging democratic order. The institutional adaptation made by the army during World War I suggests that a military caste is not necessarily professionally hidebound, ingrown, and self-referencing.

–DENNIS SHOWALTER,
COLORADO COLLEGE

References

Bruce I. Gudmundsson, *Stormtroop Tactics: Innovation in the German Army, 1914–1918* (New York: Praeger, 1989).

Hubert C. Johnson, *Breakthrough! Tactics, Technology, and the Search for Victory on the Western Front in World War I* (Novato, Cal.: Presidio Press, 1994).

John Keegan, *The First World War* (London: Hutchinson, 1998).

G. C. Wynne, *If Germany Attacks: The Battle in Depth in the West* (London: Faber & Faber, 1940).

David T. Zabecki, *Steel Wind: Colonel Georg Bruchmüller and the Birth of Modern Artillery* (Westport, Conn.: Praeger, 1994).

GERMAN TACTICS

HABSBURGS

Did Austria-Hungary fall victim to conflicting nationalisms?

Viewpoint: Yes. Ethnic groups throughout the empire sought their own salvation outside the crumbling imperial framework.

Viewpoint: No. The nationalities of the Austro-Hungarian Empire held together remarkably well throughout the war, and they sought independence only after they had discovered that the Allies had no interest in sustaining the Habsburg system.

In 1914 Austria-Hungary was widely regarded as the successor to the Ottoman Empire in holding the unpromising status of "the sick man of Europe." Its demise was seen as sufficiently imminent to be discussed not merely in Balkan capitals but in Paris and St. Petersburg as well. In Germany, the principal ally of the empire, the Habsburg connection was widely dismissed as political poison. During the war Austria-Hungary did little to dispel its image. Its armies were driven out of Serbia and met repeated disaster on the Galician plains and in the Carpathian Mountains. German troops were so regularly sent to shore up Austrian collapses that the reinforcements gave themselves the nickname "corset stays."

Austrian soldiers not only surrendered in wholesale lots, they turned their coats as well, fighting with former prisoners of war (POWs) under Allied command on every major front. Most of these traitors were Slavs, northern and southern, whose initial desertion was frequently inspired by mistrust and ill-treatment by a military system dominated by Germans and Magyars. The Austrian economy collapsed as early as 1916—chiefly because of internal tensions exacerbated by a drain of resources from the countryside that between 1914 and 1916 cut grain production in half. As early as 1915 the kingdom of Hungary forbade the shipment of foodstuffs to the Cisleithanian provinces of the Dual Monarchy.

Efforts to mobilize a society priding itself on its easygoing casualness were too late and too little. By 1917 industrial output was falling steeply. An overworked transportation network was gridlocking—as much from the deaths of horses by starvation as from the breakdown of locomotives through overwork. POWs returning from a revolutionizing Russia spread discontent fueled by hunger. In early 1918 a wave of strikes swept the monarchy. Disaffection spread to a harbor-bound navy, to the rear echelons of the army, and into the front lines.

The Allies contributed to the decline of Austria-Hungary by playing the nationalist card in an effort to mobilize support from Slavic dissidents—and in the United States, from emigrants—by promising postwar self-determination. Germany increasingly treated the Habsburg monarchy as a client rather than an ally, disregarding both its interests and its complaints with an insouciance that sparked the fury of helplessness. Austria-Hungary began disintegrating even before the Armistice of 1918, as its component provinces and peoples sought to salvage what they could from the wreck. Did the empire collapse because of its internal contradictions and tensions or was it victimized by four years of war that stressed its institutions and its loyalties past the breaking point?

Viewpoint:
Yes. Ethnic groups throughout the empire sought their own salvation outside the crumbling imperial framework.

The dual monarchy of Austria-Hungary was an anomaly among European states. The historical trend, accelerating since the French Revolution, was for nations to form around common cultural and linguistic identities, as Germany and Italy had done most recently in the 1870s. Austria-Hungary by contrast had for four hundred years been assimilating a dozen different cultures with various languages and identities. The empire included regions with historic ties to Germany, Italy, Poland, Russia, and the Ottoman Empire. There were no common customs, religions, or languages, except for Germanic high culture that critics described as an artificial construction. There was not even a legacy of conquest to serve as an integrating memory. The Habsburgs had achieved their empire less on the battlefield than in the bridal suite, by a structure of dynastic marriages.

The Austro-Hungarian army, although by many accounts no real menace to anyone (the last time it had been on the winning side of a major war was in the final months before Napoleon Bonaparte's surrender in 1814, and then as part of a coalition), was probably the best functioning governmental body. In the military reorganization of the 1870s the Dual Monarchy had developed a remarkably efficient, well-integrated "common army" that combined multicultural elements and dynastic loyalty. Its regiments were recruited territorially, by geographic districts, to enhance cohesion and facilitate mobilization. The officers, drawn from all of the national groups, including Jews, in the empire were required to be proficient in the languages of the regiment to which they were assigned, which might be Romanian, Polish, Czech, Ruthenian, or a combination of two or three tongues—some of which had only recently acquired dictionaries and written grammar.

Noncommissioned officers (NCOs), the glue of any army, were doubly important in Austria-Hungary. To facilitate communication among themselves they devised a language known as "soldier's German." This method consisted of several regulation words and phrases every soldier was required to know, supplemented by an unofficial body of army slang that enabled NCOs of differing ethnic origins to communicate among themselves, with the troops, and with the officers. It could be a cumbersome system. Some accounts describe periods of as long as an hour for an infantry unit to communicate with an artillery unit of a different nationality. Other observers speak of replacements with the "wrong" language being given orders by gestures and grimaces while under fire.

The first consequent gestures of nationalism came from the Magyars of Hungary, who had always perceived themselves as different from their European neighbors. Even their language had no cognates across cultural boundaries, and the new science of comparative linguistics demonstrated scientifically that it was not European in origin. In 1848 a Magyar rebellion was bloodily suppressed with Russian aid. Faced with continuing Magyar discontent, escalating periodically into a renewed threat of open rebellion in the powerful and strategically located community, Emperor Francis Joseph I in 1867 recognized the Crown of St. Stephen, the national symbol of Hungary, and established a Dual Monarchy, giving Hungary equal status with Austria. None of the other peoples of the empire had enough strength or potential to negotiate a similar outcome before 1914. The ideas of self-determination and self-government, however, were insidious and enduring. Francis Joseph I was right to fear their spread.

From 1914 to 1916 the giant armies that clashed over the endless plains of eastern Poland and western Russia brought no military results. The Poles, however, divided for more than a century among Germany, Russia, and Austria-Hungary, began to view the war as an opportunity to regain independence by playing the belligerents against each other. Czech and south Slav nationalists began recruiting exile legions in Russian prisoner of war camps. An increasingly comprehensive Allied propaganda campaign attacked the legitimacy of Habsburg rule and the existence of Austria-Hungary.

On 21 November 1916 Francis Joseph I, having ruled since 1848, died. He was the last link holding together the four-hundred-year-old empire. His successor, Karl I, though possibly competent, was unknown, unloved, unrespected—and unable to hold back the centrifugal forces of modern nationalism.

By now the supply system was breaking down rapidly for both the military and civilian populations. Food and ammunition were becoming scarce at the front. Soldiers lacked boots, shirts, and even underwear. Soldiers and civilians,

**Austrian mountain troops
in the Tyrol region, fall
1917**

(from Collier's New Photographic
History of the World's War [1918],
Joseph M. Bruccoli Great War
Collection, Thomas Cooper
Library, University of
South Carolina)

seeing no good outcome for their sacrifices, began questioning at the grassroots, in dugouts and taverns, the legitimacy of the state. As casualty figures rose year by year, ethnic cracks widened into chasms that grew deeper as privation increased the perception of cultural differences. Belief that one's own group was bearing a disproportionate share of the burdens of a futile war revitalized age-old feuds: Czech and German, German and Magyar, Magyar and Croat.

The army, even though it was organized on an ethnic basis, was the last Imperial institution to be affected by nationalism. Respect for the oath sworn to the emperor was reinforced by unit cohesion forged in common experiences and mutually shared hardship. Loyalty had its limits, however. In late 1917, when Russia pulled out of the war to tend to its own revolution, and Franz Conrad von Hötzendorf, the Chief of Staff, began to transfer more troops from the Eastern Front to Italy, mutinies and riots broke out throughout the empire. Put down brutally, they were a harbinger of more serious troubles to come in 1918, when Austria-Hungary expended

HEALING THE WOUNDS OF WAR

Emperor Karl I had the unenviable task of leading Austria-Hungary just as the empire was beginning to crumble as a result of nationalist pressures and war. On 11 November 1918 he issued the following message to his people before he fled to Switzerland:

Since my accession I have incessantly tried to rescue my peoples from this tremendous war. I have not delayed the reestablishment of constitutional rights or the opening of a way for the people to substantial national development. Filled with an unalterable love for my peoples I will not, with my person, be a hindrance to their free development. I acknowledge the decision taken by German Austria to form a separate State. The people has by its deputies taken charge of the Government. I relinquish every participation in the administration of the State. Likewise I have released the members of the Austrian Government from their offices. May the German Austrian people realize harmony from the new adjustment. The happiness of my peoples was my aim from the beginning. My warmest wishes are that an internal peace will be able to heal the wounds of this war.

Source: Charles F. Horne, ed., Source Records of the Great War, *volume 6 (Indianapolis: American Legion, 1930), p. 385.*

---

the remnants of its strength in a vain effort to drive Italy out of the war.

Emperor Karl I was by now basically powerless, unable to get his edicts read in Vienna, let alone in outlying provinces. To replace a moribund administration, national councils began to form among the various ethnic nationalities. On 24 October 1918 Hungarian leaders urged their troops to lay down their arms and head home. On 28 October, Prague proclaimed a Czechoslovakian state. One day later Croatia, Slovenia, and Dalmatia seceded from the Dual Monarchy. The German-speaking regions of Bohemia, Moravia, and Silesia announced the creation of an independent "German Free State" on 30 October.

In order to regain its national honor, Italy attacked one more time an empire that no longer existed and an army unable to fight. They captured between 350,000 and 400,000 Austro-Hungarian troops. Thousands of other soldiers abandoned the collapsing front, crowding aboard commandeered trains heading for new homelands. Though the Hapsburgs had run a good race for more than four hundred years, the force of nationalism, exacerbated by the stresses of World War I, brought the empire to a quick and abrupt end.

—JOHN WHEATLEY,
BROOKLYN CENTER, MINNESOTA

**Viewpoint:
No. The nationalities of the Austro-Hungarian Empire held together remarkably well throughout the war, and they sought independence only after they had discovered that the Allies had no interest in sustaining the Habsburg system.**

Nationalism—or the "nationalities question" as it was called at the time—played a prominent role in fin de siècle Austria-Hungary. There is growing evidence to suggest, however, that until its dissolution in the fall of 1918 the Dual Monarchy was a resilient structure, capable of sustaining the politics of nationalism and commanding the loyalties of its citizens. In other words, the Habsburg Monarchy disappeared because it lost a long, hard-fought war and because its adversaries decided to replace it with a host of self-described nation-states (in reality almost all were also multiethnic in composition).

Austria-Hungary has often been portrayed as a country on the verge of implosion resulting from internal national pressures. British historian A. J. P. Taylor succinctly articulated this position, stating that the Habsburg monarchy was "not a device for enabling a number of nationalities to live together," while Solomon Wank more recently argued that the Habsburg imperial rulers had absolutely no interest in transforming the imperial system into a federation of autonomous national societies. Yet, this picture is misleading: in the decade before World War I national aspirations and frictions were actually being dealt with and resolved in the Austrian half of the monarchy. Although no grand scheme for reform had been implemented, national compromises were nevertheless negotiated and concluded in four Austrian Crownlands and ratified in three—Moravia (1905), Bukovina (1910), and Galicia (1914). Only Tyrol failed to ratify the measures. Moreover, the tone of Austrian politics changed considerably in the years prior to World War I. The notorious street violence that had peaked in the 1890s showed signs of abating, while social and economic issues began to occupy a central place in political discourses in both halves of the monarchy. The rise of Social Democracy in the decade before World War I is emblematic of this change.

When war broke out in the summer of 1914, the recruited citizenry of the Habsburg monarchy willingly responded to the call to mobilize and defend their home state. Despite pessimistic predictions by the *Armeeoberkommando* (Austro- Hungarian High Command, or

AOK), there were almost no recruiting difficulties and no need to impose martial law in perceived "problem areas" such as the Czech-speaking regions of Bohemia and Moravia. Although the Army Chief of Staff in the years 1914–1917, Field Marshal Franz Conrad von Hötzendorf, interpreted the setbacks of the Austro-Hungarian army as indications of disloyal behavior on the part of certain nationalities (particularly Czech, Serb, Italian, and Ukrainian), it is much more likely that these setbacks occurred because of structural deficiencies of the army, faulty planning, and mobilization blunders during the first months of war. By the end of 1914 the professional core of the military along with its officer corps were decimated, and "the Habsburg army," in the words of István Deák in *Beyond Nationalism: A Social and Political History of the Habsburg Officers Corps, 1848–1918* (1990), was "transformed into a militia."

This citizens' army suffered horrendous casualties; more than 1 million killed, 800,000 missing in action, and an astonishing 2.7 million prisoners of war (POWs). The high numbers of POWs have been attributed by the AOK and by some modern commentators to mass desertions of soldiers from "disaffected nationalities." Yet, despite two much-heralded cases of Czech-speaking infantry regiments (Infantry Regiment 28 from Prague and Infantry Regiment 36 from Mladá Boleslav/Jungbunzlau) there is little to support the thesis of mass desertions by certain nationalities. In most cases, Austro-Hungarian soldiers became POWs when entire sections of the front collapsed or when mass surrenders were negotiated by their generals. When, for example, the fortress of Przemysl was surrendered in March 1915 to the Russians, 119,000 soldiers were led into captivity by the Austro-Hungarian major general Hermann Kusmanek. A year later, during the Brusilov Offensive (1916), an entire section of the Austro-Hungarian front collapsed near Lutsk and 200,000 soldiers were captured by the Russians in three days. In November 1918 the Italian army captured 360,000 Austro-Hungarian soldiers after an armistice agreement had been signed. Thus, it is highly unlikely that soldiers captured in such circumstances had any control over the situation, which are necessary conditions of a reasonable definition of desertion. In any case, the ethnic distribution of Habsburg POWs mirrors that of the general population. If there was overrepresentation of certain nationalities among the POW population, it occurred among those considered "loyal," such as the Austro-Germans and the Magyars.

In the same vein, the civilian population of Austria-Hungary mobilized despite increasing shortages caused by the war and the Entente blockade. Women workers of various ethnic backgrounds assumed an important role in the armaments industry (especially in Bohemia, Lower Austria, and Vienna) and money was raised through the issuance of war bonds. As occurred in Germany and Russia, there was labor unrest in the final two years of the war (culminating in the January 1918 strikes), but it did not have a distinct ethnic profile, and economic demands were not cast in national terms. Despite having a much weaker economy than Germany, France, or Britain, and experiencing severe supply problems in foodstuffs and other basic commodities, the Dual Monarchy managed to keep its citizenry committed to the effort until the end of the war. A country on the brink of implosion would not have been able to do so.

It is worth noting that unlike two other multinational states, Russia and the Ottoman Empire, Austria-Hungary did not engage in acts of collective discrimination against perceived "disloyal" nationalities. It did not deport "suspect groups" from border areas (as had been done in Russia regarding millions of Poles, Germans, Jews, and Lithuanians), nor did it commit genocide (as had been the case in Turkey regarding the Armenians). Despite facing a more heterogeneous population than Russia and the Ottoman Empire, and having to deal with the politics of nationalism longer than other multinational states, Austria-Hungarian leaders did not consider extreme national oppression.

Austria-Hungary fell apart in October–November 1918 after losing a prolonged war and after the victorious Entente decided to carve the state along national lines. Although pressured by émigré politicians since the beginning of the war, Entente leaders decided to adopt the policy of national self-determination only in the winter of 1917–1918. This decision was in no small measure an attempt to lure the population of Central Europe away from what was perceived a far bigger menace—Bolshevism. The impetus for dissolution came from abroad rather than from within. Robert A. Kann, in *A History of the Habsburg Empire, 1526–1918* (1974), argues that "two privileged national groups, Austro-Germans and Magyars, took no initiative to secede until the last weeks of the war. . . . For all other national groups, the decisive actions for secession were engineered by outside forces."

During the last seven decades of its existence, the Habsburg monarchy had a checkered record in dealing with national issues. The *Ausgleich* agreement (1867) is perhaps the prime example: it sought to appease Magyar nationalists by dividing the country into two halves but managed at the same time to antagonize other national movements (without truly appeasing Magyar nationalists). Although these antagonisms reached a high pitch at certain junctures, most noticeably during the Badeni crisis (1897), they seemed to be weakening before the war. The Habsburg Monarchy was neither a paradise on earth nor was it a "prison of nations." However, until the final days of its existence the empire had a real emotional appeal for a significant part of its populace. Among the 360,000 soldiers who fought the Italian army until the end and who were captured in November 1918 (after the state had been broken up into successor states), an overwhelming majority—estimated at three-quarters— came from nationalities long considered "suspect."

—ALON RACHAMIMOV,
TEL AVIV UNIVERSITY

References

István Deák, *Beyond Nationalism: A Social and Political History of the Habsburg Officers Corps, 1848–1918* (New York: Oxford University Press, 1990).

Robert A. Kann, *A History of the Habsburg Empire, 1526–1918* (Berkeley: University of California Press, 1974).

Alon Rachamimov, *POWs and the Great War: Captivity on the Eastern Front* (Oxford & New York: Berg, 2002).

Rachamimov, "Provincial Compromises and State Patriotism in fin-de-Siècle Austria-Hungary," *Tel Aviver Jahrbuch für deutsche Geschichte*, 30 (2001): pp. 120–132.

Alan Sked, *The Decline and Fall of the Habsburg Empire, 1815–1918* (London & New York: Longman, 1989).

Graydon A. Tunstall Jr., *Planning for War against Russia and Serbia: Austro-Hungarian and German Military Strategies, 1871–1914* (Boulder, Colo.: Social Science Monographs, 1993).

Soloman Wank, "Some Reflections on the Habsburg Empire and Its Legacy in the Nationalities Question," *Austrian History Yearbook*, 28 (1997): 131–146.

HIGH SEAS FLEET

Was the strategic concept of the German High Seas Fleet sound?

Viewpoint: Yes. The High Seas Fleet represented a reasonable-risk response to the geographic and political situation of Germany, and it performed well in the first two years of the war.

Viewpoint: No. The German battle fleet produced a small return for the investment of manpower, money, and resources.

The decision by the German Empire to build a battle fleet capable of challenging the Royal Navy has been excoriated from both military and academic perspectives. Soldiers argued from the beginning that the vital interests of Germany lay with its land forces and that resources diverted to anything but coast defense represented a mistake that would be realized in the next war. Naval analysts argued that Germany built the wrong kinds of ships for the kind of war that modern technology was determining. In a developing era of undersea and aerial war, the Kaiser's battleships and battle cruisers were obsolescent on launching. They were also "sacred vessels," incorporating too much German prestige to be committed to the kind of high-risk operations necessary to challenge a superior Royal Navy successfully.

Aside from technical and tactical issues, the German battle fleet was to critics the most vital factor contributing to establishing the Triple Entente and for increased British militarization. Britain could not negotiate the challenge to its maritime superiority—especially when the challenger was also the greatest military power on the Continent. As a result, the island empire not only increased its defense budget but also grew increasingly ready to consider war as a first option. That fact, if not immediately obvious in Berlin, should have become plain enough in the first years of the century to make Kaiser Wilhelm II's dreams of naval power something at most to be traded for the sake of improved Anglo-German relations.

Yet, the German navy was more than a "luxury fleet," more than a tribute to a monarch's vanity or a means of stabilizing and integrating a "restless Reich." At the turn of the century, Germany was in fact a world power with global interests that were not best defended by threatening all-out continental war at every challenge. A fleet, moreover, provided strategic and diplomatic flexibility in an increasingly tight international climate. With a navy it was possible to pose a broader spectrum of threats to potential enemies and to obtain a correspondingly wider area of negotiations. The failures characteristic of the prewar Reich, such as inadequate coordination of strategic planning and neglecting to calculate risks and obligations, had nothing to do with the navy as such. The Anglo-German rivalry was a product of long-standing, complicated factors among which the naval race practically had to jostle for place. The problem was not the fleet—but the inability to use it.

**Viewpoint:
Yes. The High Seas Fleet
represented a reasonable-risk
response to the geographic and
political situation of Germany, and it
performed well in the first two years
of the war.**

Kaiser Wilhelm II believed that Germany was nothing without a grand navy. That advocacy was crucial in the decision to construct a High Seas Fleet. Guided by the visionary naval minister, Admiral Alfred von Tirpitz, the High Seas Fleet grew to be a threat that Great Britain could not ignore. When the mighty British battle fleet passed by in review at Spithead in 1897, observers saw seven miles of steel that protected the sea commerce of a global empire with colonies in every corner of the globe. This display was the Royal Navy at its apogee. Every battleship returned home to commemorate Queen Victoria's Diamond Jubilee and to affirm that command of the sea was for Britain a necessity. The nation could no longer feed its population from its land alone and relied on a worldwide network of trade and colonies to finance its might.

Britain had acquired empire through a shrewd balancing act between seagoing commerce and sea power, each complementing and extending the other. The first serious challenge to its maritime supremacy since the eighteenth century came in 1898, with passage of the first German Naval Bill. Kaiser Wilhelm II was inspired by reading Alfred Thayer Mahan's *Influence of Sea Power Upon History, 1793–1812* (1890), a book the Kaiser made required reading for his naval officers and placed on every warship.

Mahan's inspiration came while pondering another historian's lecture on the Second Punic War (218–202 B.C.E.), when Carthage could only move armies from Spain to Italy overland with great effort and massive attrition, while Rome used its navy to land an army at any place of its choosing and always in good order. Mahan then reviewed history through a prism—understanding the sea as a highway. Only fleets, Mahan argued, could control the sea, and by defeating enemy fleets guarantee the passage of seaborne commerce.

The location of a nation determined its relationship to the sea, conferring advantages and disadvantages that are difficult to undo. The British Isles were blessed by nature; landlocked Germany was cursed. German routes to open ocean were flanked by England. Merchantmen departing from the North Sea coast of Germany could reach the Atlantic Ocean through the English Channel, a mere twenty miles wide between Dover and Calais, or could go north through the Scotland-Norway Gap. Either way German ships could be interdicted by English fleets operating close to home.

England also had a massive head start in naval construction; how was Germany ever to catch up? English grand strategy called for a "two power standard"—a fleet as big as two rival fleets combined. But Tirpitz saw a weakness: England, as a world power, was required to station many warships around the world to protect its trade. What evolved was a "Risk Theory." If Germany could build a fleet that was roughly two-thirds of what Britain could bring to bear in the North Sea, then it could win a measure of respect and reduce the threat to the movement of its shipping. If the pace of naval construction could be kept slow and steady for about two decades, Germany would have forty battleships and twenty battle cruisers to mount this challenge. Even when outnumbered three to two by the Royal Navy in Tirpitz's scenario, Germany would still fight an even battle—assuming its fleet had better ships and better crews.

Central to Mahan's strategic view is the concept of the decisive battle, from which control of the sea goes to the victor. Assuming that Britain accepted a similar doctrine, Tirpitz expected the future war with England to begin with the British Grand Fleet steaming into German waters to execute a close blockade. U-boats and destroyers would reply by fighting hit-and-run actions, using torpedoes to whittle down the British, whose increasingly depleted numbers would eventually be easy prey for an almost equal number of German battleships.

Tirpitz crafted his strategy narrowly to fit a specific set of circumstances. Britain responded by finding ways to concentrate its fleet, using diplomacy to lessen the need for its warships having to be stationed elsewhere. England negotiated its Western Hemisphere interests with the United States, thus lessening the potential for naval conflict in the Caribbean. An alliance with Japan in 1902 allowed England to consolidate its stations in the Far East. In 1904–1905 First Sea Lord John Fisher redeployed his capital ships, trimming the long-dominant Mediterranean fleet to place eight battleships on the Atlantic station and more than double his Channel fleet to seventeen capital ships. Rapprochement with France and Russia also lanced the threat of their combined fleets, ceding to the French fleet the responsibility of policing the Mediterranean to protect British interests and hold in check the fleets of Italy and Austria-Hungary. In return, Britain guaranteed the safety of the Channel

German newspaper picture of a battleship gun crew in action, circa 1916

(from John Keegan, An Illustrated History of the First World War *[2001])*

coast of France against the German naval threat. By 1912 Britain had concentrated thirty-three capital ships in its home waters.

With the launching of HMS *Dreadnought* in 1906, the Royal Navy threw down a technological gauntlet—the modern heavily armed battleship. Germany now had to match Britain in a renewed naval arms race, and the tempo of construction continued. By the outbreak of war in 1914, Germany could only muster eighteen modern capital ships to twenty-six of the British. Not only had England easily constructed more vessels than the Germans in less than a decade, technology was undermining many of the premises Mahan established in his study of naval history. Commerce raiding never won a naval war, wrote Mahan—but the potential of the submarine questioned that premise. Blockade was the persistent force that eroded nations by strangling their trade—but how does a fleet blockade a railroad far inland? Freight trains can move and supply

armies overland with the same ease merchantmen enjoyed at sea.

Nor did Tirpitz think beyond the naval sphere. No joint planning took place between the German navy and army. The navy sought its decisive battle in the North Sea. The army looked toward executing the Schlieffen Plan, cutting through Belgium to get at Paris—not staging in Belgium to get at London. Grand Fleet admiral John Jellicoe labored under the pressure of being the only man who could lose the war for England in one afternoon. Tirpitz had no plan to exploit the opportunities that would have resulted from defeating the Royal Navy.

As war began in 1914 the strengths and weaknesses of both sides became quickly apparent. The German navy commenced commerce raiding. A squadron of cruisers won a quick victory over an inferior British force at Coronel (1914) but was in turn destroyed by a squadron of battle cruisers at the Falklands (1914). Still, the fight was a tough one—not a single German warship struck its colors, the sailors preferring death to dishonor. On the other side of the world, German U-boats proved effective against the Royal Navy. Cruisers HMS *Aboukir, Cressy,* and *Hogue* were sunk on 22 September 1914 by the *U-9,* while the *U-24* sank the predreadnought HMS *Formidable* in December.

The threat of U-boats and mines precluded any British repeat of close blockade. Instead, the Royal Navy divided its fleet, leaving one group of warships to block the English Channel while holding the Scotland-Norway gap with the bulk of its capital ship fleet based at Scapa Flow and Rosyth. The capture of German naval codes (1915) allowed the Grand Fleet to deploy as soon as the German High Seas Fleet did. German forays were thwarted at Heligoland Bight (1914) and Dogger Bank (1915), both British victories.

In the year following these actions, the High Seas Fleet saw much turnover at the top ranks, as Admiral von Ingehol was replaced by the more-timid von Pohl. By mid 1916, leadership of the High Seas Fleet had passed to the more aggressive Admiral Reinhard Scheer, who gave Tirpitz's Risk Theory its best test, taking out the High Seas Fleet on 31 May to clash with the Royal Navy at Jutland, near the entrance to the Baltic Sea.

Scheer brought sixteen dreadnoughts and five battle cruisers against Jellicoe's twenty-eight dreadnoughts and nine battle cruisers. The battle was inconclusive. The High Seas Fleet sank three modern battleships, compared to its loss of one modern dreadnought. Both sides lost a lesser assortment of cruisers and destroyers, and a few German capital ships returned badly damaged. Yet, the Grand Fleet won by maintaining its stranglehold on sea-lanes exiting to the Atlantic Ocean. Scheer, in his after-action report, acknowledged this strategic failure.

Inferior fleets need not always fight battles to influence war. Failing to force battle on its terms, the High Seas Fleet became a "fleet in being," whose existence forced Britain to maintain its battle fleet at a level of strength and effectiveness that absorbed a disproportionate share of national resources. A fleet in port, however, loses its effectiveness quickly. Germany shifted its strategic emphasis to sea denial in 1917 with unrestricted U-boat warfare, and for lack of a mission, morale in the High Seas Fleet plummeted. Two more post–Jutland sorties amounted to nothing. Crews got by on short rations while officers dined well, further increasing resentment. By the fall of 1918, symptoms of mutiny and disaffection were undermining the High Seas Fleet.

After Germany began negotiating for an armistice in the fall of 1918, the High Seas Fleet was ordered to sortie once again on 27 October, this time on what was expected to be its "death ride." This deployment was throttled by the passive resistance of sailors, while officers looked the other way. Red flags flew from the masts of mighty dreadnoughts while sailors formed councils and took to the streets of Kiel and fomented revolution. In the end, the fleet surrendered without firing a shot and later was ignominiously scuttled by skeleton crews. Nonetheless, the limited results it achieved did not make the strategic concept that inspired it a bad idea. The failure of the High Seas Fleet indicates rather that even a good tool is ineffective in the hands of those who cannot use it properly—or will not use it at all.

—WILLIAM TERDOSLAVICH,
NEW YORK, NEW YORK

Viewpoint:
No. The German battle fleet produced a small return for the investment of manpower, money, and resources.

In 1898 Germany began a serious expansion of its fleet. Until then the German navy consisted of a few cruisers and some coast-defense ships, but the new navy minister, Admiral Alfred von Tirpitz, persuaded the Kaiser and the Reichstag to build a large fleet. Tirpitz's goal was, however, not to fight and win battles directly; it was to gain strategic leverage against Great Britain in the race for colonies. Since it was the fastest developing nation, and national power and prestige were measured in terms of colonies, Germany wanted more than the few it had. The Germans were also worried about the growing inclination of Britain to introduce preferential tariffs across the British Empire—and there was a serious debate in Britain about this policy, despite a history of supporting free trade. The overseas markets that Germany was developing might be cut off at the stroke of a pen.

German strategy, however, misfired badly. The British saw it as bullying, although, to be fair, the Germans were also worried by the growing Russian fleet in the Baltic. The British had long felt that, as an island nation relying on imports, they must have clear naval superiority. Thus, they reacted to the German challenge by building more and (eventually) much better battleships, and at a faster pace. Indeed, the Germans not only drove the British to build a larger fleet but also to form a hazy alliance with the French, precisely what the Germans did not want. Instead of making the British respect Ger-

CREATING SEA POWER

In his memoirs, German admiral Alfred von Tirpitz defends his policy of building a battle fleet:

The reproach which is levelled at me from time to time of having pursued a one-sided and obtuse battle-fleet policy, is based upon an error. In comparison with the historical progress of our empire, we were late in going out into the world and upon the sea. In the bustle of the world, however, we had to expect conflicts of interest. It was important that we should avoid such things, and indeed impose no restrictions upon our activity so long as the understructure of our power was not secure. Until this was strengthened by our fleet and by our political support, we could not move with any freedom upon the seas of the world and demand equal rights. Our, and particularly my, personal task therefore lay primarily in the creation of this sea-power, and this could only be done by the institution of the battle fleet. Moreover, we were compelled by the threats of the British in the first decade of this century to concentrate our fleet in force in home waters. Under these conditions trans-Atlantic expeditions, such as the China campaign, the action against Venezuela or the Agadir affair seemed to me altogether undesirable, quite apart from their particular disadvantages, for they only gave rise to jealousy of a State which could not yet be regarded as an equal at sea. During the last few years before the war, however, I saw the time approaching in which England's inclination to attack us would cease, and give place to an attitude which would invite trade on an equal footing. This opened up a prospect of greater liberty of movement, which I also considered advisable for reasons affecting the service. The Prussian military spirit on which the whole national existence and the higher economic life of our people was founded, and will also have to be founded in the future, has one weak spot; the tendency to routine. It needs great personalities and keen judges of human nature like Moltke, Roon, and the old Emperor, to keep the live spirit going in the machine. The Prussian must have his pig-tail cut from time to time or else it will grow too long. Thus a certain rigidity in diligent, correct but subordinate work threatened to deprive the over-strained officers of the navy of any width of horizon. Particularly owing to the short period of service in our military organization, the life of our battle fleet in home waters ran the danger of losing through continual drill its enlivening contact with peoples and countries overseas. I not only wanted to train the officers in navy routine, but I also wanted to enable them to feel at home in Berlin society and the great world. Further, as I have said before, the gathering together of Germanism over the whole world required the support of the fleet more strongly than ever. Finally it was in my view our fleet's mission to react fruitfully upon the narrow horizon of many Germans at home by means of the experiences which it had collected abroad. In conjunction with Germans abroad, the fleet was to deepen the understanding for our national existence, which, in consequence of the increasing population and industry, was no longer confined between the Rhine and the Vistula, but had to sink its roots more and more in activities overseas.

Source: Alfred von Tirpitz, My Memoirs, volume 1 (New York: Dodd, Mead, 1919), pp. 196–199.

many and work with it, Britain was now lined up as an enemy. As costs of ever-larger battleships spiraled higher, furthermore, the Germans found they had lost control of the arms race and were trying to slow things down (effectively admitting defeat) even before war broke out.

Therefore the big-navy policy was a diplomatic failure. Although the increased naval strength of Germany won it some minor colonial concessions, these additions were not nearly enough to balance having antagonized Britain. Nor was it a military success. Tirpitz gave more thought to his theories of political leverage than how the fleet would operate in wartime. While he correctly assumed the British would institute a blockade, he wrongly thought that it would be near to land, with the blockaders a few miles off the German coast and thus vulnerable to raids by surface ships and attrition from submarines. In order to maintain their blockade, the British would have to keep a constant stream of ships going to sea, remaining on station, and returning home to refuel; the Germans could easily time a raid to pounce on part of the enemy fleet. Instead, the British established a distant blockade, intercepting inbound merchantmen before they got to the North Sea and risking some raids by holding their warships well back from the German coast. They had realized, as Tirpitz had not, that this form of blockade would be just as effective and much less risky.

Tirpitz's diplomatic failure might have been redeemed in a successful battle, but the British were too careful. It was obvious that the Germans planned to divide and conquer rather than risk a showdown with the larger British Grand Fleet. The British remedy was equally obvious: stay together. Since the distant blockade worked, the British had no need to divide their fleet, which left the Germans at a loss as to how to make them disperse. By raiding the English coast they hoped to force the British to keep some ships at sea as a rapid-reaction force, but the Royal Navy declined the bait. In only one action did the Germans come close to getting their raiding force in the position they needed to catch the British. In fact, over the course of the war, battleships on both sides spent more time in port than at sea. There was only one significant battle between them—and it was indecisive.

What eventually developed in the North Sea was a tense standoff, with squabbles at the boundaries of a watery "no man's land." The Germans laid minefields to protect their ports, while keeping lanes open to let submarines out—and through which they could always sortie the fleet. The British also laid minefields to try to seal the Germans in. German minelayers and minesweepers eventually were operating 150 miles from their coast; these small craft needed support or British ships would sink them. So the Germans used destroyers to keep watch for British warships, with light cruisers ready to support the destroyers and bigger ships kept ready to support the cruisers. Without battleships to support the minelayers and minesweepers, the German North Sea ports could have been blocked by British mines. This strategy, however, inverted the prewar naval expectations. Big ships did not exist to support little ships; they were supposed to be the top of the pyramid. In addition, the German heavy ships played a role in deterring various British plans to invade the Baltic or occupy small islands in the North Sea as advanced blockade bases.

British plans for either a North Sea or Baltic invasion were consistently scuppered not by fear of German battleships but by the dual problems of supplying the landing force and the threat of mines and submarines attacking follow-up forces. The British always expected to have to defeat the German battle fleet before entering the Baltic; after doing so, they might well have forced their way in and landed several infantry divisions. But unless that landing won the war, the Germans could lay mines and station submarines to prevent supplies from reaching the invasion force until it was compelled to surrender. The real problem for amphibious operations did not come from battleships but from mines and torpedoes.

While the Germans needed some battleships to protect their North Sea minelayers and minesweepers, they could probably have managed with many fewer vessels. In a battle where the British sought to interfere with the German small craft, the Germans would only have needed to avoid defeat, not score a decisive victory. How many battleships would the British have been willing to trade for a few minesweepers?

Furthermore, could the Germans have used the resources (financial, industrial, and manpower) that went into the battleships more effectively? If the effort had been put into naval forces, it would have required adopting a strategy that avoided big battles and instead looked to attack British shipping. More cruisers would have been stationed in the few German colonies to raid enemy shipping. This policy would admit the obvious: German colonies and ships were eventually doomed against the more powerful Royal Navy. It could only last a relatively short time, since a British blockade and campaign against German colonial bases would eventually eliminate the commerce raiders. Thus, it made little sense to adopt this strategy for the short war that everybody expected for a host of military, political, diplomatic, and economic reasons.

Meanwhile, in the North Sea the Germans would have had to utilize more light cruisers, more destroyers, and possibly more submarines and zeppelins. These weapons would have been effective defensive forces but by prewar standards had little offensive punch. Of course, submarines would have had the same potential that historically developed, but before 1914 nobody anticipated using them against commercial shipping. It is more likely that German strategy would have followed a similar course and that U-boats would eventually have been used against merchant shipping, but they would have had more of these weapons at the start of the war. Such a policy would have been unpalatable for the German navy: in its budget battles it would have only an unexciting claim to coast defense, not a dramatic, offensive rationale that would justify substantial spending.

Did Germany need an aggressive naval strategy as well as a large land army? Probably not, because its long-standing enemies were France and Russia, neither of which posed a major naval threat nor was susceptible to substantial naval pressure. If a portion of the manufacturing effort that went into building the second-largest fleet in the world had been devoted to the army, Germany could have had more artillery and more shells at the start of the war, perhaps more trucks to carry supplies, and possibly a larger army. In fact, had the German government focused on a Continental strategy, the army would have been stronger and its enemies possibly weaker. Expansion of the German fleet provoked Britain; without that policy, Britain might not have lined up against Germany in 1914. The German government decided to build more battleships in 1912 rather than add four divisions to the army; with hindsight, those divisions might have been the margin between victory and defeat in France.

—SANDERS MARBLE,
SMITHSONIAN INSTITUTION

References

Paul G. Halpern, *A Naval History of World War I* (Annapolis, Md.: Naval Institute Press, 1994).

Holger H. Herwig, *"Luxury Fleet": The German Imperial Navy, 1888–1918* (London: Allen & Unwin, 1980).

Paul M. Kennedy, *The Rise of the Anglo-German Antagonism, 1860–1914* (London & Boston: Allen & Unwin, 1980).

Jonathan Steinberg, *Yesterday's Deterrent: Tirpitz and the Birth of the German Battle Fleet* (London: Macdonald, 1965).

Wolfgang Wegener, *The Naval Strategy of the World War,* translated by Herwig (Annapolis, Md.: Naval Institute Press, 1989).

HIGH SEAS FLEET

HOMOSEXUALITY

Did the war experience foster awareness and acceptance of homosexuality and homoeroticism?

Viewpoint: Yes. World War I provided a context for men to express erotic conceptions of virile masculinity and misogyny.

Viewpoint: No. War was the province of conventionally defined masculinity that made little room for unconventional sexuality.

The relationship of sex and war is so generally acknowledged that it seems redundant to say homosexuality as well as heterosexuality was influenced by the events of 1914–1918. World War I brought together millions of males between the ages of eighteen and forty, under conditions of common living that as a rule mocked notions of "Victorian reticence" that in any case were usually manifestations of middle-class status or aspirations. Washing and bathing facilities were public. One German regimental history published a picture of several men perched companionably together on an open pole latrine. Apart from direct sexual activity—the "red lamps" so often mentioned in British soldiers' memoirs, or the "tolerated houses" that shocked more-prudish members of the American Expeditionary Force (AEF)—the sexualization of language and conversation was one way of asserting masculinity and claiming status in an affinity group.

Sexualization developed but not sexuality. "The love that dares not speak its name" had been "coming out" in Europe well before the Great War. From Oscar Wilde to Kaiser Wilhelm II, rumor vied with truth in the tabloid press, in courtrooms, and in bedrooms as well. Illegal in every country of Europe, homosexuality was frequently denounced by its critics as "demasculinizing" future generations of soldiers, not only directly but also by fostering a climate of effeminacy in everything from artistic tastes to smoking habits.

Among the more interesting social consequences of World War I is the transformation of the cigarette from a symbol of sissiness to a trope of masculinity. That process had much less to do with the artifact itself than with the ease of keeping cigarettes alight under difficult conditions, the welcome deadening effect of nicotine on the senses of taste and smell, and the widespread acceptance of sharing cigarettes and lights both as a social icebreaker among strangers and a gesture of solidarity between officers and men that did not challenge the limits of discipline.

In those contexts, cigarettes may well stand as a signifier for the impact of the Great War on homosexuality. Paul Fussell in *The Great War and Modern Memory* (1975) argues for the significance of "homoeroticism": a sublimated, desexualized attraction of males for males he describes as "temporary homosexuality." His relatively limited database, chiefly literary evidence provided by a particular section of British officers, has been challenged by later research making a case that the intensity and intimacy of wartime male relationships was a more complex reaction to circumstances that European men had never experienced.

Peacetime environments favored male isolation: in the nuclear family and through competition for success. The "solidarity" of the trade union and socialist movements was always somewhat artificial. In the army, especially at the front, the solidarity and comradeship was real—a facilitator of survival and a barrier to insanity. It could and did become "a love surpassing the love of women." It was also a love circumstantial and conditional, linking men who would never have come together in their civilian lives. Its temporary instrumental nature inhibited the development of sexual dimensions, sublimated or overt. So did the severe penalties all armies provided for that offense—discipline reflecting less a principled homophobia than concern for abuse of superior/subordinate relationships.

The appetite of the war for men was indifferent to sexual orientation, and circumstances left little energy for gay-bashing at the front or behind the lines. One might indeed speak of the "invisible homosexual," reduced to anonymity by his uniform and by an environment fostering indifference to sexual orientation, as long as its manifestations were not seen as threatening group identities as vital as they were fragile. What counted was not whom someone preferred to kiss in private but his public performance and persona.

Viewpoint:
Yes. World War I provided a context for men to express erotic conceptions of virile masculinity and misogyny.

The closest ties between soldiers on both sides of "no man's land" were the relationships men developed with their comrades. The vast majority of these friendships were defined by conventional norms: sharing rations, mail, clothing, and equipment, as well as offering boon companionship in the face of an uncertain fate. Less-common fraternal association could and often did translate into the expression of romantic love between men in service together. Such associations were certainly disapproved of by structured social organizations in Western society as an immoral refutation of the established, heterosexual bourgeois order. They were also considered anathema to the morale and combat efficiency of military structures. Yet, despite efforts undertaken in concert by military, political, and social authorities, homoeroticism and homosexuality persisted among soldiers engaged in the war effort. Such behavior, however, was not the result of World War I. It was the extension of the gender identification of middle- and upper-class youth imparted by cultural institutions—public schools, artistic venues, and male-oriented socialization—in the decades prior to August 1914. These cultural values were not forgotten in the midst of war but were often the only means for participants to contextualize the war. Or, as Eric J. Leed observes in *No Man's Land: Combat and Identity in World War I* (1979), "It is simply inconceivable that those who fought on both sides of No Man's Land were not, initially at least, the products of their respective cultures." If homosocial interaction was valued in civilian society before the war, it is not implausible that some soldiers retained this cultural attachment even in the midst of the war.

According to Michael C. C. Adams, author of *The Great Adventure: Male Desire and the Coming of World War I* (1990), maleness in Edwardian Britain and America was tied to a trope of masculine activity developed in public schools and reinforced in games, scouting activities, and communal living. One's measure as a man was defined by bravery, discipline, chivalric honor, physical strength and toughness, and rugged stoicism in the face of tribulation. Buttressing these values was a suspicion of feminized behaviors, including the wanton expression of emotion, nervousness, a lazy and dreaming disposition, and an overall lack of moral rectitude. School texts and lessons, popular books and novels, and public entertainment reinforced this gendered perceptual framework. Tales of plucky lads roughing it in the wilderness or assuming their masculine prerogative to venture forth against the heathen in the name of God, Empire, or Republic were important components of the creation of male identity. Team and individual sport, at times violent, emphasized the importance of a strong body and moral fairness in the pursuit of life's reward. "Play up, play the game," was not a mere poetic device; it was a call to young men to take the rules and zeal of the playing field beyond adolescence into manhood.

Male-oriented associations were introduced to young men as children and were imbued with value that transcended adolescence. Throughout Europe and America the Boy Scouts and other outdoor youth associations offered a chance for young men to experience the adventure and male companionship they had only encountered in novels. In Wilhelmine Germany, another masculine venue is described by Ute Frevert in *Men of Honour: A Social and Cultural History of the Duel* (1995): the university dueling societies. Here young men tested their courage, skill, and fortitude in potentially mortal combat. Dueling clubs fulfilled other roles as well. Not only did they provide fertile

APOLOGIA PRO POEMATE MEO

Wilfred Owen, a British poet and soldier, wrote this poem in late 1917; he was killed in battle on 4 November 1918.

I, too, saw God through mud,—
  The mud that cracked on cheeks when wretches
    smiled.
  War brought more glory to their eyes than blood,
  And gave their laughs more glee than shakes a child.

Merry it was to laugh there—
  Where death becomes absurd and life absurder.
  For power was on us as we slashed bones bare
  Not to feel sickness or remorse of murder.

I, too, have dropped off fear—
  Behind the barrage, dead as my platoon,
  And sailed my spirit surging, light and clear
  Past the entanglement where hopes lay strewn;

And witnessed exultation—
  Faces that used to curse me, scowl for scowl,
  Shine and lift up with passion of oblation,
  Seraphic for an hour; though they were foul.

I have made fellowships—
  Untold of happy lovers in old song.
  For love is not the binding of fair lips
  With the soft silk of eyes that look and long,

By Joy, whose ribbon slips,—
  But wound with war's hard wire whose stakes are
    strong;
  Bound with the bandage of the arm that drips;
  Knit in the welding of the rifle-thong.

I have perceived much beauty
  In the hoarse oaths that kept our courage straight;
  Heard music in the silentness of duty;
  Found peace where shell-storms spouted reddest
    spate.

Nevertheless, except you share
  With them in hell the sorrowful dark of hell,
  Whose world is but the trembling of a flare,
  And heaven but as the highway for a shell,

You shall not hear their mirth:
  You shall not come to think them well content
  By any jest of mine. These men are worth
  Your tears. You are not worth their merriment.

Source: *Wilfred Owen,* The Poems of Wilfred Owen, *edited by Edmund Blunden (London: Chatto & Windus, 1946), pp. 85–86.*

ground for the instillation of a militarized *denk-stil* (style of thinking) that identified honor with blood, the dueling associations also commodified and denigrated femininity. Women were transformed from partners into objects to be simultaneously scorned and fought over, and dueling scars became marks of virility and honor in the eyes of the holder.

The flip side of virile masculinity was virulent misogyny. As youths were schooled in the vitality of their bodies and character, they were also instructed that women were to be distrusted. Adams describes how femininity was viewed as the parasitic partner of the sexual dyad. On the one side, marriage was valued as essential to the survival not only of the bloodline but also of the state as well. Preserving the name and the state, however, came with a price. Close association with women eroded the barrier between the genders and could put men in mortal danger of losing their virility and masculinity. Klaus Theweleit, in *Male Fantasies* (1987–1989), places this relationship in a more Freudian context, postulating the presence of an Oedipal relationship transfixing German men that translated into an incapacity to experience normative relationships with women.

The ideal of virile masculinity and the fear of femininity also found artistic and literary voice in the fin de siècle decadence movement. Fascinated with themes of seduction, corruption, decay, and death, participants frequently portrayed iconographic representations of masculinity cast into mortal contest with femininity. According to Bram Dijkstra, in *Idols of Perversity: Fantasies of Feminine Evil in Fin-de-Siècle Culture* (1986), one way this portrayal was achieved was by imbuing women with mythic roles reflecting the danger of their alleged sexual power. As siren, they lured men to their destruction through the promise of lust. As vampire, they sapped the essences of their victims while polluting their blood with venereal disease. As George L. Mosse observes in *The Image of Man: The Creation of Modern Masculinity* (1996), the decadents offered a public venue for artistic homosexuals such as Oscar Wilde, Aubrey Beardsley, and Charles-Pierre Baudelaire to express their sexual identities as they also rejected society's expectations.

The decadents were but one artistic voice in fin de siècle society that appealed to a thriving subculture of homosexuality. Every major urban center in the West contained a small community of men and women who participated in same-sex lifestyles. By necessity, however, these communities existed in a shadowy periphery. In the eyes of mainstream European society, the homosexual was an aberrant creature that defied nature and morality. Politically, homosexuals were criminalized by legislation and criminal codes that classified sodomy and other lewd acts as felonious offenses. In addition to the cultural and political censure applied against it, homosexuality was judged as a biological flaw. The weight of medical authority was also levered against same-sex orientation. Homosexuals were classified as victims of sexual inversion, their normal masculine aspect subverted by an internalized femininity, constituting a "third sex" distinct from the male/female dyad. Furthermore, in a society obsessed with social Darwinism, homosexuality also offered evidence of the inexorable process of race degeneration, the participant's sexual inclination evidencing a physical and moral dissipation. Thus, once uncovered, practicing homosexuals faced confinement either in prison, as moral criminals, or in hospitals, as mental degenerates.

In addition to those who were already identified as homosexuals, the war provided a catalyst through which other individuals encountered the nature of their sexual orientation. For some participants, being placed within the exclusive community of men for a prolonged period validated the homosocial experiences of childhood and adolescence. The communal relationships with other soldiers held reminders of the scouting forays and collegial interactivities of youth, while mundane activities such as bathing called up artistic images of masculine nudes. The act of combat itself was endowed with erotic overtones as well, the most noted examples remaining the imagery of British war poets such as Wilfred Owen and Rupert Brooke, as well as the deification of war by German author Ernst Jünger. Much of this writing was later categorized as the expression of *frontgemeinschaft,* the front community that united soldiers on both sides in a shared experience of war. For those who participated in it, homosexual interaction was a refinement of this shared identity, the total expression of the brotherhood of service in war.

Added to the homosocial and homoerotic facets of military service was the liminality of war itself. Leed describes how the war experience produced a series of disjointed estrangements from normalcy that transformed the participant. Different forms of coping with these points of separation with cultural and traditional values were pursued, including the fleeting sanctuary of romantic love and sexual contact between willing partners. Facing the prospect not merely of death in battle but total physical annihilation in the storm of steel, individuals turned to the comfort of a romanticized personal past, rejecting the uncertain future modernity held. For some, this past included the poetic expression of manly love, an affirmation acted out and given life in the shadow of death.

Fussell has described the homoeroticism in the works of the British war poets as a literary device employed by a select group of English literati to express their own tortured reactions to the war, which was not representative of the mass experience. Thus, homosexuality, either as the subject of fantasy or active participation, is reduced to a small and vocal minority. This point has since been taken up to marginalize the reality of same-sex relations between men in uniform. Support is offered in reviews of British court martial hearings, which indicate that homosexuality was almost nonexistent. The problem with relying exclusively upon the paucity of indictments for sodomy or other acts of indecency is the omission of the primary mechanism of the military for regulating sexual behavior. For much of the twentieth century, homosexuality was not only considered a crime, it was also perceived to be a mental illness, officially classified by physicians as a psychopathic state. The U.S. Army Medical Department study of neuropsychiatry in the war indicates that 209 out of 8,772 soldiers who passed through General Hospital No. 214, one of the American Expeditionary Force (AEF) neuropsychiatric hospitals, between 1 January 1918 and 1 July 1919 were diagnosed with sexual pathology, one of the constitutional psychopathic states that were the institutional metaphors for homosexuality. The combined actions undertaken by the dual pillars of military discipline and authority—the judge advocate and the medical officer—to identify and classify homosexuals as socially and medically unfit for service reveal a higher incidence of homosexuality in the uniformed services than alleged by those seeking to marginalize the behavior.

Overlooked as well by the focus of attention on the British war poets and men of letters is the experience of other combatants. In his study of sexuality in wartime, *The Sexual History of the World War* (1934), Magnus Hirschfeld described how the prewar homosexual community in Germany sought justification and repeal of legislation outlawing them through military service. Mosse observes how soldiers and officers in Germany idealized the virility of the masculinized community in the trenches, transferring these values in the 1920s to the different nationalist political movements. Theweleit also describes how German officers with homoerotic and homosexual inclinations, fighting after the armistice with *Freikorps* companies in the East, transferred their desire into a ferocious misogyny that identified women with death, blood, and bolshevism. Such imagery, Theweleit says, persisted in the National Socialist vision of virile, heroic, and racially pure German masculinity, to which femininity was made submissive and subservient.

HOMOSEXUALITY

It is difficult to make an objective reckoning of the extent to which British, German, French, and other soldiers expressed and acted upon their desires for other men. British officers such as Siegfried Sassoon, Robert Graves, and T. E. Lawrence notwithstanding, homosexuals were reluctant to record their deepest feelings, let alone share them with their peers, out of the fear of prosecution or hospitalization. Indeed, for many, their wartime trysts with other men were just that—a temporary distraction or reaching out for companionship, to be repressed as they returned to civilian life and the stability of family life. It is clear, however, that homosexuality was not only experienced by a sizable, if indeterminate, group of uniformed men in World War I, but that many retained their sexual identity after the war. Postwar Berlin especially acquired a near-mythic reputation for its alleged permissiveness with regard to same-sex liaisons and relationships, but homosexual men and lesbians alike partook of the relaxed atmosphere toward sexual mores in cities such as Paris and London in the 1920s. Yet, self-recognition and the freedom to express one's sexual identity did not necessarily translate into broad cultural acceptance. The social turmoil of the Great Depression and conservative reaction—not only in National Socialist Germany but also in the Western democracies as well—to economic and political distress forced homosexuals back into the shadows.

—BOBBY A. WINTERMUTE,
TEMPLE UNIVERSITY

Viewpoint:
No. War was the province of conventionally defined masculinity that made little room for unconventional sexuality.

Close friendships among soldiers developed as a result of their common experiences in World War I. These relationships may have included some homosexual and homoerotic aspects. The existing evidence yields no unqualified conclusions. Less-conventional manifestations of masculinity can be found in allusions to homosexuality and homoeroticism by authors such as Robert Graves, Wilfred Owen, Siegfried Sassoon, and T. E. Lawrence writing about the conflict. Extending these authors' words to the rest of the armed services in World War I stretches the limits of logic. According to cultural historian George

L. Mosse in *The Image of Man: The Creation of Modern Masculinity* (1996), World War I added no new feature to the existing construction of masculinity. The war experience, however, strengthened some aspects of that existing masculinity.

Prior to World War I, men occupied the public, political, and economic spheres. Their masculine duties included that of provider and protector, both for their families and their nations. In schools in both Germany and Britain, boys were taught that men dutifully met the challenge of any situation. War represented a cultural process in which males were transformed from boys into adults. This transition excluded women. Indeed, it was from the Victorian feminine virtues of softness, supportiveness, and passivity that boys tried to break away. Men had to remain war-like to avoid slipping back into a boyish condition or falling into feminine ways. Those effeminate men could be homosexuals who possessed unmasculine or deviant traits such as weakness, cowardice, and decadence. Heterosexual men, on the contrary, exhibited the following masculine virtues: courage, self-sacrifice, self-control, decisiveness, vigor, stoicism, resolve, and quiet strength. According to Freudian psychology, even "straight" men might have some hidden anxieties about their sexuality. Certainly, men felt the need to define their collective status as adult males in opposition to boys, women, and homosexuals. World War I emerged as an opportunity for both the rite of passage to manhood and the guarantee of that passage.

In every European nation, the overwhelming majority of people—regardless of class, gender, ideology, or sexual orientation—rallied to the colors in 1914. Men served a cause greater than themselves. Parades and rallies occurred in all the capital cities, while the standing armies mobilized. Nationalistic and militaristic fervor gripped European nations. The fervor emphasized masculinity as well as misogyny. Propaganda played up the masculine symbols of a given nation. Posters portrayed the enemy as effeminate or barbaric, who could be defeated only by soldiers who possessed proper masculine qualities.

Once the fighting started, the horrors of trench warfare drew men together, causing a sincere and heartfelt camaraderie to develop. Sometimes labeled as small-unit cohesion, group identification, or male bonding, the camaraderie among soldiers leveled class distinctions, ethnic backgrounds, and even national allegiances. Soldiers gradually lost their individual identity as "me" and replaced it with the collective identity of "us." Time and time again, veterans made references in novels and memoirs to their great loyalty

German soldiers opening a Christmas parcel, circa 1916

(from Grosser Bilderatlas des Weltkrieges [1915–1919], Joseph M. Bruccoli Great War Collection, Thomas Cooper Library, University of South Carolina)

to their squad of fellow soldiers. Every bombardment, every charge, every retreat, every meal, and every death brought these men closer together. They would fight, die, or kill to save their close friends. They treated their wounded and dying comrades with great compassion and gentleness. The small groups of soldiers became surrogate families. Soldiers "loved" one another—but not necessarily in the physical sense.

The love among soldiers grew out of no mere romantic fancies. On the contrary, theirs was a community of martyrs who shared their own rituals and way of thinking about life and

death. A darker side to combat also existed. World War I required men to prove their manhood by brutally killing other men not unlike themselves. Theirs was a community of devoted friends—a brotherhood. In part, their camaraderie intensified because the soldiers had been removed from their homes, families, and civilian lives. That estrangement, with its loneliness and alienation, drove men still closer together. Theirs was a homosocial community. Whatever homoerotic motifs or homosexual activities might be made, they were within the context of nonphysical love.

HOMOSEXUALITY

Many sexual allusions can be found in the language and activities of war. For example, military vocabulary includes terms such as assault, thrust, and penetration. These terms all connote aggressive and offensive actions, whether with another human being or against an enemy. Indeed, in the case of the first, sexuality, coercion, and violence combine in cases of rape. The rape victim is therefore assaulted, just as soldiers might assault trenches where enemy soldiers unwillingly awaited thrusts and penetrations of bayonets. Still, the analogy between a physical assault and a military assault can only be taken so far, because those enemy soldiers often repelled the advance and counterattacked themselves.

According to Paul Fussell, in *The Great War and Modern Memory* (1975), homoeroticism also existed in the trenches. He believes that homoerotic experiences occurred in part because the front lines contained few or no women. Without available objects of their sexual urges, homoeroticism became more and more prevalent among soldiers on the front lines. Fussell uses the term "homoerotic" to describe chaste, idealistic, sublimated crushes among soldiers—"a form of temporary homosexuality." Such relationships had been fostered, for example, among the middle- and upper-class boys while they were in English public schools before the war. These soldiers carried their experiences from boyhood into adulthood. Developing crushes on and affections for other men yielded means to cope with the loneliness and terror of the front. These homoerotic longings among soldiers notwithstanding, Fussell is careful to point out that few longings for other men extended into physical relationships.

Authors such as Graves, Owen, Sassoon, and Lawrence included homoerotic motifs in their works and heightened the awareness of homosexuality in World War I. Certainly, their works were acknowledged as worthy of inclusion in the literary canon. Some authors were themselves homosexuals or had engaged in homosexual acts. They portrayed their lovers or would-be lovers in idealistic terms. The object of affection might have been a youthful soldier with chiseled features, relative cleanliness, and golden hair. These young men possessed aesthetic beauty and purity about them. This idealism, however, did not correspond to the reality of death, filth, stench, and misery in the trenches. Perhaps the pervasiveness of homosexuality and homoeroticism in some postwar literature may also have been just as idealized, leaving a wide gap between fiction and nonfiction.

Aside from the flowery language used by authors, finding hard evidence for the acceptance and practice of homosexuality in World War I is no easy task. Statistics, where available, allow few concrete conclusions to be drawn regarding the number and frequency of homosexual activity. Authors and others brought their cultural biases to their wartime experiences and postwar writings. They tended to come from middle- and upper-class backgrounds that held certain, often Victorian, views of homosexuality.

Available evidence regarding sexuality among soldiers strongly suggests that heterosexuality was pervasive, rather than homosexuality. Massive numbers of soldiers of all combatant nations had intercourse with women, whether it was consensual, forcible, or compensatory. Women were therefore the objects of war and often the sexual conquests or rewards of war.

Whether old or young, married or single, soldiers frequently visited brothels and employed prostitutes during World War I. Their activities often had a medical penalty. In the British army alone, 27 percent of all diagnosed diseases were classified "social diseases" or, in modern terms, venereal diseases. More than four hundred thousand British men required treatment for their conditions. Elsewhere in Paris in 1914 and 1915, almost four thousand French girls were arrested for prostitution; about half of these girls had contracted venereal diseases. If these large numbers of hospitalized and diagnosed cases allow any inference about the orientation of sexual activity, then there must have been millions of additional male soldiers engaging in heterosexual intercourse.

As for those cases involving homosexuality, the numbers of cases were miniscule. Between 1914 and 1919 in the British army, 22 officers and 270 enlisted men were court-martialed for acts of "indecency" with other soldiers. Once again, if this low number of convictions for homosexual activities allows any inferences about this supposedly deviant activity, then sexual relations between male soldiers may not have occurred very often. Even those homosexual activities that did occur may have been little more than experimentation by soldiers who were curious, lonely, or confused, rather than a wholesale acceptance of homosexuality.

The comparative statistics on heterosexual and homosexual activities point to a relatively insignificant level of the latter relative to the former in World War I. Although homosexuality and homoeroticism achieved a higher level of visibility and acceptance as a result of the war, this fact does not mean that any level of tolerance was achieved. Political and cultural reactions to the Great Depression pushed homosexuals back into closets because they represented a challenge to the sexual status quo and thus to social order in those nations.

—DAVID J. ULBRICH, TEMPLE UNIVERSITY

References

Michael C. C. Adams, *The Great Adventure: Male Desire and the Coming of World War I* (Bloomington: Indiana University Press, 1990).

Bram Dijkstra, *Idols of Perversity: Fantasies of Feminine Evil in Fin-de-Siècle Culture* (New York: Oxford University Press, 1986).

Modris Eksteins, *Rites of Spring: The Great War and the Birth of the Modern Age* (Toronto: Lester & Orpen Dennys, 1989).

John Ellis, *Eye-Deep in Hell: Trench Warfare in World War I* (London: Croom Helm, 1976).

Jean Bethke Elshtain, *Women and War* (New York: Basic Books, 1987).

Niall Ferguson, *The Pity of War* (London: Penguin, 1989).

Ute Frevert, *Men of Honour: A Social and Cultural History of the Duel,* translated by Anthony Williams (Cambridge: Polity Press & Cambridge, Mass.: Blackwell, 1995).

Paul Fussell, *The Great War and Modern Memory* (New York: Oxford University Press, 1975).

Lesley A. Hall, *Hidden Anxieties: Male Sexuality, 1900–1950* (Cambridge: Polity Press, 1991).

Margaret Randolph Higonnet and others, eds., *Behind the Lines: Gender and the Two World Wars* (New Haven: Yale University Press, 1987).

Magnus Hirschfeld, *The Sexual History of the World War,* 3 volumes (New York: Panurge Press, 1934).

Eric J. Leed, *No Man's Land: Combat and Identity in World War I* (Cambridge & New York: Cambridge University Press, 1979).

George L. Mosse, *Fallen Soldiers: Reshaping the Memory of the World Wars* (New York: Oxford University Press, 1990).

Mosse, *The Image of Man: The Creation of Modern Masculinity* (New York: Oxford University Press, 1996).

Klaus Theweleit, *Male Fantasies,* translated by Stephen Conway and others, 2 volumes (Cambridge: Polity Press, 1987–1989; Minneapolis: University of Minnesota Press, 1987–1989).

HOMOSEXUALITY

IMPERIAL RUSSIA

Was Imperial Russia's gradual dissolution in 1914–1915 a manifestation of structural weaknesses exacerbated by the war?

Viewpoint: Yes. The tsarist policy of centralizing power, limiting reforms, and ignoring the suggestions of advisers ensured that Russia could not effectively wage war and remedy its internal problems.

Viewpoint: No. The crisis in Russia was a function of military defeats that reflected the incompetence of the high military command.

The first two years of the Great War strained tsarist Russia to its breaking point. Vladimir Lenin described the war as massively accelerating the process of revolution, and after nearly a century of hindsight it is difficult to establish a credible counterfactual scenario in which Russia might have avoided at least something along the lines of the February 1916 collapse of the monarchy. Was the war itself the cause of the collapse of Imperial Russia? Or did the war merely exacerbate fundamental weaknesses that had been previously demonstrated yet never effectively addressed?

Adherents of the latter position highlight drastic changes of prewar Russian political and economic systems. The Duma, the parliament established after the abortive revolution of 1904–1905, was admittedly far from French or British levels of power and effectiveness. It marked, however, an irrevocable step away from the bureaucratized absolutism that had defined Russia since the days of Peter the Great. The armed forces had been significantly improved since their debacles in the Russo-Japanese War (1904–1905). The Russian economy was developing exponentially, despite being in only the early stages of utilizing the vast natural resources of the country. Its industrial sector in particular was rapidly overhauling its Western counterparts in the production of such key indicators as machine tools and proved able to keep the army effectively supplied for most of the war. The cultural malaise that had alienated so many of the young intellectuals and academicians from the existing order involved as much posturing as conviction and was more dangerous in hindsight than in prewar reality.

From this perspective, Russia was brought down by the shortcomings of its army. Its high command proved unable to develop a coherent strategy. Unwilling to choose between Germany and Austria-Hungary as the primary enemy, it dissipated its forces against the two foes. Russian generals, indeed the officer corps as a whole, were at best mediocre in field command. Pitting the bodies of their men against the technology of the Central Powers, in the end they bled Russia white at the front.

An alternative position argues that the Russian army was no worse than its counterparts—it was not that much less effective in adjusting to the demands of industrial mass war. The Eastern Front, moreover, was unlike the Western Front in offering greater relative opportunity for mobile operations. Russian generals had their successes, from the battles of Gumbinnen and Lemberg (1914) to the Brusilov offensive (1916). In contrast to the governments in the West and the Central Powers, however, the Russian government refused to mobilize either its society or its industry to sustain the war effort. It ignored or marginalized political processes at all levels. By the time the government began to mend its ways, in mid 1915, it had sacrificed so many lives that it had also lost its claim to public trust.

The failure of the government was in turn significant because of the deeper weaknesses in the system. Prewar economic improvements had been relative. Faced with the absolute demands of war, industry could not meet the minimal needs of the army. Nor could the railroads move raw materials and finished products on the scales modern war demanded. Nor could politicians inexperienced even in the role of loyal opposition contribute effectively to the making and critiquing of policy. Young people from the educated classes whose alienation from the system had been only theoretical experienced its shortcomings directly, as junior officers, war workers, and nurses. The relatively thin "crust of competence" that had enabled a still-backward Russia to function as a modern state prior to August 1914 was within a year broken beyond repair.

Had the tsar and his advisers been willing or able to accept the immediate risk of refusing war in 1914, they might have averted the collapse of 1916. In fact, however, the negative synergy between structural defects and military defeat spelled doom for the Romanov empire.

Viewpoint:
Yes. The tsarist policy of centralizing power, limiting reforms, and ignoring the suggestions of advisers ensured that Russia could not effectively wage war and remedy its internal problems.

The problems in Imperial Russia had been evident since its defeat in the Crimean War (1853–1856). From that time, various tsars tried to repair the problems that had led to that setback, but they only achieved minimal and temporary success. By 1914 Russian political, economic, and social structures had deteriorated significantly and were continuing to do so. The onset of World War I simply sped up the process.

Russia missed the spurt of growth experienced by the West in the first half of the nineteenth century because it was so cut off from western developments by the censorship of Nicholas I. While western Europe developed new military, communication, and industrial technology, Russia essentially stayed in the eighteenth century. In addition, the political, social, and intellectual revolutions of early nineteenth-century Europe missed Russia entirely and resulted in a society profoundly behind the rest of Europe in virtually every area.

After losing the Crimean War, Alexander II tried to compensate for Russian backwardness through his Great Reforms, but even he tried to limit change to the areas that he perceived as crucial—military, judicial, and economic—and his reforms were designed to keep as much of the traditional structure of Russian society as possible. He recognized that the serfs had to be free in order for any of his reforms to work, but even this monumental change was limited and implemented in such a way as to maintain tight control over peasants, severely curtailing their freedom of movement and seriously undermining the chances of Russia for industrialization or agricultural advancement. Subsequent tsars tried to tighten control over the population even more, reinforcing traditional social relationships and reasserting the authority of the tsar over every aspect of society. While all the tsars of the nineteenth century understood the need for technological and industrial advancement, none of them were willing to allow the social change that accompanies these developments. The Imperial government tried desperately to find a way to foster technological progress and allow the necessary (if evil) industrial growth without any of the social or political upheaval that had accompanied these processes in the West. They believed that by insisting on the absolute power of the autocracy, refusing to allow any political changes, and limiting as much as possible the social changes that industrialization encouraged, they could learn from the "mistakes" of the West and eventually have a wealthy, technologically advanced country populated by docile peasants and workers under the supervision of kindly but firm gentry and industrialists, all with absolute faith in the omniscience of the tsar. This plan failed.

Despite the attempts of the government to limit social change, the demographic upheaval caused by industrialization in the late nineteenth and early twentieth centuries was just as significant as in any western country. Traditional ties were broken, and with them the customary restraints on behavior. Peasants who moved to the city developed a new relationship to work, to their families, and to the upper classes. The same clashes between industrialists and workers that occurred in western Europe emerged in Russia. The government had two responses: it either ignored the problems or sent in the army. Neither action resolved the situation.

By the turn of the century, Russia was seething with social, political, and economic problems. Russian workers in 1900 had the worst housing in Europe and the poorest working conditions. Russian peasants still farmed using the severely outdated techniques that they had practiced two hundred years before—the limits placed on them by the commune discouraged anyone from trying new techniques, buying any new equipment, or even investing in fertilizer—and Russia endured a series of famines as a result. Even the upper classes found fault with the system: industrialists clamored for more freedom and incentives to expand their businesses while the gentry and professional classes yearned for a political voice. The defeat of the Russians in the Russo-Japanese War (1904–1905), like the Crimean War fifty years earlier, threw Russian problems into high relief. Russia did not have the technology, the economy, or the will to compete in the twentieth-century world.

Nicholas II was forced to recognize these problems during 1905, but he did not have even the limited vision of his grandfather to help him deal with the shortcomings of Russia. Indeed, it would have taken monumental changes for Russia to recover sufficiently to enter the coming world war with any hope of victory, but Nicholas was reluctant to undertake even moderate changes. Instead, he made empty promises and attempted to deal with the problems by fiat. He was committed above all to maintaining the autocracy and, in that commitment, lost sight of everything else. The few modifications he tried, such as the agrarian reforms of Premier Pyotr Stolypin, reflected his desire to maintain control and his ambivalence to any real change that could pull Russia out of its financial, technological, and social quagmire. In addition to the tsar's reluctance, the people of Russia (particularly the peasants)—conditioned by centuries of heavy-handed traditions—were also reluctant to change. The hope of the Stolypin plan was to build a country of hardworking, independent farmers, but the peasants were loathe to give up the minimal security provided by the communal system. They also saw the futility of destroying the commune when there was not enough land to go around and resisted the reforms. Russia was in a mess: the cities were hotbeds of social unrest as workers grew increasingly angry with their conditions and the upper classes chafed under the firm but misguided management of the tsar. The countryside was also in turmoil as peasants tried to eke out a living on the exhausted soil and to hold on to the only security they knew—their traditional commune.

This was the situation when Russia declared war in 1914. It had been suffering from economic and social decline (at least relative to the progress of the West) for more than fifty years. The people were frustrated by the halfhearted attempts of the government to deal with these problems and by the tsar's insistence on his absolute authority despite the evidence that he could not solve the problems of Russia. As the war unfolded, it became increasingly clear that progress had been slight: the transportation system was wholly inadequate to the challenge of supplying the war, the mobilization plan was uncoordinated (it took workers first, leaving only newly recruited, unskilled peasants to fumble around in the factories, which resulted in a steep drop in production at a time when the government needed peak performance), and the tsar proved himself once again to be completely out of touch with the problems or desires of his people—most notably by refusing to allow independent groups to help supply the troops with much-needed food and clothing. A government that is too frightened to take advantage of patriotic fervor is in serious trouble indeed.

The huge losses early in the war did nothing to help the situation. As Russian men died at the front, many without guns or boots, the political and economic situation at home deteriorated rapidly. But the problems that Russia experienced were not new, they were simply intensified and accelerated by the war. The nineteenth-century tsars' continued reluctance to allow significant change, to relinquish any power, or to listen to the advice of experts had led to an impasse. Russia could not cope with the war and its internal structural problems.

—GRETA BUCHER,
U.S. MILITARY ACADEMY

Viewpoint:
No. The crisis in Russia was a function of military defeats that reflected the incompetence of the high military command.

Many historians who study Russia have argued that the events of 1917 were inevitable. Because of growing social and economic instability, they argue, Imperial Russia was doomed

IMPERIAL RUSSIA

NICHOLAS II TAKES THE REINS

On 5 September 1915 Tsar Nicholas II assumed command of the Russian army and spelled out his reasons for doing so in an address to his uncle and former army commander in chief, Grand Duke Nicholas:

At the beginning of the war I was unavoidably prevented from following the inclination of my soul to put myself at the head of the army. That was why I intrusted you with then Commandership-in-Chief of all the land and sea forces.

Under the eyes of the whole of Russia your Imperial Highness has given proof during the war of steadfast bravery which caused a feeling of profound confidence, and called forth the sincere good wishes of all who followed your operations through the inevitable vicissitudes of fortune of war.

My duty to my country, which has been intrusted to me by God, impels me to-day, when the enemy has penetrated into the interior of the Empire, to take the supreme command of the active forces and to share with my army the fatigues of war, and to safeguard with it Russian soil from the attempts of the enemy.

The ways of Providence are inscrutable, but my duty and my desire determine me in my resolution for the good of the State.

The invasion of the enemy on the Western front necessitates the greatest possible concentration of the civil and military authorities, as well as the unification of the command in the field, and has turned our attention from the southern front. At this moment I recognize the necessity of your assistance and counsels on our southern front, and I appoint you Viceroy of the Caucasus and Commander-in-Chief of the valiant Caucasian Army.

I express to your Imperial Highness my profound gratitude and that of the country for your labors during the war.

On 23 October the tsar amended his proclamation:

From May to October the Russian Army was subjected to uninterrupted blows along a front of 700 miles. The Austro-Hungarians applied every possible means, not excepting such as are forbidden by international treaties, in order to increase the pressure against us. Masses of their troops were flung against this front and sent to destruction regardless of losses. Military history does not afford another example of such pressure.

During these months of continuous and prolonged action the high qualities and mettle of our troops under the difficulties and arduous conditions of the retreat were demonstrated afresh. Notwithstanding his obstinacy in fighting and his persistency in carrying out maneuvers, the enemy is still confronted by an army which fully retains its strength, morale, and its ability, not only to offer a stanch and successful resistance, but to assume the offensive and inflict blows which have been demonstrated by the events of recent days. This affords the best proof that the Austro-Germans failed to destroy, or even to disorganize, our army.

Seeing that they have failed in that effort during the five months which were most favorable to them, it would be impossible for them to repeat the Galician and Vistula exploits now that the successes of the Allies in the west have complicated the strategic position. The crisis has passed favorably for us. We issued safely from the difficult position in the advanced Vistula theater, where we were enveloped on three sides, and now stand based upon the center of our empire, unexhausted by war.

It is true that there is still much fierce and determined fighting ahead. There may be movements rearward, but there will certainly be advances also. Our army lives in the expectation of a general offensive and looks with full confidence to the armies of its allies. It will march boldly and cheerfully forward, conscious that in doing so it is defending the interests of our country and the interests of our allies. Stern struggle with the forces of nature have schooled the Russians to hardships and ingrained in them the instinct to hasten to the succor and relief of a brother in need. Hence an appeal from our allies will always find a warm response from the Russian Army.

Source: *Charles F. Horne, ed.,* The Great Events of the Great War, *volume 3 (New York: National Alumni, 1923), pp. 320–322.*

to military defeat and revolutionary catastrophe. A careful study of the first two years of World War I indicates that this situation was not necessarily the case, however. Rather, Russian woes were caused by a leadership that was almost universally bad. Incompetence, anachronism, and unprofessional conduct characterized much of the Russian military hierarchy and the upper echelon of civilian officials responsible for war matters. This fact doomed Russia to its crushing defeats in 1914 and 1915, and to the instability that led to the catastrophic events of 1917. It was the consequences of the war, rather than structural features of Imperial Russia, that led to the triumph of communism.

The most central military problem for Russia in 1914 was its thoroughly outdated approach to warfare. Although observers have frequently remarked that this case was generally true for all the combatant powers and that military tactics everywhere lagged behind technological innovation, the situation in Russia was a case unto itself. Much progress had been made since the embarrassing defeat of Russia in the Crimean War (1853–1856). In the reign of the reformist Tsar Alexander II (1855–1881), the Imperial armies were modernized and professionalized in much the same way as those of the other European powers. The combat experience of Russia in its 1904–1905 war with Japan had even given it some advantages over European armies. Unlike the German and Austro-Hungarian armies, for example, Russia had adapted a mobilization strategy that allowed forward elements of its armies to attack before all units were in place. Because of this development, Russian armies were able to enter East Prussia within two weeks of the opening of hostilities in 1914, rather than the widely expected six weeks, and frustrate German plans to deliver a knockout blow to France before turning their attention to Russia.

In several critical categories, however, Russia lagged far behind its competitors. In a land where the social prestige of the aristocracy continued to dominate public life into the twentieth century, the elegant and traditional cavalry remained prominent in the ranks of the military. Unlike most other modern European armies, Russian cavalry had not been exclusively relegated to logistical support, irregular combat with frontier peoples, or ceremonial duties. In the first weeks of 1914 the Imperial army fielded no fewer than thirty-seven cavalry divisions against Austria and Germany. In an age when rapidly advancing troops had to be supplied by train, transportation requirements for horses, fodder, and other materials

not needed by infantry meant that Russia had to use the same number of trains to supply a cavalry division of four thousand men that it did to supply its infantry divisions of sixteen thousand. The Russian rail network, which was actually modern and well developed in the western provinces of the empire, if not anywhere else, was thus utilized in a thoroughly inefficient way.

The aristocratic ethos of the officer corps also affected Russian battlefield tactics. In the first weeks of the war a substantial number of the elite officer corps was killed because its training prized gallantry and bravery to such an extreme that caution was considered cowardly. The attitude resembled the commitment of the French army to *offensive à outrance* and the élan of attack, but it had much more in common with the traditional ideas of battlefield honor that dated back to Napoleonic times. The Russian War Minister in 1914, General Vladimir Sukhomlinov, once stated with pride that he had not read a military manual in twenty-five years and routinely castigated his subordinates for showing interest in the techniques of modern warfare. In 1913 he fired several instructors at the prestigious General Staff Academy because they insisted on teaching modern tactics. Early in the war, Tsar Nicholas II even had to appear before young officer cadets to assure them that there was no dishonor in taking cover. British, French, and German officers may have led direct infantry assaults across open fields, but they had no shame about digging in and dodging bullets.

Grand strategy was also permeated by antiquated thinking. Although the Russians had developed an unexpectedly fast schedule for the advance of their forces into East Prussia, the character of their deployment was out of step with modern warfare. The armies stationed in Russian Poland far outnumbered the German Eighth Army in East Prussia, but their effectiveness was diminished by the decision of their commander, General Yakov Zhilinskii, to maintain huge fortress garrisons to protect the Russian frontiers.

As any responsible general should have known by 1914, strategic fortresses were no longer insuperable obstacles to large mobile armies that could bypass them and to high-caliber guns that could blast them to pieces. This fact had been known for at least half a century, with examples going back to the American Civil War (1861–1865). Even though German artillery had easily demolished all the "impregnable" Belgian forts around Liège in the two weeks before the Russian attack began, Zhilinskii still persisted with his backward strategy. Before the Russian armies moved into East

**Russian troops preparing
an artillery piece to fire in
southern Silesia. The
soldier in the foreground
is signaling another unit**

(from The Illustrated War News,
*17 January 1917, page 27, Joseph
M. Bruccoli Great War Collection,
Thomas Cooper Library, University
of South Carolina).*

Prussia, a significant number of troops and heavy guns were siphoned off for duty in strategic fortresses. As much as one-third of the infantry strength of General Aleksandr Samsonov's Second Army, and nearly 40 percent of his artillery, were lost to this useless purpose. On the German side of the border, General Max von Prittwitz und Gaffron, the Eighth Army commander usually dismissed as inexperienced and timid, systematically emptied German fortifications of their garrisons and stripped them of literally every gun to ensure the maximum possible battlefield presence. In a modern war that depended on large and highly mobile armies, the Russians willingly surrendered much of their numerical advantage. As it happened, all of the Russian border fortresses were reduced and captured by the Germans with relative ease in the summer of 1915.

As it became apparent that Russia was losing control of the military situation, Russian strategic planners made another crucial mistake. Rather than fight the Germans on an extended front in the salient formed by Russian Poland, the High Command decided to effect a strategic withdrawal to shorten the front. This decision was not a bad one in itself, for it avoided a large-scale envelopment operation that General Erich Ludendorff, the German Eastern Front chief of staff, was advocating at the time. It had an adverse impact on Russian strategy, however, because it involved the abandonment of the critical industrial centers of Lodz, Lublin, Vilnius, and the Polish capital of Warsaw, as well as

much of the strategic rail network, to German and Austrian control. Looking back on their victory over Napoleon Bonaparte in 1812, the Russians also initiated a scorched-earth policy to deny war materials, foodstuffs, and other commodities to the advancing enemy. The problem with this approach, however, was that in 1812 the destruction had been confined to the narrow corridor of Napoleon's route to Moscow. In 1914–1915 it was applied along the entire front and created enormous dislocations of people, communications, and economic activity.

If strategy and tactics were subpar, the leading military personnel were completely incompetent. Sukhomlinov's refusal to acknowledge modern military realities had been noted. His tenure as Minister of War in 1909–1915 was a disaster for other reasons as well. To begin with, he scandalously misappropriated ministerial funds to keep himself and his young fourth wife living a luxurious lifestyle. His lack of probity encouraged people to offer bribes and sweet perquisites in exchange for favors. While most of these dealings were not of great significance, it later came to light that Sukhomlinov's corruption led him into close relationships with many dubious figures, including the top Austro-Hungarian agent in Russia before the war and the infamous German spy, Colonel Miasoedov. Disbelieving in modern warfare, Sukhomlinov also crucially failed to build up the Russian armaments industry. When the Russian army experienced chronic shortages of heavy guns, artillery shells, rifles, and cartridges in World War I, it

IMPERIAL RUSSIA

was not because Russia was a benighted land with an uncompetitive military-industrial base. In September 1915—three months after Sukhomlinov's dismissal—Russia produced almost exactly as many artillery shells as Great Britain. The flaw, rather, lay with the failure of Sukhomlinov and those around him to realize the full military potential of the country before it was too late.

Command assignments were also poorly chosen. The two army commanders ordered to invade East Prussia in August 1914, Samsonov and First Army commander General Pavel Rennenkampf, had battle experience as division commanders in the Russo-Japanese War but belonged to rival factions in the army. The Russian High Command overlooked that fact when it ordered them to carry out a joint operation to surround the German forces in East Prussia. When Samsonov moved north from Warsaw in August 1914, Rennenkampf's army marched to support him after a delay of several days, and then only slowly. After overcoming initial German resistance, Rennenkampf halted and then moved his forces away from Samsonov's beleaguered army, which was fighting the German Eighth Army on its own around the Masurian Lakes. While he blamed his lackluster performance on bad intelligence and other misunderstandings, Rennenkampf may have allowed his disdain for his fellow commander to supersede sound military operations. The catastrophic defeat of the Russians at what became known as the Battle of Tannenberg originated in no small way with a poor personnel decision.

An unprofessional approach to military assignments reached even the highest levels. Grand Duke Nicholas (Nikolay Nikolayevich), the tsar's first cousin, was a forward-thinking man who had led the Imperial cavalry in the Russo-Japanese War and advocated military modernization. His progressive ideas, which also extended into the political arena, prejudiced Sukhomlinov and several other conservative courtiers against him. In the years leading up to 1914, his opponents effectively blocked his career advancement and marginalized his influence by confining him to regional commands. Although he served as supreme commander in 1914–1915, he only replaced Zhilinskii after the disaster at Tannenberg, and was himself promptly sacked in August 1915, as much out of envy and political suspicion as for military reverses.

The worst, however, was yet to come. After Grand Duke Nicholas was dismissed in 1915, Tsar Nicholas II assumed personal supreme command of the Russian armed forces, even though his only military experience was the two easy years he had spent as a regimental cavalry officer. He also took supreme command in spite of the direct opposition of most of his own ministers—men whom he himself had appointed and who served at his pleasure. In sharp contrast to all other heads of state, even the self-absorbed German emperor Wilhelm II, the tsar consistently took a major role in military planning and most tactical decisions. His limited training and experience translated into uninspired military leadership, but as the dissenting ministers pointed out, his personal command now brought all responsibility for the failure of the Russian army on him personally and on the monarchy as an institution. The tsar's absence from his capital, moreover, kept him fatally out of touch with the domestic political situation, which increasingly came under the control of the widely disliked and inconveniently German-born Empress Alexandra. Even more alarming was the growing influence of the Siberian mystic Grigory Rasputin. Possessing an unexplained ability to soothe the pain of the tsar's hemophiliac heir, Rasputin rose to a position of serious influence at court. The correspondence of Nicholas and Alexandra included many letters in which the empress related Rasputin's instinctual advice on military strategy and several replies in which the emperor promised to act on it. While historians debate the true extent of Rasputin's influence, the fact of its existence cannot be denied, and public notice of his role at court discredited the monarchy in a major way.

The woes of Imperial Russia had much more to do with military mismanagement than long-term structural problems. The magnitude of the events of 1917 has led much of the historiography to argue that since revolution broke out, every aspect of the Imperial government and society must have been fatally flawed. All roads, in other words, led to 1917. A closer examination reveals, however, that mass disillusionment with the monarchy came as a result of its military failures and the political crises caused by Nicholas II's foolhardy personal involvement in the war. The antiwar riots that broke out in Petrograd in February 1917 were caused by temporary food shortages resulting from the exhaustion of the railway system, not by principled mass opposition to the current social and economic order. The subsequent collapse of the Imperial system had much more to do with the tsar's absence from the capital and inability to bring the situation there under control at a critical time. Seeing both military disaster and domestic crisis, the army command deserted the forlorn tsar and hoped for the best. The tragic descent of Russia into communist dictatorship followed from the incompetent leadership of its Provisional Government after March 1917. The dissolution of the Imperial system, however, was firmly rooted in the poor military decisions of 1914 and 1915.

–PAUL DU QUENOY,
GEORGETOWN UNIVERSITY

References

Marc Ferro, *Nicholas II: The Last of the Tsars,* translated by Brian Pearce (New York: Oxford University Press, 1993).

Martin Gilbert, *The First World War: A Complete History* (New York: Holt, 1994).

John Keegan, *The First World War* (New York: Knopf, 1999).

Dominic Lieven, *Nicholas II: Emperor of all the Russias* (London: Murray, 1993).

W. Bruce Lincoln, *Passage Through Armageddon: The Russians in War and Revolution, 1914–1918* (New York: Simon & Schuster, 1986).

Robert K. Massie, *Nicholas and Alexandra* (New York: Atheneum, 1967).

Bruce W. Menning, *Bayonets Before Bullets: The Imperial Russian Army, 1861–1914* (Bloomington: Indiana University Press, 1992).

Alexander Rabinowitch, *Prelude to Revolution: The Petrograd Bolsheviks and the July 1917 Uprising* (Bloomington: Indiana University Press, 1968).

Hans Rogger, *Russia in the Age of Modernisation, 1881–1917* (London & New York: Longman, 1983).

Dennis E. Showalter, *Tannenberg: Clash of Empires* (Hamden, Conn.: Archon, 1991).

Barbara Tuchman, *The Guns of August* (New York: Macmillan, 1962).

Avrahm Yavmolinsky, *Road to Revolution: A Century of Russian Radicalism* (London: Cassell, 1957).

JAPAN

Was Japan's role during World War I essentially imperialistic?

Viewpoint: Yes. Japan took advantage of the Western powers' withdrawal from Asia to seek its own empire on the mainland and in the western Pacific.

Viewpoint: No. The Japanese goal was not hegemony but "intimate cooperation" with China and Manchuria.

Japanese policies in World War I were shaped by a long-standing resentment against the unequal treaties imposed by the Western powers after the opening of Japan to foreign trade, combined with a growing ambition to extend its power in Asia and the Pacific. As early as the 1870s an emerging generation of diplomats and theorists argued that to survive in its new environment, Japan would have to emulate the colonial powers and develop its own imperium. Commerce, colonization, and settlement—these were the prerequisites of national identity and national greatness. An island poor in raw materials needed secure sources of the imports on which its industrialization and prosperity depended.

Two problems confronted this theory. First, almost every area of Asia with anything worth exploiting was either under Western influence or able to defend itself. The creation of a sphere of influence in Korea (1876) and the occupation of Formosa (1895) added nothing to the power of Japan and in some ways subtracted from it by creating strategic hostages, requiring defense but contributing nothing in return. Gains made in China after the war of 1894–1895, and in Manchuria after the Russo-Japanese War (1904–1905), similarly proved marginal compared to perceived requirements for Japanese greatness. These advances were, however, costly in other respects. The national economy was strained to the limit, especially by the conflict with Russia, and burdened by large foreign loans. The kind of navy required to maintain great-power status in the Pacific was not built cheaply. Not only did taxes become increasingly oppressive on a still largely agricultural populace, but the developing industry was distorted by the need to produce guns, engines, and armor plate domestically. The battleships and armored cruisers that won Tsushima (1905) had been largely built in foreign yards. Ten years later Japan was constructing its own dreadnoughts, but at disproportionate expense. An expanding army found its new units committed to overseas garrison duty. The Western powers continued to compete financially in Manchuria, which Japan regarded as its particular sphere of influence, while China remained nearly immune to Japanese economic penetration.

In the years before World War I, opinion makers were increasingly recommending peaceful alternatives, such as trade and immigration, to influence based on force. If the United States and Australia were insultingly hostile to the notion of Japanese settlers, that opposition was best addressed by diplomacy. The year 1914 changed the Japanese approach. Japan entered the war on the Allied side. Its ships patrolled Pacific trade routes and occupied German island possessions. Its soldiers overran the German sphere of influence on the Chinese mainland. Its diplomats put increasing pressure on the Chinese government, which was the unstable creation of recent revolution. In

1918 Japan even sent forces into Siberia as part of the anti-Bolshevik initiative undertaken by the Allies in the final months of the war. When the peace conference was assembled at Versailles, Japan was recognized as a player in the executive game. Whether Japan could sustain its gains, and what domestic and international prices had to be paid for them, were other stories.

Viewpoint:
Yes. Japan took advantage of the Western powers' withdrawal from Asia to seek its own empire on the mainland and in the western Pacific.

World War I gave Japan both the diplomatic and military opportunity to create new bilateral relationships with the Asian mainland and the nations of the southern Pacific that fell outside the multilateral norms of imperialism typical of the turn-of-the-century Pacific Rim. Prior to the outbreak of World War I, from 1905 to 1914, the defense of the empire constituted the basis of Japanese strategic and diplomatic policies in the Far East. The outbreak of the Great War radically altered the diplomatic and military context in East Asia and afforded the empire an excellent opportunity to expand on the continent and in the northern half of the South Pacific at the expense of the Western powers.

The expansion of the Japanese Empire took place in two distinct phases: 1914–1916 and 1916–1921. Under the cabinet of Okuma Shigenobu, the Foreign Ministry and Military General Staffs, and then the Advisory Council on Foreign Relations pursued territorial expansion and bilateral negotiations that secured a new position for Japan in China and the Pacific. Under General Terauchi Masatake, with support of the upper echelons of Japanese society and the *genro* (powerful nobles left over from the reign of the Meiji emperor), the Japanese government consolidated these gains and sought further expansion on the Asian mainland based on secret treaties with the Western powers. This territorial expansion came at the direct expense of the Western imperial powers—Germany, Great Britain, France, Russia, and the United States—because of their preoccupation with the European war effort.

It was apparent from the beginning that hostilities in Europe would upset the balance of power in East Asia, leaving Japan free to pursue its ambitions almost without check. Great Britain tried to limit potential Japanese expansion in Asia by asking Japan to join the Allied war effort. According to Roy Hidemichi Akagi, in *Japan's Foreign Relations, 1542–1936, A Short History* (1936), the British ambassador, appealing to the Anglo-Japanese alliance that had

existed since 1902, made a formal request on 7 August that "the Japanese fleet should if possible hunt out and destroy the armed German merchant cruisers who are now attacking our [British] commerce." The ambassador added that such a course "means an act of war against Germany but this is, in our opinion, unavoidable." The British changed their tone, however, by issuing a second memorandum on 12 August to the effect that Japanese actions should not extend beyond the China Seas to the Pacific Ocean or to any foreign territory, with the exception of that on the continent of East Asia immediately occupied by Germany. Great Britain obviously did not preclude Japanese gains at German expense in China, but they tried to delimit what the Japanese government could do in Asia and the South Pacific using the Anglo-Japanese Alliance.

The cabinet of Okuma, however, had other things in mind regarding Japanese actions in Asia. Largely made up of individuals related to the political parties in power in Japan, the cabinet bypassed the political position and advice of the ruling *genro*. This move would cause the eventual downfall of the Okuma cabinet, but not before it accomplished its imperialistic goals and further influenced the expansion of the Japanese Empire under *genro* leadership in the latter part of World War I.

In the summer of 1914 the Okuma cabinet created the Council on National Defense to coordinate the budgets and planning of the two military services (army and navy) to deal with German forces in East Asia and the South Pacific. While the British sought only limited help in East Asia, the Okuma cabinet elected to go to war in order to seize the German base in Tsingtao, as well as the lease by Germany of Shantung province (Kiaochow), and to establish control over the German islands in the Pacific.

Okuma's cabinet accomplished these objectives rather quickly by utilizing a Council on National Defense. This body was composed of various leaders of the government ministries and the chiefs of the Army and Navy General Staffs. They agreed upon a defense program that sanctioned an increase in forces stationed in Korea, an expanded naval program, and a greatly increased financial package for military expenditures. By November the Japanese had captured the former German holdings in Shantung and by January of 1915 controlled German Micronesia north of the Equator. Other than these limited

JAPAN

Yoshihito Harunomiya, emperor of Japan from 1912 to 1926

(from Collier's New Photographic History of the World's War [1918], Joseph M. Bruccoli Great War Collection, Thomas Cooper Library, University of South Carolina)

actions, the active role of Japan as an "Ally" in World War I was limited to the use of its warships to patrol the Mediterranean Sea toward the latter part of the war.

In opposition to Okuma's agenda, certain elements of the Japanese Imperial government, particularly the *genro,* especially Yamagata Aritomo and his powerful political clique, sought reappraisal of the initial Japanese wartime China policy on a basis of racial and cultural affinities, a kind of Pan-Asianism. Instead, the Okuma cabinet and Foreign Minister Kat. Takaakira issued in 1915 the "Twenty-One Demands," a set of proposals intended to give Japan a great deal more actual power in China vis-à-vis the Western states and the existing Chinese government.

The Twenty-One Demands reflected on the surface the Japanese government's desire to extend its influence in the provinces of Shantung, south Manchuria, Inner Mongolia, and Fukien. Economic, and to a lesser extent military, expansion into these provinces also brought together elements of an imperialist policy toward China that Japan had been unable to pursue because of the intervention of the Western powers.

As Ian Nish in *Japanese Foreign Policy, 1869–1942: Kasumigaseki to Miyakezaka* (1977) elaborates, the Twenty-One Demands were grouped under five general headings. The first had to do with the transfer of German rights in Shantung Province to Japan as well as the right to construct a rail line there. The second concerned the recognition of the special position of Japan in south Manchuria and eastern Inner Mongolia. The third group dealt with the establishment of a Sino-Japanese company, under the supervision of the Japanese government, which would grant extensive and exclusive rights to mine in certain areas of the Yangtze River valley. The fourth group asked that no further harbors, bays, or islands along the coast of China be ceded or leased to any other imperial power, especially the Fukien coastline opposite Taiwan. Group five asked several things specifically of the Chinese government: to employ Japanese political, financial, and military advisers; to establish joint Chinese-Japanese police forces where the Japanese felt them necessary; to purchase 50 percent or more of Chinese arms and armaments from the Japanese, or establish joint Chinese-Japanese arsenals that would employ Japanese engineers and use Japanese materials; and grant Japan the right to build railroads in southern China.

In effect, these demands strengthened the military position of Japan in the environs of Korea and Taiwan and furnished the basis for a rapid extension of Japanese commercial activities on the mainland. For these reasons they met with strong approval in Japan, but they caused serious ire in China and among the Western powers, especially the United States and Great Britain. In particular, group five of the demands indicated Japanese aspirations to extend an overall protectorate over China. By dropping this group of demands, Japan was able to secure acceptance of the rest. In May of 1915, China signed treaties embodying, with minor modifications, the remaining demands.

Kato and Okuma sought to create for Japan a strong position from which to deal with the Western powers at the close of World War I. Instead, the violent anti-Japanese movement in China following the Twenty-One Demands, and disapproval of the United States and Great Britain, spelled the end of the Okuma cabinet in October 1916. Protecting its imperialist gains and laying grounds for further expansion remained, however, major goals of the Japanese government.

The next stage came under the auspices of the Terauchi government from 1916 to 1918. General Terauchi Masatake and his "transcendental cabinet" set out to consolidate the privileges acquired by the Twenty-One Demands. This course meant pursuing and exploiting new concessions in Manchuria and Shantung and securing recognition for the Sino-Japanese treaties.

At this time Great Britain needed Japanese naval assistance in the Mediterranean Sea to combat the highly successful German submarine campaign. The Terauchi government agreed to supply naval support in return for recognition of the Japanese position in Shantung and rights to the German Micronesian islands north of the Equator. By threatening to cut back on its contribution to the war effort against Germany, the Japanese government was also able to obtain a secret agreement with Great Britain, recognizing all of their gains in China and the South Pacific.

Japan was then able to obtain similar secret agreements from the other Allies, with the exception of the United States.

The Terauchi government, understanding that the United States would not enter into such a secret agreement, sent Ishii Kikojiru to Washington, D.C., during the autumn of 1917 in the hope that some sort of agreement could be reached. The result was the Lansing-Ishii agreement, in which both countries reaffirmed the economic principles of the Open Door Policy (1899) and the integrity of China as a political entity. This agreement recognized both the freedom of the powers to trade freely in China and the "special interests" that Japan had with China based on territorial congruity.

With this agreement and the secret treaties with the European powers, the Terauchi government felt it had consolidated almost all of its imperial gains in Asia. The Russian Revolution (1917), however, opened unexpected further possibilities. In 1917 the military general staffs pushed for a move into the Amur River basin. Utilizing a military alliance with China, the Terauchi government felt it could obtain northern Sakhalin and further expand Japanese influence in northeastern Asia, thus establishing its predominant position in the Orient.

Little was accomplished until July 1918, when the United States proposed a limited joint intervention in Siberia to rescue Czech elements of the White Russian Army trapped in Bolshevik Siberia. The Japanese government agreed to the American proposal and eventually dispatched more than 72,000 soldiers to Siberia. The Americans were out of Siberia by 1920, but the Japanese remained until the latter part of 1922 and only withdrew when international pressure and the consolidation of the Soviet government made it necessary.

The Siberian Expedition cost Japan a great deal of money, increased friction with the United States and among factions in the Japanese government, and caused domestic disturbances outweighing its lack of substantial gains. However, it demonstrated the willingness of the Japanese government at the close of World War I to continue to further its interests and gain territories in East Asia at the expense of the Western powers.

In September 1918 Hara Takashi established the first "party" government in Japanese history. His cabinet continued the policies of the Okuma cabinet and the *genro*-dominated Terauchi government and was strongly committed to preserving the new position of Japan in Asia. At the Paris Peace Conference (1918), the Japanese delegation refused to give up its "wartime gains" on mainland China and in the South Pacific. The Hara cabinet also created a new domestic plat-

EXPANSION

In 1919 Japanese author Kiyoshi Karl Kawakami published a defense of Japanese expansion, including the implementation of the Twenty-One Demands (1915):

It is, therefore, mainly dictates of self-preservation which impelled Japan to enter into the Ishii-Lansing agreement, and which urges her to secure her position in Manchuria, Shan-tung, and Fukien. Had China had a well organized government, capable of developing her own resources, and fully prepared to protect her own interests against Western onslaught, Japan's policy in those sections would have taken a totally different course.

There is another factor which must be recognized in discussing Japanese activities in China. The teeming millions of Nippon, confined within their own narrow precincts, and forbidden, by the mandate of western nations, to emigrate to any of the territories occupied or controlled by the white races, must perforce find a field of activity within their own sphere. With this in view Japan is eager to convert herself into a great industrial and commercial nation. If she fails in this attempt, she must eventually perish from congestion, stagnation and inanition. And in order to become a foremost industrial nation, she must have the essential materials of modern industry such as iron and coal.

To her great disadvantage, Japan has little of such materials in her own country. The volume of iron ores produced at home is but a fraction of what Japan actually consumes. Of coal she has a considerable output, but none that is available for coking purposes. Without coke the steel industry is impossible. China is the country to which Japan must logically and naturally look for the supply of iron ores and coking coal. That is why Japan is anxious to secure mining concessions in China, before China's mines and collieries, unutilized by herself, will be all but mortgaged to Western nations—nations which have already secured vast colonies in different parts of the world, and which have plenty of raw materials and mineral supplies in their own territories.

The American embargo intensified Japan's national desire, long uppermost in the minds of her industrial leaders, for the independence of her steel industry from foreign mills. That desire soon became a national slogan. And yet how is Japan to translate that slogan into a reality? She has but scant supply of ores at home. What she is at present getting from China and Manchuria is far from commensurate with her demand. Unless Japan succeeds in entering into a satisfactory agreement with China for the further development of China's iron resources, her industrial structure will never be placed upon a secure foundation.

What iron Japan has been getting from China comes almost exclusively from the Tayeh mines on the Yang-tsu river. These mines are owned and operated by a Chinese corporation called the Han Yeh Ping Company, which also operates the Han q Yang Iron Works and the Ping Shang coal mines. Ever since its establishment, in 1898, its finances have been in such an unhappy condition that it has contracted with the Yokohama Specie Bank of Japan various loans totalling $40,000,000. In spite of the huge loan it has advanced, the Japanese bank has no voice in the management of the business of the Han Yeh Ping Company. All it is permitted to do is to oversee the expenditures of the company.

In these conditions can we not find a factor impelling Japan to seek greater sources of iron and coal supply in China, untrammeled by the obstacles of China's domestic and foreign politics? Whether Japan succeeds in this attempt is not a question of aggrandizement, but a question of life or death.

With her growing population forbidden to seek opportunities in countries where profitable employment awaits their toil, with her food product inadequate to supply her own need, Japan must perforce become an industrial country. Surely the Western nations, which have agreed among themselves to exclude the Japanese from their own territories, will not conspire to block Japan's way in that part of Eastern Asia where she seeks nothing more than the means of self-preservation.

Source: *K. K. Kawakami, Japan and World Peace (New York: Macmillan, 1919), pp. 160–179.*

JAPAN

form designed to bolster "national defense." The fulfillment of national defense called for revamping education to fight bolshevism and expanding industrial capacity. The latter policy was directly tied to expanding the navy to protect Japanese interests in Asia and enhance the Japanese economic position in Asia at the expense of the other powers.

Based on the secret treaties of 1917 and the Lansing-Ishii agreement, Japan retained almost all of the territories and privileges it gained during the war. The United States insisted that Japan accept a compromise formula that would eventually return Shantung to China but at an unspecified date. In the final analysis, Japan gained a major foothold on mainland China, attained new rights and privileges in Manchuria and Fukien Province, and gained most of the islands north of the Equator that Germany had held. All of this expansion came at the expense of European power and interests in Asia.

The Japanese also acted the role of the concerned ally in the European theater without committing significant forces or expending troops. The Japanese government showed its willingness to work directly with the United States in Siberia while simultaneously trying to expand its interests in that sphere. These actions would have been highly unlikely unless Great Britain, and then the United States, were not distracted by other concerns in Europe. The Japanese Empire nevertheless flexed its diplomatic and military muscles and pursued its own interests separate from Anglo-European desires.

—JACK HAYES, COLORADO COLLEGE

Viewpoint:
No. The Japanese goal was not hegemony but "intimate cooperation" with China and Manchuria.

The Great War was a crucial factor in a central aspect of Japanese history: the search for a modern identity. That quest in turn was closely linked to a concept of the modern state as defined in the nineteenth-century West: a power system focused on authority, armed force, and empire. Well before the outbreak of war in 1914, key elements of the Japanese military/administrative elite sought primacy, if not hegemony, in Asia, as well as control over the Diet and the political parties it incorporated.

In that context, China assumed particular significance as an historic center of Asian civilization and a fellow object of Western imperialism.

To Marshal Yamagata Aritomo, founder of the Japanese army and influential confidential adviser to the throne, relations with Western powers, especially Britain, were essentially limiting and correspondingly temporary. At the same time, these "Asianists" were something other than imperialists in the Western sense. They saw the future of north Asia in terms of a developing "intimate cooperation" among China, Japan, and Manchuria, acting together against external interference. Initially, Japan would be the focal point of the relationship—ideologically, economically, and militarily. Force would be necessary to break down what remained of a decadent Chinese imperial order and to convince dissidents that resistance was futile. Eventually, however, the connection would be of siblings: the elder brother and younger siblings, joint heirs of a common tradition.

Reasonable parallels might be drawn with concepts developing about the same time in the United States regarding appropriate relations with Latin America. Beginning with the Wilson administration (1913–1921), direct gunboat diplomacy was making place, if not yet giving way, to an alternate vision of mutually profitable economic relations based on free trade. A cynic might indeed suggest that the Japanese vision was more generous in that it made room for economic development on the Chinese mainland rather than regarding it as a permanent source of raw materials, and based the relationship on a concept of common culture as opposed to the increasingly conscious ethnic racism of the Americans.

Yamagata's plan, moreover, was not the only Japanese approach to national identity during the Great War era. An alternate position was taken by Foreign Minister Kato Taakakiri. Kato was anything but a quietist. He regarded international relations as a high-stakes game conducted in a state of anarchy. He believed Japan had vital interests in Manchuria and special interests in China. Kato, however, was as much an Anglophile as Yamagata was an admirer of Germany. In particular, he had internalized British notions that the best guarantor of the interests and security of individual states was a balance of power based on alliances among nations with common interests. From Kato's perspective, the natural ally of Japan was Great Britain. Both were island states, relatively poor in resources, and lying off the coast of rich hinterlands. Kato understood—better than many Britons—that British prosperity depended less on its global empire than on its economic connections with Europe. He perceived China in a similar context. The British alliance negotiated in 1902 was the best guarantee Japan had against a challenge to a mainland position whose existence required understanding that

Japan was only one of several contestants for influence over Chinese resources and markets.

Kato, however, is not appropriately understood as an imperialist in the conventional sense. His vision instead invites comparison with the contemporary position known as postimperialism. Kato understood more clearly than the Yamagata faction the difficulty of imposing Japanese influence on China directly by military means, even for a relatively short period. He sought instead a kind of enforced cooperation on the part of the Chinese government, which saw close relations with Japan as its best—or only—practical policy. Here again, parallels might be drawn with the United States, only this time to Theodore Roosevelt—with his more robust view of the use of force in Latin American affairs—or to Woodrow Wilson's relations with Mexico.

The outbreak of war in 1914 was for both factions an opportunity to shape Japanese identity by reinforcing their Asian position. The wars against China (1894–1895) and Russia (1904–1905) had gained Japan a strong foothold on the mainland. The national exhaustion following the latter conflict, and the Chinese revolution (1912), had combined to demonstrate the limits of the Japanese position relative to the Western powers. Kato moved quickly, seizing the German concessions in China, increasing the sphere of Japanese security operations in Manchuria, and in January 1915 presenting the Chinese government with a laundry list of "negotiating points" history has legitimately recorded as the "Twenty-One Demands."

Kato's initiatives marked a long step toward the development in Japan of a syncretized concept of regionalism. Differences in ethnic and cultural patterns between Japan and the West, far from diminishing in the prewar years, had been revitalized by American and Australian hostility to Japanese immigration. Increasing numbers of political leaders across the ideological spectrum saw the Great War as merely the first stage in an ethnically based Darwinian struggle, with the winners eventually turning on the Asian peoples. President Wilson's Fourteen Points was widely interpreted in Japanese decision-making circles as rhetorical camouflage for an American-led Western conspiracy against the only non-Caucasian world power. Against this apocalyptic vision developed the concept of what was often called an "Asian Monroe Doctrine," based on "coexistence and co-prosperity"—with Japan playing the role the United States assumed in the Western hemisphere. Increasingly during the war, concepts of a pan-Asian order based on a common Sinic culture took a back seat to concrete, pragmatic visions of regionalism that assigned to China the role of providing raw materials and labor, to Manchuria the mission of furnishing living space to an overcrowded Japan, and to Japan itself the provision of leadership and protection.

That last point is significant. Japan took seriously the military challenge posed to Asia by the West. During the war it began a naval construction program designed to provide by 1927 a fleet of sixteen capital ships, with cruisers and destroyers in proportion—a fleet not only strong enough to guarantee the regional position of Japan, but if necessary to challenge for mastery of the Pacific the United States, which was increasingly critical of Japanese policies and behaviors in China. The army, however, was falling behind the curve established on the Western Front. It remained a horse-powered, infantry-based force in an era of the industrialized battlefield. Since the constitution established the army and navy as separate entities, neither answerable to anyone except the Emperor, the imbalance exacerbated endemic tensions.

The strategic anxieties of Japan were further increased by the fact that, though some areas profited short-term by filling Allied orders for munitions, the economy as a whole missed the synergies of stimuli that moved the Western states into advanced industrial powers. Japan, moreover, lacked human resources, such as doctors, scientists, engineers, and technicians of all sorts. What it possessed was people. Even during the war, a samurai ethic originally applied to fewer than one-tenth of the population was being extended to the entire population. Military training, always rigorous and demanding by Western standards, crossed the line into comprehensive brutalization, with the aim of mass-producing soldiers and sailors willing to compensate for material shortages with sweat, blood, and spirit.

The Japanese economy nevertheless proved unable to stand the immediate strains of pursuing an assertive Asian policy. In the aftermath of the Great War, proponents of moderation gained enough influence in parliament and the administration to keep the military services in check: to secure withdrawal of Japanese troops from the old German concessions on the Shantung Peninsula, and from Siberia, where they had been committed in response to the Bolshevik Revolution (1917). The army was reduced by four divisions. The navy was cut back in accordance with the Washington Treaty (1922). Successive party-based cabinets pursued cooperative diplomacy with the other powers in China, while simultaneously seeking to improve their position among indigenous factions in Japan. The links between expansionism and national identity, in short, were substantially diminished.

What remained were two other prewar mentalities significantly weakened in the West by the events of 1914–1918. One was the continued postulating of war as a normal continuation of state policy. The other was an acceptance of war as an affirmative national experience. They would surface again—but in later years and under different circumstances.

-DENNIS SHOWALTER,
COLORADO COLLEGE,
AND
-KEVIN CLARK, U.S.
MILITARY ACADEMY

References

Roy Hidemichi Akagi, *Japan's Foreign Relations, 1542–1936, A Short History* (Tokyo: Hokuseido Press, 1936).

W. G. Beasley, *Japanese Imperialism, 1894–1945* (Oxford: Clarendon Press; New York: Oxford University Press, 1987).

James B. Crowley, "Japan's Military Foreign Policies," in *Japan's Foreign Policy, 1868–1941: A Research Guide,* edited by James William Morley (New York: Columbia University Press, 1974), pp. 3–117.

Russell H. Fifield, *Woodrow Wilson and the Far East: The Diplomacy of the Shantung Question* (New York: Crowell, 1952).

Mikiso Hane, *Modern Japan: A Historical Survey,* third edition (Boulder, Colo.: Westview Press, 2001).

James William Morley, *The Japanese Thrust Into Siberia, 1918* (New York: Columbia University Press, 1954).

Ian Nish, *Japanese Foreign Policy, 1869–1942: Kasumigaseki to Miyakezaka* (London & Boston: Routlege & Kegan Paul, 1977).

Mark R. Peattie, *Nanyo: The Rise and Fall of the Japanese in Micronesia, 1885–1945* (Honolulu: University of Hawaii Press, 1988).

Charles Nelson Spinks, "Japan's Entrance into the World War," *Pacific Historical Review,* 5 (1936): 297–311.

Tatsuji Takeuchi, *War and Diplomacy in the Japanese Empire* (Garden City, N.J.: Doubleday, Doran, 1935).

JAPAN

LEAGUE OF NATIONS

Did the League of Nations live up to its mandate to insure peace through collective security?

Viewpoint: Yes. The League provided an effective problem-solving forum in the immediate postwar years.

Viewpoint: No. The structure and mandates of the League gave it authority without power and made it ultimately dependent on the goodwill of the great powers.

The League of Nations remains one of the more tantalizing might have beens to come out of the Great War. Seen from an optimistic perspective, it offered a revolutionary promise of collective security and international solidarity as an alternative to the zero-sum anarchy that had defined international relations since the emergence of the modern state. The League institutionalized mechanisms for cooperation in every aspect of interaction that might cause conflict among states. Primarily remembered for its work on nationalist matters, it addressed social issues as well: the rights of labor, public health, and arms sales. The League sought to establish new economic and commercial parameters to replace those disrupted or discredited by war. It promoted equitable treatment for the ethnic, cultural, and religious minorities it knew would inevitably appear in many countries given the comprehensive redrawing of boundaries after 1918. The machinery of a new European order was put in place. The failure to use it rests with states that were unwilling to abridge their rights and claims—even theoretically.

"Never seek to run before you can walk," reply critics who see the key failure of the League in its inability to address the central issue behind its creation: security. Its weakness in this area reflects an emphasis on structure as opposed to substance. International organizations can contribute much to defusing crises and normalizing interactions. To do so, however, they must operate from a matrix of mutual trust. The degree of trust may be minimal, but it nevertheless must be present. The initial exclusion of Germany from the League, as well as the absence of the United States and the Soviet Union from its high councils during the crucial early years, denied both legitimacy and power to the organization.

Throughout its existence the League of Nations never lost the image of being the wartime creation of an addled American idealist, Woodrow Wilson, who had been unable to sell his idea to his own country. As the League evolved, it was viewed—however mistakenly—as a stalking horse for France and Britain and as a platform for small states to play a role in world politics. In great-power terms the League of Nations never became more than a useful clearinghouse for discussing—and frequently resolving—secondary grievances. That last accomplishment is not to be despised, given the high levels of tension characteristic of postwar diplomacy. It was not, however, enough to provide legitimacy to such an untested institution.

Viewpoint:
Yes. The League provided an effective problem-solving forum in the immediate postwar years.

If ever an organization was universally disparaged, it was the League of Nations. The child of the Paris Peace Conference (1919)—born to save the world from another bloodbath such as the debacle of World War I—the League has since been deemed to have been stillborn, to have been abandoned, hamstrung, or misguided. These judgments, however, does not stand up to scrutiny. Though, of course, some charges could be leveled against the League, the claim that it stood no chance at all is utterly false. The achievements of the League between the wars and the viability of international multilateral cooperation, as has since been amply demonstrated by its successor the United Nations, are proof that such an organization could have been successful. In the first decade of existence of the League, the organization displayed a vigor and vitality that could well have continued, if only the leading members had not withdrawn their political support.

The League is sometimes seen as having been stillborn because important major powers were not members, particularly the United States. The story of American isolationism in the 1920s is greatly exaggerated. In fact, the United States sent a permanent observer to League headquarters in Geneva and participated in negotiations there despite the putatively isolationist stance of the Harding, Coolidge, and Hoover administrations. Generally, charges of American isolation are vastly overplayed, as Washington remained interested and active in disarmament, financial restructuring, and economic development in Europe. U.S. policy toward Europe was akin to that of many contemporary Republicans who advocate that the private sector should lead American policy abroad. In the 1920s, American business and finance was aggressively involved in Europe, and the Dawes (1924) and Young (1929) Plans successfully solved the greatest political problem facing Europe: how to finance war reparations. Like the United States, Russia and Germany, the two other major powers excluded from the League, were admitted in time.

Nor was the League, as its critics have claimed, designed from the outset to be ineffective. The League was only able to act when there was consensus among its members on steps to be taken. That there would be consensus on any given issue is far too much to expect from a multilateral organization. There were occasions when consensus was reached and action taken. There were several occasions in which the League was able to settle international disputes. The ancient quarrel between Norway and Denmark concerning sovereignty over Greenland, for example, was resolved by the League, as were rows between Bulgaria and Greece and a disagreement about the Iraqi border. The League also was effective in monitoring border disputes and in administering referenda and plebiscites dealing with German adjustments for Silesia, Schleswig, and the Saar. These actions may not necessarily be the greatest achievements of mankind, yet lesser disputes had certainly caused wars before.

The League proved to be a useful clearinghouse for the general cooperation of states. Business, regulation, commerce, and public health were areas where the League succeeded rather well. So too did it succeed in the area of international justice. The World Court was under the umbrella of the League, where it functioned well. The utility and obvious public good of such efforts are manifestly clear. That these activities continue under the United Nations indicates that the League served durable and desirable purposes. These initiatives continue to operate rather well, five decades after the end of World War II (1945).

Similarly, the flexibility of the League would eventually have allowed it to overcome some of its early weaknesses. It certainly showed some signs of vitality. Smaller nations, as well as some of the larger ones, were enthusiastic about the promise of the League. The admission of Germany was accompanied by recognition of its western borders, a testimony to the value Germany placed upon membership in the League. Germany was particularly keen to get into "the Club" because they desired to have the same rights and privileges of other states. The entry of the Soviet Union in 1935 was also a sign that the League retained some appeal to great powers. Legitimacy had its attractions, even to those who might not love the status quo.

What ultimately doomed the League was the hypocrisy of both France and Britain, who paid lip service to the ideals and goals of the organization yet never blinked when an opportunity arose to abandon the League in favor of selfish goals. One of the chief tenets of international relations is that a state must limit itself because of "enlightened self-interest"; this self-restraint was absent on too many important occasions. In fact, the League was—and the United Nations is—an institutionalization of "enlightened self-interest." In the aftermath of World War I, it was difficult for states to keep self-restraint in the proper perspective.

–PHIL GILTNER,
U.S. MILITARY ACADEMY

Sir James Eric Drummond, first secretary general of the League of Nations from 1919 to 1933

(U.S. Library of Congress)

Viewpoint:
No. The structure and mandates of the League gave it authority without power and made it ultimately dependent on the goodwill of the great powers.

In January 1920 the original thirty-two members of the League of Nations held their first meeting. Created by Article 1 of the Treaty of Versailles (1919), the League was intended to insure peace through collective security. From the start, however, the League lacked the resources to insure that the status quo could be maintained because it relied on the support of the Great Powers to make an impact on the international stage. The Manchurian (1931–1932) and Ethiopian (1935) Crises demonstrated that the League was unable to counter aggressive maneuvers, even by its own members. Many members, including Great Britain, saw the League as only a tool, and hardly the most important one, in maintaining peace.

In 1919 there was much debate about the ability of the League to meet challenges to peace. Because of its charter to administer and distribute territorial mandates the League had great

responsibility, but it lacked independent and active organizations to carry out its measures. France had argued for a League military to enforce the peace imposed by the Paris Peace Conference, but the United States and the United Kingdom would not support an international navy or army. Lacking teeth, the League had few options in the face of aggression. It was forced to rely on the military resources of member nations. Countries were inclined, however, to utilize their resources solely for themselves and not for the collective good, thereby putting the League at the mercy of its members, especially those nations seen as Great Powers. In order to organize any effective action, the resources of the largest members of the alliance were essential. Without the Great Powers, the League could not act forcibly. If the League could not mobilize its members for military action, only economic sanctions remained. Again, members worked only for their own interests, and the United Kingdom, for example, could hardly be expected to impose economic sanctions that would hurt its own position. Finally, even if the members cooperated on military or economic sanctions, the League could only react to situations. It lacked the ability to preempt challenges to collective security. The only real power the League had over an offending power was to take away the mandates it controlled, a sanction that it lacked force to implement.

The British public initially supported a League concept. The concept of the League originated with Goldsworthy Dickinson, a classics scholar at Cambridge, who thought of it long before World War I started. Dickinson joined the Union of Democratic Control, which became the League of Nations Society. The Society allied itself with other liberal special-interest groups in the United Kingdom to convince the public to support a League concept for the preservation of peace. Following the British example, American societies also began to spring up. David Lloyd George utilized the excitement for a League to help propel himself into the office of prime minister. Lord Robert Cecil in 1918 led a government study on the League concept, and the Foreign Office established a new office for handling issues related to a possible League.

For British politicians and ordinary citizens, a League made sense. It could be used to supplement traditional British strategies: naval hegemony, imperial strength, and continental commitment. The League could be used to uphold the European order without the use of the British army on the Continent. Likewise, a League focused on maintaining peace and the status quo would help to strengthen the British hold over its empire—in short, it would mean cheap peace and prestige.

Even if the public supported the League, the British army and Royal Navy would not. Both military branches refused to rely on the power of a third party to preserve British security. They were concerned about the trustworthiness of an international body, especially if it might rule against British interests. Even if the British were members of a League, they would still need to act unilaterally or in concert with a few key powers. Though the British were the greatest supporters of the League, they still desired alternatives in the face of negative League actions. British membership was enthusiastic but conditional.

The British saw the League as a tool. Although they planned to use the League to gain naval concessions from the Americans, it was far from their most important association used to insure British security. The empire was worth a thousand Leagues of Nations because it provided security in case of an attack. Therefore, the British had to have a League that would support the empire, not dismantle it. They would never allow small powers to dominate the agenda. If formerly colonial nations were able to hijack control of the League, it might be used as a means to force decolonization. Britain, therefore, kept control of the League through finances. Throughout the existence of the League, the United Kingdom was its largest financial contributor, on average supplying 11 percent of the budget. With taxpayer dollars at a premium, it is clear that the British saw the League as a body under their control.

Though Britain was the most supportive nation of the League after its establishment, during World War I the most prominent spokesman for the organization was U.S. president Woodrow Wilson. Yet, after World War I, Wilson was unable to get the Republican-dominated U.S. Senate to ratify the Treaty of Versailles and to support the creation of the League. The United States did not join the League, a fatal flaw in its conception.

The United States remained inconsistent in its policy toward the League of Nations. Overall, Department of State officials saw the League as a positive influence on international relations, but they preferred that the organization remain unobtrusive in the spheres of U.S. interest, such as in Latin America. Without American support, the League could not significantly influence the nations in South America and the Caribbean, which were dominated by the United States. In crises in other regions, such as in Manchuria, the United States might be sympathetic to League goals, but it remained noncommittal to its programs. The United States could work with the League, but only on its own terms, much like other Great Powers dealt with the organization.

The lack of U.S. participation was a fundamental weakness that hindered League action from the beginning. British politicians such as Lloyd George had hoped the League would keep the Americans linked to collective security in Europe. Without American participation, the British determined that their defense rested solely in their own hands. The British would consider themselves first. The League of Nations was doomed to fail the moment the U.S. Senate refused to ratify the Treaty of Versailles. Without the newly emerging power of the United States linked to the League, no other Great Power was willing to curtail its own freedom of action.

Even during the founding process there were several American reservations concerning the League. What if its sanctions contradicted U.S. policies in the Americas, which could be a direct assault on the Monroe Doctrine (1823)? What if the British Dominions were given full voting rights in the League assembly? The British would then lead a bloc—including Canada, Australia, and New Zealand—that would have more collective power within the League than the Americans. Even those people who were enthusiastic about the League believed that solutions beneficial to the United States had to be found.

Some rising powers of the world were destined from the start to be unsupportive of the League. Japan had rallied behind a statement of racial equality in the League of Nations Covenant. Australia and New Zealand actively worked to block any statement on race that could bring an end to their whites-only immigration policies. Japan was not even able to accomplish a statement on the equality of nations in the charter. This failed effort gave the Japanese an initial bitter attitude toward the League. To them, the League seemed committed to enforcing the superiority of the white world. Since the League would not even support the equality of nations, it lost the full support of the Japanese. This loss of a rising power was disastrous for the League. Instead of supporting peace in Asia, Japan attempted to increase its own prosperity. The League needed the support of all powers it could gather. Even the loss of a non-European, rising middle power helped lead to the destruction of the League.

From the signing of the League Covenant, none of the victorious Little Entente powers intended to let the League interfere in their own interests. Italy, Britain, France, and Japan all utilized the Allied Supreme Council from the war years to discuss shared diplomatic issues. This body, along with the Conference of Ambassadors and the Inter-Allied Reparations Committee, provided the Allied members of the League an avenue to another Great Power absent from

LEAGUE OF ROBBERS

On 6 October 1931 the Chinese Soviet government complained about the findings of the League of Nations, through the Lytton commission, on the Japanese takeover of Manchuria:

The Provisional Central Government of the Chinese Soviet Republic long ago told the popular masses of the whole country that the League of Nations is a League of Robbers by which the various imperialisms are dismembering China. The principal task of the Lytton Commission of Enquiry sent to China by the League was to prepare the dismemberment of China and the repression of all the revolutionary movements that have raised the flag of the Chinese Soviets.

Now the Commission of Enquiry of the league of imperialist robbers—the Lytton Commission—has already published its report regarding the dismemberment of China. This report is an admirable document shown to the Chinese popular masses by the imperialists regarding the dismemberment they propose to inflict on China, and yet the Kuomintang, which is selling out and dishonouring the country, as well as the government which is the emanation of the Kuomintang, have accepted it completely!

The Lytton Report is the bill of sale by which imperialism reduced the Chinese people to slavery! The Soviet Government calls on the popular masses of the whole country to participate in an armed uprising under the direction of the Soviet Government, to wage a national revolutionary war in order to tear to shreds the Lytton Report, and to oppose all the new projects of the imperialists for dismembering China, repressing the Chinese revolution, and attacking the Soviet regions and the Soviet union. Let us hurl out of China, Japanese imperialism and all other imperialisms in order to obtain the complete liberation and independence of the Chinese people! Let us defend the Soviet Union with arms in our hands, let us establish a close alliance between the toiling masses of China and of the Soviet Union.

The Soviet Government proclaims to the workers, peasants, and soldiers of the whole country, and to all the exploited popular masses, that if we really want to wage national revolutionary war and oppose the dismemberment of China by the imperialists, we must first overthrow the reactionary domination of the Kuomintang, these scavengers who pick up the scraps of the imperialist dismemberment of China, and who are repressing the national war!

Source: "The League of Nations Is a League of Robbers!" The Maoist Documentation Project, <http://www.maoism.org/msw/vol6/mswv6_14.htm>.

the League, the United States. As long as the Americans were willing to work in concert with the European Great Powers outside of the League, its position as the final arbiter of peace was not secure. In the end, most matters brought to the League for judgment were related to the League itself or brought to the League by individual countries. The Great Powers allowed the League to exist as a possible tool, but it never had their full confidence as long as the Americans were not participants.

The United States was not the only important power outside of the League. The Soviet Union did not participate in the Paris Peace Conference, the Treaty of Versailles, or the formation of the League of Nations. It was not until 1934 that the Soviets entered the League. Even then the Soviet Union appeared divided in action, using the League to attack fascist states and also independently making cooperative agreements with Nazi Germany. Germany was seen by many as the cause of World War I. The United Kingdom had hoped that German membership in the League would help to restrain German aggression. In 1926 Germany entered the League. With the rise of Adolf Hitler, Germany began to violate clauses of the Treaty of Versailles and eventually left the League, never committing to collective security.

In September 1931 the ability of the League to maintain collective security was tested. After a series of incidents along the South Manchuria Railway, the Japanese army occupied the town of Mukden and began to gobble up the Chinese province of Manchuria. The Japanese organized the Chinese puppet state of Manchukuo in order to consolidate its victories. On 21 September 1931 the Chinese appealed to the Council of the League under Article 11 of the League Covenant for aid. However, the Great Power members resisted giving League aid. No effective action followed.

The United States and the Soviet Union appeared to be the two nations best able to influence the region, but both were nonmembers of the League. France, a member, was willing to provide the Chinese with moral support but unwilling to contribute firm action. The United Kingdom was hesitant to support any plan, such as economic sanctions, that would threaten British investments in Japan. Additionally, some British politicians were willing to support the Japanese in their acquisition of an economic colony. Would it not be better to have Japan, a League member, dominating resource-rich Manchuria instead of the Soviet Union? Sir John Simon actually acted as an advocate in the Council of the League, insuring that no firm action could be taken immediately. It was difficult for

LEAGUE OF NATIONS

the Great Powers, who held their own colonies, to criticize the actions of Japan.

In January 1932 the League appointed Lord Lytton to study the situation. The Lytton Commission determined that the Japanese had indisputably and forcibly seized Chinese territory. When the League Assembly was called to study Lytton's findings in December 1932, Simon again acted as the Japanese spokesman, painting their actions in a positive light. In the end, the League would not order the Japanese to do anything. The Council and the Assembly both agreed that Japan was an aggressor. Both called for all nations to acknowledge the sovereignty of China over Manchuria and asked that members not recognize Manchukuo. No member did. Japan left the League and kept Manchuria instead of agreeing to the verdict. Some theorized that if the Great Powers, such as Britain, had supported firm action by the League that Japan would have surrendered Manchuria. Others, such as Italian dictator Benito Mussolini, believed that if the Great Powers would not support action against Japan, perhaps other aggressive actions could be taken without serious League penalties.

Mussolini had dreams of reestablishing Rome as a great power. In order for Italy to return to prominence, Mussolini needed colonies. In Ethiopia (Abyssinia), Mussolini saw his own Manchukuo. He could acquire new natural resources, while at the same time avenging the Italian defeat by the Ethiopians at Adowa (1 March 1896). Italy would gain a new market and Rome would live again. The Japanese had provided Mussolini with the model.

On 3 October 1935 Italian armies attacked the weak government of Ethiopian emperor Haile Selassie. The month before, the British had declared support for Ethiopia in the League in anticipation of an Italian attack. With the British spearheading the effort, the League actually imposed economic sanctions on Italy, including an oil embargo. Early on, however, another Great Power, France, sabotaged sanctions. They negotiated with the British outside of the League in December to create the Hoare-Laval Pact. In this agreement, Britain and France determined that Ethiopia would be divided into an Italian protectorate and colony. In the end, the British pulled out of the agreement because of public opinion, but the Italians preserved their victory over Ethiopia.

By the time sanctions could begin to affect the Italian invasion, Italy had already gained complete control over the new colony. With the Italian victory complete, the League withdrew its sanctions. Mussolini had learned well. The League of Nations had yet again been proven a failure in insuring collective security.

In December 1939 the League expelled the Soviet Union for its invasion of Finland. By then, it was clear that the League had failed to maintain the peace. In the fires of World War II, the League died. Even before the invasion of Poland, the Great Powers attempted to avoid a European war outside the League, such as in Munich in 1938. The League of Nations had no real power, was unable to maintain the peace, and could operate internationally only with the goodwill of the Great Powers. Without the consistent support of nations such as the United States, Germany, and the Soviet Union, the League was fatally wounded. With only partial support from its Great Power members, for instance the United Kingdom, the League was destined to be powerless.

–DANIEL BUTCHER,
KANSAS STATE UNIVERSITY

References

Elmer Bendiner, *A Time for Angels: The Tragicomic History of the League of Nations* (New York: Knopf, 1975).

Donald S. Birn, *The League of Nations Union, 1918–1945* (Oxford: Clarendon Press; New York: Oxford University Press, 1981).

Warren F. Kuehl and Lynne K. Dunn, *Keeping the Covenant: American Internationalists and the League of Nations, 1920–1939* (Kent, Ohio: Kent State University Press, 1997).

F. S. Northedge, *The League of Nations: Its Life and Times 1920–1946* (Leicester, U.K.: Leicester University Press; New York: Holmes & Meier, 1986).

Christian Raitz von Frentz, *A Lesson Forgotten: Minority Protection Under the League of Nations: The Case of the German Minority in Poland, 1920–1934* (Münster: Lit Verlag, 1998).

MARITIME TECHNOLOGY

Did unreliable technology handicap navies during World War I?

Viewpoint: Yes. Naval vessels suffered from poor designs and communications.

Viewpoint: No. Naval operations during the Great War were hindered by the failure of the admirals to develop strategic and operational doctrines that utilized the capabilities of their warships.

Naval technology has generally advanced at a slow pace. An eighteenth-century ship of the line could and did remain an effective fighting instrument for more than half a century. A contemporary U.S. aircraft carrier has an expected life almost as long. Beginning in the mid nineteenth century, steam propulsion and armor protection created a state of technical confusion that left even the Royal Navy convinced that the best policy was to construct a "fleet of samples": build only a few of each improved design and wait for the wave to crest.

By the 1890s present patterns and future trends seemed sufficiently clear for navies to concentrate on standardized types and designs. The battleship and its thin-skinned cousin the armored cruiser; the "protected cruiser" for imperial policing and trade protection; the torpedo boat and its emerging successor the destroyer—all began assuming familiar outlines. British introduction of the all-big-gun battleship, the HMS *Dreadnought,* in 1906 further homogenized fleet composition and naval construction. Each navy essentially employed similar types of ships, and while each had its design differences, the casual reader is likely to find difficulty in distinguishing among a German, a British, or a U.S. battleship of the Great War era, to say nothing of less familiar types such as cruisers and destroyers.

The rapid development and corresponding homogenization of designs was accompanied by comprehensive, rapid changes in every other aspect of naval architecture and technology. Coal gave way to oil as a fuel. Reciprocating engines were challenged and replaced by turbines. Propellants and fuses changed the nature of ammunition as improvements in gun design enhanced range and accuracy. It is not enough for the student of naval warfare in the early twentieth century to know that a certain class of cruiser was armed with a specific number of six-inch guns. The critical question is what "mark" of gun was carried: how recent was the design? A new four-inch gun might compensate for a lighter shell by longer range and superior rate of fire. For battleships, the purported advantages to be gained by increasing the elevation of the main battery guns was sufficient to merit extensive discussion in arms-limitation conferences.

A predictable underside of this technological revolution was unreliability. In personnel terms, navies had historically depended on seamen, not engineers. The "typical" sailor of any navy had never been expected to be a technician. Now, not only armament imposed new criteria. Introduction of electric power in warships created whole new specialties for enlisted men. The development of mechanical range finders made new demands on mathematical skills and mental alertness. Even when more or less properly maintained, the new technology was risky. Deteriorated ammunition destroyed several capital ships riding peacefully at anchor. Engine failure kept others "redlined" even as their fleets prepared to sortie. For admirals, the question was less how many ships were on the order of battle than how many could get under way at a given time. For captains, bringing their guns on target and keeping them there was more critical than the weight of the shells in a broadside. Naval technology in the Great War was a sword that cut both ways.

Viewpoint:
Yes. Naval vessels suffered from poor designs and communications.

Fighting ships of World War I utilized the best technologies available. However, these new systems, from engines to methods of communication, were untried in battle. This newness made them dangerous for both the men and ships that relied on them. At Jutland (1916) HMS *Queen Mary* exploded after taking a shell in one of her turrets. Admiral Sir David Beatty, while watching the battle cruiser burst into flames, was heard to say in stoic British fashion, "There seems to be something wrong with our bloody ships today." He was correct. Flaws in each of the new systems added considerable danger when ships came under fire.

World War I provided a testing ground for the latest advances in naval armament and technology. Crews who serviced those systems found that their training was insufficient preparation for war. Systems that worked well in training exercises failed repeatedly during wartime operations. The size and complexity of the ships magnified errors in design and in the application of new technology. When these ships put to sea, they became laboratories in ship design and development.

Most of the ships active in World War I used diesel or steam turbine engines. Diesel engines offered higher top speeds and greater fuel efficiency. There was, however, a trade-off for those improvements. The higher the top speed required, the more cylinders that had to be added. Additional cylinders lengthened the crankshaft necessary to drive the propellers. Longer crankshafts increased the vibration within the ship and, more important, along the drive shaft. If enough outside vibration was added, by a nonpenetrating shell hit, for example, it could cause the gears and shaft to fly apart. The traveling vibratory force, speed of the ship, and natural undulation of the ocean affected other stations throughout the entire ship. Lieutenant George Mountbatten of the HMS *New Zealand* noted that during the Battle of Dogger Bank (1915) his range finder operator could not assess the range of enemy ships because of the vibration coming from the engines.

In battle the shell propellant aboard the vessel was often more dangerous than incoming enemy fire. When the two were combined, the effects could quickly turn a ship into a charnel house. There is an ongoing debate among academics about whether flash suppressors on British ships were adequate for the job. Some scholars blame the gunners for lax safety precautions and for taking risks to increase the rate of fire. Other historians place the blame on the delivery system for shells and propellant. The Germans used similar systems to the Allies but changed them early in the war, realizing the danger after a near-fatal fire on the SMS *Seydlitz*. It took the Battle of Jutland to make the British consider that cordite flashes within the turret were a problem.

In the turrets, temperatures rose, and the loading of shells became a race to beat the enemy in scoring the first hit. Means of clearing the heat generated by expended shells was almost nonexistent, as was protection from muzzle flash. Smoke from the guns blurred men's vision. Sailors raced to stop hot, ejected shell cartridges from flying across the turret. The hectic pace, coupled with unforeseen problems in ship design, created a highly dangerous environment. Mountbatten again, in his after-action report from the Battle of Dogger Bank, described the problems shared by gun crews throughout the Royal Navy. Improper drainage led to water rushing into the turret, down into the magazine, and even into the cordite hoppers. Gun sights were covered in water. Electric lights shorted out, plunging the turret crew into darkness. All these obstacles occurred while the battle cruiser engaged the enemy. Such delays, even for only a few seconds, could lead to disaster. As in the Age of Sail, naval warfare was still a matter of who hit the fastest. When gun crews on the *New Zealand* should have been operating at optimum efficiency, design flaws hampered their best efforts.

Communication among ships in battle was essential for both the coordination of fire and the issuing of movement orders. The standard methods in use proved inadequate and dangerous; the Battle of Jutland illustrated their weaknesses. British admiral Sir John Jellicoe reported

A British trawler bringing in a mine

(from The Illustrated War News, *26 December 1917, page 15, Joseph M. Bruccoli Great War Collection, Thomas Cooper Library, University of South Carolina)*

that delays in relaying wireless coded messages were a considerable problem. According to Jellicoe, this interval included "the time taken to write out the report, transmit it to the wireless office or signal bridge, code it, signal it, decode it on board the receiving ship, write it out and transmit it to the bridge." The process of relaying a wireless message included as well a significant time lapse from reception of the message to implementation of the order.

Delays inherent in coded radio communication forced ships to fall back on older methods: visual signals. Flags and light signals were used in battle to send movement and firing orders. These methods proved unreliable and dangerous in battle. At the Battle of Jutland,

British commanders continually misread flags. These lapses were primarily responsible for the escape of the German fleet. Lights were the method of choice for nighttime communication because of their visibility, but they made the sending ship a target for enemy guns. Misread light signals led to several collisions during the destroyer action at Jutland.

Jellicoe notes in *The Grand Fleet, 1914–1916: Its Creation, Development, and Work* (1919) that German ships were better armed than their British counterparts. Turret hits were particularly dangerous. At Jutland three British battle cruisers—*Queen Mary, Indefatigable,* and *Invincible*—were sunk as a result of armor-penetrating hits. The explosions set off the cordite, which then caused another explosion to rip into the magazine. The resulting third explosions then tore into the engines, sending gears and cylinders flying and ripping through bulkheads and men, tearing the ships apart in minutes.

Optical sighting in the turrets and conning towers also brought further problems that would only be discovered in battle. The British used coincident optical range finders. These sighting mechanisms took two separate images that were then manually brought into focus. Inaccuracies in the British system could lead to errors by as much as +/-165 meters at a range of 20,000 meters. The closer the target the less the margin of error. At 2,000 meters the margin of error would be only +/- 2.6 meters. Battles such as Jutland and Dogger Bank began at ranges in excess of 18,000 meters, creating a margin of error of approximately +/-100 meters. Most accepted naval strategies formulated before the war, however, stated that battle would take place at much closer ranges.

German optical range finders operated on a different principle than British instruments. Their systems were stereoscopic and more accurate in finding the initial range of a target. They could not be fooled by changes in target angle. Yet, they also had critical problems in their use. Operators needed to undergo continuous and difficult testing in order to ensure that they could maintain a fix on a target. Their accuracy was tested on a daily basis, which was psychologically taxing. Similar systems were used in World War II, and German range finder operators were given permanent psychological support to help them cope with the stress.

All of these factors contributed to low hit rates compared to the number of shells expended during a battle. At Jutland the British fired 1,784 shells with only 100 hitting a target. The Germans faired slightly worse, expending more than 2,400 shells with only 120 hits. Accuracy ratings of under 10 percent were not uncommon. Most of the shells expended were used to find the range of enemy ships. Once the ranges were ascertained with some degree of certainty, problems within the turret contributed to critical delays in firing the guns, which translated into increasing the risk of being hit by enemy shells. In combat the inadequacies of these critical systems cost lives and ships.

The ships of World War I were a patchwork of new technologies that were never tested in battle until the outbreak of war. Errors in design, implementation, and execution were magnified while under enemy fire. Unstable propellants and poorly designed gunnery systems were more dangerous to the men who operated them than was incoming fire from enemy ships. Unreliable communication sys-tems caused confusion and collision. Over the course of the war many of these issues were solved, although often purchased with much bloodshed.

–VINCENT J. SCUTARO,
NEW YORK, NEW YORK

Viewpoint:
No. Naval operations during the Great War were hindered by the failure of the admirals to develop strategic and operational doctrines that utilized the capabilities of their warships.

Many new weapons were first used in action in World War I, prominent among them the dreadnought battleship, submarine, and air-plane. Others, such as mines and torpedoes, quickly developed beyond anything that had previously existed. All of these advances had serious effects on the naval battlefield. Further-more, the capabilities of most weapons changed even during the war, and tactics were altered in response to technical innovations. Senior offic-ers redesigned strategies and tactics "on the fly" when old ideas had to be discarded.

Not quite a decade before the outbreak of World War I the battleship was reinvented with the launch of the HMS *Dreadnought,* the fast-est, best-protected, best-armed battleship in the world. Suddenly the British had a qualitative edge—and their efficient shipyards would out-build their rivals. All major powers (and some minor ones) started building dreadnoughts; in fact, they did so because these ships were almost as much a symbol of power as an actual implement of battle.

Naval officers generally assumed that shortly after war broke out there would be a decisive engagement between the battle fleets, and the victor would then exploit their advan-tage. Admirals also thought about battleships as the centerpieces of the navy, with smaller ships scurrying around the margins of battle in a sup-porting role. Battleships, however, had flaws. Their armor was arranged mainly to protect against relatively short-range direct fire rather than long-range fire on plunging trajectories. Guns were increased in range and hitting power, and aiming systems were improved, so chances were slim that battle would actually be at close range where this armor would be most effective.

Battleships were also highly vulnerable to underwater attack by both mines and torpedoes.

A SMOKING HEAP OF RUINS

The following selection is a description of the Battle of Jutland (31 May 1916) from the viewpoint of a sailor aboard the German battlecruiser Lützow, *which was hit by twenty-four large shells and several torpedoes during the engagement and was so badly damaged that the Germans later scuttled it.*

Suddenly the entire ship is roughly shaken. The colossus heaves far over, and everything that is not fixed is upset. The first direct hit! The torpedo pierces the fore part of the ship. Its effects are terrible. Iron, wood, metal, parts of bodies, and smashed ships, implements are all intermixed, and the electric light, by chance spared, continues to shine upon this sight.

Two decks lower, in the Diesel dynamo room, there is still life. That compartment has not been hit, and twenty-seven men, in the prime of life, have been spared, but the chamber is shut off from all others, for the water is rushing into all sections. They are doomed to death. Several 38-centimeter shells squarely hit their mark, working terrible havoc. The first hit the wireless department. Of the twelve living men who a moment ago were seated before the apparatus, there is nothing more to be seen. Nothing is left but a smoking heap of ruins. The second shot again pierced the fore part of the ship. The entire forepart of the vessel, as far as the Diesel motor room, was past saving.

Another broadside meant for the *Lützow* fell short, but a torpedo boat close by disappeared, leaving only a few odd pieces of wood and a smashed lifeboat drifting around. It is now half-past 7, and the hostile circle grows ever smaller. The *Lützow* and the *Seydlitz* lie with their bows deep in the water; both are badly mauled. The forepart of the *Lützow* was in flames. Shells burst against the ship's side in rapid succession. A terrible sight is presented on board the *Lützow*, and it needs iron nerves to look upon it cooly. Hundreds have lost their lives, while many have lain for hours in torture, and the fight is not yet over. The bow is now crushed in and is entirely submerged. The four screws are already sticking half out of the water, so that the *Lützow* can only make eight to ten knots an hour, as against the normal thirty-two.

The Admiral decides to transfer to the *Moltke.* He gives orders to turn and get away from the scene of the fight, but the *Lützow* has not gone a mile before she receives a broadside of 38-centimeter shells. The entire ship was filled with the poisonous fumes of the shells, and any one who failed to affix his gas mask was doomed to be suffocated.

It was three-quarters of an hour before the lighting installation was restored. Then for the first time could the extent of the damage wrought by the salvo be seen. One of the shells had landed in the sick bay. Here there were only three doctors and fifteen attendants, besides 160 to 180 wounded. Of all those, only four remained alive. These four were hurled into the next compartment by the air pressure; there they lay unconscious.

The *Lützow* was now a complete wreck. Corpses drifted past. From the bows up to the first 30-centimeter gun turret the ship lay submerged. The other gun turrets were completely disabled, with the guns sticking out in all directions. On deck lay the bodies of the sailors in their torn uniforms, in the midst of the empty shell cases. From the masts fluttered torn flags, twisted signal lines, and pieces of wire of the wireless installation. Had not the lookout man and the three officers on the commander's bridge given signs of life, the *Lützow* would have truly resembled a ship of the dead. Below, on the battery deck, there still lay innumerable wounded, but there was no longer a doctor to attend to them.

Source: Charles F. Horne, ed., Source Records of the Great War, *volume 4 (Indianapolis: The American Legion, 1930), pp. 179–180.*

Much of this vulnerability could have been predicted, and some of it was: from the beginning, battleships seldom went close inshore, near potential minefields. Few thought ahead to the next step, though: minefields would be laid further and further from the coast. What was more, submarines were not as fragile as most experts thought and could patrol much further from their bases. Once a few warships were sunk by mines or torpedo hits, strategists became even more cautious. Battleships were escorted everywhere they went, and they started supporting (from safe distances) the smaller ships, inverting conventional strategy. Battleship admirals did not like this strategy, but they were quickly forced to adapt.

A practical submarine prototype dipped below the waves twenty years before World War I began. It had no periscope, no weapons, could only stay underwater a few hours, and needed to be towed in windy weather. It was more of a publicity stunt than a weapon—but it had potential. By 1914 that potential began to develop, and submarine technology was advanced in the next few years, to the point that submarines could attack shipping off the U.S. coast and sink ships one hundred times bigger than themselves. Everyone was left scrambling to catch up: senior naval officers, politicians, diplomats, and the public. Naval strategy adapted fairly quickly, at least with respect to warships. No big ship was left without a cloud of screening destroyers to keep the subs out of range. Another effect on strategy had already been forecast: submarines could operate against invasion forces, and even if the troops landed safely, the submarines could attack supply ships that followed behind. This situation deterred most amphibious operations.

Another question quickly arose: What would submarines do against merchant shipping? The tactics of submarine attacks were simple; arguments against their use revolved around legal and diplomatic concerns. No one had foreseen a role for submarines in attacking civilian ships, and international law did not address the question. In 1914 the Germans started sinking merchantmen (in small numbers); they continued in 1915, with better results (before the howls of American protest over the sinking of the *Lusitania*). In 1916 (to minimize diplomatic risks) the Germans implemented different rules, but in 1917 they cast off the restraints and nearly strangled British supply lines.

Since there was no effective way to seek out and destroy a U-boat unless it attacked, it was the defenders who had the real problems. Their tactical advantage meant subs were frequently successful; patrolling warships could only respond to where the sub had been rather than where it was. Indeed, for years all navies (aggressive use of U-boats did not give the Germans any special insights into how to defend against them) were obsessed with fighting an "offensive" war against subs rather than defending merchantmen by sailing them in convoys. The dogma "attacking is good, defending is bad" had been bred into generations of sailors, and they could not work it out of their hearts.

Mines, a much more pedestrian weapon, were thought of as defensive (a ship had to hit the mine—the mine did not attack the ship), but they were extremely effective. Only a decade before World War I, during the Russo-Japanese War (1904–1905), three battleships were sunk by mines, and others were damaged—yet, in the interval, little was done to protect vessels from these weapons. Minesweeping and mine technology remained low priorities, and ships were not redesigned to withstand mine damage. The

same admirals who expected a big battleship duel once the war began apparently expected it to happen in the middle of the ocean where mines would not get in the way, rather than in any of the shallow seas near Europe. Mines took a heavy toll, from a modern Royal Navy dreadnought to a dozen older battleships of various nations through the war—and many humble cargo ships were also sunk. Mines made protracted operations in coastal waters extremely hazardous, and this danger scuttled many ambitious plans for amphibious operations in the North Sea, the Adriatic, and even the Baltic. Only gradually were more (and newer) ships turned into minesweepers, and the losses declined, but strategy did not change. Both sides worked feverishly to lay minefields (to constrict the enemy, even if they sank nothing) or sweep channels (and retain some freedom of movement). This policy sometimes required the minelaying craft to be covered by destroyers and supported by cruisers, which were in turn supported by battleships. Tactics had been turned around, with the big supporting the small, but the strategy stayed the same.

If dreadnoughts and submarines seemed newfangled, aircraft were a more futuristic advance. The first powered flight took place in 1903 and the first flight over the English Channel was completed in 1909. A bare five years later visionaries could see airplanes changing the world in many ways—but World War I military strategists had to deal with the here and now. Underpowered aircraft could not lift large payloads, and no twenty-five-pound bomb aimed by the Mark I eyeball posed much danger to a warship. The obvious use of aircraft was as scouts, and all countries made good use of them. The Germans counted on their zeppelins to give them a substantial edge, since the "gasbags" could carry wireless transmitters and receivers while shadowing an enemy fleet for several days, but they proved fragile in rough weather, and the North Sea was too harsh for them to be reliable.

Land and naval aircraft developed many specialized functions as fighters, scouts, and bombers; by 1917 there were torpedo planes as well as flying boats that could hunt U-boats far out into the Atlantic. The British and Russians both worked hard at taking aircraft to sea by building seaplane carriers. The Russians used their aircraft in raids in the Black Sea, while the British planned something more ambitious. They envisioned an air raid against German bases to lure (or force) the German fleet to sea—where the main British fleet could finally destroy it.

There are, of course, other areas where technology made World War I substantially different from previous wars. No single technology was a "war winner"; victory depended on how skillfully adaptations were made to constantly evolving technologies. To make the situation even more complex, changes on one's own side interacted and had to be integrated: for example, better optical technology meant warships could fire at longer ranges, but it also meant that their armor should be in different places. In addition, there was always the question of what the enemy was doing—what surprise might they be about to spring on the world? So technologies (the plural is important) were a multivariable equation.

Senior naval officers were, certainly, always behind the curve: technology was moving too fast for anyone to keep up. To make predictions about where things were moving was liable to be embarrassing and also likely to be wrong—and in war, "wrong" costs lives. There was, instead, a generalized caution about the risks that developed, along with a constant series of little steps as strategists reacted to smaller changes. Although strategies became cautious, tactics (especially of smaller, and thus expendable, ships) changed rapidly, and by the end of the war there were some operational plans that were not just bold but visionary.

–SANDERS MARBLE,
SMITHSONIAN INSTITUTION

References

Paul G. Halpern, *A Naval History of World War I* (Annapolis, Md.: Naval Institute Press, 1994).

Admiral Viscount Jellicoe of Scapa, *The Grand Fleet, 1914–1916: Its Creation, Development, and Work* (London & New York: Cassell, 1919).

John Keegan, *The Price of Admiralty: War at Sea From Man of War to Submarine* (London: Hutchinson, 1988).

Ronald H. Spector, *At War, at Sea: Sailors and Naval Combat in the Twentieth Century* (New York: Viking, 2001).

Jon Tetsuro Sumida, *In Defence of Naval Supremacy: Finance, Technology, and British Naval Policy, 1899–1914* (Boston: Unwin Hyman, 1989).

John Terraine, *Business in Great Waters: The U-boat Wars, 1916–1945* (London: Cooper, 1989).

MARITIME TECHNOLOGY

Did the British use of armed merchant vessels inadvertently stimulate the German development of unrestricted submarine warfare?

Viewpoint: Yes. The possible presence of Q-ships (armed merchant vessels) made U-boats less willing to surface and warn merchant crews before sinking their vessels.

Viewpoint: No. The logic of submarine attacks worked against traditional rules of naval warfare, and the presence or absence of Q-ships had no bearing on the situation.

In the course of the nineteenth century, international law on the subject of captures at sea grew increasingly complex and increasingly precise. This situation in good part reflected consistent pressure from the United States, whose foreign policy emphasized freedom of the seas even during wartime. It reflected as well the increasing numbers of passengers, emigrants, tourists, and business travelers carried by shipping lines that replaced sail and approximate schedules with steam and predictable arrivals. By 1914 the rules were plain. Any hostile merchantman was subject to capture. Any neutral ship could be stopped and searched for contraband. If it was carrying forbidden or questionable goods, it too could be seized and brought into port. In both cases the ship could be sunk if the captor could not provide a prize crew—and international law gave captains wide discretion in deciding whether they could spare men. In such cases, however, the safety of the crew and passengers was paramount. They must be taken on board the capturing vessel, or some equivalent provision had to be made. Otherwise, international law required the ship to be sent on its way.

Any set of regulations less suited to submarines can scarcely be imagined. Submarines carried small crews, and every man was needed to run the boat. There was no room for supernumeraries. Submarines were most effective when they were able to remain hidden under water and when using torpedoes, as opposed to surfacing and using their deck guns. On the surface they were extremely vulnerable to ramming and gunfire—even from small-caliber weapons. Submarines in the early years of World War I carried relatively few torpedoes, and they were so powerful relative to the normal merchant target that using them often seemed wasteful. As a result, U-boat captains regularly surfaced and used their deck guns against merchantmen. For that tactic to be a common one, however, the merchant crew had to be obliging enough to make no resistance and sufficiently passive to prefer the risks of a long voyage in open boats to those of putting up a fight or trying to run.

Civilian crews did both in early 1915, but only occasionally. German laws of war, moreover, provided harsh penalties for civilians who resisted in any way, even by using a ship as a weapon. The Royal Navy responded by commandeering merchantmen, giving them concealed medium-caliber guns, and calling them Q-ships. When the U-boat surfaced, this Q-ship would hoist the naval ensign and open fire. It was all perfectly legal—and perfectly counterproductive—as the German captains simply replaced surface gunfire with submerged torpedo attacks in a long step toward comprehensive unrestricted submarine warfare.

**Viewpoint:
Yes. The possible presence of
Q-ships (armed merchant vessels)
made U-boats less willing to surface
and warn merchant crews before
sinking their vessels.**

Beginning in 1915 the British Royal Navy sent Q-ships to sea to aid in the defeat of the German U-boat menace. The British Q-ship, also known as a "mystery ship," was far more than an armed merchant vessel. It concealed a variety of guns, depth-charge launchers, torpedo tubes, and small arms behind camouflaged, collapsible panels and underneath deckside equipment such as lifeboats and cargo containers. Q-ship captains trained their Royal Navy crewmen to act like a merchantman crew and look the part as well. Beards and shabby clothes for the crewmembers, as well as non-naval daily routine, made the disguise complete. Additionally, all empty spaces within the hull of the ship were packed with wood in order to slow the sinking process if struck by a torpedo.

Q-ships sailed singly or in convoy. When in convoy, they normally either placed themselves in the front of the formation, where an awaiting U-boat could attack them, or at the rear, where they could act as a straggler. Needless to say, the strictest secrecy kept even the naval escort guessing which of the merchantmen in the convoy was a Q-ship. By 1917 there were twenty to thirty Q-ships at sea, mimicking various types of commercial vessels.

The key tactic in the playbook of the Q-ship was to allow the submarine to get as close as possible, maintaining the disguise until the last moment. Once the U-boat entered the kill zone, the Q-ship would let loose with every available weapon. The slightest damage to the hull of the U-boat would keep her from diving and ensure a "kill."

Word of the Q-ship threat soon spread throughout the German submarine force. Q-ship crews had to resort to even more sinister tactics to lure the U-boat closer, since no submarine skipper would surface unless he was sure his prey was a helpless merchantman. German submarines often surfaced to obtain the papers of the targeted ship—proof of a kill and

therefore important documentation to bring home. After being hit by a torpedo, part of the Q-ship crew would feign panic and escape to lifeboats. Ideally, the Q-ship would stay afloat long enough to allow the remaining concealed gun crews to let off a shot when the U-boat surfaced to finish off the ship with shellfire.

Throughout the course of the war, Q-ships claimed only eleven U-boats destroyed. They provided an additional reason—with the standard threats from British warships, aircraft, and merchant vessel gunners—for U-boat commanders to make submerged attacks without warning. As Admiral William Sims, World War I commander of American naval forces in European waters, wrote in *The Victory at Sea* (1920):

> . . . the most important accomplishment of the mystery ships was not the actual sinking of submarines, but their profound influence upon the tactics of the U-boats. It was manifest in the beginning that . . . it would cause all submarines to be wary of all mercantile craft. They were therefore obliged largely to abandon the easy, safe, and cheap methods of sinking ships by bombs [charges placed by the crew] or gun fire, and were consequently forced to incur the danger of attacking with the scarce and expensive torpedo.

According to Paul G. Halpern, in *A Naval History of World War I* (1994), some evidence demonstrates that U-boat skippers made deliberate attempts to find and destroy Q-ships in 1917, when sixteen were lost in a single year to submarine attack. Submarine captains soon learned how to recognize the traits of a Q-ship, such as the seams for collapsible walls. As the war continued, the value of the Q-ship was essentially in its deterrent nature rather than in its ability to kill submarines.

The overriding concern for the U-boat skipper was the safety of his own boat; his orders confirmed that fact. The Q-ships were such a dangerous threat that submarine commanders had to use extreme care in every attack. The use of submerged attack without warning grew tremendously during the war. In 1915 and 1916 the annual percentage of attacks without warning did not exceed 29 percent. By January 1917 the monthly figures showed that 37.5 percent of attacks were made without warning and by April had risen to 60 percent. For the submarine, the basic advan-

ACTION-STATIONS!

Harold Auten, skipper of the Q-ship Heather, *recalls in his memoirs his first command:*

At the same moment the look-out reported: "Periscope on the port bow, sir."

Simultaneously the rattlers went; for the officer of the watch has to be always on the alert. There was a rush to action-stations as a hundred men sorted themselves out, one running one way and one running another; yet in a few seconds absolute silence reigned, everybody had reached their action-stations.

On the upper deck nothing to the outward eye had occurred. Two or three men had lounged along, picking up something, and had gone on—beyond that, nothing. The men at action-stations rapidly loaded their guns, and the officer in command of each had reported to me on the bridge that their quarters were correct.

Depth charges were got ready and also reported correct. Tube-belts were gleefully buckled on by the men whose duty it was to place the tube in the cartridge, while a great glow of expectation descended upon everybody. Every man felt a tingle of delight running through him. Here was the great chance coming, here was he going to shine and again, here he was going to battle with the undersea pirates, whom he had been hoping to meet for many weary months.

I ordered the engineers to stand by and prepare for full speed, which was about eighteen knots, but to maintain the steady nine which the ship had been doing throughout.

The "Heather" went plugging along comfortably, no one on the upper deck appearing to take the slightest interest in life, but everybody was keeping his eyes as wide open as he could. I had my eye fixed on the periscope and was watching its every movement. Fritz appeared to have stopped, and it would take over a quarter of an hour to reach him, provided, of course, that he stayed where he was and that the ship held on at her present speed.

It appeared very certain that Fritz was lying in wait, and as the ship approached would take a favourable opportunity to torpedo her. However, the "Heather" stood her course. It appeared almost incredible that the submarine could keep her periscope awash in this fashion, and I decided to go full speed ahead and depth charge this pest. . . .

To anybody who knew anything of the Hun's methods, his intentions were pretty obvious. The distance was still shortened, and the ship bounded on with the intention of either ramming or dropping a quantity of depth charges on the submarine. Everybody was, in the sailor's phraseology, "on the top line." Fritz now appeared to come a little closer, as though he intended to shorten his range as we passed, and make sure of torpedoing the ship.

"Stand by depth charges and lance bomb," I cried through the voice-pipes.

The ship leapt forward, and I directed the helmsman to steer direct for the periscope. Away aloft flew the white ensign, flapping madly as the ship tore through the water straight for the Hun. The men with the lance bombs were at their stations, two on either side of the bridge and one right forward in the very stem of the ship, with his bomb already aloft like a harpoon ready to strike.

Suddenly there was a frantic scream from the man in the bows. "Hard a port," he yelled. "It's the top of the mast."

I had, however, seen it before him, and had ordered the helmsman to put his helm hard a-port.

The ship gave one sickening lurch to starboard, as her helm was put over and spun round at right angles. At the same time the engines were slowed down. It was a narrow squeak. I then took a right detour at slow speed and approached the supposed periscope. It proved to be the mast of a large ship sticking out of the water, not more than a couple of feet.

It was indeed lucky that we had spotted what it was, or the ship would have undoubtedly torn over the sunken wreck and ripped her bottom through.

Source: Harold Auten, "Q" Boat Adventures: The Exploits of the Famous Mystery Ships By a "Q" Boat Commander *(London: Jenkins, 1919), pp. 165–168.*

Q-SHIPS

tage of stealth, in attacking submerged, had to be used as a matter of survival as opposed to using more-risky surface attacks.

—JOHN ABBATIELLO,
U.S. AIR FORCE ACADEMY

Viewpoint:
No. The logic of submarine attacks worked against traditional rules of naval warfare, and the presence or absence of Q-ships had no bearing on the situation.

The submarine from its earliest conceptions was a device of subterfuge and stealth. Surfacing to destroy enemy shipping by using the deck gun was a matter of satisfying international law and the more practical reason of conserving a limited supply of torpedoes aboard the German U-boat. This approach was changed as the British blockade of the North Sea egresses bade increasingly fair to drive the Germans into starvation. The change in U-boat strategy was therefore a result of necessity and the fundamental tactics that submarines dictated by their nature. The use of Q-ships by Britain was a peripheral factor. Instead, the German Naval Staff (*Admiralstab*), came to realize that every British ship was part of the British war machine. More important, in a naval war founded on blockades, sinking enemy supplies outweighed the advantages of hunting enemy warships and following international law.

The German Naval Staff did not initially see their nascent U-boat arm as playing more than a peripheral role in overall naval strategy. Submarines were to be used in the defense of the German coastline. By 1914 Germany commanded a force of twenty-eight primarily obsolete U-boats. These were divided into two flotillas, with the mission of preventing the British Grand Fleet from penetrating the Heligoland Bight and engaging the outnumbered German High Seas Fleet.

The Royal Navy, however, did not act as anticipated. British strategy was based on blockading Germany. The British Grand Fleet patrolled blockade routes in the North Sea, attempting to starve Germany. Furthermore, England did not want to engage the Germans in a large-scale battle that could cripple British naval superiority. British and German naval operations quickly stagnated into a series of inconclusive limited engagements.

While the German High Seas Fleet was held at bay, the U-boat became the only credible means of offense at sea. The original U-boat flotillas were expanded and new flotillas created. With few warships available, the *Admiralstab* sought new targets for the U-boats: the British merchant fleet—but there were problems in successfully executing this new strategy in the face of international law, which called for ships flying a neutral flag, or unarmed enemy merchantmen, to be stopped, boarded, and if found to be carrying contraband, taken over with a prize crew. If that operation was not possible, the crew of the offending vessel could be captured and the vessel sunk.

Germany, not wanting to offend neutral nations (particularly the United States), attempted to follow the letter of these conventions. That strategy, however, greatly hampered the U-boat as an offensive weapon by forcing them to surface every time they encountered a noncombatant ship. It quickly became apparent that the submarine was ill equipped, too fragile, and too small to carry out this role. To be effective, U-boats needed cause to violate international law and to strike without warning from below the waves.

Britain, in an effort to tighten its blockade, violated established treaties by declaring the entire North Sea a war zone, flying the flags of neutral countries on its merchantmen, and arming civilian ships. This last act, the creation of the Q-ship, was one of the first attempts at antisubmarine warfare. The idea behind the Q-ship was simple. The British navy hid armament on fishing trawlers and light merchant ships in an attempt to lure a U-boat to the surface. When the unsuspecting U-boat emerged, the Q-ship would open fire.

While seemingly an ingenious strategy, the Q-ships only brought limited success. According to V. E. Tarrant, in *The U-Boat Offensive 1914–1945* (1989), of the 178 U-boat losses only 11 were caused by Q-ships. U-boats had more to fear from enemy warships and being rammed, regardless of ship type, than they had from Q-ships. The British Q-ship strategy also failed in that the armed fishing boats and trawlers lost more than twice their number than the number of U-boats sunk. The exposure of U-boats to ramming and surface fire by any ship was equally and often more dangerous than any action by ships with the Q designation. Q-ships were not effective at destroying U-boats, nor did they affect German deployment of U-boats near the British Isles.

The Q-ship failed for several reasons. Some of the problems the British inadvertently brought on themselves. By breaking established naval conventions in the first place, they allowed other nations to do so as well. When the British declared the North Sea a war zone and dis-

Q-SHIPS

**The Q-ship
Penshurst, 1916**

(from E. Keble Chatterton,
Q-Ships and Their Story,
[1972])

guised their ships as neutrals, it allowed the Germans the latitude to declare a campaign of unrestricted submarine warfare. Since no ship could positively be identified as neutral or hostile, all ships would be considered hostile. Even before their deployment, the chance for Q-ships to play a significant role was gone.

World War I taught the *Admiralstab* and U-boat commanders several important lessons. The average submarine carried a crew of about thirty men. Because of the smaller size of submarines, relative to other warships, all hands were necessary for the successful operation of the U-boat. No men could be spared, nor could any extras be carried aboard, to man a prize crew. Furthermore, a submarine that was relatively successful on a patrol could spare no space for prisoners. When a submarine confronted a merchant ship that chose to resist or escape, submarines could rarely overtake it or submerge in time to avoid being rammed. Early in the war the passenger vessel *Colchester* was able to outrun a surfaced U-boat. Even submerged boats were not safe. Attempting to exit Scapa Flow, the U–*18* was rammed twice: first by a trawler and then fatally by a British destroyer. In a combat zone, submariners were correspondingly disinclined to surface and were probably relieved when the second U-boat offensive made surfacing unnecessary.

Surface attacks not only endangered the submarine and its crew, but they also hampered its effectiveness as a fighting vessel. During the first unrestricted warfare campaign (1915), U-boats attacked 274 British merchant ships. Attacks made while submerged were successful 58 percent of the time. Those victims that escaped could thank for their survival two factors: inaccurate firing solutions and/or torpedo failure. The majority of attacks on merchantmen (163) were done on the surface. These types of attacks were only 46 percent successful. Failures here were generally caused by ships that outran submarines or decided to counterattack.

Most U-boats were configured with four torpedo tubes, usually two bow and two stern. Early U-boats were rarely commissioned with a deck gun. Later models, such as the U–*19*, carried an 8.8 centimeter gun. Some coastal submarines carried a single machine gun or a 5 centimeter gun. Older U-boat models would be refitted to carry a deck gun, but they often lacked the firepower necessary to be effective against anything but the smallest and lightly armored ships.

The emergence of the British Q-ship did not change the military or political circumstances surrounding U-boat employment. Germany began to feel the effects of the British blockade as early as 1915. Its first U-boat offensive ended in response to saber-rattling by the United States. Naval engagements such as Jutland (1916) only brought home the point that the British outnumbered and outgunned the German surface fleet. The second U-boat offensive, and the tactic of sinking the enemy without warning, were born out of the desperation of Germany to end the war before its economy collapsed.

U-boat strategies, especially during the second offensive, were based on diplomatic risks and best-strategy considerations. They reflected as well the increasingly clear fact that U-boats, and submarines in general, were most effective when strikes were based on stealth and hit-and-run tactics. In order to use their best naval weapon effectively and decisively, the Germans gambled diplomatically and lost. The successful development of U-boat tactics by the *Admiralstab* and its commanders at sea, however, is often forgotten because of strategic defeat of the boats.

–VINCENT J. SCUTARO,
NEW YORK, NEW YORK

References

John Ellis and Mike Cox, *The World War One Data Book: The Essential Facts and Figures For All the Combatants* (London: Aurum, 2001).

Niall Ferguson, *The Pity of War* (London: Penguin, 1998).

German Warships of World War I: The Royal Navy's Official Guide to the Capital Ships, Cruisers, Destroyers, Submarines and Small Craft, 1914–1918 (London: Greenhill, 1992).

Paul G. Halpern, *A Naval History of World War I* (Annapolis, Md.: Naval Institute Press, 1994).

John Keegan, *The Price of Admiralty: War at Sea From Man of War to Submarine* (London: Hutchinson, 1988).

William Sowden Sims, *The Victory at Sea* (Garden City, N.Y.: Doubleday, Page, 1920).

V. E. Tarrant, *The U-Boat Offensive 1914–1945* (London: Arms & Armour, 1989).

John Terraine, *Business in Great Waters: The U-boat Wars, 1916–1945* (London: Cooper, 1989).

Q-SHIPS

RUSSIAN LOGISTICS

Did Russia have an efficient logistical system during the Great War?

Viewpoint: Yes. Although Russia did suffer some shortages during the conflict, it produced and received enough matériel to sustain its war effort.

Viewpoint: No. The Russian logistical system was able to only sustain the material demands of the war for a few months before sliding into gridlock and eventual collapse.

Among the most enduring images of the Russian effort in the Great War is a lack of the tools of modern war—not merely artillery pieces, shells, and aircraft but also basic requirements, such as small arms. Accounts are replete with stories of replacements being sent unarmed to the front and told to pick up the rifles of casualties, or of bayonets being used to do the work that more-sophisticated armies entrusted to shells and bullets.

This explanation was useful during and after the war for those associated with the tsarist system to explain away the defeat of Russian armies. On one level it nurtured an image of Russia as entering into a conflict for which it was unprepared in order to support ungrateful allies. Some versions go so far as to accuse France and Britain of bad faith, or at least indifference to the fate of Russia, in that the Western Allies failed to make a sufficient effort to deliver the war matériel Russia needed so badly. The Communist government also found the shortage motif useful both as an indictment of the old order and a justification for the heavy concentration on military spending. Finally, scholars of all cultures have found the arms shortage a useful focal point for discussions of the Russian failure to develop an industrial society before 1914.

Norman Stone in *The Eastern Front, 1914–1917* (1975), his seminal analysis of the Russo-German conflict during World War I, challenged conventional wisdom on a statistical level. He made a strong case that domestic Russian production, combined with the Allied delivery of munitions, showed that Russia was on the whole no worse off than the other major combatants for most of the war. Subsequent research has focused less on figures than on infrastructures. The material results cited by Stone were the product of a national mobilization that depended for financing on borrowing and on printing money—both the causes of runaway inflation. The new and expanded factories drew labor from unskilled men and women, taken largely from the farms. That employment diminished productivity both in the cities and in an agricultural system that was increasingly labor-intensive as work animals were requisitioned by the army. Finally, the Russian administrative system was less and less able to move either food or manufactured goods where they were needed. The prewar "crust of competence," people who could make trains run on time and keep records accurately, was thin at best. The losses and sacrifices of war diminished Russian industry and overstrained the survivors to a point where, well before the Revolution of 1917, the decisive problem was not shortages but gridlock.

Viewpoint:
Yes. Although Russia did suffer some shortages during the conflict, it produced and received enough matériel to sustain its war effort.

Russia achieved remarkable growth in the production of war matériel, with a continuous improvement in quantities of supplies from 1914 through 1916. Machine-gun production, for example, rose from 165 units per month in 1914 to more than 1,200 per month by December 1916. In addition, over that same period of time Russia received more than 32,000 machine guns from its allies, mostly from the United States. Even more important than sheer quantitative increases such as this one, however, was the improvement in the Russian production system during the first two years of World War I.

In an unprecedented event private Russian citizens and agencies of what might be termed "civil" society joined forces with government ministries and industrialists in two forums to address Russian supply needs. The first of these, the *Zemstva* Union, provided critical supplies and humanitarian aid to the army during the chaos of the opening months of the war and the Great Retreat of 1915. Under Prince Georgy Lvov, who had earned a heroic reputation in Russia for his assistance to veterans of the Russo-Japanese War (1904–1905), the *Zemstva* Union provided 7.5 million suits of underwear, 250,000 tents, fur winter clothing for 250,000, and more than 180,000 hospital beds from privately funded sources in the first six months of the conflict. The Union represented a voluntary effort to coordinate the efforts of local Russian officials. Limited in its scope, the *Zemstva* had originally been formed by the Great Reforms of Tsar Alexander II in the 1860s. Despite restrictions placed on its activity by an untrusting central government, the *Zemstva* raised more than 25,000,000 rubles in 1914 and more than 100,000,000 in 1915, all of which was spent on supplies and medical aid. When Commander-in-Chief Grand Duke Nikolay Nikolayevich begged the visiting president of the Duma in September of 1915 to "Get my army shod!" the *Zemstva* Union led the response, buying more than 5,000,000 pairs of boots from the United States.

The second, more-formal forum that mobilized Russian society and production to meet war needs was the "Special Conference on National Defense." This agency, a mixture unprecedented in Russian history, brought together government ministers, private industrialists, technical experts, supply and weapons specialists in the army, and patriotic citizens. A combination of political and bureaucratic authority with technical expertise enabled this agency to drastically improve Russian industrial production to meet the needs of the army. Under its leadership, Russian rifle production soared from 41 total rifles produced in the first seven months of 1914 to more than 40,000 each month by the end of 1915. By the spring of 1916 every Russian rifle had a reserve of about 400 rounds, as Russia produced 1.3 million rifles and 1.5 billion cartridges per year. Shell production, which had limited Russian artillery to 2 or 3 rounds per gun per day early in the war, rose to more than 1.5 million shells per month by early 1916, an increase of more than twelve times from the opening days of the war. Gun production increased just as dramatically. From 1900 to 1914, including the period of the Russo-Japanese War, Russia produced an average of 1,237 field guns per year. In 1916 alone it produced more than 5,000 field pieces. In fact, Russian production of field guns was, by 1917, greater than that of either Britain or France. In summary, the "Special Conference" greatly enhanced Russian production, despite the many obstacles it faced. In so doing, it reduced (but did not eliminate) the dependence of Russia upon foreign sources of supply.

The Allies provided Russia with prodigious quantities of equipment as well. The relative calm on the Western Front in 1915 enabled British and French sources to deliver more than 150 heavy guns, 500 trench mortars, 2,000,000 hand grenades, 75,000,000 rifle cartridges, 2,500,000 pounds of explosives, and 50 airplanes, as well as armored cars, barbed wire, and other supplies to the port of Archangel. According to W. Bruce Lincoln, in *Passage Through Armageddon: The Russians in War and Revolution, 1914–1918* (1986), British military observer General Alfred Knox noted that "The Russian military position had improved by the commencement of summer 1916 far beyond the expectations of any foreign observer who had taken part in the retreat of the previous year."

That improvement also included food, the most critical supply of any army. By mid 1916 Russian grain reserves were more than twice that of the previous year. Keeping grain that would have been exported in peacetime boosted Russian reserves. Lincoln noted that Russia had "grain to spare" as 1916 drew to a close.

Thus, it was not matériel shortages per se that crippled the Russian effort and set it on the path to defeat and revolution. Instead, incompetent military and civilian leaders mis-

Russian soldiers in fall 1917

(from Collier's New Photographic History of the World's War [1918], Joseph M. Bruccoli Great War Collection, Thomas Cooper Library, University of South Carolina)

managed domestic material production and reserves and failed to properly deliver the Allied aid it received.

Russian war plans were fundamentally flawed. On its frontier with Germany, Russia relied heavily upon massive fortress complexes, such as Novo-Georgievsk and Ivangorod on the Vistula and Brest-Litovsk, supported by smaller fortresses such as Grodno, Kovno, and Osowiec. Such bastions hearkened back to an earlier age of warfare and failed to account for the mobility and speed of the modern German army, not to mention the awesome power of siege artillery in the twentieth century. Most critically, however, these fortresses tied up massive quantities of weapons, supplies, and troops that could not be made available to the hard-pressed Russian field army in the opening months of the war. The arsenals of those field armies contained only about two-thirds of the (profoundly outmoded) estimates by the Russian General Staff of cartridge reserves in August 1914. Thus, while the troops of the Third Army fought hand-to-hand, using bayonets fixed on empty rifles in the spring of 1915, more than 75,000,000 rifle cartridges were locked away in the fortresses of Kovno, Grodno, Osowiec, and Brest-Litovsk. As the Germans drove eastward, the armies that faced them begged for shells and supplies. Nine thousand pieces of artillery, including 900 heavy guns, 1,000,000 shells, and more than 100,000,000 rounds of rifle and machine-gun ammunition were lost in the fall of Ivangorod and Novo-Georgievsk. Russian commanders could not marshal the trains to move those supplies to the field armies, even if they had taken the decision to do so, during the German offensives in spring 1915.

Perhaps nowhere was the mismanagement of resources so pronounced as in that of grain. Russian peasants refused to sell their bumper crops of 1915 and 1916. Artificially low prices set by the government and the lack, or complete absence, of consumer goods provided absolutely no incentive for peasants to deliver grain that the urban workers and the army so desperately needed. By 1916 peasant protests and riots signaled the first ominous steps toward collapse and revolution.

One final aspect of the Russian supply situation was also critical. The transportation system faced impossible challenges in trying to deliver the enormous wartime volumes of matériel over the vast distances of Russia. When both domestic and Allied sources of supply are considered, each bullet fired by a Russian soldier had to be brought more than 4,000 kilometers from source to front. Each artillery shell was transported more than

AND THE SILENCE OF MY BATTERIES

In his memoirs Russian general Anton Denikin, commander of the Fourth Rifle "Iron" Brigade, recounts the lack of adequate supplies on the Eastern Front:

By late 1914 there was already a keen shortage of supplies and cartridges, but the careless and ignorant war minister, Sukhomlinov, succeeded in convincing the sovereign, the Duma, and the public that all was well. Toward the spring of 1915 a terrible crisis became evident in equipment and especially in military stores. The strain of artillery fire in that war reached unprecedented and unexpected dimensions, upsetting all the theoretical calculations made by both our and western European military science. But while industry in the western countries, by extraordinary effort, coped with the critical task of creating huge arsenals and stocks, we were unable to do so.

Only toward the spring of 1916 did we manage, by colossal effort and foreign orders, to acquire heavy artillery and replenish our stock of cartridges and supplies. Of course it was still not on a scale with that of our allies but it was sufficient for prolonging the war with some hope of victory. . . .

I recall that in the 8th Army that summer we had only two hundred shells remaining for each gun and had not been promised supply replacement from the artillery department before early fall. Batteries consisting of eight guns each were reduced to six guns and empty ordinance depots were dispatched to the rear as unnecessary.

The spring of 1915 will remain in my memory forever. Grievously bloody battles. Neither cartridges nor shells. The battle near Peremyshl in mid-May meant eleven days of cruel fighting for the Iron Brigade. Eleven days of the dreadful boom of German heavy artillery, literally razing whole rows of trenches along with their defenders. And the silence of my batteries.

We were unable to answer. There was nothing with which to answer. Even rifle shells were rationed. Nearly exhausted regiments repulsed one attack after another with bayonets or, in extreme cases, by firing point blank. I watched as the ranks of my brave riflemen diminished, and I experienced despair as I realized my absurd helplessness. Two regiments were almost annihilated by one burst of enemy fire. When after three days' silence our six-gun batteries received fifty shells, it was reported by telephone to all the regiments. And all companies, all the riflemen, breathed more easily. Under such circumstances no strategic plan toward either Berlin or Budapest would or could be carried out.

Source: *Anton I. Denikin,* The Career of a Tsarist Officer: Memoirs, 1872–1916, *translated by Margaret Patoski (Minneapolis: University of Minnesota Press, 1975), pp. 252–253.*

6,500 kilometers from manufacturer to gun. Combined with the impossibly scrambled Russian distribution system (for example, it was more efficient to import iron ore and coal from Baltic sources to Petersburg industries than to move domestic sources from Krivoy Rog in the south), these distances overwhelmed the transportation system.

Thus, mismanagement, incompetence, and geography were the crippling factors of Russian wartime logistics. Ample quantities of supplies and material were produced by Russia or received from the Allies, but the inability to deliver them where they were most needed fatally undermined the army and the regime, paving the road to defeat and revolution.

—DAVID L. RUFFLEY,
U.S. AIR FORCE ACADEMY

Viewpoint:
No. The Russian logistical system was able to only sustain the material demands of the war for a few months before sliding into gridlock and eventual collapse.

In addition to its many other structural problems, Imperial Russia never developed an adequate infrastructure to supply its armies with the materials needed to fight a modern war. Entering World War I as the least-developed great power, its factories could neither compete with those of its enemies nor equal those of its allies, at least not in proportion to its wartime responsibilities. Chronic mismanagement in the top echelons of the government prevented Russia from reaching its full potential. Such related factors as weak war finance, poor railroad construction and maintenance, and political instability damaged the ability of Russia to build and stockpile armaments all the more.

The main problem with Russian military preparation actually preceded the outbreak of war in 1914. Rather than taking constructive steps to make the army a competitive force in Europe, Vladimir Sukhomlinov proved to be an absolute disaster as Imperial War Minister. In addition to habitual personal malfeasance, dubious associations with people who later turned out to be enemy agents, and backward thinking about strategy and tactics, Sukhomlinov did a terrible job of equipping the army. In the years leading up to 1914, a time characterized by increasing diplomatic and strategic tension with Austria-Hungary and Germany, he actually underspent the allotted annual funding of his ministry. Although military spending increased in the years before 1814, Sukhomlinov did a poor job.

Because of sloth and general incompetence the Russians allowed their stockpiles of shells, small arms, artillery, and other important war materials to decrease. When the Russian army went to war in 1914 the inadequacy of its preparations became immediately apparent. A significant percentage of its infantry (approaching one-third in some units) went into combat unarmed. When the poorly equipped soldiers were sent into battle, they were told to pick up the weapons dropped by their fallen comrades. Russian artillery units were so undersupplied that they often stood silent in the face of German bombardments and infantry assaults or fired off only a few token rounds each day. Infantry attacks against German positions could not be supported by coordinated fire from heavy guns, and defensive positions could not be supported by artillery fire. In a war that came to be dominated by fortified front lines, the swift exhaustion of Russian ammunition stockpiles allowed the Germans to conduct effective campaigns and conquer significant amounts of enemy territory. When Germany opened its offensive in Russian Poland in the spring of 1915, the only realistic strategic option for the Russian general staff was to conduct a withdrawal to a shorter and more defensible line.

Once the magnitude of the supply disaster was identified, however, the Russian government took several steps in the right direction. In 1915 Tsar Nicholas II finally dismissed the ineffectual Sukhomlinov and replaced him with General Alexei Polivanov, an industrious, technocratic modernizer. The tsar also allowed the formation of "special councils" to address problems of production and supply on the home front. A group of distinguished industrialists and financiers formed a War Industries Committee, led by the moderate right-wing political figure Aleksandr Guchkov, to coordinate the efforts of the special councils and to rationalize military production. The Russian government appealed to the Allied powers, domestic investors, and their own growing banking sector for loans to facilitate further development. It also communicated news of its shortages to the Western Allies (Sukhomlinov never mentioned it to them) and accepted their offers of material and technical assistance.

Despite the improvements brought about by these efforts, however, the Russian system of war supply remained a lost cause. Production increased, but even its most dramatic growth was inadequate for the needs of the army. Russia was producing as many artillery shells as Great Britain by September 1915, but statistics such as these were misleading for several reasons. First, Russia mobilized thirteen million men over the course of the war, compared with the relatively smaller totals of Britain and France. Even if it produced equivalent quantities of war materials by the autumn of 1915, its per-capita production remained only a fraction of what the British and French were realizing, and Russia could make correspondingly less material available to its troops. The technological sophistication of Russian weaponry, furthermore, lagged significantly behind that of most other major combatants, and Russia never developed emerging military technologies such as tanks, planes, and telephone communications on a competitive scale.

Second, Russia had to defend single-handedly a one-thousand-mile front against both Germany and Austria-Hungary, as well as another significant front against the Ottoman Empire. Britain and France had imperial commitments and engaged in small campaigns on other fronts, but the overwhelming majority of their strength was concentrated in the geographically small area of the Western Front. They shared the burden of defense there, moreover, with the tenacious Belgian army, troops from their colonial empires, and ultimately with the might of the American Expeditionary Force (AEF). With the exception of Serbia and Romania, the first of which was effectively eliminated as a combatant by the autumn of 1915 and the second of which entered and left the war in a three-month period in late 1916, Russia stood alone in the East.

Although some historians point out that the initial successes of the Brusilov offensive, launched in Galicia in the summer of 1916, were possible because Russian artillery batteries had higher reserves of shells than those of their opponents, this logistical feat was hardly spectacular for a country that had not taken the offensive for nearly two years and had offered only token resistance in the meantime. German and Austrian forces opposing General Aleksey Brusilov were less well supplied because their counterparts on the Western Front were more heavily engaged. Indeed, a significant part of the Battle of Verdun, where German guns often fired several hundred thousand shells a day, was concomitant with the whole duration of the Brusilov offensive. Despite early successes, the Russian effort collapsed as soon as German reinforcements and supplies arrived. Even if Russia had consistently produced a comparable amount of armaments to its Western allies, the armaments still would have been insufficient to satisy its military responsibilities.

Third, while British and French war production was significant, these countries were also in a much better position to expand their arsenals through trade and purchase than Russia was. London and Paris started buying military munitions from the United States well before America entered the war in April 1917. American banks extended generous credits and loans to the Western Allies almost from the beginning of the conflict. British ownership of half the merchant marine in the world, its possession of the largest navy, and—despite the German U-boat blockade—the relative ease of access to ports in the British Isles and France for transatlantic shipping made importing war matériels quite easy. Although Russia received foreign war materials, its infrastructure was totally unprepared to handle either their receipt on an adequate scale or their transport to the front. German control of access to the Baltic Sea and Turkish control of the entry to the Black Sea meant that Russia could only receive supplies through three ports—Murmansk on the Arctic Sea, Archangel on the White Sea, and Vladivostok on the Pacific. Frozen Archangel could only be used for a maximum of six months out of the year, while construction of the Murmansk and Trans-Siberian railroads was only completed in 1916. The strain that the war placed on Russian railroads overall led to frequent breakdowns and chronic congestion, especially since the most sophisticated segments of its rail network and much of its rolling stock—together with much industry— were lost in the Polish territories that fell to the Germans in 1915. By 1917 the situation was so difficult that Russian railroads could barely move domestically produced matériels to the front or, ominously, even supply the major cities with food. A large amount of Allied war supplies simply sat on the loading docks of distant ports; some supplies sat long after Russia left the war.

Russian war production had a myriad of other persistent problems as well. In addition to the geographic factors of its isolation, it did not enjoy financial resources comparable to those of its allies. While it possessed a modern banking system and a generally competent ministry of finance, it already had huge foreign debts that dated back to the industrial growth of the late nineteenth century and had only increased in the years leading up to the war. France and Belgium, the largest prewar creditors to Russia, were now fighting for their lives and had no available capital to lend out. Like Britain, both countries had to borrow abroad just to keep themselves supplied and fighting.

While America lent freely to Britain and France, its political leaders and capital markets distrusted Tsarist Russia almost as much as they distrusted Imperial Germany and had little inclination—or practical ability, for that matter—to help it financially. Relative to its European allies, the ability of Russia to borrow abroad was sharply curtailed.

State revenue for industrial development and military production was also problematic. Without its regular peacetime infusions of foreign capital, and having to compensate for its serious initial lack of supply, the Russian government embarked on an inflationary course that dramatically cut the value of its currency and its people's real wages. While inflation was a problem throughout Europe, the situation in Russia, where cost of living rose three times faster than wages by late 1916, was truly catastrophic. Uniquely among the combatant powers, the Russian tax base suffered, for the government had not adopted the modern revenue-generating schemes of direct taxation of property and income, practices that had become common in Europe and the United States in the decade before the war. Most of the Imperial budget was still supported by excise taxes on goods that people were less likely to buy in an economy of high prices and scarcity and by customs duties on imports that had vanished because of the geographic isolation of the empire in wartime.

Perhaps the greatest threat to steady war production came from the political turbulence of 1917. After the monarchy was toppled in February of that year, the management of labor and production questions by the Provisional Government was, like so many of its other initiatives, a dismal failure. In addition to its inheritance of the structural problems of the Old Regime, Russia neither completely succeeded in reestablishing law and order nor effectively challenged radical challenges to its economic policy.

Although Russian industrial workers had many legitimate grievances and were in many ways manipulated by socialist agitators and political parties, their increased radicalization was catastrophic for war production. Identifying political controversies closely with the nature of their work and the general economic situation, sprouting workers' committees presented industrial owners and managers with demands for shorter hours, higher wages, and better working conditions. Such demands were sometimes modest, reasonable, and acceptable to management, but in many cases—especially in the overworked war industries—they were radical, unrealistic, and violent. Among other things, radical workers frequently demanded broad worker participation in managerial decisions, the removal of unpopular managers and foremen (regardless of their actual qualifications or effectiveness), impossibly high pay increases, and abstract political reforms that business owners were simply incapable of bringing about. The physical intimidation and violence that accompanied many of these labor-management confrontations frequently scared owners and managers into accepting any demand presented to them, however absurd or economically unsound, or into shutting their plants down altogether. In short, Russian industry became simultaneously less productive and more expensive to operate.

After the Bolsheviks seized power in October 1917, moreover, their wholesale expropriation of industry created an even bigger disaster. Their initial policy of giving over nationalized industrial assets to "worker control" merely resulted in workers voting for even higher wages, still shorter hours, and worse production decisions than they had originally demanded. Already having asked Germany for an armistice, Bolshevik hopes for maintaining some leverage in the Brest-Litovsk peace negotiations were made impossible by the almost total disintegration of the Russian industrial base, as well as the continuing disintegration of the military. Only the imposition of a full command economy based on central planning, ruthless coercion, and political terror could eventually restore some semblance of order to Russian industry. By then, of course, Russia had lost World War I and had begun its descent into civil war and communist dictatorship.

–PAUL DU QUENOY,
GEORGETOWN UNIVERSITY

References

Orlando Figes, *A People's Tragedy: The Russian Revolution, 1891–1924* (London: Cape, 1996).

Martin Gilbert, *The First World War: A Complete History* (New York: Holt, 1994).

John Keegan, *The First World War* (London: Hutchinson, 1998).

W. Bruce Lincoln, *Passage Through Armageddon: The Russians in War and Revolution, 1914–1918* (New York: Simon & Schuster, 1986).

Bernard Pares, *The Fall of the Russian Monarchy: A Study of the Evidence* (London: Cape, 1939; New York: Knopf, 1939).

Richard Pipes, *The Russian Revolution* (New York: Knopf, 1990).

Dennis E. Showalter, *Tannenberg: Clash of Empires* (Hamden, Conn.: Archon, 1991).

Norman Stone, *The Eastern Front, 1914–1917* (New York: Scribners, 1975).

Barbara W. Tuchman, *The Guns of August* (New York: Macmillan, 1962).

Rex A. Wade, *The Russian Revolution, 1917* (Cambridge & New York: Cambridge University Press, 2000).

Allan K. Wildman, *The End of the Russian Imperial Army: The Old Army and the Soldiers' Revolt*, volume 1, *The Old Army and the Soldiers' Revolt (March–April 1917)* (Princeton: Princeton University Press, 1980).

RUSSIAN REVOLUTION

Was the return of Vladimir Lenin and several other exiled Bolshevik leaders in 1917 decisive to the development of the Russian Revolution?

Viewpoint: Yes. Without Lenin the Bolsheviks had no reasonable chance of imposing their particular structure on the revolutionary process.

Viewpoint: No. The Russian Revolution was well on its course before Lenin's return.

In early 1917 the German High Command agreed to transport three dozen exiled Russian revolutionaries from Switzerland across Germany to the newly renamed Petrograd. The purpose of the exercise was to foment revolution in Russia and thereby achieve through politics what for two and a half years had proven impossible militarily: drive Russia out of a war Germany was a long way from winning.

The Germans were well aware of the risks they ran—so much so that Vladimir Lenin's insistence that the train be given extraterritorial rights on its passage through Germany, with no one entering or leaving it, has been processed into legend as an external "sealing" to prevent contagion by the plague of revolution. Yet, how decisive was the presence of Lenin and his associates in the final process of replacing the tsar's government with a Bolshevik one? Revolution had been well under way before Lenin's famous arrival at the Finland Station. The Provisional Government formed in March 1916 had been able to do little about the problems generated and exacerbated by eighteen months of war. The erosion of Russian infrastructure had continued, with everything from the railway system to local administrations either gridlocking or dissolving. Allied pressure to launch new offensives canceled the benefits, material and moral, that the new government received from its democratic orientation. Well before the government established committees to consider soldiers' grievances, military discipline at the front and in the rear became symbolic as fewer superiors risked giving orders that might be challenged or ignored.

Opposition to the Provisional Government was, however, as diffuse as it was powerful. The various parties and factions supporting revolution had long histories of mutual enmity, personal and ideological. Those with a Marxist base found their situation further complicated by Karl Marx's insistence that a bourgeois revolution based on a developed capitalist system was a necessary precondition for the final triumph of Communism. It required a good deal of exegesis and even more logic chopping to argue that these conditions had been fulfilled in the Russia of 1917.

Lenin had argued before the war that Russia under the right circumstances could omit the bourgeois-democratic revolution and proceed directly to a dictatorship of the proletariat supported by its natural ally, the peasantry. From the first days of his return, Lenin's clarity of vision and his ruthless determination galvanized the still-small Bolshevik movement, attracted supporters, and inhibited rivals. As the grip of the Provisional Government slackened and Russia slid toward chaos, someone who was that sure of himself reassured others as well. The Bolshevik coup of November 1917 was remarkable not for its immediate success—by that time power was almost literally lying in the streets—but for the subsequent lack of resistance, from any quarter: a circumstance that endured for the first crucial weeks the Bolsheviks consolidated their position and began steering Russia down Lenin's path.

Viewpoint:
Yes. Without Lenin the Bolsheviks had no reasonable chance of imposing their particular structure on the revolutionary process.

When the Imperial German government allowed a trainload of exiled Russian radicals to cross its territory and return home in the spring of 1917, it condemned Russia to a firestorm of revolution and civil conflict that outlived World War I by many years. Although the Germans intended the repatriation of Vladimir Lenin and several other Bolshevik leaders to benefit the position of Germany in the war by provoking domestic strife in Russia, they unleashed forces with long-range consequences that they failed to comprehend. Without Lenin's decisive and fanatical leadership at a critical time in 1917, the Bolshevik Party could never have entertained serious pretensions to national leadership.

One of the critical problems that had beset the Bolshevik Party was that its radical Marxist leadership, uncompromising in its devotion to communist revolution, had long been a special target for the tsarist authorities. Lenin, its undisputed leader, had been jailed for helping found a revolutionary political organization in 1895 and was then exiled to Siberia in 1897. When his sentence expired in 1900, he left Russia and spent the next seventeen years in various West European cosmopolitan centers, where he cultivated his position as the leader of the Bolshevik Party and supported himself by "borrowing" party funds and living off the income of his mother's estate. The revolutionary careers of many other Bolshevik leaders and lesser party members paralleled Lenin's. Many of them spent years abroad to escape the consequences of their subversive activities in Russia and lost touch with the political realities in the country. At the same time, other prominent Bolsheviks remained in Russia. A handful even sat in the protoparliamentary Duma (representative council) after an initial boycott of its elections. Yet, these Bolsheviks also had their problems. Roman Malinovsky, the most prominent domestic Bolshevik leader and probably the second most important leader in the party after Lenin, turned out to be a tsarist

police informer. Several other prominent Bolshevik agitators, most of whom had also spent at least some time abroad, were apprehended and sentenced to prison terms or Siberian exile.

Despite the respect that Lenin commanded and his unchallenged leadership, the Bolshevik Party was diffuse, disorganized, and unpopular in the first months of 1917. Before the collapse of tsarism in March, none of the Bolshevik leaders—or most other radicals for that matter—predicted that a communist revolution would be a real possibility in the foreseeable future. In January 1917, only a few weeks before the popular disturbances in Petrograd brought down the monarchy, Lenin himself told an audience that the older generation of the socialist movement (in which he included himself, at age forty-six) might not live to see the revolution. Within Russia, the Bolshevik Party had one tortured newspaper (*Pravda*), subject to constant police surveillance and censorship, and only a few thousand active members.

The collapse of tsarism offered a partial solution for this organizational problem. Shortly after the weak Provisional Government assumed power, it issued a full amnesty for political offenders against the Old Regime. Exiled and imprisoned revolutionary leaders were free to return to the political centers of European Russia without restrictions and regardless of the nature of their crimes, provided, of course, that they could travel there. For the scattered Bolsheviks, this amnesty meant that they could now assemble openly in Petrograd and work for the vision of a communist future. Political freedom, however, did not by itself promise to consolidate the Bolshevik Party or enable it to mount a serious campaign for national leadership. In the first weeks of democratic revolution in Russia, during February–March 1917, the now openly operating Bolshevik Party organization in Petrograd was timid in its approach to revolution. Under the editorial leadership of Lev Kamenev and Iosif Dzhugashvili (a young revolutionary known by his party alias, Stalin), who had returned from Siberian exile under the amnesty, *Pravda* declared its unreserved solidarity with the Provisional Government and support for its authority.

In a classically Marxist sense this stand was the correct policy to follow. Marx and his major disciples had predicted that a socialist

A FRENCH AMBASSADOR ON LENIN

French diplomat Georges Maurice Paléologue, in his memoirs, recalls the resilience and power of Vladimir Lenin during the initial days of the Russian Revolution:

Saturday, April 21, 1917.

When Miliukov assured me that Lenin had been hopelessly discredited in the eyes of the *Soviet* by the extravagance of his "defeatism," he was once more the victim of an optimistic illusion.

On the contrary, Lenin's influence seems to have been increasing greatly in the last few days. One point of which there can be no doubt is that he has already gathered round him, or under his orders, all the hot-heads of the revolution; he is now established as a strong leader.

Born on the 23rd April, 1870, at Simbirsk on the Volga, Vladimir Flitch Ulianov, known as Lenin, is a pure Russian. His father, who belonged to the provincial *petite noblesse,* was employed in the department of education. In 1887 his eldest brother, implicated in a plot against Alexander III, was condemned to death and hung. This tragedy determined the whole course of life of young Vladimir Flitch, who was finishing his education at Kazan University: he threw himself heart and soul into the revolutionary movement. The destruction of tsarism was thereafter an obsession with him, and the gospel of Karl Marx became his breviary. In January, 1897, the police, who were keeping an eye on him, exiled him for three years to Minuschinsk, on the Upper Jenissei, near the Mongolian frontier. On the expiration of his sentence, he was permitted to leave Russia and he made his home in Switzerland, from which he frequently visited Paris. Tireless in his activities, he soon formed an enthusiastic sect which he fired with the cult of international Marxism. During the seditious disorders of 1905 he thought for a moment that his hour had come, and secretly returned to Russia. But the crisis passed; it was only a prelude, the first stirring of popular passions, and he went back into exile.

Lenin, utopian dreamer and fanatic, prophet and metaphysician, blind to any idea of the impossible or the absurd, a stranger to all feelings of justice or mercy, violent, machiavellian and crazy with vanity, places at the service of his messianic visions a strong unemotional will, pitiless logic and amazing powers of persuasion and command. Judging by the reports I have received of his first speeches, he is insisting on the revolutionary dictatorship of the working and rural masses; he is preaching that the proletariat has no country and proclaiming his longing for the defeat of the Russian armies. When anyone attacks his crude fancies with some argument drawn from the realm of reality, he replies with the gorgeous phrase: "So much the worse for reality!" Thus it is mere waste of time to endeavour to convince him that if the Russian armies are destroyed, Russia will become helpless prey in the claws of the German conqueror who, after gorging himself on her, will abandon her to the convulsions of anarchy. The man is all the more dangerous because he is said to be pure-minded, temperate and ascetic. Such as I see him in my mind's eye, he is a compound of Savanarola and Marat, Blanqui and Bakunin.

Source: Maurice Paléologue, An Ambassador's Memoirs, *volume 3, translated by F. A. Holt (New York: Doran, 1925), pp. 303–305.*

revolution would follow from a pseudoscientific historical process that moved through progressive stages of social and economic development. In this dialectic process, a successful socialist revolution could only develop within a "bourgeois" society dominated by a fully industrialized, capitalist economy. Since Russia in 1917 was still an overwhelmingly rural nation just emerging from autocratic rule, strict Marxists believed that it had only just begun to enter the necessary capitalist stage of development. Their propensity to collapse political events into theoretical categorizations led them to believe that the Provisional Government represented this essential "bourgeois democratic phase" of development. Even though the Bolsheviks were the most radical political party, their domestic leadership's decision to support the Provisional Government was in step with both Marxist theory and with the attitudes of the comparatively less radical Menshevik and Socialist Revolutionary Parties.

Socialist revolution was their shared ultimate goal, but they all believed that it could only happen after a prolonged period of industrialization and economic development.

After the German government facilitated Lenin's return in April 1917, however, the Bolsheviks changed their tune. Despite the content of Marx's teaching on the importance of the "bourgeois democratic" revolutions for the natural progression toward communism, Lenin immediately made clear that he had no time for the Provisional Government. Seeing the political crisis around him, Lenin developed an opportunistic variant of Marxist philosophy that called for immediate revolutionary action. Conscientious Bolsheviks, he proclaimed, should work to "force the hand of history." Lenin believed that through diligence and discipline they could effectively bypass the capitalist stage of development and work to build communism in the here and now rather than in some remote future. Immediately upon Lenin's arrival in Petrograd, he elaborated his "April Theses," a radical political platform calling for the replacement of the Provisional Government by the working-class Soviet institution and the radical transformation of the Russian economy and society along strictly Marxist lines.

Naturally, Lenin was working on a weak theoretical basis, even for a Marxist. The only basis he could find in Marx's writings was a cryptic passage in a letter to a Russian Populist revolutionary, in which Marx said that revolution in underdeveloped Russia could be possible if it were quickly followed by a worldwide revolution that then supplied Russia with massive material aid. This battle cry was hardly inspiring, but Lenin believed it, and that was all that mattered. By the force of his personality, he was without challenge within the Bolshevik Party. The structure of the party complemented his strong leadership position, for its founding principle—which separated it from the Menshevik faction of the Russian Social Democratic movement—was its adherence to a tightly organized and hierarchical structure of authority. Through this "democratic centralism" the party leadership exercised total authority over its lower echelons and rank and file, which were bound to obey its decisions or risk disciplinary action. When Lenin decided to pursue an activist revolutionary program in April 1917, he was out of step with more doctrinaire Marxists, including those among the Bolsheviks, but the nature of the organizational structure prevented anyone from contradicting him. Without his decisive personal leadership and immediate presence in the Russian capital, the Bolsheviks were unlikely ever to have followed the surprisingly militant course that Lenin demanded upon his return.

In the months that followed, Lenin's determination became an important factor in the fortunes of the now militant Bolshevik Party. The Provisional Government proved itself to be a consistently indecisive executive authority. By its own words it was only supposed to be a temporary regime that would hold power until a democratically elected Constituent Assembly decided the political future of Russia. It also absolved itself of responsibility for most pressing political and economic issues, which were also relegated to the future government. Unable to instill public confidence or even preserve law and order in many ways, the Provisional Government created mass disillusionment. Lenin's call for radical change presented an alternative. Although the Bolsheviks never inspired anything close to a majority of public support, even among Russians inclined toward socialism, Lenin was able to differentiate his party from the more timid socialists willing to work with the Provisional Government. By remaining in perpetual opposition, the Bolsheviks avoided any association with the failures and weaknesses of the government. Instead, the determination of the party gave it a broad reputation for revolutionary vigilance. Even if most socialists disagreed with the Bolsheviks and opposed many of their policies, they nevertheless believed—fatally as it turned out—that Lenin's party was committed to the defense of the revolution. This image was enhanced by the pronounced role played by armed Bolshevik factory workers, the so-called Red Guards, in resisting suspicious troop movements ordered by the army commander in chief, General Lavr Kornilov, in August 1917. Sharing their history of underground activity and police trouble, moreover, most socialists looked on the Bolsheviks as comrades in arms who could be trusted to work honestly and effectively for the good of the working class. It never occurred to them that their "misguided brothers" would soon pursue a one-party dictatorship based on terror and coercion, and the Bolshevik leaders cultivated their image as defenders of democracy up to and even during the October coup. Without Lenin's decisive leadership and overwhelming presence, the Bolshevik Party could never have achieved this "special" status and would have probably remained a fringe socialist party with marginal public support and no serious pretensions to government.

Lenin's most decisive moments came in September and October 1917, when it became clear that the authority of the Provisional Government was slipping away. As confidence in

Street fighting in St. Petersburg in 1917

(from Grosser Bilderatlas des Weltkrieges *[1915–1919], Joseph M. Bruccoli Great War Collection, Thomas Cooper Library, University of South Carolina)*

the government plummeted, it was widely rumored that its prime minister, Aleksandr Kerensky, or elements within the military, or both in combination, would attempt a counter-revolutionary coup. Lenin saw these rumors, which had little foundation in fact despite Kornilov's machinations, as a critical advantage in his own plot to take power. Arguing that the time had come for the Bolsheviks to depose the government, Lenin used the force of his personality and unchallengeable leadership to compel the Central Committee of the party to approve plans for a revolutionary coup. Lenin's presence was essential for its decision. In the critical weeks leading up to the uprising, he had to defuse substantial intraparty opposition to secure adherence to the plan. If he were still trying to direct revolutionary activity from cafés in Switzerland, his task would have been infinitely more difficult, if not impossible.

When the Bolsheviks overthrew the Provisional Government on 25 October 1917, their entire effort was the result of Lenin's leadership. Some historians, and the Bolsheviks themselves, later argued that the events of October 1917 were inevitably caused by the social and economic crises in Russia and that the Russian people made a conscious "choice" for communism. This analysis ignores Lenin's crucial role in shaping events. His presence in Russia, facilitated by the German government, led directly to the Bolshevik turnabout in April 1917 and its consequent advocacy of radical revolutionary transformation. As a result of this change, the Bolsheviks were sharply distinguished from the other socialist parties, which supported the ineffectual Provisional Government and lost their prestige as its fortunes declined. Lenin's important personal role was also decisive in October 1917, when he forcefully committed the party to the coup d'état that brought it to power. Without him that critical decision likely would never have been made, and the seminal event in the radicalization of the Russian Revolution would never have taken place.

—PAUL DU QUENOY,
GEORGETOWN UNIVERSITY

Viewpoint:
No. The Russian Revolution was well on its course before Lenin's return.

While Vladimir Lenin played a pivotal role in the final results of the Russian Revolution, his return in April was only one of many factors that led to the fall of the Provisional Government and the rise of the Soviets. The February Revolution was the result of a mass uprising triggered primarily by hunger and frustration with World War I. The institution of the Provisional Government did not solve these fundamental problems, and dissatisfaction with its policies mounted throughout 1917 regardless of the political stance of the leadership in the Petrograd Soviet.

The tsarist Duma reconstituted itself as the Provisional Government and took control over the country after the Tsar abdicated. This government had been elected by a small portion of the population and could not claim to represent the wishes of the Russian people. Still, these men were, by and large, highly educated liberals who wanted Russia to have a parliamentary system that would protect individual rights and freedoms. They believed in private property, education, and democracy—at least in theory. They also tended to be from the upper classes and believed that it was their duty to guide the largely uneducated Russian populace onto the right path. In addition, they understood the responsibility that their government had to its allies and the territorial claims that it could make after the war was won if it continued to fight.

Taking all these perfectly reasonable factors into consideration, the leaders of the Provisional Government were concerned that a popular election might not institute the right kind of government—they might, for example, end up with a group of populists who would succumb to mass pressure to abandon the allies and lose the territory that Russia stood to gain by staying in the war. A new government might also violate the sacred right to private property and give peasants land, distribute food among the poor, and basically destroy any hope Russia had for a western-style bourgeois democracy. For these reasons, the Provisional Government kept delaying the Constituent Assembly, apparently hoping to get through the war before making any radical changes in government. The government immediately granted wide-ranging civil rights to the population, paving the way for open and active agitation and demonstrations against its policies. It is clear that these men deeply believed in liberal government and truly wanted to do what they thought was best for

Russia. It is equally clear, however, that they did not trust the Russian people to govern themselves, nor did they understand how much the Russians deplored their continuing participation in the war. In order to contain the situation, this unpopular government needed to make concessions to public sentiment or forbid free criticism of its policies. By doing neither, it set the stage for further rebellion.

The fact that the Russians continued to lose the war did not help the Provisional Government. Problems at the front had little to do with politics; they had more to do with morale, supplies, and the mass desertions that took place before each military engagement—most notably, during the Galician campaign. As the soldiers "voted with their feet" and left the front, the Russian forces continued to lose every major battle. Returning soldiers told horrific stories of draconian discipline and huge numbers of casualties. They returned to impoverished cities and a chaotic countryside, where peasants had begun to seize land from nobles and gentry and redraw the property lines of Russia without permission from the government. Tensions were high in both town and country. The Provisional Government continued to promise future elections and imminent victory, but as bad news poured in from the front, fewer and fewer people believed the assurances of the leadership. The widespread hatred of the Provisional Government and its policies grew steadily, simply because the government refused to accede to the overwhelming desire of the Russian public to get out of the war or to deal with the complex problem of peasant landholdings. The longer the Provisional Government refused to acknowledge the importance of these issues, the angrier and more violent the people grew.

Meanwhile, the Provisional Government became increasingly unpopular with the conservative factions and with the army. The government simply looked inept—it was losing the war, the cities kept erupting into chaos, and peasants were "reclaiming" land all over the countryside. Not surprisingly, criticism started to emerge from those groups who feared that the revolution was not yet over and wanted the Provisional Government to maintain order at home and give the army more support at the front. General Lavr Kornilov's attempted coup in August did not happen in a vacuum—everyone on the Right was concerned that the government would lose control entirely and that another revolution would result in exactly the kind of popular radical leadership that the Provisional Government was trying to prevent by postponing the Constituent Assembly. These factions urged the government to crack down, to censor the press, and to arrest anyone who spoke out against state policy. While the government moved against some of the more radical and outspoken Bolsheviks, the leaders did not want the Provisional Government to become a dictatorship and so refused to implement the harsh, repressive measures that the Right demanded. By the end of the summer, the Provisional Government had managed to alienate virtually everyone in the country. Kornilov's attempted coup shows that in addition to the possibility of a popular revolt, the government was also in danger of losing power to the military.

Lenin's return in April certainly turned the tide of the revolution for the tiny Bolshevik faction of the Petrograd Soviet. He insisted that the Bolsheviks withdraw support from the Provisional Government and pursue the ultimate goal of the workers' revolution immediately, rather than waiting for the slow development of capitalism. The Bolsheviks, however, constituted only a small part of the Petrograd Soviet, which was dominated by moderate socialists who favored sticking to the historical time line outlined by Karl Marx and anticipated a long wait for capitalism to develop in Russia before a workers' revolution could occur. Not until the end of August did the Bolsheviks win a majority in the Soviet, which they eventually attained because they reflected the growing desires of the Russian people to get out of the war and to distribute land to the peasants and food to the cities. Their slogan "Bread, Peace and Land" did not create those desires—it capitalized on the already existing mood of the country. The Bolsheviks simply rode the wave of the popular revolutionary spirit, which was made abundantly clear during the July Days, when the people of Petrograd took to the streets, rioting in favor of Soviet power. While the workers demanded that the Soviet take over the Provisional Government, moderate members of the Soviet tried to explain to the workers that the moment for the workers' revolution had not arrived—they had to allow the bourgeois revolution to run its course. The mobs did not find this argument compelling. The Bolsheviks, on the other hand, hid or tried to calm down the rioters—they were not ready for the Soviet to take over since it was still controlled by moderate socialists rather than Bolsheviks; revolution was at hand, according to Lenin, but just not quite yet. The rioters did not find this line of reasoning satisfying either, but finally dispersed after three days. Clearly, the revolution had plenty of momentum even without the Bolsheviks or Lenin to guide it.

The Provisional Government was doomed to fail as long as it insisted on ignoring the wishes of the Russian people—and there is no indication that the leadership ever seriously considered getting out of the war or dealing with the issues of bread and land. Its paternalistic attitude toward the Russian people infuriated a population that was already hungry and war weary. The people became increasingly radical and revolutionary, and this sentiment played into the hands of the Bolsheviks, who managed to manipulate the coming revolution to their own ends; the movement toward a second revolution against the Provisional Government, however, had little to do with Lenin's return.

–GRETA BUCHER,
U.S. MILITARY ACADEMY

References

Edward Hallett Carr, *The Bolshevik Revolution, 1917–1923,* 3 volumes (London: Macmillan, 1950–1953).

Isaac Deutscher, *The Prophet Armed, Trotsky: 1879–1921* (New York: Oxford University Press, 1954).

Orlando Figes, *A People's Tragedy: The Russian Revolution, 1891–1924* (New York: Viking, 1997).

Figes and Boris Kolonitskii, *Interpreting the Russian Revolution: The Language and Symbols of 1917* (New Haven: Yale University Press, 1999).

Sheila Fitzpatrick, *The Russian Revolution* (Oxford & New York: Oxford University Press, 1982).

Richard Pipes, *The Russian Revolution* (New York: Knopf, 1990).

Leonard Schapiro, *The Communist Party of the Soviet Union* (New York: Random House, 1959).

Robert Service, *Lenin: A Biography* (Cambridge, Mass.: Harvard University Press, 2000).

Adam B. Ulam, *The Bolsheviks: The Intellectual and Political History of the Triumph of Communism in Russia* (New York: Macmillan, 1965).

Ulam, *Stalin: The Man and His Era* (New York: Viking, 1973).

Dmitrii Volkogonov, *Lenin: A New Biography,* translated by Harold Shukman (New York: Free Press, 1994).

Rex A. Wade, *The Russian Revolution, 1917* (Cambridge & New York: Cambridge University Press, 2000).

RUSSIAN REVOLUTION

SALONIKA

Was there a strategic value to the Allied occupation of Salonika in Greece?

Viewpoint: Yes. The Salonika expedition helped to erode the enemy position in the Balkans to the point that by the fall of 1918 the Allies were able to achieve a decisive breakthrough.

Viewpoint: No. The deployment of Allied troops in the area occurred too late to help save Serbia.

German propagandists called the fortified Allied positions around the Greek city of Salonika the largest internment center in the world. More than 250,000 British, French, African, Serb, and Greek troops spent so many months pinned in place that French premier Georges Clemenceau dubbed them "the Salonika gardeners." Salonika is justifiably dismissed as another Great War sideshow, a venture optimistically begun that wound up a dumping ground for discarded generals and a trap for divisions that might better have been employed on the Western Front. An initial commitment of two divisions to shore up Serbia, which was overwhelmed by a major Central Powers offensive, led to the introduction of a dozen more divisions at the far end of Allied supply lines, in a region whose economic and technological infrastructure was in no way suitable for sustaining modern, high-tech war.

From the perspective of the Central Powers, indeed, Salonika was for most of the war a model economy-of-force operation, sustained by a Bulgarian army of little use outside the region, with minimal German and Austrian support. Yet, soldiers at Salonika saw some of the fiercest mountain fighting of the war, the rebirth of the Serbian army, and the making of the Yugoslav state. As Allied troops swept through a collapsing opposition, the new Balkan order emerged—one determined not by words but blood—from the Salonika sector.

**Viewpoint:
Yes. The Salonika expedition helped to erode the enemy position in the Balkans to the point that by the fall of 1918 the Allies were able to achieve a decisive breakthrough.**

The historiography of the Salonika front strongly regards the Allied effort there as an unnecessary dispersion of resources that could have been more effectively used else-where. Indeed, the myth of "Germany's largest prison camp" generally supports the view that the Salonika front was a victory for the Central Powers. However, by setting up the conditions for the collapse of the Balkan position of the Central Powers, the creation of the Salonika front played a vital part in the eventual Allied triumph in 1918.

An understanding of the Balkan position held by the Central Powers begins with a discussion of the Second Balkan War (1913) and with the alienation of Bulgaria from Russia and the Balkan Christian

BREAKOUT!

In an official report (30 September 1918) by French general Louis d'Esperey, he describes the breakout of Allied troops against the Bulgarians at Salonika:

On September 15th, in the forenoon, two French divisions and one Serbian division, making an attack on the formidable mountain barrier formed by the Vetrenik, the Dobropolje, and the so-called Sokol, made a breach in the enemy front which was to bring about the falling-in of the front. By this breach, which was gradually widened, the Serbian armies and the French and Greek troops supporting them went forward with untiring energy, in spite of the exceptional difficulties of the ground and of the desperate resistance of the enemy, towards their main objective—the region of Kavadar-Demir Kapoo. They reached this region on September 22nd, cutting at one stroke the communications of the First Bulgarian Army operating on the Vardar, and those of the 11th Bulgar-German army fighting to the north of Monastir. The French and Serbian troops rivaled each other in endurance, courage and self-sacrifice.

All the Allied forces gradually took part in the attack. On September 18th the British-Greek divisions, after stubborn fighting, captured the enemy positions of Doiran, retaining in this region very important forces. From September 21st the Italian, Greek and French troops of the Allied army of Monastir moved up. On September 22nd the general pursuit commenced, and was carried out with splendid ardor and energy.

On September 23rd the Serbians crossed the Vardar towards Krivelak. On the 24th the French cavalry entered Prilep. On the 25th Ishtip was captured, as well as the formidable barrier of the Beles. The British opened up the road to Strumitza, which they entered on the 26th. On the same day the Serbians reached Kotchana and Veles, and the Italian, French and Greek troops were marching on Kicovo.

By the evening of the 26th the Bulgarians asked for a suspension of hostilities, and announced the dispatch of plenipotentiaries.

In the course of these glorious operations, which the hasty throwing in of German reënforcements was unable to prevent, the Allied armies captured a great number of prisoners and immense booty. Allied air squadrons took a most active and efficient part in the battle, continually reporting to headquarters, bombarding and ceaselessly machine-gunning the enemy troops and convoys, sowing disorder among them and preventing them eluding our grasp.

Source: *Charles F. Horne, ed.,* Source Records of the Great War, *volume 6 (Indianapolis: American Legion, 1930), pp. 322–323.*

---

states. Prior to 1912 Bulgaria enjoyed the support of Russia and occupied a preeminent place in regional politics. After the end of the First Balkan War (1912–1913), clumsy Bulgarian diplomacy deprived the country of the fruits of victory, Macedonia and Salonika in particular, which went to Serbia and Greece respectively. Furthermore, Bulgaria was "stabbed in the back" by neighboring Romania and lost even more territory. Finally, Russia discarded forty years of support in favor of Serbia. These twin losses of prestige and territory infuriated the Bulgarian public and destabilized regional politics.

The first clue to the changing regional balance of power was the secret Turco-Bulgarian Treaty (August 1914), wherein Bulgaria aligned itself with the hated Turks against its erstwhile friends. This action, in many ways, sounded the death knell of Serbia and Romania. Later, in the summer of 1915, Bulgaria signed alliances with Germany and Austria-Hungary. Finally, in October 1915, Bulgaria took its revenge by joining in the destruction of Serbia. This action was an important contribution to the Central Powers' position by reestablishing land communications with Turkey; the Bulgarians also took control of Macedonia (an unfulfilled objective from the Balkan Wars).

The Bulgarian mobilization in September 1915 triggered the Anglo-French occupation of Salonika in neutral Greece. The Allied force was ordered to advance north through the Vardar Valley (in southeastern Yugoslavia and northern Greece) to assist the Serbs, but it was stopped by the Bulgarian Third Army and forced to retreat. The Allied response was to

SALONIKA

commit more troops and finally to land the evacuated remnants of the defeated Serb army there as well. By 1916 there were more than a quarter million British, French, and Serb soldiers contained in the Salonika beachhead.

The Bulgarians sent a considerable portion of their army to contain the Allies—the First, Second, and Fourth Armies; the Germans sent their Eleventh Army. By September 1916 there were nine Bulgarian and one German infantry divisions ranged against five British, four French, and six Serbian infantry divisions. Although the Allies had a numerical advantage, the Bulgarians and Germans occupied the high ground in excellent defensive positions. Furthermore, conditions within the cramped Salonika beachhead fostered diseases that ravaged the Allied force. Nevertheless, the Allies maintained their presence in northern Greece.

The Bulgarians were not done yet with taking their revenge on their enemies. In August 1916 the hapless Romanians made an ill-advised decision to enter the war on the Allied side. Although it was initially successful, Romania was in an extremely bad geographical position (essentially in a giant salient wedged between the Austrians and Bulgarians). Again, Bulgaria took advantage of the opportunity and cheerfully joined in the destruction of Romania. By winter, the shattered Romanian army was forced out of its homeland and Bulgaria annexed the Dobruja (a Black Sea coastal area south of the Danube River). Thus, as the war entered its third year, Bulgaria had recouped two of three contested territories that it had regarded as its own.

The Bulgarian army was fairly highly regarded by the European powers and had performed well against the Turks in the First Balkan War. In the Second Balkan War, an unsound strategy pitted it piecemeal against the Serbs and Greeks. When the Romanians and Turks attacked the unprotected Bulgarian rear, it was forced to end the war on unfavorable terms. The human and financial cost of the war to Bulgaria was high. However, as Bulgaria entered World War I, it possessed a fighting army led by experienced commanders. Subsequent performance against the Serbs in 1915 and against the Romanians in 1916 highlighted the tactical proficiency of the Bulgarian army. Against the Allies at Salonika, the Bulgarians continued their success by containing a numerically and logistically superior enemy for nearly three years. By 1918 the Allies had approximately six hundred thousand soldiers assigned to the expanded Salonika front.

The historiography of the Salonika front suggests that these Allied soldiers might have been used more effectively elsewhere. More-over, most historians regarded the Salonika front as a peripheral sideshow that made but a small contribution to the end of the war. These speculative arguments fail to address the following points: 1) Bulgarian war aims; 2) where the small, but powerful, Bulgarian army could have been used had it not been containing the Allies in Salonika; and 3) the importance of the effect of the Allied breakout from Salonika on the Balkan position of the Central Powers.

By joining the Central Powers, Bulgaria hoped to achieve its original objective, which was the establishment of a "Greater Bulgaria." Nationalists envisioned this new superstate as including Macedonia, parts of Kosovo and Albania, and Thessaly (including the city of Salonika). Furthermore, the Bulgarians desired reclamation of the Dobruja, which had been lost to Romania in 1913. By the beginning of 1917, Bulgaria had largely achieved these objectives, with the exception of regaining Salonika and portions of northern Greece. Based on Bulgarian actions in 1915 and 1916, what might have been the likely outcome of an Allied withdrawal from the Salonika front? The Bulgarians would have been left with an incomplete agenda of its war aims. A critical aspect of the concept of "Greater Bulgaria" was strategic access to the Aegean Sea. Although Bulgaria won a tiny port on the Aegean in 1913, the real strategic prize was the cosmopolitan port city of Salonika. In fact, when the Greeks beat the Bulgarians into Salonika in 1912, friendly relations between the two countries immediately disintegrated. Retention of the city by Greece after the First Balkan War was one of the causes of the Second Balkan War. Thus, Bulgaria coveted the acquisition of Salonika and its surrounding hinterlands.

An unusual city, inhabited largely by Jews, Salonika was the main outlet for the commerce of the Vardar Valley, which was in the hands of the Bulgarians by late 1915. Three powerful Bulgarian armies and one German army surrounded Salonika and were poised for action. These combat-tested armies were full of veterans of successful campaigns. At a minimum, the Bulgarians probably would have seized the opportunity to take Salonika itself. This occupation would have been the logical next step to achieve Bulgarian war aims and would have exacted revenge on the third country that it had lost territory to in 1913. However, might the Bulgarians have gone further? The small Greek army alone could not have stopped the powerful Bulgarian army and perhaps it might have tried to conquer all of Greece. The continued Allied presence in Salonika insured that this invasion never happened and thwarted Bulgarian aspirations.

SALONIKA

Assuming that the Bulgarians had merely taken Salonika and the immediate hinterlands and made peace with Greece, what use might the army have been to the Central Powers? Maximally, the Bulgarian infantry divisions might have been brought to bear on either the Italian or Eastern Fronts. The Bulgarian army was a powerful force with a proven record of success in battle. In 1917, particularly as the Austro-Hungarian armies were declining, the weight of the army might have had a decisive effect in either theater. Minimally, five of the seven first-rate Turkish infantry divisions that were employed in the Balkans in 1916 would have been free for deployment to more-threatened theaters. These combat-hardened infantry divisions might have altered the outcome in Caucasia, Mesopotamia, or Palestine and perhaps prevented the loss of Gaza, Jerusalem, and Baghdad. In any event, if the Allies had withdrawn from Salonika, German and Bulgarian troops stationed there would have been sent elsewhere as well. Certainly the Allies would have had additional substantial forces, but since the Central Powers were generally on the defensive against the British and French, this action would have been a zero-sum gain for the Allies.

By remaining in Salonika and by constantly committing more forces there, the Allies eventually broke the powerful position of the Central Powers in the Balkans. This defeat was the decisive strategic blow from which the Central Powers could not recover and effectively ended the war. When the Allies, under French general Louis d'Esperey, finally broke out of the Salonika front in mid September 1918, the Balkan position of the Central Powers folded like a house of cards. The Bulgarian army, weakened by disease and now almost unsupported by Germany, collapsed rapidly. By 29 September 1918 the British were well into Bulgaria; the French had taken Macedonia and were advancing into Kosovo. That day Bulgaria capitulated. This result was an unanticipated strategic disaster for the Central Powers for which there was no solution. The unopposed Allies raced forward, reaching Belgrade, Bucharest, and Turkish Thrace by early November 1918. Austria-Hungary had no reserves available with which to salvage the disaster and was forced to ask for an armistice as French cavalry prepared once again to invade the empire. The Turks were in a similar strategic position, having sent their scant reserves to Palestine and to Caucasia. The arrival of General George Milne's British army at the gates of Adrianople was the final blow that propelled the Ottoman Empire to seek an armistice. With its three allies prostrate and its entire southeastern flank open to attack, Germany soon followed by requesting an armistice.

Far from being "Germany's largest prison camp," the Salonika front tied down most of the Bulgarian army (and a Turkish corps as well) and was a constant source of concern for the Central Powers. The fact that the Allies maintained a strong force in Salonika threatened the security of Austria-Hungary, Bulgaria, and the Ottoman Empire. For the manpower-rich Allies, the Salonika front was a good investment and ultimately broke the cohesion and will of the Central Powers.

—EDWARD J. ERICKSON,
NORWICH HIGH SCHOOL, NEW YORK

Viewpoint:
No. The deployment of Allied troops in the area occurred too late to help save Serbia.

The Balkan theater during the Great War defies conventional classification. The fighting there can be understood as an expansion of the regional conflict that began in 1911 between the Balkan States and the Ottoman Empire. It arguably ended not in 1918 but with the 1924 evacuation of the Greek community in Anatolia and the subsequent population exchange between Greece and Turkey. Without denying the significance of great-power policies and behaviors in motivating Balkan behavior, the states that emerged in the region during the nineteenth century were independent actors, willing and able to play autonomous roles. Serbia in particular came in the years prior to 1914 to define its role as a cross between Piedmont and Prussia: focal point for a south Slav union whose nature Serbia would define. In that context the Sarajevo crisis of 1914 for Serbia essentially launched a "Third Balkan War," whose stakes were understood as conquest or annihilation.

Austria-Hungary for its part also waged what amounted to a total war against an enemy it perceived as seeking nothing less than the destruction of the Habsburg Empire. The Austro-Hungarian invasion of Serbia in 1914 was accompanied by levels of atrocities previously unknown in modern great-power warfare. The operation was characterized as well by unusual levels of incompetence—to the point where an outnumbered, outgunned Serbia rallied and drove the Habsburgs back across the frontier in a desperate counteroffensive.

That action represented the last efforts of a state whose resources had been exhausted

even before World War I. For most of 1915 the Balkans remained militarily quiet as the Central Powers and the Entente Powers vied for support in their capital cities. The Allied attack on the Gallipoli Peninsula (1915), however, convinced German chief of staff Erich von Falkenhayn of the need to remove the Serbian thorn from the side of the Central Powers and open a Danube route to their hard-pressed Ottoman ally. In October 1915 a joint force of Germans, Austrians, and Bulgarians, whose government had entered the war in hopes of avenging earlier defeat and securing future benefits, overran an outnumbered and out-gunned Serb army.

As its troops were driven back on all fronts, Serbia called to its allies. As early as December 1914 there had been desultory talk in Paris and London of opening a Balkan front. Cooler heads, however, had correctly observed that such an operation could only be supported through the Greek port of Salonika, itself undeveloped and with no more than a single-track railway connection to Serbia. Nevertheless, in October 1915 two divisions were transferred from the Dardanelles to Salonika—over the determined protests of a Greek government determined to remain neutral. That force was too small by far to prevent the final defeat of Serbia and the subsequent retreat through the

Albanian mountains of more than a quarter million soldiers and civilians.

The survivors were initially evacuated to the island of Corfu. Eventually they would be transferred to a Salonika front formed as France and Britain steadily reinforced their troops on the ground. During 1916 the entrenched camp of Salonika absorbed more than a dozen British and French divisions in what was sarcastically described as "the war's largest internment center." Its occupants, according to French politician Georges Clemenceau, contributed nothing to the war effort, instead "cultivating their gardens" in the manner of Voltaire's *Candide* (1759). That result had not been the original intention of the French government. Premier and Foreign Minister Aristide Briand argued for the possibility of using Salonika as an entering wedge, achieving in that sector the kind of tactical victories that would encourage Greece and Romania to join the Allies. The British were more dubious. Apart from a climate so unhealthy that large numbers of men were disabled by malaria, poor terrain and logistics combined to frustrate large-scale offensives. During 1916 it became increasingly apparent that nothing could be done without the overt support of Greece.

British troops resting in their trench at Salonika, Greece, circa 1915

(Imperial War Museum, London)

SALONIKA

That support was long in coming and in the end owed more to Greek politics than to Allied threats and blandishments. Not until 1917 did a coup remove King Constantine, who was friendly to the Central Powers, in favor of his son, Alexander, and a reorganized government headed by Eleuthérios Venizélos. The Entente Powers during 1916 successfully focused their energy on bringing Romania into the war. While Romania was not as feckless and helpless as its contemporary critics asserted, it was unable to stand against the steamroller the Central Powers promptly sent against it—without interference from Salonika. With most of their country occupied, the Romanian army withdrew toward the Russian frontier and bided its time.

Neutralization of Romania shifted attention once again to Salonika. The Serbian government and army spent much of the year purging allegedly disloyal officers. The official entry of Greece into the war, however, encouraged the Serbs to put their house in order more quickly than they might otherwise have done; and Serb divisions, including former Russian prisoners of war, began taking their place on the line. Commander Louis Guillaumat, and his successor, Louis Franchet d'Esperey, supervised the introduction of new weapons and the improvement of logistical infrastructure.

The operational stalemate nevertheless continued. Political and military controversies between Paris and London, and between the Entente Powers and their local allies, over the purposes and prospects of the theater prevented the reduction of the Salonika garrison to a maintenance force. They handicapped as well its reinforcement to levels promising anything beyond tactical successes gained at high cost, in the fashion typical of the Great War.

In August 1917 a fire reduced much of Salonika to ashes. Disease continued to debilitate Allied ranks. Morale suffered from a general sense that no one knew exactly what anyone was contributing to the war effort in this backwater. Not until September 1918 did the Allies finally strike. By then they confronted primarily a Bulgarian army badly weakened by casualties and disease and shaken by the recent revolutions in Russia. Within days,

Soviets were forming in Sofia and the government was asking for an armistice. French divisions thrust up the Danube valley and the British contingent turned toward Constantinople. Serb troops reentered their devastated homeland, and on 29 October the Croat Diet in Zagreb declared its allegiance to the new state of Yugoslavia. On 11 November the last Habsburg emperor abdicated.

On balance, the Allies and the Central Powers did have one thing in common. They put enough into the Balkans as a theater of war to destabilize the region—yet not enough to facilitate reconstructing stability in new forms. In the first months of 1919 Yugoslavia clashed with Italy over Fiume and the Dalmatian coast. Romania saw its loyalty rewarded with the Judas gift of Transylvania. Greek troops landed in Smyrna, the vanguard of a doomed dream of an Asian empire. Treaties signed in the suburbs of Paris did nothing to avert a continuing descent into chaos tempered by dictatorship or modified by external conquest—a pattern that continued unabated into the next century. Salonika remains a monument to the long-term consequences of half-hearted measures.

—DENNIS SHOWALTER,
COLORADO COLLEGE

References

Lynn H. Curtright, *Muddle, Indecision, and Setback: British Policy and the Balkan States, August 1914 to the Inception of the Dardanelles Campaign* (Thessaloniki: Institute for Balkan Studies, 1986).

David Dutton, *The Politics of Diplomacy: Britain and France in the Balkans in the First World War* (London: Tauris, 1998).

Martin Gilbert, *The First World War: A Complete History* (New York: Holt, 1994).

Alan Palmer, *The Gardeners of Salonika* (New York: Simon & Schuster, 1965).

G. Ward Price, *The Story of the Salonica Army* (London: Hodder & Stoughton, 1918).

SALONIKA

SHELL SHOCK

Was the high incidence of shell shock during the Great War attributable to a failure of leadership?

Viewpoint: Yes. The failure of officers to instill esprit de corps, to maintain a paternalistic attitude, and to recognize the limits of their troops' endurance escalated the incidence of psychological breakdowns.

Viewpoint: No. The physical effects of the extraordinary volume of lethal firepower that was a normal condition of the frontline experience caused behavioral disturbances in many soldiers.

The concept of war producing mental and emotional, as well as physical, casualties antedates the twentieth century. Prussian king Frederick the Great, for example, suffered repeatedly during the Seven Years' War (1756–1763) from physical symptoms generally associated with stress. Armies recognized a condition called "nostalgia." Usually manifested as a loss of affect by recruits suddenly and completely removed from familiar environments, it appeared as well among experienced soldiers during and after combat. During the American Civil War (1861–1865) both armies discharged significant numbers of men with diagnoses of "insanity" or "paralysis." Long after the fighting ceased, veterans were being committed to hospitals for inexplicable behavior, ranging from unacceptable to dangerous, that families, doctors, and the men themselves traced to their war experiences.

Despite the increasing amount of empirical evidence, neither the military nor the medical professions were willing to make room for the concept that the ability to meet the demands of war involved anything more complex than an act of will. To a degree, that belief represented the survival and democratization of the traditional aristocratic perspective that the battlefield was properly the province of men with breeding and honor. It reflected as well the influence of a crude form of Social Darwinism that interpreted war as the supreme test of individual and racial fitness.

From the first days of August 1914, technology created strains on the frontline soldier. Earlier conflicts were limited by the inability of armies to sustain battle beyond a few days. After that time, resources were so exhausted and organizations so disrupted that both sides were compelled to stop and regroup. Nor could even the developed weapons of the mid nineteenth century produce the effects of 1914. Apart from the physical effects of shells and bullets on unprotected human bodies, as well as the stench and the filth, men were subjected to noise levels exceeding even the worst of those in factories. The comprehensive assaults on soldiers' nervous systems had no frames of reference even remotely approaching the most demanding civilian existence. Death and mutilation were random processes, defying any individual's courage or skill. Heroism, leadership, and all the other traditional martial behaviors lost relevance because their manifestations had so few witnesses. Relief from this torment amounted to no more than a few predictable days.

It was scarcely surprising that increasing numbers of men could not cope. Some men manifested physical symptoms: trembling, incontinence, and stomach pains. Others withdrew emotionally along an arc ranging from self-isolation to catatonia. Still others lapsed into overt bizarre behavior. Those who just ran away until they could run no more could be dealt with by time-tested means: the firing squad and the military prison. But in all the armies, even the least sophisticated regimental officers increasingly understood, however vaguely, that they were confronting a phenomenon outside the scope of army regulations. And a few doctors were introducing a new description and a new diagnosis: they spoke of shell shock.

Viewpoint:
Yes. The failure of officers to instill esprit de corps, to maintain a paternalistic attitude, and to recognize the limits of their troops' endurance escalated the incidence of psychological breakdowns.

For its protagonists the Great War was a new kind of conflict, dominated by artillery and high-explosive shells. New types of warfare spawned new technologies, and World War I was no exception. *Shell shock* was a term coined by the British to describe the psychological breakdown of their soldiers on this new technological battlefield. Although soldiers had suffered from psychiatric illnesses in previous conflicts, shell shock was first viewed as a new and dangerous physical illness related to the increasingly powerful high-explosive shells that pounded the trenches. It was first thought that shell bursts close to a soldier could have a physical effect on his nervous system, hence the term. As the war progressed, however, it was soon apparent that this hypothesis could not explain the varieties or incidence of shell shock among soldiers. Instead, doctors turned to prewar diagnoses to label casualties and looked beyond the new technology for wider reasons to explain the existence of war-induced psychiatric disorders manifested by previously healthy young men.

As the medical services quickly realized, the great escalation in psychiatric casualties was not merely the result of new technology physically shaking, and thus shocking, the body. A combination of factors, including the sudden death of friends, fatigue, the strain of long periods of service in poor conditions, intense fear, and the loss of belief in victory and the meaning of the war could all affect a soldier's mental attitude and, for some, contribute to their breakdown. As Charles Moran, a medical officer with the First Battalion of the Royal Fusiliers between 1914 and 1917, explained in *The Anatomy of Courage* (1945), "men wear out in war like clothes." What he meant by this statement was that soldiers could not continue to function indefinitely in difficult conditions. He claimed that each soldier had but a limited stock of willpower, which he constantly expended during his time in the front line. When he had drawn too heavily, for too long, on his stock of courage, a soldier would finally break down.

This testimony suggests that most men could survive on the technological battlefield, but each had his limit. What armies needed in World War I were leaders with the insight to identify and extend that limit. Too many leaders, in all armies, failed to support their men and manage their manpower resources effectively. The result was an explosion in psychiatric casualties. Prevention of shell shock required skillful leadership, from the general to the junior officer, and at all levels in World War I the leaders were found wanting. In the higher echelons of the army, leadership failures were associated mainly with the conception and direction of battles. First, on all sides, there was an assumption that high casualties were an inevitable and tolerable byproduct of any attack. Such assumptions contributed to the German strategy of attrition and the bloodbath of Verdun (1916) and permitted the massacre of the British army on the Somme (1916) that resulted in the total decimation of scores of battalions. For the soldiers who survived these battles, the high casualties had a damaging effect on morale. In the aftermath of an attack, soldiers were psychologically vulnerable, having lost their close comrades who had provided their support, comfort, and obligation to continue in times of stress. Moreover, survivors also suffered from guilt and bewilderment that they were still physically unscathed when so many of their friends were dead or injured.

High casualties also undermined the soldiers' faith in their commanders. The survivors felt that they were regarded as expendable and lost hope in the ability of their high command to succeed and in the possibility of their surviving the war intact. Hope was an important commodity in war, being identified as the best preservative by medical officers such as Moran. Its loss could have devastating consequences for the individual, as it removed reasons to continue to endure in the trenches.

Second, those directing the war behind the lines remained relatively ignorant of the state of their troops and the conditions under which they were fighting. As a result, they continued to prosecute offensives long after they had ceased to have any prospect of success. This strategy required units to be rotated through the battle zones more frequently, pushing fatigued soldiers beyond the limits of their physical and mental endurance.

The failure to understand the problems facing troops in the trenches is certainly a criticism that has been leveled at Field Marshal Douglas Haig and his leadership of the British army. In part, this critique arose because of the culture and organization of the army itself. As the idea of the offensive was central to British operations and promotion depended on showing fighting spirit, corps and divisional commanders felt unable to inform their superiors when their formations had exceeded their fighting limit. Rather than interpreting a refusal to attack as a positive way of conserving manpower by preserving the mental and physical health of soldiers, the high command compounded the problem by viewing it as an admission of weakness and punished such leaders by removing them from their commands. As a result, the high command was unaware it was asking more of its soldiers than they were able to give. It was unable to identify the limits of their soldiers' endurance until it was too late and psychological casualties had spiraled out of control.

At the level of the junior officer in the trenches, leadership failures were also apparent. According to Lord Gort, who gave evidence to the British Southborough Committee investigating shell shock, it was possible to control its incidence through effective "man mastership." It was the role of battalion officers to understand the needs of their men and to take steps to maintain their morale and will to fight. Officers could bolster the will of their men by fostering an esprit de corps within their unit and an attitude that frowned on shell shock. If soldiers subscribed to this culture and retained pride in their formation and its history, they were more likely to feel an obligation to uphold past reputations and thus less likely to give way when the fighting became tough.

The paternalistic relationship between officer and soldier was also important. An officer could help to organize sports and other relaxing activities behind the lines that allowed his men to release tensions that inevitably built up in the trenches. Once in the line he could treat his men with understanding and preempt psychological problems by identifying those who needed to be rested. Often the signs of potential breakdown were not obvious to the outsider. For example, a previously boisterous man could become quieter and more introverted, and only an officer who had taken care to get to know his men would be able to identify such changes in character and take the necessary action.

The regimental medical officer obviously also had a vital part to play in managing shell shock. It was within his authority to keep a man behind the lines for a few days or even to recommend that he be sent on a training course, for there were many ways in which a man could be given a rest. However, he had to tread a fine line between identifying those who could give no more and opening the floodgates to those who simply wanted to evade trench duty. If the medical officer was too lenient, he risked encouraging the development of shell shock in his unit as it became seen as a way of leaving the trenches, and consciously or unconsciously men under stress naturally reacted to an escape route.

By fostering esprit de corps, maintaining a paternalistic attitude, and, above all, resting those who were clearly in need, officers had the opportunity to bolster the psychological reserves of their men and extend their limits of endurance. Too often, however, battalion officers, preoccupied with their own situation or lacking the moral courage needed to rest a proportion of the battalion in the face of opposition from above, failed to grasp this opportunity and lost men to shell shock as a result.

American psychiatrist Thomas W. Salmon in *The Care and Treatment of Mental Diseases and War Neuroses ("Shell Shock") in the British Army* (1917) described shell shock as the flight from an unbearable situation to a place made more tolerable by illness. New technologies presented soldiers with frightening and horrifying experiences. The shelling experienced by soldiers of World War I was of a type and intensity that was new and shocking, and it unsurprisingly provided a convenient label for psychiatric breakdown, at least in the English language. Nevertheless, it was ultimately the dramatic failures in leadership that created the unbearable situations from which men fled. Each unit and each man had their own limits of endurance, and a failure to identify these limits and to manage the soldiers accordingly ensured that some men were required to give more than they were able. The inevitable outcome was an escalation in the incidence of psychiatric illness during the Great War.

–H. B. MCCARTNEY, KING'S
COLLEGE, LONDON

Viewpoint:
No. The physical effects of the extraordinary volume of lethal firepower that was a normal condition of the frontline experience caused behavioral disturbances in many soldiers.

Before defending the premise that shell shock was caused by the unendurable psychological stress of shelling, it makes sense to ask what other explanation there might be. For example, to posit that shell shock was the indirect result of bad leadership—bungling by strategic planners or callousness in battalion and company commanders—ignores historical and medical evidence. Certainly there were botches and butchery from the start, as in the impractical defense of Mons (1914) and the subsequent retreat, or in the too-optimistic original French line of defense, the collapse of which necessitated the frantic heroism of the First Marne (1914). However humiliating, the retreats and consolidations of 1914 were episodes of rapid movement with low incidence of combat hysteria, desertion, or poor morale. Yet, what soldier by December would not have agreed that the first year had been a failure?

Nor at home did early reverses diminish confidence in government and brass; in Britain there was a jolly willingness to fight that persisted long enough for British field marshal Horatio Kitchener to raise some two million volunteers in 1915 and to delay the institution of a draft until after the Somme (1916). In the most desperate year, 1917, Englishmen, Anzacs, and Canadians were wasted at Passchendaele and Vimy; the French, having experienced the *abbatoir* of Verdun the year before, were now asked by General Robert Nivelle to retake the heights along the Chemin des Dames. By 1917 the ineptitude of British and French generals was an open joke; jibes about Red Hats and general headquarters (GHQ) were traded among the frontline troops; and there were shake-ups at the top of the French hierarchy. One could argue that doubtless by now there was ample cause for widespread demoralization, but that is not what happened. Psychiatric casualties were fewer in 1917 than in 1916. Under horrendous conditions, the Allies fighting before Ypres (1917) did not break, and when the French mutinied that same year, the disruption—far from hysteria, cowardice, or irrationality—had instead the hallmarks of a *grève,* in which rank and file demonstrate to management that the master plan will not work.

In fact, the generals' most egregious errors and outrageous demands on human endurance did not provoke widespread psychological trauma, not in 1917 when there were fewer men than ever sent back tagged NYDN, or "Not Yet Diagnosed, Nervous," nor at any other time. Perhaps by 1917 those most susceptible to shell shock had already become casualties, or medical officers had become more adept at detecting malingerering, alcoholism, and other problems, so that the effective rate dropped. Or perhaps men were simply being given rest in greater numbers. Such explanations are plausible and probably describe minor contributory causes. The most reasonable explanation is that the human response to the maelstrom was changing. Why and when men's minds broke were better understood, and so preventive measures and early interventions among the "windy" were more efficacious. Certainly, the conditions of 1917 were not better. The Somme (1916) was not less violent than Passchendaele, and perhaps it was militarily better conceived (if by such a polite phrase one can distinguish the waste of the Somme from the cruel imbecility of Passchendaele). At the Somme the troops had hopes for a breakthrough that no one in the fight in Flanders (1917) would have expected. Similarly, at Verdun (1916), the Golgotha on which French manhood demonstrated its determination that the Boche would not pass, troops motivated by God, necessity, and unquestionable valor suffered combat fatigue in a measure unequaled before or after, or so one is convinced by Pierre Miquel in *Mourir à Verdun* (1995). Indeed, the substantial difference seems to be that 1916 convinced most that shell shock was not a question of brain injury or failure of character; rather, it was a natural response of the mind to incessant threat of sudden annihilation.

All manner of evidence, from medical case studies to literary memoirs such as those of Siegfried Sassoon, Edmund Blunden, and Georges Duhamel, or R. C. Sherriff's play *Journey's End* (1929) and novels such as Henri Barbusse's *Under Fire: The Story of a Squad* (1916) and Erich Maria Remarque's *All Quiet on the Western Front* (1929), show that while many men snapped, they did not predictably snap when the bombardment was at its worst. In fact, Ernst Jünger's combat classics *The Storm of Steel: From the Diary of a German Storm-Troop Officer on the Western Front* (1929) and *Copse 125: A Chronicle From the Trench Warfare of 1918* (1930), and his astonishingly titled *Battle as Inner Experience* (1926), suggest that men are unlikely to break when the fire is heaviest. Most men held together until such a moment that their nervous collapse would neither pro-

DIAGNOSIS

A 1917 volume on shell shock by Grafton Elliot Smith and Tom Hatherly Pear describes some of the manifestations of the condition:

The most obvious phenomena are undoubtedly the disturbances of sensation and movement. A soldier may be struck blind, deaf or dumb by a bursting shell: in rare cases he may exhibit all three disorders simultaneously or even successively. It should be added that these troubles often vanish after a short space of time, as suddenly and dramatically as they appeared. Thus one of the blinded soldier survivors of the *Hesperian* recovered his sight on being thrown into the water. Other blind patients have had their sight restored under the action of hypnosis. Mutism is often conquered by the shock of a violent emotion, produced accidentally or purposely. Examples of such "shocking" events taken at random from our experience were the sight of another patient slipping from the arms of an orderly, the "going under" chloroform, the application of a faradic current to the neck, the announcement at a "picture house" of Rumania's entry into the war (this cured two cases simultaneously), and the sight of the antics of our most popular film comedian. The latter agency cured a case of functional deaf-mutism, the patient's first auditory sensations being the sound of his own laugh.

The muscular system may be affected in an equally striking manner. Contractures often occur in which a man's fist may be immovably clenched for months; or his back may be bent almost at right angles to his lower limbs, there being in neither case any bodily change discoverable by the neurologist which can account for such a condition. These contractures, though curable, often prove very obstinate, and at present their nature remains somewhat of a mystery.

Other distressing and long continued disturbances take the form of muscular twitchings and tremors or loss of power in the limbs.

Not every nerve-case, however, presents such striking and objective signs as those which we have just been describing. The *subjective* disturbances, which are apt to go undiscovered in a cursory examination of the patient, are frequently more serious than the objective, and are experienced by thousands of patients who to the mere casual observer may present no more signs of abnormality than a slight tremor, a stammer, or a depressed or excited expression. These afflictions: loss of memory, insomnia, terrifying dreams, pains, emotional instability, diminution of self-confidence and self-control, attacks of unconsciousness or of changed consciousness sometimes accompanied by convulsive movements resembling those characteristic of epileptic fits, incapacity to understand any but the simplest matters, obsessive thoughts, usually of the gloomiest and most painful kind, even in some cases hallucinations and incipient delusions—make life for some of their victims a veritable hell. Such patients may have recovered from sensory or motor disturbances and yet may suffer from any or all of these afflictions as a residuum from the original "shock-complex"; they may suffer from them as a complication of the discomfort attending upon a wound or an illness, or, on the other hand, they may have no overt bodily disorder: their malady then being usually given the simple but all-inclusive (and blessed) description "neurasthenia."

Source: G. Elliot Smith and T. H. Pear, Shell Shock and Its Lessons *(Manchester, U.K.: University Press; New York: Longmans, Green, 1917), The Medical History of World War I, Internet website, <http://www.ukans.edu/~kansite/ww_one/medical/medindex.htm#PSYCHIATRY>.*

---

voke their summary execution by a line officer nor, more often, cause them to abandon their comrades in the moment of great danger. Given the conditions and the now standard assumption that after two hundred hours of exposure to combat all men will have broken, it is astonishing how few men suffered long-lasting mental casualty in the Great War. British psychiatrist Grafton Elliot Smith estimated in *Shell Shock and Its Lessons* (1917) that incidence of shell shock at its peak accounted for about one third of all battlefield injuries. Most of these casualties could be returned fit to units after several weeks of rest, sound nutrition, and repeated cheerful and firm assertions that they would get over their fears. In other words, much shell shock was transient dementia, mental confusion exacerbated by violence (or fear) and prolonged physical hardship, something other victims, sympathetic nurses, or the padre

SHELL SHOCK

SHELL SHOCK

The HYDRA

Journal of the Craiglockhart War Hospital

No. 7   JULY 21ST, 1917   PRICE 6D

CONTENTS

H. & J. Pillans & Wilson, Printers, Edinburgh.

could often address with as much success as the medical officer.

Originally, of course, shell shock was assumed to display a spectrum of symptoms indicative of physiological damage to the brain. As late as 1919, American E. E. Southard, in his book *Shellshock and Other Neuropsychiatric Problems Presented in Five Hundred and Eighty-nine Case Histories from the War Literature, 1914–1918* (1919), included photographs from microscope slides showing "capillary punctate haemorrhages" in the corpus callosum of the brain. No doubt there were many instances of grave damage to hearing as well as concussions caused by explosions that led to ephemeral or permanent impairment of motor abilities or cognition. However, someone who is punch drunk or brain damaged ought to be fairly easy to distinguish from a syphilitic, imbecile, schizophrenic, or malingerer unless one's diagnostic skills are crude, as they tended to be, or one wants to blame apparent failure of character on physical cause, which was also often the case. Shell shock, conceived of as a primarily physical problem, concealed the immaturity of psychiatry and served to fend off the erosion of morale that might occur were troops to seize upon the idea that a threshold of nervous collapse exists for each person.

Still, to understand that shell shock was not caused exclusively (or even largely) by damage to the brain and spinal cord does not explain how it was the direct result of combat conditions. Yet, if the problem was physical, why did physical intervention tend to be the least efficacious therapy, especially in the long run? As doctors slammed doors to convince a man he could hear, electrocuted the throat to prove that he could utter cries of pain, or used winches and pulleys to unfold muscles frozen in terror, they assumed that physical solutions either demonstrated physical etiology or proved that psychosomatic conditions were shallow or sham. Either way, the altered soldier could be shipped on or sent back to the front. Often these soldiers were soon back with the same complaint, or their psyches were crippled for life. Inevitably, men who were "cured" too fast, or returned too soon to the conditions that had provoked mental crises, found that their traumas became deeper and more apt to be characterized by psychosomatic paralysis or acute psychotic states. For many such men what might have been episodes of temporary abjection became intractable psychiatric handicaps.

Doctors such as Smith and William Halse R. Rivers, who preferred patience and talk therapy, achieved the best results. The slow, kind cure of clean linens, wholesome food, and long rambles in the countryside was not just the most humane therapy, it was the most efficacious. Practitioners of the kinder method shared the conviction that the most important ingredient in a soldier's recovery was the promise that he would recover. These same psychiatrists found that the most common barrier to recovery was not contempt of authority or fear of death, as one might expect were bad leadership the source of the problem. Rather, the crux was repression of guilt, specifically the feeling that the victim had let down his mates. Men, it seems, unconsciously prefer terror to a sanity that includes recognition that one may have failed in solidarity with one's friends. Thus, Rivers saw no paradox in the idea that recovering the courage to return to the fight was usually far more effective in healing a man's psyche than offering him the prospect of a medical discharge. (No brain damage can create guilt as efficiently as the feeling one has left one's comrades in the field of fire.)

Also, it seems men wanted to shed their disabilities, during and after the war, and that desire to be healed was a major therapeutic advantage. Lyn MacDonald, in *The Roses of No Man's Land* (1980), mentions that in 1921 in Britain there were 65,000 pensioners for shell shock, and 50,000 the following year; 30,000 were still being paid just before the outbreak of World War II. While these numbers are significant in absolute terms, compared to 750,000 British dead, and considerably more than that figure maimed, the rate suggests success in returning men to mental balance. There is no psychological logic—evident, occluded, or perverse—that can explain why men, potentially loaded with shame and fully exposed to hideous conditions, would want to return either to trenches or to the responsibilities of civil life if they hold the belief that too much had been asked of them. Nor would cerebral trauma be likely to go away years later, for brain injuries generally either subside in the first forty-eight hours, or they never do. Indeed, shell shock, as a mischievous or involuntary form of insubordination, can in no way explain the mutiny of French soldiers in 1917, perhaps the sanest event in the entire war. Nor does bitterness about the complicity of the nation in soldiers' trauma suggest why 15,000 should get off the pension rolls four years after the war, by which time one might reasonably consider men's infirmities permanent or "institutional."

Exposure to conditions for which bombardment is both sign and substance is the only coherent way to explain the psychopathology of shell shock. While grainy footage of men going over the top into machine-gun fire may characterize the modern impression of trench war, in fact men only left the trenches after prolonged—

usually days-long—preparatory and retaliatory shelling. Compared to long periods of anticipation punctuated by random shell bursts, instances of direct infantry assault were rare, and sustained bombardments were not as common as desultory periods of patrol, prelude, and incidental harassing fire. Still, 70 percent of the casualties in the Great War came from artillery, and 70 percent suffered often ghastly head and neck injuries. Sometimes shells singly shrieked out of a clear and quiet sky, reminding men that they were never and nowhere safe; sometimes tons of ordnance landed in small areas and kept exploding for hours. Conditions in the trenches were tumultuous, murderous, and exposed. Men were invested with nightmare images that filled long stretches of inactivity. In the mud, among the rats and the stinking dead, assailed by lice, a man could lose composure even over the imagined noise of an incoming round. The waiting silence or the wailing maelstrom defined the sounds of an inner hell for which the topography of "no man's land" was outward gloss.

Considering the actual and psychic landscape that soldiers inhabited, it is small wonder some infantry became unnerved and no wonder artillery was despised. Artillery defined the war. For this reason it is appropriate to consider shell shock an accurate figure of the spiritual and mental harm the war inflicted on those whom it did not kill. Tactically, artillery accounts for why the front lines held with little change for four years. It explains why troops could not be allowed to outdistance the ability of support artillery barrages to inch along ahead of them; therefore, attacks were ponderously slow and gains often had to be renounced by nightfall. Artillery created the apocalyptic terrain of craters and body parts that haunted the imagination of combatants. The modernity of artillery rendered contemptible the dash of cavalry and the stalwart courage of the infantry. Artillery created the overwhelming sense that one's adversary was anonymous, industrial, and omnipotent. Since artillery is shorthand for the whole bloody mess, shell shock is the sufficient and cogent metonymy for the entire war and its human costs.

—MARK A. R. FACKNITZ,
JAMES MADISON UNIVERSITY

References

Ted Bogacz, "War Neurosis and Cultural Change in England, 1914–22: The Work of the War Office Committee of Enquiry into 'Shell-Shock'," *Journal of Contemporary History,* 24 (1989): 227–256.

Joanna Bourke, *Dismembering the Male: Men's Bodies, Britain and the Great War* (London: Reaktion, 1996; Chicago: University of Chicago Press, 1996).

John Bourne, *Britain and the Great War, 1914–1918* (London & New York: Arnold, 1989).

Wendy Holden, *Shell Shock* (London: Channel 4 Books, 1998).

Edgar Jones and Simon Wessely, "Psychiatric Battle Casualties: An Intra- and Interwar Comparison," *British Journal of Psychiatry,* 178 (2001): 242–247.

Paul Lerner, "Psychiatry and Casualties of War in Germany, 1914–18," *Journal of Contemporary History,* 35 (2000): 13–28.

Lyn MacDonald, *The Roses of No Man's Land* (London: Joseph, 1980).

David H. Marlowe, *Psychological and Psychosocial Consequences of Combat and Deployment with Special Emphasis on the Gulf War* (Santa Monica, Cal.: Rand, 2000).

Pierre Miquel, *Mourir à Verdun* (Paris: Tallandier, 1995).

Charles McMoran Wilson Moran, *The Anatomy of Courage* (London: Constable, 1945).

Daniel Pick, *War Machine: The Rationalisation of Slaughter in the Modern Age* (New Haven: Yale University Press, 1993).

William Halse R. Rivers, "The Repression of War Experience," *The Lancet,* 194 (February 1918): 173–177.

Thomas W. Salmon, *The Care and Treatment of Mental Diseases and War Neuroses ("Shell Shock") in the British Army* (New York: War Work Committee of the National Committee for Mental Hygiene, 1917).

Ben Shephard, *A War of Nerves: Soldiers and Psychiatrists in the Twentieth Century* (Cambridge, Mass.: Harvard University Press, 2001).

G. Elliot Smith and T. H. Pear, *Shell Shock and Its Lessons* (Manchester, U.K.: University Press; New York: Longmans, Green, 1917).

E. E. Southard, *Shellshock and Other Neuropsychiatric Problems Presented in Five Hundred and Eighty-nine Case Histories from the War Literature, 1914–1918* (Boston: Leonard, 1919).

Jay Winter, "Shellshock and the Cultural History of the Great War," *Journal of Contemporary History,* 35 (2000): 7–11.

STRATEGIC BOMBING

Did the strategic bombing of cities by the British and Germans lead to total war?

Viewpoint: Yes. Both sides hoped that bombings would depress civilian morale and drive the enemy to the negotiating table.

Viewpoint: No. Technological, doctrinal, and organizational limitations relegated strategic bombing to a nuisance weapon throughout the war.

Robin Higham, in *Air Power: A Concise History* (1972), perceptively notes that strategic bombardment during World War I involved two kinds of attacks. One set of targets was clearly military. Supply dumps, railroad facilities, and factories were out of reach of surface forces. Other targets were enemy cities, which were bombed essentially for psychological reasons. The first category of attacks began in 1914–1915 with Allied strikes on German airship and submarine bases and construction facilities, as well as raids against industrial targets in the Rhineland. British aircraft even flew from Belfort, in the far south of France, to hit a zeppelin factory on Lake Constance.

The limited success of these operations, reflecting the poor load-carrying capacity of available aircraft, led to an increase in the numbers of planes involved. That change in turn generated an increasing randomization of bombing patterns. Improved defenses had the same consequences: antiaircraft guns did not have to be particularly accurate to encourage crews without parachutes to fly higher and formations to attack at night.

Early German raids, also ostensibly directed against military targets, had exponentially less success. Zeppelins, which were the initial attack vehicles, were large, vulnerable gasbags that tended to unload their bombs from heights, making accuracy impossible. German military doctrine favored as well a certain obscuring of the lines between civilians in general and those civilians directly assisting the enemy war effort. When the French government proclaimed certain towns immediately behind the lines as "open," that is, undefended and unoccupied, German military and legal authorities dismissed this move as a transparent ruse and continued attacking them from the air.

The zeppelin strikes on Britain in 1915–1916, however, escalated air warfare to a new level. While actual damage and casualties inflicted were limited, the raids raised a political storm impossible for censorship to conceal. Correspondingly encouraged, the Germans continued their attacks, increasingly concentrating on breaking British morale, which seemed invitingly vulnerable and whose apparent weakness under pressure reinforced prewar German stereotypes about the degeneracy of Britain. The zeppelins were joined by long-range aircraft, which took over the campaign when airship losses grew intolerable. The planes in turn switched from day to night attacks as defenses improved and then in 1918 were withdrawn as their loss rates also climbed beyond acceptability.

The Allies responded by establishing in 1917 their own strategic striking forces. French night bombers regularly crossed the Rhine, striking increasing numbers of towns and cities, and continuing their raids in 1918 as a complement to the shorter-ranged interdiction operations of the Air Division. The British Royal Flying Corps/Royal Air Force formed what eventually became the

Independent Force, mounting day and night attacks from French territory; by the armistice it was receiving planes able to reach Berlin from southeast English airfields. Italy followed a similar path as Britain; America intended to join the strategic air war in 1919.

The primary target of these later organizations was morale. On one level they were retaliation for enemy attacks—and on another for enemy stubbornness in continuing the war. In positive terms, the raids were intended to inflict enough damage and cause enough disruption to first disturb, then paralyze, the war effort of the Central Powers. Their actual successes were limited by technology and by the unexpectedly quick end of the war. The concept of strategic bombing, however, endured and flourished for the rest of the twentieth century.

Viewpoint:
Yes. Both sides hoped that bombings would depress civilian morale and drive the enemy to the negotiating table.

Before World War I there had been some fanciful science-fiction accounts of bombing cities from the air—but political and military leaders did not take such ideas seriously. Prior to August 1914 the political/military leadership of the major combatant nations were sure that any war would be over with a few major battles in several weeks. When the war degenerated into a bloody stalemate in late 1914, German and British leaders looked to long-term strategies to win the war. Since battlefield victory was a far more difficult proposition than anyone had ever imagined, both sides looked for means to strike at the enemy population in order to weaken the will of the nation to continue the fight. The British struck first by instituting a strict naval blockade that cut off food imports into Germany; by 1916 the country was desperately short of food and the morale of the civilian population was under great stress.

The German navy was not in a position to institute the same type of blockade against Britain but its submarine force had the potential to affect the British civilian population in a similar manner if enough of its merchant fleet were sunk. By instituting ruthless naval blockades, Britain and Germany had taken the first great step toward total war. Escalation in warfare is not usually conducted by giant leaps but rather by smaller steps. Bombing cities was the last, and perhaps most decisive, step in making World War I a truly total war.

One reason the German army and navy had not seriously considered bombing enemy cities prior to 1914 was the state of aviation technology at the time. Most airplanes were fairly light and short-ranged machines with one-hundred-horsepower engines. Such craft were capable of carrying a pilot, an observer, and perhaps a few light (twenty-pound) bombs. The idea of long-distance bombing with such weapons was simply impractical. The one aircraft that was capable of long

range and a heavy bomb load, the dirigible, possessed a lot of disadvantages. They were expensive, difficult to build and maintain, slow, and highly vulnerable to weather and enemy fire. In short, they were not likely to last long in combat. The German army, which disliked the zeppelins for the above reasons, lost most of its small fleet in reconnaissance missions in the first weeks of the campaign. The navy, on the other hand, had a lot of confidence in the zeppelins, built up its force, and designed new airships that could fly at high altitude and reduce their vulnerability to enemy fire. While the German army placed its faith in the airplane, the navy possessed an airship force of 3,740 men and nine bases by December 1914. That same month a memo to the Kaiser and government from the naval staff argued that using the zeppelins to bomb London would "diminish the enemy's determination to prosecute the war."

The army and navy prepared their airships for a bombing offensive against Great Britain during the winter of 1914–1915. In the late fall of 1914 the high command received a proposal from Major Wilhelm Siegert, one of the senior officers of the *Luftstreitkräfte* (army air service), to create a special airplane bomber force for strategic missions that would be directly under the command and control of the high command, which quickly approved Siegert's proposal and started forming an elite bomber force in Flanders under the code name "Carrier Pigeon Detachment-Ostende."

At the same time that a long-range bomber force of zeppelins was being formed, German aviation pioneer Ferdinand von Zeppelin and aircraft designer Claudius Dornier began developing a multiengine airplane that could carry a large bomb load for a long distance. By the fall of 1914 not only Zeppelin but also other aircraft companies, such as AEG, were making heavy bombers. The army was skeptical at first, but by mid 1915 AEG had produced a two-engine bomber that could comfortably carry a 250-pound bomb load for two hundred to three hundred kilometers. Zeppelin's multi-engine aircraft successfully flew in August 1915. The high command was impressed and ordered that several wings of heavy bombers be built as soon as possible. Technological breakthroughs in aircraft and engine design since the

STRATEGIC BOMBING

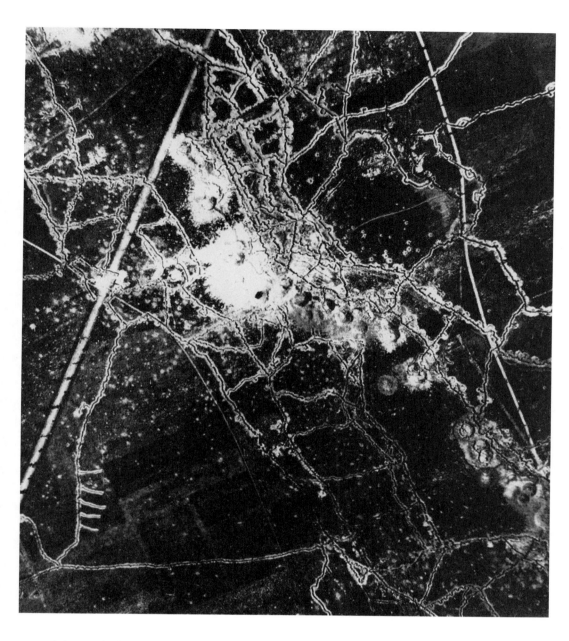

Aerial view of the trenches near Auchy-les-Labassee, France, 1915. The white area in the center of the picture indicates land devastated by heavy artillery barrages

(Imperial War Museum, London).

start of the war had opened up the possibility of long-range bombing.

The first strategic bombing offensive in history was the attack of German zeppelins against Great Britain on 31 May 1915. Three zeppelins appeared directly over London in daylight, unleashed several tons of bombs, and killed dozens of civilians. The airships sailed majestically away without being engaged by British defenses. The English public was at first panicked and then outraged that the Germans could so brazenly attack them. This effect on British morale was precisely what the German high command had intended.

The imperial capital was chosen because it was recognized as the Allied strategic center of gravity. Britain had a small army but was the industrial and financial powerhouse of the Entente. Britain was also perceived as having less at stake in the war than France and Russia, which

were fighting on their national territory. If British civilians were demoralized and disillusioned with the war the Germans might compel the British government to make a separate peace. With Britain out of the war, the Entente had little chance of victory. It was, in fact, a sound strategic concept and worth the risk of the international outrage that followed this direct attack upon civilians.

While the airship bombing had dramatic effects at the start, the British quickly built up a defense system that made such operations highly dangerous and difficult. The raids were stopped in the spring of 1916 after 222 sorties; German airships had dropped 175 tons of bombs on England, killed 557 civilians, and wounded another 1,358 people. Airship losses were simply too heavy for the benefits gained.

The concept of demoralizing the enemy by attacking civilians behind the lines, however, was not discarded or discredited. It was simply recognized that the technology of delivering bombs was ineffective. By the spring of 1917 the German air service had fashioned an aerial weapon that they believed would be effective in attacking Britain. A large force of more than forty Gotha G IV two-engine bombers, each capable of carrying 1,100 pounds of bombs a considerable distance, was assembled and stationed on the Flanders coast within range of London. The airplane was in most respects a far more effective means of bomb delivery than the airship. The "England Wing" of the *Luftstreitkräfte* was directed to bomb London as part of a two-pronged offensive against British morale. The other part of the offensive was resumption of unrestricted submarine warfare. The German high command determined that if the food supply of Britain was cut off and its civilians subjected to aerial bombardment that morale might break and Britain might be forced to make a separate peace.

As in the zeppelin raids of 1915, the first attacks by Gotha bombers in May 1917 caused considerable panic and set off a crisis in confidence in the government. At first the Germans were able to attack without opposition, but soon the British had effective defenses in place and forced the Germans to fly at night—with a consequent high accident rate. In a few months, it was clear that the strategy had failed, although Germany would bomb London until May 1918, killing 836 civilians and wounding 1,982. The offensive was called off because of heavy bomber losses. At the same time, Paris was bombed on several occasions as the Germans attempted to demoralize the French; however, their civilian morale apparently held up better than that of the British.

The German air attacks in 1915 had let the proverbial genie out of the bottle. From the first months of war the French air service bombed German towns containing rail yards and industrial centers. With the bombing of London the British Royal Flying Corps, which became the Royal Air Force (RAF) in 1918, was determined to wreak similar havoc in German cities. Although Berlin was far out of range to British bombers, some major German industrial cities were more accessible. By 1917 the RAF had a force of more than one hundred heavy bombers ready to fly over Germany. Throughout 1918 the British bomber force, known as the Independent Force, attacked dozens of cities, ostensibly to destroy vital industrial centers but primarily to weaken the morale on the German home front. In 353 raids in 1917 and 1918 the British dropped more than seven thousand bombs on German cities, killing 797 civilians and wounding 380. As with the German bombing campaigns, the price in lost British aircraft and aircrew had not been worth the damage inflicted.

Italian aviation theorist Giulio Douhet is usually credited with developing, in the 1920s, the theory of breaking the morale of the enemy by bombing their cities. Yet, this result was precisely the intent of both the German and British leadership from 1915 to 1918 when they ordered enemy cities bombed. Prior to World War I the only civilians subject to direct attack under the acknowledged rules of war were those individuals caught up in the siege of a city. When civilians were made a primary target in 1915 the fundamental rules of warfare were changed. World War I was the most "total" form of war that Europe had seen since the Thirty Years' War of the seventeenth century. Casualties inflicted by the German and Allied city-bombing campaigns were actually quite small. A psychological and legal barrier, however, had been crossed that would make it relatively easy for both sides to inflict mass casualties in World War II. In World War I the leaders of Germany and Britain had a fairly comprehensive and rational strategy to demoralize each other's home fronts by using airpower. The means were just too primitive for the strategy.

-JAMES CORUM,
USAF SCHOOL OF ADVANCED
AIRPOWER STUDIES

Viewpoint:
No. Technological, doctrinal, and organizational limitations relegated strategic bombing to a nuisance weapon throughout the war.

On 25 August 1914, with the war less than a month old, a German zeppelin lumbered over Antwerp and dropped several bombs. Witnessing the raid, American newspaper correspondent E. Alexander Powell described how "weak and nauseated" he felt upon entering a home struck by the indiscriminate load, as the woman sleeping inside "had literally been blown to fragments." He grimly concluded, "Her remains could only be collected with a shovel." The horrors of such an attack led one historian to liken the zeppelin to "the H-bomb of its day, an awesome Sword of Damocles to be held over the cowering heads of Germany's enemies." Disturbing sentiments aside, however, one must ask if the bomber, in both its lighter and heavier-than-air variants and presaged by H. G. Wells's *The War in the Air* (1908), was truly as destructive as one may think. To be sure, all of the expressions of modern airpower were present in World War I in seed form; a significant fact given the airplane was only a decade old at the start of the conflict. Nevertheless, the efforts to employ air-

BOMBING RAID

Belgian pilot Willy Coppens de Houthulst describes in his memoirs a 1917 bombing raid he participated in against German billets:

On April 26, I went across the lines for the first time by night to bomb the German billets at Zarren, making two separate trips. Surprise is essential for this type of attack; for the occupants leave their billets on the first alarm and take to shelter. And yet the whole squadron was sent over, as I have said, twice; in any case, Zarren, being within range of our artillery, did not justify this air method of attack.

I was rather astonished to discover that, when flying at night, at a height of about 1,000 feet, visibility was quite good. The eye can only penetrate darkness, or for that matter, mist, at any angle very close to the vertical. It is therefore necessary to gain a certain height in order to command a sufficient area of the ground beneath one.

Below, a few points of light could be seen coming from unshuttered windows, betraying the homes of beings for ever unidentified. Near the front, coloured lights rose in curves, their momentary reflections visible in the flood-waters. Other flares, attached to silken parachutes, threw patches of sky into dazzling light, making the stars appear pale by contrast.

Soon we entered the danger-zone. As we droned our way across the lines, clusters of incendiary balls of fire came winding up to meet us, and anti-aircraft shells burst around us for all the world like the bubbles breaking on the surface of a glass of champagne. Searchlight beams, giants' fingers groping sinisterly for us, cut the firmament into so many wedges of blackness, and, now and then, like a moth crossing in front of a headlight, an aeroplane would emerge into a beam from one of these wedges and turn into a thing of silver, while the giant's finger, trembling with excitement, essayed to hold it, and other beams converged to assist, and the guns below concentrated their fury on the target, filling the sky with detonating high-explosive; until the aeroplane, diving and twisting this way and that, plunged back into the obscurity whence it had come.

In the pattern of the carpet moving in beneath me, I could see our objective. As we drew near, the enemy's fire became fiercer and the fan-like glow from our bombs, bursting at the end of their unseen fall, added itself to the pyrotechnic display.

I could visualize the stir being caused down there: the gunners and the machine-gun crews sweating at their weapons, and the "*embusqués*" fleeing for their lives and going to ground to the huge delight of the combatant troops present. That was what invariably happened on our side, and I could see no good reason for a similar comedy not being enacted here.

The first time I released my load of bombs, I was astonished at the extremely slight movement imparted to my machine, which went on its way undisturbed. I had expected the sudden release of a hundred-weight or more of cargo to have more effect on an aeroplane.

Source: Willy Coppens de Houthulst, Days on the Wing, *translated by A. J. Insall (New York: Arno, 1980), pp. 73–75.*

---

power in the form of strategic bombing—to bring a swift end to the stalemate on the ground—revealed more of the vain hopes of the belligerents than the real capabilities of such a weapon.

The most determined strategic-bombing campaigns of the war where levied by the Germans and the British, with the former enjoying an initial advantage by way of a mature airship program at the beginning of the war; by 1914 zeppelins had logged some one hundred thousand miles and carried 35,000 passengers on 1,600 flights without a single accident. Early aircraft were too flimsy to carry any serious load apart from the necessary crew, nor did they enjoy a significant long-range capability—traits that were characteristic strengths of Count Ferdinand von Zeppelin's dirigibles. Thus, while the substantial British bombing efforts would not begin in earnest until 1917, the German campaign was launched much earlier.

As early as 1912 the Germans had devised plans to bomb "Fortress London" with both dirigibles and fixed-wing aircraft. Despite early misgivings at the prospect of bombing unarmed civilians, German naval commander Alfred von Tirpitz rationalized that "if one could set fire to London in thirty places, then the repulsiveness would be lost sight of in the immensity of effect." Nevertheless, the war was a year old before Kaiser Wilhelm II authorized the bombing of "military" targets in and around London, though the piecemeal attacks did little real damage. The attackers were often blown off course by winds aloft; army airships suffered their worst losses in 1916, as six dirigibles were downed in the span of three months. The program was turned over to the navy, which launched its largest attack on 19 October 1917; eleven zeppelins dropped 275 bombs, killing 33 Londoners, but the Germans lost five airships in the process as poor weather and enemy ground and air defenses made them pay a high cost for the bombing. In the end, the German navy, which had constructed some eighty zeppelins during the span of the war, lost twenty-three to enemy gunfire and another thirty-one to accidents or storms, killing more than 400 crew members.

Despite the abysmal results of the zeppelin attacks—which ultimately claimed the lives of only 500 British civilians, injuring an additional 1,300—the Germans formed a new heavy bombing unit (*Kagohl 3*) in late 1916 with the intention of bringing Britain to its knees by coupling the attacks of *Gotha* bombers with unrestricted submarine warfare. The massive bombers were designed to fly above British antiaircraft defenses, dropping their bombs with impunity from sixteen thousand feet—but again, the results were poorer than expected. The first *Kagohl 3* raid was launched on 25 May 1917, with the intention of striking the heart of the city, but all twenty-two bombers were forced to drop their ordnance on Folkstone because of poor weather over the capital. The attacks continued with varying degrees of success for the next four months, eventually changing to night raids and then tapering off in September. In the final analysis, the *Gotha* raids were less prone to the hazards of poor weather over Great Britain, enjoying a definite improvement over their airship cousins; but the paucity of real material damage produced by these raids prompted German leadership to question the utility of the attacks. Total property damage suffered came to just more than £2 million, less than half of what the British spent on the war each day. Nevertheless, whatever may have been absent in terms of physical damage levied was recovered in terms of psychological impact.

By late summer 1917 the British population was frenzied by this foreshadow to the Blitz of 1940, as a week of raids drove some 300,000 Londoners to seek refuge in the Underground. The government went so far as to persuade newspaper editors to curtail publishing grisly photos in an effort to allay panic. The *Gotha* attacks of 1917–1918 killed some 800 civilians and wounded another 1,500, forcing the War Cabinet to form a committee, headed by Lieutenant General Jan Smuts, to deliberate on the issue of home defense. Smuts's report, which served as the driving force behind the eventual formation of the independent Royal Air Force (RAF), also inspired the formation of the Allies' strategic bomber corps, the Independent Force (IF), headed by Air Marshal Hugh Trenchard.

Despite the doctrinal immaturity of the IF, three particular target sets were identified: population centers (usually attacked under the auspices of reprisal raids), "nerve centers" (government buildings and infrastructure), and industry. Large Handley Page 0/400s and Sopwith 1 1/2 Strutters were used to strike targets deep within Germany, as Prime Minister David Lloyd George sought to "bomb Germany with compound interest." Although intended to be an Allied effort, including a French, Italian, and American contingent, Trenchard's force was almost exclusively British. Even its name infuriated Allied ground commanders who eschewed the concept of aerial operations conducted apart from the ground war. Nevertheless, the IF got under way by the summer of 1918, with Trenchard devising grand plans for the following year, which included proliferation of the huge Handley Page 1500, use of newly designed two-thousand pound bombs, and employment of poison-gas air attacks. These efforts were shortened by the Armistice in November, with authorities questioning its effectiveness in the midst of the campaign.

These doubts, however, were calmed under the guise of psychological effect, as Trenchard claimed that "the moral effect of bombing stands undoubtedly to the material in the proportion of 20 to 1." Trenchard's force dropped a total of 550 tons of bombs in the final six months of the war, as a small group of IF intelligence officers, led by RAF major Paul, were dispatched to western Germany in December 1918 to survey the damage wrought by the bombing. Paul's team spent six weeks gathering data by surveying locations up to the east bank of the Rhine; he submitted his final report at the end of February 1919. As historian George K. Williams notes in *Biplanes and Bombsights: British Bombers in World War I* (1999), "Paul very likely touched a bureaucratic nerve" as "his assessments were severely edited" when compiled into the final official report released by the IF in January 1920, as bomber proponents seemed more committed to service advocacy than reporting accuracy. In addition to Paul's unpopular assessment, the U.S. Air Service made its own postwar bombing survey, covering much of the same territory as that of the RAF. The American assessment was as unflattering as Paul's; it stated that though "the decision to 'bomb something up there' might have appealed to one's sporting blood, it did not work with greatest efficiency against the German fighting machine." Also, the bombers were likened to long-range artillery—and a costly form at that—as during a five-month period in 1918 three squadrons of planes (numbering nearly three hundred total craft) dropped, in terms of average daily weight, the same amount of ordnance as eight 155-millimeter guns fired in the same period. In contrast to the morale-bombing advocates, the U.S. report concluded, "This investigation has decidedly shown that the enemy's morale was not sufficiently affected to handicap the enemy's fighting forces in the field." Thus, even though bomber advocates comforted themselves with the notion of "moral effect"—materiel damage of British bombing in 1918 accounted for less than one-tenth of 1 percent of the German war expenditure—the only morale altered was that of the British. The average citizen took comfort in the fact that the RAF was striking back at the German menace that proved so unsettling over the skies of London.

Strategic bombing was born during the Great War. In a war where defense prevailed, bombing offered the hope of breeching the deadlock, but that hope was never realized as technological, doctrinal, and organizational advances had not yet caught up with the dreams of the early airpower prophets. To be sure, the gospels of the Douhet, Trenchard, and American William Mitchell would each be refined, with proselytizing beginning in earnest once the war was over, but the fact remains that the "bombing experiment" was cut short by the Armistice. This end forced theorists to extrapolate the potentials of the weapon, rather than analyze its real wartime impact, and it is this fabled speculation that has largely replaced the facts of the actual performance of strategic bombing from 1914 to 1918. Additionally, the bold claims of World War II bomber advocates in the conduct of the Combined Bomber Offensive have served to further cloud the realities of this weapon in World War I; the early promises of strategic airpower did not match the reality of what it could bring to the fight.

–JOHN D. PLATING,
U.S. AIR FORCE ACADEMY

References

Martin Gilbert, *Atlas of World War I* (New York: Oxford University Press, 1994).

Gilbert, *The First World War: A Complete History* (New York: Holt, 1994).

Robin Higham, *Air Power: A Concise History* (London: Macdonald, 1972).

Jane's Fighting Aircraft of World War I (London: Jane's Publishing, 1946).

Lee Kennett, *The First Air War, 1914–1918* (New York: Free Press, 1991).

Kennett, *A History of Strategic Bombing* (New York: Scribners, 1982).

John H. Morrow Jr., *The Great War in the Air: Military Aviation from 1909 to 1921* (Washington, D.C.: Smithsonian Institution Press, 1993).

Walter Raleigh, *The War in the Air: Being the Story of the Part Played in the Great War by the Royal Air Force,* volume 1 (Oxford: Clarendon Press, 1922).

Douglas H. Robinson, *The Zeppelin in Combat: A History of the German Naval Airship Division, 1912–1918* (London: Foulis, 1962).

George K. Williams, *Biplanes and Bombsights: British Bombers in World War I* (Maxwell Air Force Base, Ala.: Air University Press, 1999).

STRUCTURAL FLAWS

Was World War I the result of structural flaws in the European political system that developed after 1871?

Viewpoint: Yes. Increasing nationalism and militarism in the last half of the nineteenth century made the war inevitable.

Viewpoint: No. The Great War was triggered by specific events, beginning with the assassination of Archduke Franz Ferdinand, and fueled by a series of short-sighted decisions by national leaders.

The outbreak of the Great War can be explained in simple terms: the European system of managing interstate relations broke down. A conflict in the Balkans began a chain reaction as states honored their alliance commitments and pursued their perceived self-interests. Was that breakdown an accident, or did the conflict reflect underlying stresses that fractured when put to a stronger-than-usual test?

Advocates of a "long fuse" interpretation of the causes of World War I go back to the foundation of the Second German Empire in 1871. The "restless Reich" that resulted from the war of 1870–1871 was the dominant power in Europe, but especially after the fall of Chancellor Otto von Bismarck in 1890 Germany lacked the judgment and stability to exercise its power wisely. The consequences of that failure were exacerbated as other great powers, especially France and Russia, grew dissatisfied with the Continental status quo and sought to modify it in their favor. Imperialism, with its accompanying rivalries, and alliances whose escape clauses made them undependable in crises combined to increase antagonisms and foster a general arms race. The growing increase in the size and deadliness of European armies and fleets in turn gave them a trump-card status, making conflict a first option rather than a last one.

The status quo of Europe faced domestic as well as international challenges. The liberal order that had dominated the Continent since the mid nineteenth century was under attack by a socialist movement that challenged the fundamental legitimacy of private-property capitalism. An emerging feminist movement and a parallel youth culture attacked patriarchy and gerontocracy. Nationalism based on self-defined ethnic identity claimed a right to fulfill destinies abridged by existing frontiers. Social Darwinism proclaimed a gospel of survival of the fittest. Intellectually and culturally the vitalism of German philosopher Friedrich Nietzsche and French philosopher Henri-Louis Bergson offered alternatives to the everyday rationalism of the Industrial Revolution. Even science was breaking its enlightened, Newtonian boundaries. Small wonder, as the new century progressed, that many welcomed the outbreak of war as a chance to escape confining routines.

When, however, all of the underlying factors are evaluated, the most that can be said is that Europe did not have to be forced into what became the Great War. Popular support and enthusiasm may sustain conflicts, but they cannot start them. That process is the result of concrete decisions made by individual actors. Europe was not dragged to war in 1914 by peoples; it was committed by governments.

Viewpoint:
Yes. Increasing nationalism and militarism in the last half of the nineteenth century made the war inevitable.

The catastrophe of the Western Front naturally led any thinker to question why the ostensibly most advanced civilization in the world at the turn of the century, Europe, had by 1914 fallen to killing millions of its sons for the sake of a few yards of mud. The initial spark that caused the war, the assassination of Archduke Franz Ferdinand and his wife in an obscure Balkan town, could not possibly have caused such a colossal horror show. Indeed, the roots of World War I run much deeper than an inflexible alliance system, the Schlieffen Plan, or the ongoing Balkan crisis. The horror of World War I was the result of festering nationalism, militarized public discourse, and politics—all of which were symptoms of the generally undelivered promises of modern life in the wake of industrialization and urbanization.

Nationalism is perhaps the best known of these root causes and was a major problem even before the war. This difficulty took two forms. First was the matter of unresolved national aspirations of minorities across Europe, most famously the case in the Habsburg Empire. Germanic Austria and Magyar Hungary lorded over a score of different languages and national groups, and by 1914 the empire was held together only by the prestige of the royal house. Neighboring powers wished to pluck away bits of the empire. Serbian aspirations motivated Gavrilo Princip to murder Ferdinand, whose intent to solve the nationalist question in the polyglot Austro-Hungarian Empire had already alienated the heir to the throne from the elite of his own empire. Cases of unrealized national sovereignty were in the minds of many people around the world, and U.S. president Woodrow Wilson's Fourteen Points spoke squarely to this desire. One cannot underestimate the power of nationalism: Wilson's promise still stirs the hearts of suppressed nationalists everywhere.

On another level, the development of nationalism over the course of the nineteenth century informed the decisions driving Europe to war in 1914. This kind of nationalism emphasized competition between nations: it was almost as if international relations had filled the same position in people's lives as following sports teams. European leaders eagerly promoted such aggressive loyalty. By 1871 Prussia and Piedmont Sardinia had successfully cloaked their conquest of their neighbors in the mantle of national self-determination. Italian statesman Camillo Benso, Conte di Cavour, famously noted that now that they had created an Italy, they needed to create Italians. Imperial Germany also struggled with the nature of a new German identity. This process unfolded in other, more-established states, as French and British identities were developed through the increase in public schooling and the spread of media. Though states have always sought prestige, in the last half of the century the audience for this struggle had changed. Whereas in the past, national prestige had been aimed at the monarchs, ministers, and other elite, now it was aimed at those whom these targets had deemed "the rabble." Given that this message was still being produced by these same elite, it should come as no surprise that it was more often presented in the form of invective, chest thumping, and saber rattling. International trade, the race for colonies, and national reputation were all packaged in a way that more often than not precluded compromise and accommodation.

This message was often expressed in the most militaristic tone. Bismarck's aggressive and forceful policies set a norm. Military victory over Denmark, Austria, and France provided the model for states to emulate. These quick, relatively painless, and seemingly easy victories convinced both casual and professional observers that military solutions were not only possible but also preferable. The mythology of the nineteenth century holds that it was a peaceful century, but wars in Italy, the Balkans, Germany, the Crimea, Africa, Asia, and India all indicate that Europeans remained as aggressive as ever. Individuals internalized the fantasy of clean and profitable warfare and eagerly sought reserve officer's commissions. A German cartoon of the era depicted a bourgeois man who had just lost his leg in a train accident. As he holds his leg in the air, he declares, "Oh No! I'm no longer eligible for war duty!" The caption was: "His first thought." By 1914 war was widely glorified. Is it any wonder that crowds thronged the squares and cheered the outbreak of World War I?

All across the Continent, European leaders promoted bellicosity. In a world where governments had not learned how to deal with the new realities of mass society, it is no wonder that the leaders played the war drums for support. The old elite were positively frightened by the masses and sought to bring them into the fold. This tendency was partly because the changes wrought by industrialization, urbanization, and the development of mass society had not yet delivered the world they promised. Only France, after a series of rebellions and revolutions, had even approached a working democracy with nearly universal suffrage and responsible government. Britain was still trying to remove the hold of the elite and had not yet extended the vote to women. The situation was worse in the powers that had formed the old Holy Alliance. Though enfranchised, German subjects had a sham constitution from Bismarck: though voted into office, the people's representatives had no real power, which actually lay in the hands of the landed elite and the royal house. Austria and Russia had nothing approaching democracy. It perhaps should not be surprising that the pressure of war forced Germany, Austria, and Russia to collapse into revolutionary anarchy. Such developments are not spontaneous. Though Britain and France had problems by the end of the war, neither had the pervasive, and in the end lethal, difficulties experienced by the other three great powers.

Europe was psychologically ready and eager for a war in 1914. Much to the surprise of many people, however, the war they got was neither quick nor easy. The state of mind in Europe, its expectations and grievances, had been festering for at least fifty years. The changes of the nineteenth century only appeared to have come easily, but in fact, the frictions that came with development had been there all along. Though warfare often can be viewed in isolation, World War I cannot. Any understanding of the origins, development, and conclusion of World War I needs to consider the totality of European civilization.

—PHIL GILTNER,
U.S. MILITARY ACADEMY

Viewpoint:
No. The Great War was triggered by specific events, beginning with the assassination of Archduke Franz Ferdinand, and fueled by a series of short-sighted decisions by national leaders.

Great events, even wars, do not always demand equally great causes. One of the chief ironies of the Great War was that Europe was

more structurally resilient in 1914 than it had been in the previous five decades. Earlier crises had forced the resolution of contentious imperial disputes. Even tensions resulting from the naval rivalry between Germany and Great Britain had abated; English prime minister David Lloyd George noted in July 1914 that relations between Britain and Germany had rarely been more amicable. War came in August primarily because statesmen and their military advisers decided it was an opportune time to settle accounts. The spark, of course, was the Bosnian Serb nationalist Gavrilo Princip's assassination of Archduke Franz Ferdinand. Yet, the assassination merely provided a pretext to set already well-oiled machines of war into motion. Specific contingencies, blunders, and misapprehensions—not inherent structural flaws—produced World War I.

Several crises could have led to general war. These included (among others) the Moroccan crises of 1905–1906 and 1911 (the Agadir incident), the Bosnian Annexation crisis of 1908, and the First and Second Balkan Wars of 1912–1913. In each crisis, military leaders demonstrated restraint as diplomats engaged in backroom horse-trading to forge compromises that left contending parties reasonably satisfied. By 1914, French and British colonial rivalries had been resolved in Africa and Asia, with Siam recognized as a buffer state separating their respective possessions in Asia. The two rivals also resolved their century-long naval competition in 1912 and formed an Entente Cordiale that provided a modus vivendi for future cooperation.

Meanwhile, French tensions with Germany concerning Morocco had abated, as Germany recognized French claims in exchange for territory in the Congo. Also resolved were colonial rivalries between Britain and Russia, with Afghanistan serving as a neutral buffer between imperial possessions in India and Persia. (The latter had previously been partitioned with Russia controlling the north and Britain the south with the central region serving as a buffer.) The Anglo-Russian Entente (1907) cleared the way for the creation of the Triple Entente. With France, Britain, and Russia working in concert to restrain a bellicose Kaiser Wilhelm II and the Second Reich, the balance of power in Europe established at the Congress of Vienna (1815) rarely seemed more sound or stable.

As various European powers contended for the spoils of a declining Ottoman Empire, however, tensions rose and fell in the Balkans with pan-Slavic unpredictability. Nevertheless, European diplomats showed considerable skill in localizing and alleviating these tensions. In the

Annexation Crisis (1908) the Austro-Hungarian Empire grabbed Bosnia, which contained a sizable Bosnian Serb population. As Serbia mobilized for war with Russian support, Germany threw its support to Austria-Hungary, leading the tsar to back down. Having recently lost a war against Japan (1904–1905) and recovering still from the Revolution of 1905, the tsar dared not risk war in 1908 merely for pan-Slavic unity. Similarly, in 1913 Serbia occupied Albania, in part to gain access to the sea denied by the London Congress (1912). Again, an Austro-Hungarian ultimatum sufficed to check Serbian ambition, with Russia acquiescing since Serbian territorial integrity remained uncompromised.

Set within this context, the crisis of July 1914 initially seemed a minor annoyance. It instead came to mark the failure of European crisis management. Yet, failure was neither structural nor systemic but rather a product of local contingencies, misunderstandings, and willful choices. Following Ferdinand's assassination, Austria-Hungary demanded an investigation and full accounting by Serbia of the apparent conspiracy—a demand to which Serbia refused to accede since prominent army and government officials were implicated in the plot. With a "blank check" of support from the kaiser, Austria-Hungary ordered the mobilization of Army Group South—not its entire army—for a punitive campaign to punish Serbia for its complicity in the assassination and its continued support of the "Black Hand" terrorist organization.

Escalation of this minor Balkan dispute was hardly inevitable. If the Habsburg military had clearly stated its intent to respect Serbian territorial integrity during its punitive campaign, Russia may have remained on the sideline. If the kaiser had not been so eager to issue the Habsburgs a "blank check" of support, Emperor Franz Josef may have scaled back his demands to acceptable levels. Instead, emboldened by the kaiser's blanket promise to keep the Russian bear at bay, Austria-Hungary embarked on sweeping retaliatory measures to eliminate once and for all Serbian pretensions to Balkan hegemony.

Faced with a potentially catastrophic loss of prestige if he lodged merely a diplomatic protest, the tsar asked his military advisers if he could order only partial mobilization of the Russian army. Unprepared for this contingency, his advisers insisted that the only option was full mobilization. Once he gave the order, the die was cast. Diplomats struggled manfully, but unsuccessfully, against rigid war plans that confined them to policy straitjackets.

These plans encapsulated and enshrined a preference for attacking first and talking later.

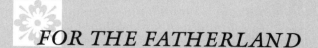

FOR THE FATHERLAND

On 23 November 1893, Kaiser Wilhelm II inducted a new class of recruits at ceremonies held at the Garrison Church of Potsdam, where he declared:

You are assembled here from all quarters of my realm in order to meet your military obligation and have in this holy place sworn loyalty to your kaiser even unto your last breath. You are still too young to understand all of this, but little by little it will be made known to you. Do not bother yourselves too greatly about all this but trust in God, now and again say an "Our Father," which has many a time renewed a warrior's courage.

Children of my Guards, from this day you are incorporated into my army. Now you stand under my command and have been permitted the privilege of wearing my uniform. Wear it with honor. Think on our fatherland's glorious history. Think also that the German army must be armed against the inner foe as well as the foreign. More than ever unbelief and discontent raise their head in the fatherland, *and it may come about that you will have to shoot or bayonet your own relatives and brothers*. Then seal your loyalty with the offering up of your heart's blood. Now, go home and fulfill your duty.

Source: *Ernst Johann, ed.,* Reden des Kaisers: Ansprachen, Predigten und Trinksprüche Wilhelms II *(Munich: Deutscher Taschenbuch Verlag, 1966), pp. 55–56.*

Germany responded to full Russian mobilization by implementing the Schlieffen Plan and attacking France. Like his cousin the tsar, the kaiser had asked his chief military adviser whether partial mobilization against Russia was possible, only to be told by Helmut von Moltke (the Younger) that the Schlieffen Plan was all or nothing. The kaiser's reply that "your uncle would have answered differently" was both cutting and telling.

Yet, the July Crisis seemed propitious to Germany because, whereas Russia was regaining its strength and industrializing at a fairly rapid pace, it still lagged behind Germany in industrial output and military efficiency. Wait two or three more years, however, and Russia might imperil the intricate and delicate timetable of the Schlieffen Plan. If this delicate timetable was disrupted and war prolonged, the chief German ally—the multiethnic Austro-Hungarian Empire—might collapse under the strain of prolonged fighting and economic disruption, as in fact it did.

France made similar calculations about the propitiousness of the July Crisis. In the years leading up to the Great War, the French worried they were falling irreversibly behind

Bosnian Serb student Gavrilo Princip being apprehended after shooting Archduke Franz Ferdinand and his wife in Sarajevo on 28 June 1914

their Teutonic neighbors. They knew Germany had 28 million more people and a larger, more efficient military. The longer they waited to attack, the wider the demographic gap and the longer the odds of success. The French further believed that, in their embrace of élan and the *offensive à outrance,* they finally had developed a war-winning formula. A headlong offensive, the French had concluded, was also the best means of spurring Russia to attack Germany in the east.

Even the empire concerned most with preserving the status quo found war advantageous. A decisive German victory on the Continent, the British concluded, would fundamentally upset the European balance of power, leading eventually to direct military threats against the Home Islands. Better to destroy the German High Seas Fleet in 1914 and reduce the German army to a more manageable size than to wait to strike until the German navy had attained rough parity with the Royal Navy.

Reinforcing front-loaded, rigid, "doomsday machine" war plans were sociocultural attitudes toward war. In some sense Britain, France, Germany, Russia, and other European nations marched to war simply because they wanted to. Germans were not the only Europeans who saw war as a harsh, yet ultimately necessary and rewarding, manifestation of Hegelian dialectic. Social Darwinism ran rampant

throughout Europe. War benefited humans as a species, or so British eugenicist Karl Pearson claimed. Edwardian England, with its enervating cultural practices and ennui, needed an energizing dose of vigor that a short, sharp war would give, or so militant enthusiasts argued that summer.

War enthusiasm drew strength from a well nigh universal belief that any conflict would be brief, certainly over in fewer than six months. In the idyllic summer of 1914, thinking the unthinkable—that nations and empires might be embarking on a grievously destructive war over which generals and statesmen would exercise only limited control—proved literally impossible. Most commentators subscribed to the sentiments in Norman Angell's *The Great Illusion* (1910) that war was unprofitable and increasingly futile because of the linkage and interdependence of world economic markets. The book quickly sold two million copies, and Angell nearly won a Nobel Peace Prize. Perhaps his book was too persuasive; as generals and statesmen concluded, it was best to strike quickly before war became obsolete.

Tragically, war was not obsolete in 1914, but neither was it inevitable nor a systemic outcome of structural flaws. Rather, it was a product of specific contingencies that included assassination, misapprehensions about Habsburg intentions, overly rigid and even fatalistic war plans, and specific sociocultural attitudes that favored recourse to what most everyone believed would be a brief, glorious, possibly even the last, war. Brevity was not a quality of the Great War, nor was it "the war to end all wars." Instead, military effort drove nations to extreme political demands, further prolonging the agony of what became in its horror and lack of finality the defining event of the twentieth century.

–WILLIAM J. ASTORE,
U.S. AIR FORCE ACADEMY

References

Fritz Fischer, *Germany's Aims in the First World War* (New York: Norton, 1967).

Michael Howard, *The Lessons of History* (New Haven: Yale University Press, 1991).

James Joll, *The Origins of the First World War*, second edition (New York: Longman, 1984).

Donald Kagan, *On the Origins of War and the Preservation of Peace* (New York: Doubleday, 1995).

Paul M. Kennedy, ed., *The War Plans of the Great Powers, 1880–1914* (London & Boston: Allen & Unwin, 1979).

Dwight E. Lee, *Europe's Crucial Years: The Diplomatic Background of World War I, 1902–1914* (Hanover, N.H.: University Press of New England, 1974).

Gerhard Ritter, *The Sword and the Sceptre: The Problem of Militarism in Germany*, 3 volumes, translated by Heinz Norden (Coral Gables, Fla.: University of Miami Press, 1969–1973).

L. C. B. Seaman, *From Vienna to Versailles* (London: Methuen, 1955).

Hew Strachan, ed., *The First World War*, volume 1, *To Arms* (Oxford & New York: Oxford University Press, 1998).

Samuel R. Williamson Jr., *The Politics of Grand Strategy: Britain and France Prepare for War, 1904–1914* (Cambridge, Mass.: Harvard University Press, 1969).

TRENCH WARFARE

Did trench warfare lead to pointless slaughter?

Viewpoint: Yes. The trench experience reduced soldiers to levels of passivity.

Viewpoint: No. Trench warfare actually held men out of the line in support or reserve most of the time, and its defining experiences, barrages and attacks, were unusual.

The defining experience of the Great War on all fronts was trench warfare. In earlier centuries armies had faced each other from fixed positions—but never for years at a time and never under the physical and psychological circumstances of 1914–1918. For men whose peacetime routines were increasingly free of random violence, the daily physical risks that accompanied being under direct enemy observation were in themselves a shock. Even to men from factories and mines, the noise could be overpowering. The weapons, steadily improving in range, accuracy, and destructive power, challenged human identity. The Great War pitted steel against flesh directly, in a dichotomy impossible to avoid or misunderstand.

At the same time, men adapted. One response was fatalism: accepting the concept that one's destiny was beyond one's control. That attitude had been so influential before the nineteenth century in broad segments of the European population that a strong cultural memory of it remained to resurface at the fronts. Another approach involved "domesticating" industrialized war: anthropomorphizing weapons by giving them names and nicknames, linking their sounds with those found in nature. A third solution emphasized overcoming technology by mastering it. Pilots in the air and storm troopers on the ground perceived themselves as interacting with, and ultimately transcending, the machines of war. The citizen soldier as archetype increasingly made place for the technowarrior, an aristocrat of performance defined by violence.

On a more mundane level, the nature of trench warfare encouraged normalization. The combination of static fronts and improved administration meant that armies on the whole managed their daily affairs competently relative to their respective previous standards. Rations arrived on time; mail was delivered regularly; and systems of passes and furloughs were implemented predictably.

In the front line a principle of "live and let live" was widely applied, even in the "hottest" sectors and by units with deserved reputations for aggressiveness. The British Expeditionary Force (BEF) practice of large-scale raiding, often and defensibly described as wasting lives for no proportionate end, grew in part from Canadian officers' concern that their men were becoming too "comfortable" in the trenches. Even the fire-eaters, however, tacitly admitted that such practices as sniping, targeting latrines, and interrupting ration parties could not be carried to mutual extremes without making trench life impossible.

The length of operations in the Great War meant that pitched battles were not the norm. It was more usual for a division to suffer heavy casualties, be assigned to quiet sectors and "fattened up" for the next phase, then once more take ruinous losses in a few days or weeks, and begin the process again. In such a context, "going over the top" could be processed as an occasional catastrophe in a general environment of routine.

The high force-to-space ratios that facilitated trench war enabled processes of regular rotation away from the front. A given battalion in any army might spend as much as three-fourths of its time in support or reserve, often for months and years in the same sector.

Formal and informal cultures of entertainment and activity correspondingly developed to absorb off-duty attention and energy. The British took the lead in that process—a logical outcome of a prewar military experience that often left units in isolated locations, thrown on their own resources. But the French and Germans as well authorized or accepted soldiers' newspapers and came to see the value of other similar grassroots initiatives. The comradeship veterans of the war describe so favorably was arguably less a product of service at the front itself than of the life behind the lines that structured experience and memory by providing routines.

Viewpoint:
Yes. The trench experience reduced soldiers to levels of passivity.

In every war ordinary soldiers are unable to control their own fates. Superiors order them wherever they please; the enemy compels certain actions and prohibits others; weather and terrain dictate the ground rules of their lives; and technology can make men feel powerless when confronted with its unyielding steel. The Great War on the Western Front, however, took this helplessness to new heights. Here soldiers were bound to trenches, enduring long stretches of inactivity, suffering the random bombing or sniper attack, then undertaking terrifying charges where the increased firepower of new technology mowed down the defenseless victims in large numbers. Faced with this overwhelming threat and unable to act against it, men became little more than passive victims in a war machine that ground on endlessly.

This style of warfare was not how it was supposed to be. When war broke out in August 1914 the nations of Europe knew exactly how their armies—the most advanced in the world—would fight the first major conflict of the new century. Using the latest technology, their cavalry, infantry, and artillery would conduct a quick war of maneuver, speeding through enemy territory to take their opponent's capital before they even had time to react. These expectations made the stalemate that developed in France and Flanders so shocking and prevented soldiers from preparing themselves for the unearthly conditions on the Western Front. For rather than permitting the fast, clean conflict of the future, technology betrayed its masters and instead forced the creation of a vast system of trenches that rent the Continent in two.

Technology had in fact created the conditions for one of the most ancient sorts of warfare—a siege, rather than a war of mechanically enhanced maneuver. The Germans, properly prepared and supplied, simply sat down behind their defenses of wire and earth and waited out years of futile attacks by the Allies. There were, however, two sides to the trench coin. While the deep holes helped to protect Allies and Germans alike, they also confined them, kept them from moving where they pleased, and stopped them from escaping both their enemies and the terrible technology of war. It was, then, the trenches themselves that began to turn soldiers into passive objects destined for destruction rather than free actors in the war of their dreams.

There were other factors at work as well. In this siege warfare, the terms offensive and defensive lost all meaning, for although the Germans were nominally on the defensive most of the war, and the Allies supposedly conducted continuous offensive operations to expel the invaders from Flanders and France, in truth neither side could advance nor would they yield ground. Locked in this eternal stalemate, unable to move forward and win victory or to retreat and at least end the war, ordinary soldiers were frozen in place by their physical surroundings, by the threat of court-martial, by deeply felt ideals of duty, and by the terms of the war itself.

Men caught up in the surreal new battleground were also forced to contend each day with the technological innovations that had created the stalemate. Heavy artillery, machine guns, quick-firing rifles, and, later, mortars increased firepower and the strength of the defensive, making easy movement forward a thing of the past. These marvels of the modern world had a quite unintentional side effect that increased the passivity of soldiers—the enemy became invisible, a faceless threat that, like Jove, hurled lightning bolts from the blue to strike good and evil alike.

How soldiers experienced the war shows the power of the brute forces that they faced in the trenches—and how their responses were necessarily limited by their straitened circumstances.

British soldier firing a Lewis Gun from a trench in the summer of 1916

(from The Illustrated War News, 2 August 1916, page 22, Joseph M. Bruccoli Great War Collection, Thomas Cooper Library, University of South Carolina)

First, they were assaulted by the enemy whom they could not see and struck down from afar by shells that often blew one man to bits and left his neighbor untouched. With no one to strike back at, men were forced to stand impotently and to simply take the punishment delivered from on high. Then there was the sheer randomness of shelling, its most devastating aspect, which prevented reasoned action to stop one's own injury or death. Many of the soldiers who fought in the war remembered the accidental stop, turn, or even stumble that saved their lives. Chance thus seemed a more authentic explanation for who lived and died in the trenches than did training, skill, or any particular act at all. Belief in chance, however, led to a debilitating fatalism that caused many men to abandon hope and concern for the greater purposes of the war, as well as active participation in combat. Soldiers did what they had to do to survive, and no more.

The routines of war, meant to keep men moving and involved in the fight, actually contributed to this sense of futility and to the passivity of the men. Each day soldiers on the Western Front carried out exactly the same actions: they "stood to," fired off shells, shot at the enemy trenches, and were shot at in turn. Each day the results were the same: more casualties and no change in the war. Soldiers were not fooled at all into thinking that their activity had accomplished anything—other than to keep them busy so that they would not think about the larger picture. According to Carroll Carstairs, in A *Generation Missing* (1930), they understood the war, especially after the Somme

(1916), as an "endless affair," an eternal cycle of repetitive actions that achieved nothing.

The war thus became something that happened to one rather than an activity in which one participated. One particularly astute soldier, Rudolf Georg Binding, in A *Fatalist at War* (1929), described the war as something like a glacier, with men at the front little more than the hapless moraine pushed ahead of its inexorable destructive power. For others it was Armageddon, the final battle that would end in the destruction of the entire world; the final conflict that was, significantly, ordained in Scripture and therefore destined to happen no matter what mortal man might do. Frontline soldiers imagined shelling in particular as an avalanche, a tornado, or a storm of steel. Like any natural disaster, it was something that one could not predict or control and that one could only hope to survive. An offensive, the operation designed to snap men out of this passivity, was known to the British as "the show," and they learned that their true role was as spectators in this theater of war, rather than actors. Finally, the powerful reaction of trench soldiers to air battles, their enthusiasm for airmen and the war above them, underlined the dichotomy between their own helpless condition and the freedom of action that the "knights" of the air enjoyed.

The terms that soldiers used for themselves, and even for the enemy at the front, showed an awareness of their own passivity. The British soldiers saw themselves as the "poor bloody infantrymen," forced to do the dirtiest work, but deserving compassion for their suffering as well. In the same vein, participants on both sides in the war, such as Guy Chapman, in *A Passionate Prodigality: Fragments of Autobiography* (1933), described themselves, and even soldiers on the other side, as "victims," the state of ultimate passivity. Condemned to die for the sins of their nations, their part in the war was lamented by one soldier as the "long crucifixion." Other soldiers no longer even saw themselves as people; they had become ants and other defenseless creatures, powerless in their attempts to stop the tremendous material forces amassed against them.

Some of the ways that trench soldiers sought to cope with their hellish conditions show just how impotent they were. One absolute truth underlay all their responses: no one would escape the trenches unscathed. The most that one could hope for was not victory in battle but rather a "cushy" wound that would give a soldier the much-desired trip home to "Blighty." The many cases of self-inflicted wounds attests to the number of soldiers whose only action in the war was to hurt themselves rather than the enemy. To prevent more-serious injuries, soldiers depended not on their own actions but rather on charms, spells, and superstitions. Even highly educated officers understood that they were unable to affect their own fates and therefore carried various medallions, crosses, and talismans with them at all times. Another reaction to the war was even more extreme, yet it shows more clearly the helplessness of the frontline soldier. Incapable of advance, unable to retreat, and bound to the trench as surely as a prisoner is confined to a cell, a large number of men simply retreated into their own minds. It is no coincidence that the term "shell shock" was invented during this war, for the immobile stalemate on the Western Front pushed many men to insanity.

Yet, it would be a mistake to see these men as completely without moral resources in their passive condition. Neither the British nor the Germans ever mutinied, and the French only did so when asked to carry out an offensive, not because they would no longer endure the terrible conditions on the front. The reasons for this situation are many: a strong sense of duty to country and one's comrades; fears of being thought a coward; and the threat of courts-martial. Just as importantly, however, over time the trench soldiers came to believe that if one could do nothing but stand in the face of certain death, then to stand without giving in might be the bravest deed of all.

—MARY HABECK,
YALE UNIVERSITY

Viewpoint:
No. Trench warfare actually held men out of the line in support or reserve most of the time, and its defining experiences, barrages and attacks, were unusual.

For many cultural historians the soldiers of the Great War have been viewed as victims, powerless in the extreme, caught in the grip of an impersonal, industrial war that dispensed death from great distances. Eric J. Leed's influential work, *No Man's Land: Combat and Identity in World War I* (1979), exemplified this interpretation. He argued that on the outbreak of war men joined the army to escape modernity and a mechanistic, repressive mode of civilian living. It was to be a new start, a reawakening for them and for the societies from which they were drawn. However, instead of finding new freedoms, the soldier found himself powerless as an individual, crouching in trenches for days on end, simply waiting to be destroyed from afar. Such a sustained experience resulted in passive soldiers rejecting aggression, embracing superstition, and, in a minority of cases, retreating into neurosis.

This portrayal of the Great War soldier's experience of trench warfare is, nonetheless, far from the norm and differs from the experience of the ordinary soldier in three fundamental ways. First, the tasks soldiers had to perform while occupying frontline trenches ensured that they remained too busy to simply wait around pondering death. Secondly, the routine of trench warfare ensured that a unit was rotated frequently, so soldiers were rarely subjected to sustained periods of attack, active defense, or bombardment. Finally, the soldiers did not react to life in the trenches in the way that Leed describes. Rather than tending toward passivity and powerlessness, World War I soldiers sought to exert a degree of control over their lives within the confines of the military system.

Although the threat of death was ever present, the daily routine of the frontline trench helped to militate against feelings of powerlessness and the inevitability of death. Half an hour before sunrise and sunset, soldiers would "stand to" on the firestep of the trench, as dawn and dusk were the times of choice for an attack. For the rest of the day soldiers would be subject to inspections, perform sentry duty, and undertake repair work on the trenches. At night, patrols might be sent out into "no man's land" or parties detailed to strengthen the wire in front of the trench. Snipers and occasionally

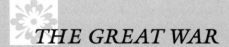

THE GREAT WAR

The following passage was written by poet James Dickey in 1993 for an exhibition commemorating the seventy-fifth anniversary of the armistice ending World War I:

Of all the wars that have been fought by the human race from the time of caves, and most likely before them, the trees, World War I brought in a far greater degree of aggression, mutilation, blood and death than had existed in all the previous wars combined. The landscape of Hell itself could not compare in terror and ugliness with the trenches, with no-man's-land. Here, human creatures were brought abruptly face-to-face with the misery and degradation that they and their own inventions had created. The machine had turned on its inventors, with a cold and callous fury quite literally beyond words, as men struggled desperately to live among the high-speed metals, the rats and the slime. The human sensibility changed permanently toward its darker, more pessimistic side, and this was reflected in its art in such startling ways that art was given, in a grim sense, a new release, a new beginning. It is not necessary for the artist to have been a participant, though many of them were. One is not required to ponder the tank, the bomber, the battleship, the long-range artillery piece or the machine gun, all stemming from that war. All that is needed to understand World War I in its philosophical and historical meaning is to examine barbed wire—a single strand will do— and to meditate on who made it, what it is for, why it is like it is.

Source: *James Dickey, keepsake for the Joseph M. Bruccoli Great War Collection, Alderman Library, University of Virginia, 11 November 1993 – 28 February 1994 (1993).*

trench mortars could enliven these proceedings, while raiding parties to gather intelligence and harass the enemy were organized periodically. Many of these activities endowed the soldier with a feeling of purpose, even a sense of adventure, which helps to explain why for some soldiers, service in the trenches was viewed as a positive, life-enhancing experience. Thus, authors such as Graham H. Greenwell could write, in *An Infant in Arms: War Letters of a Company Officer, 1914–1918* (1935), "I have to confess that I look back on the years 1914–1918 as among the happiest I have ever spent."

While memories of active frontline experience are prominent features of postwar memoirs and histories, one must remember that throughout World War I all units were regularly rotated through the frontline and support trenches and to rear and reserve areas in order to maintain unit efficiency and troop morale. For British infantry units, the amount of time they spent at rest behind the lines was calculated to be, on average, three-fifths of the total time spent on the Western Front. To be sure, the term "rest" proved something of a misnomer, particularly for the British soldier, who was often required to perform tedious fatigues, including the unloading of railway trucks and the transporting of stores, in addition to performing drills and completing training, while behind the lines. French soldiers had more time allocated for complete rest and recovery, particularly after the mutinies of 1917, but were also required to train hard during periods out of the front line. Nevertheless, the fact remains that for the majority of their service, soldiers were not under constant pressure in the trenches of being bombarded by shells and pinned down by snipers.

The world behind the lines often provided a complete contrast with the reality of the trenches. Even a few miles behind the battle zone the countryside could be unspoiled, with French or Belgian civilians continuing with their daily lives in small villages and hamlets. Such villages provided a degree of normality for the soldiers. Alongside the grinding fatigues there were opportunities to eat and drink in small cafés that provided an alternative to army fare and the welcome prospect of contact with women. Moreover, as the war progressed, a range of leisure activities was instituted behind the lines. The British were particularly successful in organizing diverting activities, in part because their soldiers received the least opportunity for leave. Drawing on civilian popular culture, a variety of sporting teams was arranged and competitions were played between units. Football leagues became an important part of life behind the lines, as well as horse racing, seaside excursions, and divisional canteens. While some of these pastimes were peculiarly British, concert parties, theater, and the cinema have been well documented as providing an escape for men of all armies. Indeed, the German High Command made great efforts to provide concerts and plays for their soldiers preparing for the offensive of March 1918. It is clear that time behind the lines was deemed essential by all armies for sustaining the morale and motivation of soldiers and became an integral part of the routine of trench warfare.

Not only were units constantly moved between front and rear, they were rotated between active and quiet fronts. Between 1914 and 1918 the trench system of the Western Front stretched for 475 miles. At any one time battle would be waged in discrete areas while other lengths of the front would be quiet. This situation allowed units that had experienced heavy fighting in one sector to be moved to a quieter area to recover.

It was at Verdun (1916) that the French instituted their policy of rotating fighting divisions through the battle sectors, a strategy that was adopted by the British, who sent all their available divisions, with the exception of one, through the Battle of the Somme between July and November 1916. Generals were aware that during great battles the intensity of fighting and shelling, and the scale of the casualties, was such that their units could spend only a finite period in the frontline trenches before they stopped functioning effectively and had to be withdrawn and reconstituted. This was most effective on a quiet front where the damaged unit could absorb drafts and regain its cohesion and fighting strength while performing routine trench warfare. Thus, although the experience of battle and artillery bombardment was shocking and could easily induce feelings of powerlessness in the face of failed attacks and high casualties, it actually formed only a small part of the average soldier's war experience.

More common was routine trench warfare on quiet fronts. In many sectors soldiers on both sides agreed to live and let live. In other words, they agreed to tacit truces, or the ritualization of firing patterns to minimize the danger to each other. This rejection of aggression should not be interpreted as a reaction to feelings of powerlessness. It was not a product of soldierly passivity, but rather an active choice. The soldier of World War I could, within certain parameters, influence the level of aggression at the front. Soldiers did not always choose to minimize the levels of violence. Troops on both sides wanted to win the war and were equally capable of choosing active resistance if it was deemed to be militarily beneficial. However, on quiet fronts, it was generally counterproductive to provoke the enemy for little military gain.

Such attitudes toward the conduct of warfare helped to precipitate the French mutinies of May and June 1917. With the failure of the Chemin des Dames offensive, nearly half of French divisions refused to move up to the front to attack in a protest against the conduct of offensive tactics that were resulting in the slaughter of French units for little military purpose. The soldiers returned to the trenches only when the high command conceded, among other things, to alter their tactics and to abandon large-scale offensives, at least until the arrival of the Americans.

The French were not the only army to suffer disorder and disruption. With the disaster at Caporetto (1917), Italian forces suffered from mass desertions and the German army hemorrhaged deserters toward the end of the war. These desertions were the extreme ways in which a soldier could shape his life once in uniform. Less extreme were the many forms of resistance that occurred within units of all nationalities. From malingering and grousing to trade-union-inspired "go slows," soldiers found myriad ways of exerting their own views, values, and beliefs within the army system and thus retained a degree of control over their fate.

Life in the trenches of World War I could be a horrifying and overwhelming experience, particularly during periods of fierce fighting. It is therefore understandable that events that triggered intense emotions in soldiers should overshadow descriptions of routine trench warfare in postwar memoirs. Nevertheless, this emphasis should not blind one to the fact that heavy barrage and attack, and the feelings of powerlessness that they could sometimes induce, were, in fact, unusual. The routine of trench warfare ensured that soldiers spent only a limited period of time in the front line and units were quickly rotated out of active sectors. Moreover, troops fighting in the trenches were citizen soldiers. Although serving in the army, they were reluctant to relinquish their rights as citizens and sought to challenge authority and exert their opinions throughout the war. Thus, the majority of soldiers serving in World War I did not become cowed, passive victims rendered helpless by the experience of trench warfare.

–H. B. MCCARTNEY,
KING'S COLLEGE, LONDON

References

Bernard Adams, *Nothing of Importance: Eight Months at the Front with a Welsh Battalion, October, 1915, to June, 1916* (London: Methuen, 1917).

Tony Ashworth, *Trench Warfare, 1914–1918: The Live and Let Live System* (London: Macmillan, 1980; New York: Holmes & Meier, 1980).

Stéphane Audoin-Rouzeau, *Men at War, 1914–1918: National Sentiment and Trench Journalism in France during the First World War,* translated by Helen McPhail (Providence, R.I.: Berg, 1992).

Rudolf Georg Binding, *A Fatalist at War,* translated by Ian F. D. Morrow (Boston & New York: Houghton Mifflin, 1929).

Carroll Carstairs, *A Generation Missing* (Garden City, N.Y.: Doubleday, Doran, 1930; London: Heinemann, 1930).

Hugh Cecil and Peter H. Liddle, eds., *Facing Armageddon: The First World War Experienced* (London: Cooper, 1996).

Guy Chapman, *A Passionate Prodigality: Fragments of Autobiography* (London: Nicholson & Watson, 1933).

Giles E. M. Eyre, *Somme Harvest: Memories of a P.B.I. in the Summer of 1916* (London: London Stamp Exchange, 1938).

J. G. Fuller, *Troop Morale and Popular Culture in the British and Dominion Armies* (Oxford: Clarendon Press; New York: Oxford University Press, 1990).

Graham H. Greenwell, *An Infant in Arms: War Letters of a Company Officer, 1914–1918* (London: Dickson & Thompson, 1935).

Eric J. Leed, *No Man's Land: Combat and Identity in World War I* (Cambridge & New York: Cambridge University Press, 1979).

Erich Maria Remarque, *All Quiet on the Western Front,* translated by A. W. Wheen (London: Putnam, 1929).

Leonard V. Smith, *Between Mutiny and Obedience: The Case of the French Fifth Infantry Division during World War 1* (Princeton: Princeton University Press, 1994).

Hew Strachan, ed., *The Oxford Illustrated History of the First World War* (Oxford & New York: Oxford University Press, 1998).

TRENCH WARFARE

TSAR NICHOLAS II

Did the decision of Tsar Nicholas II to take personal command at the front accelerate the fall of the Russian Empire?

Viewpoint: Yes. The tsar was unqualified to command at the front, and he exacerbated an already bad situation by a series of poor decisions.

Viewpoint: No. The Russian military situation was so bad by late 1915 that decisions made by the tsar after that point had little bearing on the collapse of the empire.

Russian tsar Nicholas II left the newly renamed city of Petrograd (formerly St. Petersburg) in 1915 to assume personal command of the armies at the front. He did so against the urgent advice of his ministers, who argued that an already disrupted administration would be strained to the collapsing point if the autocrat ultimately responsible for decision making was five hundred miles out of touch. They contended that it was foolish to take such a step after the series of defeats Russia had suffered during the summer: setbacks resulting in the loss of Warsaw, the sacrifice of two million casualties, and the virtual exhaustion of Russian reserves of weapons and ammunition. Instead of being the rallying point of the Russian people at war, the monarchy would become their scapegoat by accepting de facto responsibility for anything else that might go wrong with the conduct of operations.

Nicholas was adamant. Since August 1914 he had wanted to take the field at the head of his troops. He spent as much time as possible at army headquarters, frequently accompanied by his son, playing the roles of a loving father and an interested spectator. His own military skills were best illustrated by his personally testing a new design of uniform and pack in a nine-hour march before the war. If Tsar Nicholas manifested the virtues of a storekeeper, as a soldier he showed the qualities of a supply sergeant. Nor did the tsar possess the force of character to impress the senior staff officers who now did the real work of command. None of the military decisions made between his assumption of command and his abdication in 1916 owed anything to his input. Instead, familiarity bred neglect. The tsar was no longer a figure of awe and mystery—just the unassuming middle-aged man in an unpretentious uniform who waited every day for the regular letters from his wife.

Nicholas's gesture had international consequences. The French and British governments interpreted it as nailing the flag to the mast: the tsar's government would stand or fall with the outcome of the war. Germany too processed the decision as a signifier, ending any possibility of a negotiated peace. The real significance of Nicholas's decision, however, was as his advisers predicted. His physical removal from Petrograd left the threads of government hanging. They were taken up by the tsarina. German-born and lacking the intellectual development to shape her driving energy, which was increasingly in thrall to her sinister adviser monk, Grigory Rasputin, Alexandra would complete the catastrophe of the empire.

Viewpoint:
Yes. The tsar was unqualified to command at the front, and he exacerbated an already bad situation by a series of poor decisions.

Tsar Nicholas II's decision to take personal command of the armed forces in August 1915 was one of the most disastrous decisions in Russian history. At a stroke he both removed effective leadership from the war effort and absented himself from the seat of the political power in the empire. As the war on the Eastern Front dragged on, both of these factors conspired to lead Russia into catastrophe. A significant amount of responsibility for the military defeat of Russia and its descent into the horrors of revolution and communism must be laid at the feet of its last emperor.

From a military standpoint Nicholas II's arrival at headquarters made positively no sense. Apart from his brief service as a cavalry officer when he was still heir to the throne, he had no education in military affairs. Unlike his ancestor Peter I (the Great), who had patiently educated himself in the arts of war and based all promotions and assignments—including his own—on strict meritocracy, the unprepared Nicholas merely appointed himself to the Supreme Command. This decision was especially disastrous in the emerging school of modern warfare, where no army could take the field effectively without high-quality professional leadership. This reality had been recognized even in underdeveloped Russia, where the reformist Tsar Alexander II had dramatically reformed and modernized officer training and military techniques after the defeat of his country in the Crimean War (1853–1856). Nicholas, who modeled his relationship with the nation after the power scenarios of the Romanovs of the seventeenth century, showed his disregard for military professionalism by placing himself at the head of his army despite his lack of qualifications.

From a sound, professional perspective, moreover, such a transition was unnecessary. Despite antiquated strategic thinking and incompetence in the ranks of its officer corps, Russia fielded enough reliable commanders in World War I to obviate the emperor's need for his presence at headquarters. The commander in chief whom Nicholas replaced, his cousin Grand Duke Nicholas (Nikolay Nikolayevich), was a career officer and one of the most modern and progressive thinkers in the Russian military. The initial success of Russia in mobi-

lizing the forward elements of its army fast enough to defy prewar predictions of its effectiveness was largely his doing. The early reversal at Tannenberg in August 1914 resulted much more from the incompetence of the responsible field commanders than from the Grand Duke's command. The shortages of weapons and ammunition that bedeviled the Russian army thereafter were brought on by the incompetence of the corrupt war minister Vladimir Sukhomlinov. When Grand Duke Nicholas had the opportunity, moreover, he proved his command abilities amply. Despite the terrible defeat in East Prussia, the Russian armies arrayed against the Austro-Hungarian forces in Galicia inflicted a high number of casualties and made impressive gains in the autumn of 1914. Combined German and Austrian attacks in Russian Poland later in the year were checked. Even the great retreat of the summer of 1915, which surrendered much ground to the Central Powers and was the immediate pretext for Grand Duke Nicholas's dismissal, was conducted skillfully and for sound strategic reasons.

Nicholas II's personal assumption of command grew out of one of the critical weaknesses of his reign: his own shortsightedness as a ruler and as an individual. In addition to his naive belief that he shared a personal communion with the Russian people, he ruled over a political system that could not function without his immediate presence. This fact was not merely perceived in hindsight. When the Emperor announced his decision to his cabinet, ten of the twelve ministers of state objected and tried to convince him to reconsider. Tellingly, ministers in Imperial Russia served only at the pleasure of the tsar and had no responsibility to the *Duma* (protoparliament), which had existed since 1906, or to any other institution. That Nicholas was about to make a catastrophic mistake was clear even to his own placemen.

What was the content of their objections? First of all, the already delicate domestic political situation in Russia would be endangered by the tsar's personal association with the military fortunes of his country. Any other military commander could be blamed for a disaster and then dismissed, but by taking personal command the Emperor would now bear personal as well as political responsibility for all military failures. The deterioration of the Russian position in the field after he assumed command made such an outcome unavoidable regardless of the myriad of other problems faced by the war effort. Indeed, one of the leading criticisms of Nicholas's leadership has been that he single-handedly lost the war and caused the deaths of millions of Russian soldiers. As unfair as that opinion may be, Nicholas's own foolishness made it stick.

The larger and more obvious problem was that the Emperor's near-permanent move from the capital, Petrograd, to Supreme Headquarters (*Stavka*) in the provincial town of Mogilev took him away from his paramount responsibilities as head of state. In an age before radio and other "real time" means of communication, the communications infrastructure of Russia was incapable of keeping the tsar in regular touch with events elsewhere. Even though the telephone had been invented and came into regular use on the Western Front, none was ever installed at the tsar's military headquarters. To communicate with the capital, he had to rely on correspondence by telegram and regular mail. As a result he became less and less in touch with the political realities of the home front. Domestic political issues either eluded his attention altogether or reached him in a grossly distorted form.

The growing disconnect between the tsar and the capital was especially dangerous because Nicholas tried to compensate for his absence by entrusting more and more authority to his wife, Empress Alexandra. There were indeed few reasons why he should have done so. The Empress was herself not Russian, but rather a princess of the German Grand Duchy of Hesse-Darmstadt, who was thought to be personally cold and uncomfortable in her husband's country. At a time when Russia was engaged in a mortal struggle with Germany, public opinion and even many in the elite shared the view that Alexandra was actively working against Russia. While the various conspiracy theories and rumors about her pro-German machinations were untrue, they nevertheless spread like wildfire as the war continued, and acquired more credibility with each new military reverse. As a matter of principle, moreover, the Russian empress had no traditional or other kind of role in government, and many saw the enhancement of Alexandra's role as a subversion or usurpation of the tsar's rightful authority. After a few months of her de facto government, court circles and even relatives of the tsar began to talk about a minor coup d'état to deprive her of power and to place her under house arrest.

To make matters worse, the Empress found herself incapable of making many government decisions and came to rely with increasing desperation on the shady Siberian mystic Grigory Rasputin, a peasant who had an inexplicable ability to soothe the suffering of the hemophiliac heir to the throne. After his appearance at court became well estab-

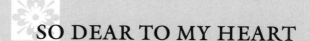

SO DEAR TO MY HEART

On 22 March 1917 Tsar Nicholas II was arrested; the following is his final order of the day to the Russian army he had led, as recorded by French ambassador Georges Maurice Paléoloque:

I address you for the last time, you soldiers who are so dear to my heart. Since I renounced the throne of Russia for myself and my son, power has been transferred to the Provisional Government which has been set up on the initiative of the Imperial Duma.

May God help that Government to lead Russia to glory and prosperity! And may God also help you, my brave soldiers, to defend your country against a cruel foe! For more than two years and a half you have continuously borne the hardships of an arduous service; much blood has been spilt, enormous efforts have been made and already the hour is at hand in which Russia and her glorious allies will break down the enemy's last desperate resistance in one mighty common effort.

This unprecedented war must be carried through to final victory. He who thinks of peace at the present moment is a traitor to Russia.

I am firmly convinced that the boundless love you bear our beautiful Fatherland is not dead in your hearts. May God bless you and Saint George, the great martyr, lead you to victory!

NICHOLAS

Source: *Maurice Paléoloque, An Ambassador's Memoirs, volume three (New York: Doran, 1923), p. 259.*

lished in the tsar's absence, Rasputin brought further disgrace on the Romanov dynasty. Quite simply, he used the trust of the Imperial family and his access to the Empress to peddle influence for money and sexual favors and frequently boasted in public about how much power he exercised over the imperial family. Because of the tsar's absence and Rasputin's salacious reputation, it was widely rumored that the mystic and the Empress were having an affair. While this innuendo was certainly untrue, it was nevertheless circulated and believed. Much of the antimonarchy propaganda that developed during the war involved pornographic depictions and insinuations involving the Empress and the mystic.

Publ ic perceptions of the monarchy were worsened by the plain fact that Rasputin's input had a serious impact on policy decisions and appointments. It is clear that the Empress trusted him implicitly, and together the two worked to oust responsible officials who objected to Rasputin's influence and presence at court, or who advocated reforms that would threaten the power of the throne. Unfortunately for Russia, many of these individuals were competent modernizers whose talents were sorely needed for the good of the country. Indeed, the mystic's chicanery contributed to the dismissal of Grand Duke Nicholas, who had once threatened to hang Rasputin if he came to headquarters. Although historians debate how deep Rasputin's influence truly was, there was nevertheless a pronounced correlation between Alexandra's conveyance of his advice to the tsar and Nicholas II's actual decisions about government appointments and sometimes even military matters. Before Tsar Nicholas had taken command of the army, Rasputin's presence at court had been barely tolerated and his political influence was nearly nonexistent. When Rasputin was eventually assassinated in December 1916, the murder was carried out by conservative defenders of the throne who included a first cousin of the tsar, his nephew by marriage, and a prominent right-wing politician.

The events of February 1917 revealed exactly how much the tsar's authority had deteriorated. When a series of strikes, bread riots, and political demonstrations created mass unrest in Petrograd toward the end of the month, the response of the government was totally inadequate. Unseasonably warm weather added to the crowds, and the situation quickly got out of hand. Nicholas II's response was a pure product of his absence at the front and the lack of effective communications. In the first critical days of the disturbances, when his personal leadership might still have made an impact, the tsar received only limited information from the capital and simply responded that the crowds should be dispersed. In other words, he reacted as if Petrograd were experiencing the same type of run-of-the-mill demonstrations that had happened before and could be controlled with relative ease. What he did not know was that there were hundreds of thousands of people in the streets and that neither the overwhelmed police nor the green army units in the capital were capable of restoring order or were even particularly willing to do so for his sake. By the time Nicholas realized that he should return to the capital, already several days after the initial reports had reached him, it was too late. Striking railroad workers stopped his train from approaching Petrograd. Isolated in the provincial city of Pskov in western Russia, he suddenly found himself confronted with delegations from his army commanders and the Duma informing him that he had no choice but to abdicate from the throne. Even before Nicholas issued his abdication manifesto, however, a committee of high-profile Duma members took "temporary power" as a Provisional Government. Most military units in the capital, including one commanded by another first cousin of the tsar, had already sworn allegiance to it, and most other army units quickly recognized its authority after the abdication. The traditional tsarist police and administrative apparatus disappeared almost overnight. The Russian monarchy had vanished.

Nicholas II was in many ways responsible for his own fall from power. Removing himself to military headquarters was foremost among his mistakes. Closed off to the home front, the crucial domestic political leadership that Russia needed was no longer forthcoming from its only recognized authority. In Nicholas's absence real power flowed from his suspiciously German wife and an unsavory peasant mystic, while total responsibility for military reverses rested squarely on the tsar's shoulders. Nicholas's effective departure from domestic government also surrendered ever more authority and legitimacy to the heretofore strictly controlled Duma and to other institutions of burgeoning civil society in late Imperial Russia. The final nail in the coffin came during the abdication crisis itself, when popular demonstrations with no far-reaching political goals revealed the inefficacy of the autocracy and provided an entrée for a new form of government. No one knew in early 1917 what that transition would mean for Russia and the world, but much of it originated with Nicholas II's de facto abdication from serious leadership in August 1915.

—PAUL DU QUENOY,
GEORGETOWN UNIVERSITY

Viewpoint:
No. The Russian military situation was so bad by late 1915 that decisions made by the tsar after that point had little bearing on the collapse of the empire.

When news of Nicholas II's decision to assume command of the Russian army reached his Council of Ministers, they warned him, almost unanimously, that this move was a grave error. The Russian ministers feared Nicholas's decision not only because the tsar was unschooled in military tactics and strategy but also because of the enormity of the crisis that confronted the Russian army by late summer 1915. Even worse than Nicholas's decision was his timing. The Great Retreat, begun under the

TSAR NICHOLAS II

blows of German general August von Mackensen's offensives in May, was nearing its climax. The withdrawal, or perhaps more accurately the evacuation, of Russian Poland and the westernmost lands of Russia was nearly complete. Only the fall *rasputitsa,* the quagmire of mud that defined Russian roads with the start of the seasonal rains, brought the German advance to a halt.

Since the opening of World War I, catastrophic losses had eviscerated the Russian army as a fighting force. The Russian system of divided command, replete with competing fronts, contradictory strategies, and jealous generals, was fatally flawed and the war all but lost by September of 1915 when Nicholas assumed command. Rifts between "traditionalists" (usually nobles) in the artillery and cavalry versus "innovators" (often of "plebian" origin) in the infantry seriously undermined combat operations. Army commanders often refused to talk to each other and sometimes even to their own chiefs of staff because of loyalty to one of these perspectives. Most infamously, the antagonism between Aleksandr Samsonov (an innovator) and Pavel Rennenkampf (a traditionalist) prevented their coordination of their advance into East Prussia with the tragedies of Tannenberg (1914) and the Masurian Lakes (1914) as the result.

Russian casualties in the first full year of war were staggering—1.5 million Russian troops had been killed, wounded, or taken prisoner by the end of 1914. Allan K. Wildman, in *The End of the Russian Imperial Army: The Old Army and the Soldiers' Revolt* (1980), noted that this figure represented nearly half of the prewar trained manpower and was especially devastating to the officer corps. Russia could never make good these losses. It could replace private soldiers with new conscripts, but the experience and training of both officers and men was never successfully duplicated. Even a commander in chief vastly more talented than Nicholas II could not provide men with the experience lost in the first year of the war. The most successful Russian general, Aleksey Brusilov, described the loss: "In a year of war, the regular army had vanished. It was replaced by an army of ignoramuses." By the end of 1915, before Nicholas's own actions and decisions could bear fruit for good or ill, total Russian casualties reached 3.8 million, an unimaginable figure made more concrete by one general's calculation that Russia had lost 300,000 men per month since the start of the war.

Even more crippling than the physical loss of such prodigious numbers of men was the psychological devastation. Dennis E. Showalter, in *Tannenberg: Clash of Empires* (1991), noted that such psychological damage was apparent as early as Tannenberg: the commanders and troops of the Northwest Front had marched into East Prussia confident in their two-to-one numerical superiority and believed in their forthcoming overwhelming victory. Therefore the disaster at Tannenberg was even more devastating to the Russian psyche than the physical loss alone.

Before Nicholas assumed command, replacements were rushed into combat without sufficient training, and frequently without weapons. Not surprisingly, these raw troops retreated rapidly before the well-oiled military machine of Germany. How they retreated revealed their commanders' (not the tsar's) incompetence.

In an illusory analogy to the Napoleonic invasion, Russian commanders incorporated "Moscow tactics" into their withdrawals in 1914–1915. These tactics included a scorched-earth policy that destroyed the best industry in Russia and generated an endless stream of refugees who streamed eastward, clogging roads, draining resources, and demoralizing citizens and soldiers alike.

This demoralization, however, was not the only problem Russia faced. Nicholas's political decision making before assuming military command had already hopelessly isolated him from his own government and alienated him from his people to a degree that made his subsequent military role inconsequential.

Despite the Great Retreat, patriotic Russians of genuine talent, ability, and loyalty rallied to the Russian cause. National, provincial, and municipal leaders developed plans to assist the state in its time of need; Nicholas's own ministers overcame their rivalries to present to him a united plan of action.

Members of the *Duma* (protoparliament), infamous for political infighting, overcame their differences to form a "Progressive Bloc" in early 1915. Oriented toward mobilizing the Russian economy and industry to support the war effort, this group represented an unprecedented union of almost 75 percent of the deputies into one alliance. By August the Bloc had developed a program of action that might have alleviated some of the worst logistics problems. At least cooperation with the Bloc might have reduced the growing rift between the tsar and his people, but Nicholas's prime minister refused to even hold conversations with Bloc representatives.

At the same time, the Union of Municipalities and the Zemstva Union, representatives of cities and provinces of Russia, convened a congress in Moscow to devise methods of supporting the war effort. Prince Georgy Lvov, renowned throughout Russia for his work in providing medical aid to wounded troops, called this congress "The moment . . . to establish a true alliance between the tsar and the people."

Prince Lvov was not the only prominent Russian to note the vitality of these movements or their decisive potential. Nicholas's own ministers urged compromise with the Bloc and the congress. They urged Nicholas to replace the aged Prime Minister Ivan Goremykin and at least negotiate to involve these popular representatives in solving the problems of the country. Instead, Nicholas replaced the most outspoken ministers and refused to talk to either the Bloc or the congress. This action made cooperation with the Duma impossible, alienated many of the last, most able supporters in the regime, and began the process of inserting malleable mediocrities into ministerial posts under the influence of Empress Alexandra and Grigory Rasputin—the infamous "ministerial leapfrog."

Nicholas's assumption of command is often condemned for increasing Alexandra's, and thereby Rasputin's, influence in government affairs. Her domination of Nicholas, and Rasputin's power over her, however, were already well established before his departure. She was Goremykin's champion and the Grand Duke Nicholas's (Nikolay Nikolayevich) enemy, with the devastating consequences of alienation and isolation shown by the Bloc and Congress decisions. Alexandra's alienation from the people, largely based on her German ancestry, was so pronounced that not even her genuinely dedicated hospital work for wounded soldiers could endear her to them. To argue that she would have had less influence over Nicholas and government affairs had he remained in the capital is moot.

Political decisions alienated the tsar from his people and isolated him from his own government. But it was the desperate inability of Russia to mobilize its industry to a war footing, at a cost of hundreds of thousands of casualties, that gutted the morale and ability of the army and ultimately broke its loyalty to the throne.

Russian soldiers marched into combat in 1914–1915 blind, dismounted, and, incredibly, often unarmed. Aerial reconnaissance, so vital given the vast distances and rapid pace of operations on the Eastern Front, was nearly impossible. Cavalry could no longer perform this traditional function rapidly enough. Even though Russia had 250 airplanes at the start of the war, lack of spare parts (and frequent shootdowns by Russian troops, who believed that only Germans could use such infernal contraptions) kept most aircraft grounded and Russian commanders blind.

Equally disabling was the complete absence of motorized transport. All supplies for the army were moved by horse and human power once they reached the railhead. No trucks of any kind existed in any significant numbers, and if they had, the complete lack of all-weather roads would have rendered them useless. Even German commanders remarked at how incredibly difficult logistics operations became once they advanced into railless and roadless Russian territory. Unlike the Germans, Russian quartermasters had nearly impossible problems of distance to solve as well. The average rifle bullet destined for a Russian soldier had to travel 4,000 kilometers from its source, and the average artillery shell 6,500 kilometers. These incredible distances were aggravated by the fact that two of every three artillery shells and one third of the rifle bullets fired by Russian troops through the end of 1916 came from Allied, not Russian, factories. No commander in chief could solve these problems alone.

The one great successful Russian effort, the Brusilov Offensive, came after Nicholas assumed command. War Minister Alexis Polivanov, under Nicholas's command, worked energetically with the War Industries committees and the Zemgor (Red Cross) to dramatically improve conditions in the Russian army during the winter of 1915–1916. By early 1916 well-trained recruits were armed, clothed, and fed better than their predecessors, and the troops' confidence was restored. A half million of these *Polivanovtsy* spearheaded Brusilov's thrust in the summer of 1916. That offensive ultimately failed because of the same problems of incompetent command (Generals Alexei Evert and Aleksey Kuropatkin to Brusilov's right) and impossible logistics that had plagued the army before Nicholas took charge. The last, best Russian effort at victory ground up the *Polivanovtsy* and their supplies, and the criminal incompetence of Evert, Kuropatkin, the Guards' commanders, and others finally broke the will of the long-suffering peasant troops. W. Bruce Lincoln, in *Passage Through Armageddon: The Russians in War and Revolution, 1914–1918* (1986), noted the testimony of one Guards' lieutenant about himself and his men: "We are willing to give our lives for Russia, for our Motherland, but not for the whims of generals." By the end of 1916 the army was broken, fully and irreparably. It was destroyed by incompetent generals, failed logistics, and the horrendous, grinding casualties it suffered from the opening days of the war. Nicholas's decision to take command paled in comparison.

–DAVID L. RUFFLEY,
U.S. AIR FORCE ACADEMY

References

Marc Ferro, *Nicholas II: The Last of the Tsars,* translated by Brian Pearce (New York: Viking, 1991).

Orlando Figes, *A People's Tragedy: The Russian Revolution, 1891–1924* (London: Cape, 1996).

Figes and Boris Kolonitskii, *Interpreting the Russian Revolution: The Language and Symbols of 1917* (New Haven: Yale University Press, 1999).

Martin Gilbert, *The First World War: A Complete History* (New York: Holt, 1994).

John Keegan, *The First World War* (London: Hutchinson, 1998).

W. Bruce Lincoln, *Passage Through Armageddon: The Russians in War and Revolution, 1914–1918* (New York: Simon & Schuster, 1986).

Robert K. Massie, *Nicholas and Alexandra* (New York: Atheneum, 1967).

Bernard Pares, *The Fall of the Russian Monarchy: A Study of the Evidence* (London: Cape, 1939; New York: Knopf, 1939).

Richard Pipes, *The Russian Revolution* (New York: Knopf, 1990).

Dennis E. Showalter, *Tannenberg: Clash of Empires* (Hamden, Conn.: Archon, 1991).

Allan K. Wildman, *The End of the Russian Imperial Army: The Old Army and the Soldiers' Revolt,* volume 1, *The Old Army and the Soldiers' Revolt (March–April 1917)* (Princeton: Princeton University Press, 1980).

U.S. ENTRY

Was the United States motivated to enter the war by self-interest?

Viewpoint: Yes. The Wilson administration realized that U.S. geopolitical interests were not best served by German hegemony in Europe.

Viewpoint: No. Woodrow Wilson believed that American entry into the Great War was a moral commitment to restructuring the world order so that a conflict of this nature could never happen again.

From the beginning of the Great War there was never a real chance of American participation on the side of the Central Powers. German-American support for the Fatherland and Irish-American distaste for the Sassenach (the Gaelic name for the "Saxon," or English, inhabitants of Great Britain) remained at rhetorical levels. For all the prewar rhetoric of comity between "the two great branches of the Anglo-Saxon race," no significant interventionist movement developed in the White Anglo-Saxon Protestant (WASP) sanctuaries of the East Coast. Despite an increasingly sophisticated Allied propaganda campaign, the American people manifested only moderate interest in World War I for its first two and a half years.

Nor was U.S. entry into the war determined by its economic relationship with the Allies. American involvement and contributions were important. By mid 1916, for example, the British Expeditionary Force (BEF) was receiving three-fourths of its light artillery shells from U.S. sources. France was nevertheless the real "arsenal of democracy" in World War I, with America valued as much for its ability to provide raw materials and its supply of finished goods. What brought the United States into the war were the calculated policies of President Woodrow Wilson.

Initially espousing neutrality, Wilson grew committed as the war progressed not only to shaping a peace but also to developing a future world order preventing similar conflicts by making the world safe for democracy and business. Wilson saw no contradiction between the two, but rather a symbiosis benefiting all participants. The president's focus was sharpened by an increasing conviction that U.S. security was vitally threatened by German domination of Europe. Steam had made the Atlantic Ocean for the United States what the English Channel had been for Britain: a barrier that could all too easily be overcome. Any expectations that a victorious Reich would prove a benevolent hegemon were challenged by a pattern of direct provocations that were both deliberate and clumsy. The submarine campaign; the Zimmermann telegram, with its rhetoric of undoing the results of the Mexican War (1846–1848); and the heavy-handed contempt with which the German government reacted to protests—by 1917 these factors had become impossible to ignore in an international climate offering no institutional means of resolving such issues and behaviors short of war.

On entering the war the Wilson administration continued to assert an independent status. The United States became not an allied state but an "associated power." The Fourteen Points that by late 1918 had achieved exalted status as far away as Bulgaria were issued as a distinctly American statement. Germany turned to the United States in its initial efforts to secure an armistice. Wilson's policy, however, depended ultimately on force rather than documents—in other words, on substantial, direct military participation in the principal theater of the war. Both to establish good faith during the war and to provide leverage for shaping the postwar settlement, millions of Americans were sent "over there."

Viewpoint:
Yes. The Wilson administration realized that U.S. geopolitical interests were not best served by German hegemony in Europe.

A great cliché of American history is that President Woodrow Wilson revolutionized foreign affairs by predicating the involvement of his country with the world on high moral and ethical convictions. Although the cerebral, sober, and academic Wilson was doubtlessly a man of high principle and determined moral conviction, many treatments of the foreign policy of his administration belie the sharp pragmatism of his approach. U.S. entry into World War I in 1917 was a foregone conclusion and an action that greatly served American military, political, and economic interests. Wilson's decision to side with the Allies was made almost exclusively with these considerations in mind.

As the leader of an emerging world power, Wilson found himself in a difficult position in 1914. The outbreak of war in Europe had enormous consequences for the burgeoning global role of the United States; yet, in many ways the American people had little inclination to go against President James Monroe's admonition in the early nineteenth century against looking for foreign monsters to slay. To many American observers, the war in Europe seemed to be a purely European affair, a conflict on the traditional European model with causes and stakes that had absolutely nothing to do with the United States and were certainly not worth American lives.

Nevertheless, a significant strain of public thought recognized the implicit danger of a reorganization of the international polity uninfluenced by U.S. interests and concerns. As soon as war broke out, former president Theodore Roosevelt called strenuously for American entry on the Allied side. For Roosevelt and many others, the prospect of a German victory was as horrible as it appeared to be likely. During his own presidency (1901–1909) he had to use "gunboat diplomacy" to prevent Germany from building economic, and possibly strategic, positions in Latin America and the Caribbean. He had also been in a position to observe the

growing German presence in China, a country where America wanted to keep an "open door" to free international trade. If Germany were willing to take steps toward violating the Monroe Doctrine (1823) when it was only one of several imperial powers, what might it try to do if it achieved a pan-European hegemony as a result of World War I? The international preeminence enjoyed by Britain in the decades before the war, moreover, had been remarkably free of confrontation with the United States, and in many instances the interests of the two maritime powers were complementary. How peaceful the international situation would remain should Germany supersede the British Empire was a difficult question.

Sitting in the Oval Office, Wilson could not ignore these concerns. Yet, he still had to perform a delicate balancing act. He was keenly aware that American public opinion would never support war unless there were either a clear provocation or an unambiguous threat to U.S. security. This sentiment characterized not only public opinion but also the belief of a significant faction of the Democratic Party, a grouping that included the chief cabinet official responsible for foreign affairs, Secretary of State William Jennings Bryan. In the absence of a clear reason to go to war, Wilson had to maintain American neutrality in order to secure reelection in 1916—a campaign that prominently featured the slogan "He Kept Us Out of War!" A unilateral and apparently uncalled-for entry into the conflict would have damaged Wilson's political credibility and led to a dangerous lack of domestic unity. Indeed, until Germany reintroduced unrestricted submarine warfare and attacked American ships in early 1917, Wilson almost certainly could not have received the necessary congressional mandate for a declaration of war.

His proneutrality rhetoric notwithstanding, Wilson's conduct of foreign affairs favored the Allies and prepared America for war on their side from the outset of the European conflict. As a growing maritime and commercial power, the United States could not avoid the effects of the conflict on international shipping and the law of the seas. The first involvement of the United States in the war grew out of its responses to the British naval blockade of German ports and to the German submarine cam-

American troops donning gas masks

(postcard in scrapbook, Joseph M. Bruccoli Great War Collection, Thomas Cooper Library, University of South Carolina)

paign against maritime traffic inbound to Britain. From the first days of the war the Royal Navy stopped and searched neutral ships, including U.S. vessels, for contraband goods in transit to the Central Powers. Although this practice represented a clear violation of neutral rights, particularly as the list of contraband goods was expanded to include food and other materials intended purely for civilian use, the Wilson administration made only muted protests. Its international law expert, State Department official Robert Lansing, later admitted that he unnecessarily complicated and prolonged blockade disputes with Britain deliberately so that the British could extricate themselves and continue to strangle German international trade.

While the British encountered practically no resistance from the United States to their blockade tactics, Germany resorted with increasing desperation to submarine attacks on British shipping. Even before American lives were lost to German U-boats, Wilson categorically declared that Germany would be held accountable for endangering U.S. citizens. The deaths of 128 Americans traveling on the British passenger ship *Lusitania*, sunk on 7 May 1915, drew sharp condemnation from Wilson; he demanded that Germany refrain from attacking civilian passenger ships. Although any American president is bound to defend the lives of his countrymen through diplomacy, Wil-

son's response was disingenuous in several ways. The *Lusitania* was carrying contraband ammunition to Britain (one of the reasons it sank so easily), and the Germans had published an open letter in *The New York Times* informing the traveling public that the ship was a target for submarine attacks. The imbalance between Wilson's response to the *Lusitania* sinking and the tightening British blockade, furthermore, became obvious even to proneutrality members of the administration. Secretary of State Bryan resigned when Wilson refused to balance his condemnation of Germany with an equally sharp condemnation of British activity. Lansing, who made no secret of his pro-Allied bias, was appointed to replace him.

With Bryan's departure, the Wilson administration quickly began to talk of war. When the Germans sank another passenger liner in August 1915, an incident in which two Americans died, Lansing tartly informed the German government that if it failed to stop its submarine policy, it could expect a declaration of war. Germany immediately apologized and promised to comply with Lansing's demand, but when the passenger liner *Sussex* was sunk the following spring (24 March), President Wilson made the even stronger demand that Germany refrain from attacking merchant ships, too. If the German government failed to comply, Wilson threatened to break diplomatic relations. For a time the German government moderated its submarine attacks, believing that it might achieve a decisive victory in 1916 (the year of Verdun) without having to rely on a full, provocative blockade of Britain. By January 1917, however, unsuccessful in its land operations, Germany again reinstituted unrestricted submarine warfare, this time believing that if it could not force a decision in France, it could at least starve Britain to the breaking point before any potential American intervention could occur. Without even waiting for another ship to be sunk, Wilson made good on his pledge to break diplomatic relations. After the loss of five ships in March 1917, he asked Congress for a declaration of war.

Wilson's conduct between the *Sussex* incident and the declaration of war is revealing, for it betrays his implicit willingness to involve the United States in the conflict. In the summer of 1916 he used all political means at his disposal to defeat a congressional measure to bar Americans from sailing on the ships of combatant powers. In March 1917, after he severed relations with Germany, Wilson ignored congressional prohibitions and ordered the arming of American merchant ships. In the first instance Wilson worked to allow Americans to continue traveling abroad in harm's way. In the second he defied Congress to place American ships in potential firefights with German naval units. Neither policy was characteristic of a man who wanted to preserve the neutrality of his country and only reluctantly stirred to teach the world a moral lesson.

If the situation at sea indicated a clear American bias against the Central Powers and, therefore, against the prospective hegemony of Germany over continental Europe, the approach of the United States to international economics was also an important indication of where its sympathies lay and what its interests truly were. When the scale and cost of World War I grew beyond all expectations, the combatants had to look to world financial markets for loans and credits. As the most prosperous neutral power (and, arguably, the greatest economic power overall), the United States had the potential to become the chief creditor to belligerent nations. Indeed, by 1918 America completely reversed its prewar financial position, erased its substantial foreign debts, and had actually lent the world slightly more than it had owed four years earlier.

Wilson's policies did much to contribute to this transformation, and he carried out the necessary policies knowing that they would benefit the Allies to an inestimably greater degree than the Central Powers. Before the war American banks had conducted much more trade and maintained much closer financial relationships with Allied businesses and institutions than they had with those of Germany and Austria-Hungary. The chief architect of American war finance, the banker and industrialist John Pierpont Morgan, had openly favored the Allied cause from the beginning. Therefore the Allies would be expected to benefit in an unbalanced way from American financial help. After Wilson allowed U.S. banks to offer credits to the combatant nations at the outbreak of war and direct loans after October 1915, more than 90 percent of the available American lending capital—totaling more than $2 billion—flowed to Britain and France.

Even as Wilson's willingness to overlook diplomatic incidents and fill the British and French war chests helped the Allied cause, the health of the American industrial and manufacturing economy became a major factor influencing his decision to go to war. America had always conducted more trade with the Allies—the British Empire was its largest trading partner before 1914—and thus stood to lose heavily if those nations were either defeated by Germany or too drained by standing alone in the conflict to carry on as major economic powers afterward. Preferential treatment for Britain and France was therefore predetermined by existing commercial trends. American exports to the Allies roughly doubled in each year of the conflict while trade with Germany essentially stopped after war had broken out. As Wilson astutely realized, the future health of the American economy was tied to the success of the Allied war effort. The war at sea intersected with this factor, because while the British blockade of Germany was virtually impenetrable and for all practical purposes ended its maritime trade, the German submarine blockade of Britain was highly porous. Even in their most successful month of April 1917, when U-boats sank more than 860,000 tons of shipping inbound to Britain, supplies still flowed across the Atlantic from American ports.

The final and most far-reaching factor that edged Wilson toward war was the prospective peace settlement and how it would have played out without American involvement in the conflict. If the Allies had been able to vanquish Germany on their own—or with only an assist from benevolent American neutrality—it would have been the traditional European powers who set the agenda in the postwar world. Despite its growing economic power, the absence of the United States from the war would have left it without a voice in international affairs. For an emerging world power, this prospect was intolerable. Surely the victorious Allies would have restructured the world to their own advantage without any regard for American interests.

A GROWING CANCER

On 13 June 1917 at Union College in New York, former president William Howard Taft, who was then a professor of law at Yale University, gave an address on U.S. involvement in the war in Europe. A portion of that address appears below:

The issue at present is drawn between the democracies of the world and the military dynasties, and people like to characterize that as the issue. It is and it isn't. What I mean by that is: The United States is not a knight-errant country going about to independent people and saying, "We do not like your form of government, we have tried our own popular government and we think it is better for you to take it." That is a very unreasonable position, in so far as that form of government deals with only their domestic pursuits and their domestic happiness. If they like to have a Czar, if they prefer it, why, it isn't for us to take away their freedom of will. Otherwise we shall go back to the logic of the Inquisition, when they burned people in this world so that they might not burn in the next.

But when their form of government involves a policy which does not confine its opinions to the people who make the government or support it, but becomes a visible policy against the welfare and happiness of the rest of the world family, we have a right and a duty, standing with other nations as we do, to see to it that such a foreign policy is stopped and stamped out forever.

I will not minimize or confuse. Germany is not exhausted. That machine which it has been creating for fifty years is a wonderful machine. . . .

This militarism is a cancer which must be cut out by a surgical operation. It shows its malignant character in the utter disregard of the rules of war. It shows itself in the violation of Belgium; in the violation of the Hague treaties, which forbid the dropping of explosives out of aërial craft, the planting of mines, the use of asphyxiating gases and flames, all spread out in The Hague treaties, and all violated promptly by this German military machine.

It is therefore a cancer which would absorb the wholesome life of the world unless it is cut out, and necessitates suffering and pain in ridding the world of it. There are other evidences of divine plan. Think of the battle of the Marne, where this matchless machine began to find France and England unprepared, and they turned at the Marne when the German hosts with their guns were heard in Paris, and by mere moral force they turned those German legions back. Think of the blindness of this absorption of gross materialism as brought into the intellect of the Germans.

They cannot understand other people. They cannot recognize a moral force that binds people together in a cause. They said England will not stand by Belgium; it has trouble with Ireland; they said France is torn with Socialism and it is a decadent nation. In both cases they made blunders. They said as regards Canada, Australia, New Zealand, and South Africa, England has no control of them by force; they are far removed from it and will follow the path of materialism and gain; they will follow where profit determines; they will not be held. And yet, nothing has been grander than this light bond which unites England with these independent dependencies, and they have rallied to the support of the mother country, responded out of gratitude for the liberty that it conferred upon them, and they have made sacrifices which call for our profound admiration.

Source: *Charles F. Horne,* Source Records of the Great War, *volume 5 (Indianapolis: American Legion, 1930), pp. 121–123.*

Their intention to do so had become known as early as May 1916, when the agenda of an inter-Allied economic conference considered responses to the American role in the postwar world. Wary of the newcomer's growing economic and political clout, the Allied representatives agreed to use aggressive protectionism in their trade and finance policies to prevent American dominance after peace was restored. Given the Allied aims in World War I, this plan was no small threat. In the event of an Allied victory, the Central Powers would almost certainly have been dismantled as states and had their colonies and other territories transferred to the administration or influence of the victorious powers. Indeed, a watered-down version of this policy was advocated even with the American presence at the peace conference. An expanded hegemony controlled by Britain, France, Italy, and Russia to the exclusion of the United States would certainly have been of no benefit to long-term American economic and strategic interests. No responsible president could ignore the magnitude of this threat to the U.S. world position in the future, and indeed Wilson did not. Almost immediately, he took steps to ease antitrust and banking laws so that American firms could become more competitive in foreign markets. Wilson's desire to influence the peace settlement played a critical role in his increasing willingness to risk conflict situations with Germany and gear American foreign and economic policy toward war.

Wilson's good intentions, honest belief in the superiority of democracy, and personal ethics did not override, nor disqualify pragmatic factors. If he had wanted to pursue a moral high ground, he would have taken quite a different course. He could have avoided the maritime controversies; kept American citizens as far out of the combat zone as possible; refused to supply any of the belligerents with arms, money, and other supplies; and disregarded the potential consequences of a world peace settlement made in the absence of American influence. Yet, to do so would have betrayed the long-term interests of the United States and over time compromised the peace and prosperity of its people. In the end Wilson chose not to do that.

—PAUL DU QUENOY,
GEORGETOWN UNIVERSITY

Viewpoint:
No. Woodrow Wilson believed that American entry into the Great War was a moral commitment to restructuring the world order so that a conflict of this nature could never happen again.

One cannot seriously argue that President Woodrow Wilson did not believe that he was on a crusade to save the world. His entire career was a testimony to his belief in the power of reform. Domestically, as one of the great figures of the Progressive Era, Wilson instituted a series of impressive reforms. Internationally, Wilson vigorously and consistently argued for and helped to create a world along the lines of his ideology. The enduring legacy of his career has been that American policy since World War I has been to establish, strengthen, and defend a Wilsonian system.

Wilson envisioned a world that was made up of liberal democratic states practicing free-market trade, submitting to the rule of law as represented in multilateral bodies, and also recognizing the right to self-determination. One may or may not agree with these principles, but they have officially stood as the basis for American policy since the signing of the Atlantic Charter (1941). They also were publicly proclaimed to be Wilson's policy on 8 January 1918, when he articulated them to the U.S. Congress in his Fourteen Points speech. He fought doggedly to protect these points as the basis of his policy until his death.

Of course, there is room to criticize Wilson for failing to live up to his professed ideals. The man who promoted liberal reforms in the United States, for example, was the same man who allowed segregation of blacks on federal property. Similarly, many of his proposed policies did not make it into the final version of the peace treaty in 1919. The call for "open covenants, openly arrived at," would be eliminated first. The sheer complexity of a peace settlement made it virtually impossible for the Paris Peace Conference to negotiate in the open. Had it been done so, no doubt the negotiations would have dragged on for years. British and French vengefulness also contributed to the exclusion of the German delegations from the negotiations at Paris. Wilson's own particularly strict morality inclined him to see the Germans as guilty for causing the war. This viewpoint colored his willingness to see the peace as one that should punish the Germans, who then would see the error of their ways and submit to the new order being drawn up among the Big Four of Wilson, David Lloyd George, Georges Clemenceau, and Vittorio Orlando.

Yet, despite the vengeful elements of the peace treaty, Wilson's actions seem to indicate that moralistic tendencies motivated him. Wilson had refused to bring along Republican representatives from the U.S. Senate as he and his panel of experts sailed off to France for the peace conference because he did not wish his vision for a better world to be sullied by others who might challenge him. Similarly, he eased up on the issue of national self-determination for British and French colonies because he wanted Paris and London to cooperate in the League of Nations. The League, in Wilson's view, was the device that would persist past the years of bitterness that naturally followed the end of war and that would, in the end, right the wrongs of the world system. This faith was what made the president willing to fight the U.S. Senate to the bitter end to ratify the treaty.

Wilson arrived on the world stage in 1917 with a program of reform to fix the problems that he believed caused the Great War. His program would remove those practices, address the grievances of the oppressed, and offer hope for the future without Great Power rivalries between the elites at the expense of ordinary people. Wilson's vision was for a new world: even the language of the treaty reflected this sense that Americans were somehow above the fray. The treaty always referred to the "Allied and Associated Powers," where the United States was understood to be the "Associated Power." The new Wilsonian world would be characterized by free trade, multilateralism, and democracy. The lack of such a system was the underlying cause of the clash of empires that eventually unleashed a world war in 1914. The message carried well in Europe, where people in all countries hoped for and believed in the Wilsonian peace plan. The German delegation fully expected that they would be part of a peace conference that would follow Wilsonian lines.

Wilson promised more than he could deliver. The war was won by the efforts of the French and British, and their wishes could not be ignored at the peace conference. National self-determination would be only something forced upon the empires of those who lost the war, not upon Britain and France. Nor could French and British aspirations for more colonies, now shrouded in the mantle of "League Mandates," be ignored. Moreover, the mandate system held the potential of actually living up to its professions of providing for eventual independence of the supervised countries. Indeed, independence was granted in a few cases. Wilson could not simply steamroll his allies and force their agreement to his program, for their cooperation in the League was crucial to its success. Just as he would with the Senate, Wilson refused to budge on the issue of the League; he was forced to compromise on other issues of his program in order to protect that which he held as most important. Because he could not deliver on all his dreams does not mean that he did not truly hold them to be proper goals. Rather, he suffered from the all-too-common problem of one's reach exceeding one's grasp.

–PHIL GILTNER,
U.S. MILITARY ACADEMY

References

John W. Coogan, *The End of Neutrality: The United States, Britain, and Maritime Rights, 1899–1915* (Ithaca, N.Y.: Cornell University Press, 1981).

Walter LaFeber, *The American Age: Foreign Policy at Home and Abroad,* volume 2, *Since 1896,* second edition (New York: Norton, 1994).

Robert Lansing, *War Memoirs of Robert Lansing, Secretary of State* (Indianapolis: Bobbs-Merrill, 1935).

Ernest R. May, *World War and American Isolation, 1914–1917* (Cambridge, Mass.: Harvard University Press, 1959).

Carl P. Parrini, *Heir to Empire: United States Economic Diplomacy, 1916–1923* (Pittsburgh: University of Pittsburgh Press, 1969).

VERDUN

Did the Germans hope to achieve a military or a political goal at the Battle of Verdun?

Viewpoint: The Battle of Verdun marked an attempt by General Erich von Falkenhayn to defeat the French army by means of attrition.

Viewpoint: The German goal at Verdun was to force France out of the war by convincing the government that victory was impossible.

The Battle of Verdun (1916) originated in German chief of staff Erich von Falkenhayn's conclusion that little chance existed in the foreseeable future of either concluding a separate peace with Russia or directly forcing England out of World War I. France was another story. In his 1919 memoirs Falkenhayn cites a "Christmas memorandum" he allegedly submitted to the Kaiser in 1915. No trace of this document has ever been recovered; the chances are good that Falkenhayn wrote it after the war. Nevertheless, it represents accurately the Chief of Staff's thinking at the turn of the year, as expressed in a series of minutes and meetings. Falkenhayn described France as being at the limits of its endurance militarily and economically. The optimal German strategy was therefore to drive France out of the war—not by seeking a decisive breakthrough in the style of the early years of the war but by choosing an objective for whose retention the French would have to commit their total remaining resources. Two such sites existed: Belfort and Verdun. The latter, close to a major German rail line, seemed a more-promising choice.

The issue of whether Falkenhayn proposed to defeat France by bleeding its army white in the trenches, or by convincing the French government and people that the war was unwinnable, remains a subject of controversy. What is certain is that on 21 February 1916 more than 1,200 German guns opened fire on French positions around the city. After a week the Germans had advanced six miles, taking Fort Douaumont without resistance. With their backs to the wall, however, the French began to develop a defense in depth that first stalled the offensive, then stalemated it. Fort Vaux, one of the keystones of the resistance, fell on 8 June. On 23 June the Germans got close enough to Verdun to bring the city under machine-gun fire. Yet, the French line held and counterattacked; on 14 July, Falkenhayn halted the operation. The British attack on the Somme and the "Brusilov offensive" on the Eastern Front were making more-pressing demands on an overstrained German war effort.

Falkenhayn paid for his miscalculation with the loss of his job, being relieved and demoted to an army command. The French army, which from first to last rotated three-fourths of its divisions through the sector, mounted a series of limited counterattacks, retaking Douaumont and Vaux and recovering most of the lost ground by mid December. Losses were roughly equal for both sides: around 300,000 for the French and 325,000 for the Germans. The moral effects of the battle, however, lasted long after the end of the Great War.

Viewpoint:
The Battle of Verdun marked an attempt by General Erich von Falkenhayn to defeat the French army by means of attrition.

In the horror of the Great War, there are several battles that stand out for their higher-than-average casualties and their seeming senselessness—Ypres (1914), the Somme (1916), Verdun (1916), and Passchendaele (1917) are all names that scar the collective consciousness of European nations even today. In these battles, soldiers on each side gave their lives on a scale profligate even by the standards of a war that demanded manpower on such an unprecedented rate. For instance, at the battle of the Somme 60,000 British soldiers were killed or wounded on the first day alone. By the time the battle had ended five months later, the British had suffered 420,000 casualties, the French around 195,000, and the Germans somewhere near 600,000. However, of these battles only one was designed from the beginning as a means of deliberately killing as many enemy soldiers as possible and, as such, was a unique approach to warfare—Verdun.

The Battle of Verdun was the brainchild of Erich von Falkenhayn, who as Chief of the German General Staff from September 1914 was the de facto commander of the German army. Falkenhayn developed his plan as a response to the difficult strategic position in which Germany found itself in 1916.

The failure of the plan for a short war in late 1914 left Germany fighting against enemies superior in manpower on two fronts. Although it could hold the lines defensively and even gain notable successes against Russia, Falkenhayn was convinced that he needed a new means of bringing the war to an end on German terms. To remain on the defensive would mean a slow defeat for Germany as food supplies and other resources were gradually running out because of the Entente blockade. In late 1915 Falkenhayn informed the chancellor, Theobold von Bethmann Hollweg, that he did not think Germany had the resources to survive another year of war. Offensives on the Eastern Front had resulted in gains of territory, but the Russian Empire steadfastly refused to form a separate peace with Germany, and its army merely retreated into the vastness of its territory to avoid being annihilated. Russia was just too big a foe to be defeated by Germany. Therefore victory, in Falkenhayn's conclusion, would have to come on the Western Front, where he believed the weakest of the Entente powers—France—was

to be found. Falkenhayn felt this way for several reasons. First, from his prewar experiences he believed French officials to be excessively sensitive to public opinion and, hence, politically weak. Second, relative to the other powers, France was low on manpower. Before the war it had conscripted 85 percent of its eligible manpower into the army. Much of this strength had been sacrificed in the war to date, and German intelligence estimated that the French army in late 1915 was smaller than it had been at the outbreak of the war. Third, France had already lost a good portion of territory and did not have the space to withdraw its troops much further. Unlike the Russians, French forces could not run away in the face of a German offensive; they would have to stand, fight, and suffer casualties that could not be replaced. Thus, by the end of 1915, Falkenhayn chose France as the target for what he hoped would be a war-deciding attack early in 1916.

After deciding on the target of his offensive, Falkenhayn needed to figure out how to conduct his attack. He knew that Germany did not have the manpower resources to put together a reserve large enough to break through the defensive lines on the Western Front and to defeat the Entente forces badly enough for them to sue for peace. Despite his best efforts, only twenty-five divisions could be assembled. Anything more than this amount and the defensive lines on both fronts would be too lightly held to withstand an enemy counterattack. The massive British and French attacks in 1915 had shown that twenty-five divisions were insufficient to break through modern field positions. Further, even if this force could break through the Entente trench lines, it would not be strong enough to engage the enemy in decisive battle before they could form new defensive positions. Therefore, another means would have to be found to bring the war to an end.

In the face of these battlefield difficulties, Falkenhayn developed a sophisticated and unique response. Rather than attempt a breakthrough and a subsequent battle to annihilate the French forces, Falkenhayn planned to make use of what he saw as German strengths against French weaknesses in a new type of battle. He planned to attack a section of the front and threaten an object for which the French command would feel compelled to throw in every last man to defend. In these counterattacks, Falkenhayn believed, the French army would "bleed itself white," to use his gruesome phraseology. He felt that by inflicting such high casualties, the French people would recognize that the war could only be won at an unacceptably high price. Falkenhayn contended that it would

**French machine-gun crew
in Fort Vaux at Verdun**

(from John Keegan, An Illustrated
History of the First World War
[2001])

force the French people to pressure their government into making peace with the Germans.

There remained the choice of where to launch his offensive. Falkenhayn toyed with the idea of attacking the fortress town of Belfort, not far from the Franco-Swiss border. However, he soon recognized that the French would not fight tooth and nail for this town. Additionally, the lines of communication leading to the area were insufficient to supply a major offensive. Instead, Falkenhayn chose the fortress city of Verdun. This town lay at the middle of a great salient in the lines of the German Fifth Army almost in the center of the Western Front. In 1914 the local French commander had refused an order from his superiors to surrender the fortress to the advancing Germans and had thus fired the popular imagination of the French people. Moreover, the loss of the fortress would weaken the entire French defensive position. It could not be surrendered in 1916 without creating a political storm in France and without causing serious harm to the defense of the country. Additionally, unlike Belfort, there were good roads and rail routes to the area, and the position of the city was favorable for a German offensive. Being in a salient meant that German artillery could fire into the area from three sides and could potentially range over the entire area.

This strategy, then, gave Falkenhayn the method by which the French would bleed themselves white.

Although the popular image of death and destruction in World War I is the machine gun, in fact, the vast majority of casualties were the result of artillery fire. Falkenhayn had seen how devastating artillery fire could be to an attacking force during the course of the German defensive battles on the Western Front in 1915. During these battles, weak German forces were able to defend themselves against far superior enemy forces by the effective use of artillery. Now, he intended to make use of this power as a means of killing French soldiers during his own offensive in 1916.

Verdun is dominated by high ground to the north and to the east of the city. Falkenhayn planned for the Fifth Army to launch a limited attack, well supported with artillery, to seize the dominating heights to the east of the city on the right bank of the Meuse River. There, the German offensive would halt. From the commanding heights, the Germans would have good defensive positions and would still be able to dominate the fortress and the surrounding area with artillery fire. The Fifth Army was to dig in and bring up additional artillery to resist the counterattacks Falkenhayn believed the

THEY SHALL NOT PASS

The next morning a formidable rumor—the Boches are coming up to assault Fort de Vaux. The newspapers have told the facts; our 75s firing for six hours, the German bodies piling up in heaps. Horrible! but we applauded. Everybody went out of the trenches to look. The Yser, said the veterans, was nothing beside this massacre.

That time I saw Germans fleeing like madmen. The next day, the same thing over again; they have the cynicism to mount a battery on the slope; the German chiefs must be hangmen to hurl their troops to death that way in masses and in broad daylight. All afternoon, a maximum bombardment; a wood is razed, a hill ravaged with shell-holes. It is maddening; continuous salvos of "big chariots": one sees the 380's and 420's falling; a continuous cloud of smoke everywhere. Trees leap into the air like wisps of straw; it is an unheard-of spectacle. It is enough to make you lose your head, yet we patiently wait for the outcome.

The barrage fire cuts our communications with the rear, literally barring off the isthmus of Death Ravine. If the attacks on our wings succeed, our two regiments are prisoners, hemmed in, but the veterans (fathers of families) declare that we shall not be taken alive, that we will all fight till we die. It is sublime.

"Keep up your courage, coolness, and morale, boys, and we will drive them back in good time."

It is magnificent to see that our last recourse is a matter of sheer will; despite this monstrous machinery of modern war, a little moral effort, a will twenty years old that refuses to weaken, suffices to frustrate the offensive! The rifles do not shoot enough, but we have machine guns, the bayonet, and we have vowed that they shall not pass. Twenty times the alarm is given; along the hillside one sees the hands gripping the rifles; the eyes are a little wild, but show an energy that refuses to give way.

A whole section shoots. But are the outposts driven in? Nobody knows. I take my rifle to go and see. I do not catch a ball. I find the sentinels flat on their faces in their holes, and run to the rear gesticulating and crying out orders to cease firing. The men obey. I return to the front, and soon, a hundred yards away, I see a bush scintillate with a rapid line of fire. This time it is they. Ta-ca-ta-ca, bzzi—bzzi. I hold my fire until they approach, but the welcome evidently does not please them, for they tumble back over the ridge, leaving some men behind. One wounded cries, "Frantchmen!"

I am drunk, mad. Something moves in the bushes to the right; I bound forward with set bayonet. It is my brave sergeant, who has been out to see whether the Boches have all run away. These are truly the most interesting moments of war; no longer the waiting, the anguish of bombardment, but the thrill of a free march into a glorious unknown—oh, that intoxication! I sing the "Marseillaise," the boys jubilate, all the successive attacks have failed. After this evening the offensive is going to slacken for several days.

Source: *Charles F. Horne, ed., Source Records of the Great War, volume 4 (Indianapolis: American Legion, 1930), pp. 227–228.*

French would inevitably launch to relieve the beleaguered fortress.

Falkenhayn, though, quickly ran into difficulties. His plan was so radical that he was never able to convey it to his subordinates fully. The commander of the Fifth Army, Crown Prince Wilhelm, and his chief of staff, Constantin Schmidt von Knobelsdorf, raised objections to Falkenhayn's plan. First, they did not have faith in Falkenhayn's planned attrition of the French. They believed that their army should conduct an operation that stuck to traditional goals—a breakthrough followed by some type of decisive battle fought in the open. In keeping with this goal, they believed that the offensive should be widened to include the heights north of Verdun on the left bank of the Meuse River. While Falkenhayn was able to order the commanders of the Fifth Army to restrict their assault to the heights on the right bank of the Meuse, he was unable to change their beliefs in what the operation should accomplish. His idea of bleeding the French army required his forces

VERDUN

to be sparing of the lives of their own troops. A breakthrough required his troops to exert themselves to the utmost to overwhelm the French defenses. Thus, Falkenhayn faced the difficult task of keeping his attacking forces in line with his mission. As the operation wore on and the French will to continue the war did not collapse as Falkenhayn had hoped it would, his goals became increasingly more ambitious as well and more in line with those of the Fifth Army. After all, if the offensive did not result in the defeat of France, he hoped that it would at least result in the capture of a strategically important site.

Falkenhayn also overestimated the abilities of German forces and underestimated those of the French forces. He had assumed that the Fifth Army would be able to take the heights on the right bank of the Meuse within several days by means of a limited offensive. The capture of these commanding heights was essential for Falkenhayn's plan. The delay of the launching of the initial assault by poor weather in mid February tipped off the French to the offensive and allowed them crucial time to reinforce their positions. When the German attack came on 21 February, they were better prepared and were able to hold up the German advance. The Fifth Army was never able to reach the heights it needed to dominate the battlefield. The French kept possession of this position and used it to call down artillery fire upon the attacking Germans. Moreover, just as the commanders of the Fifth Army had predicted, the heights on the left bank of the Meuse also proved to be positions from which the French could dominate the German attack routes. Falkenhayn was forced to widen his offensive to include these positions, but like the heights on the right bank, the Germans were never able to expel the French.

With the commanding heights not in the possession of German forces, Falkenhayn's unique plan of creating an artillery killing zone into which the French would have to attack was in ruins. Rather than abandon his offensive, however, Falkenhayn tried to salvage something from the ruins. He believed, despite the failure of his initial plan, that his goal of exhausting the French army could still be reached. Falkenhayn and members of his staff were convinced that the Fifth Army was inflicting far higher casualties upon the French than they were themselves suffering. Thus, the offensive at Verdun took a new twist once the initial plan had failed. Falkenhayn ordered the Fifth Army to continue its attacks to force the French to counterattack. In this way, he hoped that French manpower resources would be exhausted before German ranks were depleted themselves.

The fact that Falkenhayn's strategy of attrition failed at Verdun does not detract from its uniqueness. Never before in the history of warfare had one opponent striven to bring about peace by targeting the manpower resources of the enemy. Not strong enough to achieve a decisive victory in a traditional battle, Falkenhayn attempted instead to make use of German strength (artillery tactics) to strike at what was a French weakness (its manpower). Falkenhayn calculated, perhaps not wrongly given the mutinies within the French army less than a year after the end of the Battle of Verdun, that the French would not be able to sustain high casualties. He believed that the loss of so many young Frenchmen would force the populace to apply influence on their government to make peace. In Falkenhayn's plan, tactical operations were to have a strategic effect and French democracy was to be its ultimate downfall.

–ROBERT T. FOLEY,
KING'S COLLEGE, LONDON

Viewpoint:
The German goal at Verdun was to force France out of the war by convincing the government that victory was impossible.

Erich von Falkenhayn initially viewed the plans for the Battle of Verdun (1916) in a negative light. By November 1915 he was convinced the opportunity for Germany to negotiate peace with Russia had passed and that the war as a whole had degenerated into exactly the kind of protracted struggle for survival the General Staff and the War Ministry had spent decades insisting Germany could not win. The focal point of the Allied coalition was Great Britain, the state Falkenhayn had long described as the most dangerous and implacable enemy of the Second Empire. A direct blow at the island kingdom was impossible. The German navy, on which so much wealth had been lavished, was still too weak to risk a decisive battle. For the next year Falkenhayn recommended an unrestricted submarine campaign, both to diminish the imports on which the British war effort depended and perhaps to goad the Royal Navy into risking a surface encounter on German terms. That goal, however, was only one pole of his proposed strategy. France, Falkenhayn insisted, was "England's tool on the continent," its

VERDUN

"continental sword." Should it be broken, or stricken from British hands, the European position of Germany was assured.

Falkenhayn extended his argument by describing the vulnerabilities of France. With a population two-thirds that of Germany, its war losses had been even larger. Some of its major resource and industrial centers were under German occupation. The labile, emotional French people were growing collectively tired of the war. At the same time France was directly vulnerable in a way Britain and Russia were not. Within German reach, immediately behind the front, there were objectives for which the French army would have to commit every man it could muster. Paradoxically, the internal weaknesses Falkenhayn postulated would make such a commitment all the more necessary; the politicians and generals lacked the popular support for hard decisions. Germany, on the other hand, because its objectives had no moral significance, would be in a position to take as much or as little of the action as it wished.

Such an option would mean recovery of an initiative lost with the collapse of the Schlieffen Plan. It also represented a response to new operational and tactical realities. The Allied offensives in the West during 1915, Falkenhayn argued, had shown that frontal breakthroughs were no longer possible. The continuous front from the North Sea to Flanders precluded even small-scale flanking movements. In its early outline form, Falkenhayn's proposal was a feint, an economy-of-force measure. Attack on a narrow front, he insisted. Draw the French onto morally vital ground and then use German superiority in firepower and small-unit tactics to make it a killing ground.

The exact sector required careful thought. Falkenhayn ruled out Flanders as too constricted and Alsace as too mountainous. The front in central France did not offer the kinds of psychological objectives his proposed operation required. Falkenhayn's options finally came down to two fortress cities with long-standing importance—Belfort and Verdun. Belfort was too close to the Swiss border to provide the geographic flexibility for the kind of cut-and-thrust fighting Falkenhayn initially desired. Verdun won by default.

The more Falkenhayn considered it, the better the Verdun option appeared. The fortress had been demilitarized at the start of the war; only the concrete shells of the outer defenses remained. German advances in 1914, however, had left Verdun in an operational salient, susceptible to attack on two sides. Its road and rail links to the rest of France were minimal. Germany, on the other hand, controlled more than a dozen rail lines on its side of the front.

Political factors may have influenced the Chief of Staff as well. Since the start of the war, German emperor Wilhelm II had been reduced to a figurehead—so much so that there had been talk of appointing Falkenhayn's bitter rival Paul von Hindenburg as "Reich caretaker." Verdun lay in the sector of the army group nominally commanded by Wilhelm's heir. A war-deciding victory won under the auspices of Crown Prince Wilhelm would give the Hohenzollern dynasty a badly needed lift.

Falkenhayn's plans for Verdun, in short, must be understood in policy contexts to make sense of their military aspects. Verdun was what movie director Alfred Hitchcock would later call a "Macguffin": an object valueless in itself around which the real story could be constructed. Falkenhayn later stated that he never intended to capture Verdun at all. His instructions spoke of an attack "in the direction of" Verdun. His frequently stated idea of bleeding the French army to death was not intended to weaken the front directly to a point where a breakthrough became possible. He therefore rejected the original proposal of the Crown Prince and his staff to mount an attack on a larger scale than Falkenhayn intended, an attack on both sides of the Meuse River. By Falkenhayn's calculation an expanded offensive would cost Germany as many lives and resources as it would France. That option was one Germany could not afford in the overall context of the war. Victory to Falkenhayn meant disrupting the government and destabilizing society—perhaps to a point of actual collapse but in any case to an extent compelling France to see reason and seek peace on German terms.

Seen from a perspective nearly a century later, Falkenhayn's strategy worked better than perhaps even he realized. Verdun, a previously obscure frontier city, became almost overnight a symbol of France at war. Three-fourths of the French army eventually passed through the Verdun sector, following a policy designed to share the strain among divisions as opposed to feeding replacements into units on the spot. Certainly, neither public nor political morale cracked immediately. There is a solid connection between the experiences of the nation at Verdun and a growing general disillusion with the war, which nurtured General Robert Nivelle's promise in the spring of 1917 to bring victory by just one more general offensive—which came close to breaking the army and badly shook the home front as well.

What went wrong was arguably Falkenhayn's own lack of moral courage. He expected high casualties—very high casualties. And he never mustered the will to tell his generals, much less his soldiers, that the terrain they fought for was meaningless. Had he done so, the offensive might have lacked the intensity Falkenhayn's plan required. There was no obvious reason for him to assume in the first place that Verdun represented "sacred soil" France would hold to a finish. Instead the reverse was true: Verdun acquired totemic status in France because the Boche, the Germans, appeared to want it so badly. As the fighting progressed, places such as Fort Douaumont and Fort Vaux, Dead Man's Hill, and Wood of the Crows became symbols for Germans as well as French. Instead of managing his battle like a usurer, carefully weighing general risks and advantages and costs and gains, Falkenhayn himself came to resemble a gambler who seeks to recoup an initial loss by increasing his bets, then increasing them again. He found a comfort zone in micromanaging the details of a failing campaign, until events on other fronts finally impelled him to close down an operation that had strayed far from its original concept. Verdun became a disaster for the German army, the German state, and the German people in good part because the man who shaped it abandoned control of his creation.

–DENNIS SHOWALTER,
COLORADO COLLEGE

References

Holger Afflerbach, "Planning Total War? Falkenhayn and the Battle of Verdun, 1916," in *Great War, Total War: Combat and Mobilization on the Western Front, 1914–1918,* edited by Roger Chickering and Stig Förster (Cambridge & New York: Cambridge University Press, 2000), pp. 113–131.

Erich von Falkenhayn, *General Headquarters, 1914–1916, and Its Critical Decisions* (London: Hutchinson, 1919).

Robert T. Foley, "Attrition: Its Theory and Application in German Strategy, 1880–1916," dissertation, University of London, 1999.

Alistair Horne, *The Price of Glory: Verdun 1916* (New York: St. Martin's Press, 1962).

VERDUN

Did the Germans needlessly sacrifice students and underage volunteers at the Battle of Ypres?

Viewpoint: Yes. The German army and government were shortsighted in committing so many potential officers to battle as ordinary infantrymen in newly raised units.

Viewpoint: No. German planning was based on a war of short duration, and victory seemed close enough in 1914 to justify using every available resource in a massive offensive.

In October 1914 the German army launched a series of all-out attacks around the Belgian city of Ypres in its drive for Calais and the Channel ports. Prominently featured in this offensive were several army corps, organized after the outbreak of war, that included a relatively large number of volunteers—many of them students or members of youth groups. On one hand, for a country whose armed forces were based on conscription, the volunteers were a phenomenon. On the other hand, they harked back to an earlier heroic period in Prussian and German history: the Wars of Liberation against Napoleon Bonaparte (1813–1815). In that conflict, according to popular mythology, young men had risen of their own accord against tyranny. Students had followed their teachers, and apprentices their masters, into battle. Though reality had been considerably more pedestrian, recently completed centennial celebrations confirmed the myth.

In fact, the new units were poorly trained, poorly equipped, and poorly commanded. Far from being composed of youthful volunteers whose energy and vigor might have compensated for their lack of preparation, the regiments and battalions included an average of more than 80 percent reservists, who were largely from the older generations. Many had spent no time in uniform. The others, who thought their army days were long behind them, had forgotten most of their training, much of which in any case was based on doctrines and weapons long obsolete. Their physical fitness as well left much to be desired and had not been significantly improved by a brief training regimen consisting mostly of close-order drills. The officers and noncommissioned officers were overwhelmingly drawn from the retired lists; their skills and energy were correspondingly atrophied. The few regular soldiers were often men their parent units had not wanted to take to the front.

It was scarcely remarkable that these formations achieved nothing of significance operationally. Nor was it remarkable that their casualties were ruinous—higher than even the norms of 1914. What was unexpected was the transformation of this military catastrophe into a myth that between the wars became a national cult. The older men, most of whom were working-class fathers snatched from the ways of peace to fight in the ditches of Flanders, were conveniently forgotten. The volunteers, despite their relatively small numbers, came to symbolize patriotism, heroism, and self-sacrifice—all the virtues nationalists and Nazis described as neglected in the Weimar Republic. Their deaths helped Germany claim a moral victory as compensation for defeat in arms—and helped as well to condition the country for a second try.

Viewpoint: Yes. The German army and government were shortsighted in committing so many potential officers to battle as ordinary infantrymen in newly raised units.

On 18 October 1914 the Germans began a massive assault near Ypres, Belgium. Its aim was to break through to the Channel ports, cutting off the British Expeditionary Force (BEF) from supplies and reinforcements. Key to the German hopes was a reorganized Fourth Army. The eight divisions that were its core did not belong to the prewar order of battle. Instead, they were new formations, their organization authorized only on 16 August. They had less than two months of training and were armed and equipped with the scrapings and castoffs from German magazines and arsenals. Their officers were middle-aged reservists; their noncoms were long retired from active duty. The regiments and divisions, however, had enthusiasm—passion generated by the presence in their ranks of teenage volunteers, members of youth organizations as well as high school and university students, who were unwilling to await their call to arms and had pestered depots and recruiting offices until a place was made for them in a war everyone expected would end before the year turned.

In later years, German mythology described these regiments as being entirely drawn from the ranks of these adolescent volunteers. Reality was a good deal more pedestrian. In most of the battalions the proportion of students and their counterparts ranged from 10 to 20 percent—less in some cases. The balance of the rank and file came from *Ersatz* (supplementary) reservists, with no training at all, and older reservists of varying status who had not been immediately needed to fill out originally mobilized units. They regarded the enthusiasm of their teenage comrades with various mixtures of amusement and cynicism. The youngsters, however, set the tone, burst into patriotic songs at every opportunity on the march or in camp, found profound meaning in the inefficiencies and stupidities of army life, and led the way into a series of attacks that one by one collapsed with ruinous losses.

Dixmude, Beselare, Bixschoote, and, above all, Langemarck—these heretofore quiet villages became the graveyards of the new corps and divisions. It was recognized almost from the beginning at higher headquarters that these inexperienced, poorly trained men had been sacrificed by officers ignorant of modern war and generals innocent of any plan beyond throwing battalions and regiments at objectives amounting to little more than coordinates on a map. During the war, the army and the nationalists transformed the catastrophe into a legend of young heroes—heedless of death, joy in their hearts, and a song on their lips—storming forward into enemy fire. An army communiqué even reported a successful attack undertaken to the tune of "Deutschland über Alles" ("Germany above All"), the national anthem of the Second Reich.

Modern German historians, anxious to demythologize the national experience, take pains to argue that singing during the charge was a post facto construction, part of a broader militarist myth. Nevertheless, contemporary Allied accounts repeatedly mention confronting attacks carried forth by singing German soldiers all along the sectors of the front occupied by the new divisions. The picture is further complicated by the importance of group singing both in the German army and in youth and student organizations. It is highly unlikely that men in their first actions, charging over the sticky clay of Flanders beet fields, had breath or energy for song on a regular basis. It is, however, plausible that singing was used as a means of identification when more conventional methods failed or to sustain small-group morale in desperate situations.

The myth of soldiers singing in battle is scarcely confined to Germany. It is a central aspect, for example, of the British movie classic *Zulu* (1964). Accounts of at least one counterattack at Dien Bien Phu (1954) have French Foreign Legionnaires and Vietnamese paratroopers singing as they advanced into Viet Minh fire. For millions of Germans during and after World War I, however, the heroic youth of Langemarck became a symbol of the unconquerable spirit of their country. The Nazis made Langemarck a central feature of their militaristic ideology. Survivors who had participated in the battles seldom raised questions or challenged a legend that gave purpose

to their own sacrifices and sanctified the deaths of their comrades.

Yet, considered in a pragmatic context, the losses at Langemarck had consequences that ran deeper than the immediate casualty lists. Imperial Germany was a class society. Its officer corps in particular was drawn from the higher levels: not so much from the aristocracy by 1914, but from the upper-middle classes. Within that parameter, an essential criterion for obtaining a commission was education. Under peacetime circumstances a significant number of the young men who volunteered from school for the front in 1914 would have spent a year in the active army as volunteers, paying their own expenses. At the end of their service they would have been eligible to apply for a reserve commission. Even if not selected, they would have remained in a pool of potential candidates available in an emergency. Instead, by January 1915, hundreds were dead and even more were crippled.

The maxim of "no officer rather than a poor officer" meant the wartime army refused to expand significantly its criteria for a commission. Losses among the "war volunteers" of 1914 diminished the pool from which to draw. The German army began suffering from a chronic shortage of officers, especially junior officers with the kinds of qualities and qualifications exhibited by the volunteers of 1914. That erosion of command structures at company levels contributed no little amount to the steady decline of the army's effectiveness as the war progressed.

In a wider context as well, the misuse of the "Langemarck generation" highlighted the haphazard and halfhearted preparations of Imperial Germany for a war its generals and politicians alike were sure must eventually

British soldier (center) standing between two German officers during the Christmas truce at Ypres in 1914

(Imperial War Museum, London)

YPRES

come. The peacetime military budget stretched to provide for the conscription and training of only about one-half of the men who became eligible each year. Most of the rest were assigned immediately to the supplementary reserve. Many of these men in their early twenties were recalled and assigned to the new corps in 1914, reinforcing the image that the units were composed of inexperienced youth. Other superfluous conscripts were declared medically unfit for one of an increasingly broad spectrum of reasons (flat feet was a common one), or deferred because of family obligations or academic status. In practice the German conscription system before 1914 resembled the U.S. Selective Service System prior to the Vietnam War (ended 1975) in containing so many loopholes that almost anybody could find one—especially a son of the middle classes who really did not want to wear an actual uniform.

Within the army itself, budgetary considerations did as much as social ones to limit the size of the officer corps. Noncommissioned officers too were difficult to recruit and retain in an increasingly affluent society. Equipment was purchased and allocated in the context of force structures developed for a short war. As a result, when the high command decided to expand its order of battle in the fall of 1914, everything was lacking for fielding effective units. One reason the newly formed units did so much parade-ground drill was a scarcity of rifles, knapsacks, and other personal gear necessary for field exercises. Saluting drills and classes in foot care were held less from the pedantry of superannuated officers and sergeants than for want of alternatives. These soldiers often did not know how to care for or control horses. During the fighting around Langemarck, one artillery battery was put out of action when the horses of its ammunition column stampeded under fire. Companies and regiments went haphazardly into action, not knowing even where they were, much less where the enemy was, not because incompetent captains and colonels were unable to read maps but because there were no maps to give them. Men went hungry for days at a time because first sergeants, a decade too old and fifty pounds too heavy for frontline duty collapsed under the burdens of administration.

The army learned from experience. The next group of war-raised divisions received a better chance. Their cadres were larger and stronger, including many experienced officers and NCOs who had recuperated from wounds. Their training included much more practice in fieldcraft and infantry-artillery

cooperation. The fate of the young volunteers of 1914 nevertheless epitomized the failure of the Second Reich to prepare consequently for the war that it, more than any other power in Europe, had expected and welcomed.

—DENNIS SHOWALTER,
COLORADO COLLEGE

Viewpoint:
No. German planning was based on a war of short duration, and victory seemed close enough in 1914 to justify using every available resource in a massive offensive.

On 11 November 1914 the *Oberste Heeresleitung* (OHL), the German High Command, issued the following statement that described the bloody battle fought by units of the four army corps hastily raised by the German Ministry of War upon the outbreak of war:

> On the Yser front, we made good progress yesterday. . . .West of Langemarck, the new regiments charged against the first line of the enemy's position singing "Deutschland, Deutschland über alles" and took it. Around 2,000 men of the French line infantry were taken prisoner and 6 machineguns were captured.

Like many official statements made during World War I, this statement was composed of half-truths. It was true that the young soldiers of the new German corps had taken the first line of the French position and had taken some prisoners. However, this result was only part of the tale of the inconclusive battle that has become known as the First Battle of Ypres. The OHL omitted to release the number of casualties suffered by the inexperienced young troops who had been carrying out the assaults against the Entente line since late October. The German commanders failed to let on in their official announcements that between 19 October and 11 November the units of the two attacking armies, Duke Albrecht's Fourth Army and Crown Prince Rupprecht's Sixth Army, had suffered close to 100,000 casualties and that the new units had suffered disproportionately. Prior to the First Battle of Ypres, Regiment 243, raised only in September, had been at full strength with 67 officers, 242 noncommissioned officers, and 2,011 soldiers. On 1 December 1914 it counted 19 officers, 70 noncommissioned officers, and 605 soldiers.

Corresponding regiments suffered similarly in the battle.

Despite the half-truths of the official announcement, the OHL could not keep such serious losses quiet. As notification of the wounded, missing, and dead worked its way back to the families on the home front, all of Germany soon knew of the sacrifice of the young men who had volunteered at the outbreak of war in August. While a virtue was made of their "heroic" loss by the German propaganda machine, Erich von Falkenhayn, who as Minister of War had ordered the formation of the new army corps and who as Chief of the General Staff had ordered their use in October, came under intense criticism. Falkenhayn's contemporaries, as well as historians, criticized him for using the inexperienced troops so soon after their formation and for not giving them sufficient time to train for the realities of modern war. Indeed, many censured him for using the manpower available to Germany in late 1914 to construct new units rather than as replacements for casualties in old units. In keeping with this harsh interpretation, the First Battle of Ypres has come to be called in Germany the "*Kindermord von Ypren*" (massacre of the innocents at Ypres).

Like all interpretations, however, this damning criticism of Falkenhayn was taken with the benefit of hindsight. A closer examination of the circumstances under which the reserve corps were formed and how they were initially intended to be used casts a different light on the decisions made by Falkenhayn in late 1914.

When war broke out in August 1914, Falkenhayn took to the field with the German Imperial Headquarters as the Prussian Minister of War. In obedience to an agreement reached between the Ministry of War and the General Staff in 1896, Falkenhayn ordered the creation of five new reserve corps on 16 August to "make use of the remaining powerful strength of the people for the defense of the nation." The troops for these new corps were to be found from two sources. First, they were to be drawn from surplus manpower in the depots of the German peacetime army corps. Many units possessed troops that did not fit into the order of battle of the German field army, and these could be readily formed into the core of the new units. Second, the troops were to be drawn from the ranks of those young Germans who had not been called up for service with their annual classes. Although Germany had conscription since the Napoleonic Wars, not every able-bodied male served his term. The German government simply could not afford to call up all its available manpower. As the German population grew, so too did the numbers of young men exempted from service. It had long been planned that these fit, but untrained, men were to form the bulk of the reserve corps to be formed at the start of a war.

In order for this new force to have any effect on a war that most soldiers in the summer of 1914 believed would be over "before the leaves fell" in autumn, the new units would have to be formed and put into the field rapidly. Before the war, German strategists had planned that these units would be used to help the field army administer the "coup de grâce" to an enemy it expected to be already largely defeated. As such, speed of deployment was more important than quality of training or armament. After all, even a scratch force should have no difficulty in defeating disorganized and demoralized enemy units, the leadership believed, particularly if the new German units were well commanded.

When Falkenhayn ordered the creation of these five corps, the German armies had yet to begin properly their advance into France. However, within a few weeks of his signing the order, the French advance into Alsace/Lorraine had been defeated and enemy units seemed to be running away as quickly as they could. Everything appeared to be proceeding to plan, and the Minister of War had no reason to deviate from the policy drawn up before the war for the creation of new army corps. Indeed, to begin changing plans at this point in the war risked throwing the entire process into confusion and doing more harm than good.

After the defeat of the German war plan at the Battle of the Marne, Falkenhayn also took over as Chief of the General Staff from the luckless Helmuth von Moltke the Younger. Falkenhayn inherited an army that was tired, if not yet completely exhausted, from a rapid fighting advance across Belgium and northern France. He desperately needed fresh forces to renew this advance and hopefully to finish off the Entente forces. One of Falkenhayn's first acts as Chief was to order the transfer of forces from Alsace/Lorraine to the German right wing in northern France in order to renew the German outflanking maneuver. These troops, however, proved insufficient, and the competing Entente and German flanking maneuvers were halted when they reached the Channel coast. With the flanks secured, Falkenhayn now faced the more difficult prospect of having to break through the enemy's hastily prepared defensive positions in order to restore mobility to the battlefield and to secure victory.

With hindsight, it is possible to say that the prospects for piercing the Entente line in

Adolf Hitler, later the leader of Nazi Germany, served as a young soldier in Flanders during World War I. He recalls his early military service in Mein Kampf (1925). Many historians question the accuracy of this account, as the myth of singing soldiers and glorification of the sacrifice made by youthful volunteers was used by the Nazis to promote a militaristic society.

Thus, as probably for every German, there began for me the most unforgettable and the greatest period of my mortal life. In the face of the events of this mighty struggle the entire past fell back into shallow oblivion. It is now ten years since this mighty event happened, and with proud sadness I think back to those weeks of the beginning of the heroic fight of our people which Fate had graciously permitted me to share.

As if it were yesterday, one picture after the other passes before my eyes: I see myself donning the uniform in the circle of my dear comrades, turning out for the first time, drilling, etc., till finally the day came when we marched.

There was only one thing that worried me at the time, like so many others also: that was whether we would not arrive at the front too late. This alone disturbed my peace again and again. Thus in every jubilation over a new heroic deed there seemed to be a hidden drop of bitterness as with every new victory the danger of our being delayed seemed to increase.

Finally, the day came when we left Munich in order to start fulfilling our duty. Now for the first time I saw the Rhine as we were riding towards the west along its quiet waters, the German river of all rivers, in order to protect it against the greed of the old enemy. When through the delicate veil of the dawn's mist the mild rays of the early sun set the Niederwalddenkmal shimmering before our eyes, the "Watch on the Rhine" roared up to the morning sky from the interminably long transport train and I had a feeling as though my chest would burst.

Then at last came a damp, cold night in Flanders through which we marched silently, and when the day began to emerge from the fog, suddenly an iron salute came whizzing over our heads towards us and with a sharp report the small bullets struck between our rows, whipping up the wet earth; but before the small cloud had dispersed, out of two hundred throats the first hurrah roared a welcome to the first messenger of death. But then it began to crackle and roar, to sing and howl, and with feverish eyes each one of us was drawn forward faster and faster over turnip fields and hedges till suddenly the fight began, the fight of man against man. But from the distance the sounds of a song met our ears, coming nearer and nearer, passing from company to company, and then, while Death busily plunged his hand into our rows, the song reached also us, and now we passed it on: *"Deutschland, Deutschland über alles, über alles in der Welt!"*

After four days we came back. Even our step had become different. Boys of seventeen now resembled men.

The volunteers of the regiment had perhaps not yet learned to fight properly, but they knew how to die like old soldiers.

This was the beginning.

Source: *Adolf Hitler,* Mein Kampf, *edited by John Chamberlain and others (New York: Reynal & Hitchcock, 1939), pp. 213–214.*

Flanders were not good. However, to Falkenhayn in late October 1914, the chances did not look so bad. First, at this point in the war, no one had ever attempted to break through field positions. The fieldworks thrown up by the English and French soldiers did not look so solid: their trenches were shallow, their positions weak, and they lacked reserves. Moreover, if the state of his own troops was any guide, Falkenhayn assumed the Entente forces were exhausted from the nearly continuous combat in which they had been engaged since mid August. The Entente lacked the fresh forces that Falkenhayn had at his disposal—the newly formed Fourth Army with its four brand new reserve corps. If these forces were untested in combat, at least they were placed under experienced command and were reinforced by an additional reserve corps and by heavy artillery freed by the fall of Antwerp on 9 October. If they were not well trained tactically, he believed that their youthful enthusiasm would make them aggressive in the attack and impervious to casualties. The combination of a thinly held line manned by an exhausted enemy and the new, five-corps-strong army convinced Falkenhayn that one last push would be sufficient to collapse Entente resistance and at least gain for Germany the Channel ports, if not final victory.

Falkenhayn, however, had calculated incorrectly. The Entente forces were nowhere near as exhausted as he had assumed, and he seriously underestimated the strength of field fortifications in the hands of troops armed with rapid-fire rifles and machine guns. Even under the cover of fire from superior artillery, the antiquated close-order tactics employed by the ill-trained new reserve corps resulted in appalling casualties. Their enthusiasm did not lead to the expected rapid capture of enemy positions, but merely to higher casualties; and, in the course of a few short weeks, the initial manpower reserve of Germany was frittered away for no real gain.

Given the appalling casualties suffered by the young German troops, discussions of Falkenhayn's decisions in the First Battle of Ypres have been dominated by emotion rather than reason. With the benefit of knowledge of the toll trench warfare took on attacking units, historians can now argue that Falkenhayn's offensive was doomed before the first German war volunteer had left the safety of his own defenses. However, in these early days of the war, the issue was not so clear. Falkenhayn knew how tired his own army was from fighting its way across Belgium and France. Based upon this knowledge and the limited intelligence reaching him about the Entente forces, he concluded quite reasonably that they were in a similar, if not worse, state. Additionally, prewar ideas about the importance of morale in the attack convinced not only Falkenhayn, but most officers, that highly motivated troops could overwhelm modern defenses and take field positions. Thus, the new army, composed as it was of young, fit, and eager troops, seemed the ideal force to administer the coup de grâce to the weakened, worn-out Entente forces defending Flanders. Falkenhayn made the decision that any competent commander would have made in his place. If his offensive had been successful, the deaths of the war volunteers would no doubt have been considered by observers to be "glorious" rather than "tragic."

–ROBERT T. FOLEY,
KING'S COLLEGE, LONDON

References

Holger Afflerbach, *Falkenhayn: Politisches Denken und Handeln im Kaiserreich* (Munich: Oldenbourg, 1994).

Erich von Falkenhayn, *General Headquarters, 1914–1916, and Its Critical Decisions* (London: Hutchinson, 1919).

Bruce I. Gudmundsson, *Stormtroop Tactics: Innovation in the German Army, 1914–1918* (New York: Praeger, 1989).

Karl Unruh, *Langemarck: Legende und Wirklichkeit* (Koblenz: Bernard & Graefe, 1986).

YUGOSLAVIA

Was the new state of Yugoslavia simply "Greater Serbia"?

Viewpoint: Yes. Serb leader Nicola Pašić intended to create a centralized state dominated by Serbia.

Viewpoint: No. The South Slavic federation proclaimed at the end of the war began with a mutual determination to establish ethnic cooperation.

Yugoslavia—the Kingdom of the Serbs, Croats, and Slovenes—was arguably the most unnatural creation of a war ostensibly justified on the principle of national autonomy. Serbs, Croats, Slovenes, Magyars, and other groups jostled for control in a state without a numerically dominant nationality, let alone a majority one. Yet, in the context of Great War politics, the legitimacy of Yugoslavia was as great as any successor state and its mandate for existence clearer than most.

It began with Serbia, the "Balkan Piedmont," whose nationalists well before 1914 saw their state as a focal point for a South Slav kingdom that would incorporate the smaller ethnic groups emancipated from centuries of alien occupation and governance. During World War I a Serb government, in exile after Serbia was overrun by the Central Powers in 1915, made a case for compensation as both a victim of Teutonic aggression and a guarantor of postwar stability in southeastern Europe. Almost simultaneously, Croat and Slovene members of the Austrian Parliament, increasingly conscious of the weakness of Austria-Hungary, called for the integration of Habsburg South Slav territory into a single state under Habsburg rule. This "trialist" approach to the Habsburg problem had been discussed before the war. Now it seemed promising enough that the Serb government and an ephemeral "Yugoslav Committee," formed from South Slav exiles in London, joined forces to call for a Serb, Croat, and Slovene state—without Habsburg involvement. When Austria-Hungary disintegrated in October 1918, a breakaway faction from the Habsburg South Slav parties accepted the latter solution. In the face of increasing chaos, the remaining groups followed more or less grudgingly, accepting union with Serbia and the subsequent proclamation of a South Slav kingdom with the Serbian dynasty at its head.

The new state had a government with excellent connections in the Allied capitals. It had an army that had proved its effectiveness in the Salonika campaign. It had bureaucrats with practice in administration. Not least, its creators had some experience with compromise. What Yugoslavia lacked was trust. Most Croats and Slovenes were more or less suspicious of Serb intentions. Many Serbs saw their new countrymen as lackeys of the Habsburgs, whose ethnic consciousness needed stimulating. Serbs tended to dominate the formative processes of the new state, and Croats responded with overt, constant opposition. The result was a mutual pattern of electoral and administrative abuses, waste, fraud, and corruption far beyond the fears of prewar critics of South Slav unity—and a long way from wartime promises.

Viewpoint:
Yes. Serb leader Nicola Pašić intended to create a centralized state dominated by Serbia.

Clearly, proponents of the "Yugoslav Idea," the union of Habsburg Slavs with independent Serbia, faced enormous challenges given the diverse ethnic, geographical, cultural, and historical background of the South Slavs under Austrian and Hungarian tutelage. The key Serbian and Croatian leaders, however, showed no mutual determination to overcome the particularism and chauvinism necessary to create a genuine federalist state. Although the South Slav political agreement proclaimed at the end of World War I reflected the language of federalism, ethnic nationalism had already paved the way for a centralized state dominated by Serbia.

The Yugoslav Idea had emerged during the nationalist fervor of the 1860s with the Dalmatian Croats of the Habsburg Empire, led by Ante Trumbić. The difficulties facing Trumbić were clearly visible at the Fiume Congress (1905) of Habsburg Serbs and Croats, where Croat opposition scuttled a united front. This conference witnessed the first foray into politics of Stjepan Radić, who soon would be the voice of Croat intransigence.

On 29 July 1914, the day following the Austrian declaration of war on Serbia, the government of Nicola Pašić issued a strongly nationalist manifesto calling on all Serbs to defend their homeland. Only under extreme pressure did he declare the overall objective of Serbia to be the liberation and unification of all South Slavs. From the start, Pašić could never conceive of a future Yugoslav state other than Greater Serbia, and his wartime statements and agreements to the contrary were merely tactical moves that reflected the desperate military situation of Serbia. This small country suffered fully 1 million killed of its 4.5 million subjects. For Pašić and his followers, their wartime sacrifice justified Serb domination of any future postwar South Slav state.

When war broke out, Trumbić went to then-neutral Italy and established a "Yugoslav Committee." His campaign for Yugoslavism remained one-sided until July 1917, when he and Pašić met on the island of Corfu and declared their support for establishing a common state after the war under the Serbian Karageorgević dynasty. The new state would be democratic, provide guarantees for religious freedom and equality, and receive a constitution from a Constituent Assembly whose members would be chosen by universal suffrage and secret ballot. At this time the Serbian leader proved amenable to compromise, with his country occupied and his major ally, tsarist Russia, in the throes of revolution. Subsequent relations between the Yugoslav Committee and the Serb government, however, remained strained.

In August 1918 the Habsburg Slavs met in Zagreb and agreed to form a Yugoslav National Council (YNC) of Slovenes, Croats, and Serbs under the leadership of Father Anton Korošec, leader of the Catholic Slovenian Populist Party. The YNC soon received the support of the Croatian diet and the governor of Bosnia-Herzegovina, but the Slovenes affirmed their own independence. Although Korošec went to Geneva to elicit support for the YNC cause after the Habsburg military authorities transferred authority to the YNC on 28 October, he failed to gain international legal recognition from the Allies. Meanwhile, despite the Corfu Pact (20 July 1917), differences between Trumbić and Pašić prevented formation of any joint Yugoslav government. The Serb leader clearly pursued his aim to have Serbia represent all South Slavs and liberate and absorb the Habsburg Slavic territories.

Yet, wartime events compelled Pašić to continue to compromise in the short term. Italians had moved into territory claimed by the YNC, rampaging peasants were seizing land, and the specter of Bolshevism had raised its ugly head. These events, along with Allied pressure, led him to agree on 11 November to what became known as the Declaration of Geneva. By terms of this agreement, Pašić, Trumbić, and Korošec sanctioned the establishment of "one state, formed of Serbs, Croats and Slovenes," to be ruled by both the Serbian government and YNC until a Constituent Assembly created permanent institutions for a combined state. Despite Pašić's action, this federalist declaration was never willingly accepted by his own government in Corfu or by the Serbian army, which, in effect, destroyed the basis for a genuine federalist state. At the same time, Croatian leaders in the YNC back in Zagreb expressed grave reservations as well. Under pressure from the advancing Italian army, they succumbed to Habsburg Serbs in the YNC who, on 23 November, seized the initiative and convinced the Council to proclaim unity with Serbia in a Serbo-Croato-Slovene state, under the Serbian dynasty, without conditions. On 26 November, Montenegro declared its union with Serbia. Then, on 1 December, the same day the Serb army entered Zagreb, representatives of all South Slav territories convened in Belgrade and officially declared the formation of the Kingdom of the Serbs, Croats, and Slovenes.

Even though a genuine South Slav federation seemed achievable at last, conflicting viewpoints remained to be accommodated. Pašić had not given up his Greater Serbia views, and equally unsettling, the mercurial Croatian peasant leader, Radić, refused to sanction the political arrangement; instead, he called for an independent peasant Croatian republic. In the elections for the Constituent

YUGOSLAVIA

Assembly in 1921, Radić emerged as master of Croatia in opposition to the new Yugoslav state. In the Assembly the forces of centralism, led by Pašić, proved victorious over the supporters of federalism, and the so-called Vidovdan Constitution (28 June 1921) established a centralized administration for the entire state under the Serb monarch, King Alexander I.

The failure to establish a federal structure for union set the stage for the interwar turmoil ahead and the civil war that developed after the state disintegrated during World War II. In the early 1920s Radić remained intransigent, yet stubbornly refused to state his terms for Croatian acceptance of the state. Following Radić's assassination in Parliament in 1928, Croatian members left the legislature, and relations with the Serbs deteriorated further. Radić's successor, Vladimir Maćek, proved more cooperative, but his terms for Croatian support would have meant the disintegration of the state. Under these circumstances, King Alexander I proclaimed in 1929 a royal dictatorship and named the state the Kingdom of Yugoslavia. As one observer noted at the time, there seemed to be everyone in Yugoslavia but a Yugoslavian. Although the king fostered what he called a new "Yugoslav patriotism" in place of Serb and Croat particularism, his dictatorship became openly anti-Croatian. In 1934 he, too, died at the hands of an assassin, and the Croatian Question remained unresolved during the remainder of the interwar period. Meanwhile, extremists on both sides gained ground, and the hatred represented by groups such as the Ustashi, a Croatian terrorist organization, burst forth during World War II and established a legacy of ethnic divisiveness that continued to haunt the Yugoslav future.

Reviewing the course of events during and immediately following the Great War, it is clear that the Yugoslav Idea never attracted genuine support from the two main South Slav leaders and their constituents. The Serb leader, Pašić, never abandoned his Greater Serbia program despite the tactical compromises represented by the Corfu Pact, the Geneva Declaration, and the proclamation after the war of what appeared to be a federal union. Radić, for his part, also refused to accept a federal union of South Slavs that would mean defeat for his aim of an independent Croatia. Because these two leaders represented the feelings of most Serbs and Croats, the efforts of the federalists within the Yugoslav Committee and Yugoslav National Council were doomed to fail from the outset. The record clearly shows that there was no mutual determination to overcome ethnic particularism. From its beginning, the new state of Yugoslavia was Serbia written large.

—DAVID N. SPIRES, UNIVERSITY OF COLORADO, BOULDER

Viewpoint:
No. The South Slavic federation proclaimed at the end of the war began with a mutual determination to establish ethnic cooperation.

Many myths emerged from the smoky proceedings of the Versailles Peace Conference (1919) at the end of World War I. One of the most persistent myths, and least grounded in reality, involves the creation of Yugoslavia. A popular misconception is that Yugoslavia was little more than "Greater Serbia," an extension of the victorious Allied Kingdom of Serbia. This conclusion is far from the truth. Yugoslavia, the state of the South Slavs, was no Serbian Empire. Serbian national interests were not paramount; Serbs did not benefit more than other constituent members. An ad hoc solution opposed by many Serbs and favored by non-Serbs, the political entity lacked any of the hallmarks of an empire and appeared more like an uneasy group home where the leaseholder grudgingly accepted former enemies as lodgers who promised to pay their way.

Serbia did not gain much from being included in the Yugoslav project. The position of Serbs was not dominant relative to the Croats and Slovenes (who had just lost the war fighting as part of the Austro-Hungarian Empire). Furthermore, the concept of a Greater Serbia does not take into account the good reasons Croatia and Slovenia had for joining Yugoslavia. The major nations involved in the creation of Yugoslavia were the Serbs (including the Montenegrins), Croats, and Slovenes. They all had long histories and vibrant cultures. The only independent peoples before World War I were the Serbs and Montenegrins. They were both mainly Orthodox Christians who spoke Serbian and had similar cultures. A relatively small number of Serbs (and Croats) had been converted to Islam through centuries of Turkish domination, most of them living in the major towns of Bosnia-Herzegovina. Later, mainly under Josip Broz Tito's divisive Communist regime (1953–1980), the "Bosnian Muslims" developed a separate political identity, but prior to and during World War I they largely saw themselves (and were seen by others) as either Serbs or Croats. Though Serbs established their kingdom decades before the war, not all Serbs lived in Serbia; many Serbs lived in Bosnia-Herzegovina, Vojvodina, and Krajina within the Austro-Hungarian Empire.

Croats and Slovenes were also part of Austria-Hungary but had restricted local autonomy and were by and large not permitted to govern themselves. Both are Roman Catholics; Croats speak Croatian, while Slovenian is a separate and more distinct Slavic language. National movements

CORFU PACT

On 20 July 1917 the Serbs, Croats, and Slovenes declared the formation of a new state:

In the first place the representatives of the Serbs, Croats, and Slovenes declare anew and most categorically that our people constitutes but one nation, and that it is one in blood, one by the spoken and written language, by the continuity and unity of the territory in which it lives, and finally in virtue of the common and vital interests of its national existence and the general development of its moral and material life. The idea of its national unity has never suffered extinction, although all the intellectual forces of its enemy were directed against its unification, its liberty, and its national existence. Divided between several States, our nation is in Austria-Hungary alone split up into eleven provincial administrations coming under thirteen legislative bodies. The feeling of national unity, together with the spirit of liberty and independence, have supported it in the never-ending struggles of centuries against the Turks in the East and against the Magyars in the West.

Being numerically inferior to its enemies in the East and West, it was impossible for it to safeguard its unity as a nation and a State, its liberty and its independence against the brutal maxim of "might goes before right" militating against it both East and West. But the moment has come when our people is no longer isolated. The war imposed by German militarism upon Russia, upon France and upon England for the defence of their honor as well as for the liberty and independence of small nations, has developed into a struggle for the Liberty of the World and the Triumph of Right over Might. All nations which love liberty and independence have allied themselves together for their common defense, to save civilization and liberty at the cost of every sacrifice, to establish a new international order based upon justice and upon the right of every nation to dispose of itself and so organize its independent life; finally to establish a durable peace consecrated to the progress and development of humanity and to secure the world against a catastrophe similar to that which the conquering lust of the German Imperialism has provoked.

To noble France, who has proclaimed the liberty of nations, and to England, the hearth of liberty, the Great American Republic and the new, free, and democratic Russia have joined themselves in proclaiming as their principal war aim the triumph of liberty and democracy and as basis of the new international order the right of free self-determination for every nation. Our nation of the three names, which has been the greatest sufferer under brute force and injustice, and which has made the greatest sacrifices to preserve its right of self-determination, has with enthusiasm accepted this sublime principle put forward as the chief aim of this atrocious war, provoked by the violation of this very principle.

The authorized representatives of the Serbs, Croats, and Slovenes, in declaring that it is the desire of our people to free itself from every foreign yoke and to constitute itself a free, national, and independent State, a desire based on the principle that every nation has the right to decide upon its own destiny, are agreed in judging that this State should be founded on the following modern and democratic principles.

The pact included:

1. The State of the Serbs, Croats, and Slovenes, who are also known as the Southern Slavs or Jugoslavs, will be a free and independent kingdom, with indivisible territory and unity of allegiance . . .

2. This State will be named "The Kingdom of the Serbs, Croats, and Slovenes . . ."

5. The three national designations—Serbs, Croats, and Slovenes—are equal before the law throughout the territory of the Kingdom, . . .

7. All recognized religions may be freely and publicly exercised . . .

9. The territory of the Kingdom of the Serbs, Croats, and Slovenes will include all the territory inhabited compactly and in territorial continuity by our nation of the three names . . .

Source: "The Pact of Corfu & The Formation of Yugoslavia, 1917," *Modern History SourceBook* <http://www.fordham.edu/halsall/mod/1917yugoslavia1.html>.

among these two peoples had failed to win independence before World War I. Croats and Slovenes fought against the Allies on the side of the Central Powers; Serbia and Montenegro were Allied countries. Despite initial victories, Serbia could not withstand the combined weight of Austria-Hungary, Germany, and finally Bulgaria, and Serbian forces were forced into general retreat across Albania to the Adriatic Sea. The remnant of the army eventually regrouped, landing with the French and British at Salonika (Thessaloniki) in Greece, opening up a new front. By November 1918 Serbian troops had pushed into Croatia, Hungary, and Austria and had freed vast tracts of Macedonia and Bosnia-Herzegovina.

Yugoslavia was unique of all the countries created at the end of the war, in that it was composed of both victor and vanquished. In effect, the victims were asked to absorb aggressors into a larger state and peacefully coexist with them. Serbia sought first and foremost to bring all Serbs within its borders but had conflicting opinions regarding absorbing non-Serbs. (Serbian war aims shifted with the fortunes of war: from small border adjustments to the final settlement and creation of the new Yugoslavia.) Many Serbs eventually believed that the benefits of a unified Serbia outweighed the dangers of joining with Croatia and Slovenia and absorbing the inevitable smaller populations of Germans, Hungarians, Bulgarians, Romanians, and Albanians. Other Serbs, particularly those with some experience in government, argued that national minorities were a tremendous liability and the seed of future wars; the easiest way to avoid conflict over minorities was not to have them. They also raised a strategic objection to enlarging the state: absorbing all of Croatia and Slovenia would bring Serbian borders north to Italy and Austria—frontiers where fighting was still going on in 1919.

The threat of being absorbed into larger, hostile Latin and Germanic neighbors gave the Slovenes a different perspective on redrawing the Balkan map: any Slavic entity was preferable. Moreover, if they did not participate in a Balkan solution, they would be punished by the Allies as defeated Central Powers—maybe even given to the Italians as spoils of war. A united Yugoslavia, however, would be treated as part of the winning side and its members could avoid penalties such as reparations. This fear of annihilation and punishment was a motivating factor for the Croatians, as well. Both they and the Slovenes had faced for some time the threat of "Germanization" or "Magyarization," the process by which these larger peoples (Austrians and Hungarians) sought to erode other national identities.

After the war, Serbs again expressed several views on absorbing Slovenia and Croatia. From one Serb perspective, reuniting with Bosnia-Herzegovina and annexing Vojvodina was a natural outcome of the war, something for which they had been fighting. After all, these regions were primarily peopled by Serbs, who in turn wanted to join their brothers across the border. Croatia and Slovenia, however, would be serious liabilities: the Kingdom of Serbia was an established, independent state with its own government and institutions. The Serb government in exile was not enthusiastic about creating a large country of more than 12 million people, fewer than half of whom would be Serbs. They favored U.S. president Woodrow Wilson's stance of independence and self-determination for all the peoples of the region. Serbia should grow to encompass Serbian lands and people, they thought; but beyond that belief there was little incentive to house alien populations, especially when they had, until a few weeks before, been shooting at each other.

Another Serbian perspective favored South Slav unity. At the least, many Serbian idealists looked eagerly forward to union with their Slavic brothers. Even before World War I began, many Serbs saw themselves as the liberators of the Balkans. After all, they had virtually single-handedly challenged Turkish rule, and alone among Balkan peoples achieved their own independence; they were the first to break their own chains. Once it was clear that the Serbian army was going to recover from defeat and retreat in 1915, this goal of liberating the other subjugated Slavs grew even more popular.

Ultimately, however, the London exiles, and not troops on the battlefield, established the reality of Yugoslavia. A large "lobby" of Croats and Slovenes had already formed to oppose the Austro-Hungarian monarchy, and the prospect of independence was an alluring one. The idea of Yugoslavia was embraced wholeheartedly by many influential Croats and Slovenes living in Britain during the war, especially as it became clear that Germany and its allies would lose. Neither people had fared well as subjects of the Germans and Hungarians, so anyone looking to the future (and to the next potential war) sought a stable alternative. Intellectually and emotionally, the ideal of South Slav unity went back much farther than 1918. The great nationalist revivals of the nineteenth century inspired the "Illyrian Movement," a loose affiliation that advocated unity for all people living in the ancient Roman province of Illyria (roughly what was planned for Yugoslavia). Many writers, poets, and thinkers saw a South Slav union as the only possible protection against further domination by outside powers, and they became more outspoken as World War I dragged on.

While the beginnings of the "Yugoslav" movement as an alternative to Austro-Hungarian domination may explain the affinity Croatian and Slovene intellectuals had for the creation of a new state, it is only half the picture. Regardless of the

Serbian troops in autumn 1916

(from Collier's New Photographic History of the World's War *[1918], Joseph M. Bruccoli Great War Collection, Thomas Cooper Library, University of South Carolina)*

thoughts of poets, the Serbian government was largely opposed to creating a new superstate wherein they would go from an independent kingdom to one member of a larger multinational unit. It was a difficult subject, and no one wanted to rush blindly forward.

Nevertheless, in December 1918 the Kingdom of the Serbs, Croats, and Slovenes officially came into being, declaring itself an independent state, governed from Belgrade and headed by Serbian Regent Alexander (who did not become king until 1921). The biggest challenge facing all the new postwar states was to create a government and constitution that would reconcile all the conflicting elements. Yugoslavia had more of these elements than perhaps any other new state: multiple nations, with differing religions and different political traditions and cultural histories, who had recently been fighting on opposite sides. All national groups were made up of individuals who bitterly opposed or wholeheartedly wished for one, united Yugoslavia; there were also large numbers of people in the middle, either unconcerned or as yet unconvinced of what would be best.

Regent Alexander was also opposed to a "Greater Serbia." He had seen how Serbs had struggled for independence as a minority in foreign empires and had no desire to create an empire of his own. Even if one discounts the altruistic aspects of this decision, postwar Serbia was in no condition to rule an empire. One-fifth of its population had been killed or had died of typhus and other diseases, and Serbian agriculture and fledgling industry had been largely destroyed. Instead of establishing a Greater Serbia through conquest, Alexander set up local governments and largely encouraged Croats and Slovenes (and even Hungarians, Germans, Rumanians, and Albanians) to create their own institutions where they were the majority. Indeed, Alexander's solicitousness toward the Croatians proved especially detrimental to Serbs. In Krajina, Serbs had enjoyed autonomy under Imperial protection since the eighteenth century. The new Belgrade government abrogated this long-standing treaty and placed the Serbs of Krajina under Croatian jurisdiction. There are many other examples of the favored position non-Serbs enjoyed in the early Yugoslavia. All but the highest-ranking former Austro-Hungarian officers were accepted immediately into the Yugoslav army. Service in the Austro-Hungarian army counted toward pensions from the Serbian Royal Government— even when those years were spent at war with Serbia. By any standards this treatment was more than fair. Some Serbian officers resigned in protest over having former enemies promoted over their heads. The civil administration, too, retained much of the Austro-Hungarian apparatus of state. There were only a handful of Serbs moved into government positions in the newly freed territories, and these officials were mainly technicians brought in for such things as large engineering projects.

The investment strategy of the new Belgrade government is perhaps the strongest piece of evidence against the Greater Serbia thesis. Even with all the damage done to Serbia during the war, most of the money Belgrade invested went into the non-Serb territories. Clearly, the first step in creating Greater Serbia would be to raise the Serb standard of living, most likely at the expense of non-Serbs. It seems quite the opposite happened. In the interest of unity, the Belgrade government allowed the

YUGOSLAVIA

position of Serbs outside of pre-war Serbian territory to deteriorate very quickly. In addition to the loss of legal status in Krajina, Serbs also lost the right in many places to worship in Orthodox churches.

The first and greatest challenges to the Yugoslav state, indeed to the very ideal of South Slav unity, came from Croatia. As early as December 1918 there was fighting in Zagreb between Serbian troops and local radicals demanding independence. This minority, led by Stjepan Radić of the Croatian Peasant Party, thought the formation of Yugoslavia was "overly hasty and ill-prepared," and they claimed to have more than one hundred thousand signatures on an appeal to the Allies to recognize an independent Croatia. Croat politicians continued obstructionist tactics with a resulting relative lack of material or political progress in Croatia, compared to other newly liberated regions in the interwar period, such as Czechoslovakia. Though Yugoslavia was arguably a product of Croatian lobbying, the politicians who initially favored its creation were not prepared for the actual event. The more time passed from the end of the War and the fall of the Habsburg Empire, the worse the situation in Croatia became. Croats who enthusiastically supported the creation of Yugoslavia had almost no voice by the mid-1920s.

Slovenia proved a much more amicable partner than Croatia. Slovene political leaders tended to side with the Belgrade government, especially during the first decade after the war. They had much to gain: leverage with neighboring countries dealing with Slovenian minorities in Italy and Austria, protection from those same neighbors, and economic stimulus from the royal government.

Macedonia, too, proved a viable addition, with only minor incidents with Bulgarian nationals caught within the new borders. In Vojvodina and surrounding areas there were problems with the nearly half million Hungarians that the Allies had assigned to Yugoslavia. Much like the Germans in the Sudetenland (controlled by Czechoslovakia), the Hungarian minority in Yugoslavia had really only one political aim: reunification with Hungary. This goal led to increasing tensions as the interwar period progressed. Initially, however, the Hungarians (and the Germans, Albanians, and Romanians) relied heavily on the central government and allied themselves politically with the Yugoslav royalist parties.

Throughout the early period of Yugoslavia, through investment in the former Imperial regions, establishment of local political and cultural institutions, integration of the military, lenient treatment of local terrorists and even the naming of his second son after a Croatian medieval hero, Alexander attempted to forge a new state with a new identity. When this policy failed to win over the Croatians,

he even offered them independence in 1928. Yet this effort, too, failed; alternatives to Yugoslav unity were bleak. Serbian national interests were frequently sacrificed to Yugoslavia, but to no avail.

It is significant that the greatest challenges to the existence of Yugoslavia came from the Croats and Serbs; for the seventy-five-year history of this country spun on the axis of relations between these two peoples. The other nations and groups had little power either to split the country or to hold it together. It seems clear that if the Serbs had rejected Croatian overtures that Yugoslavia would never have come to be; it is equally apparent that if Croats had cooperated with the Serbian government, Yugoslavia would never have come apart.

–LAWRENCE A. HELM,
NASA HEADQUARTERS
AND
–JULIJANA BUDJEVAC,
GEORGE WASHINGTON UNIVERSITY

References

Milos Acin-Kosta, *Yugoslavia in Our Time* (Washington, D.C.: Ravnogorski Venac, 1991).

Melville Chater, "Jugoslavia–Ten Years After," *National Geographic* 58 (September 1930): 257–309.

Dimitrije Djordjevic, ed., *The Creation of Yugoslavia, 1914–1918* (Santa Barbara, Cal.: Clio, 1980).

Robert A. Kann, *A History of the Habsburg Empire 1526–1918* (Berkeley: University of California Press, 1974).

R. G. D. Laffan, *The Guardians of the Gate: Historical Lectures on the Serbe* (Oxford: Clarendon Press, 1918), republished as *The Serbs: Guardians of the Gate* (New York: Dorset Press, 1989).

Ivo J. Lederer, *Yugoslavia at the Paris Peace Conference: A Study in Frontiermaking* (New Haven: Yale University Press, 1963).

Harold Nicolson, *Diaries and Letters,* 3 volumes, edited by Nigel Nicolson (London: Collins, 1966–1968).

Nicolson, *Peacemaking 1919* (London: Constable, 1933).

Robin Okey, *Eastern Europe 1740–1985: Feudalism to Communism* (London: Hutchinson, 1982; Minneapolis: University of Minnesota Press, 1982).

Joseph Rothschild, *East Central Europe Between the Two World Wars* (Seattle: University of Washington Press, 1974).

Alan Sked, *The Decline and Fall of the Habsburg Monarchy, 1815–1918* (London & New York: Longman, 1989).

YUGOSLAVIA

APPENDIX

The degree of public participation and the level of popular endurance demanded by the Great War nurtured the first systematic, general use of propaganda. To a degree it was based in prewar nationalist and patriotic rhetoric that was the material of newspaper editorials, school textbooks, and Sunday sermons. It combined xenophobia and defensiveness: mistrusting "the other" and legitimating arms races and cultural chauvinism. That defensiveness dominated wartime propaganda in the early years as well. Each combatant sought to ensure that its people understood that it had been first provoked beyond endurance then treacherously attacked. Beginning in 1916, however, war aims played an increasing role. The sacrifices of the trenches demanded recompense, and retribution demanded the other side pay for its perfidy.

Initially, the military played a significant role in orchestrating the propaganda campaigns—not least because they controlled the primary sources of information from the front. War correspondents such as Philip Gibbs of Great Britain were encouraged to write favorably—not much of a challenge given their usually high levels of patriotism and their nearly complete ignorance of modern war. By the middle of the war, government agencies were taking center stage, orchestrating comprehensive programs of information and disinformation ranging from atrocity stories to children's tales. This mobilization of minds depended heavily on mass culture: the popular press; posters and placards; and the cinema, where feature films and newsreels told the national story and stars such as Charlie Chaplin and Douglas Fairbanks supported the war effort by selling bonds. The artifacts of daily life were brought to the war's service, as playing cards, ashtrays, and beer mugs sported patriotic motifs. In some circles even sex became a matter of patriotism: supporting men home from the front and replacing casualties by winning "the battle of the cradle."

Propaganda increasingly assumed moral as well as military dimensions. In France, Britain, and Germany the moral dimension was most frequently expressed in an intensified rhetoric of "no compromise" and of "seeing it through" at any cost. In the United States the war was also widely interpreted as a springboard for reform and for state-supported righteousness both against the Hun abroad and in pursuit of middle-class causes like suffrage and prohibition. In Russia the fall of the Empire inspired campaigns against oppression whose initial tones were quasi-religious. To its early adherents Bolshevism was a crusade, as much as the war was a crusade to those Americans hoping to carry the banner of reform across the Atlantic Ocean. It was that crusading impulse that in 1918 began outflanking other state propaganda systems, instead appealing directly and viscerally to the people themselves.

Italian cartoon with the caption: "Toward peace. . . . forever"

(from Grosser Bilderatlas des Weltkrieges *[1915–1919], Joseph M. Bruccoli Great War Collection, Thomas Cooper Library, University of South Carolina)*

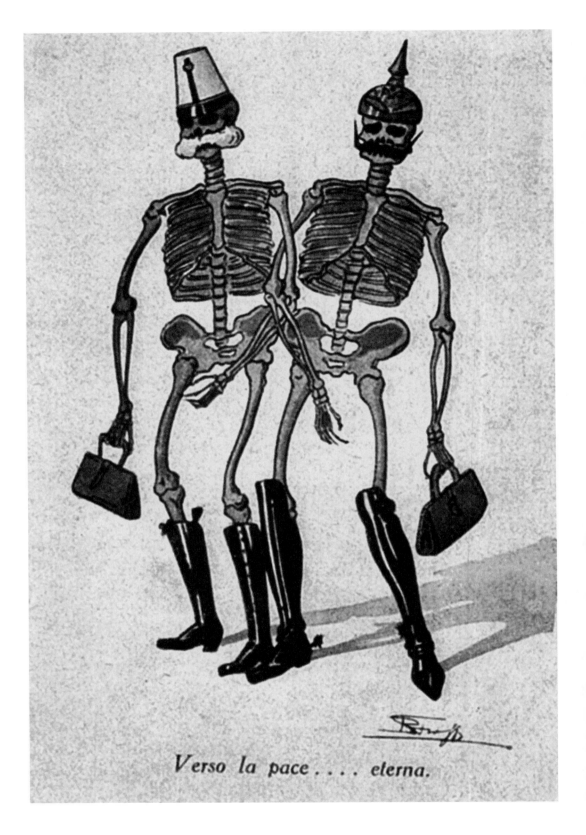

Verso la pace . . . . eterna.

French war-bond poster with an allegorical depiction of American troops coming to assist French, Belgian, and British soldiers. The translation reads: "Give money for victory and the triumph of liberty!"

(Joseph M. Bruccoli Great War Collection, Thomas Cooper Library, University of South Carolina).

French illustration of a mother and child dying during a German gas attack. The caption reads: "The benefits of culture"

(from Les Crimes des Barbares *[1918], Joseph M. Bruccoli Great War Collection, Thomas Cooper Library, University of South Carolina).*

LES BIENFAITS DE LA " KULTUR "

LES GAZ ASPHYXIANTS

« *Est-il un procédé plus conforme au droit des gens que ce nuage de vapeur qu'un vent léger emporte doucement vers l'ennemi ? »* (Gazette de Cologne).

Composition de J. SIMONT.

Illustration showing a French village destroyed by the Germans

(from Les Crimes des Barbares [1918], Joseph M. Bruccoli Great War Collection, Thomas Cooper Library, University of South Carolina)

APPENDIX

**Cover for a French
publication about
German atrocities**

(from Les Crimes des Barbares
*[1918], Joseph M. Bruccoli Great
War Collection, Thomas Cooper
Library, University of
South Carolina)*

APPENDIX

French poster with the warning: "Be silent, the German is on the line" (above) and an Allied poster lampooning German military might (below)

(both from Grosser Bilderatlas des Weltkrieges *[1915–1919], Joseph M. Bruccoli Great War Collection, Thomas Cooper Library, University of South Carolina)*

LES CRIMES DES BARBARES

AU NOM DU " BON VIEUX DIEU ALLEMAND ! "
Composition de Ch. LÉANDRE.

LA MISSION DIVINE DU KAISER

« Rappelez-vous que vous êtes le peuple élu. L'esprit du Seigneur est descendu sur moi, parce que je suis l'Empereur des Germains. Je suis l'instrument du Très-Haut. Je suis son glaive, son représentant.

« Malheur et mort à tous ceux qui résisteront à ma volonté ! Malheur à ceux qui ne croient pas en ma mission ! Malheur et mort aux lâches !

« Qu'ils périssent, tous les ennemis du peuple allemand ! Dieu exige leur destruction, Dieu qui, par ma bouche, vous commande d'exécuter sa volonté !

(PROCLAMATION DE GUILLAUME II A SON ARMÉE DE L'EST.)

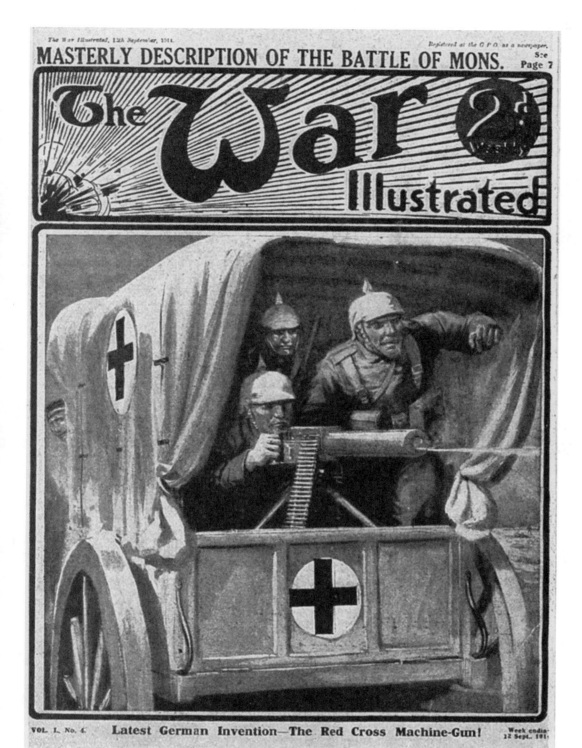

Cover of a British periodical depicting Germans firing a machine gun from the back of an ambulance

(from Grosser Bilderatlas des Weltkrieges *[1915–1919], Joseph M. Bruccoli Great War Collection, Thomas Cooper Library, University of South Carolina)*

British poster warning of German intentions

(from Grosser Bilderatlas des Weltkrieges *[1915–1919], Joseph M. Bruccoli Great War Collection, Thomas Cooper Library, University of South Carolina)*

APPENDIX

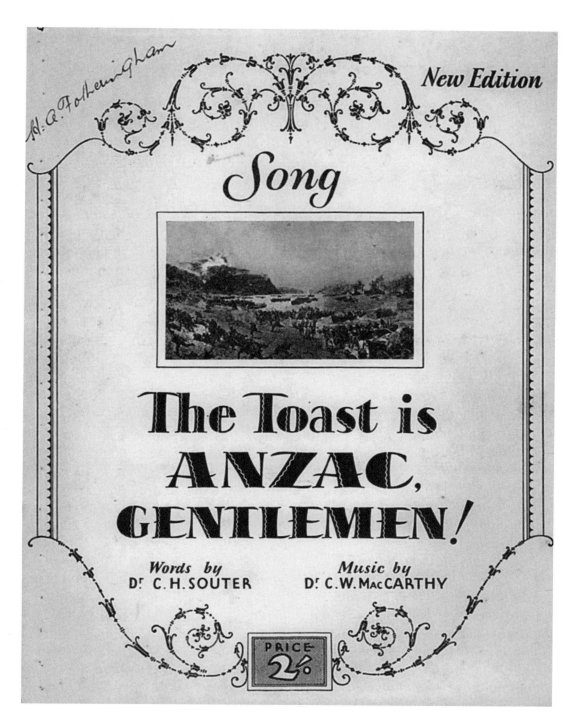

Sheet music celebrating the soldiers of the Australian and New Zealand Army Corps, circa 1915

(Joseph M. Bruccoli Great War Collection, Thomas Cooper Library, University of South Carolina)

APPENDIX

APPENDIX

The Beast Breaks Loose: Kultur as it Appears to Edmund J. Sullivan

Sheet music honoring the mothers of U.S. military personnel, 1918

(Joseph M. Bruccoli Great War Collection, Thomas Cooper Library, University of South Carolina)

APPENDIX

APPENDIX

Sheet music celebrating the arrival of U.S. troops in Europe, 1918

(Joseph M. Bruccoli Great War Collection, Thomas Cooper Library, University of South Carolina)

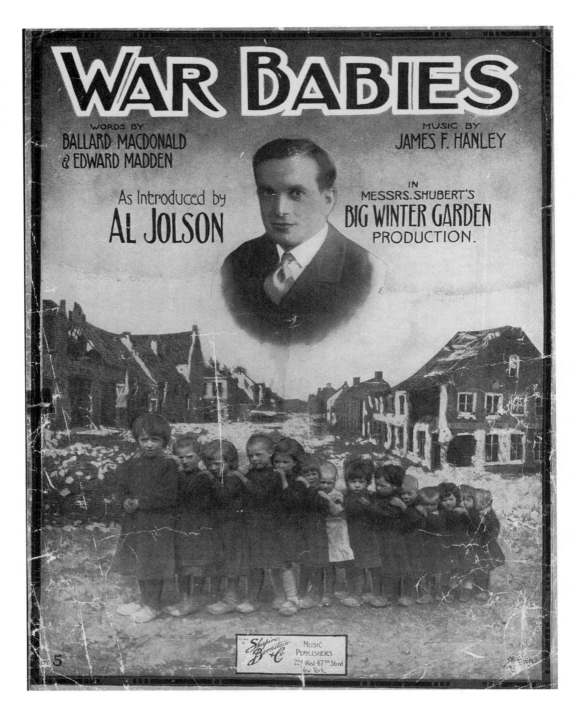

Sheet music for a song about U.S. idealism, 1914

(Joseph M. Bruccoli Great War Collection, Thomas Cooper Library, University of South Carolina)

U.S. poster urging immediate support of the Allied war effort

(Joseph M. Bruccoli Great War Collection, Thomas Cooper Library, University of South Carolina)

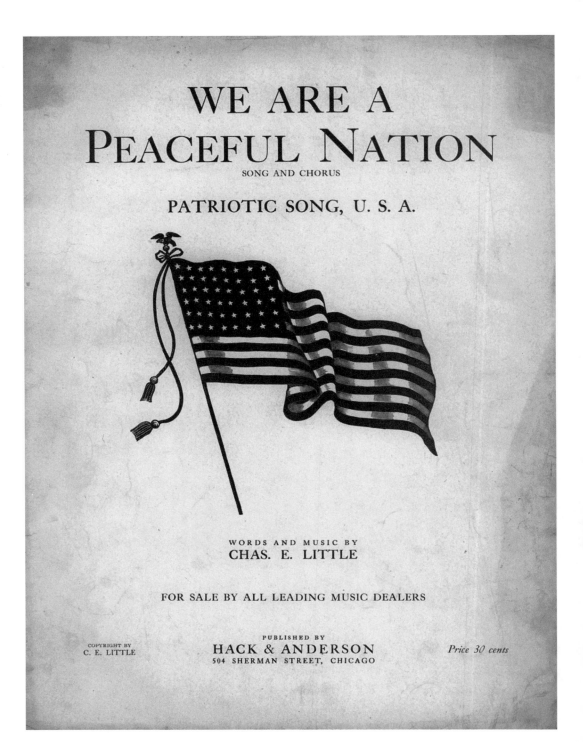

Sheet music for a song about the American symbol of freedom, 1917

(Joseph M. Bruccoli Great War Collection, Thomas Cooper Library, University of South Carolina)

APPENDIX

Sheet music for a
humorous song about
the martial spirit, 1918

*(Joseph M. Bruccoli Great War
Collection, Thomas Cooper
Library, University of
South Carolina)*

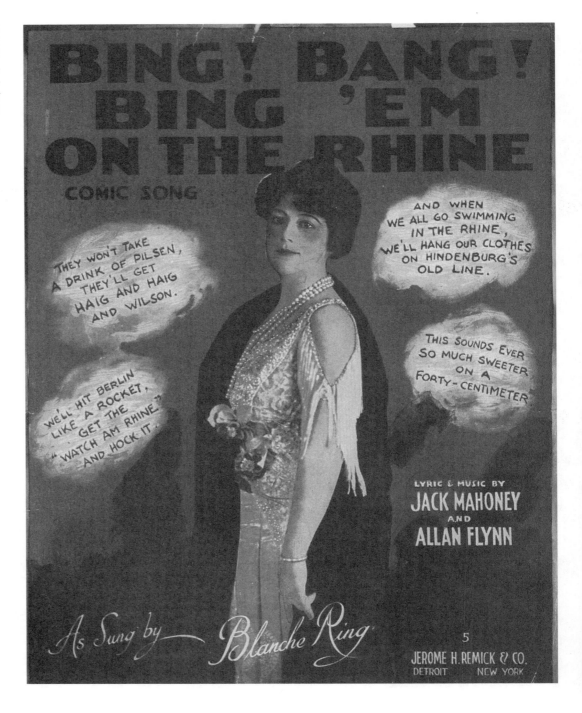

Sheet music celebrating American determination to defeat Germany, 1918

(Joseph M. Bruccoli Great War Collection, Thomas Cooper Library, University of South Carolina)

APPENDIX

APPENDIX

Sheet music for a popular song expressing the desire of many Americans in 1915 to keep out of the war

(Joseph M. Bruccoli Great War Collection, Thomas Cooper Library, University of South Carolina)

Sheet music commending the sacrifice of U.S. mothers, 1917

(Joseph M. Bruccoli Great War Collection, Thomas Cooper Library, University of South Carolina)

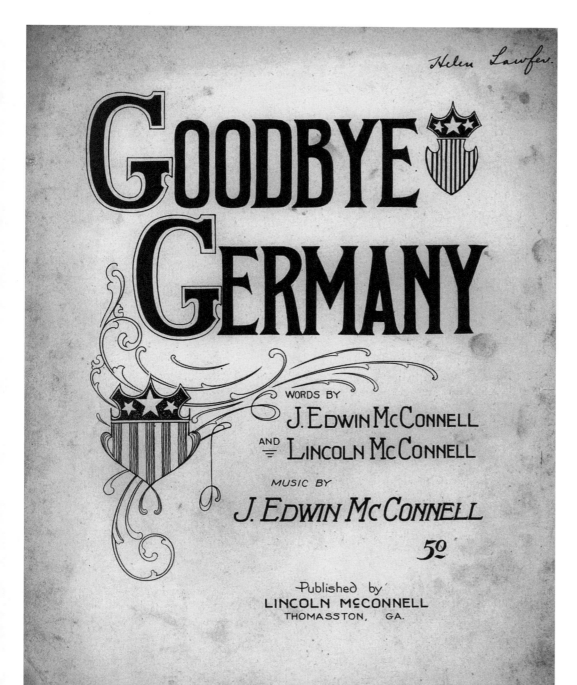

Sheet music for a song predicting the defeat of Germany, 1917

(Joseph M. Bruccoli Great War Collection, Thomas Cooper Library, University of South Carolina)

HALT the HUN!

BUY U.S. GOVERNMENT BONDS
THIRD LIBERTY LOAN

APPENDIX

Sheet music for a song about the U.S. military spirit, 1918

(Joseph M. Bruccoli Great War Collection, Thomas Cooper Library, University of South Carolina)

Sheet music ridiculing the German leader, 1918

(Joseph M. Bruccoli Great War Collection, Thomas Cooper Library, University of South Carolina)

APPENDIX

**Sheet music for a song
celebrating U.S. troops
being sent to Europe, 1917**

*(Joseph M. Bruccoli Great War
Collection, Thomas Cooper
Library, University of
South Carolina)*

APPENDIX

Sheet music for a song hailing the Allied wartime spirit, 1918

(Joseph M. Bruccoli Great War Collection, Thomas Cooper Library, University of South Carolina)

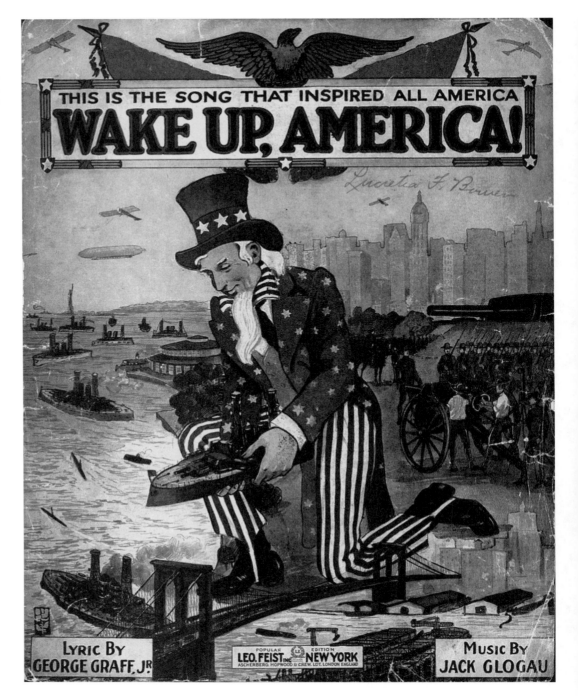

APPENDIX

REFERENCES

1. AFRICA

Clayton, Anthony. *France, Soldiers, and Africa.* London & New York: Brassey's Defence Publishers, 1988.

Echenberg, Myron. *Colonial Conscripts: The Tirailleurs Sénégalais in French West Africa, 1857–1960.* Portsmouth, N.H.: Heinemann, 1991; London: Currey, 1991.

Page, Melvin E., ed. *Africa and the First World War.* London: Macmillan, 1987; New York: St. Martin's Press, 1987.

2. AFRICAN AMERICANS

Barbeau, Arthur E. and Florette Henri. *The Unknown Soldiers: Black American Troops in World War I.* Philadelphia: Temple University Press, 1974.

Brink, William and Louis Harris. *The Negro Revolution in America: What Negroes Want, Why and How They are Fighting, Whom They Support, What Whites Think of Them and Their Demands.* New York: Simon & Schuster, 1964.

Foner, Jack. *Blacks and the Military in American History: A New Perspective.* New York: Praeger, 1974.

Fredrickson, George M. *Black Liberation: A Comparative History of Black Ideologies in the United States and South Africa.* New York: Oxford University Press, 1995.

Goings, Kenneth W. *The NAACP Comes of Age: The Defeat of Judge John J. Parker.* Bloomington: Indiana University Press, 1990.

Gottlieb, Peter. *Making Their Own Way: Southern Blacks' Migration to Pittsburgh, 1916–30.* Urbana: University of Illinois Press, 1987.

Grimshaw, Allen D., ed. *Racial Violence in the United States.* Chicago: Aldine, 1969.

Grossman, James R. *Land of Hope: Chicago, Black Southerners, and the Great Migration.* Chicago: University of Chicago Press, 1989.

Kellogg, Charles Flint. *NAACP: A History of the National Association for the Advancement of Colored People.* Baltimore: Johns Hopkins University Press, 1967.

Marks, Carole and Diana Edkins. *The Power of Pride: Stylemakers and Rulebreakers of the Harlem Renaissance.* New York: Crown, 1999.

Meier, August and Elliott Rudwick. *From Plantation to Ghetto,* third edition. New York: Hill & Wang, 1976.

Nalty, Bernard C. *Strength for the Fight: A History of Black Americans in the Military.* New York: Free Press; London: Collier-Macmillan, 1986.

Silberman, Charles E. *Crisis in Black and White.* New York: Random House, 1964.

Sloan, Irving J. *Blacks in America: 1492–1970: A Chronology & Fact Book,* third edition. Dobbs Ferry, N.Y.: Oceana, 1971.

Taylor, Arnold H. *Travail and Triumph: Black Life and Culture in the South Since the Civil War.* Westport, Conn.: Greenwood Press, 1976.

Weinstein, Allen and Frank Otto Gatell, eds. *The Segregation Era, 1863–1954: A Modern Reader.* New York: Oxford University Press, 1970.

3. AIR WAR

Buckley, John. *Air Power in the Age of Total War.* London: UCL Press, 1999; Bloomington: Indiana University Press, 1999.

Corum, James S. *The Luftwaffe: Creating the Operational Air War, 1918–1940.* Lawrence: University Press of Kansas, 1997.

Gorrell, Edgar S. *The Measure of America's World War Aeronautical Effort.* Northfield, Vt.: Norwich University, 1940.

Hallion, Richard. *Rise of the Fighter Aircraft, 1914–1918.* Annapolis, Md.: Nautical and Aviation Publishing Company of America, 1984.

Higham, Robin. *Air Power: A Concise History.* London: Macdonald, 1972.

Hudson, James J. *Hostile Skies: A Combat History of the American Army Air Service in World War I.* Syracuse, N.Y.: Syracuse University Press, 1968.

Jane's Fighting Aircraft of World War I. London: Jane's Publishing, 1946.

Kennett, Lee. *The First Air War, 1914–1918.* New York: Free Press, 1991.

Kennett. *A History of Strategic Bombing.* New York: Scribners, 1982.

Lawson, Eric and Jane. *The First Air Campaign, August 1914–November 1918.* Conshohocken, Pa.: Combined Books, 1996.

Morrow, John H., Jr. *German Air Power in World War I.* Lincoln: University of Nebraska Press, 1982.

Morrow. *The Great War in the Air: Military Aviation from 1909 to 1921.* Washington, D.C.: Smithsonian Institution Press, 1993.

Raleigh, Walter. *The War in the Air: Being the Story of the Part Played in the Great War by the Royal Air Force.* Oxford: Clarendon Press, 1922.

Robinson, Douglas H. *The Zeppelin in Combat: A History of the German Naval Airship Division, 1912–1918.* London: Foulis, 1962.

Wells, Mark K. ed. *Airpower: Promise and Reality.* Chicago: Imprint Publications, 2000.

Williams, George K. *Biplanes and Bombsights: British Bombers in World War I.* Maxwell Air Force Base, Ala.: Air University Press, 1999.

4. ASIA

Akagi, Roy Hidemichi. *Japan's Foreign Relations, 1542–1936, A Short History.* Tokyo: Hokuseido Press, 1936.

Beasley, W. G. *Japanese Imperialism, 1894–1945.* Oxford: Clarendon Press; New York: Oxford University Press, 1987.

Hane, Mikiso. *Modern Japan: A Historical Survey,* third edition. Boulder, Colo.: Westview Press, 2001.

Morley, James William, ed. *Japan's Foreign Policy, 1868–1941: A Research Guide.* New York: Columbia University Press, 1974.

Morley. *The Japanese Thrust Into Siberia, 1918.* New York: Columbia University Press, 1954.

Nish, Ian. *Japanese Foreign Policy, 1869–1942: Kasumigaseki to Miyakezaka.* London & Boston: Routledge & Kegan Paul, 1977.

Peattie, Mark R. *Nanyo: The Rise and Fall of the Japanese in Micronesia, 1885–1945.* Honolulu: University of Hawaii Press, 1988.

Takeuchi, Tatsuji. *War and Diplomacy in the Japanese Empire.* Garden City, N.J.: Doubleday, Doran, 1935.

5. BIOGRAPHIES

Abraham, Richard. *Alexander Kerensky: The First Love of the Revolution.* New York: Columbia University Press, 1987.

Afflerbach, Holger. *Falkenhayn: Politisches Denken und Handeln im Kaiserreich.* Munich: Oldenbourg, 1994.

Bond, Brian and Nigel Cave, eds. *Haig, A Reappraisal 70 Years On.* London: Cooper, 1999.

Cooke, James J. *Pershing and His Generals: Command and Staff in the AEF.* Westport, Conn.: Praeger, 1997.

Ferro, Marc. *Nicholas II: The Last of the Tsars,* translated by Brian Pearce. New York: Oxford University Press, 1993.

Gilbert, Bentley Brinkerhoff. *David Lloyd George, A Political Life,* volume 2: *The Organizer of Victory, 1912–16.* London: Batsford, 1992.

Hantsch, Hugo. *Leopold Graf Berchtold: Grandseigneur und Staatsman.* 2 volumes. Graz: Verlag Styria, 1963.

Mango, Andrew. *Atatürk: The Biography of the Founder of Modern Turkey.* Woodstock, N.Y.: Overlook Press, 2000.

Owen, Frank. *Tempestuous Journey: Lloyd George, His Life and Times.* London: Hutchinson, 1954.

Powell, Geoffrey. *Plumer: The Soldier's General: A Biography of Field-Marshal Viscount Plumer of Messines.* London: Cooper, 1990.

Prior, Robin and Trevor Wilson. *Command on the Western Front: The Military Career of Sir Henry Rawlinson, 1914–18.* Oxford & Cambridge, Mass.: Blackwell, 1991.

Robertson, William. *Soldiers and Statesmen, 1914–1918.* 2 volumes. London: Cassell, 1926; New York: Scribners, 1926.

Rowland, Peter. *David Lloyd George: A Biography.* New York: Macmillan, 1975.

Service, Robert. *Lenin: A Biography.* Cambridge, Mass.: Harvard University Press, 2000.

Smythe, Donald. *Pershing: General of the Armies.* Bloomington: Indiana University Press, 1986.

Terraine, John. *Douglas Haig: The Educated Soldier.* London: Hutchinson, 1963.

Ulam, Adam B. *Stalin: The Man and His Era.* New York: Viking, 1973.

Volkogonov, Dmitrii. *Lenin: A New Biography,* translated by Harold Shukman. New York: Free Press, 1994.

6. COMBAT EXPERIENCE

Adams, Bernard. *Nothing of Importance: Eight Months at the Front with a Welsh Battalion, October, 1915, to June, 1916.* London: Methuen, 1917.

Ashworth, Tony. *Trench Warfare, 1914–1918: The Live and Let Live System.* London: Macmillan, 1980; New York: Holmes & Meier, 1980.

Audoin-Rouzeau, Stéphane. *Men at War, 1914–1918: National Sentiment and Trench Journalism in France during the First World War,* translated by Helen McPhail. Providence, R.I.: Berg, 1992.

Cecil, Hugh and Peter H. Liddle, eds. *Facing Armageddon: The First World War Experienced.* London: Cooper, 1996.

Denizot, Alain. *Verdun, 1914–1918.* Paris: Nouvelles Editions Latines, 1996.

Ellis, John. *Eye-Deep in Hell: Trench Warfare in World War I.* London: Croom Helm, 1976.

Horne, Alistair. *The Price of Glory: Verdun 1916.* New York: St. Martin's Press, 1962.

Hynes, Samuel. *The Soldiers' Tale: Bearing Witness to Modern War.* New York: John Lane, 1997.

Leed, Eric J. *No Man's Land: Combat and Identity in World War I.* Cambridge & New York: Cambridge University Press, 1979.

Marquess of Anglesey. *A History of the British Cavalry, 1816 to 1919,* 4 volumes. London: Cooper, 1986.

Pick, Daniel. *War Machine: The Rationalisation of Slaughter in the Modern Age.* New Haven: Yale University Press, 1993.

Simpson, Andy, ed. *Hot Blood and Cold Steel: Life and Death in the Trenches of the First World War.* London: Donovan, 1993.

Winter, Denis. *Death's Men: Soldiers of the Great War.* London: John Lane, 1978.

7. DIPLOMACY AND INTERNATIONAL RELATIONS

Bendiner, Elmer. *A Time for Angels: The Tragicomic History of the League of Nations.* New York: Knopf, 1975.

Birn, Donald S. *The League of Nations Union, 1918–1945.* Oxford: Clarendon Press; New York: Oxford University Press, 1981.

Coogan, John W. *The End of Neutrality: The United States, Britain, and Maritime Rights, 1899–1915.* Ithaca, N.Y.: Cornell University Press, 1981.

Fifield, Russell H. *Woodrow Wilson and the Far East: The Diplomacy of the Shantung Question.* New York: Crowell, 1952.

Kennedy, Paul M. *The Rise of the Anglo-German Antagonism, 1860–1914.* London & Boston: Allen & Unwin, 1980.

Kuehl, Warren F. and Lynne K. Dunn. *Keeping the Covenant: American Internationalists and the League of Nations, 1920–1939.* Kent, Ohio: Kent State University Press, 1997.

LaFeber, Walter. *The American Age: Foreign Policy at Home and Abroad,* volume 2: *Since 1896,* second edition. New York: Norton, 1994.

May, Ernest R. *World War and American Isolation, 1914–1917.* Cambridge, Mass.: Harvard University Press, 1959.

Nicolson, Harold. *Peacemaking 1919.* London: Constable, 1933.

Northedge, F. S. *The League of Nations: Its Life and Times 1920–1946.* Leicester, U.K.: Leicester University Press; New York: Holmes & Meier, 1986.

Parrini, Carl P. *Heir to Empire: United States Economic Diplomacy, 1916–1923.* Pittsburgh: University of Pittsburgh Press, 1969.

Raitz von Frentz, Christian. *A Lesson Forgotten: Minority Protection Under the League of Nations: The Case of the German Minority in Poland, 1920–1934.* New York: St. Martin's Press; Münster: Lit Verlag, 1999.

8. FRANCE

Autin, Jean. *Foch, ou, le Triomphe de la Volonté.* Paris: Perrin, 1987.

Fridenson, Patrick, ed. *The French Home Front 1914–1918,* translated by Bruce Little. Providence, R.I.: Berg, 1992.

Laffargue, André Charles Victor. *Foch et la Bataille de 1918.* Paris: Arthaud, 1967.

Laure, Auguste Marie Emile. *Le Commandement en Chef des Armées Françaises du 15 mai 1917 a l'armistice.* Paris: Editions Berger-Levrault, 1937.

McPhail, Helen. *The Long Silence: Civilian Life Under the German Occupation of Northern France, 1914–1918.* London & New York: Taurus, 1999.

Pedroncini, Guy. *Pétain: Géneral en Chef, 1917–1918.* Paris: Presses Universitaires de France, 1974.

Porch, Douglas. *The March to the Marne: The French Army, 1871–1914.* Cambridge & New York: Cambridge University Press, 1981.

Smith, Leonard V. *Between Mutiny and Obedience: The Case of the French Fifth Infantry Division During World War I.* Princeton: Princeton University Press, 1994.

9. GENERAL HISTORIES

Adams, R. J. Q., ed. *The Great War, 1914–18: Essays on the Military, Political, and Social History of the First World War.* College Station: Texas A&M University Press, 1990.

Barzun, Jacques. *From Dawn to Decadence: 500 Years of European Cultural Life, 1500 to the Present.* New York: HarperCollins, 2000.

Carstairs, Carroll. *A Generation Missing.* Garden City, N.Y.: Doubleday, Doran, 1930; London: Heinemann, 1930.

Chickering, Roger and Stig Förster, eds. *Great War, Total War: Combat and Mobilization on the Western Front, 1914–1918.* Cambridge & New York: Cambridge University Press, 2000.

Craig, Gordon A. and others. *World War I: A Turning Point in Modern History, Essays in the Significance of the War,* edited by Jack J. Roth. New York: Knopf, 1967.

Eksteins, Modris. *The Rites of Spring: The Great War and the Birth of the Modern Age.* New York: Houghton Mifflin, 1989.

Ellis, John and Mike Cox. *The World War One Data Book: The Essential Facts and Figures For All the Combatants.* London: Aurum, 2001.

Ferguson, Niall. *The Pity of War.* London: Penguin, 1998.

Fussell, Paul. *The Great War and Modern Memory.* New York: Oxford University Press, 1975.

Gilbert, Martin. *Atlas of World War I.* New York: Oxford University Press, 1994.

Gilbert. *The First World War: A Complete History.* New York: Holt, 1994.

Gilbert. *The Jews in the Twentieth Century: An Illustrated History.* New York: Schocken Books, 2001.

Horne, John, ed. *State, Society, and Mobilization in Europe During the First World War.* Cambridge & New York: Cambridge University Press, 1997.

Howard, Michael. *The Lessons of History.* New Haven: Yale University Press, 1991.

Howard. *War in European History.* London & New York: Oxford University Press, 1976.

Howard and William Roger Louis, eds. *The Oxford History of the Twentieth Century.* Oxford & New York: Oxford University Press, 1998.

Johnson, Paul. *A History of the Jews.* New York: Harper & Row, 1987.

Keegan, John. *The First World War.* London: Hutchinson, 1998.

Kennedy, Paul. *The Rise and Fall of the Great Powers: Economic Change and Military Conflict from 1500 to 2000.* New York: Random House, 1987.

Lichtheim, George. *Europe in the Twentieth Century.* London: Weidenfeld & Nicolson, 1972; New York: Praeger, 1972.

Liddell Hart, B. H. *The Real War, 1914–1918.* Boston: Little, Brown, 1930.

Liddell Hart. *Reputations: Ten Years After.* Boston: Little, Brown, 1928.

Maier, Charles S. *Recasting Bourgeois Europe: Stabilization in France, Germany, and Italy in the Decade After World War I.* Princeton: Princeton University Press, 1975.

Marwick, Arthur, ed. *Total War and Social Change.* Houndsmills, U.K.: Macmillan, 1988; New York: St. Martin's Press, 1988.

Mayer, Arno J. *The Persistence of the Old Regime: Europe to the Great War.* New York: Pantheon, 1981.

Mazower, Mark. *Dark Continent: Europe's Twentieth Century.* New York: Knopf, 1998.

Mosier, John. *The Myth of the Great War: A New Military History of World War I.* New York: HarperCollins, 2001.

Mosse, George L. *Fallen Soldiers: Reshaping the Memory of the World Wars.* New York: Oxford University Press, 1990.

Offer, Avner. *The First World War: An Agrarian Interpretation.* Oxford: Clarendon Press, 1989; New York: Oxford University Press, 1989.

Pound, Reginald. *The Lost Generation of 1914.* New York: Coward-McCann, 1964.

Roshwald, Aviel and Richard Stites, eds. *European Culture in the Great War: The Arts, Entertainment, and Propaganda, 1914–1918.* Cambridge & New York: Cambridge University Press, 1999.

Sachar, Howard Morley. *The Course of Modern Jewish History.* Cleveland: World, 1958.

Sheffield, Gary. *Forgotten Victory: The First World War, Myths and Realities.* London: Headline, 2001.

Sternhell, Zeev and others. *The Birth of Fascist Ideology: From Cultural Rebellion to Political Revolution,* translated by David Maisel. Princeton: Princeton University Press, 1994.

Strachan, Hew, ed. *The Oxford Illustrated History of the First World War.* Oxford & New York: Oxford University Press, 1998.

Strachan, ed. *World War I: A History.* Oxford & New York: Oxford University Press, 1998.

Terraine, John. *To Win a War: 1918, the Year of Victory.* London: Sidgwick & Jackson, 1978.

Tuchman, Barbara W. *The Guns of August.* New York: Macmillan, 1962.

Vital, David. *A People Apart: The Jews in Europe, 1789–1939.* Oxford & New York: Oxford University Press, 1999.

Winter, Jay. *Sites of Memory, Sites of Mourning: The Great War in European Cultural History.* Cambridge & New York: Cambridge University Press, 1995.

10. GERMANY & AUSTRIA-HUNGARY

Bell, A. C. *A History of the Blockade of Germany and of the Countries Associated with Her in the Great War Austria-Hungary, Bulgaria, and Turkey, 1914–1918.* London: HMSO, 1937.

Deák, István. *Beyond Nationalism: A Social and Political History of the Habsburg Officers Corps, 1848–1918.* New York: Oxford University Press, 1990.

Fischer, Fritz. *Germany's Aims in the First World War.* New York: Norton, 1967.

Herwig, Holger H. *The First World War: Germany and Austria-Hungary, 1914–1918.* London & New York: Arnold, 1997.

Kann, Robert A. *A History of the Habsburg Empire, 1526–1918.* Berkeley: University of California Press, 1974.

Kühl, Stefan. *The Nazi Connection: Eugenics, American Racism, and German National Socialism.* New York: Oxford University Press, 1994.

Lupfer, Timothy T. *The Dynamics of Doctrine: The Changes in German Tactical Doctrine During the First World War.* Fort Leavenworth, Kans.: Combat Studies Institute, U.S. Army Command and General Staff College, 1981.

Lutz, Ralph Haswell, comp. *The Causes of the German Collapse in 1918,* translated by W. L. Campbell. Stanford: Stanford University Press, 1934; London: H. Milford, Oxford University Press, 1934.

Paschall, Rod. *The Defeat of Imperial Germany, 1917–1918.* Chapel Hill, N.C.: Algonquin, 1989.

Rachamimov, Alon. *POWs and the Great War: Captivity on the Eastern Front.* Oxford & New York: Berg, forthcoming.

Ritter, Gerhard. *The Sword and the Sceptre: The Problem of Militarism in Germany,* 3 volumes, translated by Heinz Norden. Coral Gables, Fla.: University of Miami Press, 1969–1973.

Sked, Alan. *The Decline and Fall of the Habsburg Empire, 1815–1918.* London & New York: Longman, 1989.

Tunstall, Graydon A., Jr. *Planning for War against Russia and Serbia: Austro-Hungarian and German Military Strategies, 1871–1914.* Boulder, Colo.: Social Science Monographs, 1993.

Whalen, Robert Weldon. *Bitter Wounds: German Victims of the Great War, 1914–1939.* Ithaca, N.Y.: Cornell University Press, 1984.

11. GREAT BRITAIN AND THE EMPIRE

Bond, Brian. *The Victorian Army and the Staff College, 1854–1914.* London: Eyre Methuen, 1972.

Bourne, John. *Britain and the Great War, 1914–1918.* London & New York: Arnold, 1989.

Brown, Ian Malcolm. *British Logistics on the Western Front, 1914–1919.* Westport, Conn.: Praeger, 1998.

Cannadine, David. *The Decline and Fall of the British Aristocracy.* New Haven: Yale University Press, 1990.

Cassar, George H. *The Tragedy of Sir John French.* Newark: University of Delaware Press; London: Associated University Presses, 1985.

Constantine, Stephen, Maurice W. Kirby, and Mary B. Rose, eds. *The First World War in British History.* London & New York: Arnold, 1995.

Dewey, Peter. *War and Progress: Britain, 1914–1945.* London & New York: Longman, 1997.

Fuller, J. G. *Troop Morale and Popular Culture in the British and Dominion Armies.* Oxford: Clarendon Press; New York: Oxford University Press, 1990.

Graves, Robert and Alan Hodge. *The Long Week-end: A Social History of Great Britain, 1918–1939.* London: Faber & Faber, 1940.

Griffith, Paddy. *Battle Tactics of the Western Front: The British Army's Art of Attack, 1916–18.* New Haven: Yale University Press, 1994.

Griffith, ed. *British Fighting Methods in the Great War.* London: Cass, 1996.

Harris, J. P. and Niall Barr. *Amiens to the Armistice: The BEF in the Hundred Days' Campaign, 8 August–11 November 1918.* London & Washington: Brassey's, 1998.

Laffin, John. *British Butchers and Bunglers of World War One.* Gloucester: Sutton, 1988.

Pollard, Sidney. *The Development of the British Economy, 1914–1990,* fourth edition. London: Arnold, 1992.

Turner, John. *British Politics and the Great War: Coalition and Conflict, 1915–1918.* New Haven: Yale University Press, 1992.

12. INTERNET WEBSITES

Encyclopaedia of the First World War <http://www.spartacus.schoolnet.co.uk/FWW.htm>

The Great War (1914–1918) <http://www.pitt.edu/~pugachev/greatwar/www1.html>

The Great War and the Shaping of the 20th Century <http://www.pbs.org/greatwar/>

The World War I Document Archive <http://www.lib.byu.edu/~vdh/wwi/>

World War I: Trenches on the Web <http://www.worldwar1.com/>

13. IMPERIALISM

Aldrich, Robert. *Greater France: A History of French Overseas Expansion.* Basingstoke, U.K.: Macmillan, 1996; New York: St. Martin's Press, 1996.

Baumgart, Winfried. *Imperialism: The Idea and Reality of British and French Colonial Expansion, 1880–1914,* translated by Baumgart and Ben V. Mast. Revised edition. New York: Oxford University Press, 1982.

Betts, Raymond. *Tricouleur: The French Overseas Empire.* London: Gordon & Cremonesi, 1978.

Mangin, Louis-Eugene. *Le Général Mangin.* Paris: Lanore, 1986.

14. LIBRARY HOLDINGS

Hoover Institution on War, Revolution and Peace, Stanford University, Stanford, California.

Imperial War Museum, London.

The Joseph M. Bruccoli Great War Collection, Special Collections Department, Alderman Memorial Library, University of Virginia.

The Joseph M. Bruccoli Great War Collection, Thomas Cooper Library, University of South Carolina.

15. MEMOIRS & AUTOBIOGRAPHIES

Binding, Rudolf Georg. *A Fatalist at War,* translated by Ian F. D. Morrow. Boston & New York: Houghton Mifflin, 1929.

Chapman, Guy. *A Passionate Prodigality: Fragments of Autobiography.* London: Nicholson & Watson, 1933.

REFERENCES

Eyre, Giles E. M. *Somme Harvest: Memories of a P.B.I. in the Summer of 1916.* London: London Stamp Exchange, 1938.

Falkenhayn, Erich von. *General Headquarters, 1914–1916, and Its Critical Decisions.* London: Hutchinson, 1919.

Foch, Ferdinand. *Memoirs of Marshal Foch,* translated by T. Bentley Mott. New York: Doubleday, Doran, 1931.

Gough, Hubert. *Soldiering On: Being the Memoirs of General Sir Hubert Gough.* London: Barker, 1954.

Knox, Alfred. *With the Russian Army, 1914–1917, Being Chiefly Extracts From the Diary of a Military Attaché.* London: Hutchinson, 1921.

Lansing, Robert. *War Memoirs of Robert Lansing, Secretary of State.* Indianapolis: Bobbs-Merrill, 1935.

Nicolson, Harold. *Diaries and Letters,* 3 volumes, edited by Nigel Nicolson. London: Collins, 1966–1968.

Priestley, J. B. *Margin Released: A Writer's Reminiscences and Reflections.* New York: Harper & Row, 1962.

Valéry, Paul. *Variety,* translated by Malcolm Cowley. New York: Harcourt, Brace, 1927.

16. NAVAL OPERATIONS

Corbett, Julian S. *Naval Operations,* 5 volumes. London & New York: Longmans, Green, 1920–1931.

German Warships of World War I: The Royal Navy's Official Guide to the Capital Ships, Cruisers, Destroyers, Submarines and Small Craft, 1914–1918. London: Greenhill, 1992.

Halpern, Paul G. *A Naval History of World War I.* Annapolis, Md.: Naval Institute Press, 1994.

Herwig, Holger H. *"Luxury Fleet": The German Imperial Navy, 1888–1918.* London: Allen & Unwin, 1980.

Hezlet, Arthur. *The Submarine and Sea Power.* London: Davies, 1967.

Keegan, John. *The Price of Admiralty: War at Sea From Man of War to Submarine.* London: Hutchinson, 1988.

Sims, William Sowden. *The Victory at Sea.* Garden City, N.Y.: Doubleday, Page, 1920.

Spector, Ronald H. *At War, At Sea: Sailors and Naval Combat in the Twentieth Century.* New York: Viking, 2001.

Steinberg, Jonathan. *Yesterday's Deterrent: Tirpitz and the Birth of the German Battle Fleet.* London: Macdonald, 1965.

Sumida, Jon Tetsuro. *In Defence of Naval Supremacy: Finance, Technology, and British Naval Policy, 1899–1914.* Boston: Unwin Hyman, 1989.

Tarrant, V. E. *The U-Boat Offensive 1914–1945.* London: Arms & Armour, 1989.

Terraine, John. *Business in Great Waters: The U-boat Wars, 1916–1945.* London: Cooper, 1989.

Wegener, Wolfgang. *The Naval Strategy of the World War,* translated by Herwig. Annapolis, Md.: Naval Institute Press, 1989.

17. ORIGINS OF WWI

Joll, James. *The Origins of the First World War.* Second edition. London & New York: Longman, 1984.

Kagan, Donald. *On the Origins of War and the Preservation of Peace.* New York: Doubleday, 1995.

Kennedy, Paul M., ed. *The War Plans of the Great Powers, 1880–1914.* London & Boston: Allen & Unwin, 1979.

Lee, Dwight E. *Europe's Crucial Years: The Diplomatic Background of World War I, 1902–1914.* Hanover, N.H.: University Press of New England, 1974.

Lee, ed. *The Outbreak of the First World War: Causes and Responsibilities,* fourth edition. Lexington, Mass.: Heath, 1975.

Seaman, L. C. B. *From Vienna to Versailles.* London: Methuen, 1955.

Stevenson, David. *Armaments and the Coming of War: Europe, 1904–1914.* Oxford & New York: Clarendon Press, 1996.

18. RUSSIA

Deutscher, Isaac. *The Prophet Armed, Trotsky: 1879–1921.* New York: Oxford University Press, 1954.

Figes, Orlando. *A People's Tragedy: The Russian Revolution, 1891–1924.* New York: Viking, 1997.

Figes and Boris Kolonitskii. *Interpreting the Russian Revolution: The Language and Symbols of 1917.* New Haven: Yale University Press, 1999.

Lieven, Dominic. *Nicholas II: Emperor of All the Russias.* London: Murray, 1993.

Lincoln, W. Bruce. *Passage Through Armageddon: The Russians in War and Revolution, 1914–1918.* New York: Simon & Schuster, 1986.

Massie, Robert K. *Nicholas and Alexandra.* New York: Atheneum, 1967.

Menning, Bruce W. *Bayonets Before Bullets: The Imperial Russian Army, 1861–1914.* Bloomington: Indiana University Press, 1992.

Pares, Bernard. *The Fall of the Russian Monarchy: A Study of the Evidence.* London: Cape, 1939; New York: Knopf, 1939.

Pipes, Richard. *The Russian Revolution.* New York: Knopf, 1990.

Schapiro, Leonard. *The Communist Party of the Soviet Union.* New York: Random House, 1959.

Showalter, Dennis E. *Tannenberg: Clash of Empires.* Hamden, Conn.: Archon, 1991.

Stites, Richard. *Revolutionary Dreams: Utopian Vision and Experimental Life in the Russian Revolution.* New York: Oxford University Press, 1989.

Ulam, Adam B. *The Bolsheviks: The Intellectual and Political History of the Triumph of Communism in Russia.* New York: Macmillan, 1965.

Wade, Rex A. *The Russian Revolution, 1917.* Cambridge & New York: Cambridge University Press, 2000.

Wildman, Allan K. *The End of the Russian Imperial Army: The Old Army and the Soldiers' Revolt,* volume 1: *The Old Army and the Soldiers' Revolt (March–April 1917).* Princeton: Princeton University Press, 1980.

19. SEXUALITY

Adams, Michael C. C. *The Great Adventure: Male Desire and the Coming of World War I.* Bloomington: Indiana University Press, 1990.

Dijkstra, Bram. *Idols of Perversity: Fantasies of Feminine Evil in Fin-de-Siecle Culture.* New York: Oxford University Press, 1986.

Frevert, Ute. *Men of Honour: A Social and Cultural History of the Duel,* translated by Anthony Williams. Cambridge: Polity Press & Cambridge, Mass.: Blackwell, 1995.

Hall, Lesley A. *Hidden Anxieties: Male Sexuality, 1900–1950.* Cambridge: Polity Press, 1991.

Hirschfeld, Magnus. *The Sexual History of the World War.* 3 volumes. New York: Panurge Press, 1934.

Mosse, George L. *The Image of Man: The Creation of Modern Masculinity.* New York: Oxford University Press, 1996.

Theweleit, Klaus. *Male Fantasies,* translated by Stephen Conway and others. 2 volumes. Cambridge: Polity

Press, 1987–1989; Minneapolis: University of Minnesota Press, 1987–1989.

20. SHELL SHOCK

Babington, Anthony. *Shell-Shock: A History of the Changing Attitudes to War Neurosis.* London: Cooper, 1997.

Holden, Wendy. *Shell Shock.* London: Channel 4 Books, 1998.

Marlowe, David H. *Psychological and Psychosocial Consequences of Combat and Deployment with Special Emphasis on the Gulf War.* Santa Monica, Cal.: Rand, 2000.

Salmon, Thomas W. *The Care and Treatment of Mental Diseases and War Neuroses ("Shell Shock") in the British Army.* New York: War Work Committee of the National Committee for Mental Hygiene, 1917.

Shephard, Ben. *A War of Nerves: Soldiers and Psychiatrists in the Twentieth Century.* Cambridge, Mass.: Harvard University Press, 2001.

Smith, G. Elliot and T. H. Pear. *Shell Shock and Its Lessons.* Manchester: University Press; New York: Longmans, Green, 1917.

Southard, E. E. *Shellshock and Other Neuropsychiatric Problems Presented in Five Hundred and Eighty-nine Case Histories from the War Literature, 1914–1918.* Boston: Leonard, 1919.

21. STRATEGY, LOGISTICS, TACTICS

Foley, Robert T. "Attrition: Its Theory and Application in German Strategy, 1880–1916." Dissertation, University of London, 1999.

Gudmundsson, Bruce I. *Stormtroop Tactics: Innovation in the German Army, 1914–1918.* New York: Praeger, 1989.

Howard, Michael, ed. *The Theory and Practice of War: Essays Presented to Captain B. H. Liddell Hart.* London: Cassell, 1965.

Johnson, Hubert C. *Breakthrough! Tactics, Technology, and the Search for Victory on the Western Front in World War I.* Novato, Cal.: Presidio Press, 1994.

22. TECHNOLOGY AND SCIENCE

Palazzo, Albert. *Seeking Victory on the Western Front: The British Army and Chemical Warfare in World War I.* Lincoln: University of Nebraska Press, 2000.

Richter, Donald. *Chemical Soldiers: British Gas Warfare in World War I.* Lawrence: University Press of Kansas, 1992.

Travers, Tim. *How the War Was Won: Command and Technology in the British Army on the Western Front, 1917–1918.* London & New York: Routledge, 1992.

Travers. *The Killing Ground: The British Army, the Western Front, and the Emergence of Modern Warfare, 1900–1918.* London & Boston: Allen & Unwin, 1987.

23. UNITED STATES

Baruch, Bernard M. *American Industry in the War: A Report of the War Industries Board (March 1921),* edited by Richard H. Hippelheuser. New York: Prentice-Hall, 1941.

Bass, Herbert J., ed. *America's Entry Into World War I: Submarines, Sentiment, or Security?* New York: Holt, Rinehart & Winston, 1964.

DeWeerd, Harvey A. *President Wilson Fights His War: World War I and the American Intervention.* New York: Macmillan, 1968.

Drew, Dennis M. and Donald M. Snow. *The Eagle's Talons: The American Experience at War.* Maxwell Air Force Base, Ala.: Air University Press, 1988.

Kennedy, David M. *Over Here: The First World War and American Society.* New York: Oxford University Press, 1980.

Koistinen, Paul A. C. *Mobilizing for Modern War: The Political Economy of American Warfare, 1865–1919.* Lawrence: University Press of Kansas, 1997.

Trask, David F. *The AEF and Coalition Warmaking, 1917–1918.* Lawrence: University Press of Kansas, 1993.

Zieger, Robert H. *America's Great War: World War I and the American Experience.* Lanham, Md.: Rowman & Littlefield, 2000.

Zimmerman, Phyllis A. *The Neck of the Bottle: George W. Goethals and the Reorganization of the U.S. Army Supply System, 1917–1918.* College Station: Texas A&M University Press, 1992.

24. YUGOSLAVIA

Acin-Kosta, Milos. *Yugoslavia in Our Time.* Washington, D.C.: Ravnogorski Venac, 1991.

Djordjevic, Dimitrije, ed. *The Creation of Yugoslavia, 1914–1918.* Santa Barbara, Cal.: Clio, 1980.

Laffan, R. G. D. *The Guardians of the Gate: Historical Lectures on the Serbe.* Oxford: Clarendon Press, 1918. Republished as *The Serbs: Guardians of the Gate.* New York: Dorset Press, 1989.

Lederer, Ivo J. *Yugoslavia at the Paris Peace Conference: A Study in Frontiermaking.* New Haven, Conn.: Yale University Press, 1963.

Okey, Robin. *Eastern Europe 1740–1985: Feudalism to Communism.* London: Hutchinson, 1982; Minneapolis: University of Minnesota Press, 1982.

Rothschild, Joseph. *East Central Europe Between the Two World Wars.* Seattle: University of Washington Press, 1974.

REFERENCES

CONTRIBUTORS' NOTES

ABBATIELLO, John: An Air Force pilot since graduation from the U.S. Air Force Academy in 1987, he completed a master's degree at King's College, London, in 1995 and subsequently taught military history as a member of the faculty at the Academy. He recently returned to King's, where he is pursuing a doctorate; his studies focus on naval aviation in World War I.

ASHLEY, Susan A.: Professor of history at Colorado College, specializing in French and intellectual history; author of many scholarly articles.

ASTORE, William J.: Associate professor and director of international history at the U.S. Air Force Academy; earned his doctor of philosophy degree from the University of Oxford in 1996; author of *Observing God: Thomas Dick, Evangelicalism, and Popular Science in Victorian Britain and America* (2001).

BRUCE, Robert B.: Assistant professor of military history at Sam Houston State University; earned his Ph.D. from Kansas State University; author of *A Fraternity of Arms: America and France in the Great War* (forthcoming) and *France and the Great War, 1914–1918: A Historical Dictionary* (forthcoming); author of articles on various aspects of French military history published in the *Journal of Military History* and *Army History*.

BUCHER, Greta: Associate professor at the U.S. Military Academy; earned her Ph.D. in Soviet history from Ohio State University; author of "Struggling to Survive: Soviet Women in the Postwar Years," *Journal of Women's History* (Spring 2000).

BUDJEVAC, Julijana: Doctoral student in Eastern European history at George Washington University.

BUTCHER, Daniel Lee: Doctoral candidate in history at Kansas State University.

CLARK, Kevin: Instructor at the U.S. Military Academy, specializing in military history.

CORUM, James S.: Professor of Comparative Military Studies at the USAF School of Advanced Airpower Studies; author of *The Roots of Blitzkrieg: Hans von Seeckt and German Military Reform* (1992), *The Luftwaffe: Creating the Operational Air War, 1918–1940* (1997), and co-author with Richard Muller, of *The Luftwaffe's Way of War* (1998).

DINARDO, Richard L.: Associate professor for National Security Affairs at the U.S. Marine Corps Command and Staff College, Quantico, Virginia; author of *Mechanized Juggernaut or Military Anachronism?: Horses and the German Army of World War II* (1991), *Germany's Panzer Arm* (1997), and "The Dysfunctional Coalition: The Axis Powers and the Eastern Front," *Journal of Military History* (1996).

ERICKSON, Lieutenant Colonel (Ret.) Edward J.: Doctoral candidate in history at the University of Leeds, Yorkshire, United Kingdom; teaches world history at Norwich High School, Norwich, New York; author of *Ordered to Die: A History of the Ottoman Army in the First World War* (2001); and co-author, with Frederick M. Lorenz, of *The Euphrates Triangle: Security Implications of the Southeast Anatolia Project* (1999).

FACKNITZ, Mark A. R.: James Madison University.

FOLEY, Robert T.: Lecturer assigned to the Joint Services Command and Staff College in the Defense Studies Department of King's College, London; completed his doctorate in German strategic thought before and during World War I at the Department of War Studies, King's College; editor and translator of *Alfred von Schlieffen's Military Writings* (forthcoming).

FORSTCHEN, William R.: Assistant professor of history at Montreat College; author of *The Lost Regiment* series.

GARDNER, Nikolas: Accepted a position as lecturer in military history at the University of Salford, Greater Manchester, U.K.; earned his Ph.D. in military history at the University of Calgary (2000); author of "Command in Crisis: The British Expeditionary Force and the Forest of Mormal, August 1914," *War & Society* (1998) and "Command and Control in the 'Great Retreat' of 1914: The Disintegration of the British Cavalry Division," *Journal of Military History* (1999); author of *Trial by Fire: Command in the British Expeditionary Force in 1914* (forthcoming).

GILTNER, Phil: Teaches at the U.S. Military Academy; author of *In the Friendliest Manner: German-Danish Economic Collaboration Under the Nazi Occupation of 1940–1949* (1998); earned his Ph.D. at the University of Toronto; researches and writes on the Danish economy during World War I.

HABECK, Mary: Assistant professor at Yale University; co-editor of *The Great War and the Twentieth Century* (2000) and *Spain Betrayed* (2001).

HAYES, Jack Patrick: Visiting instructor at Colorado College; working on his doctoral degree at the University of British Columbia; researching late-nineteenth- and early-twentieth-century political, legal, and economic development in China and Japan.

HELM, Lawrence: Holds a B.A. in East European History from George Washington University, and is currently Information Systems Lead for NASA Headquarters.

KAUTT, Captain William: U.S. Air Force, San Antonio, Texas; former assistant professor of History at the U.S. Air Force Academy; author of *The Anglo-Irish War, 1916–1921: A People's War* (1999).

MARBLE, Sanders: Instructor at American Military University and former senior historian for <www.ehistory.com>; wrote his dissertation (University of London, 1998) on artillery in World War I.

McCARTNEY, H. B.: Lecturer in Defense Studies for King's College, London, based at the Joint Services Command and Staff College; contributor to "Post Combat Syndromes from the Boer War to the Gulf," *British Medical Journal* (forthcoming); writing a book about the British Territorial Force and World War I.

McJIMSEY, Robert: Professor of history at Colorado College; author of "A Country Divided?: English Politics and the Nine Years' War," *Albion,* 23 (Spring 1991) and "Crisis Management: Parliament and Political Stability, 1692–1719," *Albion* (forthcoming).

NEIBERG, Michael S.: Assistant professor of history at the U.S. Air Force Academy; author of *Making Citizen Soldiers: ROTC and the Ideology of American Military Service* (2000) and *Warfare in World History* (2001).

PALAZZO, Albert: Research Fellow in the School of History, University of New South Wales at the Australian Defence Force Academy; completed his B.A. and M.A. at New York University and Ph.D. at Ohio State University; author of *Seeking Victory on the Western Front: The British Army and Chemical Warfare in World War I* (2000), *The Australian Army: A History of Its Organisation From 1901 to 2001* (2001), and *The History of the Royal Australian Corps of Transport, 1973–2000* (forthcoming).

PLATING, John D.: Instructor of military history at the U.S. Air Force Academy; earned his M.A. at Ohio State University; specializes in the history of airpower, technology, and warfare; couples his academic pursuits with 2,300 flying hours in military aircraft.

QUENOY, Paul du: Doctoral candidate in history at Georgetown University.

RACHAMIMOV, Alon: Tel Aviv University; author of *POWs and the Great War: Captivity on the Eastern Front* (forthcoming) and "Provincial Compromises and State Patriotism in fin-de-Siècle Austria-Hungary," *Tel Aviver Jahrbuch für deutsche Geschichte* (2001).

RUFFLEY, David L.: Instructor of history at the U.S. Air Force Academy; earned an M.A. in International Relations from Troy State University, an M.A. in Russian/Soviet Studies from the University of Washington, and a Ph.D. in Russian History from Ohio State University; author of *Children of Victory: Young Specialists and the Evolution of Soviet Society, 1965–1982* (forthcoming).

SCHMITT, Deborah A.: Associate professor of history at the U.S. Air Force Academy; earned an M.A. and a Ph.D. in African history from Indiana University under Dr. Phyllis Martin; her dissertation, "The Bechuanaland Pioneers and Gunners in the Second World War," is under review for a book contract by Greenwood Press.

SCUTARO, Vincent J.: Independent scholar, New York, New York.

SHOWALTER, Dennis: Professor of history at Colorado College; president of the Society for Military History; visiting professor at the U.S. Military Academy and U.S. Air Force Academy; author and editor of many books; joint editor of *War in History.*

SKARSTEDT, Vance R.: Holds a Ph.D. from Florida State University; assistant professor of history at the U. S. Air Force Academy, specializing in American and military history.

SPIRES, David N.: Holds a Ph.D. in military history from the University of Washington and teaches history at the University of Colorado at Boulder. As a career Air Force officer, he served on the faculty of the Air Force Academy; in intelligence assignments in Vietnam, Europe, and Turkey; and as staff historian at Headquarters United States Air Forces in Europe. His publications include articles and presentations on the German Army and Air Force Space issues, and books on the pre-Hitler German Army, U.S.-Greek military relations, and strategic defense issues. He is the author of *Beyond Horizons: A Half Century of Air Force Space Leadership* (1997) and *Air Power for Patton's Army: The XIX Tactical Air Command in the Second World War* (forthcoming). He edited *Key Documents in Air Force Space History* (forthcoming), a collection of important documents from the U.S. military space program.

TERDOSLAVICH, William: Independent scholar, New York, New York.

TERRY, Michael: Holds an M.A. from the University of North Dakota; adjunct professor at the U.S. Air Force Academy, specializing in airpower history and space studies.

THOMSEN, Paul A.: Freelance researcher and writer; received an M.A. in History from Brooklyn College in 1996; served as a research associate and archivist for Joseph A. Califano Jr. and The Benjamin J. Rosenthal Library of Queens College; completed specific assignments for various book packagers and publishers; presently serves as an historical researcher/writer for New York Parks and Recreation; author of articles in several journals, magazines and anthologies, including *Illuminations, American History Magazine, Military History Magazine,* and *A Date Which Will Live in Infamy;* he resides in New York City.

TODMAN, Daniel: Pembroke College, Cambridge University.

TUNSTALL, Graydon A.: University of South Florida; author of *Planning for War Against Russia* (1993).

ULBRICH, David J.: Doctoral student in military history at Temple University; author of "Henry S. Aurand: Student, Teacher, and Practitioner of U.S. Army Logistics, 1920–1995," in *The Human Tradition in America Between the Wars, 1920–1945* (2001).

WHEATLEY, John: Independent scholar, Brooklyn Center, Minnesota.

WINTERMUTE, Bobby A.: Doctoral candidate in history at Temple University.

INDEX

water supply system in VII 283

Chicago Daily News IX 4

Chicano Power II 94

Chief Joseph Dam (United States) VII 53

Childers, Robert IX 93

Chile I 123–128, 140, 152; VI 64, 87, 194, 265–266
  access to Import-Export Bank I 53
  Allende government I 26
  CIA activites in VI 86–87
  coup of 1960s I 26
  human rights record I 143
  U.S. intervention (early 1970s) I 15, 123–133

China I 41, 44, 54, 59, 86–91, 141, 277, 287–288, 292; II 4, 9, 36, 39–40, 47, 119, 168, 171; VI 10, 35, 42, 49, 53, 56, 59, 90, 107, 121, 136, 147, 154, 175, 178, 181, 199, 201, 203, 213–214, 243, 265, 271; IX 91, 96, 162, 164–165, 167–168, 174–175, 246
  accuses Soviets of aiding Vietnam VI 44
  as balance to U.S.S.R VI 201
  attacks on Quemoy and Matsu I 265–270, 275
  attacks Vietnam VI 43
  blue-water navy of VI 53
  bombing of embassy in Belgrade VI 54
  border clashes with Soviet Union VI 40, 43
  defense spending of VI 54
  economy VI 53, 219
  German interests in VIII 31, 137
  human-rights in VI 219
  influence on North Vietnam I 296–297
  Korean War I 273–275
  meeting with United States in Warsaw (1969) VI 43
  Nationalists I 61
  nuclear espionage of VI 219
  Nuclear Non-Proliferation Treaty I 218
  nuclear proliferation I 222–224
  nuclear weapons development I 222, 239
  purchase of Western military hardware VI 42
  rapprochement with the United States VI 38–45
  relations with Russia VI 53
  relations with Soviet Union VI 38, 113, 203
  Russian threat to British interests in VIII 33
  Shantung province siezed IX 163
  Soviet role in postwar VI 254
  support for Afghan resistance VI 166
  support for FNLA and UNITA VI 1
  Taiwan-U.S. mutual-security treaty I 268
  Tiananmen Square Massacre (1989) VI 54, 113, 121
  U.N. Security Council membership I 300
  U.S. intelligence sites in VI 43
  U.S. Ping-Pong team trip VI 43
  U.S. relations with VI 4, 88

China Hands I 58–63; VI 158

Chinese Civil War VI 150

Chinese Communist Party (CCP) VI 181

Chinese Cultural Revolution (1966–1976) VI 40

Chinese Revolution (1949) VI 177; IX 168

Chlorine gas, effects of VIII 239

Chou En-lai I 266, 269, 277

Christian Democratic Party (CDP)
  in Chile I 124, 127–130

Christmas bombing (1972) VI 28

Christian Church, evangelization of VIII 203

Christmas Truce (1914) VIII 62–63

Chunuk Bair VIII 117–118, 123

Church, Frank VI 61

Church of England
  World War I VIII 203, 208
  World War I chaplains VIII 203

Churchill, Winston I 31, 154, 201, 231, 305; II 32, 39; IV 19, 40–45, 144, 148, 210, 213; V 25, 34–46, 85, 102, 104, 109, 118, 123, 135–136, 146, 152, 168, 176, 221–222, 236; VI 8, 78, 104, 146, 173, 267, 280; VIII 33, 79, 104, 117–118, 122; IX 52, 57, 100, 103
  "balance of terror" VI 15

Balkans V 46, 69–72, 75
  "Iron Curtain" speech (1946) I 286; VI 9, 49, 250
  military background IV 41–42
  opposition to Operation Anvil/Dragoon V 238–241
  Tehran Conference (1943) I 259
  Yalta Agreement (1945) I 300–304
  Yalta Conference (1945) V 309–315

CIA. *See* Central Intelligence Agency

CIO. *See* Congress of Industrial Organizations

civil liberties I 73–81

Civil Rights Act (1964) II 25–26, 91, 141, 162, 164, 192, 277–278, 293

Civil Rights movement II 19–28, 42–48, 80, 89–96, 159, 162–163, 165, 180, 257; III 181–189, 268; VI 25, 140
  affirmative action II 143
  connections to labor movement II 189
  March for Jobs and Freedom (1963) II 27
  March on Washington (1963) II 25, 91–92
  media coverage of II 20–22
  President's Committee on Civil Rights (1946) II 42
  relationship with labor movement II 192
  resistance to II 25, 140
  Scottsboro case III 188
  "separate but equal" doctrine II 137
  use of civil disobedience II 140
  voter registration II 27

Civil War (1861–1865) VI 26, 28, 57; VIII 14, 18, 23, 25, 68, 136, 149, 199, 226, 296, 299; IX 19, 22, 116, 158, 209

Civil Works Administration (CWA, 1933) III 154

Civilian Conservation Corps (CCC, 1933) III 154

Clark, Mark W. IV 146; V 125–126, 187
  Italian campaign IV 144

Clark, William P. VI 231

Clark Amendment (1975) VI 1–4

Clay, Lucius I 35–36

Clausewitz, Carl von VIII 16, 71, 112–113, 199

Clean Air Act Amendments (1970) II 183

Clean Water Act (1972) VII 256, 258, 262–264, 267–269, 274, 303–305
  reauthorization VII 274

Clemenceau, Georges VIII 11, 19, 78, 147, 149–150, 256, 278, 283–283; IX 203, 207, 250
  assassination attempt upon VIII 278

Cleveland VII 116, 122–123, 262, 265

Clifford, Clark M. I 160; II 6, 205

Clifford-Elsey report II 205, 208

Clinton, Bill I 97–98; II 80; VI 8, 58, 61, 231, 235; VII 224; VIII 11
  abortion legislation II 223
  and dam protests VII 221
  Dayton accords II 154
  impact of 1960s on presidency II 163
  Israel I 159
  Lewinsky scandal VI 231
  pro-choice stand II 223
  re-election of II 200

Clinton administration
  arms-control agreements VI 20
  defense spending VI 220
  foreign policy of VI 58
  nuclear nonproliferation I 224
  on flood control VII 214

CNN Cold War television series VI 66

Coastal Zone Management Act (1972) II 183

Cobra helicopter VI 173

Coffin, Howard IX 21

Colautti v. *Franklin* (1979) II 222

Colby, William E. VI 257

Cold War I 27–32, 82–90, 101–106, 115–122, 148–155, 165–203, 216–224, 271–276, 300–303; II 4, 9, 30–63, 68, 104, 163; III 10, 48; V 46, 119, 145, 149, 191, 199; VI 1–6, 8–11, 30–33,

108-115, 130-133, 160-162, 168-172, 175-
178; VII 31, 53, 97, 174, 188
casualties in VI 50
causes of VI 252
conclusion of VI 47-51, 213-216
dam building in VII 29
effect of nuclear weapons I 250-257
end of VI 150, 214
impact on development of space programs II 241
impact on federal highway development II 107
impact on U.S. space program development II
257
late 1970s intensification II 172
military buildup II 43
mutual assured destruction (MAD) I 251-252
origins of I 258-264; II 30
Reagan's role in ending VI 221-241
Stalin's role in starting VI 250-252
vindicationist interpretation VI 155
Cole v. *Young* I 80
Collier, John, Commissioner of Indian affairs III 141-
142
Collins, J. Lawton I 6; V 122
Colorado VII 10, 13, 112, 181, 182
farmers' use of water in VII 13
production of crops on irrigated land in VII 11
Colorado River VII 27, 31, 151-153, 155, 168, 211, 214
dams on VII 108-115, 152
Colorado River Compact (CRC) VII 152-153
Colorado River Irrigation District VII 157
Colorado River Land Company VII 152
Colorado River Storage Project (CRSP) VII 27, 112
Columbia Basin VII 29
dams in VII 196
Columbia Basin Project VII 202
Columbia River VII 25, 27-28, 31, 51-61, 197, 199,
202, 219-220, 222, 225, 227
as salmon producer VII 53
first major navigation project on VII 52
hydroelectric dams on VII 198
Columbia River Fisherman's Protective Union VII 53
Columbia River Highway VII 57
Columbia River Inter-Tribal Fish Commission VII 61
Columbia River Packers Association VII 53
Comal River VII 70
combat effectiveness
Germany V 282, 284
Japan V 281-282
Leyte campaign V 281
Normandy invasion V 282
psychological limits IV 47-52
United States V 278-286
Combined Bomber Offensive IX 223
Combined Chiefs of Staff (CCS) V 20, 23, 25, 38, 42-
45
Commission on Polish Affairs VIII 281
Commission on Presidential Debates II 196, 199
Committee on Public Information (CPI) VIII 296; IX
78
Committee on the Present Danger VI 256, 262
Committee to Re-Elect the President (CREEP) II 177;
VI 24
Commonwealth of Independent States (CIS) VI 54
Commonwealth of Nations VI 13
communism I 148-155; II 31-32, 56-57, 160; VI 49;
IX 83
atheism of VI 176
attraction for women VI 49
China II 267
collapse of II 153
global II 130
ideology I 258-262; VI 49
infiltration of federal government II 133
world domination VI 175-182
Communist Control Act (1954) I 74, 77
Communist Information Bureau (Cominform) I 36-
113; VI 179, 246

Communist International (Comintern) I 113; III 224,
226; IV 80; VI 178, 254, 277
Communist Manifesto (1848) VI 178
Communist Party I 74; III 182, 221
in Chile I 124
in Guatemala I 123
of the Soviet Union III 224; VI 179, 276
of Yugoslavia (CPY) VI 273-278, 280-281
Communist Party of the United States of America
(CPUSA) II 46-48; III 237; VI 123, 154,
157
1932 presidential candidate III 182
Federation of Architects, Engineers, Chemists and
Technicians II 228
history of III 224
organization of Southern Tenant Farmers
Unions II 189
Community Action Programs (CAP) II 270-276
Compañía de Terrenos y Aguas de la Baja California,
S.A. VII 155
Comprehensive Immigration Law (1924) III 233
Comprehensive Test Ban Treaty (CTBT) I 224; VI 58
Comprehensive Wetlands Management and
Conservation Act VII 274
Concert of Europe VI 203
Confederate army, Zouave units in IX 116
Conference on Environmental Economics at Hyvinkää
(1998) VII 89
Congo IX 226
Congregational Church VIII 204
Congress of African People (1970) II 95; III 193, 195
Congress of Berlin IX 99
Congress of Industrial Organizations (CIO) II 188,
197; III 183-184, 191, 195
Congress on Racial Equality (CORE) II 161; III 219
Congress of Vienna (1815) IX 45, 226
Connally, John VI 257
Connolly, Thomas T. II 208; III 31; VI 151
Conrad von Hotzendorf, Franz VIII 46-47, 49, 252;
IX 64-65, 99, 135, 137
Conservation in Action Series (1947) VII 278
Conservative Party (Great Britain) VI 13
Conscription Crisis (1917) VIII 158-159
Constantine (Greek king) IX 208
Constantinople VIII 117-118, 122, 173, 212, 214-215,
228; IX 208
Contadora peace process VI 194
containment I 142, 144, 154, 158, 160, 183-184, 187,
262, 271-272, 274, 288, 293; II 30-31, 58,
269; VI 59, 80, 83, 203
Dulles criticism of I 273
during Carter administration I 13
strongpoint I 82-86
universal I 82-90
Contras VI 57, 61, 191-196, 237, 241
Convention on the Protection of the Mediterranean Sea
against Pollution VII 143-144, 305-310
conventional warfare IV 46-52
convergence theory VI 241
Coolidge, Calvin III 22, 25, 47, 176, 178, 226; IX 92
Coolidge administration IX 171
authorizes Boulder Dam VII 28
Cooper v. *Aaron* (1958) II 286
Cooper, John Sherman VI 61
Cooper-Church amendment (1970) I 44; VI 60
Coordinating Unit for the Med Plan VII 145
Coppola, Francis Ford VI 222
Cordier, Andrew VI 75
Corfu IX 207
Corn Production Act (1917) IX 59
Costa Rica I 53
invasion threats from Nicaragua (1949, 1955) I
125
U.S. intervention in mid 1950s I 15
Council of Ten VIII 282
Council on Environmental Quality Rainfall VII 214,
224
Council on Foreign Relations VI 199, 203

Index

INDEX

INDEX

Mozambique Liberation Front (*Frente da Libertação de Moçambique* or FRELIMO) VI 2, 6; VII 239
Mozambique National Resistance Movement (*Resistência Nacional Moçambicana* or RENAMO) VI, 2, 4, 6
Mubarak, Hosni I 163, 317
Mudros Armistice (1918) VIII 217
mujahidin (mujahideen) I 10–16; VI 2, 133, 165, 238
    U.S. support VI 229
Mundt, Karl E. I 74, 306; II 131, 211
Mundt-Nixon Bill I 74
Munich Agreement (1938) I 293, 300
Munich Conference (1938) IV 127
Municipality of Metropolitan Seattle (Metro) 188–195
Munitions of War Act (1915) IX 56
Murphy, Charles Francis III 262
Murphy, Justice Frank V 188
music
    "folk revival" II 214
    as political force II 214
music industry
    impact of television II 218
    record companies at Monterey Music Festival II 219
    sheet music production II 217
    technological advances II 216
    youth market II 219
Muskie, Edmund Sixtus VII 176, 261, 263–264, 268
Mussolini, Benito I 134; IV 14, 80; V 36, 108–109, 117, 135, 169, 175–177, 226, 233; VIII 95; IX 96, 175
    alliance with Hitler V 179
    downfall V 2
    invasion of Ethiopia V 118, 120
    proposal of the Four Power Pact V 120
    removal from power V 178, 179
    support of Franco IV 224, 226
Muste, A. J. II 7; III 184
Mutual Assured Destruction (MAD) I 154, 169–171, 191, 198, 202, 226–227, 230–232, 251–252; II 67; VI 31, 168, 174
Mutual Defense Assistance Act (1949) I 59
Mutual Security Act I 175
Mutual Security Program (MSP) I 175
MX missile VI 17–18

N

Nader, Ralph VII 178, 265, 269
Nagasaki I 30, 230, 239, 242–245, 249, 268; III 12, 15; V 3, 8, 49, 52, 111, 154, 192; VI 31; VII 174
Nagy, Imre VI 130–131, 134, 270
Nagymaros Dam (Hungary) VII 100–101, 104
Namibia VI 1 6; VII 7, 38, 236–237, 240–242
    as U.N. Trust Territory 236
    withdrawal of South African troops VI 7
Nanking Massacre (1937) V 151
Napoleon I IX 116
Napoleon III IX 30, 116
Napoleonic Wars (1803–1815) I 166, 259; VIII 233–234
narcotics III 133–137
    Boxer Rebellion III 136
    Foster Bill (1910) III 137
    Harrison Act (1914) III 137
    history of legal regulation III 133
    progressive movement III 135
Narmada (Sardar Sarovar) Project (India) VII 127, 132
Narmada River 9, 134
Narodny Kommissariat Vnutrennikh Del (People's Commissariat for Internal Affairs, NKVD) IV 50; V 233; VI 275, 278
Nassau Agreement (1962) VI 11, 13
Nasser, Gamal Abdel I 110, 162, 273, 277–278, 283, 314; II 117, 146–147; VI 11, 80–81, 106, 161, 246, 268, 270; VII 3
    challenges Britain I 280
    pan-Arab campaign I 281

"positive neutrality" II 148
Nation of Islam II 93–95
National Aeronautics and Space Administration (NASA) II 246, 258, 260
    creation of II 242
    funding of II 261
National Association for the Advancement of Colored People (NAACP) II 19–20, 23, 25, 27, 44–45, 90, 94, 138, 140–141; III 80, 93, 118, 121, 182, 184–186, 217, 270–274; IX 2, 4
    opposition to Model Cities housing projects II 277
    Scottsboro case III 185
National Association of Black Journalists II 96
National Association of Broadcasters II 123
National Association of Colored Women III 167
National Audubon Society VII 215
National Black Political Convention (1972) II 95, 198
National Committee of Negro Churchmen II 95
National Committee to Re-Open the Rosenberg Case II 228
National Council of Negro Churchmen (NCNC) II 94
National Council of Mayors VII 258
National Defense and Interstate Highway Act (1956) II 107
National Defense Highway Act (1956) II 249
National Education Association II 190, II 191
National Environmental Policy Act (NEPA) II 183; VII 31, 176, 266, 269,
National Farmers Process Tax Recovery Association III 159
National Front for the Liberation of Angola (*Frente Nacional de Libertação de Angola* or FNLA) VI 1, 6, 87, 165
National Guard Act (1903) VIII 301
National Industrial Recovery Act (NIRA, 1933) III 27–28, 62, 65, 149,154
    Supreme Court ruling III 25
National Intelligence Estimates (NIEs) VI 256–258, 260
National Labor Relations Act (Wagner Act, 1935) III 149, 193
National Labor Relations Board (NLRB) II 188; III 30, 62, 149, 190–191, 193, 195
National Liberation Front (NLF) I 296; II 119, 263–264, 266
National liberation movements VI 183–187
National Negro Congress (NNC) III 184
National Organization of Women (NOW) II 78
National Organization for Women v. *Joseph Scheidler* (1994) II 223
National Parks Association VII 30
National Pollutant Discharge Elimination System VII 264
National Prohibition Act (1919) III 200
National Reclamation Act (1902) III 243
National Recovery Administration (NRA, 1933) III 30, 154
National Security Act (1947) I 5, 7, 64, 69; VI 61
National Security Agency (NSA) I 74; II 230; VI 157
National Security Council (NSC) I 54, 64, 83, 121; VI 41, 90, 96, 196, 231
National Security Council memorandum 68 (NSC-68) I 83–84, 89, 149, 182, 211, 274
National Security Decision Directives (NSDD) VI 13, 32, 82, 166
National Socialist German Workers' Party (Nazi Party) I 35; IV 267; VI 49, 176, 254, 274, 277; VIII 92, 94, 167
National Union for the Total Independence of Angola (*União Nacional para a Independência Total de Angola* or UNITA) VI 1–2, 6, 87, 165
National Urban League II 94; III 80, 184; IX 2, 4
National Water Act of 1974 (Poland) 18
Native Americans VIII 23, 27
    advocate breaching dams VII 221
    and dam income VII 59
    and fishing VII 57, 197, 220

INDEX

INDEX

floods on VII 231
pollution of VII 234
Rhine-Main-Danube Canal 104, 204–210
Rhodes, James A. VII 265
Rhodesia VII 239; VIII 86
British immigration to VII 237
colonialists in VII 7
Rhodesian Unilateral Declaration of Independence VII 240
Rhône River VII 92–95, 147
Rhône River Authority VII 93, 96
Ribbentrop, Joachim von V 134
Ribbentrop-Molotov Non-Aggression Pact (1939) V 28, 30, 32
Rich, Willis VII 201
Richtofen, Manfred von IX 38
Rift Valley VII 229
Riis, Jacob August III 260
Rio Grande River VII 152
Rio Treaty I 93
riparian ecosystems in the U.S. Southwest VII 211–218
Rivers and Harbors Act (1899) VII 266
Rivers and Harbors Act (1925) VII 52
Roan Selection Trust VII 5
Robarts, John P. VII 118
Roberto, Holden VI 1, 165
Roberts, Justice Owen III 25, 28, 30; V 188
Robertson, William VIII 77, 102–108, 221
Robinson, Bestor VII 112
Robinson, James H. II 44
Rock Around the Clock (1956) II 219
Rock and Roll II 213–219
"British invasion" II 216
commercial aspects II 219
form of rebellion II 219
liberating force II 213
mass marketing of II 216
origin of term II 214
punk trends II 216
revolutionary force II 214
unifying force II 216
Rockefeller, John D. III 271
Rockefeller, Nelson A. III 48; VII 264
Rocky Boy's Reservation VII 172
Rocky Ford VII 15
Rocky Ford Ditch Company VII 13
Rocky Mountains VII 151, 181, 197
Roe v. *Wade* (1973) II 78, 220–226, 280, 284
Rogue River VII 31, 223
Romania I 110, 294; II 36, 39, 172; V 64; VI 51, 88, 175, 206, 210, 217, 245, 249, 252, 261, 265, 274, 276; VII 248–250, 252–254; VIII 43–44, 46, 93–97, 163, 216, 230, 278; IX 60–61, 66, 127, 193, 205, 207
chemical spill in VII 247–255
Department of Waters, Forests, and Environmental Protection VII 248
Environmental Protection Agency VII 248
forest clear-cutting in VII 254
relationship with Soviets I 253
Soviet Domination I 107
U.S. recognizes communist government I 303
Romanian Waters Authority VII 248
Rommel, Erwin V 123–126, 129, 135, 143, 176, 181, 226; VIII 111
legend V 175
Roosevelt, Eleanor III 150, 217, 219
Roosevelt, Franklin D. II 32, 39, 50, 52, 165, 197, 203, 280; III 10–11, 14, 45, 48, 86, 89, 109, 147, 190, 193; IV 173, 210; V 58, 236, 249; VI 8–9, 20, 36, 56–57, 78, 104, 123, 146–147, 158, 205, 254, 267; VII 28, 97, 152, 202
arsenal of democracy III 64
Asia policy IV 254
attitude toward Soviet Union III 13
belief in a cooperative relationship with the Soviet Union I 101
Brain Trust II 210

Casablanca conference (1943) V 252
election of VII 27
Executive Order 8802 (1941) III 219
Executive Order 9066 (1942) III 103–104
Fireside chats III 148, 152
Four Freedoms V 250
Good Neighbor Policy I 125; III 47
Great Depression III 54–60
Inaugural Address (1932) III 152
isolationism V 289–294
Lend Lease Act IV 160
Native American policies III 141–142
New Deal II 47, 271; III 193, 263
New Deal programs III 62–63
Operation Torch (1942) V 251
opinion of Second Front IV 213
presidential campaign (1932) III 148
previous war experience V 253
relationship with George C. Marshall V 251
Roosevelt Court II 281
State of the Union Address (1941) II 99
Scottsboro case III 188
Selective Service Act (1940) V 250
support of Great Britain V 250
support of highway building II 106
support of naval reorganization IV 3
Supreme Court III 24
unconditional surrender policy V 270–276
western irrigation VII 25
World War II strategy V 251, 253
Yalta conference V 252, 309–315
Roosevelt, Theodore I 306; II 195, 199, 271–272; III 208, 211, 240–247, 177; VIII 18, 22, 129, 205; IX 5, 168, 246
appreciation of public image III 242
Bull Moose Party III 243
conservation efforts III 243
Dominican Republic III 247
establishes federal refuges VII 271, 273
First Children III 242
labor disputes III 243
New Nationalism III 211
Nobel Peace Prize II 99, 243
racial prejudices III 246
role as a family man III 242
Rough Riders III 241
signs Newlands Reclamation Act VII 25
Spanish-American War (1898) III 245
supports western reclamation VII 26
Teddy bears III 242
views on Latin America I 132
Roosevelt (FDR) administration III 46; VI 154
dam projects VII 25
national drug policy III 135
New Deal III 163
opium trade III 137
policy toward Jews III 251
relationship with labor movement II 188
Soviet sympathizers in VI 61, 154
spurs Western growth VII 28
support of Mexican Water Treaty VII 152
Third World VI 80
War Refugee Board (WRB) III 253
Roosevelt (TR) administration
Anti-Trust Act (1890) III 242
Big Stick diplomacy III 46
corollary to the Monroe Doctrine III 247
Department of Commerce and Labor, Bureau of Corporations III 242
foreign policy III 243, 245
Hepburn Act (1906) III 243, 245
National Reclamation Act (1902) III 243
Panama Canal III 243, 247
Pure Food and Drug Act (1906) III 243
United States Forestry Service III 243
Roosevelt Corollary (1904) III 46
Roosevelt Dam (United States) VII 214, 216
Root Elihu VIII 298

Rosellini, Albert D. VII 190
Rosenberg, Alfred V 143, 216
Rosenberg, Julius and Ethel I 274; II 131, 227–234; VI
154, 156, 158, 177
and Communist Party of the United States of
America (CPUSA) II 227
arrest of II 229, 231–232
execution of II 233
forged documents II 230
Freedom of Information Act II 228
G & R Engineering Company II 229
martyrdom II 230
Meeropol, Michael and Robert, sons of II 228
possible motives for arrest of II 231
proof of espionage activity II 230
Soviet nuclear spying I 241, 243, 246–247
Young Communist League II 228
Ross, Bob VII 74
Rostow, Walt W. I 20, 294
flexible response I 120
Rowlett Act (1919) IX 93
Royal Air Force (RAF) I 235; IV 163, 168; V 86, 90,
93, 95, 124; VIII 55, 194; IX 9, 11, 217, 220,
222
attacks on civilians V 87
Royal Air Force (RAF) Mosquitoes V 60
Royal Canadian Navy V 80, 82, 85
Royal Flying Corps (RFC) IX 10, 38
Royal Navy (Britain) V 43, 82, 85, 118, 260; VI 75;
VIII 132; IX 31, 48–51, 75–77, 79, 99, 139–
142, 173, 176–177, 181, 183–184, 186, 228,
247, 256
Ruacana Diversion Wier VII 239
Ruckelshaus, William D. VII 263, 266, 268
Rundstedt, Field Marshal Karl Gerd von 125–126, 129
Rupprecht, Prince VIII 179–180, 184, 246, 274
Rural Institute in Puno, Peru VII 74
Rusk, Dean I 160, 294; VI 71, 95–96, 101
Russia
alliances before World War I VIII 35, 225–231
anti-semitism VIII 164
Constituent Assembly IX 199, 201
Crimean War (1853–1856) VIII 33
Council of Ministers IX 240
Duma IX 145, 190, 201, 238, 240
General Staff Academy IX 158
Great Retreat (1915) IX 240
Imperial state, collapse of IX 81, 154–161
Jews in VIII 164, 167
Provisional government VIII 96, 167, 170–178,
260, 261; IX 194, 196237–243202, 240
Socialists VIII 255, 258, 261
Soviet IX 82
Special Conference of national Defense IX 190
White Army VIII 168
World War I VIII 30, 44–45, 48, 69, 71–72, 76,
82, 92–101, 122, 182, 208–209, 212–213,
245–246, 251–252, 256, 277, 281, 299; IX
27, 30, 34, 43, 45, 48–49, 60–67, 84, 91–93,
99, 101, 105, 108, 120, 128, 133–137, 140,
145, 163, 171, 189–195, 204, 208, 224, 226,
228, 237–243, 250, 252–253, 267
aircraft IX 13
alliance VIII 11, 212, 223
army in VIII 69, 75, 170–171
casualties VIII 125–126, 268
cavalry IX 72
naval aircraft IX 181
Supreme headquarters IX 239
War Industries Committee IX 193, 243
women in combat VIII 125, 129
Zemstva Union IX 190, 242
Russian Federation VI 47, 53–54, 114
former communists VI 55
Russian Revolution (1917) VI 176; VIII 96, 163, 170,
211, 221, 261, 268; IX 27, 165, 168, 189,
195–202, 208, 240

Russian Civil War (1918–1920) VI 244
Russo-Japanese War (1904–1905) IV 256; VI 40; VIII
35, 44–45, 73, 75, 226, 228, 247; IX 127,
154, 156, 160, 162, 168, 181, 190, 227
Russo-Turkish War (1877–1878) VIII 73, 226
Rwanda I 289; II 101, 155; VI 51, 213
Tutsi population VI 83

S

SA (storm trooper) I 139
Sacco, Nicola and Bartolemo Vanzetti III 228–237;
VIII 301
involvement with Italian anarchist groups III 233
League for Democratic Action III 235
New England Civil Liberties Union III 235
protest over verdict III 231
trial III 231
Sacco-Vanzetti Defense Committee (SVDC) III 234
Sacramento River VII 29, 272
as-Sadat, Anwar I 159, 309, 311–314; II 150; VI 162–
164, 170
death (9 October 1981) I 317
making peace I 317
objective I 316
policies I 316
"year of decision" I 316
St. James Declaration (1942) V 264
Saimaa Lake, Finland VII 90
Saipan
fall of (1944) V 112
Sakharov, Andrei I 146; II 104
Salish Mountains VII 171
Salmon 2000 Project VII 229–235
Salsedo, Andrea III 229–231
Salt River VII 214, 216
Samsonov, Aleksandr IX 65, 159–160, 242
San Antonio River VII 70, 256
San Antonio Riverwalk VII 71
San Antonio Water System (SAWS) 70, 74
San Antonio, Texas VII 69–70, 74–75
recycling of water in VII 70
San Francisco VII 262
San Francisco Bay VII 178
San Luís Rio Colorado VII 153, 154
San Marcos River VII 70, 74
San Pedro River VII 216
Sandanistas (Nicaragua) I 48–51, 53–54, 94, 96, 125–
126; II 58; VI 61, 64, 190–191, 193, 237,
241, 265
attempting to maintain control of Nicaragua I 56
Civil Defense Committees VI 192
removed from power (1990) I 51
takeover of Nicaragua (1979) I 54, 141
Sand Dunes and Salt Marshes (1913) VII 277
Sanders, Bernard II 197, 201
Sandoz chemical spill VII 229–230, 232
Sanger, Margaret III 17–18, 171
Santa Barbara, California VII 269
oil platform blowout off of VII 265
Santa Barbara Declaration of Environmental
Rights VII 267
Sarant, Alfred II 230
Sardar Sarovar project (India) VII 9, 132, 134
Saronic Gulf VII 148
Sarraut, Albert V 116
Sassoon, Siegfried IX 150, 152, 212
Satpura Mountains, India VII 125
Saudi Arabia II 153; VI 164–165, 239; VII 79, 81
Afghan rebels VI 238
dependence on United States I 162
fundamentalist movements I 163
Iraqi bombing of I 195
Operation Desert Storm I 157
pan-Arab campaign I 281
support of United States I 158
Savage Rapids Dam (United States) VII 31
Save the Narmada Movement VII 127

Savimbi, Jonas VI 1–7, 165
Saynbach River VII 230
Scales v. *United States* I 81
Scalia, Anton II 224
Scalia, Antonin II 143
Scandinavia IX 81
Scapa Flow IX 48, 53, 142, 187
Scharnhorst, Gerhard von IX 127
Schechter Poultry Corporation v. *United States* (1935) III 28
Schecter, Jerrold L. I 243
Schecter, Leona P. I 243
Scheer, Reinhard 142
Schelling, Thomas C. I 171
    flexible response I 121
Schlieffen, Alfred von VIII 71, 75, 179–180, 182, 184–185, 245–248; IX 41–42, 46, 103, 124
Schlieffen Plan VIII 71, 110, 114, 148, 180, 183, 199, 208, 245–253; IX 42, 44–45, 225, 227, 257
Schlesinger, Arthur M., Jr. I 74; VI 56–57, 154
School busing II 292–299
    Boston opposition to II 294
    Charlotte-Mecklenburg School District II 293
    impact on white flight II 294
    integration of public schools II 293
Schmidt, Helmut VII 207
Schutzstaffeln (SS) IV 84, 118, 130, 137, 139; V 58; VIII 60, 95
Schutztruppe (protectorate forces) VIII 85, 89
Schuylkill River VII 256
Scopes Trial (1925) III 33, 37
Scopes, John III 32–34, 37, 39
Scotland VIII 134, 203; IX 53, 78
Scottsboro case III 181, 185
Scottsboro Defense Committee III 188
Sea of Cortez VII 151
Sea of Galilee VII 136
Sea of Japan VII 148
Sea of Marmara VII 79
Seaborg, Glenn T. VII 176
Seattle, Washington VII 188–195, 197
    city council votes for dam removal VII 222
Seattle Post-Intelligencer VII 191
Seattle Times VII 191
Second Anglo-Boer War (1899–1902) VIII 198
Second Balkan War (1913) IX 203
Second International (1889) VIII 260
Second London Naval Disarmament Conference (1935–1936) V 204, 208
Second National Water Act (1961, Finland) VII 85, 87
Second Naval Conference (1927) V 204
Second Reich Ix 262
Securities and Exchange Commission (SEC) III 154
Sedition Act III 229
Seecht, Hans von IX 131
Segregation II 19, 24, 26, 28, 42, 91, 137, 160, 162–163
    public facilities II 138
    U.S. armed forces IV 216–222
Selassie, Haile IX 94, 96, 175
Selective Service II 4–5
Selective Service Act (1917) VIII 296
Selective Service Act (1940) V 250
Selway River VII 29
Senate Foreign Relations Committee II 208
Senate Internal Security Subcommittee (SISS) II 131, 134
Senate Judiciary Committee III 26
Senegal IX 111, 113
    soldiers in French army IX 112, 118
Sephuma, Olive VII 243
Serageldin, Ismail VII 280
Serbia VIII 43–45, 47, 76, 95, 106, 162, 208, 212, 216, 226, 228–229; IX 99, 102, 133, 193, 203–204, 225, 227, 266–272
    defeat of IX 207
    invaded by Austria-Hungary VIII 72; IX 206
    population reduced by World War I VIII 189
Seufert Bros. v. *United States* (1919) VII 57–58

Seventeenth Amendment II 196
Sexual revolution II 235–240
    beginnings of II 238
    Commission on the Status of Women (1961) II 238
    effects of II 224
    myth of vaginal orgasm II 238
    power vs. sex II 237
Seyhan River VII 79
Shaler, Nathaniel VII 277
Shanghai Commission (1909) III 137
Shanghai Communiqué (1972) II 172–173
Sharpeville Massacre (1960) VII 239–240
Shashe River, Botswana VII 33
Shasta Dam (United States) VII 29
Shatt al Arab VII 77
Sheaffer, John VII 262
Shelley v. *Kraemer* (1948) II 141
Shelley, Mary II 86
Shellfish VII 41–50
shell shock IX 209–216
Sherman Anti-Trust Act (1890) III 242
Sherriff, R. C. IX 212
Shevardnadze, Eduard VI 116
Showa Restoration V 112
Shriver, Sargent II 271, 275
    War on Poverty involvement II 272
Shultz, George P. VI 231
Siberia IX 163, 165, 168, 197
Sicherheitsdienst der SS (SD, Security Service of the SS) V 214, 216
Sicherheitspolizei (German Security Police) IV 141
Sieg River VII 230
Sierra Club VII 27, 30–31, 108, 111–114, 177
    fights Grand Canyon dams VII 110
Sierra Nevada Mountains VII 112, 272
Sigismund Chapel, Wawel Cathedral, Poland VII 18
Silent Spring (Carson) II 183; III 7; VII 86, 160, 162
Silent Valley Project (India) VII 127
Silesia IX 136, 171
Silvermaster, Nathan VI 126
Sims, William IX 75, 184
Simsboro Aquifer VII 75
Sinai Peninsula I 308–309, 311–312, 316–317; VII 2, 135
    demilitarization I 314
    Israeli forces I 313
Sinn Féin VIII 156, 158–159, 161–162
Sino-French War (1884–1885) IX 101
Sister Carrie (Dreiser) II 239
Sit-in movement (1960s) II 27, 160; VI 25
Six-Day War (1967) I 156–157, 159, 162, 308, 314; VI 107, 163, 171; VII 135, 140
    aftermath I 312
    Gaza Strip I 314
    Golan Heights I 314
    Sinai Peninsula I 314
    West Bank of the Jordan River I 314
Sixth Amendment II 281
Skagit River VII 223
Skawina Aluminum Works VII 18–19
Skoropadsky, Pavlo VIII 99–100
Slim, William V 3, 122, 198
Slovak Green Party VII 103
Slovak Union of Nature and Landscape Protectors VII 103
Slovakia VII 248, 250, 252
    dams in VII 100–107
    environmentalists in VII 103
    importance of Gabcikovo dam VII 103
    nuclear reactor at Jaslovské Bohunice VII 103
    nuclear-power plant at Mochovce VII 103
    symbolic importance of Danube VII 102
Slovenia IX 136, 266–272
Smith Act (Alien Registration Act of 1940) I 77, 79, 81; III 11
Smith v. *Allwright*, 1944 II 141
Smith, Adam IX 54–55

Index

Smith, Bessie III 79, III 82
Smith, Holland M. "Howlin' Mad" V 297, 299
Smith, Howard Alexander II 208
Smith, Ian VI 2, 83
Smuts, Jan VIII 85–86, 89; IX 13, 222
Smyrna VIII 214, 217; IX 208
Smyth Report I 248
Smyth, Henry De Wolf I 247–248
Smythe, William A. VII 151
Snake River 27, 29, 31, 53–54, 196–197, 220, 221, 223–225, 227
    dams on VII 219–228
Social Darwinism III 260; IV 86, 123; VIII 60, 299; IX 99, 112, 209, 224, 228
Social Democratic Party I 255; VI 20, 207
Social Ecological Movement VII 20
Social Security Act (1935) III 63, 149
Socialism II 34, 60, 160; VIII 254–262; IX 83
Socialist convention (1913) III 223
Socialist Labor Party II 42
Socialist Party II 196, 199; III 222–223
    Debs, Eugene V. III 221
Socialist Unity Party (SED) VI 118, 121
Soil Conservation and Domestic Allotment Act (1936) III 157
Solidarity VI 110, 237; VII 17, 19, 20
Solzhenitzyn, Aleksandr VI 200
Somalia II 100, 155–156; VI 164, 271
    claim to Ogaden VI 165
    Ethiopian conflict VI 165
    imperialism I 151
    relations with the Soviet Union VI 165
Somoza Debayle, Anastasio I 48–49, 54, 126, 141; III 51; VI 190–191
Somocistas VI 64, 191
Sonoran Desert VII 151–152
    agriculture in VII 152
Sorensen, Ted II 275
Sorenson, Theodore C. II 117
South Africa I 51; VI 1, 2, 4, 6, 50, 54, 87, 136, 178, 215; VII 2, 5, 67, 236–237,239–241; VIII 31, 160–161, 208
    apartheid VI 13
    Bill of Rights VII 287
    British immigration to VII 237
    inequalities of water supply in VII 284
    intervention in Angola VI 7
    intervention in Mozambique VI 6
    nuclear weapons development I 219–223
    rinderpest epidemic VII 34
    use of water by upper class VII 7
    water policy in VII 286, 287
South African National Defense Force VII 7
South African War (1899–1902) IX 68
South America, introduction of species to the United States from VII 217
South Carolina
    laws on rice dams and flooding VII 272
    rice cultivation in the tidewater zone VII 272
    slaves cleared swamp forests VII 272
South Dakota VII 181
    dams in VII 29
South East Asia Treaty Organization (SEATO) II 52, 264
South Korea I 86–87, 288, 293; II 37; VI 102, 147–149, 217, 263
    domino theory I 266
    invaded by North Korea (1950) I 208; VI 28
    invasion of I 184
    nuclear weapons development I 216, 219, 223
    U.S. intervention I 158
South Vietnam I 40–46, 290, 293–299; II 5–8, 263, 266; VI 58–60, 92–99, 101, 138, 140, 201, 203, 284
    aid received from United States I 158; VI 2, 66, 142, 144
    conquered by North Vietnam I 142; VI 222
    declares independence I 290

Soviet support I 185
Southeast Asia Treaty Organization (SEATO) I 277; VI 203, 287
Southeastern Anatolia Project VII 77, 83
Southern African Hearings for Communities affected by Large Dams VII 242
Southern Baptist Convention III 38
Southern Christian Leadership Conference (SCLC) II 22, 26, 28, 89
Southern Okavango Integrated Water Development Project VII 243
Southern Pacific Railroad VII 151, 155
Southern Rhodesia VII 237, 239
Southern Tenant Farmers' Union (STFU) II 189; III 159
South-West Africa VII 237, 239
South-West African People's Organization (SWAPO) VII 239
Southwest Kansas Groundwater Management District VII 185
Soviet expansionism I 262; II 34–35, 208, 264, 267; III 10
    U.S. fear of II 129, 207
Soviet intervention
    Hungary I 278, 281
    Middle East I 277
Soviet Union I 77, 91; II 9, 56–62, 64–71, 168, 171; III 10; VI 9, 16, 20–21, 32, 35, 49, 106, 115–116, 147, 149, 161, 201, 206, 208, 236, 250–255, 260, 264; VII 55; VIII 94, 97, 99, 277, 285
    aging leadership VI 111
    aid to China V 198
    aid to Mozambique VI 2
    Angola policy VI 41, 43, 165
    annexes Estonia VII 22
    "Aviation Day" I 192
    bomber fleet I 6; VI 50
    casualties in Afghanistan (1979–1989) I 12
    Central Committee II 59
    Central Committee Plenum II 60
    challenge to U.S. dominance in Latin America I 125
    collapse I 11; VI 47, 50, 58, 108, 213, 224, 227, 235, 237; VII 17, 207; VIII 139
    Cominform I 178
    Communist Party VI 244, 247
    cooperation with Nationalist Chinese government I 304
    coup (1991) VI 114
    Cuban Missile Crisis II 116; VI 70–76
    Czechoslovakia (1948) II 130, 133
    defense spending I 197; VI 54; VI 116, 120, 226
    demographics VI 242
    demokratizatiia I 152
    development of wartime economy IV 233
    diplomatic work I 289
    domination of eastern Europe I 258, 260
    domination of other countries I 271
    drain on resources by war in Afghanistan I 13
    East Germany policy VI 115–122, 211
    Eastern Europe as defensive barrier I 303
    economy I 184; II 57, 59; VI 109, 111, 214, 242
    empire VI 243–249
    entry into war against Japan I 301
    espionage network II 130
    Estonian contribution to VII 22
    fear of the West I 181
    first Soviet atomic bomb test I 244
    forces in Afghanistan I 13
    foreign aid VI 54, 254
    gains control of Eastern Europe I 302
    glasnost I 152; VI 108–114
    government suspicion of citizens I 185
    Gross National Product II 60
    human rights record II 104; VI 35, 85, 109, 200, 244
    Hungarian uprising I 276

INDEX

HISTORY IN DISPUTE, VOLUME 9: WORLD WAR I, SECOND SERIES

357

Taylor, Maxwell D. I 119, 294; VI 95–96
Taylorism IX 22, 24
Teal, Joseph N. VII 52
Team B VI 256–263
Teapot Dome investigation (1922) III 178, 180
Teheran Conference (1943) I 110, 259, 288; II 32; V
46, 72, 236
Tehri Hydro-Electric Project (India) VII 127
Television
broadcast license II 122
commercial development II 122
impact on American society II 121
information-oriented programming II 126
noncommercial II 125
programming II 122
quiz show scandals II 123
role in American society II 125
Vietnam War II 124
Vietnam War coverage II 125
viewer demographics, 1980 II 124
Watergate hearings II 124
Teller, Edward VI 256–257
Tellico Dam (United States) VII 31
Tennessee River VII 26, 28, 31
Tennessee Valley Authority (TVA) I 27–30; III 154;
VII 1, 27–28, 130
impact on South VII 28
Tenth Inter-American Conference I 49
Tet Offensive (1968) I 40; II 5; VI 23, 29, 60
Texas VII 181–182, 185
water management policies in VII 69–75
Texas Groundwater Management District No. 1 VII
185
Texas Houston Ship Canal VII 265
Thames River VII 234
Thar Desert VII 125
Thartar Canal Project VII 77
Thatcher, Margaret VI 8, 10, 54, 195
critic of EEC VI 13
supports United States VI 13
The Dalles Dam (United States) VII 29, 51–61
The Dalles-Celilo Canal VII 52, 56–57
thermal pollution VII 175
Thessaloníki
construction of sewage works in VII 148
industry in VII 148
Third Republic IX 111
Third World VI 2–3, 35, 43, 55, 61, 63, 65, 68, 77–78,
80–81, 83, 116, 131, 133, 140, 145, 149, 160,
163, 186, 221–222, 236; VII 67
and the Cold War VI 264–272
beef imports to Europe VII 37
collapse of communist regimes in VI 239
effect on global balance of power I 14
gross national product I 14
national liberation movements in VI 188
Soviet influence VI 188
U.S. interventions I 15
U.S. policies on I 22; VI 80
water crisis in VII 286
Third World Liberation Front II 94
Tho, Le Duc I 291
Thompson, Tommy VII 57–59
Three Emperors' League VIII 225–227
Three Mile Island (1979) II 86
Three-Staged Plan for Optimum, Equitable, and
Reasonable Utilization of the Transboundary
Watercourses of the Tigris-Euphrates
Basin VII 79
Tibbets, Paul W. V 50
Tignes, France, riots at VII 99
Tigris River VII 77
Tijuana River VII 152
Tirailleurs Senegalais IX 113–115
Tirpitz, Alfred von VIII 29, 31, 34–35, 249; IX 101,
140, 142–143, 221
Tisza Club 252
Tisza River, chemical spill on VII 247–255

Title IX (1972) II 77
Tito, Josip Broz I 36, 59, 86, 108–110, 113, 273, 277,
283; VI 134, 136, 182, 217, 254, 265, 268,
271, 273–281; VIII 192; IX 268
Tojo, Hideki I 134; IV 7; V 49, 194, 264
Tonga (Batonka) people VII 5, 239, 242, 245
effect of dam on VII 4
Tokyo trials (1945–1948) V 263–269
comparison with Nuremberg trials V 266–267
dissent of Radhabinod Pal V 267
International Military Tribunal for the Far East
(IMTFE) V 266
Torrey Canyon accident (1967) VII 143
Total Strategy White Paper VII 240
Totally Equal Americans VII 172
Townsend, Charles Wendell VII 277
Trading with the Enemy Act (1917) III 223
"Tragedy of the Commons" VII 47, 48, 70, 73
Trans-Jordan VII 81; VIII 166, 214; IX 96
Treaties—
—Brest-Litovsk (1918) VIII 95–97, 141, 173, 278;
IX 27
—Bucharest (1918) VIII 95
—Dunkirk (1948) I 204
—Frankfurt (1871) VIII 278
—Lausanne (1923) VIII 214
—Locarno (1925) V 116–120
—London (1913) VIII 212
—Ouchy (1912) VIII 212
—Moscow I 107
—Sevres (1920) VIII 214, 217
—Turko-Bulgarian (1914) IX 204
—Versailles (1919). See Versailles Treaty
—Washington (1922) IX 168
Treblinka I 138; V 54, 57, 158, 161
Trees
cottonwoods VII 12, 212, 214, 215
elms VII 232
mesquites VII 212
oaks VII 212, 232
riparian importance of VII 215
salt-cedars VII 12, 215, 217
willows VII 212, 214, 215, 232
Trenchard, Hugh IX 10–11, 222
Tribal Grazing Lands Policy (TGLP) VII 34
Trident Conference (1943) V 236
Trinity River VII 223
Tripartite Pact (1940) V 294
Triple Alliance VIII 44, 46, 226, 229
Triple Entente VIII 35, 45; IX 226
Trotsky, Leon VI 179, 274–275; VIII 167
Trout Unlimited VII 31, 213
Trudeau, Pierre E., signs Great Lakes Water Quality
Agreement VII 120
Truitt, Reginald V. VII 43–44, 47
Truman, Harry S I 28, 35, 65, 69, 109, 113, 148, 159,
257, 285; II 39, 42, 44, 49–50, 197, 199,
203–204, 207–208, 280; III 10–14, 62; V
46, 98, 106; VI 20, 56, 144, 146–148, 153,
205, 231, 250, 284; IX 7
acceptance of a divided Europe I 264
adoption of containment policy I 262
anticommunism VI 155
appointment of Baruch I 27
approval of NSC-68 I 182
at Potsdam Conference I 263
atomic bombing of Japan I 239
attitude toward Stalin I 259, 261–263
containment policy I 274
Executive Order 10241 II 131
foreign policy I 58; II 205
foreign policy links to domestic ideology II 209
Interim Committee III 15
Marshall Plan I 176
response to communism II 130
restraint in use of nuclear weapons I 235
service in World War I VIII 192
Truman Doctrine II 145

Type IX V 80
Type VII V 79, V 80
Type VIIC V 83
unrestricted warfare IX 77, 120, 142, 187, 246, 248, 256
Upper Colorado River Storage Project VII 30
Upper Stillwater Dam (United States) VII 31
Urban political bosses III 259–265
Uruguay
    communist guerrilla movements I 125
    in War of the Triple Alliance I 125
    military coups I 26
    reduction of U.S. military aid I 141
Utah VII 31, 112

V

Vaal River VII 7–8, 240–241
Vance, Cyrus R. I 143, 145; VI 42, 263
Vandenberg, Arthur I 306, 203, 205, 207–208
Vandenberg, Hoyt Sanford I 6, 236
Van der Kloof Dam (South Africa) VII 243
Van Devanter, Justice Willis III 25, 27, 31
Vanishing Air (1970) VII 269
Vanzetti, Bartolomeo III 229–238
Vardar Valley IX 204–205
Vargha, Janos VII 101
Vatican VIII 208–209
V-E Day IV 62; V 60
Velsicol Chemical Company VII 162–165
Velvet Divorce (1992) VII 100
Velvet Revolution (1989) VII 101
Venereal Disease VIII 128
Venona Project I 242–243; 247; VI 123, 126, 154, 156
Ventura, Jesse II 199, 201
Venice, World War I IX 107
Vernichtungskrieg (war of annihilation) IV 88, 141
Venizelos, Eleutherios IX 208
Versailles Treaty (1919) I 255, 285, 293, 300; II 99, 145; III 99, 180; IV 17–18, 86, 164, 266–273; V 148, 202, 292; VI 176; VIII 20, 58, 95–96, 156, 166, 173, 207, 264, 277–285, 295, 298–299 ; IX 21, 27, 93, 95–96, 172–174, 268
    Article 231, War Guilt Clause IV 267; VIII 280, 282, 284
    impact on German economy IV 269
    impact on World War II IV 267
Vichy France IV 275–280; IX 84
    anti-Semitism IV 277, 280
    cooperation with Nazis IV 276, 278
    National Renewal IV 276
    Statut des juifs (Statute on the Jews) IV 277
    support of the *Wehrmacht* (German Army) IV 277
Victoria, Queen of England VIII 30, 32, 35
Vidovian Constitution (1921) IX 268
Vienna Declaration I 253
Viet Minh V 146–148; VI 106; IX 260
Vietcong I 40–42, 296–297; VI 93, 96
    attacks on U.S. bases (1965) I 291
    begins war with South Vietnam I 290
Vietnam I 41, 46, 50, 54, 82, 87, 89, 273, 290–294, 298–299; II 3–5, 7–10, 40, 173, 269; VI 32, 50, 59, 64, 80–81, 98, 101, 107, 201, 203, 229, 261, 270–272; VIII 35, 193; IX 260
    as a colony of France I 290
    Buddhist dissidents VI 92
    French withdrawal from I 213; II 266; VI 102, 106
    imperialism I 151
    peace agreement with France I 290, 297
    seventeenth parallel division II 267; VI 98
    U.S. bombing of I 183
    U.S. military buildup I 183; VI 96
Vietnam War (ended 1975) I 40, 44–45, 89, 101, 140, 142, 144, 290–299; II 3–10, 97, 177, 180, 224, 257, 260, 263–265, 273; VI 8, 23–29,

33, 38, 56–57, 61, 85, 88, 98–99, 103, 138–145, 173, 185, 202, 222, 266, 283–285; VIII 60, 188, 266; IX 262
    comparison to Soviet invasion of Afghanistan I 14
    domino theory I 266, I 297–298
    doves II 263
    folly of U.S. militarism I 183
    Gulf of Tonkin Resolution I 291
    hawks II 263
    impact on Republican and Democratic concensus II 208
    impact on U.S. domestic programs II 270; VI 185, 202
    labor movement support of II 193
    number of casualties I 291
    Operation Duck Hook II 6
    Operation Flaming Dart I 291
    Operation Rolling Thunder I 291
    reasons for U.S. involvement I 292, 295, 297–298
    result of containment policy II 265
    result of French colonial system II 267
    television coverage II 124–125; VI 145
    Tet Offensive II 9, 180, 275
    U.S. troop buildup I 291
    U.S. troops leave I 291
    Vietminh I 290
    Vietnamization VI 99
Villa, Francisco "Pancho" III 125–130; VIII 16, 18, 22; IX 6
Villard, Henry VII 57
A Vindication of the Rights of Women (Mary Wollstonecraft) II 74
Virginia
    liberalizes oyster-leasing laws VII 42
    oyster industry in VII 40–50
    privitization of oystering VII 47
    signs Chesapeake Bay 2000 Agreement VII 49
Vistula River VII 18, 20
Volksgemeinschaft (people's community) IV 80, 83
Volstead Act (1919) III 200
Volta River VII 2, 4
Volta River Project VII 4
Voltaire IX 207
Volunteers in Service to America (VISTA) II 272, 276
Voting Rights Act (1965) II 26, 91, 162–163, 165, 283

W

Wagner Act (1935) II 188; III 27–31, 63, 66, 149, 190
Waldersee, George von IX 99
Walesa, Lech VI 110; VII 20
Wallace, George C. II 180, 197, 199, 273, 281
Wallace, Henry A. I 31, 148, 287; II 197, 207, 209; III 159, 162
    Pete Seeger and the Weavers II 214
    presidential race (1948) II 211
Waller, Thomas Wright "Fats" III 79
Wannsee Conference (1942) IV 139; V 161
War Industries Board (WIB) Ix 18, 23
War of Attrition (1970) I 308, 316
War of 1812 VII 116
War of the Triple Alliance (1864–1870) I 125
War on Poverty II 270– 279; VI 141
    counter-assault to II 277
    reasons for failure of II 271
War Powers Resolution (1973) VI 58, 61, 195, 222, 283–287
War Refugees Board (WRB) III 253, 256
War Relocation Administration (WRA) III 102
Wars of Liberation (1813–1815) IX 126, 259
Wars of Unification (1866–1871) IX 126
Warhol, Andy II 216
Warm Springs Reservation VII 56, 60
Warne, William E. VII 55
Warren, Earl II 90, 136, 138, 142, 180, 280–291, 296
Warsaw Pact I 102, 154, 206, 256; II 60–61; VI 50, 110, 118, 121, 130–131, 168–170, 177, 184, 207–208, 235, 249, 267, 271

pollution control in VII 264
Wisconsin State Committee on Water Pollution VII 122
Wohlstetter, Albert J. I 213, II 65
Wollstonecraft, Mary II 74
Wolman, Abel VII 47
Women's Air Force Service Pilots (WASPs) V 303
Women's Army Corps (WAC) V 303
Women's movement II 162, 165
    and Prohibition III 198
    Progressive Era III 165-173
    and World War I VIII 124-130, 296, 298
Wood, Edward (Earl of Halifax) IX 83
Wood, Leonard IX 6
Woodstock II 257
Woodstock Dam (South Africa) VII 243
Woodwell, George M. VII 262
Woolf, Virginia VIII 130
Workers World Party II 197
Works Progress Administration (WPA), 1935 III 150, 163
World Bank I 20, 22, 124, 145; VI 120; VII 5, 7-8, 62, 83, 130, 132, 146, 241, 280, 287
    Resettlement Policy VII 244
    sets tone on water policy VII 286
World Bank Inspection Panel VII 8, 9
World Commission on Dams VII 9, 127, 130, 133, 242
    report of (2000) VII 317-332
World Commission on Water for the Twenty-First Century 286
World Court IX 171
World Health Organization (WHO) VII 143, 253
World Jewish Congress III 256; V 58
World War I (1914-1918) I 88, 112, 149, 284, 286; III 210, 223, 229, 244; VI 57, 176, 178, 267; VII 82; IX 22, 27
    African soldiers in IX 111-118
    African Americans III 268; IV 218; VIII 298, 301
    airplanes VIII 115, 193-197; IX 9-14, 38
    Allied cooperation IX 104-110
    Allied suplies to Russia IX 190
    Anglo-German naval rivalry VIII 29-36
    artillery IX 39
    arts IX 84
    balloons in IX 14
    casualties IX 30
    causes I 205; IX 224-229
    chemical warfare VIII 239-244
    combat tactics VIII 109-116
    convoys IX 74-79
    cultural watershed IX 80-90
    Balkans IX 206, 266-272
    Belgian neutrality IX 41-47
    British strategy IX 48-53
    East Africa VIII 84-90
    Eastern Front VIII 49, 60, 79, 91, 94, 110, 114, 125, 182, 240, 242, 252 IX 27; 60-66, 71, 108, 120, 124, 127, 129, 135, 154, 159, 206, 238, 243, 252-253
    European economics IX 83
    European leadership IX 98-103
    firepower and mobility VIII 109-116
    gender roles VIII 124-130
    homosexuality in IX 146-153
    impact on American business in Mexico III 128
    impact on Jews VIII 163-169
    impact on U.S. isolationism V 289; VIII 295-302
    Japan in IX 162-169
    Lost Generation VIII 186-192
    mass mobilization III 19
    Middle East VIII 37-42, 60
    military innovations VIII 193-197
    motivations of soldiers VIII 59-64, 263-269
    Ottoman Empire VIII 117-123
    naval war IX 139-142
    New Women III 168, 172
    prewar alliances VIII 225-231

prostitution in IX 146, 152
recreation for soldiers IX 234
religion VIII 202-210
Russia IX 237-243
shell shock IX 209-213
Socialists in Europe VIII 254-262
strategic bombing in IX 217-223
Supreme War Council IX 104
technology in IX 231
trench warfare IX 230-235
venereal disease IX 152
Western Front VIII 11-13, 16-19, 21, 24, 27-28, 39, 51, 56-57, 59, 61, 77-79, 90, 96, 102, 104, 106, 108-110, 112, 114, 117, 122, 177, 179-185, 187-188, 195, 197, 208, 221, 264, 272-273, 276, 282; IX 12-13, 15-16, 27, 29-31, 33-34, 38, 40, 48-49, 53, 61, 65-67, 71-73, 104-110, 114, 118, 120, 122, 124, 128, 131, 190, 193, 203, 225, 231-232, 234-235, 253-254
women in VIII 296, 298
World War II (1939-1945) I 61, 91; III 11, 50, 250-257; VI 8, 27, 31, 36, 49, 77, 79, 126, 146, 179, 267; VII 27, 29, 53, 69, 90, 93, 109, 152, 168, 174, 188, 199, 202, 204, 236-237, 257, 263-264, 273, 278, 287; IX 22, 27
    African American contributions IV 221; IX 115
    Allies V 27-33; VI 169
    Anglo-American alliance IV 208
    anti-submarine defense IX 79
    Axis powers V 62-67
    Balkans V 68-78
    Catholic Church VIII 209
    Eastern Front IV 53-60
        casualties IV 55
        Soviet advantages IV 55
    effect on Great Depression III 63
    homefront segregation IV 218
    impact on Civil Rights movement IV 220
    impact on colonial powers VI 183
    Japanese internment III 102-109
    Kyushu invasion III 13
    labor impressment IX 114
    Okinawa III 15
    Operation Olympic III 14
    Operation Overlord II 39
    Pacific theater III 13, 214; VI 254
    Pearl Harbor III 214-215
    relationship of Great Britain and U.S. II 31
    resistance movements V 243-247
    role of tanks IV 238-251
    Soviet casualties II 38
    strategy: IV 104-128; Allied V 19-26; Anglo-American disputes V 34-40; Anglo-Americn relations V 41-47; atomic bomb V 48-55; Axis V 62-67; Balkans 68-78; bomber offensive V 86-100; Eastern Front IV 53-60; Italian campaign IV 143-150; Operation Barbarossa V 226-234; Operation Dragoon V 235-242; unconditional surrender V 270-277; Yalta conference V 309-316
    submarines V 255-261
    Teheran Conference (1943) II 32
    threat of Japanese invasion III 108
    Tokyo trials (1945-1948) V 263-269
    unconditional surrender policy V 270-276
    U.S. combat effectiveness V 278-286
    U.S. Marine Corps V 295-301
    War Plan Orange III 108
    women's roles V 302-308; VIII 130
    Yalta Conference (1945) II 39
World's Fair, Chicago (1933) III 2
World's Fair, New York (1939) II 122
World's Fair, St. Louis (1904) III 242
World Water Commission VII 280, 281
World Water Forum (2000) VII 286
World Wildlife Fund (WWF) VII 107

X

Xhosa VII 67, 242

Y

Yakama Reservation VII 60
Yakovlev, Aleksandr N. I 104, 152
Yalta Conference (1945) I 73, 110, 252, 254, 256–257, 259, 273, 285, 288, 300–307; II 39, 205, 211; V 32, 75, 88, 252, 309–315; VI 126, 153, 158, 267
    "betraying" east European countries I 59
    criticism of I 302, 306
    "Declaration of Liberated Europe" I 300
    Far East I 303–304
    German war reparations I 300
    Poland V 310–311
    Stalin's promise of elections I 151
    United Nations V 310, 314
Yamagata Aritomo IX 164, 167
Yamamoto, Isoroku IV 2, 6
Yamashita, Tomoyuki
    trial of V 265
Yarmuk River VII 78, 81
Yasui, Minoru V 188–189
Yasui v. *U.S.* (1943) V 188
Yates v. *United States* (1957) I 81; II 281
Yatskov, Anatoli II 230
Year of Eating Bones VII 242
Yellow Sea VII 148
Yeltsin, Boris VI 113–114
Yemen VIII 39, 41, 212
    assasination of Ahmad I 282
    civil war (1962) II 150
    pan-Arab campaign I 281
    revolution I 158
Yom Kippur War (1973) I 162, 222, 308–317; VI 41, 43, 107, 161, 163, 166, 171, 204, 268
Yosemite National Park VII 112
Young Lords II 94, 197
Young Plan (1929) IV 270; IX 92, 171
Young Turks VIII 37, 45, 211
Yugoslav National Council (YNC) IX 267
Yugoslavia I 36, 108, 273, 277, 294; II 154, 156; VI 134, 136, 175, 181, 217, 219, 226–227, 243–

244, 265, 271, 273–275, 277; VII 248–249, 252–254; IX 93, 203, 208, 266–272
    collectivization VI 274
    NATO in VI 219
    "non-aligned" movement I 283
    Soviet domination until 1948 I 107; VI 54
    U.S. aid I 86
Yuma County Water Users Association (YCWUA) VII 154
Yuma Valley VII 151, 155

Z

Zahniser, Howard VII 112
Zaire VI 81
    support for FNLA and UNITA VI 1
Zambezi VII 5
Zambezi River VII 1–2, 4, 236–237, 239
Zambezi River Authority VII 245
Zambezi Valley Development Fund VII 245
Zambia 1, 4, 236–237, 239
    as British colony 4
    copper mines in 5
Zapata, Emilano III 125, 127, 129–130
Zemgor (Red Cross) IX 243
Zepplin, Ferdinand von IX 218, 221
Zeppelins VIII 200; IX 13, 181, 217–218, 220
Zhou En-Lai II 168, 172; VI 43
Zimbabwe VII 1, 4–5, 66, 236–237
    as British colony VII 4
    black nationalist movement in VII 9
    eviction of blacks from traditional homelands VII 8
    water extraction in VII 63
Zimbabwe African National Union (ZANU) VII 239
Zimbabwe African People's Organization (ZAPU) VII 239
Zimbabwe Electricity Supply Authority (ZESA) VII 7
Zimmermann Telegram VIII 296; IX 21, 245
Zimmerwald Conference (1915) VIII 256, 259, 261
Zionism VIII 41, 168, 208; IX 93
Zouaves IX 111, 115–116
Zola, Emile VIII 147
Zwick, David R. VII 268

Index

INDEX

ISBN 1-55862-448-1

9 781558 624481

90000